T0367144

THE I TATTI
RENAISSANCE LIBRARY

James Hankins, General Editor

PETRARCA
INVECTIVES

ITRL II

FRANCESCO
PETRARCA
◆ ◆ ◆
INVECTIVES

EDITED AND TRANSLATED BY

DAVID MARSH

THE I TATTI RENAISSANCE LIBRARY
HARVARD UNIVERSITY PRESS
CAMBRIDGE, MASSACHUSETTS
LONDON, ENGLAND
2003

Series design by Dean Bornstein

Library of Congress Cataloging-in-Publication Data

Petrarca, Francesco, 1304–1374.
[Selections. English & Latin].
Invectives / Francesco Petrarca ; edited and translated by David Marsh.
p. cm. — (The I Tatti Renaissance library ; 11)
English and Latin text; study in English.
Includes bibliographical references (p.) and index.
Contents: Invective against a physician —
Invective against a man of high rank with no knowledge or virtue —
On his own ignorance and that of many others —
Invective against a detractor of Italy.
ISBN 0-674-01154-6 (alk. paper)
I. Marsh, David, 1950 Sept. 25– II. Title. III. Series.
PQ4496.E21 2003
874'.01 — dc22   2003056663

Contents

✤✤✤

Introduction

ಕಿಲ್ಪಿಕ

Franciscus scripsit etiam invectivas, ut non solum poeta, sed etiam
   orator haberetur.
Francesco also wrote invectives so that he would be reputed an
   orator as well as a poet.
                     — Leonardo Bruni, *Dialogi ad Petrum Paulum Histrum*

The most celebrated and influential man of letters of the Trecento,
Francesco Petrarca was born in 1304 in the Tuscan town of
Arezzo, where his father had settled after being exiled from his
native Florence in 1302. His father, ser Petracco, was a notary who
soon found employment in the papal Curia, which had recently
been transferred from Rome to Avignon; and the young Francesco
grew up in nearby Carpentras. At his father's urging, he studied
law in Montpellier and Bologna, and then took minor orders. But
his main ambitions were literary. Besides the Italian poems that he
gradually assembled in the so-called *Canzoniere*, Petrarca began a
Latin epic (left unfinished) about the Roman general Scipio, titled
Africa, for which he was crowned as poet laureate in Rome in 1341.
(Later, he began, but did not complete, a series of historical and
allegorical celebrations in Italian *terzine* called *Trionfi*.) His various
friendships with scholars and potentates are recorded in his letters, assembled in the collections called *Familiar Letters* and *Letters
of Old Age*. He wrote various treatises and dialogues concerning
history and moral topics, including *On Illustrious Men*, *On Religious
Leisure*, *On the Solitary Life* and *Remedies for Good and Ill Fortune*. As
Petrarca's fame grew, his presence was requested in great cities
such as Milan and Venice; but he constantly yearned for the more
congenial setting of the countryside, and he spent his final years
near the village of Arquà outside Padua, where he died in 1374.[1]

Petrarca's literary and social success did not come without a price, and he came under attack from various quarters. As a response to such attacks, Petrarca's invectives offer a vital picture of his thought and personality which in many ways complements his other treatises and his collected letters. He evidently viewed them as important, since he took the trouble to revise and publish them in his lifetime.

In his four invectives, Petrarca assails representatives of four prestigious sources of authority in medieval Europe: the science of medicine (*Invective contra medicum*), ecclesiastical dignity (*Contra quendam magni status*), scholastic philosophy (*De sui ipsius et multorum ignorantia*), and French culture (*Contra eum qui maledixit Italie*). Together with the letters connected to them, the invectives constitute a principal source for Petrarca's biography, even if they must be read within the context of a literary tradition.

Invectives against a Physician

In December of 1351, Pope Clement VI fell seriously ill in Avignon. After a relapse in February 1352, Petrarca sent him a brief epistle (*Letters of Old Age* 16.3) urging him to rely on a single physician, rather than on the crowd of physicians attending him. The contents of this letter were apparently related in such garbled form that the pope asked Petrarca to write him a more formal letter, which the humanist did in his *Familiar Letters* 5.19, dated March of 1352. This more elaborate epistle provoked an angry response from one of the papal physicians, to whom Petrarca replied in a quickly drafted composition, which later became his first invective. The angered physician wrote a second attack, to which Petrarca again responded between January and May of 1353, before he left Vaucluse for Milan. Later, during his Milanese residence, he revised his two responses and published them as the four *Invectives against a Physician* in 1355.[2]

Petrarca articulates the argument of his invectives through a series of antitheses contrasting the values of the hostile physician to his own. Against the "mechanical" art of medicine, the humanist celebrates the liberal art of rhetoric. Against the sterile dialectic of scholastic Aristotelianism, he exalts the edifying allegory of poetry. Against the sordid practices of physicians, he vaunts his idyllic life in the country.

Invective against a Man of High Rank

Between March and August of 1355, Petrarca, now living in Milan, composed a much shorter work with a much longer title: *Invectiva contra quendam magni status hominem sed nullius scientie aut virtutis (Invective against a Man of High Rank with No Knowledge or Virtue)*. Directed against cardinal Jean de Caraman (d. 1361), the invective assails the sanctimonious arrogance of this powerful prelate, while also defending the humanist's residence at the Milanese court of the "tyrannical" Visconti. Adopting themes common in classical satire, Petrarca argues that the wealthy cardinal is a slave to his position, while he himself retains his freedom at the Milanese court.[3]

On His Own Ignorance

From 1362 onwards, Petrarca was living in Venice, where he eventually found himself under attack from an unexpected quarter, his immediate circle of friends. As he relates, he had walked into a trap set for him by four friends, who had tired of the humanist's censures of Aristotelian philosophers. Besides the element of surprise, these four men also had the advantage of their powerful standing in society, for they represented a sort of cross-section of the Venetian patriciate: the soldier Leonardo Dandolo, the merchant Tommaso Talenti, the nobleman Zaccaria Contarini, and the physician Guido da Bagnolo. (Their names, not mentioned by

Petrarca, are recorded in the margins of two manuscript sources.) In response to their attack, Petrarca composed not an invective, but an apology for his own ignorance. He wrote the first draft in 1367, revised it over the next two years, and dedicated it to Donato Albanzani in a letter of January 13, 1371.[4]

The work pits the pagan learning of Aristotelianism against Petrarca's humanism, which countenances the reading of classical authors as long as they are morally edifying. The humanist grants that both Aristotle and his beloved Cicero were great men, but with Pauline severity he denounces their limited vision as pagan authors. Despite its elements of invective, Petrarca's *On His Own Ignorance* offers an intellectual autobiography and a cultural manifesto that shaped the course of Italian Renaissance humanism.

Invective against a Detractor of Italy

In the spring of 1368, Petrarca wrote a letter to Urban V—his *Letters of Old Age* 9.1—in which he urged the pope to move the papacy from Avignon back to Rome. Petrarca's letter provoked a Latin tract by the Paris-trained cleric and theologian Jean d'Hesdin (ca. 1320–1400), who denounced Rome as a corrupt city and vaunted the superiority of France as the ideal seat of the papacy. As an Italian and a passionate student of Roman history, Petrarca could not resist confuting the friar's treatise in his *Invectiva contra eum qui maledixit Italie* (*Invective against a Detractor of Italy*), composed in 1373.[5]

As a detailed refutation of Hesdin's tract, Petrarca's last invective points the way toward the polemical exchanges of the Quattrocento, in which humanists censured the texts of their opponents. (In addition to his textual rebuttal of Hesdin, Petrarca also takes Bernard of Clairvaux to task.) Against the public denunciations of Rome, Petrarca offers a lively defense of the city's ancient glory and of ancient Romans like Cicero and Varro.

The rhetoric of vituperation

The violent language of the invectives will shock readers who are more familiar with Petrarca as the sweet celebrant of his love for Laura. Often the tone and imagery of these declamations seems closer to Dante's *Inferno* than to the *Canzoniere*, even if the latter collection includes denunciations of papal Avignon. But Petrarca is consciously drawing on the verbal license of ancient invective, which he explicitly invokes toward the end of his *Against a Physician* and *On His Own Ignorance*. Classical invective sought to denigrate an individual on the basis of birth, upbringing, "mechanical" professions, moral defects, physical shortcomings, and so on.[6] It was a branch of epideictic oratory which aimed at undermining the credibility of a judicial witness or political opponent by impugning his integrity. Accordingly, its realm was that of *ethos*, or personal character. In his 1910 study of this rhetorical theme, Wilhelm Süss lists various topics employed in denigrating an opponent, including aspersions on his father and mother, accusations of criminal and sexual misconduct, and caricatures of his physical defects.[7] These topics were obviously suited to a face-to-face encounter in a law court or public assembly, and we find examples of them in Cicero's speeches *In Vatinium* and *In Pisonem*.[8]

Yet it is precisely these topics which Petrarca avoids, preferring instead to rely on abusive epithets to denigrate his opponents. Quite strikingly, Petrarca employs far more abusive language than the Latin models that he cites as precedents: the invectives exchanged by Cicero and Sallust, and Jerome's polemics with Rufinus.[9]

At the same time, epideictic rhetoric embraces the antithetical topics of praise and blame, and invective often contrasts the adversary's vices to the author's virtues. Petrarca is at pains to establish polarities that contrast his own ethical values to the flawed ethos

of his opponents. Whereas the invectives of Cicero and Sallust begin by explicitly citing their adversary's name—an indication that the texts are forgeries—Petrarca refrains from naming his opponents. His invective against a physician, for example, begins: "Whoever you are . . ." At the beginning of his essay *On His Own Ignorance*, he purposely omits the names of the friends who have attacked him: "I am often visited by four friends, whose names you don't need to ask, since you know them all. Besides, the inviolable law of friendship does not permit us to cite our friends by name, even when their actions are unfriendly" (§5). And in his invective *Against a Physician* he insists that he must not flatter his opponent by naming him: "Clearly, my detractor will gain no fame by violating a humble and solitary country-dweller, rather than a king or temple. And I think that he should neither be named by me here, nor by others elsewhere. Is anyone engaged in such worthless affairs that he would waste his time on such a trivial reputation?" (§209). In this same invective, Petrarca pointedly contrasts the ignominious obscurity of his adversary with the celebrated figures of his historical compilation *On Illustrious Men*: "I am writing a work called *On Illustrious Men*. I don't dare say what it's like. My readers will judge. . . . It does not discuss doctors, poets, or philosophers. It only deals with men who were distinguished by their military prowess or profound dedication to the state, and whose deeds won them outstanding glory. If you think you have a rightful place in it, tell me where, and I shall comply. In it, I have assembled illustrious men from every century, as well as my poor wit allowed. Yet I am afraid that your arrival may drive them away, and that, if you alone remain, the title of the book will have to be changed from *Illustrious Men* to *The Egregious Fool*" (§64–65).

Vituperative comparisons

Petrarca's abusive language describes his adversaries with reference to three denigrating topics: human stupidity and madness, bestial traits and behavior, and repellant substances like urine, vomit, and sewage.

Let us begin with accusations of madness. In *Against a Physician*, Petrarca repeatedly calls the doctor a madman: "O fool and madman" (§75), "O madman lacking any good qualities" (§165), and "leaden brain" (§182).[10] For their devotion to Aristotle, he calls all doctors "presumptuous ignoramuses" (§109).[11] In *Against a Man of High Rank*, Petrarca likewise characterizes his adversary as a madman. He writes that "favorable fortune converted your madness to rage" (§9); and he urges the cardinal to keep some material or insanity in reserve (§15). In *Against a Detractor of Italy*, Petrarca asks rhetorically: "How can you deal with such stupidity?" (§22). Toward the end of the piece, he declares, "I no longer pursue his delirious ravings" (§87).

Comparisons to animals abound in all four invectives. Petrarca's invective *Against a Physician* is filled with denigratory animal comparisons: "You are dumbfounded, you beast: I guess you never heard this before" (§36); "O ridiculous animal, you are writing a book" (§44).[12] The physician is called an "industrious mouse" (§44), and compared to a hoopoe (§91), a bird that feeds on graves and excrement.[13] Indeed, this physician is a man who delights, like a hog, in wallowing constantly in the mud (§207).[14] But he is also a dangerous viper: "Listening to your words, I see that you are eager to bite, but being torpid with ignorance, like a cold viper, you are unable to pour forth your store of venom. But in the end, the friction of your wrath warms you up in a horrible way, and you rise up as far as my heel, more terrifying for your hiss than your bite"[15] (§32). Likewise, in *Against a Man of High Rank*, Petrarca compares the cardinal to a poisonous snake: "You harbored the

same pride when you seemed humblest, and the same venom, like a snake dormant in the winter. As soon as fortune warmed you with the blazing ray of prosperity, you burned like a poisonous reptile, and struck—first biting me, whom you used to lick, and then others, too, I'm sure" (§26).

On a lighter note, Petrarca's *Against a Physician* implicitly compares his adversary to a braying donkey (§101), and says that he belongs in Apuleius's novel *The Golden Ass*: "You should ask Apuleius of Madaura to assign you a place in his book about the ass that philosophizes" (§65). And for his disdain of Virgil, Petrarca compares this physician to a bat or an ape (§175).[16]

In fact, the opening words of the invective compare the physician to a dog whose barking has aroused a sleeping lion (§1). Later, Petrarca writes that the doctor barks at poets as a dog barks at the moon (§62). This canine imagery culminates when Petrarca compares Averroes to a dog barking at the sun. Christ, Petrarca writes, "is called a prophet by those who attribute lesser gifts to him, with the exception of this one dog who barks not at the moon, as the phrase has it, but who barks with his rabid and foaming mouth at the very sun of justice" (§85). And in *On His Own Ignorance*, Petrarca compares his friends to rabid dogs: "And so great is the power of evil that they stick out their tongues like rabid dogs and whet their fangs even against their friends, wounding the ones they love" (§11). Even Petrarca's beloved Cicero is rebuked as a pagan in terms that suggest a dog: "Here is the same Cicero later in the same book. After many weighty observations that smack of piety, he suddenly returns to his gods, like a dog to its vomit"[17] (§64).

In *Against a Detractor of Italy*, Petrarca repeatedly exploits the ambiguity of the Latin noun "Gallus," likening his French opponent to a rooster or hen:

Now let us hear our Gallic rooster, or more truly, our raven, who blackened his white feathers with dark lies . . . Let

us hear him croaking, I say, and repeating his madness in
hoarse squawks. (§33)

Now let our Gaul open his ears, and lower his insolent
cockscomb . . . and shake the dust of error from the tail-
feathers of his Gallic shallowness. (§44)

But I know full well: he is gawking at these unknown things,
which cannot be learned by Gauls or hens. (§47)

In one and the same man I have found a cock's comb and a
goose's tongue — O monstrous species! — combined with the
stubbornness of his contentious nation. . . . (§58)

I only hoped that the causes of enormous ills — the poisonous and harmful vintage of this unhappy exile — could be
eliminated. What does our Gaul squawk now? (§62)

This barnyard image of the Gaul as rooster does not preclude
comparisons to other animals, such as the following: "But our
Gaul, I see, would prefer to remain a barbarian, and gladly resides
in the mud where he was brought up . . . for hogs love mud, frogs
love the swamp, and bats love darkness" (§13).

Finally, the most repugnant denigrations allude to disagreeable
substances. In *Against a Physician*, Petrarca is most vehement when
he denounces the doctor for his constant examination of urine
samples, a sordid practice which the humanist contrasts to his
own life in the beauty of nature: "You are a manipulator of your
patients, an insincere and disgusting adulator, if I correctly judge
your nature. In the hope of a vile little gain, you frequent the latrines of both popes and paupers. By contrast, it is my custom to
frequent verdant woods and solitary hills, desiring only knowledge
or glory"[18] (§6). Petrarca even attributes the physician's sallow
complexion to the effects of this practice: "Your own wasted pallor
comes from the chamber-pots you study each day" (§98). The as-

sociation of urine with sewage inspires fierce insults: "You are a great and profound sewer, as Seneca says" (§53).[19] And in an image that anticipates the violent language of Quattrocento invectives, Petrarca imagines his foe riding triumphant through the sewer: "You might parade in a sewer, which is your notion of the Capitol, among the noisy farts of your patients and the clang of your basins" (§141). In his conclusion (§190), Petrarca assigns the doctor an unholy trinity of goddesses to worship: "I have selected three divine names for you . . . Pallor, Sewer, and Fever."

In *Against a Detractor of Italy*, Petrarca employs the vulgar language of bodily functions. "This barbarian," he writes (§10), "unable to control his bile has vomited many charges against me."[20] Like the physician denounced twenty years earlier, this Frenchman thrives in a sewer: "He goes on at length about the tranquillity and prosperous state of the Church, as he convulses in that sewer" (§14). And Petrarca accuses him, like Cicero, of "willingly returning to his own vomit" (§23).

Fortune of the Invectives

Petrarca succeeded in his endeavor of publicizing his own moral and intellectual values while consigning his detractors to oblivion. Once published, his invectives exercised considerable influence on several generations of humanists. In the decade after the author's death, his invective *Against a Physician* was translated into Italian by Domenico Silvestri, a friend of Boccaccio in Florence. More than forty manuscripts survive of the Latin original of *Against a Physician*, and more than twenty of *Against a Detractor of Italy*.

By 1400, the invectives formed part of a Petrarchan canon of Latin works which younger humanists could read with measured enthusiasm. Around 1402, Leonardo Bruni composed the first of his *Dialogues to Pier Paolo Vergerio*, in which an exacting classicist like Niccolò Niccoli cites Petrarca's invectives as a demonstration

of his rhetorical skills which ultimately must be found wanting.[21] Yet if their style appeared deficient by improving standards of Latinity, the invectives furnished arguments that Quattrocento humanists found convincing. In Bruni's dialogue, Niccoli repeats the condemnation of scholastics for making Aristotle into an irrefutable authority like Pythagoras—a point that Petrarca made in his *On His Own Ignorance*.[22] And Petrarca's combative attitude soon found imitators as humanists engaged in literary quarrels of their own. For example, the *Antidota* of Lorenzo Valla against Bartolomeo Facio and Poggio Bracciolini are filled with Petrarchan touches.[23]

I have divided the text into paragraphs mainly as a convenience to the reader in comparing the original text and translation. (In his invectives *Against a Physician* and *Against a Detractor of Italy*, Petrarca writes that subdividing a text is a hallmark of scholastic pedantry!)

I wish to thank James Hankins of Harvard University for his assistance in completing this project, and Abigail Fojas for scanning the Latin texts. Francesco Bausi, who is preparing a new critical edition of *Contra medicum*, generously offered advice on several passages.

Notes

1. See Ernest Hatch Wilkins, *Life of Petrarch* (Chicago: University of Chicago Press, 1961); Ugo Dotti, *Vita di Petrarca* (Bari: Laterza, 1987).

2. Wilkins, pp. 123–24; Dotti, pp. 252–57.

3. Wilkins, p. 147–48; Dotti, pp. 309–11.

4. Dotti, pp. 390–96.

5. Wilkins, pp. 235–36; Dotti, pp. 418–20.

6. See Lindsay Cameron Watson, "Invective," in *Oxford Classical Dictionary*, 3d ed. by Simon Hornblower and Antony Spawforth (Oxford—

New York: Oxford University Press, 1996), p. 762; Severin Koster, *Die Invektive in der griechischen und römischen Literatur* (Meisenheim am Glan: Verlag Anton Hain, 1980); Ilona Opelt, *Die lateinischen Schimpfwörter und verwandte sprachliche Erscheinungen: Eine Typologie* (Heidelberg: Carl Winter Universitätsverlag, 1965); Opelt, *Hieronymus' Streitschiften* (Heidelberg: Carl Winter Verlag, 1973), esp. "Das Portrait des Gegners," pp. 172–80.

7. Wilhelm Süss, *Ethos: Studien zur älteren griechischen Rhetorik* (Leipzig and Berlin: B. G. Teubner, 1910), pp. 247–55, lists the following topics: 1. father a slave; 2. father a foreigner; 3. father's and mother's base profession; 4. theft and crimes; 5. sexual behavior; 6. relations with relatives and foreigners, ethical breaches; 7. sullenness; 8. appearance and manner, physical defects, clothing; 9. cowardice in battle; 10. financial ruin.

8. Cf. M. Tulli Ciceronis *In Calpurnium Pisonem oratio*, edited with text, introduction, and commentary by R. G. M. Nisbet (Oxford: Clarendon Press, 1961), Appendix VI, pp. 192–97, "The *In Pisonem* as an Invective." Nisbet mentions criticisms of social background, mockery of physical appearance, accusations of immorality (hedonism, dissipation, avarice, pretention), and finally, the employment of abusive vocabulary (animal names, dirt, monstrosity, and political catchwords). See also the extensive analysis of the speech in Koster, *Invektive*, pp. 210–81.

9. On the (spurious) Cicero-Sallust exchange, see Koster, *Invektive*, pp. 177–200.

10. Cf. also §§108, 119, and 138. On *vesanus* in Cicero's speeches, see Opelt, *Schimpfwörter*, p. 142. Cicero uses *amens* and *demens* more frequently.

11. Petrarca exploits the traditional contrast in classical Latin between *idiota*, "ignorant layman," and *philosophus*, "philosopher": cf. Cicero, *Defense of Sestius* 51.110. Cf. also Cicero, *Against Verres* 2.4.2.4 or *Against Piso* 26.62 (Opelt, *Schimpfwörter*, p. 142; Koster, *Invektive*, p. 257).

12. On *belua* in Cicero's speeches, see Opelt, *Schimpfwörter*, pp. 143–44; cf. Cicero, *Against Piso* 1 and 8: *belua . . . cum hac importuna belua* (Koster, *Invektive*, p. 359).

13. The hoopoe is a European woodland bird with a prominent crest which is considered unclean in the Bible (Leviticus 11.19; Deuteronomy

14.18), and was supposed to feed on graves and human feces: cf. Isidore of Seville, *Etym.* 12.7.66.

14. Cf. (ps-) Cicero, *Invective Against Sallust* 1.3: "ut lutulentus sus cum quovis volutari" (Koster, *Invektive*, pp. 191, 359). Cf. also Jerome, *Commentary on Hosea* in *PL* 25.855: "[haeretici] instar porcorum volutantur in coeno"; the passage is cited in David Wiesen, *Jerome as a Satirist: A Study in Christian Latin Thought and Letters* (Ithaca, New York: Cornell University Press, 1964), p. 187.

15. Cf. Cicero, *In Vatinium* 4: "tamquam serpens" (a passage discussed in Koster, *Invektive*, p. 127). Opelt, *Schimpfwörter*, p. 144, notes that Cicero calls Clodius both *serpens* and *vipera* in his speech *On the Augurs' Responses*. Cf. Jerome, *Contra Vigilantium* 15: "Nec a suo studio monachi deterrendi sunt a te lingua viperea et morsu saevissimo" (*PL* 23.351); and *Adversus Jovinianum* 1.1: "Totus enim tumet, totus jacet: attollit se per singula, et qualis debilitatus coluber, in ipso conatu frangitur" (*PL* 23.211).

16. Cf. Petrarca, *On His Own Ignorance*, §141: "Hinc impune aquilam noctue, cignum corvi, leonem simie lacessunt" (two parallels in Petrarca's letters are cited in Fenzi's edition, p. 516, n. 598).

17. The expression "ad vomitum suum" derives from Proverbs 26.11: "As a dog returneth to his vomit, so a fool returneth to his folly" (*Sicut canis qui revertitur ad vomitum suum, sic imprudens qui iterat stultitiam suam*). The expression is cited as proverbial in 2 Peter 2.22, which describes believers who have relapsed into sinful pleasures: "It has happened to them according to the true proverb: 'The dog returns to its own vomit', and 'The sow is washed only to wallow in the mud'" (*Contigit enim eis illud veri proverbii: Canis revertens ad suum vomitum: et, Sus lota in volutabro luti*). In his *Adversus Jovinianum* 1.39, Jerome cites 2 Peter 9–22, and in the next chapter (1.40) he describes his adversary Jovinianus as a "canis revertens ad vomitum" (*PL* 23.267–68); cf. Wiesen, *Jerome as Satirist*, pp. 213–14.

18. Cf. Jerome, *Adversus Jovinianum* 2.12: ". . . guttur nostrum meditatorium efficitur latrinarum?" (*PL* 23.302B), cited in Wiesen, *Jerome as Satirist*, p. 52: "Our throat becomes merely a waiting room for the latrine."

19. Petrarca cites Seneca the Elder, *Controversies* 3.pr.16. Opelt, *Schimpf-wörter*, p. 233, notes this passage, and on p. 229 says that Jerome uses it as well.

20. Cf. Jerome, *Against Jovinianum* 1.1: "exordium, quod hesternam crapulam ructans, ita evomit" (*PL* 23.212). Wiesen, *Jerome as Satirist*, p. 217, calls this "abusive terminology derived from Cicero," citing *Philip-pics* 5.7.20. See also Jerome, *Against Vigilantius* 8: "post haec de barathro pectoris sui coenosam spurcitiam evomens" (*PL* 23.346).

21. Cf. Leonardo Bruni, *Dialogi ad Petrum Paulum Histrum*, ed. Stefano Ugo Baldassarri (Florence: L. S. Olschki, 1994), p. 257: "Scripsit prae-terea *Bucolicon carmen* Franciscus, scripsit etiam *Invectivas*, ut non solum poeta, sed etiam orator haberetur. Verum sic scripsit, ut neque in bu-colicis quicquam esset quod aliquid pastorale aut silvestre redoleret, neque quicquam in orationibus quod non artem rhetoricam magnopere desideraret." Niccoli's charge is not refuted later in the dialogue.

22. Ibid., p. 244: "Atque cum quidpiam confirmare opus est, proferunt dicta in his libris quos Aristotelis esse dicunt . . . Haec dicit, inquiunt, Philosophus; huic contradicere nephas est, idemque apud illos valet et *ipse dixit* et veritas. . . ." Petrarca makes the same point in *On His Own Ig-norance*, §36. Their common source is Cicero, *On the Nature of the Gods* 1.5.10.

23. Cf. the opening of Valla's *Antidotum in Facium*, ed. Mariangela Regoliosi (Padua: Antenore, 1981), p. 3: "more veterum adolescentium in causis forensibus auspicandis, qui, ut se disertos, ut probos, ut rei publice studiosos ostenderent, claros viros in iudicium vocabant, criminibus responsuros." This custom is cited by Petrarca in *Against a Physician* 209.

INVECTIVES

INVECTIVE CONTRA MEDICUM

Liber Primus

1 Quisquis es qui iacentem calamum et sopitum, ut ita dixerim, leonem importunis latratibus excitasti, iam senties aliud esse alienam famam prurienti lingua carpere, aliud propriam ratione defendere. Iniquum, fateor, inter nos certamen instituitur: ubi me percutias habeo, ubi te repercutiam non habes. Quod enim nomen habere potest mercennarius et infamis artifex? Profecto autem michi tecum non de opibus aut de imperio, sed de solo nomine pugna est, cuius te egenum atque inopem esse, etsi non admonearis, intelligis. Quia tamen cogis ad id, ad quod nunquam sponte descenderem, et loqui aliquid necesse est, ne, si — quod interdum in animum venit — propter contemptum rerum tuarum tacuero, tu tibi forsan ex mea taciturnitate complaceas, petita non a te sed a lectore venia siquid contra morem meum dixero, respondebo ad aliqua. Multa enim tam inepte dicis, ut quisquis ea responso digna duxerit, ipse merito videri possit ineptior.

2 Primum itaque, literis tuis lectis, risum me cohibere nequisse noveris. Quonam enim alio modo clarius probare poteras verum esse quod negas: te, scilicet, egressum tuis, alienis in finibus oberrare, magno cum eorum discrimine qui, nimium creduli, te sequuntur, quibus, sanitatis fructum pollicitus, nil nisi intempestivos

INVECTIVES AGAINST
A PHYSICIAN

Book I

Whoever you are, your relentless barking has roused an idle pen 1
and a sleeping lion, as it were. You shall soon learn that it is one
thing to carp at another's fame with a prurient tongue and another
to defend your own fame with reason. The struggle between us is
not fair, I confess. There are places where you may strike me, but
none where I may strike you back. How can a hireling and ill-
famed mechanic possess a good name? My battle with you does
not concern wealth or power, but only my good name, something
which you completely lack, as you know even without being reminded. Yet you force me into a contest that I would never have
entered willingly, and I must therefore speak. If I remained silent
in my contempt for your affairs — as occurs to me at times — you
might take pleasure in my silence. So I shall reply to several
charges, asking the reader's forgiveness, but not yours, if I say anything that runs counter to my nature. Most of what you write is so
foolish that anyone who dignifies it with a reply will justly appear
a greater fool.

To begin with, you should know that I couldn't help laughing 2
when I read your letter. How could you more clearly prove the
truth of what you deny? You abandon your own territory to wander in someone else's domain, thus placing in the greatest danger
those patients who blindly follow your advice. You promise them
the fruits of good health. But although they need action rather
than words, all you give them are the immature flowerets of your
worthless verbiage. How much sweat and effort it cost you to un-

flosculos inutilium verborum ingeris, cum facto non verbis opus sit? Quanto enim sudore quantoque cum studio inanem, sed ampullosam et tumidam plenamque convitiis epystolam effudisti! Sed hic vester est mos: adversus verum iurgio certatis. Et nimirum hoc ipso quantum tibi fideres apertissime declarasti. Si enim non extremus perditissimusque omnium fuisses, non desperasses fieri posse ille unus ex multis, qui, iuxta sententiam meam, esses in Romani Pontificis consilium evocandus. Imo vero generose mentis inditium est, etsi uni tantum spes glorie proposita sit, in id niti, ut unus ille tu sis. Quod si assecutus fueris, voti compos egregii; alioquin, laudabili saltem sis commendandus affectu.

3   Ego quidem (nam memini) non artificium sed artifices improbavi, eosque non omnes, sed procaces atque discordes. Mirum dictu ut, sibi conscius, tuus multorumque animus indoluit et exarsit. Nescio quid hic rei est. Argue tardos philosophos, punge inertes poetas, carpe incompositos oratores: nunquam Plato et Aristotiles, nunquam Homerus et Virgilius, nunquam Cicero aut Demosthenes irascentur; increpa medicos inutiles et ignaros: omnes prope frement et insanient.

4   Quod ante non noveram, brevi literula sum expertus: singulare quiddam hoc in genere dixerim. An forte ideo quia universali macule nemo subtrahitur? Nolo id quidem opinari; necdum despero fore aliquem medicum cui valde probetur quicquid dixi dicturus ve sum, quique suam singularem laudem in comuni ceterorum infamia recognoscat et, quod cuntis excellentibus ingeniis insitum reor, gaudeat se paucorum similem dissimilemque multorum. Quod nisi ita esse crederem, frustra suasissem unum de multis eligendum, ut verba mea repetam, 'non eloquentia, sed scientia et fide conspicuum.'

leash this vapid, bombastic, and turgid epistle filled with insults! But this is the custom of men like you: you combat the truth with abuse. Your action declares openly how much you believe in your-self. Indeed, if you hadn't been the worst and most corrupt of all, you wouldn't have despaired of being the one physician chosen from many, as I recommended, to be summoned to advise the Ro-man pontiff.[1] It is evidence of a noble mind that even when hope of glory is offered to one person only, you strive to be that one. If you succeeded, you would realize an extraordinary ambition; if not, you would at least deserve praise for your commendable aspi-ration.

For my part, I remember clearly that I did not criticize the 3 medical profession, but merely its professionals — and not all of them, but only the insolent and factious ones. Yet in your guilt you and many others were inwardly distressed and enraged to an amazing degree. I don't know what's the matter. Attack slow-witted philosophers, goad unskillful poets, and disparage inele-gant orators: Plato and Aristotle, Homer and Virgil, Cicero and Demosthenes will never be angry. But reproach ineffective and ig-norant physicians, and nearly all of them rant and rave.

Your brief little letter has taught me something I didn't know 4 before. Perhaps I should say that this is peculiar to your breed. Can the reason be that no physician is free of this universal stain? I would not like to think so. I still hope that there may be some physician who completely agrees with what I have said and shall say. Such a man would recognize that the common disrepute of his colleagues redounds to his personal praise. And he would take pride in being like the few and unlike the many — a trait that is in-grained in all great geniuses, I think. If I didn't believe this, it would have been pointless for me to argue that one physician should be chosen from many — to quote my words, "one notable for his science and good faith rather than his eloquence."[2]

5   Quo consilio cur in me tam vehementer exarseris mirarer, nisi
ignorantiam ac diffidentiam tuam noscerem, cum (ut postea didici) vestrorum quoque doctissimi egrum uni fideli medico et rari
erroris committendum dicant, ne, plurimos consulens, plurimorum incidat in errores. Tu tamen ille unus proculdubio non es,
quod si esses, nunquam discordes ac nescios medicos increpanti
tam ventosa respondisses epystola. Profundissime tangebaris, tam
graviter exclamasti.

6   Nec puduit illud etiam inter confusum murmur inserere: me
pontifici adulatum. Ego ne cuiquam adularer, cui propositum sit,
vulgo etiam non ignotum, preter virtutem ac bonam famam, uni-
versa contemnere? Quid autem me moveret, ut nunc fierem quod
ab annis tenerioribus nunquam fui? Percontare ipsum illum de
quo loquimur, et dicet tibi sepe ultro se michi obtulisse quantum
tu optare, licet sis importunissimus, non auderes, meque propter
amorem libertatis, quod tibi inexpertum et incognitum bonum est,
omnia recusasse. Desine itaque lepram tuam et ambitionis avari-
tieque malum bene valentibus imponere. Tu palpator, tu non solum blandus, sed — si es ille quem puto — tediosissimus etiam adulator, non modo pontificum sed et pauperum latrinas, vilissimi spe
lucelli, ego florentes silvas et solitarios colles ambire soleo, nonnisi
vel scientie cupiditate vel glorie.

7   Id non scripto sed cachinno refellendum arbitror quod inter
anxie conquisitas evadendi vias, quibus inenodabilem veri laqueum
tentas abrumpere, palpitando dixisti: me, forsan tui nominis invidia tactum, illud scripsisse, quo tibi gregique tuo famam eriperem.
Ego ne tibi miser invideam? Absit! avertat Deus! Qui enim misero
invidet, necesse est sit ipse miserrimus. Ego tibi nomen eripere ni-

If I weren't familiar with your ignorance and lack of confidence,   5
I would be surprised that my advice had fanned your anger against
me. As I later discovered, even the most learned of your colleagues
say that a patient should be entrusted to one trustworthy physician who seldom errs. Otherwise, by consulting many physicians,
he may be exposed to the errors of many. You are clearly not that
doctor. If you were, you would never have written such a windy
letter to answer my criticisms of factious and ignorant physicians.
You must have been cut to the quick to have cried out so loudly.

In your confused babbling, you did not scruple to insinuate that   6
I fawn on the pope. But how could I, of all people, fawn on anyone? As is commonly known, it is my policy to despise everything
but virtue and my good name. What could persuade me to change
what I have been since my early years? Ask the very man we are
discussing. He will tell you that he often volunteered to give me
more favors than you could dare to wish for, as importunate as
you are. And he will tell you that I refused them all out of my love
of freedom, a virtue of which you have no experience or knowledge. Cease, then, to infect people in good health with your lep-
rosy and with the maladies of your ambition and avarice. You are a
manipulator of your patients, an insincere and disgusting adulator,
if I correctly judge your nature.[3] In the hope of a vile little gain,
you frequent the latrines of both popes and paupers.[4] By contrast,
it is my custom to frequent verdant woods and solitary hills, desiring only knowledge or glory.

There is another charge which, I think, deserves to be refuted   7
by laughter rather than by writing. In your desperately contrived
attempts to sever the inextricable knot of truth, you groped in the
dark. You said that I had perhaps been stung by your reputation,
and that I had written my letter to rob you and your circle of your
fame. Could I, poor wretch, envy you? Never! God forbid! Whoever envies a wretch must perforce be himself most wretched.
How could I deprive *you* of your name, you obscure fellow? You

tar, inglorie? Procul ab hoc periculo es; ire potes toto securus orbe terrarum: quod ad fame iacturam attinet

cantabis vacuus coram latrone viator.

Erit qui forte nares amputet, oculos effodiat: famam tibi nullus eripiet quam non habes.

8   Quid autem intolerabilius homine insolenti, qui, ubi pudorem semel abiecerit, quicquid dixeris negabit? Magna meretricie frontis impudentia est! Negas ecce medicos discordare, que publica totius humanis generis est querela. Utinam tamen ita sit! Malim me esse mentitum, quanquam hac in re mentitus esse non possim; ceterum, salvis omnibus, errasse maluerim, quam, me veridico, periclitari tot hominum milia, qui discordi et vario et prorsus incerto medicorum imperio gubernantur. Nempe, quod in summi pontificis nuper cura dicis fuisse concordes, vide, non dico ne mentiaris—id enim iam vobis quotidianum atque vulgare est—sed ne maximis testibus veritas vos ipsa confundat. Concordastis, forte, postquam ille convaluit, qui—quod nemo, ne ipse quidem, dubitat—multo ante convaluisset, si tu saltem per totum egritudinis sue tempus in extremis Indie litoribus habitasses.

9   O si quod ominari horreo, sed, licet immortalis Dei vicarius, est tamen ipse mortalis—si ergo tunc nature debitum persolvisset, quanta fuisset inter vos et quam indecisa discordia de pulsu, de humoribus, de die cretico, de farmacis! Celum ac terram dissonis clamoribus implessetis, causam ipsam egritudinis ignorantes. Miseri qui sub auxilii vestri fidutia egrotant! Cristus autem, in cuius manu salus hominum sita est, salvum illum, ignorantibus omnibus vobis, fecit—et faciat precor quantum sibi, quantum Ecclesie, cui

are far from running such a risk, and may travel the whole world
in safety. As for the loss of your fame:

An empty-handed traveler, you'll whistle in the robber's face.[5]

Perhaps someone will cut off your nose, or rip out your eyes. But
no one will rob you of fame that you don't possess.

What could be more intolerable than an insolent fellow who   8
has renounced all shame and will deny anything you say to him?
What great impudence! What meretricious effrontery! You deny
that physicians disagree, when the whole human race openly complains of the fact. If only this were the case! I wish I were lying, although I could not lie about this. Indeed, I wish I were mistaken
and that everyone were healthy. Instead, I speak the truth, and
thousands of people are in danger because they are governed by
the factious, divergent, and uncertain authority of physicians. You
say that you physicians agreed about the pope's recent care. Beware, but not that you lie: for you physicians are all notorious for
lying every day. Beware lest the truth itself refute you with mighty
proofs. Perhaps you all agreed once the pope's health had im-
proved. But no one, including the pope, doubts that he would
have recovered much sooner, if *you* at least had spent the entire pe-
riod of his illness living on the distant shores of India.

But suppose—I shudder to think it!—that the pope had paid   9
his debt to nature. Even the vicar of immortal God is mortal.
What great and unresolved discord there would have been among
you concerning his pulse, his humors, his critical day, and his
medications![6] Ignorant of the real cause of his illness, you would
have filled heaven and earth with dissonant cries. Wretched are
the sick who trust in your aid! But Christ, who holds all human
salvation in his hands, saved him despite your ignorance. I pray
that Christ may do all that is necessary for him and the Church
he governs. You physicians appropriate the results of God's be-
neficence and the excellence of the pope's own physical constitu-

presidet, est necesse! Vos, Dei beneficium et complexionis ac nature sue laudem usurpantes, videri vultis illum a mortuis susci-
tasse, et nunc tandem, transacto periculo, concordatis (non inele-
ganti vafritie) ne, si pater ille doctissimus quique vel ingenio vel
experientia, non dicam omnia, ut tu adulator, sed multa, cognoscit
ac previdet, discordare vos senserit, precipites ancipitis vie duces
abiciat, spernat atque oderit.

10   Sed michi crede: nequiquam rete iacitur ante oculos pennato-
rum. Novit ille mores vestros; et, si me interroges, propter cuiusdam speciem honestatis et ne consuetudinem publicam damnasse
videatur, vestra potius vult ferre fastidia, quam quia ignoret aliquanto gravius esse periculum vitam suam nugis vestris, quam fragilem sine gubernaculo carinam pelago ventisque committere.

11   Quod ad me attinet, iracundiam tuam minime quidem miror.
Sciebam verum esse satyricum illud:

Accusator erit qui verum dixerit,

nec minus illud comicum:

Obsequium amicos, veritas odium parit.

Quod cum comuniter verum sit, tum, precipue inter illos qui
mendacio vivunt. Illud miror: quod ira se in rabiem furoremque
convertit. Nichil enim tibi scripseram, quippe qui nunc etiam invitus non intellecturum alloquor; at Romano Pontifici, gravi tunc
egritudine laboranti, metu ac devotione dictantibus, epystolam
scripsi brevem — sed, nisi fallor, utilem sibi, tibi forte non ita — ad-
monuique ut turbam dissidentium medicorum, necnon et medicum non scientie sed inanis eloquentie curiosum, que ingens nostris temporibus multitudo est, omni studio caveret. Quod licet
gravissime stomaceris, me tamen neque consilii mei penitet, neque
me lapidandum credidi, si sibi, licet non egenti, fidele consilium

tion, and claim to have revived him from the dead. Now that the danger is past, you all agree, with subtle cunning. In this way, our learned father will not sense your discord, even though by his insight and experience he understands and foresees many things. (I don't say he understands *all* things, as you do, flatterer.) Otherwise, he would dismiss, spurn, and detest you as reckless guides on a dangerous path.

Believe me, it's useless to cast a net before the eyes of birds. The pope knows your character. If you ask me, he prefers to tolerate your pride in order to maintain a semblance of respectability and to avoid condemning your official practice. He is aware that it is more dangerous to entrust his life to your nonsense than it is to commit a fragile vessel to the winds and open sea without a helmsman.

For my part, I am scarcely surprised by your anger. I knew the truth of the satirist's verse

For speaking the truth, you're called an informer.[7]

as well as the comedian's verse:

Complaisance makes friends, and the truth makes enemies.[8]

This general rule is especially true of people who live by lying. But I am surprised how your anger turns to furious rage. I had never written to you before, and even now I am loath to speak to someone who won't understand me. I did write a brief letter to the Roman pontiff, dictated by my fear and devotion when he was seriously ill. Unless I am mistaken, this letter was useful to him, if perhaps not to you. I warned him to avoid carefully the crowd of quarreling physicians, as well as any doctor who pays more attention to empty eloquence than to his science: for our age offers a vast multitude of such men. Even if you rage with indignation, I don't regret my advice. Nor did I think I should be stoned to death because I offered loyal advice to this man, even if he didn't

dedissem, cui omnes qui cristiano nomine gloriamur, non modo consilium sed obsequium insuper et obedientiam deberemus.

12   Debuisti, si sanus esses, non michi rescribere, qui tibi nichil scripseram, sed eidem illi scribere, si sibi forsan aromatico illo tuo ac medicinali suadere posses eloquio, ut tibi se ipsum et res suas crederet, vitam ac salutem nisi de tuis manibus non speraret, contra autem me studiisque meis deditos, nocuum atque inutile genus hominum, declinaret, seu me poetam seu quodlibet aliud dicere libuisset. Omnia enim tibi licere arbitror, ydiota, qui propter mei, quinpotius veri odium, in poetas immerito[1] es invectus. Ego tamen hac in re poetice nichil scripsi; quod ita esse, nisi plane desiperes, ipse stilus indicio est. Cogeret me forte procacitas tua poetice aliquid de te loqui teque omnibus seculis lacerandum tradere, nisi quia indignus visus es, qui per me posteris notus esses aut locum in meis opusculis invenires.

13   Sed quid colores ceco, quid surdo sonos ingero? Mechanice res tuas age, oro te; cura, si potes; si minus, interfice; et precium posce, cum occideris. Id nulli imperatori aut regi, sed tibi uni, vite necisque domino, ut iactas, humani generis cecitate permittitur. Utere funesto privilegio. Optime enim tutissimeque arti cerebrum addixisti: quisquis evaserit, tibi vitam debet; quisquis obierit, tu illi preter experientiam nichil debes; mors nature aut egroti vitium, vita tuum munus est. Iure igitur Socrates, cum factum de pictore medicum audisset: 'Caute' inquit 'artem enim deseruit que defectus suos habet in aperto, eamque complexus est cuius error terra tegitur'.

14   Quid te autem non ausurum rear, qui rethoricam medicine subicias, sacrilegio inaudito, ancille dominam, mechanice liberalem?

need it. All of us who glory in being called Christians owe him not only our advice, but our allegiance and obedience as well.

If you were sane, you should have replied to the pope, not to 12 me, since I didn't write to you. Perhaps with your herbal and medicinal eloquence, you might have persuaded him to entrust his life and his affairs to you, and to place his hopes for life and health in your hands alone. In turn, he might have shunned me and my fellow scholars as a harmful and useless breed, whether you chose to call me a poet or something else. I think you will go to any lengths, ignoramus. In your hatred of me, or rather your hatred of the truth, you unjustly inveighed against poets. In fact, I wrote nothing poetical on this subject; and if you weren't so completely stupid, my very style would prove this to be the case. Perhaps your impudence should compel me to write about you in my poetry, exposing you to be torn apart by future generations. But you seemed unworthy of a place in my little works that would make you known to posterity.

But why do I force colors on a blind man, or noises on a deaf 13 one? Ply your trade like a mechanic, I pray you. Cure your patients, if you can. If not, kill them, and demand payment when they are dead. Thanks to the blindness of the human race, you alone are the lord of life and death, as you boast, and are granted immunity that no emperor or king enjoys. Enjoy your deadly privilege. You have devoted your brain to an excellent art that offers you the greatest security. When someone survives, he owes you his life. When someone dies, you owe him nothing but the lessons of the experience. Death can be blamed on nature or on the patient. Only you bestow life. When Socrates had learned of a painter who had become a physician, he justly observed: "What prudence! He abandoned an art in which faults are exposed, and embraced one whose mistakes are buried in the earth."[9]

What may I suppose you will not presume to do, when you 14 subordinate rhetoric to medicine? With unheard-of sacrilege, you

Nisi forsan illa te cogitatio has in insanias traxit—que si unquam caput tuum potuisset irrumpere, nunquam usqueadeo asininum atque obtusum dicerem—ut scilicet, quoniam etate nostra iniquissimos homines imperitare viris optimis fato rerum pessimo videmus, ad artes quoque speciem hanc tyrannidis trahendam ac propagandam putes. Sed prius omnia, quam huiusce rei arbitrium fortune traditum videbis. Faciet illa Nerones atque Caligulas regnare, Dyonisios atque Phalaridas in patria florere, Catonem intra pestes lybicas errare, mori Regulum in carcere, in paupertate Fabritium, Marcellum in insidiis, in exilio Scipionem. Hec et his similia faciet, quotiens volet more solito iocari; medicine suppeditare rethoricam non poterit: extra suos fines imperium non habet.

15   Sed quid loquor? Nescio an, priusquam ad finem suscepti sermonis venio, libeat mutare sententiam ac fateri ius illam etiam in artibus habere. Quod nisi ita esset, nunquam tu de tanta ignorantia, tam superbus incederes, cum multi interim viri literatissimi mendicant. Verum ea non artium fortuna, sed artificum dici debet. Ad id michi respondeas velim: si, rebus omnibus fortune imperio confusis, artes quoque confundere et liberales mechanicarum servas facere—quod utrarunque prohibebaris nomine—voluisti, cur non potius navigationi quam medicine rethoricam servam faciebas?

16   Navigationem certe sui generis, hoc est mechanicarum, quidam dixere rethoricam, eo quod in primis illi cui mercatura omnis subiacet, in peragrando orbe lustrandisque litoribus atque innumerabilium nationum conciliandis ratione animis, multa fit opus eloquentia. Unde et Mercurium, quem sermonis deum vocant, inde dictum volunt: quod mercatorum *kirius*, hoc est dominus, esse videatur. Quod cum ita sit, cur non potius, ut dixi, navigationi

subject the mistress to the serving-girl, and the liberal art to the mechanical art. But perhaps this madness was inspired by a certain idea. (And if this idea had dawned in your brain, I would never have called it so asinine and obtuse.) In other words, since the disastrous fate of our age allows the worst men to rule over the best, you think this kind of tyranny should be extended and transferred to the arts. Yet the last thing you will see is Fortune granted dominion over the arts. Fortune will let Neros and Caligulas rule, let tyrants like Dionysius and Phalaris flourish in their countries, let Cato wander amid Libyan plagues; or let Regulus die in prison, Fabricius in poverty, Marcellus in an ambush, and Scipio in exile. She will do such and similar things whenever she chooses to play her usual games. But she cannot make rhetoric serve medicine, for she has no power outside her own realm.

But what am I saying? Before I come to the end of my talk, I 15 may want to change my mind and to concede that Fortune has authority over the arts, too. If this were not the case, you could never strut around so proud of your great ignorance at a time when many men of great learning go begging. In fact, Fortune should be called mistress of the artisans, not of the arts. But answer me this, please. If the rule of Fortune confuses all our affairs, and you wish to confound the arts as well by making the liberal arts the handmaids of the mechanical arts, which runs contrary to both their names, why did you not make rhetoric the handmaid of navigation, rather than of medicine?

In fact, navigation has been called by some the rhetoric of its 16 professional class, that is, of the mechanical arts. Navigation governs all commerce, and has a special need of eloquence, for merchants travel the world, exploring distant shores and using reason to win over the minds of countless nations. Some say that Mercury, who is called the god of speech, derives his name from *mercatorum kyrios*, that is, "lord of merchants."[10] If this is so, why don't you order rhetoric to become the serving-girl of navigation?

rethoricam ancillari precipis — quod equanimius propter similitu- dinem latura sit — nisi quia ruditatem illam tuam et caligantis in- genii cecitatem occultare nullo modo potes?

17 Proximis tuis literis expecto, ridiculosissime rerum censor, ut lanificio iubeas subesse grammaticam, dyaleticam armature. Quid enim te rursus non ausurum putem, qui me os in celum posuisse dicas, quoniam medicos divinum ac celeste genus attigerim, cum tu impurissimum os aperire non sis veritus in Plinium Secundum, virum ex omnibus sue etatis doctrina ingenioque prestantissi- mum? Ita enim de illo scriptum video; nec excipitur Galienus, coe- taneus (nisi fallor) suus, vir et ipse non indoctus, sed indoctorum atque loquacium abundantissimus successorum.

18 Que autem ista dementia? Que ve ista voluptas est? A pedite vulnus acceptum equiti refundis innoxio; et soluta oratione cum sis lesus, iram ulcisceris in poetas, quasi poeticum sit omne quod nescias. Id si tibi permisero, quid usquam, queso, non poeticum relinquetur? Quid enim non te penitus ignorare crediderim, qui ad exprimendum ineptissimos sensus tuos tam pueriliter desu- dasti? Deus bone, que deliramenta! Que somnia! Insultas poetice cuius nunquam faciem vidisti; laudas medicinam quam ego non improbo. Quis enim sane mentis hoc audeat?

19 Scio artem esse non inutilem, et sero licet a nostris hominibus receptam, postea tamen in honore habitam; quinetiam inventioni deorum, ut perhibent, immortalium consecratam, tam magna res visa est, ut humana non putaretur inventio. Quam opinionem cer- tioris fidei auctor in *Ecclesiastico* confirmans, 'Altissimus de terra' in- quit 'creavit medicinam.' Quamvis id omnium sit comune — quic- quid novimus, quicquid scimus, quicquid sapimus, quid nisi divina inventio Deique donum est, cum in eiusdem libri principio scrip-

Given their similarity, it would bear this role more patiently. The reason must be that you cannot hide your lack of education and the blindness of your benighted intellect.

In your next letter, O most absurd of censors, I suspect that 17 you will subordinate grammar to the wool trade, and dialectic to the manufacture of arms. Again I ask, what may I think you will not presume to do, when you say that I "set my mouth against heaven" by attacking physicians, who are a divine and heavenly race?[11] Yet you do not hesitate to open your abominable mouth against Pliny, who was a paragon of learning and intellect in his age. This is what I find written about him, with no exception made even for Galen, who was his contemporary, unless I am mistaken. But Galen, though himself not unlearned, spawned a great host of unlearned and garrulous successors.

What is this madness of yours? What self-gratification? 18 Wounded by a foot soldier, you strike an innocent cavalryman. Offended by prose, you avenge your wrath on the poets. It is as if anything you cannot understand must be poetical. If I grant you this, what, I ask, will not be poetical? Can I believe there is anything of which you are not completely ignorant, when you sweat so childishly to express your foolish notions? Good God, what ravings! What delusions! You insult the art of poetry, when you have never beheld its face; and you praise medicine, when I do not condemn it. What sane person would dare to do this?

I know that your art is useful; and although it gained accep- 19 tance late among our people, it was afterwards held in honor. Indeed, this art was attributed to the invention of the immortal gods, for it seemed too great to be a human discovery.[12] A more reliable authority confirms this opinion in *Ecclesiasticus:* "The most High has created medicine out of the earth."[13] In fact, this is true in common of everything. What are all our experience, all our knowledge, and our wisdom but a divine creation and a gift from God? It is written at the beginning of the same book: "All wisdom

tum sit: 'Omnis sapientia a domino Deo est'? At ne tibi de mechanice tue singulari ceu laude complaceas, audi quid de agricultura,
altera mechanicarum, eodem scribitur libro: 'Non oderis' inquit
'laboriosa opera et rusticationem ab Altissimo creatam.'

20   Quid habes quod super quemcunque agricolam attollas?[2] Ambe
artes uno de fonte prodeunt: ambas creavit Altissimus. Imo vero,
quid habes quo te agricole conferas, cum humanam ille vitam
adiuvet, quam tu, licet contrarium professus, oppugnas; ille humano generi laborando prosit, tu noceas quiescendo; ille nudus in
campis fame sua publicam pariat saturitatem, tu faleratus in thala-
mis voce tua publicam destruas sanitatem?

21   In eo quidem non similiter concordamus: quod effectus medicorum dicis esse mirabiles. Quos effectus? queso te. Nisi illud forsan inter miraculosa connumeras, quod vos sepius quam ceteri
hominum, imo vero quasi continue, egrotatis. Itaque magnis in
populis facies vestra solo pallore discernitur, iamque in proverbium abiit 'colorem medici' dicere, quotiens croceum hominem aut
tabescentem videris.

22   'Parum ne' hic 'miraculi est, salutem aliis quam ipse non habeas
polliceri?' Esset profecto miraculum, nisi illud extenuaret assidui-
tas mentiendi. Nisi forte ille mirabilior est effectus, quod qui se
totum vestro consilio tradiderit, sanus esse nunquam poterit. Hi
sunt medicorum non tantum miri sed stupendi etiam effectus, medicorum vero non omnium sed multorum, atque in primis tui.

23   Credo ego Ypocratem virum doctissimum fuisse; puto Galie-
num illo duce, multa primis inventionibus addidisse. Non detraho
claris viris, ne fiam tui similis, qui obtrectandi studio me cum
Plinio miscuisti, quem si intelligere posses, esses hortandus ut le-
geres, et te ipsum in eo speculo intuens, vel deformitatem tuam

is from the Lord God."[14] Lest you become complacent in the special merit of your mechanical art, hear what is written in the same book concerning the mechanical art of agriculture: "Hate not laborious works, nor the husbandry created by the most High."[15]

What do you possess that you can exalt above any farmer? 20 Both arts derive from the same source, for both were created by the Most High. Indeed, what reason do you have for comparing yourself to a farmer? He benefits human life, while you undermine it, though you profess to do the opposite. He aids humankind by his labors; you harm it by your idleness. Naked out in the fields, he keeps the people well-fed by his hunger; lavishly dressed in their bedrooms, you destroy people's health by your words.

There is another point on which we disagree. You say that phy- 21 sicians achieve miraculous results. What results? Please tell me. Perhaps you count as miraculous the fact that you doctors are sick more often than other people, indeed almost continually. Amid great crowds of people, your faces are conspicuous by their singular pallor, which has become proverbial. When we see a person with a sallow or wasted face, we call this a "physician's complexion."

"Is it a small miracle," you ask, "when you promise others the 22 health you yourself lack?" Truly it would be a miracle, if it weren't diminished by your persistent lying. Or perhaps this is an even more miraculous result: no one who completely trusts your advice will ever be healthy. Such are the marvelous and astonishing results achieved by physicians — not by all of them, but by many and especially by you.

I believe that Hippocrates was a very learned man, and that 23 with his guidance Galen added many new discoveries to his earlier ones. I will not disparage famous men, lest I resemble you, who are so eager to malign me that you confuse me with Pliny. If you could understand Pliny, I would urge you to read him. For if you viewed yourself in that mirror, you would either correct your de-

corrigeres, vel desineres superbire. Sed—crede michi—grecum hominem putares, cum tamen is inter raros latine eloquentie principes in *Saturnalibus* numeretur.

24 Si te in literis tuis video, arrogans et ignarus es: alterum facit ut nil discas, alterum ut nil scias. Quid enim de hoc tanto viro somnias? Dicis eum quod veri habet ab antiquis medicis accepisse: vos a quibus tot mendacia didiceritis non dicis. Sed quid iterum tempore gloriaris? Ignavissimorum quorundam hominum consuetudo est, ut, cum inter vitia senuerint nullique pares sint, sola se preferant senectute. Atqui ne hanc ipsam unam gloriandi tibi materiam concesserim. In singulis enim te verbis detegis nichil esse, nichil sapere, nichil nosse.

25 Computa annos et reperies virum illum omnes fere, quibus uteris, medicos precessisse. Quanquam, quid attinet medicorum antiquitate nominibusque confidere, qui si ad lucem redeant, una voce fatebuntur nullos se hostes alios habere quam vos, quorum vel turpi segnitie vel ingeniorum hebetudine sui labores ac vigilie perierunt, quique quotidie mentiendo illos arguitis fuisse mendaces?

26 Lege, si libet, et nisi ego quoque tibi grecus videor, epystolam illam totam, que cum ad hoc unum scripta esset, ut universali domino cautionem pareret, tibi nescio cui—imo quidem scio, sed dissimulo—dolorem peperit ac furorem. Illam lege, si libet: invenies me nil omnino contra medicinam nilque contra veros medicos locutum, sed contra discerptores atque adversarios Ypocratis; quod eodem plaudente fieri credidi. Tu autem non contentus in me multa dixisse, multa itidem contra poeticam ac poetas, quadam libidine vobis insita loquendi de rebus peregrinis et incognitis, evomuisti. Non legeras apud Varronem, Romanorum doctissi-

formity or cease to be proud. Believe me, you would think he was a Greek, even if in the *Saturnalia* he is counted among the rare masters of Latin eloquence.[16]

If I see you clearly from your letter, you are both arrogant and   24
ignorant. Your arrogance keeps you from learning anything, and your ignorance from knowing anything. What nonsense do you spout about this great man? You say that what truth he knew he learned from ancient physicians. But you don't say who taught you physicians so many falsehoods. And why do you repeatedly boast of your age? This is the habit of the most ignorant men. When they have grown old in their vices and are inferior to everyone, they exalt themselves solely on account of their antiquity. But I would not grant you even this reason for boasting. By your every word you reveal that you are nothing, know nothing, and understand nothing.

Count the years, and you'll find that Pliny preceded nearly all   25
the physicians that you consult. But what is the point in trusting the antiquity and reputation of physicians? If they came back to life, they would unanimously declare that you modern physicians are their only enemy. Your shameful laziness and dull intellect have destroyed their labors and vigils; and your daily lies make liars of them.

Read my entire letter, if you will, unless I too seem Greek to   26
you. My sole aim in writing was to advise our universal lord to be cautious. Instead, it stirred up pain and fury in you, whom I don't know, or rather, whom I know but pretend not to know. Read it, if you please. You'll find that I said nothing against medicine or true physicians, but only against the detractors and adversaries of Hippocrates. I believe that Hippocrates would have applauded my action. But you were not content merely to denounce me. With your innate passion for discussing foreign and unknown topics, you vomited forth a denunciation of poetry and poets. Haven't you read what was said about poets by Varro, the most learned of the

mum, neque apud Tullium, quem fidenter—licet forte obstrepas—dixerim principem Latinorum, quid de poetis scriptum est?

27   Verba enim ipsa, nequid me mutasse vel addidisse suspiceris, apposui: 'A summis,' inquit, 'hominibus eruditissimisque sic accepimus: ceterarum rerum studia et doctrina et preceptis et arte constare; poetam natura ipsa valere, et mentis viribus excitari, et quasi divino quodam spiritu inflari. Quare suo iure noster ille Ennius sanctos appellat poetas, quod quasi deorum aliquo dono atque munere commendati nobis esse videantur. Sit ergo, iudices, sanctum apud vos, humanissimos homines, hoc poete nomen, quod nulla unquam barbaria violavit.' Hec Cicero; multa sequuntur in eandem sententiam gravissima, innumerabilia etiam apud alios, que sponte pretereo.

28   Neque enim michi propositum est in auribus tuis nobilitare velle poetarum nomen, quod tibi ignobile videri ea demum summa michi nobilitas videtur. Cui autem hec narrem? Nescio an te ridiculosior sim, si asino lyram tangam. Respondebis: 'Audio, sed nichil intelligo'; et poete nomen, nulla unquam, ut modo dicebam, barbarie violatum atque omni ex parte tibi incognitum, violabis plus quam barbarica feritate.

29   Itaque peroportune audies quod cuidam nuper tue professionis homunculo, cum assensu et approbatione multorum, dixi. Cum enim, vestro more, multa contra poetas hisceret potiusquam diceret, nunc poetam Ciceronem nunc Plinium affirmans, quesivi ab eo quid poete nomine crederet importari. Quod cum se nescire non negasset, pro tempore historiam dixi non inamenam cognitu, magnis ab auctoribus relatam, quam tibi quoque dictam puta, siquid omnino aliud quam de febribus audire potes.

30   Hanibal, vir bellicosissimus, bello victus a Romanis, Ephesum ad Antiochum, regem Syrie, profugerat; a quo letissime susceptus,

Romans,[17] or by Cicero, whom despite your possible objections I would confidently call the prince of Latin authors?

I have placed here Cicero's very words, lest you suspect me of 27 changing or adding something: "The greatest and most erudite men have told us that, while the pursuit of other subjects consists of teaching, precepts, and art, a poet excels by his own nature, is inspired by the strength of his mind, and is filled with a sort of divine spirit. This is why Ennius rightly calls poets sacred, for they seem to be commended to us by the gift and favor of the gods. So let the name of poet be sacred to you, most humane judges, and never violated by barbarism."[18] Thus Cicero writes, adding many weighty observations in this vein; and thus too other writers, whose innumerable observations I intentionally omit.

I don't propose here to ennoble the name of poets in your ears, 28 for what seems ignoble to you seems to me of the highest nobility. But to whom am I speaking? If I play the lyre to an ass, I may become more ridiculous than you. You will reply: "I am listening, but I don't understand a thing." The name of poet was "never violated by barbarism," as I just noted. But being completely unknown to you, it will be violated by your ultra-barbaric savagery.

Hence, it is quite fitting that you hear something I recently said 29 to one of your petty colleagues which met with general agreement and approbation. He was muttering rather than speaking, as you physicians do; and in his long diatribe against the poets, he called both Cicero and Pliny poets. So I asked him what he thought was meant by the word "poet." When he confessed that he didn't know, to suit the occasion I told him an entertaining story that great authors have recounted. Consider it told to you as well, if you can listen to anything that doesn't involve fevers.

After the valorous general Hannibal had been defeated by the 30 Romans, he fled to the Syrian king Antiochus at Ephesus, where he was warmly received. Antiochus burned with hatred against the Romans, and could imagine no more ideal counselor than Han-

eo quod Romanorum odiis estuanti nullus usquam consultor tam
ydoneus videbatur, in summo honore apud illum erat. Contigit autem Phormionem quendam nomine, secta perypatheticum, qui ea
tempestate literarum scientia clarus habebatur, simul illic forte
apud regem esse. Ad quem, si vellet, audiendum invitatus Hanibal, dum fama viri tactus annuisset. Seniculus non indoctus et, ut
homo grecus, audax et verbosus. Phormio, credo, extimans nichil
se melius in presentia tanti ducis nichilque convenientius loqui
posse, materiam rei militaris ingressus, in plures horas sermonem
continuum protraxit. Denique dum qualiter sit ductandus exercitus, qualiter instruenda acies, qualiter capiendus castris locus,
quando signum pugne dari, quando cani receptui conveniat, postremo que ante prelium, que in prelio, que ve post prelium sint
servanda, copiose disseruisset, secutusque esset plausus omnium,
quesitumque ab Hanibale quid sibi etiam videretur de illo sapientie professore, 'Multos,' inquit ille, 'stultos delirosque senes
vidi; nullum tamen quo magis delectarer quam sene hoc, quippe
qui tam multa de rebus incognitis loqueretur.'

31   Quo dicto facete admodum et illius et vestram impudentem
notavit audaciam. De omni enim materia loqui vultis, vestre professionis obliti que est, si nescis, urinas et que nominare pudor
prohibet contemplari; nec pudet insultare his quibus virtutum
atque animi cura est. Eleganter de hoc Phormione loquens Cicero,
'Quid,' inquit, 'aut arrogantius aut loquacius fieri potuit, quam
Hanibali qui tot annis de imperio cum populo Romano, omnium
gentium victore, certasset, grecum hominem, qui nunquam castra vidisset, nunquam denique minimam partem ullius publici
muneris attigisset, precepta de re militari dare?' Quanquam non
omnino par tua et Phormionis causa, multoque iustius ego te rideo, quam illum risit Hanibal. Ille enim de rebus licet experientia

nibal, to whom he showed the highest honors. It happened that the king's court included a certain Peripatetic philosopher named Phormio, a man renowned in that age for his vast culture. Hannibal was invited to hear him speak if he wished; and impressed by the philosopher's fame, he agreed. The little old man was not without learning, and being Greek, he was impudent and verbose. I suppose Phormio thought that in the presence of such a great general the best and most suitable topic was military science. So he launched into this topic and continued his lecture uninterrupted for several hours. At great length, he discussed how to lead an army, how to form a battle line, and how to select a campsite; when it is best to signal attack, and when retreat; and what procedures to follow before, during, and after battle. When he had finished, the entire audience applauded. But when Hannibal was asked what he thought of this professor of wisdom, he replied: "I have seen many fools and crazed old men, but no one has delighted me as much as this old man, who talks at such length about topics unknown to him."[19]

This remark wittily censured the presumption shown by that fellow and by all you impudent physicians. You wish to speak about any subject whatsoever, and forget your own profession which, in case you don't know, means inspecting urine and other things that shame forbids me to mention. But you are not ashamed to insult people who are concerned with virtue and the soul. In describing Phormio, Cicero elegantly writes: "Could anything have been more arrogant or verbose than for this Greek, who had never seen a camp or taken the least role in public affairs, to teach military science to Hannibal, who had for many years fought for empire against the Roman people, the conqueror of all nations?"[20] In fact, you are not in exactly the same situation as Phormio, and I laugh at you more justly than Hannibal laughed at him. Phormio spoke about matters which were outside his personal experience, but which he knew about through his reading.

ignotis, at saltem lectione cognitis loquebatur; tu de his rebus loqueris quarum non tantum usu atque arte es indoctus, sed ingenio
etiam prorsus indocilis.

32   Hanc historiam cum illi contentioso homini narrassem, quod
erat ipse senex, sibi dictum credidit, quasi et senium ei et stultitiam exprobrassem; itaque vehementer excanduit. Tu qua etate sis
non satis scio; nisi quod delirare sepius solent senes, non quidem
omnes, sed quorum iuvenilis etas vilibus curis et obsceno artificio
acta est. Quo autem ingenio sis, michi incognitum esse noluisti.
Audiens, ergo, te video mordendi avidum, sed ignorantia torpen-
tem, algentis more aspidis, coactum virus non posse diffundere,
nisi quod in finem, multo irarum attritu terrifice concalescens,
neque tamen tam morsu quam sibilo metuendus, in me calcaneo-
tenus erigeris.

33   Ubi, scilicet, Boetium Severinum adversus sacras Pyerides testem citas atque, ut testimonio fidem queras, cautissimus disputator, patritium illum vocas, quasi de pretura vel consolatu questio
sit, et quasi non multi testes, licet minime patritii sint, hac in re
multum Boetio preferendi. Verum absit ut huius vel alterius fide
digni hominis testimonium recusem: ad inquisitionem veri omne
genus studiosorum hominum admitto, mechanicis duntaxat exclu-
sis. Ille igitur quid? Ab egrotantis cura scenicas meretriculas philosophico procul arcet edicto. Vive, bellator egregie: universam poesim letali iaculo transfixisti. Certe siquid eorum de quibus tam
temerarie disputas didicisses, scires scenicam illam quam Boetius
notat, ipsos inter poetas in precio non haberi.

34   Non autem vidisti, cece, quod iuxta erat, licet id ipsum literis
tuis ignoranter insereres. Quid enim ait? 'Veris eum Musis curan-
dum sanandumque relinquite'. Hee sunt Muse quibus, si qui usquam hodie supersunt, poete gloriantur ac fidunt, quarum ope

You speak about matters in which you not only lack any practical or theoretical learning, but which your intellect could not possibly grasp.

When I told this story to the contentious physician, he believed   32
it was directed at him, since he too was an old man. And he exploded with rage, as if I had reproached him for both his senility and his silliness. Now, I'm not sure how old you are. Old men often dote—not all of them, to be sure, but certainly those who have spent their youth in base pursuits and an unseemly trade. But you wanted me to know how smart you are. So, listening to your words, I see that you are eager to bite, but being torpid with ignorance, like a cold viper, you are unable to pour forth your store of venom. But in the end, the friction of your wrath warms you up in a horrible way, and you rise up as far as my heel, more terrifying for your hiss than your bite.

When you cite Boethius as a witness against the holy Pierian   33
Muses, O most wary disputant, you seek to make his testimony credible by calling him a patrician. As though the issue were one that concerned a praetor or a consul, and as if there were not many better witnesses than Boethius who are by no means patricians! But let me not reject the testimony of any person worthy of credence. In the search for truth, I admit every kind of learned man. I exclude only those who practice mechanical arts. What does he say, then? By philosophical edict, Boethius banishes the "harlots of the stage" far from a patient's care.[21] Live on, famous warrior! You have thrust your deadly dart through all of poetry. Of course, if you had learned something about the subject of your dispute, you would know that the "harlots of the stage" censured by Boethius enjoy no esteem even among poets.

Blind man, you overlooked the rest of the passage, even though   34
you ignorantly quote it in your letter. What does he say? "Leave him to be tended and healed by the true Muses."[22] These are the Muses in which the poets glory and trust, if there are any poets

non egra corpora mactare, sed egris animis succurrere didicerunt. De quibus si loqui velim, donec cerebro humido ac fluenti tanta res insideat, amens ero. Neque enim vel Amphionis vel Orphei citara tam duram silicem movere posset, neque tam hirsutam tigridem lenire.

35   Quas tu atque omnes id genus fictiones, veluti vero adversas, mira plebei artificis temeritate condemnas. In quibus, tibi tuique similibus studiose abditus, allegoricus sapidissimus ac iucundissimus sensus inest, quo fere omnis Sacrarum etiam Scripturarum textus abundat; quas te animo irridere non dubito, sed supplicium times. Quam ob rem feram equo animo te poetis, quos ignoras, vanitate notissima insultantem, idque michi alicuius bone spei argumentum fuerit, si tibi valde displiceam. Cur autem indigner audere te aliquid adversum me, cum adversus Cristum, si impune liceat, sis ausurus, cui Averroym, tacito licet iudicio, pretulisti? Scis quod non mentior, quamvis aliud verbo clames. Cesset pene metus: profecto, ut sciolus videaris, esse voles hereticus.

36   Sed ad fictiones, quas carpebas, redeo. Audi ergo quid Lactantius, vir et poetarum et philosophorum notitia et ciceroniana facundia et, quod cunta trascendit, catholica religione clarissimus, primo suarum *Institutionum* libro ait: 'Nesciunt qui sit poetice licentie modus, quousque progredi fingendo liceat, cum officium poete in eo sit, ut que vera sunt in alia specie obliquis figurationibus cum decore aliquo conversa traducat; totum autem quod referas fingere, idest ineptum esse et mendacem potiusquam poetam.' Stupes, belua: nunquam, puto, istud audieras.

37   Mentiri vobis liquimus; quodque gravissimum mendacii genus est, mentiri summo cum discrimine damnoque credentium. Id si

left on earth. With their aid, poets have learned not to slaughter ailing bodies, but to treat ailing souls. If I chose to speak about the Muses until this great topic penetrated your watery and dissolute brain, I would go mad. The lyre of Amphion or Orpheus could neither move so hard a rock, nor tame so shaggy a tiger.

With the astounding temerity of a lowly craftsman, you con- 35 demn these fictions and all others of this kind as contradicting the truth. Yet they contain a judicious and delightful allegorical sense which is purposely hidden from you and your ilk. This allegorical sense also abounds in nearly every text of the Holy Scriptures, but I have no doubt that you would like to mock them, except that you fear punishment. I shall therefore patiently allow you, with your notorious vanity, to insult poets you don't know. And your great dislike for me will confirm my high hopes. Why should I be indignant that you dare to challenge me? If you could, you would dare to challenge Christ, to whom you privately prefer Averroes.[23] You know that I am not lying, even though your words proclaim something else. Suppose fear of punishment were to cease; you would choose to be a heretic in order to appear a know-it-all.

But I return to the fictions that you were criticizing. Listen to 36 Lactantius, a man who was famed for his knowledge of poets and philosophers, for his Ciceronian eloquence, and for his Catholic faith, which surpasses everything else. In the first book of his *Institutes* he writes: "They don't know the limits of poetic license, or how far one may go in inventing fictions. Yet the poet's function consists in translating actual truths into different forms using indirect and figural language with a certain decorum. But to invent everything you write down is to be a fool or a liar rather than a poet."[24] You are dumbfounded, you beast. I guess you never heard this before.

I leave lying to you physicians, including the worst kind of lie, 37 one that causes great peril and harm to those who believe it. If you don't believe me, ask the common people, who have made such be-

michi non credis, vulgus interroga, cui et illud in proverbium versum est, ut apertissime mentienti dicant: 'Mentiris ut medicus.' Poete—neque enim me hoc nomine dignari ausim, quod tu michi, demens, ad infamiam obiecisti—poete, inquam, studium est veritatem rerum pulcris velaminibus adornare, ut vulgus insulsum, cuius tu pars ultima es, lateat, ingeniosis autem studiosisque lectoribus et quesitu difficilior et dulcior sit inventu.

38   Alioquin, si tibi falso persuades—quod quidam indocti solent, qui quod consequi nequeunt execrantur—ut scilicet poete officium sit mentiri, illud tibi consequenter persuadeas velim: esse te poetarum maximum, cuius prope plura mendacia sunt quam verba. Ultro tibi meonius senex cedet, victus cedet Euripides, cedet Maro, vacuus tibi Elicon linquetur, indecerpta laurea illibatusque castalius fons.

39   Sed expergiscere, si potes, lippientesque oculos aperi: videbis poetas raros quidem, natura rerum disponente ut rara quelibet cara simul et clara sint. Videbis eos gloria et nominis immortalitate fulgentes, quam non sibi tantum, sed et aliis peperere, ut quibus ante alios perituris[3] consulere nominibus datum est, et quorum adminiculo ipsa etiam virtus eget, non equidem in se ipsa, sed in eo quod habet cum tempore et cum oblivione certamen. Te vero cum tuis nudos videbis omni vera laude, vanitatibus obsitos obrutosque mendaciis.[4]

40   Hec non adversus medicinam—quod sepe testatus sum—neque adversus excellentes medicos, qui irasci non debent si, semper rari, nostra sint etate rarissimi, sed adversus te delirantesque similiter dicta sint. In quibus illud forte mirabitur quispiam, quod libellum pro epystola remisi. Sed meminisse conveniet facilius infligi vulnus quam curari, et citius dici convitia quam repelli.

havior proverbial. They tell a patent liar: "You lie like a physician."
As for the poets — and I hardly dare dignify myself with this
name, which you in your madness cast at me as a reproach — the
poets, I say, strive to adorn the truths of the world with beautiful
veils. In this way, the truth eludes the ignorant masses, of which
you are "the very dregs."[25] But for perceptive and diligent readers,
it is just as delightful to discover as it is difficult to find.

By contrast, if you are wrongly persuaded — as is the custom   38
of some ignorant people, who detest what they cannot comprehend — that the poet's function is to lie, then I hope you will persuade yourself that you are the greatest of poets, since you utter almost more lies than words. The defeated poets will gladly yield
to you: the old man of Maeonia, Euripides, and Virgil.[26] Helicon
will be left empty for you, the laurel wreath unplucked, and the
Castalian fount untasted.

Wake up, if you can, and open your bleary eyes. You will see   39
that poets are quite rare. Nature ordains that all precious and famous things are rare. You will see the poets resplendent with glory
and immortal fame, which they win not only for themselves but
for others as well. It is their task above all else to preserve names
that would perish; and even virtue itself needs their aid, not for its
own sake, but in its struggle against time and oblivion. But you
will see yourself and your colleagues stripped of all true praise,
mired in vanities, and buried in lies.

As I have often said, my remarks are not directed at medicine,   40
nor at excellent physicians, who should not be angered that they
are so rare in this age, when they have always been rare. My remarks are directed against you and your raving colleagues. Some
people will perhaps be surprised that I answered your letter with a
treatise. But they must remember that it is easier to inflict a
wound than to cure it, and that insults are more quickly spoken
than rebuffed. Thus, the defense of Demosthenes is longer than

Ideoque et maior defensio Demosthenis quam Eschinis accusatio est, et longior Ciceronis quam Salustii invectiva.

41   Hactenus hec; cetera in tempus aliud reservo. Nolo enim putes me lacessiti stili et iustissime indignationis aculeos, more apium, in vulnere reliquisse. Experiere iterum, cum voles, quid inter ingenium et ingenium, quid inter calamum et calamum intersit. Illud verendum: ne, dum per abruta distractus, multumque huic tue ridiculose eloquentie intentus, in insuetis conflictationibus tempus teris, his, quos pecunia pariter ac sanitate spolias, magni periculi causa sim. De hoc tamen ipse videris; ego michi quicquid attentaveris ad cumulum glorie ascribam. Alta petentibus non semper quies; sed eorum sepe, qui sine gravi periculo vinci possunt, optanda rebellio est.

42   Si bene dixisses, audisses bene. Audisti autem non quod ego loqui solitus, sed quod tu meritus audire. Sile parumper et rumina, et tibi ipsi da veniam, qui cepisti. Verum ego satis: ne sanus sim, si diutius tecum loquar, qui — quod ridiculum omne supergreditur — Medicine nomine mortem michi literarum tuarum in fine denuncies. Ad quam differendam Medicina forte aliquid, tu profecto nichil; ad celerandum vero quamplurimum conferre potes. Preclarum sortitus artificium: longevis corpusculum scis expedire langoribus. Certe ipsa michi vivas, modo voces habeat, Medicina grates actura sit, si eorum presentem infamiam fando nudavero, qui antiquam illius gloriam novis erroribus extinxerunt.

the accusation of Aeschines, and the invective by Cicero is longer than that by Sallust.

But enough on this topic. I reserve the rest for another time. 41 Don't think that, like a bee, I left in the wound all those stinging barbs that were provoked by attacks on my style and by my just indignation. When you choose, you will discover what a difference there is between one intellect and another, between one pen and another. You must beware one thing. While you waste your time in unfamiliar conflicts—led astray on rough paths, and obsessed with your ridiculous eloquence—I may pose a great danger to those patients whom you despoil of both their money and their health. But that is your concern. For myself, I shall consider all your attacks as adding to my glory. People who pursue high goals do not always find rest. But an insurrection is often to be wished for on the part of those who can be conquered without grave danger.

If you had spoken kind words, you would have heard kind 42 words. Instead, you heard what you deserved to hear, not what I usually write. Remain silent for a while and reflect. Forgive yourself for starting this quarrel. I have said enough. I would be mad to speak longer with you. At the end of your letter, you transcend the ridiculous by serving notice of my death in the name of Medicine. Medicine might do something to postpone my death; you can do nothing. Indeed, you can do much to hasten it. You have been blessed with a famous trade: you know how to deliver a body from the diseases of old age. If Medicine could speak, I am sure she would thank me warmly for exposing the infamy of today's physicians, whose modern errors have extinguished her ancient glory.

43 Habes unde michi perpetuo gratias agas: de muto et elingui, argu-
tulus atque facetulus factus es. Disertissime Ypocras, nescis quantum huic calamo debeas. Ecce iam prosam scriptitas: cito facies
carmina; iam hymnos incipis balbutiendo contexere: boni ingenii
puer eris. Imo vero, stulte senex et ignare, multo consultius tacuis-
ses, non ut ideo philosophum te probares, sed ut ignorantiam saltem tuam silentio velares. Tacendo enim latere poteras, loquendo
non potes. Lingua animi sera est; hanc tu, nullo ad ostium pul-
sante, nescio cur movisti, tenebricosam fedamque pectoris tui domum omnibus aperiens, quo melius semper clausa mansisset, nisi
quia dementiam diutius occultare difficile est. Credo non legeras
quod scriptum est: 'Stultus quoque si tacuerit, sapiens reputabi-
tur; et si compresserit labia sua, intelligens.' Bene Socrates, cum
decorum adolescentem tacitum vidisset, 'Loquere,' inquit, 'ut te videam': non tam in vultu putabat videri hominem, quam in verbis.

44   Ecce, locutus es: vidimus te; iamque si milies taceas, videmus.
Voluisti apparere, et multis, quos latere poteras, esse ludibrio.
In quod—gaude, prepotens orator—externa ope non eges; nullo
opus est indice, operose mus: tuo te prodis inditio, tam late tristis
male coagulati eloqui fumus manat. O ridiculum animal—vole-
bam dicere—librum scribis; rectius dixerim quod tue professionis
est proprium: aromatum lenta fedas involucra; et ubi periculosis

Book II

You have good reason to thank me forever. You have been changed   43
from a mute, voiceless creature into a clever, witty little fellow.
Most eloquent Hippocrates, you don't know how much you owe
to my pen. Behold, now you're scribbling prose! Soon you'll be
writing verses, and shortly you'll start to stammer out hymns.
You'll be a talented little lad. Yet in fact, foolish and ignorant old
man, you would have been wiser to remain silent, not in order to
prove that you are a philosopher, but to cloak your ignorance in silence. Remaining silent, you could have gone unnoticed; speaking,
you cannot. The tongue is the latch of the mind. Though no one
knocked at your door, for some reason you released it and opened
to all the dark and foul dwelling of your soul. It should have remained forever closed, though it is difficult to hide madness for a
long time. Apparently you hadn't read what is written: "Even a
fool, if he holds his peace, will be counted wise; and if he closes
his lips, he is esteemed a man of understanding."[27] On seeing a
handsome but silent youth, Socrates wisely said: "Speak, so that I
may see you."[28] For he thought that a person is revealed less by his
face than by his words.

Behold, you have spoken, and we see you. Now, even if you fall   44
silent a thousand times, we still see you. You chose to appear and
to be mocked by many who might not have noticed you. Rejoice,
all-powerful orator, that you require no one's aid to do this! You
need no informer, O industrious mouse. You betray yourself by
your own evidence as the noxious fumes of your ill-curdled eloquence spread far and wide. O ridiculous animal, I was going to
say: You are writing a book. But let me speak more correctly, using
the terms of your profession. You are befouling the sticky wrap-
pers for your spices. In your work, you often use dangerous hocus-
pocus to prescribe the deaths of your wretched patients. And you

ambagibus dictare soles miserorum mortes, utque vilia magno
constent fallasque licentius, radicibus nostri orbis imponere peregrina vocabula, ibi nunc, ut tibi videtur, philosophicos locos, ut
ego sentio, tabificos iocos scribis.

45   Sed ut libri formam habeant, versutus opifex, distinguis in partes; et forsitan victor eris: apothecarii scripsisse te librum dicent.
Quid ni igitur exclamem? Accurrite philosophi, accurrite poete,
accurrite studiosi, quicunque usquam scribendis libris operam da-
tis, accurrite; vestra res agitur: mechanicus libros scribit, penitusque verum fit illud Sapientis Hebrei: 'Faciendi libros nullus
est finis.' Quid enim fiet si mechanici passim calamos arripiunt?
Actum est: ipsi boves, ipsique lapides scribent; nilotica biblus non
sufficiet. Siquis est pudor, dimittite illam literatis; vos, si glorie cupiditate tangimini, in vento et aqua scribite, ut ad posteros fama
citius vestra perveniat.

46   Quid querar? quid eloquar? quid dicam? Desinite, queso, qui
papiros arte conficitis, quique tenues in membranas cesorum ani-
malium terga convertitis: etruscis expiandum sacris infaustum et
infame monstrum incidit. Quid enim bicipitem puerum aut quadrupedem miramur? Quid obstupescimus mule partum, tac-
tumque de celo templum Iovis, aut sub nubibus visas faces? Quid
ethneis vaporibus ardens equor et cruentos amnes, imbremque la-
pideum, aut siquid tale in annalibus veterum reperitur? Habent
suum secula nostra portentum: mechanicus etiam libros arat.

47   Quis non Roscio deinceps artis histrionice librum donet? Erat
et ille mechanicus, sed insignis, ingenioque promeritus non modo
maximorum ducum gratiam, sed ipsius quoque familiaritatem
atque amicitiam Ciceronis. Mulcebat ille oculos: mechanicus nos-

often graft foreign names on roots from our soil, so that you can charge a high price for such rubbish and cheat your patients more easily. Just so, now you are writing what you think are metaphysical notions, but what I consider mephitical nothings.

To give them the shape of a book, O wily craftsman, you divide them in various sections. Perhaps you will succeed, and the shopkeepers will say you have written a book. Naturally, I shall exclaim: "Hurry, philosophers! Hurry, poets! Hurry, scholars! Hurry, everyone who writes books anywhere! Your business is at stake. A mechanic is writing books." The words of the Hebrew sage have come true: "Of making books there is no end."[29] What will happen if mechanics everywhere take up the pen? We're done for. Even cattle and stones will write. All the papyrus of the Nile will not suffice. But if you have any shame, leave papyrus to the learned. And if you are moved by a desire for glory, write in the wind and on the water, so that your fame may reach posterity more swiftly.

Why do I complain? How shall I speak? What shall I say? Cease, I pray, all of you who manufacture paper, and who transform the hides of slaughtered animals into fine parchment. A monstrous omen, ill-fated and ill-famed, has occurred, one that must be expiated with Etruscan rites. Why are we amazed by a child with two heads or four feet? Why do we gape at a mule giving birth, at Jupiter's temple struck by lightning, or at torches that appear in the clouds? Why gape at plains aflame with Etna's steaming lava, rivers of blood, rains of stone, or any such wonder found in the ancient annals? Our generation has its own portent: a mechanic scribbling a book.

Who would begrudge Roscius his book on the actor's art?[30] He too was a mechanic, but he was outstanding; and his wit won him both the favor of great generals and the intimate friendship of Cicero. Roscius charmed one's eyes; this mechanic wounds our

45

46

47

ter aures vulnerat; agebat ille quod placeret omnibus: hic quod nulli.

48 Aut quis coquine magistrum indignetur Apitium suam literis disciplinam inserere? Cur enim inter culinas non scribatur? Inter latrinas scribitur: cognatas res esse nomen arguit. Aut cur non inter epulas libri fiant? Inter urinas fiunt, ad quas stilo celebrandas florentissima artium rethorica captiva perducitur, et que populos moderatur, inque animis regum regnat, inter medicos ancillatur.

49 Sed queso te, philosophie atque artium domine: quo animo Tullius rethoricam tot voluminibus tantoque studio tractasset, si futuram talis ingenii servam sciret? Quam vero, non dicam servam, sed familiaris etiam tua sit, si aliunde nescirem, abunde quidem artificiosus et hybleo melle dulcior orationis tue textus insinuat. Certe, quod scolis omnibus est notum, rethorice facultatis officium est 'apposite dicere ad persuadendum, finis persuadere dictione'.

50 Quanta autem illud arte facias, quanta hoc felicitate perficias, qui te semel audierit non ignorat. Sed ista suum locum invenient: nunc a primordiis inchoandum. Excuset autem prolixitatem mei sermonis tue ignorantie magnitudo, de qua aut nichil omnino dici debuit aut parum dici non debuit.

51 Prima quidem libri tui pars de te ipso agit: quis qualis ve tu sis. Iam id ipsum caute. Sciebas te incognitum, nisi tabellionum more de te ipso aliquid loquereris, atque ita qua scriberes autoritate constaret. 'Qui sim,' inquis, 'perlecto hoc toto iam nosces opusculo'. O magne vir, nimis humiliter de te sentis: imo vero confestim accepto in manus opusculo novi te, quem et ante noveram.

ears. The acting of Roscius pleased everyone; this fellow's actions please no one.

Who would resent it if the master chef Apicius put his art in writing? Why can't one write in pantries? Some people write in their privies. (The nouns show that the two things are related.) May not books be written while feasting? Some write amid feces and urine samples. And in order to celebrate these with the pen, they enslave the distinguished art of rhetoric, which usually governs peoples and rules the minds of kings, but now serves as a handmaid to physicians. 48

Let me ask you this, O lord of philosophy and the arts. If Cicero had known that rhetoric would become the slavegirl of such an intellect, how enthusiastically would he have treated it in his many volumes of intense study? Now, if I didn't know that rhetoric was, if not your slavegirl, at least your intimate friend, the fact is made abundantly clear by the artistic construction of your discourse, which is sweeter than Hyblean honey. Clearly, as is known in every school, "the function of the rhetorical art is to speak aptly with a view to persuading, and its end is to persuade by one's speech."[31] 49

How artistically you perform, and how felicitously you succeed, is obvious to anyone who has ever heard you. But such topics must await later treatment. For now, we must begin at the beginning. The prolixity of my discourse is excused by the magnitude of your ignorance. On such a great topic, one must either say nothing at all, or avoid saying too little. 50

The first part of your book deals with you: who you are and what you are like. How prudent! You knew you would be unknown unless, like a notary, you said something about yourself and thus established the authority by which you write. "When you have read all of my little work," you say, "you will know who I am." O great man, you judge yourself too humbly. In fact, as soon as I picked up your book, I knew you as I had known you before. 51

Sed nunc scientiam tuam omnem funditus detexisti, et, ut scriptum est in Psalmo, 'denudasti fundamentum eius usque ad collum'.

52   Quid autem de te dicas, quem te facias audiamus: 'Sum,' inquis, 'medicus'. Audis hec, medicine repertor, Apollo, vel amplificator, Esculapi? 'Consequenter et philosophus'. Audis ista, Pithagoras, qui nomen hoc primus omnium invenisti? Flete repertores artium: fines vestros proterit asinus infulatus, non se modo philosophum, sed philosophiam insuper suam iactans. 'Philosophia nostra,' inquit. Heu, quid hoc est? Peiora sunt audienda, si vivimus. Iam, ut suspicor, ad finem seculi propinquamus. 'Erunt signa in sole et luna et stellis'; hoc signum in Evangelio non fuit: quando asinus philosophabitur, celum ruet. Quid vis dicam? Iam philosophie misereor, si tua est; sed meo periculo iurare ausim, nescire te quid sit esse philosophum. At ne omnia unam in partem congeram, multa etiam nunc de hac re tecum loqui habeo. Premisi autem hoc, ut scires apud me philosophum te non esse.

53   Quid vero, quid deinde intulit audax stultus? Se his artibus armatum, non tantum corporis sed animi vitia curaturum. Venite huc qui egrotatis: salus non semper ex Iudeis est; adest semibarbarus sospitator. Et me superbum vocitas! Relege nunc epystolam illam meam que te furere fecit, et faciet mori: quando ego vel philosophiam vel poesim meam, quando me aut philosophum aut poetam dixi, aut aliud quidquam, quam tuorum morum et ingenii contemptorem, quod michi non modo licitum sed debitum rebar? Verecunde se solius rethorice magistrum dicit Augustinus: tu te philosophum dicis ac medicum; addis et tertium: rethorice dominum. Quartum licet addere, postquam titulis gaudes: cloaca es

But now you have revealed all your knowledge to the very bottom. As it is written in the Psalm: "You have stripped bare his foundation unto the neck."[32]

Let us hear what you say, and how you present yourself: "I am a physician." Do you hear this, Apollo, who discovered medicine, or you Aesculapius, who enlarged it? "Consequently, I am a philosopher." Do you hear this, Pythagoras, who first invented this name? Weep, discoverers of the arts! Graced with a priestly fillet, an ass tramples your territory, boasting that he is a philosopher and claiming philosophy for his own. "Our philosophy," he says. Alas, what is this? We shall hear worse if we live longer. By now, I suspect, we are approaching the end of the world. "There shall be signs in the sun, and in the moon, and in the stars."[33] But this sign is not found in the Gospel: when an ass can philosophize, the heavens will fall. What can I tell you? I feel sorry for philosophy, if it belongs to you. But at my peril I would go so far as to swear that you don't know what a philosopher is. Let me not pile up all my arguments on this single point. I have many things to discuss with you on this subject. But I have prefaced my remarks in this way so that you know that I don't consider you a philosopher.

And then, what is the next thing adduced by this presumptuous fool? Armed with these arts, he claims that he can cure not only bodily maladies, but those of the soul as well. Come hither, all you who are sick! Health and salvation do not always come from the Jews. Here is a half-barbarian savior. And you call me proud! Read my letter again. It made you rage, and now it will make you die. When did I claim philosophy or poetry as mine? When did I call myself a philosopher or poet? When was I anything but a scorner of your character and intellect—a role I deemed not merely legitimate, but my obligation? In his modesty, Augustine merely calls himself a master of rhetoric.[34] You call yourself a philosopher and a physician; and then you add a third title: lord of rhetoric. Since you delight in titles, we may add a

52

53

41

magna quidem, ut est apud Senecam, et profunda. En quod ad primam tui gloriosi partem operis modo responsum velim.

54   Secunda apologetici tui pars de me erat, cuius in cognitione si falleris, non mirror. Quid enim non tibi alius videri possit, cum tu tibi philosophus videaris? Dixisti equidem: 'Philosophus sum'. Tam hoc verum quam quod sequitur; tam philosophus tu quam ego ambitiosus, arrogans, superbus. Nunquam michi, fateor, cum populo convenit; tanta tamen animi securitas est, ut iudicem populum non recusem. Quos honores ambierim, et non potius spreverim oblatos? Quid michi unquam arrogaverim? Ubi superbe me gesserim? De qua re et dictum est aliquid, et plusculum dicere est animus.

55   Loquar autem tibi iam, non ut adversario procaci et infesto, sed ut homini, nescio tamen an rationis ullum vestigium habenti; et dicam quod, ut puto, non intelliges, quoniam vicinarum rerum nedum ydiotis, sed doctis etiam laboriosa discretio est. Sed dicam clarius, quam dici soleat, ut, si non intellexeris, cerebri tui non stili mei vitium accusetur. Audi ergo: superbo libertas omnis superbia videtur; sapiens vero inter superbiam fidutiamque discernit, et scit largiter referre quo animo quid dicatur aut fiat. Hinc ille vir optime sibi conscius, dum in publico peroranti populus obstreperet, 'Tacete,' inquit, 'melius ego unus novi quid reipublice expediat, quam vos omnes'. Quod, ut animose, sic vere dictum, aliquos qui ad superbiam traherent fuisse, a vulgi moribus non abhorret; docti autem generose fidutie ascribunt.

56   Scipio, ille vir maximus, qui famosum primus agnomen ex Africa reportavit, capitalem causam dicturus, primo quidem die

fourth: you are a large and deep sewer, as Seneca says.[35] This, then, is my reply to the first part of your glorious work.

The second part of your apology deals with me. I am not surprised that you misjudge me. What will you think of others if you think yourself a philosopher? Indeed, you said: "I am a philosopher." This is just as true as what comes next. You are as much a philosopher as I am "ambitious, arrogant, and haughty." Now, I admit that I never agree with the people, but my self-confidence is great enough to allow the people to judge me. What honors did I solicit? What honors did I not spurn when offered? What arrogant claims did I ever make for myself? When did I conduct myself with pride? This subject has already been addressed, but I intend to say more about it.

I shall not address you now as an insolent and hostile opponent, but as a human being, even if I'm not sure whether you have even a trace of reason. And I shall say things that you will not understand, I think. For discernment in matters close to us is difficult even for the learned, not to mention the ignorant. But I shall speak more clearly than usual. In this way, even if you don't understand, people will blame the shortcomings of your brain, rather than of my style. Hear me, then. A proud man thinks that any form of independence is pride. But the wise man distinguishes between pride and self-confidence, and can generously account for the intention behind someone's words or deeds. Thus, when the people jeered at his public address, a famous man who was conscious of his own merit replied: "Silence! I alone know the interests of the state better than all of you."[36] If some have imputed his courageous and truthful words to pride, their view reflects the habits of the mob. Scholars ascribe them to his noble self-confidence.

When the great Scipio, who was the first to win his famous surname from an African campaign, was accused of capital crimes, he undertook his own defense. On the first day of the trial, "with-

54

55

56

'sine ulla criminum mentione' ut ait Livius, 'orationem adeo magnificam de rebus a se gestis est exorsus, ut satis constaret neminem unquam neque melius neque verius laudatum esse'. Quid ergo? Nunquid in proprio laus ore sordebat? Audi: 'Dicebantur,' inquit, 'ab eodem animo ingenioque quo gesta erant, et aurium fastidium aberat, quia pro periculo, non in gloriam referebantur'.

57   Secundo autem dicende cause die, dum acrius urgeretur, non modo sordidam et obsoletam vestem reorum more non induit aut submisse iudicum misericordiam imploravit, sed cum forte, revolutis annis, dies esset quo ipse bello punico secundo, periculosissimo omnium atque gravissimo, supremam manum imposuerat, virtutis ac felicitatis proprie recordatus, et ob hoc conscientie fidutia evectus, victricem capiti lauream imposuit, testatusque eo die litibus ac iurgiis abstinendum propter diei illius anniversarium honorem, quo ipse olim cum Hanibale et Carthaginiensibus bene ac feliciter decertasset, agendasque potius deis grates precandosque ut populo Romano semper sui similes duces darent, desertis in curia accusatoribus atque iudicibus, favente ac prosequente universo populo, Capitolium et deorum templa triumphantis in morem circuivit, non minus gloriosus civium reus quam fuerat hostium triumphator.

58   Rem notissimam narro, tuis licet ab auctoribus non tractatam. Nec cuiquam dubium esse potest quin inaniter effusa laudatio turpiter sonuisset, nisi eam natura rerum et quedam quasi veri necessitas extorsisset. Si leonem latratibus excitatum dixi, si me omnia preter virtutem et bonam famam solere contemnere arroganter tibi

out even mentioning the charges against him," Livy writes, "he began such a magnificent speech about his own accomplishments that it was quite clear that no one had ever been praised more finely or more truly."[37] What then? Did these praises seem sordid in his mouth? Hear what Livy says: "He recounted his deeds with the same courage and genius with which they were achieved; and no one's ears were offended, for he retold them in the context of his trial, rather than to win glory."[38]

On the second day of the trial, when he was more savagely attacked, he did not wear sordid and tattered clothing like a defendant, nor did he humbly implore the judges' mercy. It happened to be the anniversary of the day on which, many years before, he had concluded the second Punic War, the most dangerous and arduous of all Roman wars. Recalling his own virtue and good fortune, and elevated by trust in his own good conscience, he placed a victor's laurel wreath on his own head. To honor the anniversary of the day when he had fought bravely and successfully against Hannibal and the Carthaginians, he declared that everyone should abstain from trials and disputes, and instead give thanks to the gods, praying that they might always grant Rome generals like himself. Leaving behind both his accusers and the judges, and followed by the cheers of the entire people, he made the rounds of the Capitoline Hill and the temples of the gods as if celebrating a triumph. In this way, the defendant Scipio triumphed no less gloriously over his fellow citizens than he had over his wartime enemy.[39]

I recount this tale as well-known, even if your authors don't discuss it. No one can doubt that empty effusions of praise would have sounded base, unless they were required by the course of events and, as it were, by the necessity of the truth. If you think I spoke arrogantly when I called myself a "lion roused by your barking," or when I claimed to despise everything but virtue and my good name, then you are mistaken, as you are in many things. You

57

58

videor locutus, falleris ut in multis. Neque enim insolenter me locutum noveris, sed fidenter, ut te ipsum, vel gravi rugitu experge-
factus, agnosceres. Quid enim putas, aut quid ais? Nonne iam,
precor, erubesceres, nisi ruborem tuus ille letheus et immedicabilis
pallor excluderet?

59   Nonne iam, tacitus saltem ac pallidus, recognoscere incipis—
quod dixisse tibi iterum videor insolenter—quantum inter ingenium et ingenium, quantum inter calamum et calamum intersit?
Profecto autem ille, quem michi adsumpsisse videor, virtutis amor
ac laudis non otiose iactantie est, sed eo pertinet, ut scias me ab ea
quam michi obiectabas adulatoris infamia remotum, cum cesset
illa cupiditas que tuam et multorum linguas docuit adulari. 'Sed
hec turpiter, quamvis vere, proprio ex ore sonuerunt.' Iam responsum habes: tunc id vere diceres, quando nulla iusta causa sed
inanis tantum glorie studio dicerentur. Nunc non magis pro mei
nominis, quam pro ipsius defensione veri, dicta ferre debebis equa-
nimiter, et tibi parcere quod in me arguis, Cato ultime, gravissime
morum censor.

60   Adde quod ego non michi scientiam aut gloriam esse, sed earum cupiditatem, neque me virtutem aut bonam famam habere
dixi, sed optare vel, quod minus est, non spernere. Quid hic, oro,
tam superbum notas, nisi quia tibi res insueta est aliquid preter
pecunias optari vel amari? Accingere quicquid potes calumnie:
preter desiderium et affectum boni nichil michi tribuo, quibus qui
caret sibi et aliis inutilis vivit, si tamen dicendus est vivere qui op-
timarum sensu rerum eget, pessimarum passionibus abundat.

61   Accedit quod et hec et siquid in me laudabile aut siquid penitus
boni est, quamvis id tibi, doliture invide, in oculos ingesserim ut

must know that I did not speak with insolence, but with assurance so that, roused by my deep roar, you would understand your true self. What do you think, or what do you say? At this point, I ask, surely you would blush, if your fatal and irremediable pallor did not prevent your blushing?

If only in pallid silence, surely you begin now to understand 59 "what a difference there is between one intellect and another, and between one pen and another." (Here again you will think my words insolent.) In truth, my claim to love virtue and praise does not spring from idle boasting. Rather, it serves to warn you that I am free of the disgraceful adulation of which you accuse me. For I have none of the greed that has instructed your tongue and the tongues of others in the arts of adulation. "Yet even if true, such claims sound disgraceful in one's own mouth." Here you have my reply: You would be right to say this, if my claims were inspired by a desire for empty glory, rather than by a just cause. So now you must patiently bear what I say in defending the truth itself as much as my good name. And you must spare yourself these accusations against me, O latter-day Cato and most severe censor of morality.

What's more, I did not say that I possess knowledge or glory, 60 but merely a desire for them. Nor did I say that I have virtue or a good name, but that I wish for them, or at least don't spurn them. Why then, pray, do you censure me as a proud man, unless you think it unusual to desire or love something besides money? You may arm yourself with any sort of calumny. The only claim I make for myself is a keen desire for the good. Lacking this desire, one's life is harmful to oneself and to others—assuming that there exists a living being who lacks an awareness of the highest things, but abounds in passions for the lowest.

Moreover, as my conscience is my witness, if I possess anything 61 praiseworthy and good—which I have thrust before your eyes, O envious one, to cause you pain—I praise not myself but God, who

doleres, teste tamen conscientia, non inde me sed auctorem omnis boni Deum laudo, neque in me ipso glorior, sed in illo ad quem omnia refero preter defectus erroresque meos, quos michi imputo. Scit ipse me verum loqui. Ecce ut in Psalmo centesimo quadragesimo quarto ait Augustinus: 'Inventum est quomodo et me laudare possim et arrogans non sim'.

62 Verum ut de poetis, quibus ut canis ad lunam latras, aliquid immisceam, apud Virgilium Eneas, de se interrogatus, inter cetera quid ait?

Sum pius Eneas fama super ethera notus.

Idem apud Homerum respondisse novimus Ulixem. Ad hoc responsum num tu atque alii, qui nichil de vobis loqui verum simul ac magnificum potestis, vel superbe dictum ab Ulixe atque ab Enea, vel turpiter fictum ab Homero ac Virgilio clamaretis. Sed doctiores excusant, quia scilicet ut ignorantem alloquens laude propria pro inditio sit usus, et fuerit ea sibi necessitas, non voluptas.

63 Quid autem? Nonne ego etiam ignoranti loquor, ignoranti se, ignoranti me, ignoranti omnia? Equidem si vel te vel me vel aliquid boni nosses, nunquam me nil tibi dicentem, aut dicere cogitantem, nullam tui notitiam habentem aut habere cupientem, tam importunis, ut repetam quod te premit, latratibus excitasses. Cuius te hodie puto peniteat, sed tumor animi retrahere pedem vetat. Anxius itaque ridiculusque luctator, alienam, quod michi forsan credis incognitum, in tuis responsiunculis opem queris; piget hinc cepisse; pudet inde desinere: ita tergiversaris et incertus heres, atque, ut est in antiquo proverbio, auribus lupum tenes.

64 Unum hoc loco preterire noluerim quod inter superbias meas ponis: indignum te michi visum qui in meis opusculis scribereris.

is the source of all good things. Nor do I glory in myself, but in Him to whom I ascribe all things except for my defects and errors, which I claim as my own. He Himself knows that I speak the truth. Here is what Augustine says in his commentary on Psalm 144: "I have discovered a way to praise myself without being arrogant."[40]

At this point, let me cite something from the poets, at whom   62
you bark like a dog at the moon. In Virgil, when Aeneas is asked who he is, he replies: "I am dutiful Aeneas; my fame is known in the heavens above."[41] And we know that Homer's Ulysses replied in the same way.[42] Concerning their replies, you and others like you, who can say nothing about themselves that is both boastful and true, will exclaim that Ulysses and Aeneas spoke out of pride, or that Homer and Virgil invented unseemly fictions. But more learned readers will excuse them. Addressing ignorant strangers, these heroes cited their own fame to reveal their identity, and they spoke out of necessity rather than self-gratification.

Well, then? Am I not likewise addressing an ignorant person,   63
one ignorant of yourself, of me, and of everything? For if you knew yourself, or me, or anything good, you would never have roused me with your importunate "barking"—to repeat the expression that grieves you. I was not talking to you, nor was I thinking of doing so. I had no knowledge of you, nor did I seek any. Today you regret your act, I think; but your swollen pride forbids you to turn back. An anxious and ridiculous combatant, you seek outside help in your silly little replies, perhaps thinking that I don't notice. On the one hand, you are sorry you began; on the other, you are ashamed to quit. So you hang back and hesitate in your uncertainty. As the ancient proverb says, "You're holding a wolf by the ears."[43]

At this point, I must mention one of the charges you list   64
among my acts of pride, that I didn't think you worthy of mention in my writings. Be careful, please. If you think the opposite, this

Vide autem, queso, ne inter tuas potius numerandum sit, si tibi contrarium videatur. Scripsi aliqua, nec desino aut unquam desinam, dum hic digitus calamum feret. Sed, omissis aliis, ne me rursum de me ipso magnifice loqui dicas, scribo de viris illustribus. Que non ausim dicere: iudicent qui legent; de quantitate pronuntio: haud dubie magnum opus multarumque vigiliarum et, si non ab auctore, certe a subiecta materia nominandum. Nichil ibi de medicis nec de poetis quidem aut philosophis agitur, sed de his tantum qui bellicis virtutibus aut magno reipublice studio floruerunt, et preclaram rerum gestarum gloriam consecuti sunt.

65   Illic, si tibi debitum locum putas, dic ubi vis inseri: parebitur; sed verendum est ne quos ex omnibus seculis illustres, quantum hac ingenii paupertate licuit, in unum contraxi adventu tuo diffugiant, teque ibi solo remanente, mutandus libri titulus, neque *De viris illustribus* sed *De insigni fatuo* inscribendum sit. Si audire me velles, petendum potius ab Apuleio madaurensi ut in libro philosophantis asini locum habeas, vel orandus Plautus ut alicubi in *Amphytrione* te collocet, ubi sillogismos tuos explicans probes Birriam nichil esse, magnoque animo contemnas quod in meis locus tibi desit opusculis, cum et alibi aptius esse possis, et ego nullum in tuis operibus locum queram.

66   Illud quoque locus hic exigit: quam certe sit tutum de veritate tecum colloqui, quamque tranquillum, vide. Stantibus enim scriptis obstrepere et insidiari non pudet, quid faceres inter verba volantia? Quid est autem quod inter multa dixisti, me senectutem detestari? Nichil hoc falso falsius. Nemo me reverentior senectutis, nemo qui etatis illam partem pluris faciat, qui eam equiori animo complectatur, si iam adest, si appropinquat, expectet. Sed ita demum apud me venerabilis est senectus, si ab honestis pro-

may rather be counted among *your* acts of pride. I have written various works, and as long as my fingers can hold a pen, I shall not cease to write. Now, to leave aside other works, which might cause you to say that I am boasting again, I am writing a work called *On Illustrious Men*. I don't dare say what it's like. My readers will judge. As for its quantity, I will affirm that it is quite a large work, the fruit of many scholarly vigils, and it takes its name from its subject, not its author. It does not discuss doctors, poets, or philosophers. It only deals with men who were distinguished by their military prowess or profound dedication to the state, and whose deeds won them outstanding glory.

If you think you have a rightful place in it, tell me where, and I 65 shall comply. In it, I have assembled illustrious men from every century, as well as my poor wit allowed. Yet I am afraid that your arrival may drive them away, and that, if you alone remain, the title of the book will have to be changed from *Illustrious Men* to *The Egregious Fool*. If you want my advice, you should ask Apuleius of Madaura to assign you a place in his book about the ass that philosophizes.[44] Or you should beg Plautus to place you somewhere in his *Amphitryon*, so that by your syllogisms you can prove that Birria does not exist.[45] Then you could haughtily disdain my little works for not including you. You would fit in better elsewhere, and I would not ask for a place in your works.

This topic calls for another observation. Consider how safely 66 and calmly one may discuss the truth with you. In dealing with written texts, you are not ashamed to bawl protests and set traps. So how will you act in a spoken exchange? Why do you claim, among your many other charges, that I detest old age? Nothing could be falser than this falsehood. No one is more reverent of old age than I, or values this time of life more. No one more serenely embraces it if it has already come, or awaits it if it approaches. But in my view old age is only venerable when it has developed from honorable origins to attain something more glorious than wrin-

gressa primordiis gloriosum habet aliquid preter rugas. In libro *Sa-pientie*, siqua tibi talium cura esset, hanc sententiam invenisses: 'Senectus,' inquit 'venerabilis est'. Tecum sentiebat, nisi addidisset: 'non diuturna neque numero annorum computata'. Ecce, iam de-sentire incipit. Quid ergo? 'Cani sunt autem,' inquit, 'sensus homi-nis, et etas senectutis vita immaculata'.

67   Cato ille senex famosissimus, qui etatis huius apud Tullium patronus ac laudator inducitur, dum senectutem operosam sem-perque aliquid agentem dixisset, addidit: 'Tale scilicet quale cuiusque studium in superiore vita fuit'. Et iterum: 'In omni ora-tione,' inquit, 'mementote me eam senectutem laudare que funda-mentis adolescentie constituta sit'. Si hunc, philosophe, reprehen-dis, et me reprehende; secum enim sentio, nec contrarium dixi. Prorsus mutare scripta mea non potes, quippe nec ego ipse qui condidi ; postquam in publicum exierunt, mei iuris esse desierunt. Quid igitur dixi? 'Delirare sepius solent senes'. Hinc calumnie ra-dix. Sed procede; noli subsistere; lege quod sequitur: 'Non quidem omnes, sed quorum iuvenilis etas vilibus curis et obsceno artificio acta est'. Id forte verbo tu verum negas, facto autem probas esse verissimum. Itaque deum testor me nichil aliud quam te unum, dum id scriberem, cogitasse. Qualis enim senex esse poterit qui mentiendo, blandiendo, fallendoque consenuit?

68   Stultorum senum ingens copia est. Scis quare: quia sapientum iuvenum immensa penuria; qui autem inter vitia senuerunt, quo ad metam propius accedunt, eo magis insaniunt. Hos ego sepius delirantes dixi, nec mirum si ex his in quibus usque in finem vivi-tur senectus, ultima vite pars, plus impressionis accipit quam re-lique, et si densiores in imum sordes suo more descendunt. Prop-ter eandem causam, qui in virtute per omnem vitam delectati sunt, in senectute mirabiles retroacti temporis fructus legunt; et tum

kles. In the Book of Wisdom (if you cared about such things), you would find this sentence: "Old age is venerable."[46] Its author would have been agreeing with you, if he hadn't added: "not for length of time or measured by number of years."[47] See, he begins to disagree. What then? "But understanding is gray hair for anyone," he says, "and a blameless life is ripe old age."[48]

In Cicero's dialogue, the famous old man Cato is presented as defending and praising this age. After calling old age active and continually busy, he adds: "Naturally it resembles the interests of a person's early years."[49] And later he says: "Remember that throughout my discourse I praise old age that builds on the foundations of adolescence."[50] If you reprove Cato, philosopher, reprove me as well. I agree with him, and have said nothing to the contrary. You can in no way alter my writings, nor can I myself, who penned them. For once they were published, they ceased to belong to me. What did I say, then? "Old men often dote." This is the root of your slander. But keep going; don't stop. Read what follows: "Not all of them, to be sure, but those who spent their youth in base pursuits and an unseemly trade." Your words may perhaps deny that this is true, but your deeds show that it is absolutely true. As God is my witness, you were the only one I had in mind when I wrote this. What kind of old man can we expect from a person who has grown old while lying, flattering, and deceiving?

There is a vast supply of foolish old men. You know why: because there is an immense dearth of wise young people. And people who have grown old amid vices become more insane as they approach their end. Such people, I said, are quite often crazy. It is no wonder that their lifelong vices stamp the final stage of life, old age, more deeply than the other stages. And it is no wonder that the densest impurities customarily sink to the bottom. For the same reason, people who have taken lifelong delight in virtue will in their old age reap the marvelous fruits of their past. They are

67

68

maxime felices sunt, dum esse desinunt, ut incipiant esse perenniter. Hos autem constat esse rarissimos, horumque est illa quam dicis venerabilem senectutem. Reliqui vero, qui medium locum tenent, ut plus minus ve in hanc aut in illam partem inclinati vixerunt, sic in senectute meliores aut peiores fiunt.

69   Itaque mille varietates et morum infinita distantia, nec senum modo sed iuvenum, quorum omnium naturas bene, nisi fallor, et Aristotiles in *Rethoricis* et in *Arte poetica* descripsit Horatius. Hec michi nunc senum distinctio probatur, que si tibi non placet, scribe aliam, summe philosophorum, quam in marmoribus incidamus. Certe, ut ad stultos senes redeam, nunquam tu prima etate, quanquam semper temeritate notabili fueris, ausus fuisses garrire ista tam stolide, etsi in animo habuisses: solet enim adolescentie familiaris esse verecundia. Crede igitur michi, nil stulto turpique sene molestius, cui et stultitia puerilis superest et senilis accessisse videtur autoritas.

70   Sed ego iam hinc ordinem tuum amplius non sequar, quippe qui nullo modo michi videor ordinatius dicturus, quam si longissime discesserim ab ordine libri illius quem michi serio, ut asseris, remisisti, ut aperte conicerem qualis tibi repentinus ac tumultuarius stilus esset si lucubratus ac serius talis est. Pessimum quidem in primis hominum genus, summoque studio declinandum, quibus est stultitie mixta calliditas. Quia vero cum huiuscemodi adversario michi negotium sciebam, satis, ut puto, nequam tibi iustam mordendi materiam loquendo tribuerem, circumspexi.

71   Crebro igitur dixi non me medicine detrahere — sed tibi loquor improprie: nichilo detrahi nichil potest; sed intelligitur quid velim — protestationem humilem ac veram, superbe mendax, reicis; credo non aliam ob causam nisi ut indignitate ipsa exacuas et irri-

happiest when their happiness ceases on earth, and begins to be eternal. It is clear that such people are extremely rare, and it is they who enjoy what you call venerable old age. As for old people who steer a middle course, they become better or worse in old age, according to the direction they have tended to follow in life.

Hence, human character displays a thousand varieties and in- 69 finite differences in people both old and young. Unless I am mistaken, all of these natures have been well described in Aristotle's *Rhetoric* and in Horace's *Art of Poetry*.[51] I approve of their distinction between old men. But if you don't like it, write your own, O mighty philosopher, that we may carve it in stone. Let me return to old fools. Even though you have always displayed notable temerity, as a youth you would not have dared to chatter so stupidly, even if you had intended to; for adolescence is attended by modesty. Believe me, then: there is nothing more obnoxious than a foolish and shameful old man who retains his boyish folly while seeming to have acquired the authority of age.

From now on, I shall no longer follow the order of your argu- 70 ments. Indeed, I believe that the only way to write in orderly fashion will be to depart as far as possible from the order of your book. Yet you assert that you sent me this book quite earnestly so that its solemn and studied prose would allow me to imagine clearly what your extempore and improvised style would be like. Now, the worst kind of people, whom we should avoid at all cost, are those who combine cunning and folly. But since I knew I was dealing with just such an opponent, I was rather careful, I think, to avoid writing anything that might justify your censure.

As a result, I repeatedly said that I am no detractor of medi- 71 cine. (But I am speaking imprecisely. Nothing can be detracted from nothing. Still, my meaning is clear.) You reject this humble and true protest, O proud liar. I believe your sole purpose is to goad me with indignities and to provoke me to say things I would prefer not to say. But you will never induce me to condemn noble

tes ad dicendum quod dixisse nolim. Nunquam tamen efficies ut
odio turpium pulcra condemnem; quinetiam medicinam ipsam
michi feceris cariorem, quod tu eam dehonestas ac polluis. Scio, ut
dixi, non inutile artificium, auxilioque caduci corporis inventum.
Quid hoc prohibet, illudque simul verum esse te cum tuis falso
illam violare cognomine? Sophista ridicule, equitator arguitur,
equum laudas: extra propositum versaris.

72   Sed nullum excipio? imo aliquos. 'Et quos?' inquies. Ad tribunal pretoris urbani res agatur: quis me ad hoc coget respondere, si
nolim? Non est nunc aliis gratificandi locus: tecum michi res est.
Novi mores tuos, quos si tu eque nosses, odio tibi esses. Si scribam quod sentio, compatriotis aut amicis meis me blanditum dices; nichil est enim quod non simile sibi fingat vilis ac venalis animus: qualem se novit, tales alios opinatur, qua nulla inter homines
cecitas maior. Mensura vestra, fatui, cunta metimini: nec gigantem
nanus edificans nec formica cogitat elephantem. Aliquot, ni fallor,
medicos veros novi, et ingenio et ea que in omnium artium arte
ponenda est discretione pollentes, quibus, ut arbitror, eo molestior
es quo te pressius intuentur, et professionem suam tua non ambi-
gunt ignorantia deformari.

73   Esto autem: nullos norim medicos, nullos exceperim; quid vetat
esse aliquos ignotos michi, presertim studiis longe aliis vacanti, et
sanitatem corporis debenti non medicis, sed nature? Utcunque se
res habeat, nichil ego aut adversus medicinam, aut adversus minis-
trum eius locutus inveniar, licet (ut soleo) cuiuslibet artificii cor-
ruptores lingua forsan liberiore percusserim, quorum in turba te

things simply because I loathe unseemly ones. Rather, by dishonoring and polluting medicine, you make me value it even more. I am aware, as I said, that medicine is a useful trade, devised to aid our mortal bodies. What prevents this from being true, while it is also true that you and your colleagues defile medicine under a false name? O ridiculous sophist, you praise the horse when it is the rider who is being blamed. You completely miss the point.

Don't I make exceptions for any physician? Yes, for a number 72 of them. "Who are they?" you ask. Let the case be brought before the local judge. Who will force me to reply against my will? This is not the place for me to gratify others. I am dealing with you. I know your character; if you yourself knew it, you too would hate it. If I write what I feel, you will say that I am flattering my friends and compatriots. A vile and venal mind imagines that everything resembles itself. It believes that everyone has the character it sees in itself—which is humankind's greatest blindness. Fools, you measure everything by your own measure. When a dwarf builds, he doesn't imagine a giant; nor does an ant imagine an elephant. Unless I am mistaken, I know several true physicians who possess superior intelligence and the discrimination that is essential in all of the sciences. But I think that the closer they examine you, the more you distress them. They see clearly that your ignorance disgraces their profession.

But let's suppose that I didn't know any physicians or make any 73 exceptions. Why shouldn't there be some good ones unknown to me? I spend my time on far different studies and owe my health to nature rather than to physicians. In any case, no one will find that I said anything against medicine or its practitioners. Of course, as I often do, I may have too freely censured those who corrupt their trade, and I may therefore have wounded you as you hid unrecognized in their midst. Spare me, O philosopher, I pray. I was not prosecuting you, but ignorance, and not every form of ignorance. For if the ignorance of the proud must be trampled underfoot, the

latitantem et incognitum vulneravi. Parce, oro, philosophe: non te, sed ignorantiam persequebar; eamque non omnem. Calcanda est enim ignorantia superborum, humilium sublevanda. Si in hac insectatione publica singulariter es lesus, veniam merui, quia ignorans feci. Gaudes nunc, superbe, quasi affusus supplicem. Rideo potius ineptias tuas: ignorantium infamiam ad te trahis, cum tibi doctissimus videaris. Imo vero ignorantie tibi conscius extreme, quicquid ignorantibus obicitur tibi merito dictum putas et quod dissimulando fieri poterat alienum, impatientia tuum facis.

74   Quid vero si paucos medicos, quid si paucissimos dicam? Non hoc ad artis infamiam, sed ad gloriam spectat. Nonne debuerat generosus animus, difficultate non territus sed accensus, ad ipsum nomen gloriose paucitatis assurgere, seque in partem rare laudis accitum credere? Sed certe id non omnibus datum est, et paucissimorum prorsus ingeniorum ea raritas est amica. Quam ob rem ubi nobilis exultasset spiritus, plebeius ingemuit. Cur? queso. An et hic fallor? An mentior? Profecto non solum hodie, sed semper raros ingeniosos, rarissimos sapientes fuisse nemo est qui dubitet, nisi qui nunquam oculos vel in etatem suam intenderit, vel ad antiqua reflexerit.

75   Stulte — nolo enim qui sis excidat — stulte, inquam, et insane, vix ulla unquam etas vel ingeniorum vel virtutum fuit egentior quam nostra, sive id culpis hominum accidit, sive fato — si tamen eo nomine uti licet, et non rectius Dei voluntas seu providentia dici debet in sermone catholico — sive denique, quod tu fabulam putas, mundus, iam senescens et ad extremum vergens, more senescentis hominis piger ac frigidus, in sua operatione lentescit. Et tamen hac ipsa etate nulla ingeniorum penuria prestabit, ut tuo ingenio locus fiat. Frustra te contentionibus implicas, frustra te ingeris duello non tuo, quasi aut ego — quod nunquam cogitavi — me-

ignorance of the humble should be relieved. If you were particularly wounded by this general polemic, I deserved pardon because
I acted in ignorance. You rejoice now, O proud one, as if I fall
prostrate in supplication. But in fact I laugh at your folly. You
bring on yourself the disgrace of the ignorant while thinking yourself most learned. In fact, you are aware of your extreme ignorance, and rightly think that any charge of ignorance applies to
you. By dissembling, you might have left such charges to others;
but in your impatience you have made them your own.

So what if I say there are few good physicians, or even very few   74
of them? This is not said to the profession's disgrace, but to its
glory. Shouldn't a noble spirit, one that is inspired by difficulty
rather than frightened by it, rise up at the very mention of a glorious few, and consider itself summoned to share in this rare fame?
Clearly, such spirit is not given to everyone, and such excep-
tionality is congenial to only a few minds. Hence, where a noble
spirit would have exulted, a plebeian spirit merely groaned. Why?
I ask. Am I mistaken here too? Am I lying? Truly, no one can
doubt that both now and always the gifted have been rare, and the
wise rarest of all—no one, that is, but a person who has never
taken a good look at his own age or reflected on the past.

O fool—I won't let you forget what you are—O fool and mad-   75
man, I say, practically no age has been so poor in genius and virtue
as our own. The fault may lie with people or with fate, if one may
use the term. It would be more correct to use the language of Ca-
tholicism and to speak of God's will or providence. Or it may
be—and you'll think this a fable—that the world has grown old
and totters toward its end; sluggish and cold like an aging person,
it slows in its activity. Still, not even the dearth of genius in the
present age can create a place for your genius. It is pointless for
you to engage in disputes, and pointless for you to interfere in
someone else's duel. You act as if I were verbally assaulting medicine—which never occurred to me—or as if medicine would not

dicinam verbis aggrediar, aut ipsa non a quolibet opprimi malit, quam a te defendi, qui eam et exercendo violas, et opprimis defendendo. Incassum ergo niteris: nullus usquam fame tue locus est. Nemo te clamoribus tuis noscet, nisi quos, elusos verbis inanibus aut peregrinis medicaminibus infectos, tui memores in perpetuum effecisti.

76   Duo hic, antequam ad maiores illos tue criminationis insultus venio, leviter exufflanda sunt, quo dixisse me fingis an somnias: nonnunquam contra verum medicos certare, eosque non semper curare. Utrunque enim magnis sudoribus excusas. Sed ubi, precor, id dixi? Excute epystolam meam, quod, puto, propter veritatis odium graviter facis. Certe ego, illam relegens, horum nichil invenio. Et de medicis quidem alias, de te michi nunc sermo est, hostis Ypocratis, pestis egrorum, dedecus medicorum, de te michi nunc sermo est.

77   Dico igitur, si non dixi, non te contra veritatem interdum de industria vel iocandi experiendique studio certare, in quo stultissime gloriaris, sed sola semper ingenii cecitate; neque te interdum non curare, quod cupide profers quasi clipeum inscitie pestilentis, sed passim sanos in morbum, egros in mortem agere. Hoc dico. Ad hoc michi respondeas velim, hoc rethorice, serve tue, patrocinio excuses. Si enim negas, contentione dimissa populum testem voco. Nota quippe negantibus, ut veritas ingerenda, sic subtrahenda est verbose altercationis occasio. Scio quid nunc cogitas: popellus infelix, et consilii semper inops, frustra tot malis admonitus ad te redit. Quem igitur ignorantie tue in testimonium adduco? Nempe

prefer being ruined by someone else, rather than defended by you. Your practice violates it, and your defense ruins it. Your efforts are wasted, since there is no place for your fame. You cry out, but no one recognizes you, except the patients who were deceived by your empty words or poisoned by your exotic medications. They will always remember you.

Before I address the greatest insults in your allegations, I must 76 lightly brush off two alleged remarks of mine that you fabricated or dreamed up, namely, that doctors sometimes fight against the truth, and that they do not always cure their patients. You make heavy weather over both charges. But tell me, please, where did I say that? Examine my letter, as I presume that in your hatred of the truth you do earnestly. When I re-read my letter, I find nothing of the kind. While I have written about physicians elsewhere, here I am speaking of you, O enemy of Hippocrates, plague of the sick, and disgrace of physicians! I am speaking about you.

Let me say this, then, if I didn't say it already. You fight against 77 the truth, but not occasionally and on purpose because you wish to jest or, as you foolishly boast, to experiment. You fight against the truth all the time because of the sheer blindness of your intellect. Nor did I say that you occasionally fail to cure patients, as you eagerly claim to shield your pestilent incompetence. I say that you consistently drive healthy people into illness, and sick people to their death. This is what I say. Reply to this, if you please. Excuse *this*, using your servant rhetoric to plead your case. If you deny it, I'll terminate our dispute and summon the people as witness. In order to thrust the truth upon those who deny the obvious, one must remove any opportunity for wordy arguments. I know what you are thinking now: that the rabble, unhappy and clueless as ever, will ignore the danger signs and return to you. Then whom shall I summon as witness to your ignorance? No one but the people. No one else. And I won't change my mind. Both things are true. From experience, the people know your incompe-

non alium, neque sententiam muto: utrunque verum est. Inscitiam tuam populus novit expertus; idem a te poscit auxilium. Gaude, stulte insolens: iam non medicus tantum, sed Deo simillimus evasisti. De quo scriptum est in Psalmo: 'Cum occideret eos, querebant eum'. Ille quidem suscitare poterat; et tu potes, ut dicis. Quid enim sonat aliud quod inter inanes ridiculasque iactantias effudisti: 'vestra sepe opera homines velut a mortuis suscitatos'? Quantum abfuit quin te deum faceres? Sed expecta: ego te ante huius ludi finem in concilio deorum ponam et divinitate tua dignum, si potero, nomen inveniam.

78   Nunc propositum sequor. Impune occidis, ergo, cum suscites. Sed omissis prophanis et fine carentibus nugis tuis, cur hoc populus faciat, si me roges: facit hoc prudenter ut reliqua. Sapientis est verbum: 'Stultorum infinitus est numerus'. Eorum vero que a talibus fiunt, frustra ratio inquiritur. Si penitus causam petis, illa vera est quam affert amicus medicorum, Plinius, quem tu spernis ignotum et quam ego olim posui in epystola illa ad Clementem papam unde tota ista lis oritur. 'In hac,' enim ait, 'sola artium evenire, ut unicuique se medicum profitenti statim credatur, cum sit periculum in nullo mendacio maius'. Mox ex persona populi loquens: 'Non tamen,' inquit, 'illud intuemur, adeo blanda est sperandi pro se cuique dulcedo'.

79   Hec est causa que te populo, quem interimis, forte commendat, notissimosque defectus tuos cogit interim oblivisci, dum ab ardenter optantibus inconsulteque sperantibus salus queritur, ubi mors est. Tanta est spei humane pertinacia, sic in animis miserorum re-

tence; yet the same people seek your aid. Rejoice, insolent fool. No longer merely a doctor, you have become almost like God, of whom the Psalm says: "When he killed them, they sought for him."[52] God could raise the dead, and so can you, you say. What else can you mean when, amid your empty and ridiculous boasts, you blurt out: "With our help, people have been raised from the dead, so to speak"? How far was this from making yourself into God? But wait. Before this farce is over, I shall place you in the council of the gods; and if I can, I shall devise a name worthy of your divinity.

Now I return to my topic. You kill with impunity, then, while you raise from the dead. Let us leave aside your impious and interminable nonsense. If you ask me why the people act this way, I answer that they do so prudently, as in other matters. Recall the wise man's saying: "The number of fools is infinite."[53] It is pointless to seek the reason behind the actions of such people. If you look deeply, you will find that the true cause is the one I cited in my letter to pope Clement, which was the source of our dispute. Pliny, that friend of physicians whom you spurn in your ignorance, cites this cause, saying: "This is the only profession in which anybody professing to be a physician is at once trusted, although nowhere else is an untruth more dangerous."[54] Then he speaks as one of the people, and adds: "But we pay no attention to the danger, so great for each of us is the seductive sweetness of wishful thinking."[55]

This may be the reason that commends you to the very people you destroy, and that often compels them to forget your notorious shortcomings. With ardent prayers and ill-advised hopes, these people seek health where death is found. So great is the tenacity of human hope, and such the forgetfulness that reigns in the minds of wretches. Relying on such weakness, you have prematurely sent many people to Tartarus. If they returned, they could pass true judgment on you. You are safe from that place, since it is a land

78

79

gnat oblivio, qua fretus multos ante diem in Tartarum premisisti, qui si redeant illi veram de te potuerint ferre sententiam! Sed inde quidem tutus es: irremeabilis est regio. Nolo tamen speres latere superstites: notus es publice et, puto, doctos frustra tentabis; ceterorum strages minime flenda est. Quod si forte doctos aliquot turbe miscueris, et idcirco dicas illos a mortuis suscitatos, quoniam, ut ait Cicero, hec nostra 'que dicitur vita mors est', et quia huius vite finis melioris vite principium est bonis, plane verus esto, me plaudente, philosophus. Sed absit ut tale aliquid cogitare valeas aut loqui. Illud itaque verius: omnes qui evadunt tribuis tibi, omnes qui pereunt nature, ut semper habeas unde glorieris et gaudeas; miseris autem tuis nunquam desit unde tristentur et lugeant.

80   Quid nunc dicam ad reliqua? Multas tremulas sententias in me vibras, multa levium verborum tela contorques. Quis non metuat cum tanto hoste concurrere? Nichil, scito, nisi verborum tuorum fetores metuo. Si tibi improprie locutus videor, quod verborum dixerim fetores, Cesari parces Augusto quem sic loqui solitum scimus.

81   Dicis in primis me logica carere. Non credo michi rethoricam aut grammaticam interdicas, que logice nomine continentur, quamvis et id iure tuo posses, summum totius specimen barbarismi, sed eam solam, in qua te longe precellere sillogismi tui ostendunt, michi subtrahis dyaleticam, quam logicam vocas. 'En crimen, o indices!' Quod si fateri libeat, possim illustres philosophos proferre hanc ipsam qua carere arguor dyaleticam irridentes, eademque possim apud Ciceronem ostendere clarissimam philosophorum sectam, veteres perypatheticos, caruisse.

82   Sed, o stulte, non hac careo: verum scio quid ei, quid ceteris liberalibus artibus dandum sit; didici a philosophis nullam earum

without return. But you mustn't hope to hide from those who have survived. You are known to the public. It is in vain that you will make an attempt on the lives of learned men. (We scarcely need weep if you slaughter others.) Perhaps you have mixed some learned men in with the mob, and therefore claim to raise them from the dead. For as Cicero says, "our so-called life is really death,"[56] and the end of this life is the beginning of a better life for good souls. So be a true philosopher, then, with my approval. But God forbid that you are capable of thinking or saying such things! We may more truly say that you take credit for yourself when your patients live, and blame nature when they die. In this way, you always have cause to gloat and glory, while your wretched patients never lack a reason to grieve and mourn.

How shall I reply to the rest of your charges? You hurl many 80 shaky arguments at me, and launch many missiles of idle words. Who would not be afraid to engage so great an enemy in battle? Mind you, I fear nothing but the foul stench of your words. If you think I speak improperly in using the phrase "foul stench of words," you must pardon the emperor Augustus, who we know was accustomed to speak in this way.[57]

First of all, you say that I lack logic. I'm sure you don't forbid 81 me rhetoric or grammar, which are linked with the name of logic — even if that would be within your rights as the supreme paragon of all barbarism.[58] No, you only deny me dialectic, which you call logic and in which you excel, as your syllogisms show. "Behold the accusation, O judges!"[59] If I chose to allow the charge, I could cite illustrious philosophers who mocked the very dialectic that you accuse me of lacking. And I could cite Cicero to show that the ancient Peripatetics, a celebrated philosophical school, lacked it as well.[60]

But I don't lack logic, you fool. In fact, I know how much re- 82 spect should be shown to dialectic, as to the other liberal arts. But I have learned from the philosophers that I should not unduly re-

valde suspicere. Equidem, ut eas didicisse laudabile, sic in eisdem senescere puerile est. Via sunt nempe, non terminus, nisi errantibus ac vagis quibus nullus est vite portus. Tibi nobiliorem terminum non habenti, terminus est quicquid occurrit. In summo te felicitatis gradu situm reris, quotiens unum forte fragilem sillogismum, et nichil ex nichilo concludentem, multa cerebri vertigine tota insomni nocte texueris.

83   Tunc in corde tuo dicis, insipiens: 'Non est Deus, neque est altius aspirandum. Quid enim scimus? Plato et Aristotiles, magni viri, de mundo de anima de ydeis litigant; Democritus innumerabiles mundos facit; Epycurus deum nullum et mortalem animam; hanc Pithagoras in girum ducit; sunt qui eam contrahant ad suum corpus, sunt qui eam spargant in corporibus animantum, sunt qui celo reddant, sunt qui circa terras exulare cogant, sunt qui inferos asserant, sunt qui negent, sunt qui unamquanque per se, sunt qui simul omnes animas creatas putent; fuit et qui mirabilius quiddam dicere auderet, siquidem unitatem intellectus attulit dux noster Averrois'.

84   Hec tecum dicis, si tamen nosti hec. Et addis: 'Quis inter ista discernat? Quid michi autem nescio quis Cristus comminatur, quem ipse Averrois diffamavit impune, quod nemo unquam poetarum fecit, imo vero nemo mortalium?' Multa quidem a multis et scribuntur et scripta sunt nec ullus erit finis. Scribendi enim, ut quibusdam placet, insanabilis egritudo est, et velut animi febris quedam ossibus insidens; atqui nemo unquam, vel ante vel multo minus post temporalem Cristi originem, de Cristo nisi summa cum reverentia loqui seu scribere aliquid ausus est; eorum quoque qui hereses et contraria dogmata peperere, non ipse tantorum princeps hostium, Maometus, deterrente scilicet omnium linguas ac calamos nominis maiestate.[5]

vere any of them. Indeed, just as it is admirable to learn these arts, so it is childish to grow old with them. For they are a path, rather than a goal, except for those aimless wanderers who have no destination in life. Since you seek no nobler goal, whatever happens becomes your goal. You think you have reached the height of felicity whenever you spend all night, sleepless and with your brain reeling, to spin out one feeble syllogism that argues nothing from nothing.

Then, like the fool you say in your heart: "There is no God.[61] 83 We must not aspire any higher. What do we know? Great men like Plato and Aristotle argue about the world, about the soul, about ideas. Democritus postulates countless worlds. Epicurus says there is no God and that the soul is mortal. Pythagoras has the soul migrate. Some restrict the soul to its own body; others scatter it among the bodies of living creatures. Some assign it to heaven; others force it to wander in exile on earth. Some assert the existence of the underworld; others deny it. Some think each soul created by itself; others think all souls are created together. Some have even dared to say more amazing things. Thus, our master Averroes asserted the unity of the intellect."

This is what you say to yourself, if you actually understand 84 such things. And you add: "Who can distinguish between these doctrines? How can someone named Christ threaten me? Averroes defamed him with impunity, as no poet or indeed any mortal had done." Many people are writing and have written many books, and of them there will be no end.[62] According to some, writing is an "incurable disease," a fever of the mind that invades the bones.[63] Yet neither before nor much less after Christ's birth into the world did anyone dare speak or write about him without the greatest reverence, including the founders of heresies and opposing doctrines, not even the very prince of these great enemies, Mahomet himself. Evidently, the majesty of Christ's name restrained their tongues and pens.

85   Itaque quidam Deum sed non hominem, alii hominem sed non
Deum, et hominem quidem perfectissimum, ineffabilem, incomparabilem, virgineo natum partu. Qui minus illi tribuunt, prophetam dicunt, preter hunc unum canem, qui non ad lunam, ut vulgo
dicitur, sed rabido ac spumanti ore, contra ipsum solem iustitie la-
trat, summam libertatem et eximium ratus ingenium, si in illud
sacratissimum atque adorandum regibus ac gentibus nomen audeat quod nulla prorsus impietas, nulla unquam temeritas ausa
est. Hunc vos colitis, hunc amatis, hunc sectamini, non aliam ob
causam nisi quia Cristum, veritatem vivam, adversamini atque
odistis. Et quoniam blasphemare quem mundus adorat publice
non audetis, hostem eius sacrilegum ac blasphemum paulominus
adoratis. Livoris ac malivolentie mos inertis, ut cui detrahere me-
tuas, detrahentibus plaudas.

86   Hec hactenus; nec ignoro graviter te laturum, quod tuo detraham semideo. Fer autem equo animo: Deo ille meo detrahit; non
suo, fateor, nec tuo, sed meo, et omnium quos alterius vite spes et
amor tuto tramite dirigit ad felicem metam. At tu, miser, erroneus
post ydolum tuum confragosis anfractibus delectare, venturus ad
finem impietati debitum, ad quem tuus venit Averrois. Interim illi
fide, et innitere, et, quod omnes soletis, dicito: 'Quis resistet illi ingenio? Quis nudam veritatem teget inter tot armata mendacia?
Quid autem tanto viro catholici simplices respondebunt, qui, si ad
contentionem ventum fuerit, sillogismorum cumulis obruentur?
Ecce ego, qui nudiustertius nichil eram, iam magnus esse incipio:
iam sillogismos facio, iam dyaletica mea est. Ad quid aliud natus
eram? Habeo quod petebam: iam disputare non vereor, collocuto-

Some consider Christ divine rather than human. Others con- 85
sider him human rather than divine, but a human being who was
perfect, ineffable, incomparable, and born of a virgin birth. He is
called a prophet even by those who attribute lesser qualities to
him, with the exception of this one dog who barks not at the
moon, as the phrase has it, but who barks with his rabid and
foaming mouth at the very sun of justice. For he thinks it supreme
liberty and extraordinary genius if he dares assail this most sacred
name, worshiped by kings and nations, in ways that no impiety or
temerity ever dared. You physicians worship Averroes; you love
him; and you follow him simply because you oppose and hate
Christ, who is the living truth. Since you do not dare to blaspheme publicly the one whom the world worships, you practically
worship his sacrilegious and blasphemous enemy. This is the way
of spite and cowardly malevolence: when you are afraid to disparage someone, you applaud his detractors.

Enough of this topic. I am aware how ill you will bear my criti- 86
cisms of your demigod. But bear them patiently. He is disparaging
my God — not his own, I grant, nor yours — but my God. This is
the God of everyone who, guided by love and hope in another life,
travels the safe path to the goal of happiness. But you, O wretch,
wander in error after your idol, and delight in uneven and twisting
trails. You will meet the end that impiety deserves, the same end
that your Averroes met. Meanwhile, trust and rely on him, and
say, as all you physicians are wont to say: "Who can oppose his intellect? Who can protect the naked truth in the midst of so many
well-armed lies? What reply to this great man can be made by
simple Catholics who will be buried under piles of syllogisms if
they enter the contest? Look at me. Two days ago I was nothing.
Now I am beginning to be great. Now I am shaping syllogisms.
Now dialectic belongs to me. Was I born to do anything else? I
have what I sought. Now I fear no debate. If I choose, I can prove

remque meum, si libet, asinum probo'. Crede autem michi: multo
facilius te ipsum.

87   Inter hec ergo, male nate homuncio, senuisti, nec pudet vivere
nichil in vita aliud agentem. Discite, miseri, non spernere Cristum: sepe ille vobis quis esset et quid posset ostendit. O infelix!
Vilem tibi metam, dyaleticam, statuisti, ad quam tamen mira via-
toris insania, cum nunquam propinquaveris, pervenisse te putas.
Sed perveneris, sed a tergo liqueris Crisippum. Quid inde tibi nisi
miserum pudendumque? Quid enim stultitia peius? Et que stultitia maior quam totos dies inter puerilia volutari senem; dumque
sero domum redeas, nichil scire; atque has ineptias non ante di-
mittere, quam tibi conclusiunculas meditanti raptim mors impro-
visa concluserit?

88   Illam certe premeditari, contra illam armari, ad illius contemptum ac patientiam componi, illi si res exigat occurrere, et pro
eterna vita, pro felicitate, pro gloria brevem hanc miseramque
vitam alto animo pacisci, ea demum vera philosophia est, quam
quidam nichil aliud nisi cogitationem mortis esse dixerunt. Que
philosophie descriptio, quamvis a paganis inventa, Cristianorum
tamen est propria, quibus et huius vite contemptus et spes eterne
et dissolutionis desiderium esse debet. Que si tu, qui te tumido
vocas ore philosophum, vel semel in etate tam longa, senex deli-
rantissime, cogitasses, nunquam aut te philosophum dicere ausus
esses aut ibi gressum vite figeres ubi nunc figis, aut artificium
tuum quod verbis attollis, rebus opprimens, te ipsum parva pecunia tam turpiter venditares.

89   Philosophi enim, si nescis, pecunias spernunt: philosophiam
venalem facere non potes. Quis enim vendit quod non habet? Si

that my opponent is an ass." Believe me: you'll more easily prove that you yourself are an ass.

Misbegotten little man, you've grown old with such pursuits, 87 and feel no shame at living for nothing else in life. Learn not to spurn Christ, you wretches, for he has often shown you who he is and what he can do. Unhappy man! You have set yourself a base goal, dialectic, and with the traveler's strange madness, you think you have arrived there when you haven't even approached it. But suppose you had arrived, and left Chrysippus behind.[64] What will you gain from this besides misery and shame? What is worse than stupidity? And what stupidity is greater than an old man spending entire days in puerile studies? When you come home in the evening, you know nothing. And you won't abandon these trifles until sudden death abruptly concludes the flimsy conclusions that you are pondering.

Now, to meditate about death, to arm oneself against it, to pre- 88 pare oneself to disdain and accept it, to meet it when necessary, and to exchange with sublime resolve this brief and wretched life for eternal life, for blessedness, and for glory—all these things are true philosophy, which has been simply described as the contemplation of death.[65] Even though this definition was invented by pagans, it belongs to Christians.[66] For they should despise the present life, and in their hope for eternal life, they should desire its dissolution. O crazed old man, you pompously call yourself a philosopher. But if even once in your long life you had reflected on death, you would never had dared call yourself a philosopher. Nor would you have taken the path in life you now take, or sold yourself so basely and cheaply, debasing by your actions the trade you praise in words.

Philosophers spurn money, in case you don't know. You cannot 89 put philosophy up for sale. Who can sell what he does not possess? Even if you did possess philosophy, you could not put it up for sale; rather, philosophy would prohibit you from selling your-

eam haberes, non tu illam ideo venalem faceres, sed illa te venalem esse non sineret. Nunc nec ipsa te honestat, nec tu eam, sed nomen eius turpi avaritia dehonestas. Audis me, sophista ventose — parce, queso, logice nobilis, parce, si te sophistam voco: res ipsa me cogit; ubi enim res video, verbis contrariis fidem non habeo — cornutum michi enthimema perducito; admove ad eculeum: cogere poteris fortassis ut fatear; ut assentiar, nunquam coges.

90   Quomodo ego te philosophum credam cum mercennarium mechanicum sciam? Repeto libenter hoc nomen, quia novi quod nullo magis ureris convitio; non casu, sed sciens sepe te mechanicum voco, et, quo gravius doleas, non primum. Percontare qui mechanica literis mandaverunt: ab illis digito tibi monstrabitur locus tuus. Tu tamen respuis, et philosophus vis videri; quod ut assequaris — ludus risu comico prosequendus — non semel methodi vocabulo usus es. O callidum ingenium! Ad optatum compendio pervenisti: iam philosophum te alii forte dicent; ego enim non si singulas lineas methodis multis infarcias, philosophum te putabo. Inest quidem, fateor, sepe etiam stultorum animis glorie quedam preceps et inconsulta cupiditas: hanc tibi detrahere non possum. Est enim voluntas indomita precipueque dementium.

91   Id scito certissime: nec esse te philosophum, nec videri. Proinde omnium sophismatum et totius logice auxilium implora: michi prius upupam quam philosophum te probabis. Miraris, indocte, et 'Quid michi,' inquis, 'atque upupe simile est?' Nil profecto similius. Volucris galeata est, cristatique verticis, et que pueris aliquid videatur; re autem vera impurissima est avis, victusque fedissimi. Nolo aliquid obscenum loqui, non quidem propter te, qui non horres earum rerum mentionem quarum odoribus delectaris, sed propter eos qui legent ista vel audient. Sciscitare aliquem qui natu-

self. As it is, philosophy does not bring you honor, nor do you bring honor to philosophy. Instead, by your base greed you dishonor her name. Listen to me, you windy sophist. (Pardon me if I call you a sophist, O noble logician, but I am compelled by reality. When I see the facts, I cannot use words at odds with them.) Spin out a sophistical argument.[67] Place me on the rack. You may force me to confess, but never to agree.

How can I believe that you are a philosopher, when I know you 90 are a mercenary mechanic? I gladly repeat this term, since I know that no other reproach stings you more. I often call you a mechanic, not by chance but by choice; and I call you a second-rate one, to cause you more pain. Ask the authors who have discussed the mechanical trades. They will point you to your rightful place there. But you spurn them, and wish to appear a philosopher. To achieve this — a farce that calls for comic laughter — you repeatedly use the word "method." What a crafty intellect! You arrive at your goal by a shortcut. By now, others may be calling you a philosopher. But I shall not consider you a philosopher, no matter how many "methods" you cram into every line you write. Often, I grant you, even the minds of fools can conceive a reckless and precipitous desire for glory. I can't remove this desire from you. For the human will is indomitable, especially in madmen.

Make no mistake. You are neither a philosopher, nor do you 91 seem one. So implore the aid of all your sophistries and all your logic. You'll sooner prove to me that you are a hoopoe than a philosopher.[68] You are surprised, O ignoramus, and ask: "How do I resemble a hoopoe?" The resemblance is perfect. The hoopoe is a bird with a plumed crest, which children think is quite something. But in truth it is very unclean and eats a filthy diet.[69] I don't wish to speak obscenely — not for your sake, since you aren't squeamish about mentioning such things, whose odors delight you — but for the sake of others who read or hear my words. Ask someone who knows about natural philosophy, and he will describe the bird's

ras rerum noverit: dicet tibi avis illius cibos. Inde te moresque tuos inspice, teque ipsum noli fallere—nulla enim pernitiosior, nulla capitalior fraus est, quam que proprium fallit auctorem—videbis te eisdem quibus illam rebus ali.

92   Oro iam, upupa: noli philosophari; citius philosophabitur asellus. Certe preclarus platonicus Apuleius, cuius supra memini, qui, accepto veneno, asinum factum se, ut ait Augustinus, 'aut indicavit, aut finxit,' in eo statu philosophatum se iocando commemorat; philosophantem upupam nulla habet historia. Eia, upupa, fac quod soles: rimare tumulos (cetera sileo); philosophiam linque philosophis. Putabas te philosophum: fallebaris. Philosophus, quod ipsum nomen ostendit, sapientie amator: tu pecunie servus es. Sentis, logice, quam[6] sint ista contraria: sine magno apparatu conclusum arbitror esse te aliud quam putabas.

93   Quid autem in somniis philosophando non audeas, qui colorem medici negando perstringere oculos, vel excusando rationem hebetare non sis veritus? In primis pallorem negas: ita nec oculi nobis sunt nec speculum tibi. Deinde, si pallor sit, illum reipublice imputas; nec excusasse contentus, gloriari incipis, quasi philosophicum sit pallere. Quam dulce, Deus bone, verum philosophie nomen est doctis, cum falsum tibi tam dulce sit, ut inter multa ludicra te philosophice coloratum dicas!

94   Certe pallorem amantibus magister amorum tribuit; unde est illud:

Palleat omnis amans: hic est color aptus amanti

et illud alterius:

Tinctus viola pallor amantium.

diet. Then examine yourself and your character. Don't deceive yourself, for no fraud is more destructive or deadly than self-deceit. You will see that you and the hoopoe feed on the same diet.

I beg you, hoopoe, don't philosophize. An ass will sooner philosophize. The famed Platonist Apuleius, whom I mentioned earlier, took a potion and "either declared or imagined" that he became an ass, as Augustine says.[70] And he humorously records that he philosophized while in that state.[71] But history nowhere records a philosophical hoopoe. Come now, hoopoe, do what you usually do. Scratch and rummage around in burial-mounds, and in other things I won't mention. Leave philosophy to the philosophers. You thought yourself a philosopher, but you were deceived. As the name indicates, a philosopher is a lover of wisdom, but you are a slave of money. You see, O logician, how the two are contradictory. Without elaborate proofs I believe we may conclude that you are not what you thought.

Since you philosophize in your dreams, what won't you dare to do? You did not scruple to deny your physician's complexion by closing your eyes, or to excuse it by dulling your reason. First of all, you deny that you are pale. Evidently, I have no eyes, and you have no mirror. Then, admitting your pallor, you blame it on your public service. Not just content to excuse it, you begin to boast, as if being pale were philosophical. Good God, how sweet the true name of philosophy must be to men of learning! Its false name is so sweet to you that, among other ludicrous merits, you claim you have a philosopher's complexion!

The master of love affairs attributes pallor to lovers, whence his famous verse:

Let every lover be pale: such a complexion is suited to lovers.[72]

And another poet writes:

The pallor of lovers stained with violet.[73]

Sed vester longe alius pallor, et, ut statim audies, aliunde pro-
veniens. Hunc pallorem non ego, non unus aliquis scriptorum
veterum, sed res ipsa vobis tribuit, et omnium mortalium
\<iudicium\> et comune proverbium.[7] Hunc tu negare vis, et quia
non potes, ad philosophos transfers, quasi consorte vitium levatu-
rus. At quia philosophorum principes[8] utriusque lingue preclara
facie fuisse vulgatum est, non tamen hec magnifacio.

95   Sed quecunque fuerit philosophorum facies, tu ne te rursum ingeris, impudentissime hominum, tu ne michi totiens philosophorum cetibus excludendus occurris? Respondebo igitur rursum tibi
quod cuidam tui generis respondit facundissimus quidam vir:
'Barbam,' inquit, 'ac pallium' — addam ego, si libet, et egritudinem
et pallorem — 'video: philosophum non video'. Elegans plane responsio. Quid enim ad philosophiam habitus corporis aut color?
Habitus colorque, ut ita dicam, animi requiritur. Tu de philosopho
preter opinionem tuam propriam ac ridiculam nichil habes. Non
famam certe; non aspectum, quamvis palleas; non incessum: ille
fatuum potius quam philosophum representat. Male tutus esses
inter canes, si tam bene lepus aut cervus quam fatuus videreris.
Postremo, eorum que[9] certius probant philosophum, nichil habes:
non vitam, non animum, non mores, non ingenium, non linguam.

96   Vide quam nullo modo sim passurus ut philosophi nomen
usurpando commacules. Persuasisti autem tibi, ut intelligo, prorsus te esse magnum aliquid. Bene est. Satis est tibi quidem ut gaudeas, nobis ut rideamus. Sin etiam ut credamus vis efficere, facto
est opus: philosophie pars nobilior in rebus est. Quando te contemptorem rerum caducarum videro, cultoremque virtutum, studiosum vere laudis, pecunie negligentem, inhiantem celestibus, a
latrinis divitum exulantem, tunc credere potero quicquid voles.
'Porro enim,' ut Platonem sequens ait Augustinus, 'si sapientia

But your pallor is quite different, and has a different source, as you shall now hear. You physicians don't get your pallor from me or some ancient writer. It is imputed to you by reality, by the judgment of humankind, and by the common proverb. You want to deny this pallor; but since you can't, you blame the philosophers, as if you lessen your defect by sharing it. In fact, it is commonly said that the foremost Greek and Latin philosophers had handsome faces, but I won't overstate the case.[74]

Let us leave aside the appearance of the philosophers. O most 95 shameless of men, are you going to thrust yourself forward again and accost me, when you should be barred on every occasion from the company of philosophers? I shall again reply to you just as a witty man replied to one of your kind: "I see your beard and cloak" — as well as your sickliness and pallor, I might add — "but I do not see a philosopher."[75] What do physical demeanor and complexion have to do with philosophy? What is required is a spiritual appearance and complexion, so to speak. You have nothing of the philosopher but your own ridiculous opinion. You clearly don't have the fame. You don't have the aspect, though you *are* pale. And you don't have the bearing, for yours resembles a buffoon more than a philosopher. If you played a hare or stag as well as you play the fool, you'd scarcely be safe among hounds. In sum, you have none of those things that give clear evidence of a philosopher: not his life, mind, character, intellect, or language.

See how little I will allow you to besmirch the name of philoso- 96 pher by usurping it. Yet you are convinced, as I perceive, that you are really important. Fine. That suffices to make you rejoice, and us laugh. But if you want to persuade us, you need to act: for the nobler part of philosophy consists in deeds. When I see you despise transitory things, cultivate virtue, pursue true praise, ignore money, aspire to heavenly goals, and abandon rich men's latrines — then I shall believe whatever you wish. As Augustine says, echoing Plato, "If wisdom is God, who created all things, as divine author-

Deus est per quem facta sunt omnia, sicut divina autoritas veritasque monstravit, verus philosophus est amator Dei'.

97   Tu igitur, amens vage, intra cubiculum tuum redi; ibi philosophum illum quere, quem tam temerarie profiteris: nusquam invenies. Verum ista celestis et tibi hactenus inaudita philosophia est. Agamus itaque iuxta vetus proverbium: 'Pingui Minerva'; sic enim pingue tuum poscit ingenium. Si comunia illa terrene philosophie aut siquid eorum prestiteris, dignus esto qui iuxta Platonem sedeas, Aristotilem doceas, Socratem celebres, cum Xenophonte contendas. Nunc vero inops omnium que philosophum faciunt, qua fronte philosophicum nomen tibi, sive, ut cepto hereram, venerandum nocturnisque contractum chartis philosophici oris arrogas pallorem?

98   Tuus nempe diurnis pelvibus contractus et marcidus pallor est, quem si tibi vel amicitie affectus, vel pauperum miseratio, vel quam tu fingis reipublice caritas aspersisset, posset non modo non infamis, sed gloriosus etiam videri. Nunc modici fames auri per omnes cloacas miserum trahit, et talem facit, ut tu te ipsum si videas, horrere merito possis ac fugere. Noli ergo reipublice, sed cupiditatibus tuis ascribere quod talis es; neque studium infamare, sed vitam tuam. Proculdubio enim, acutissime philosophe, veram rei causam in aperto positam non vidisti. Et vis videre quid in imo viscerum ac fibrarum lateat? Quod est ante oculos non vides!

99   Ostendam tibi, ego qui non sum medicus et logica careo, palloris tui causam, quam veram esse senties vel invitus. Is per loca atra,

ity and truth have shown, then the true philosopher is one who loves God."[76]

Therefore, O erratic madman, return to your chamber, and 97 look there for the philosopher you so rashly claim to be. You won't find him there. This philosophy is a heavenly one that you have never heard of. So let us proceed "with a slow-witted Minerva," as the ancient proverb says:[77] for that is what your slow wit requires. When you have displayed the common attainments of earthly philosophy, or at least some of them, then consider yourself worthy to sit next to Plato, to teach Aristotle, to extol Socrates, and to debate Xenophon. But since at present you lack everything that makes a philosopher, how can you brazenly usurp the name of philosopher? Or, to stay with my topic, how can you claim the venerable pallor of a philosopher's face, which comes from nocturnal studies?

Your own wasted pallor comes from the chamber-pots you 98 study every day. If it were inspired by the sympathy of friendship, by compassion for the poor, or by the love you feign for the commonwealth, such pallor would not be disgraceful, but glorious. But now it is your greed for a handful of gold that drags you miserably through all the sewers, and changes you into such a creature that, if you saw yourself, you would flee in terror, and rightly so. Don't blame your public service for what you are, but your desires. Don't denigrate your studies, but your way of life. Without a doubt, O perceptive philosopher, you haven't seen the true cause of your pallor, although it lies open to view. And you seek to see what is hidden in organs and tissues? You don't see what lies in plain sight!

Even though I am no physician and lack dialectic, I shall show 99 you the cause of your pallor. Even against your will, you shall realize that this is true. You move in dark, livid, fetid, and pallid places. You rummage around in sloshing chamber-pots. You examine the urine of the sick. You think about gold. Is it any wonder if

livida, fetida, pallida, undantes pelves rimaris, egrotantium urinas
aspicis, aurum cogitas. Quid hic igitur miri est si tot circum palli-
dis, atris ac croceis ipse quoque sis pallidus, ater ac croceus?
Et si grex ille quondam providentissimi patriarche colorem traxit
obiectu virgarum variarum, quid novi accidit si tu quoque? Expectas ut ab auro dicam. Imo vero ab obiectis.

100   Multum distuli, et libentius tacerem; sed materia verum nomen
exigit, quod si sepe in Literis Sacris est, semel in his scriptum tole-
rabitur. Ab obiectis inquam stercoribus et colorem et odorem
traxeris et saporem.

in the midst of pallid, dark, and sallow places you yourself become pallid, dark, and sallow? If the wisest patriarch's flock changed color when it was exposed to mottled branches, is it strange that the same thing happens to you?[78] You're waiting for me to say that your color comes from gold. No, it comes from what you are exposed to.

I have spoken at great length, and would rather have been silent. But the subject demands its true name which may be tolerated here a single time—a name which is often found in the Holy Scriptures. I say that your color, smell and taste come from the stuff to which you are exposed—shit.

100

101   Aut ego fallor, Ypocras et Aristotiles secunde, aut in hoc certamine, quod tecum, convitiis tuis cogentibus, suscepi, prima iam levis armature tue acies fusa est. Venio nunc ad armatos et graves sillogismorum cuneos, in quibus, velut in equitatu electo, totam victorie spem reponis, ut hic quoque quid possis appareat; ubi illud primum occurrit, quod unum dementie tue sufficiens argumentum erat, quando, digressus a medicine laudibus, que sunt multe, nisi tu eas non tam loquendo quam rudendo minueres, subito furore correptus, sine ulla causa irruis in poetas, et more tuo nota atque ignota permiscens, iterum cogis ut rideam.

102   Ante omnia quidem possem calumniam tuam paucis verbis eludere. Poetas impetis: quid ad me? Poete respondeant, vel, quod est rectius, contemnant. Non enim aut tu tanti es, ut tibi sit magnopere resistendum, aut poesis auxilio meo eget, aut ego me poetam facio. Neque enim 'tali dignor honore' ut est apud Virgilium; et, si tu me dicas, aut alii poetam forte dicere voluerint, nichil tamen omnino michi tecum poetice rei est. Sed quoniam hoc in aliis meis ad te literis capere nequivisti, et ingenio fatigato nonnunquam diverticula huiuscemodi et cum stultis quoque colloquia grata sunt, insistam non moleste, audiamque quicquid ineptire libuerit.

103   Illud primum quero, cum lingua illa temeraria et pigra et viscosa et farmacis delibuta multa ructaveris in poetas, quasi vere fidei adversos vitandosque fidelibus et ab Ecclesia relegatos: quid de Ambrosio, Augustino et Ieronimo, quid de Cypriano, Victorinoque martire, quid de Lactantio ceterisque catholicis scriptoribus sentias; apud quos nullum pene mansurum opus sine poetarum

Book III

Unless I am mistaken, O latter-day Hippocrates and Aristotle, your lightly-armed front line has been routed in this battle that your insults forced me to enter. Now I face the heavily-armed wedge formations of your syllogisms. To show your power in this field, you place all your hopes of victory in these forces, as if in a hand-picked cavalry. But the very first wave of the attack suffices to demonstrate your madness. Digressing from the praises of medicine, which would be numerous if you didn't diminish them by braying rather than speaking, you are seized by sudden fury and with no reason attack the poets, mixing the known and unknown in your usual way, and forcing me once again to laugh.

To begin with, I could have ridiculed your slander with a few words. You assail the poets. What does that have to with me? Let the poets answer you, or let them despise you, as is more just. You are not important enough to merit great resistance. Besides, poetry does not need my help; I don't even claim to be a poet. As Virgil says, "I claim no such honor."[79] Even if you or others call me a poet, we have nothing poetic in common. But since you couldn't grasp this in my previous letters to you, I shall spend some time on the topic, and listen to the nonsense you are pleased to write. A weary brain sometimes takes pleasure in such pastimes, even in conversations with fools.

First, let me ask you one thing. As you wag your reckless, idle, slimy, and drug-smeared tongue, you belch forth many accusations against poets, as if they were enemies of the true faith, who should be shunned by the faithful and banished by the Church. But what then do you think about Ambrose, Augustine, and Jerome? What about Cyprian, Victorinus the Martyr, Lactantius, and other Catholic writers? Practically all of their enduring works are built using mortar furnished by the poets. By contrast, extremely few of

calce construitur, cum contra fere nullus hereticorum poeticum
aliquid opusculis suis inseruerit, seu ignorantia, seu quod ibi suis
erroribus consonum nichil esset. Quamvis enim deorum nomina
multa commemorent, quod temporum qualitatem gentiumque potius quam suum iudicium secutos fecisse credendum est, quod ipsum et philosophi fecerunt, qui, ut in *Rethoricis* legimus, deos esse
non arbitrantur, tamen poetarum clarissimi unum omnipotentem,
omnia creantem, omnia regentem, opificem rerum Deum in suis
operibus sunt confessi.

104   Respondebis autem nescire te quid apud catholicos agatur,
quippe qui Galieni *Terapenticam* tantum legas, quam non legisse
me dicis. Ad quod illud Marii, ducis eximii, responsum accipe:
'Neque literas grecas,' inquit, 'didici: parum placebat eas discere,
quippe que ad virtutem doctoribus nichil profuerant'. Certe si te
tua illa *Terapentica* vel meliorem vel doctiorem vel saltem corpore
saniorem effecisset, dolerem me eas literas non legisse. Nunc dum
te intus et extra contueor, multum vel iuditio[10] vel fortune mee
gratulor, per quam ab ea lectione remotus sum, que te talem fecit,
si talis michi futura erat qualis est tibi.

105   Sed ad poetas redeo. Que sit poetice utilitas et quis finis inter-
rogas. Larga quidem, nec inamena forte, nec inutilis respondendi
materia. Poteram, si non tibi, saltem vero satisfacere, et pauca tibi,
non ut intelligeres, sed quia quesieras, verba proicere; sed non sinis, et, more lymphatici festinans, questionem ipse tuam precipi-
tanter absolvis, aliis quidem pluribus et unctioribus verbis, sed hac
plane sententia, finem poetice statuens valde mirabilem: mulcendo
fallere. Non sunt vates unguentarii: mulcere et fallere vestrum est.
Sed his satis supra responsum puto.

106   Quo, deinde, quo philosophus noster ruit? Poesim non necessariam probat sillogismo terribili. Pudet inserere: nichil in meis lite-

the heretics ever cite poetry in their works—either because of their ignorance, or because poetry is incompatible with their errors. Of course, the poets record the names of many gods. But we must regard them as observing the conditions of their times and their races rather than their personal views: the same is true of the philosophers, who denied the existence of the gods, as we read in Cicero's *Rhetoric*.[80] By contrast, the most famous poets profess one omnipotent God as the creator and ruler of all things and as the maker of the world.

You will reply that you don't know anything about Catholic authors, because you spend so much time reading Galen's *Therapeutica*, a work you say I have never read.[81] Hear the reply of the great general Marius: "I did not care to learn Greek letters, since they had not taught their teachers virtue."[82] If reading the *Therapeutica* had made you better, wiser, or at least healthier, I would regret not having read it. But now, when I observe you both inside and out, I thank either my good judgment or my good fortune for keeping me far from this text, which might have rendered me such as you are. 104

But I return to the poets. You ask what use or purpose poetry serves. To answer you, I could cite a vast amount of material which is perhaps both pleasant and useful. I could satisfy the truth, if not you; and could toss off a few words on the subject, not to make you understand, but because you asked. But you don't let me; you rush in with frenetic haste to answer your own question in many unctuous words. Still, your point is simple. You assign poetry a truly surprising purpose—to deceive soothingly. But poets are not dealers in ointments. Salves and deceptions are *your* arts.[83] However, I think I sufficiently answered these charges above. 105

Where does our philosopher rush next? With a terrible syllogism, he proves that poetry is not necessary. I am ashamed to cite it here, since I don't want people to find anything so frivolous in 106

ris velim tam frivolum inveniri. Verte eum, tu qui multis hunc mensibus fabricatus es, probabitque contrarium. Malo tamen nichil immutes, perficiasque quod intendis: hoc volo, hic tecum sentio, ipsique tecum sentiunt poete. Quid enim aliud vult Flaccus in *Arte Poetica*, clarissimis quidem verbis, sed que tibi barbarica viderentur, ideoque illa non inserui? Ceterum, ut in re ipsa tecum sentio, sic in causis effectibusque dissentio; nec solus ego, sed veritas. Neque enim propter causam quam tu putas non necessaria poesis est; neque ex eo quod non necessariam fatemur sequitur quod tu putas.

107   Locus requirere videtur, ut repetam eam que michi ante multos annos fuit cum quodam dyaletico sene siculo similem questionem, gravissime quidem sed tamen aliquanto tolerabilius delirante. Ille enim, stili conscius, scribere non audebat; tu ad omnem stultitiam promptus ac preceps, auderes ipsum verbis invadere Ciceronem, aut ipsum scriptis lacerare Demosthenem; modo aliquid videri posses, quamvis imparia, temptare certamina, prerupte temeritatis homullule, non timeres. Abstinebat ille igitur scriptis: hoc saltem verecundie inerat; multa tamen ad unius amici mei aurem quotidie murmurabat, que ad me usque huc ipsius amici calamo preferebantur. Inter multa quidem hoc erat, quod ex te nunc audio: minime necessariam poesim. Quod cum nemo presentium negasset, conclusit ille enthimemate claudicante et rauco, ut illum prorsus ex verbis aut scolarem aut preceptorem tuum suspicer, et ait: 'Ergo ignobilis et indigna'.

108   Idem vel dicis certe, vel cogitas. Quid enim aliud sibi vult operosa illa et futilis et ante medium fessa deductio? Sed quod uni fa-

my writings. You spent many months constructing this syllogism. But just turn it around, and it will prove the opposite. Still, I'd rather you didn't change anything, but finished what you intended. This is what I want; here I agree with you, and here the poets themselves agree with you. What else did Horace mean in his *Art of Poetry*, where he uses the clearest words, which I shall not cite because you would think them barbarous?[84] Besides, while I agree on this point, I disagree concerning its causes and effects; and the truth is on my side. Poetry is not necessary, but not for the reason that you think; and your conclusion does not follow from the fact that I accept this.

In this context, I think I should recount a similar dispute I had 107 many years ago with an aged Sicilian logician, who was also profoundly deranged, if more tolerably so.[85] This man was so ashamed of his style that he didn't dare write anything. By contrast, you are so quick to plunge into folly that you would dare assail Cicero himself with your words, or to tear at Demosthenes in your writings. As long as it makes you seem important, you do not scruple to engage in struggles beyond your power, O you puny fellow with your headstrong temerity! Now, this Sicilian fellow refrained from writing because he at least had some modesty. But every day he would grumble about many things to one of my friends, who sent his comments to me in writing.[86] Among the many things he said was the same charge I hear from you: "Poetry is completely unnecessary." He used a syllogism so lame and harsh that its terms made me suspect that you were either his student or his teacher. Since no one present denied his premise, he concluded: "Therefore poetry is ignoble and unworthy."

Clearly, you say the same thing, or at least think it. What else 108 can be the meaning of this laborious and futile syllogism that sags in the middle? Still, a reply to one fool will suffice for many. O madman! You think that an art's necessity proves its nobility. The reverse is true. Otherwise, a farmer will be the noblest of crafts-

tuo dicitur, sufficiet multis. O insane! Igitur putas necessitas artium nobilitatem arguat. Contra est; alioquin nobilissimus artificum erit agricola; sutor quoque et pistor et tu, si mactare desieris, in precio eritis. Absit! Nulla vos necessitas in precio ponet, nulla faciet non esse mechanicos. Nescitis quod servus domesticus sepe quo vilior eo magis necessarius? Clibanarius et lanista quam necessarii sunt, quam viles! Citius philosophie scolis et militari cingulo, quam macello et balneis, sit caritura plebecula!

109 Ite nunc, dyaletici senes, et ex necessitate nobilitatem arguite, si videtur; nisi forte aliud sentitis in rebus vita sensu et ratione carentibus, temptate hic etiam, si libet, vestre artis effectum. Asinus magis est necessarius quam leo, gallina quam aquila: ergo nobiliores; ficulnea magis necessaria quam laurus, mola quam iaspis: ergo nobiliores. Male concluditis, falsum dicitis, pueriliter loquimini: quod nature vestre et moribus et studio convenit, non etati. Ydiote procaces, in ore semper habetis Aristotilem, qui credo in ore vestro quam in inferno esse tristius ducat, et puto dextram suam oderit, qua illa scripsit que, paucis intellecta, per ora multorum ignorantium volitarent. Ille certe vestram conclusiunculam non probabat, ubi ait: 'Necessariores quidem omnes, dignior vero nulla'. Locum non signo: nam et famosissimus locus est, et tu aristotelicus insignis.

110 Quod vero poesim inter liberalia non admittis, potes id quidem, philosophie atque artium dominus, iure tuo, sed te Homerus ac Virgilius precantur, ut eos saltem a mechanicis non excludas, cum, quod dissimulare non potes, sis et ipse mechanicus. Hoc tantum refert: quod philosophiam tuam esse tu dicis, mechanicum te esse dicunt alii. An in ordine vestro poetas non recipis? Si eos etiam inde repuleris, durus eris. Verum, ut omittam iocos, numera liberales artes: nunquid ibi non dico medicinam, que alibi habitat

men. The tailor and the miller will be highly valued, and you physicians, too—provided you stop killing people. God forbid! No necessity can give you physicians value, or prevent you from being mechanics. Aren't you aware that a domestic servant is often the more necessary the baser his function is? Consider the baker and the wool worker: how necessary they are, and how base![87] The masses would sooner forego philosophical schools and knightly garters than their food markets and public baths.

Go then, senile logicians, and argue that nobility derives from 109 necessity, if you will. If you feel the same about inanimate, insensate, and irrational things, test the efficacy of your technique on these too. The ass is more necessary than the lion, and the hen than the eagle: therefore, they are nobler. The fig tree is more necessary than the laurel, the millstone than jasper: therefore, they are nobler. You draw the wrong conclusions, you utter falsehoods, and you speak like children. All this suits your nature, character, and studies, but not your age. Presumptuous ignoramuses, you are always mouthing Aristotle. Yet I believe he would think it worse to be in your mouths than in hell. And I think he would loathe his right hand for writing things that would fly from the mouths of the many ignorant, when only a few understood them. Certainly, he would not approve your flimsy conclusion, for he writes: "The other arts are more necessary, but none of them is nobler."[88] I don't cite chapter and verse, for it is a famous passage, and you are an egregious Aristotelian.

Now, if you don't admit poetry to the liberal arts, that's your 110 right, O lord of philosophy and the arts. But Homer and Virgil beg you not to exclude them, at least, from the mechanical arts, since you yourself are a mechanic, a fact you cannot disguise. Here is what matters: you claim philosophy as your own, while others call you a mechanic. But won't you receive poets in your order? If you expel them, you are hardhearted. Joking aside, count the liberal arts. Do you find medicine among them—its home is else-

et inter mechanicas sexta est, sed ipsum philosophie nomen invenies?

III   Sepe inter magna non poni cuiusdam eximie magnitudinis argumentum est. Dabo tibi illustre exemplum ex historiis. Audires, credo, libentius fabellas, quas post cenam ante focum de orco et lamiis audire soles, sed annis certe iam non puer, si potes, adsuesce melioribus. Apud Titum Livium Hanibal ipse, vir profecto in sua arte doctissimus, dum interrogatus quos fuisse bellorum duces omnium gentium clarissimos extimaret, Alexandrum Macedonie regem primo, Pyrrum Epyrotam secundo, et — quod eius de qua multa dixi fidutie, non superbie fuit — se se tertio nominasset, admonitus ubi Africanum, a quo victum eum esse constabat, preterisset, ita certe respondet, ut appareat eum non oblivione vel invidia, sed ad singularem laudem inter magnos maximum, sive inter maximos incomparabilem siluisse, et Africanum 'e grege' aliorum 'imperatorum,' ut ipsius Livii verba ponam, 'velut inextimabilem secrevisse'. De qua re multa dici possent; sed intelligenti satis, non intelligenti autem nimis est dictum.

II2   Ad omnes quidem eas nugas, ad quas Aristotilem trahere vis invitum, non respondeo. Pudet enim me tui: nimis in propatulo ignorantiam habes; sed fidentissime unum dicam: nescire te quid sit tragedia, aut quid de tetrametris in iambicos transisse, cum tamen turpe sit docto viro proferre quod nesciat. Redi ad cor: fateberis me verum dicere. Hoc michi satis est. Dicas licet in publico me mentitum, scis tu te nichil horum intelligere, neque hoc tibi ad crimen obicerem, modo ne, te talibus implicando, et te ipsum perderes et egros tuos occideres, quia a te non tragedias, non tetrame-

where, as the sixth of the mechanical arts — or *a fortiori* any mention of philosophy?[89]

Often having no place amid great things is a sign of extraordinary greatness. I shall give you a notable example from history. I suppose you'd rather hear fables of ogres and witches, such as you are used to hear by the fire after dinner. But now that you are no longer a child in years, learn to appreciate higher things, if you can. Livy relates that Hannibal, who was the greatest expert on the art of war, was once asked whom he considered the greatest generals in the world. He named king Alexander of Macedon as the first; Pyrrhus of Epirus as the second; and himself as the third — an instance not of pride, but of the self-assurance that I have described at length. He was reminded that he had overlooked Scipio Africanus, who everyone knew had defeated him. He replied in such a way as to make it seem that he had not omitted Scipio out of envy or forgetfulness, but in order to pay singular honor to the greatest among the great, or rather to a man who was incomparable among the greatest. To cite Livy's words, he had "separated Scipio from the mass of commanders as being inestimably superior."[90] More could be said on this topic. But this will suffice for my intelligent readers, as it is superfluous for ignorant ones.

As for all the nonsense that you foist on Aristotle without his consent, I make no reply. I am ashamed of you. You display your ignorance too openly. But let me boldly say one thing. You know nothing about tragedy, or the transition from tetrameters to iambs. And yet it is disgraceful for a learned man to talk about something he doesn't know. Look in your heart: you will confess that I speak the truth. That's enough for me. In public, you may say that I am lying. But you know that you don't understand any of these matters. I wouldn't consider this ignorance criminal behavior, provided your involvement in such questions didn't damn you and kill your patients, who are not seeking tragedies, tetrame-

tra, non iambicos exigunt, sed salutem, quam si haberent, puto, sillogizando corrumperes.

113   Quis enim sine dolore capitis audiat quid est quod hinc arguis? Dicis scientiam esse firmam et impermutabilem, nec mentiris; et addis poeticam uti metris et nominibus quo pro tempore variantur; hinc infers consortio scientiarum sive artium excludendam. O ydiota, omnium tediosissime quos unquam audierim, quid hic contra poeticam singulare? Que scientia sine verbis? Et in quibus verbis non tantundem usus potest? An non audisti quod in ipsa, de qua loquimur, *Arte Poetica* scriptum est?

> Multa renascentur que iam cecidere, cadentque
> que nunc sunt in honore vocabula, si volet usus
> quem penes arbitrium est et ius et norma loquendi

114   Pauca exempli causa ponenda sunt; non tibi quidem, cervicose nescie, sed lectori. Romulus, Romane Urbis conditor, Quirinus dictus est. Cur? Quia hasta in preliis utebatur, que Sabinorum lingua *quiris* dicitur. Cesar Augustus, cum supremo vite tempore statua eius fulmine disiecta esset, in qua scriptum erat Cesar, et prima litera cecidisset, remanentibus quattuor sequentibus, consuluit aruspices quid sperandum sibi. Illi autem dixerunt, centum diebus victurum et non amplius: quod ea litera significaretur quam fulmen excusserat; ipsum vero post mortem in deorum numerum referendum: id enim significare quod remanserat, quoniam lingua Tuscorum, *esar* deus diceretur.

115   Percurre nunc Tusciam ac Sabinam, quere ostiatim quid est *esar*, quid est *quiris*: arabice te locutum credent. Mille sunt talia,

AGAINST A PHYSICIAN · BOOK III ·

ters, or iambs from you, but good health. And if they had their
health, I suspect you'd ruin it with your syllogisms.

Could anyone listen to your line of reasoning without getting a   113
headache? You say that science is fixed and immutable. In this,
you don't speak falsely. Then you add that poetry uses meters and
vocabulary that vary over time. From this, you conclude that poetry must be excluded from the company of the arts and sciences.[91] You are an ignoramus, the most tedious of all I have ever
heard. Is this accusation peculiar to poetry? Is there any science
without words? And are there words completely unaffected by usage? Haven't you heard what Horace wrote in his *Art of Poetry*,
which we are discussing:

> Many terms that have fallen out of use shall be born again,
> And those shall fall that now are in repute, if usage so wills it,
> In whose hands lies the judgment, the right, and the rule of
> speech.[92]

I must cite a few examples for the reader, if not for you, you   114
stiff-necked dullard. Romulus, who founded the city of Rome, was
called Quirinus. Why? Because in battle he used a spear, which in
the Sabine language was called a *quiris*.[93] As Augustus neared the
end of his life, a statue of him was torn asunder by lightning,
which destroyed the first letter of his name "Caesar," which was
inscribed on it. When he consulted the soothsayers to learn what
to expect, they told him that he would only live a hundred days:
for that was the meaning of the destroyed letter C. But they added
that after his death he would be numbered among the gods: for
the remaining letters spelled *aesar*, which in the Etruscan language
meant "god."[94]

Travel through Tuscany and the Sabine hills today, and go door   115
to door asking the meaning of *aesar* and *quiris*. They'll think you're
speaking Arabic. There are a thousand such words, which I intentionally leave aside. A single reason explains all of them. Words

que sciens sileo; omnium una ratio est: mutantur verba, manent res, in quibus scientie fundate sunt. Sed Aristotiles, grecus homo, mutationem poetarum forte suorum aliquam reprehendebat, qualia multa hodie videmus in theologis nostris. Hec autem apud latinos poetas mutatio nulla est. Quis enim nostrorum a Virgilii calle descivit, nisi fortasse Statius Pampinius, qui *Thebaydi* sue imperat ut virgilianam *Eneydem* sequatur et vestigia semper adoret?

116   Lege, miser, et relege locum illum aristotelicum tertio *Rethorice* unde male tornatum sillogismum elicis; neque hoc aut illud verbum excerpas, nichil intelligens, ut videaris Aristotilem legisse, sed totum locum excute. Invenies, si tamen intelliges, hominem illum ardentis ingenii et complecti omnia cupientem, de eloquentia, oratoria, et poetica, et quid inter eas intersit, et de his que utrique vitanda sunt, et utriusque vitiis atque defectibus, more suo multa disseruisse; de his autem que tu somnias, nichil penitus cogitasse, unde concludens ait: 'Manifestum est quod non omnia, quecunque de elocutione dicere est, pertractandum est nobis, sed quecunque de tali qualem dicimus'—hoc est de oratoria; de hac enim in *Rethoricis* agitur—et sequitur ratio: 'De illa autem,' inquit, 'dictum est in his que de poetica'.

117   Ab Aristotile desertus, rursus ad Boetium fugis, relativorumque ope subniteris. Quod ita ridiculum est, ut michi iam non magis ebrius quam freneticus videaris. Quo enim tua hec impertinens et absurda relatio? Ubi, undique victus, ac consternatus animo, et oblitus tui—quis non risu pereat?—ad inimicum tandem fugiens, minime latinis quidem aut congruis, sed maternis atque vulgaribus verbis, ydiota rudissime, Priscianum in auxilium tuum vocas. Magna profecto necessitas est, que cogit ut ab hoste etiam poscas auxilium.

118   Sed certe post eam quam, naufragi more, palpitando arripis relationem, longeque post 'scenicas' illas 'meretriculas' abire iussas,

change, but things endure; and the sciences are based on things. Aristotle, who was Greek, reproached some of the random changes introduced by the poets of his day.[95] And we see our Latin theologians making similar changes today. But the Latin poets exhibit no such changes. Which of our poets ever deviated from Virgil's path, with the possible exception of Statius? And even he commands his *Thebaid* to follow the *Aeneid* of Virgil and to worship his footsteps.[96]

Go, wretch; read and re-read that passage in Book Three of Aristotle's *Rhetoric*, from which you derive your misshapen syllogism. Don't cull a single word here or there in ignorance, pretending to have read Aristotle. Examine the whole passage. If you can understand it, you will find that this man of ardent genius desired to embrace all disciplines. In his fashion, he amply discusses the eloquence proper to oratory and to poetry, the differences between the two, what to avoid in them, and the flaws and defects peculiar to each. But he has given no thought at all to the notions you have dreamed up. Thus he concludes: "It is clear that we need not treat everything that can be said about eloquence, but only what concerns the kind of eloquence we are discussing here" — by which he means oratorical eloquence, the subject of the *Rhetoric* — and then he gives his reason: "the other kind is discussed in the *Poetics*."[97]

Abandoned by Aristotle, you again take refuge in Boethius, and fall back on the aid of analogies.[98] This maneuver is so ridiculous that you seem as drunk as you are mad. Where does this irrelevant and absurd analogy lead? It leads you — routed on every side, in shock and confused — to call on Priscian's help, you boorish dabbler, fleeing at last to your enemy, using your vulgar native vocabulary rather than proper Latin. Who wouldn't die laughing at that? Truly it is a great emergency that forces you to seek help from your enemy.

Now, after this analogy, at which you grope like a drowning castaway, and long after the "harlots of the stage" have been dis-

'veris,' inquit, seu 'meis', hoc est philosophicis, 'Musis, eum curan-
dum sanandumque relinquite'. Hoc est igitur quod dicebam,
quodque extra omnis relationis tue terminos sedet: nulla ibi est relatio, sed penitus diversa sententia est. Frustra te digito occultas:
male tegitur omnis ignorantia, nisi inter indoctos. Hec ne inter indoctos quidem bene tegitur? Hanc enim quis non grammatice limen ingressus puer agnosceret? Sed ei qui Philosophiam tam temere violavit, cur non liceat incestare Grammaticam?

119   Verte te ipsum quocunque libet: Muse poetarum sunt; quod
nemo quidem dubitat. At—quod, insane, non respicis—Philosophia suas illas Musas, et earum merito suum dixit Euripidem; Lucanum quoque familiarem suum non erubuit confiteri. Quod nisi
ita esset, nunquam Aristotiles, paulo te minor philosophus, librum
de poetica edidisset, quem, ut auguror, non vidisti, ut scio, non in-
tellexisti, nec intelligere potuisti. Nunquam aut Homerum poetam
Aristotiles idem exposuisset, aut Cicero transtulisset, aut clari quidam scriptores magnis illum philosophis pretulissent; nunquam
aut tragedias Anneus Seneca tanto studio dictasset, aut Solon ille,
princeps Grecie sapientum, carminibus delectatus, tam cupide
post Athenis conditas leges et etate iam provecta, fuisset poeticam
executus. Cui studio si vacare quantum instituerat in illa civilis
dissensionis intemperie licuisset, opinor, ut Timei platonici verbis
utar, 'non minorem Hesiodo vel Homero futurum fuisse'.

120   Nimis multa de re certa, tibi licet inopinabili et ignota, et in
qua perdi operam non dubito. Verum ego non tibi, sed lectori loquor, cui tam gratus fieri cupio, quam molestus tibi. Nichil sane
horum omnium necessarium erat, si vel per te ipsum nosses, vel

missed, Philosophy then clearly says: "Leave him to be tended and healed by the true Muses" — meaning her philosophical Muses.[99] As I said before, this has absolutely nothing to do with the terms of your analogy. There is no analogy here, but a completely different notion. It is pointless for you to bury your face in your hands. It is difficult to conceal ignorance, except from the unlearned. Can it be safely hidden even from the unlearned? Wouldn't a schoolboy recognize it, even if he had just begun to study grammar? Why shouldn't a man who has raped Philosophy so recklessly be allowed to commit incest with Grammar?

Turn wherever you like. The Muses belong to the poets, and no 119 one doubts it. Philosophy called the Muses "her own," but you fail to consider this, madman. Thanks to the merits of the Muses, she also called Euripides her own, and did not blush to acknowledge Lucan as her intimate.[100] If this were not the case, Aristotle — a less important philosopher than you! — would not have published his book on poetics, which I surmise you have never seen, and which I know you have not understood, and could never understand. If this were not the case, Aristotle would never have expounded Homer, Cicero would never have translated him, and famed writers would never have preferred him to great philosophers. Seneca would never have taken such pains to compose his tragedies.[101] And great Solon, the foremost of Greece's sages and an enthusiast of verse, would never have pursued poetry so avidly in his final years. If, after he had framed the laws of Athens, the tempest of civil strife had allowed him more time to study poetry as he wished to, I believe that "he would have equaled Hesiod and Homer" — to cite the words of the Platonist Timaeus.[102]

I have said too much about an indisputable matter which you 120 find unfamiliar and inconceivable, so that I am undoubtedly wasting my time. But I speak not for you, but for the reader, whom I wish to please as much as I wish to annoy you. In fact, none of these remarks would have been necessary if, either by yourself or

capere posses ab alio, que de hac scenica parte poetice dicuntur a multis, et a me ipso iam in precedentibus tacta sunt, quantum ve inter illam et heroycam intersit.

121   Nec enim negaverim, ut in vino fex et in oleo amurca, sic in rebus fere omnibus, etiam incorporeis, esse suam fecem. Itaque et philosophie quedam species et philosophi quidam vulgo habentur infames, ut Epycurus totusque epycureus ille grex: Aristippum, dico, Hermacumque et Metrodorum et Ieronimum illum senem, non hunc qui quartum inter doctores Ecclesie locum tenet. Quin et ex illustrioribus quidam in multis optimo iure carpuntur. Unde Paulus apostolus, verus Cristi philosophus, et post eum clarissimus eius interpres Augustinus, multique quos enumerare non est necesse, philosophiam laudatam ab aliis execrantur; cum tamen nulla unquam philosophia altior fuerit, aut esse possit, quam que ducit ad verum, qua nostri, celesti munere potius quam humano studio, ante omnium philosophorum vigilias ac labores eminentissime floruerunt.

122   Quid ergo? Quomodo hec sibi invicem adversa connectimus: philosophiam a philosopho reprobari? Laudatur philosophia, sed non omnis: laudatur verax, fallax carpitur. 'Illa vero non est philosophia, si fallax est'. Non infitior id quidem, sed philosophie nomen habet falsum, quo nequis nos forte seduceret, fidelissimus ac previdentissimus Paulus admonuit: 'Cavete.' inquit, 'nequis vos decipiat per philosophiam et inanem seductionem, secundum elementa mundi'. Quem secutus Augustinus, cum in libro celestis reipublice octavo hec ad literam scripsisset: 'Deinde,' inquit, 'ne quis omnes tales esse arbitraretur, audit ab eodem apostolo dici de quibusdam: quia quod notum est Dei, manifestum est illis; Deus enim illis manifestavit. Invisibilia enim eius, a constitutione

with someone's help, you had understood the nature of dramatic poetry, which many have discussed and I have already touched upon, and how much it differs from epic poetry.

Now, just as wine has dregs and oil has lees, I won't deny that 121 there are impurities in nearly all things, even in nonphysical ones. Certain sects of philosophy and certain philosophers are popularly regarded as infamous: witness Epicurus and the entire herd of Epicureans,[103] meaning Aristippus, Hermarchus, Metrodorus, and the aged Hieronymus, whom we must not confuse with the Jerome who was the fourth of the Doctors of the Church. Indeed, many of the very best philosophers have been justly reproved for various reasons. This is why the ancient philosophy that others had praised was abhorrent to the apostle Paul, a true philosopher of Christ, and later to his illustrious interpreter Augustine, as well as to many whom I need not name. Of course, there never was, and never could be, any philosophy higher than the one leading to the truth. In this, our own Christian philosophers prominently surpassed the vigils and labors of all others, if more through heavenly favor than by their human efforts.

What then? How shall we resolve this contradiction, that a 122 philosopher reproaches philosophy? Philosophy is praised, but not all of philosophy. The true one is praised, and the false one is reproved. "But if it is false, it is not truly philosophy." I don't deny this, but it still retains the false name of philosophy. Hence, the very faithful and provident Paul warns us not to be seduced by it: "Beware lest anyone deceive you through philosophy and vain seduction according to the rudiments of the world."[104] Following him, Augustine cites these words in Book Eight of his *City of God* and adds: "Then, lest the Christian think that all philosophers are like that, he hears the same apostle saying of some: 'For what can be known of God is plain to them, because God has shown it to them. Ever since the creation of the world, his eternal power and

mundi, per ea que facta sunt, intellecta conspiciuntur: sempiterna quoque virtus eius ac divinitas'.

123 Itaque, cum sepe Augustinus ipse, Paulum sequens, 'philosophorum scripta plena fallaciarum et deceptionum' diceret, putas ne de omnibus loqueretur? Absit! Ibidem enim statim platonicum dogma commendat. Et eodem libro octavo Apostolum ipsum inducit Atheniensibus loquentem: 'Cum rem magnam de Deo dixisset et que a paucis posset intelligi: quod in illo vivimus, movemur et sumus,' adiecisse et dixisse: 'sicut et vestri quidam dixerunt,' et tamen corundem rursus platonicorum sacrificia detestatur, 'quoniam cognoscentes Deum non glorificaverunt aut gratias egerunt, sed evanuerunt in cognitionibus suis, et obscuratum est insipiens cor eorum; dicentes enim se esse sapientes, stulti facti sunt, et immutaverunt gloriam incorruptibilis Dei in similitudinem imaginis corruptibilis hominis et volucrum et quadrupedum et serpentum'.

124 Quorsum hec? Ut videas philosophie totius partem unicam laudari, eamque non integram, neque tam ferociter insultes. Ad hanc enim formam et cetera rediguntur. Sed ut, omissis aliis, ceptum sequar, in ultimo agmine poetarum quidam sunt quos scenicos vocant, ad quos pertinet illud Boetii, et quicquid a quolibet contra poetas vere dicitur; et hi quidem ipsos inter poetas contemnuntur, qui quales essent Plato ipse declaravit in sua *Republica*, quando eos censuit urbe pellendos. Ut enim constet non de omnibus eum sensisse, sed de scenicis tantum, ipsius Platonis ratio audienda est ab Augustino posita: quia, scilicet, ludos scenicos 'indignos deorum maiestate ac bonitate' censebat. In quo multos sui temporis notavit eius generis poetas. Ita enim fere accidit, ut vilia quelibet multa sint. Id tamen Platonis iudicium non modo heroycis atque aliis nil nocebat, imo vero multum proderat, quoniam, velut excussor poe-

divine nature, invisible though they are, have been understood and seen through the things he has made.'"[105]

Thus, when Augustine himself follows Paul in saying that "the philosophers' writings are full of deceits and deceptions," do you think he is speaking about all of them?[106] God forbid! Soon thereafter he praises the teachings of Plato. And again, in Book Eight of his *City of God*, he presents the apostle Paul preaching to the Athenians: "After stating a great truth about God, one that only a few can understand, namely: 'In him we live, and move, and have our being,' he added: 'as certain also of your number have said.'"[107] At the same time, Paul abhorred the sacrifices of the Platonists and said: "Knowing God, they have refused to honor him as God, or to render him thanks. Hence all their thinking has ended in futility, and their misguided minds are plunged in darkness. They boast of their wisdom, but they have made fools of themselves, exchanging the glory of the immortal God for an image shaped like mortal man, even for images like birds, beasts, and reptiles."[108]

What is my point? I want you to see that only one part of philosophy is praised, and not all of it. So don't attack it so fiercely. Other disciplines conform to this model as well. Leaving others aside, I return to my topic. The so-called dramatic poets are placed in the last rank of poets. It is they who are criticized by Boethius and by others who have justly censured poetry. Even among the poets, they were despised. Plato himself declared their nature in his *Republic* when he wrote that they should be banished from his city.[109] To see clearly that he felt this way solely about dramatic poets, rather than all of them, we need only hear Plato's arguments as cited by Augustine. Plato judged stage plays "unworthy of the majesty and goodness of the gods."[110] In this passage, he censured many contemporary poets in the genre, for it often happens that worthless things are quite numerous. Yet Plato's judgment, rather than harming epic poets and others, was of great benefit to them. He entered the poetic threshing floor like a

123

124

ticam ingressus in aream, valido verbi flabro grana discrevit a pa-
leis.

125   Quando autem Homerus apud illos, quando Virgilius apud
nos, aut alii illustres scenicis ludis operam dederunt? Profecto
nunquam, sed de virtutibus, de naturis hominum ac rerum omnium, atque omnino de perfectione humana, stilo mirabili et quem
frustra tibi aperire moliar, tractaverunt. Nec tamen nichil in his
ipsis reprehensibile dixerim, quippe cum et in philosophorum
principibus multa videam reprehensa iustissime, hec sane non artis
sed ingenii culpa est. Quis igitur nescit, aut quis negat quosdam ut
philosophorum sic et poetarum in cogitationibus evanuisse? Aut
quis miretur ante veritatis adventum licuisse aliquid errori, cum
post agnitam veritatem quidam quoque catholici magni viri ita de-
viarint, ut ipsa veritas unquam acrius oppugnata non fuerit, quam
ab eis fuit?

126   Solet hoc interdum acutioribus ingeniis evenire, ut, dum penetrare volunt supervacua, nimium illud acumen in medio conamine
retundatur, atque ita vel necessaria non attingat. Siquis autem, veritatis amicus—sine qua nichil verum dici potest, quoniam, ut ait
Augustinus, omne verum a veritate verum est—siquis ergo talis,
pio instigatus affectu, ad ipsius veritatis ornatum Musarum presi-
dio niteretur, et vel stilo clarissimo Cristi vitam vel sacrum aliud
vel prophanum etiam, modo non vetitum, celebraret—quod nostrorum quidam fecerunt quamvis preter legem carminis nullo
poetico artificio usi sint—quis putas id melius posset implere?
Responde michi, vir doctissime, oro te, et quid sis responsurus
examina. An poeta talis, qualem tibi describo, et qualem esse
posse, et forsitan esse non est incredibile, an Ypocras ipse, si vive-
ret, vel medicorum unus, qui de urinis semper, non superficietenus

winnower; and with the powerful gusts of his word, he separated the grain from the chaff.

When did any illustrious poets dedicate themselves to stage 125 plays, including Homer among the Greeks, or Virgil among the Latins? Absolutely never. Instead, with their marvelous style, which I would labor in vain to explain to you, they treated the nature of people and the world, the virtues, and human perfection. I can find nothing to reproach in them, for I see that many sayings of the leading philosophers have also been reproached with great justice. This is not the fault of their discipline, but of their intellect. Can anyone ignore or deny that some of the reflections, both of the philosophers and of the poets, proved vain? Can anyone wonder that such error was tolerated before the advent of the truth? Even after the truth was recognized, some great Catholics went so far astray that they assailed the truth more fiercely than anyone else.

This often happens to persons with acute minds. By seeking to 126 fathom unessential problems, they dull their great acumen in the attempt, so that they cannot arrive even at what is essential. But let us imagine a friend of the truth. For without the truth nothing true can be expressed since, as Augustine says, everything true is true by virtue of the truth.[111] Suppose that such a person, driven by pious desire, strives to illustrate the truth with the aid of the Muses. Suppose that in a noble style he celebrates the life of Christ, or some other sacred or profane subject that is not forbidden, as some of our Latin writers have done with no poetic devices apart from meter. Who do you think can better achieve this? Answer me, most learned man, and consider well your answer. Would it be a poet such as I have described? It is not incredible that such a poet could exist or does exist. Or would it be Hippocrates himself, if he were alive? Or one of your physicians who has always lectured on urine samples with great profundity, and not superficially as you do? I believe that no one could hesitate in an-

ut tu, sed profundissime disputasset? Puto: nemo est, nisi omnino depuduit, qui in respondendo hereat. Noli ergo contemnere in aliis quod assequi non potes, qui miserrime impudentie mos est, sed venerare potius et mirare non tam scientificos aut scientiam ipsam, quam scientie largitorem, qui dona sua distribuit ut libet, et his quidem dedit numero, his autem singularitate precellere.

127   Gloriare, si placet: neque enim obluctor et magis necessarios et plures esse medicos quam poetas. Contra illi glorientur et minus necessarios et pauciores esse poetas quam medicos; quinetiam nullius generis ingeniosorum tantam semper fuisse raritatem, quanta poetarum excellentium fuit, preter oratores solos qui ex omnibus seculis paucissimi numerantur. De qua re in *Oratore* Ciceronis clarissime disputatum est. Illud in poetica singulare: quod cum in cuntis artibus mediocritas admittatur, in hac una secus est, quoniam, ut eleganter ait Flaccus,

> mediocribus esse poetis
non homines, non dii, non concessere columne.

Que, meo iudicio, non ultima raritatis poetice ratio esse potest. Tibi vero, cum primum turba hominum et necessitate artificii gloriari ceperis, illud occurrat: multis quidem, sed ante alios agricolis, in hac gloria cedendum; illi vos utroque superant. Nolo autem indigneris quod vos et agricolas iuxta pono; fecit idem Aristotiles: 'Non ex duobus medicis fit commutatio,' inquit, 'sed ex medico et agricola'. Audi ut, tanquam paria, verbis equat. Tacitus credo hec propter reverentiam Aristotelis passus sis.

128   Illud impatientius feres, si ad propositum reversus, cepta peregero; et tamen loqui oportet. Urget enim veritas calamum reluctantem, nec stomacari conveniet, si de philosophis ac poetis dicta ad mechanicos traham. Habent igitur et mechanici fecem suam.

swering, unless he has lost all sense of shame. Do not despise in others what you cannot yourself achieve, which is the custom of the basest effrontery. Rather, you should revere and admire, not scientists or their science, but the Bestower of science. He allots his gifts as He pleases. Some He allows to excel in the number, others in the uniqueness of their gifts.

Boast, if you like. I won't contest that doctors are more neces- 127 sary and numerous than poets. But let the poets boast that they are less necessary and numerous than doctors. Indeed, in no other field has genius been so rare as in the case of excellent poets — with the sole exception of orators, of whom only a handful are counted across the ages, as Cicero has brilliantly shown in *On the Orator*.[112] Poetry is unique. In all the other arts, mediocrity is allowed, but in poetry alone, as Horace elegantly puts it,

> That poets be of middling rank,
> Neither men nor gods nor booksellers have allowed.[113]

In my opinion, this may be the primary reason for the rarity of poets. You undertake to glory in your great numbers and in the necessity of your trade. But consider this: you must yield this glory to many others, and especially to farmers, who surpass you in both respects. Spare me your indignation if I juxtapose doctors and farmers. Aristotle did the same when he wrote: "It is not two doctors who exchange, but a doctor and a farmer."[114] You hear how he places the two terms as equals on the same plane. I think you should have suffered this comparison in silence out of respect for Aristotle.

You will show less patience if I return to my subject and finish 128 what I began. All the same, I must speak, for the truth urges my reluctant pen. Besides, there is no reason for indignation if I apply to mechanics what I said about philosophers and poets. In short, mechanics have their dregs too. "What do you mean by dregs?" you will cry to the heavens. Let me say it. *You* are the dregs of the

'Quenam vero ea fex est?' clamabis ad sidera. Dicam tamen: tu es fex ipsa mechanicorum. Vis hoc statim sine ambagibus probem? In fundo es; imo iaces: is proprius fecis est locus. Numera mechanicos: nullum sub te nisi theatricum videbis, nec tamen ideo, sicut preceps oris tui nobilissimis artibus insultat audacia, sic ego quamvis humilibus insulto.

129   Scio enim necessitates hominum multiplices et graves, ut non immerito propheta idem et rex clamet ad Dominum: 'De necessitatibus meis erue me'. Et undecunque necessitatibus nostris veniens, auxilium a Deo est; cuius dona gratanter reverenterque suscipi debere quis nesciat? Sive ergo ille nobis per se ipsum sanitatem dederit, sive ad id expertus medicus, sive herbarum conscia tremula anus accesserit, et ars et arte quesita vel servata sanitas munera Dei sunt. Itaque contra medicinam nichil omnino: quod milies dixi et, ut video, non sufficit. Siquid autem contra medicos locutus videor, clamo et cupio ⟨ut⟩ me studiosum omne genus audiat: contra te tantum tuique similes dictum est, diceturque quod restat.

130   Superest ut illi calumnie respondeam, qua obscuris delectari arguor, quasi notitiam rerum vulgo invidens debilioris ingenii; ad quod illud etiam affers: Deos humano generi invidere a poetis scriptum esse, sed ab Aristotile reprehensum. Ego quidem, ut pro me ipse loquar, nil cuiquam prorsus invideo, magisque vereor ne alienus michi livor officiat, quam ne me meus inficiat. Sed sub meo nomine notasti forsan invidiam poetarum. Eo enim spectat quod de deorum invidia dixisti: tanquam minime mirum sit, inter eos precipue regnare illam, qui eam usque ad superos extulerunt.

131   Qua in re, morem tuum non deserens, multum a veritate discedis. Nusquam fere vel minus invidie, vel innocentie magis, vel ami-

mechanics. Would you like me to prove this at once without beat-
ing around the bush? You are at the bottom, and lie at the lowest
point. This is the place peculiar to dregs. Enumerate the mechanical arts, and you'll see that only actors are below you.[115] But I shall
not insult the arts, however humble, even though the reckless audacity of your mouth insults the noblest ones.

I know that human necessities are manifold and burdensome.   129
Hence, David, who was both prophet and king, justly calls to the
Lord: "Bring me out of my necessities."[116] And from whatever
source our necessities come, our help is from God. And is there
anyone who does not know that we must receive His gifts with
gratitude and reverence? Whether our health comes from Him,
from an expert physician, or from a doddering crone versed in
herbals, the science of medicine is a gift of God, together with the
health it restores or maintains. Thus, I have absolutely nothing
against medicine. I have said this a thousand times, but apparently
it doesn't suffice. So if I seem to have spoken again physicians, I
shout it out passionately so that the whole class of the learned may
hear me. Against you alone, and men like you, have I spoken and
will speak in what follows.

I must still reply to your slanderous accusation that I delight in   130
obscurity, as if I were envious of granting knowledge to people of
weaker intellect. To this, you add that poets have written that the
gods are envious of the human race, and that Aristotle reproached
them for this.[117] To speak for myself, I envy no one at all. I am
more afraid of being afflicted by someone else's spite than of being
infected by my own. But perhaps you merely used my name in order to censure the envy of the poets. That is why you spoke about
the envy of the gods. It is hardly surprising that envy reigns over
those who have deified it.

On this point, faithful to your custom, you wander far from the   131
truth. There is practically no other group that exhibits less envy,
more innocence, or as much friendship. This is not the place for

citie tantundem. Non capit hic locus poetarum vitas. Quanta Virgilii integritas! quenam Statii urbanitas! que facetie Nasonis! que fides Ennii! que Pacuvii gravitas! quis Vari candor! que Flacci discretio! que Persii pietas! que modestia Lucani! que libertas atque constantia Iuvenalis! Longum est singulos attingere, nec oportet. Et sileo Grecos, sileo multos e principibus nostris huic studio deditos, atque in primis pyerii spiritus Augustum, quo nil clarius in temporalis imperii solio sol vidit.

132   Hic michi quisquam nominare audeat invidiam? aut in tam altos animos tantorumque nominum splendorem, iners et nubilosus livor tentet ascendere? Quod, si forte stilus insuetis videatur occultior, non ea invidia est, sed intentioris animi stimulus, et exercitii nobilioris occasio. Quid vero philosophi? An non Aristotiles, et qui luculentissimus omnium habetur, Plato ipse, loqui posset apertius, ut sileam reliquos, atque ante omnes Heraclitum, qui agnomen ab obscuritate sortitus est? Quid sermo ipse divinus, quem et si valde oderis, tamen aperte calumniari propter metum incendii non audebis? Quam in multis obscurus atque perplexus est! cum prolatus sit ab eo Spiritu qui homines ipsos mundumque creaverat, nedum, si vellet, et verba nova reperire, et repertis clarioribus uti posset? Certe Augustinus, ingenio illo suo, quo se et multarum artium notitiam, et quecunque de decem cathegoriis philosophi tradunt, sine magistro precepisse gloriatur, *Ysaie* principium fatetur intelligere nequivisse. Unde autem hoc, nisi forte spiritum ipsum sanctum invidisse dicas, et non potius providisse legentibus?

133   De qua obscuritate loquens Augustinus idem libro *De civitate Dei* undecimo: 'Divini,' inquit, 'sermonis obscuritas etiam ad hoc

biographies of poets. Consider the magnitude of Virgil's integrity, Statius's urbanity, Ovid's wit, Ennius's honesty, Pacuvius's gravity, Varius's candor, Horace's discretion, Persius's piety, Lucan's modesty, and Juvenal's candor and constancy![118] It would be tedious and superfluous to describe them singly. And I won't mention the Greek poets or many of our rulers who were devoted to poetry, especially Augustus who, filled with the spirit of the Muses, was the most illustrious ruler that the sun has ever seen on the throne of a secular empire.

Who would dare mention envy in this context? Can idle and   132
drab spite attempt to take its place among such exalted spirits and the splendor of such great names? Now, if readers unfamiliar with the poets perhaps find their style obscure, the reason is not envy. Poetic style serves as a stimulus to more intense reflection and as an opportunity for nobler studies. What about the philosophers? Could not Aristotle speak more clearly, or even Plato, who is considered the most lucid of all? I won't mention the rest, especially Heraclitus, whose obscurity won him his famous nickname.[119] What about the Word of God itself, which you may fiercely hate, but which you dare not openly slander for fear of burning? How many obscure and perplexing passages it contains! And yet it was uttered by the same Spirit that created humankind and the world, and that certainly could, if it wished, both invent new words and then, use the words it had invented with greater clarity. Even Augustine, who boasts that his genius mastered many arts and the philosophers' doctrine of the ten categories without a teacher, confesses that he failed to understand the beginning of Isaiah.[120] How can this be, unless perhaps you claim that the Holy Spirit was jealous rather than zealous in aiding its readers?[121]

In Book Eleven of his *City of God*, Augustine speaks about such   133
obscurity: "The obscurity of the divine word actually has the advantage of engendering more than one interpretation of the truth and of bringing these interpretations into the bright light of

est utilis, quod plures sententias veritatis parit et in lucem notitie producit, dum alius eum sic, alius sic intelligit'. Idem in Psalmo centesimo vicesimo sexto: 'Ideo enim,' inquit, 'forte obscurius positum est, ut multos intellectus generet et ditiores discedant homines, qui clausum invenerunt quod multis modis aperiretur, quam si uno modo apertum invenirent'. Idem in Psalmo centesimo quadragesimo sexto, de Scripturis Sacris agens: 'Perversum hic,' inquit, 'nichil est, obscurum autem aliquid est, non ut tibi negetur, sed ut exerceat accepturum'. Et post pauca: 'Noli,' ait, 'recalcitrare adversus obscura et dicere: melius diceretur, si sic diceretur; quomodo enim potes tu sic dicere aut iudicare quomodo dici expediat?' Quem secutus Gregorius super Ezechielem: 'Magne,' inquit, 'utilitatis est ipsa obscuritas eloquiorum Dei, quia exercet sensum, ut fatigatione dilatetur et exercitatus capiat quod capere non posset otiosus. Habet quoque adhuc maius aliud, quia Scripture Sacre intelligentia, que si in cuntis esset aperta vilesceret, in quibusdam locis obscurioribus tanto maiori dulcedine inventa reficit, quanto maiori labore castigat animum quesita'.

134   Non sequor omnia que ab illo et ab aliis in hanc sententiam scripta sunt. Que, si de Scripturis illis recte dicuntur, que sunt omnibus proposite, quanto rectius de illis que paucissimis? Apud poetas, igitur, o nimium rudis, stili maiestas retinetur ac dignitas, nec capere valentibus invidetur, sed, dulci labore proposito, delectationi simul memorieque consulitur. Cariora sunt, enim, que cum difficultate quesivimus, accuratiusque servantur, et non capacibus providetur, dum ne frustra se atterant ipsa rerum facie, si sapiunt, a limine deterrentur.

general knowledge, different readers offering different interpretations."[122] In his commentary on Psalm 126, he says: "This is perhaps expressed more obscurely so that it will engender many interpretations and so that readers will be more richly rewarded if they find closed what may be open to many interpretations, than if they find something open to one interpretation alone."[123] Then, discussing Holy Scripture in his commentary on Psalm 146, he says: "There is nothing perverse in this passage; but there is something obscure, not to deny you comprehension, but to make you work to achieve it."[124] And soon thereafter, he says: "Do not fight against what is obscure, saying 'It could be better said thus': for how can you say or judge what is right to say?"[125] Following Augustine, Gregory the Great writes in his commentary on Ezechiel: "The very obscurity of God's word is a great advantage, for it makes the understanding work so that it increases by exertion, and can grasp with training what it could not in idleness. And this obscurity has a greater benefit. If the understanding of Holy Scripture were open to all, it would be cheapened; but when it is attained in certain obscure passages, it restores us with a sweetness equal to the effort which the problem cost our mind."[126]

I shall not pursue everything that Gregory and others have   134
written in this vein. If what they say is true of the Scriptures, which are offered to all people, is it not even truer of works destined for a very few? This is why, O great ignoramus, poets maintain the majesty and dignity of their style. Rather than begrudging those who can grasp our work, we offer them this pleasant labor in order to promote their enjoyment and recollection of it. For when people acquire something with difficulty, they hold it more dear and retain it more diligently. We make sure that uncomprehending readers are frightened away from our doorstep. In this way, if they know what is best, they will not pointlessly wear themselves out with superficial learning.

III

135   Unde fit ut hic repulsi, alias vias teneant, presertim postquam
numerare ceperint, et hic quidem oblectationem animi, claritatem
nominis, lucri nichil aspexerint. Non est enim omnium studia ista
sectari, sed eorum tantum, quibus et ingenium et natura et rerum
vite necessariarum vel fortuna sufficientiam dederit, vel contemptum virtus. Itaque alter ad agriculturam, alter ad navigationem, alter ad medicinam transit. Nam quid exempli causa eventurum putas, si caput illud ubi habitat ingenium tuum, se se ad poeticam
applicuisset? Quantam in primis egestatem? Nichil enim hic ve-
nale, nullus fraudibus locus. Quot deinde passurum fuisse ludi-
bria? Quot comitum iocos, priusquam cuius uxor esset Eneas
apud Virgilium didicisset?

136   Hec est quidem vera rei ratio, non quia latere expedit, de quo
ruinosum et undique fatiscentem sillogismum extruis, sed quia
nullum fallere, paucis placere propositum est. Pauci autem docti.
Vis videre ita esse ut dico? Nempe tum demum auctor in precio
est, cum amenis ex latebris dulcis sensus eruperit, nec est dubium
non aliam ob causam tibi tuique similibus odiosam esse poeticam,
nisi quia vobis inaccessibilis et ignota est. Quod, fateor, in lucro
ponimus, non in damno. Noli igitur stilum reprobare ingenio per-
vium, memorie habilem ignor[i]antieque terribilem. Nam et sanctum canibus dare et ante porcos proicere margaritas divino etiam
eloquio prohibemur. Sane illa, quam memoras, poetica deorum invidia, altioris cuiusdam secretiorisque misterii est, quam putas;
neque solum invidie deorum, sed fraudes, bella, libidines apud
poetas sunt. Vicisti, cavillator acutissime: plus confiteor quam accuses. Sed cum dicaris animal rationale mortale, quamvis alterum
tantum sis, si placet, querenda ratio rerum est.

After such readers have been driven hence, they follow other 135
paths, especially when they begin to calculate, and find that poetry
offers spiritual delights and glorious renown, but no material gain.
(Not everyone can pursue such studies, but only those who have
suitable intelligence and disposition, and who have received an
abundance of life's necessities from fortune, or a contempt for
them from virtue.) Hence, one person will turn to agriculture, another to navigation, and another to medicine. Suppose, for example, that head of yours, where your intellect dwells, were to dedicate itself to poetry. What do you think would happen? First,
think how poor you would be! In poetry, nothing is for sale, and
there is no place for fraud. And how many jests you would suffer!
How many jokes your companions would make before you learned
whose wife Aeneas was in Virgil![127]

Here is the true reason for all this. Poets seek to please only a 136
few, not because it suits them to conceal their meaning—a charge
on which you build your ruinous and tottering syllogism—but because they seek to deceive no one. Yet people of learning are few.
Do you want proof of what I say? Clearly, we value a writer when
an agreeable sense emerges from his obscure but charming depths.
And it's obvious that you and your colleagues detest poetry solely
because you find it inaccessible and incomprehensible. We poets
consider this a benefit, I confess, rather than a loss. So don't reprove poetic style for being accessible to the gifted, convenient for
the memory, and daunting to the ignorant. The word of God likewise forbids us to feed what is holy to dogs and to "cast pearls before swine."[128] In fact, the poetic envy of the gods that you mention is a sign of a mystery more profound and secret than you
think. In poetry we find not only the envy of the gods, but also
their deceits, wars, and lusts. You have conquered, O keen sophist.
I confess to more than your accusations. Since you are said to be a
rational and mortal animal—but in fact you are merely the latter—let us seek the reason for this, if you please.

137   Primos nempe theologos apud gentes fuisse poetas et philosophorum maximi testantur et sanctorum confirmat autoritas et ipsum, si nescis, poete nomen indicat. In quibus maxime nobilitatus
Orpheus, cuius decimoctavo civitatis eterne libro Augustinus meminit. 'At nequiverunt quo destinaverant pervenire,' dicet aliquis.
Fatebor. Nam perfecta cognitio veri Dei non humani studii, sed
celestis est gratie. Laudandus tamen animus studiosissimorum hominum, qui certe quibus poterant viis ad optatam veri celsitudi-
nem anhelabant, adeo ut ipsos quoque philosophos in hac tanta et
tam necessaria inquisitione precederent. Credibile est etiam hos
ardentissimos inquisitores veri ad id saltem pervenisse, quo humano perveniri poterat ingenio, ut — secundum illud Apostoli supra relatum — per ea que facta sunt, invisibilibus intellectis atque
conspectis, prime cause et unius Dei qualemcunque notitiam sor-
tirentur; atque ita deinceps omnibus modis id egisse, ut — quod
publice non audebant, eo quod nondum viva veritas terris illuxerat — clam suaderent falsos deos esse, quos illusa plebs coleret.
Quod et philosophos postea fecisse in libro *Vere religionis* ostendit.

138   Quis enim nisi amens adulteros aut fallaces veneraretur deos?
Aut quis penitus crederet deos esse, quorum ea flagitia audiret,
que nec in hominibus tolerabilia iudicaret? Cui preterea dubium
esse posset, quin peccata que humanitatem ipsam hominibus erep-
tura essent, eadem multo magis diis talibus preriperent deitatem?
Belligerantes deos invicem Homerus et Virgilius fecerunt; propter
quod Athenis Homerum pro insano habitum Cornelius Nepos refert. Credo nimirum apud vulgus; docti autem intelligunt, si plu-

Among the pagan nations, the first theologians were poets. 137
This is attested by the greatest philosophers, confirmed by the authority of saints, and indicated by the very name of poet, if you
don't know.[129] The most renowned of these poets was Orpheus,
whom Augustine mentions in Book Eighteen of his *City of God*.[130]
"But they did not attain the goal they sought," someone will object. I admit it. For the perfect knowledge of the true God is not
the result of human study, but of heavenly grace. Still, we must
praise the spirit of these zealous people. For they clearly yearned
to attain the coveted heights of truth by the paths available to
them. In fact, in this great and necessary inquiry they even surpassed the philosophers. We may believe that these ardent inquir-
ers of the truth attained at least as much as human intelligence can
attain. In the words of the Apostle cited above, "through the
things he has created, what was invisible was understood and
seen," so that these poets acquired some kind of knowledge of the
first cause and of the one God. Then they tried in every possible
way to persuade others secretly that the gods worshiped by the de-
luded masses were false gods. But they dared not do this in public,
since the living truth had not yet illuminated the world. In his
book *On True Religion*, Augustine shows that later philosophers
acted in the same way.[131]

Would anyone but a madman venerate gods that practice adul- 138
tery and deceit? Who would truly believe that they were gods, after he had learned of their crimes, which would be judged intolerable in human beings? And who could doubt that the same sins
which deprived human beings of their humanity must *a fortiori*
strip the gods of their divinity? Homer and Virgil portrayed the
gods as warring with each other, and Cornelius Nepos tells us that
for this very reason the Athenians thought Homer was mad.[132] I
believe of course that the common people thought so. But learned
men understand that, if many gods exist, there may be discord
and warring among them. It follows that when one party is victori-

res sunt dii, et discordare illos et bella inter eos esse posse, et necesse esse ut, altero victore, alter victus, atque ita nec sit
immortalis nec omnipotens, consequenterque ne deus quidem;
unum esse igitur Deum et non plures; vulgus autem falli.

139   Et siquis interroget cur non potius palam vulgi vesaniam incre-
parent, possum cum Augustino respondere: quod utrum timore
an aliqua cognitione temporum fecerint, iudicare non est meum.
Ego tamen, etsi sola timoris causa fuerit, non mirabor, cum videam Cristi quoque temporibus, ante Sancti Spiritus infusionem,
ipsos etiam apostolos timuisse. Enimvero quod a te de invidia deorum dicitur, eodem quo cetera referendum est, nec mirari conveniet, memorantem illud Psalmiste: 'Omnes dii gentium demonia,'
et quod scriptum est: 'Invidia diaboli mors introivit in orbem terrarum'. Quenam igitur admiratio ista est, invidisse deos, qui nunquam sine invidia fuerunt? Quenam preterea poetarum culpa, rem
veram, si intelligatur, salubremque narrantium? Aut quenam aristotelica illa reprehensio? Si tamen ita est; neque enim michi nunc
aut eius loci memoria recens, aut inter hos montes liber ipse me-
thaphisicus est presens. Quomodo autem consentaneum sit, vel
poetas in hac lingue libertate reprehendere, vel deorum invidiam
excusare—in eo libro presertim in quo, principatuum pluralitate
damnata, unus omnium princeps asseritur—non video; sed addu-
cor ut credam te locum illum non melius intellexisse quam reliqua.

140   Hoc ego nunc de poetis antiquis opinabile verisimillimumque
protulerim: qui, si unum Deum crediderunt, hoc ne in illis accuses;[11] si unum credentes, plures nominaverunt seu etiam coluer-
unt, habes plane quod accuses. Nec ego quidem illos excuso, sed
comune cum philosophis crimen dico, quod, ut audisti, publici

ous, the other must be vanquished. Such a deity cannot be either immortal or omnipotent, and consequently not even a god. Therefore, there is one God, rather than many; and the masses are deceived.

If I am asked why the poets did not openly rebuke the madness 139 of the masses, I shall reply with Augustine: "Whether this was due to fear or to the influence of the times, it is not for me to judge."[133] Even if the only reason was their fear, I would not be surprised, since I see that in Christ's day even the apostles were afraid before they had received the Holy Spirit. As for what you write about the gods' envy, it all leads to the same conclusion, and should surprise no one who recalls the words of the Psalmist, "All the gods of the nations are demons"[134] or that other passage in Scripture, "By the devil's envy death entered into the world."[135] So what reason is there to wonder why the gods displayed envy, who were never without envy? Besides, how are the poets guilty if they relate what is true and salutary when properly understood? And what does Aristotle censure, if he in fact does so? I don't have a recent recollection of the passage, and I don't have a copy of the *Metaphysics* among my mountains of books. At any rate, I don't see how it makes sense to reprove poets for their verbal license and then to excuse the envy of the gods, especially in a book that condemns any plurality of ruling powers and asserts the supremacy of a single ruler over all.[136] But I am led to believe that you understood this passage no better than the others.

As for the ancient poets, let me state here what seems most 140 credible and plausible. If they believed in one God, you cannot blame them for this. If they believed in one God, but named or even worshipped several gods, you may clearly blame them. I myself don't excuse them, but the philosophers share in this offense which, as you have heard, was extenuated by their fear of public opinion, which has often shaken even the most steadfast spirits. But I shall never be persuaded that men of such genius truly be-

iudicii metus levat, qui firmissima etiam interdum corda concussit. Vere autem plures deos tanta ingenia credidisse nunquam michi persuadebitur. Sed esto; crediderint; erraverunt (nichil est enim quod disceptator indoctus et pertinax non presumat): non id certe poeticum, sed humanum fuerit, temporumque crimen vel ingenii, non artis, ut est dictum, neque quod, alio tempore atque alio ingenio et ampliori gratia, poetam esse pium disertumque prohibeat.

141   Sed nonne ego poetas, adversus fragilem et inermem hostem dum defendere videor, offendo? Risus et silentium et contemptus poterant adversus tua tela sufficere: nullis opus erat verbis. Sed tacere non potui, ne ipse tecum forsan in aliqua cloaca—id enim tibi Capitolii instar est—inter egri ventris crepitus et raucas pelves—hee tube tue sunt, hic plaudentis conclamantisque favor exercitus—velut de musarum ruina et sacrorum studiorum excidio triumphares. 'Ne respondeas stulto iuxta stultitiam suam, ne efficiaris similis ei'. Hoc cum Sapiens dixisset, statim addidit: 'Responde stulto iuxta stultitiam suam, ne sibi sapiens esse videatur'. Primum me parumper tacitum tenuit, secundum coegit ut loquerer; frustra quidem, ut puto. Si enim desieris tibi sapiens videri, incipies, quod impossibile arbitror, esse forte non stultus. Doctus fieri non potest, nisi qui se noverit atque oderit ignorantem: defectus proprii cum dolore notitia principium est profectus.

142   Et ad hos quidem sermones, non fame proprie periculum, non mei nominis offensa, quamvis gravis, tantum me, fateor, accendit, quantum hinc veri zelus, hinc tue loquacitatis inflammavit indignitas. Quantum enim ego tangebar, quicquid in poetas invectus eras, poteram, ut dixi, dissimulando transire. Nam nec michi poete nomen arrogo—quod scio quibusdam magnis viris multo studio non

lieved in a plurality of gods. Still, suppose that they did believe this. (An ignorant and obstinate debater will assume anything.) If so, the offense lay not in poetry but in human nature — it was the fault of their age or their mentality, not of their art, as I said before. In a different age, with a different mentality, and blessed by ampler grace, such an error would not prevent a poet from being pious and eloquent.

But even as I seem to defend the poets against a fragile and un- 141 armed enemy, don't I offend them? Against your weapons, laughter and silence and contempt would have sufficed. There was no need for words. But I could not be silent. Otherwise you might have held a one-man triumph in some sewer — your idea of the Capitol — among the banging of bed-pans and the farting of the sick — for such would be your trumpets, such your cheering army — to celebrate the ruin of the Muses and the destruction of sacred studies. "Answer not a fool according to his folly, lest thou also be like unto him."[137] After saying this, the Sage immediately adds: "Answer a fool according to his folly, lest he be wise in his own conceit."[138] The first saying kept me silent for a while. The second forced me to speak, but in vain, I think. Now, if you ceased to think yourself wise, you would begin perhaps to be less than foolish. But this strikes me as impossible. One becomes learned only by knowing oneself and detesting one's own ignorance. For the beginning of progress is the painful awareness of one's own shortcomings.

In writing this response, I am not so much goaded by the 142 threats to my reputation and the insults to my name, however grave they may be, as I am inflamed both by my zeal for the truth and by my indignation at your loquacity. Insofar as it affects me personally, I could pretend to ignore your invectives against poets, as I said. For one thing, I do not presume to call myself a poet. (I know that despite their intense efforts certain great men could not win this title. If it fell to me, I would not reject it; and in fact, I

potuisse contingere, quamvis, si michi forsan ultro contigerit, non respuam, et ad id me olim iuveniliter aspirasse non negem — nec convitiis tuis presens hodierne lectionis mee studium tangebatur. Poteram, ut aiunt, de calumnia iurare me poetarum libros ante hoc septennium clausisse, ita ut eos inde non legerim, non quod legisse peniteat, sed quia legere iam quasi supervacuum videtur. Legi eos dum tulit etas; et ita michi medullitus sunt infixi, ut ne divelli quidem possint, et si velim.

143   Ac ne me gloriari iterum graviter feras, non ea laus memorie sed etatis est. Tener admodum illos edidici, expertusque sum in omnibus, fere, quod in vestibulo *Civitatis Dei*, de Virgilio loquens, Augustinus: 'Quem propterea,' inquit, 'parvuli legunt, ut videlicet poeta magnus, omniumque preclarissimus atque optimus, teneris ebibitus annis, non facile oblivione possit aboleri, secundum illud Horatii

quo semel est imbuta recens servabit odorem
testa diu.

144   Accedit quod in eisdem studiis agere senectutem, in quibus adolescentia acta est, minime michi magnificum videtur. Maturitas quedam, ut pomorum, ut frugum, sic studiorum ac mentium debet esse; eoque magis, quo turpior damnosiorque, multo est animorum acerbitas quam pomorum. Si ergo poetas hodie non lego, forsan interroges quid agam. Solet enim stultitia aliene vite curiosa esse, sue negligens. Respondebo tibi, prefatus ne quod dicam superbie ascribas: 'Melior fieri studeo, si possim.' Et quia impotentiam meam novi, posco auxilium de celo et in Sacris Literis delector. Que si Victorino, pagano homini iam seni, Deo per illas alloquente, pectusque durissimum moliente, veram infuderunt[12] fidem, cur michi, cristiano homini, non possunt vere fidei firmitatem et opera et amorem vite felicioris infundere?

don't deny that in my youth I aspired to it.) For another, your insults did not affect my present studies and my daily reading. I
could swear without perjury, as they say, that I closed the poets'
books seven years ago.[139] Hence, I haven't read them since, not because I regretted reading them, but because at this point it seems a
waste of time. I read the poets as long as my age allowed, and they
are so deeply ingrained in my mind that I could not eradicate
them even if I wanted.

Don't be vexed that I am boasting again. This is no tribute to   143
my memory. but to my age. I studied the poets when I was quite
young; and in reading nearly all of them, I experienced what Augustine describes, when he speaks about Virgil early in his *City of
God*: "Young boys read him for this reason: having in their early
years imbibed this great poet, the most illustrious and excellent of
all, he can hardly be forgotten, as Horace says:

> The jar will long keep the fragrance of what it was once
> steeped in when new."[140]

What's more, I think it is quite inglorious to spend your old age   144
in the same studies as your youth. Like fruit and grain, our studies
and our minds should ripen and mature, and the more so as un-
ripe minds are more shameful and ruinous than green fruit. If I
don't read the poets nowadays, perhaps you will ask what I do.
(Folly is curious about the lives of others, and indifferent to its
own.) I shall reply to you: "I strive to improve myself if I can." But
first I shall ask you not to attribute my words to pride. Since I
know my own shortcomings, I ask heaven for help, and take delight in the Holy Scriptures. Through the Scriptures, God once
spoke to Victorinus, though a pagan and already aged, softening
his hardened heart and instilling in him the true faith.[141] So why
should they not instill in me, who am a Christian, the steadfast-
ness and good works of the true faith and the love of a more
blessed life?

145   Queris quid agam. Nitor non sine multo labore preteriti temporis errata corrigere; quodsi michi contigerit, felix ero; sed adhuc, fateor, ab eo quo suspirat animus longe absum. Queris quid
agam. Non poetas lego, sed scribo quod legant qui post me nas-
centur, et, raro plausore contentus, acies insanorum sperno. Et si
votive successerit quod ago, bene est; alioquin voluntas ipsa lauda-
bitur. Postremo, ut aliud nichil agam, maturescere saltem cupio, si
nondum forte maturavi. Tu autem, 'puer centum annorum', male-
dictus a Deo, et elementarius senex irrisus a Seneca, ibi senectutem agis, ubi pueritiam exegisti, et fluxos nunc etiam sillogismos
filo marcente conglutinas, quos queat anus quelibet temulenta
confringere; quicquid vero aliud quam puerile stramen redoluerit
adversaris.

146   Itaque libellos meos omelias vocas, quasi nomen infame meditatus, quod sanctissimis tamen atque doctissimis viris placuisse
notum est. At minime mirandum si, quorum actus despicis, et
verba contemnis. Omelia, porro, grece originis nomen est, quod
latine dici potest sermo prolatus ad populum. Ego sane in his literis ad populum nichil, sed ad ignorantiam tuam loquor, si quo
pacto possem, non dico illam tibi, sed illi superbiam extorquere.
Quis autem, queso, peregrine lingue a te nunc notitiam requirebat,
cum proprie sis ignarus? Sentis ut causam tuam ago, quo scilicet
insolentem honesti nominis contemptum excuset ignorantia?

147   O semper scolastice literator, nunquam literatus aut magister —
quis enim literatus ita scriberet? — lege philosophorum libros, vel
interroga qui legerunt: quis unquam hunc scribendi morem tenuit? Inest quidem verbis illorum vis ingens sillogistica: sillogis-
mus nunquam aut perraro; quippe, pueritiam pretergressi, loquuntur ut viri. Efficacior est autem dissimulata callide, quam inaniter

You ask what I do. I strive with considerable toil to correct the   145
errors of my past. If I attain this, I shall be happy; but so far, I
confess, I am far from the goal to which my mind aspires. I don't
read the poets, but I write things that will be read by people born
after me. Content with occasional approbation, I disdain hosts of
madmen. If my actions fulfill my wishes, I am happy; if not, my
good intentions will be praised. In sum, if I don't do anything else,
I hope at least to mature, if I haven't already matured. But you,
who are the "child of a hundred years" cursed by God, and the "old
man in first grade" mocked by Seneca, you spend your old age
where you spent your childhood.[142] Even now, you paste together
rotten strands to form flimsy syllogisms that any bibulous crone
could tear apart; and you declare war on anything that does not
reek of childish straw.[143]

You call my works homilies, as if it were a term of opprobrium.   146
In fact, everyone knows that the holiest and most learned of men
were pleased to use it. But it's hardly surprising that you contemn
the words of men whose actions you despise. Homily is a word of
Greek origin; in Latin we might call it a "sermon spoken to the
people."[144] Of course, in these letters I am not speaking to the people, but to your ignorance, hoping somehow, if not to purge you of
it, at least to purge it of pride. Yet who, I ask, required you to
know a foreign language when you are ignorant of your own? Do
you see how I take your side by allowing your ignorance to excuse
your insolent contempt of an honorable title?

You are still a schoolroom teacher of the ABCs, and have never   147
become a man of letters or a professor — for what man of letters
would write so badly? Go read the philosophers' books, or ask the
people who do read them. Who ever wrote in this fashion? The
philosophers' words reveal great syllogistic power, but they seldom
or never use syllogisms. Having grown out of childhood, they
speak like adults. Subtlety is more effective when it is shrewdly
disguised than when it is pointlessly flaunted. But here too I help

ostentata subtilitas. Sed et hic excusator, licet irrequisitus, adsum tibi: illi enim ut se, tu autem loqueris ut te decet.

148   Ecce, iurgator improbe, extorsisti ut non tantum maledictis tuis, sed et cogitatibus responderem. Quedam sponte preterii. Misereor enim tui; nam quid superbo ignorante miserius? Sed ne plene miserear, tu facis. Ita namque iactanter atque fastidiose miseria tua abuteris, ut nulla tibi miseratio debeatur. Quomodo vero dissimulem, aut quid illi faciam vanitati, qua probare niteris cuius contrarium apparet in te ipso, dumque tu loqui poteris, occultari nunquam poterit? Quanta mechanici temeritas? Rethoricam prorsus in servitutem asseris. Iam non castigandus sed urendus es, nec verbis sed verberibus coercendus.

149   Nimis insanis, medice. Crede michi: medico eges. Mirum quod medicorum nullus est, qui curam tui suscipiat; puto sis omnibus odiosus, teque perditum velint omnes. Medicine, inquam, rethoricam servam facis: de medicina viderimus. Certe ipse rethoricam in tuam servitutem aut amicitiam nunquam trahes. Quid autem probes et qualiter audiamus. 'Per medicinam,' inquis, 'et ethicam docemur recte vivere'. Dii te perdant, fugitive! Male incipis. Medicine nichil comune cum ethica, sed multa contraria. Quid vero ad vivendum recte medicina, nisi quantum agricultura? Forte etiam longe minus. Nisi putas male vixisse olim Rome tot milia virorum fortium, per quos orbis terrarum domitus, virtus culta, vitia calcata sunt; qui tamen longum in evum sine medico vixerunt. Vixerunt, fateor, male; non quia medicus temporalis, sed quia vivificator eternus illis defuit. Alioquin nulla gens melius, vel nisi male

by excusing you, without being asked. The philosophers speak as befits them, and you speak as befits you.

Behold, O shameless reviler, you have wrung from me an an- 148 swer not only to your curses, but to your thoughts as well. I intentionally pass over certain topics, since I commiserate with you. For what is more miserable than a proud ignoramus? But your actions keep me from pitying you completely. You exploit your misery so boastfully and irritatingly that you deserve no commiseration. How can I turn a blind eye to your vanity? What should I make of it? You strive to prove the opposite of what is so evident in you, which can never be hidden as long as you can speak. You have a great deal of presumption for someone who works with his hands! You even place rhetoric in your service. It is too late to reprimand you. At this point you should be incinerated rather than casti-gated; coerced with whips, not words.

Your madness is too great, O physician. Believe me, *you* need a 149 physician. It's surprising that no physician will undertake to cure you. I suspect you are odious to all of them, and that all of them desire your damnation. As I say, you make rhetoric the handmaid of medicine. We shall see about medicine. Clearly you will never force rhetoric into your service or friendship. But let us hear how you argue and what you prove. "Medicine and ethics," you say, "teach us how to live well." May the gods curse you, O runaway slave! You begin badly. Medicine has nothing in common with ethics, and is in many ways contrary to it. What has medicine got to do with living well? As much as agriculture, or perhaps much less, unless you think that thousands of brave men in Rome once lived badly. But the Romans conquered the globe, cultivated vir-tue, spurned vice, and lived to a ripe old age without the aid of physicians.[145] I confess that they lived badly. The reason was not that they lacked physicians here on earth, but that they lacked the eternal Giver of Life. Otherwise, no people lived better, unless our

vivebat virgo illa mirabilis, que carnalem suo corpori medicinam nunquam adhibuerat.

150   Cur autem, queso, medicinam ethice permisces? Tene te loco, neque fines tuos excesseris. Quamvis nec ethica prestare possit recte vivere, cum id potentioris alterius donum sit. Verum et longior operosiorque disputatio, nec propositi huius est. Prosequere igitur ludum tuum; ita, tamen, ut deinceps ethicam non molestes, sed memineris quid sutori terminos suos excedenti respondit pictorum famosissimus Apelles. Age res tuas ut medicus.

151   'Per medicinam docemur,' ais, 'recte vivere; non ut congrue loquamur vel ornate, sed potius congrue et ornate loquendi artes discimus, ut vivamus recte. Sic non medicina ad has artes refertur, sed hee potius ad illam et propter illam sunt'. Hinc concludis: 'Serve igitur eius sunt'. O male digesta conclusio! Sic iam longius feris quam minatus eras. Neque solum rethorica, sed omnes, quotcunque sunt, honeste artes, ipsa quoque philosophia et theologia, scientiarum omnium regina, tibi servient. O mechanice, si hoc michi probaveris: quod per medicinam recte vivere doceamur—omnes enim huc referuntur, et omnium unus est finis ultimus, non dico ut prestent recte vivere, sed ut ad recte vivendum adiuvent—iure ergo illi servient, que id prestat, ad quod omnes relique aspirant.

152   Certe ego nunc risu et verecundia impedior sillogismum tibi tuo parem mittere, quo probem te vilissime servum rei. Quod urbanius possum dicam: si quod alio spectat, et ad aliud refertur, et propter aliud est inventum, illi serviat oportet, ut tu vis. Medicina autem tua pecuniam spectat et ad illam refertur et propter illam est. Conclude, dyaletice: ergo pecunie serva est. Bene tibi accidit; turpioris rei servum te facere meditabar; pudor obstitit.

miraculous Virgin lived badly because she never applied medicines of the flesh to her body.

And why, I ask, do you confuse medicine with ethics? Stay in 150 your own place, and don't overstep your bounds. (In fact, not even ethics can insure that we live well. That is the gift of a more powerful one. But this would be a long and laborious discussion, and is not part of my topic.) Continue your game, then, but do so without troubling ethics. And remember what the most famous of all painters, Apelles, told the cobbler who overstepped his bounds.[146] Ply your trade like a physician.

"By medicine," you say, "we are taught to live well, but not so 151 that we may speak aptly and ornately. Instead, we learn the arts of speaking aptly and ornately so that we may live well. Thus medicine is not subordinate to these arts. Instead, these arts are subordinate to medicine and exist for its sake." From this you conclude: "Therefore they are its servants." O ill-digested conclusion! Now you are lashing out even farther than you threatened. Not only rhetoric, but every single one of the liberal arts—even philosophy and theology, the queen of the sciences—are in your service. O mechanic, if you can prove to me that medicine teaches us to live well, then the arts will justly serve medicine because it insures what all the rest aspire to. For all the arts are subordinate to one end, and have a single and ultimate goal: not to provide us with the good life, but to aid us in living well.

Ridicule and shame keep me from sending you a syllogism 152 equal to yours that would prove that you are the servant of the vilest trade. I shall speak as politely as I can. Now, if one thing has another as its goal, is subordinate to it, and was devised for its sake, then it must serve it, as you say. Your medicine has money as its goal, is subordinate to it, and exists for its sake. Draw the conclusion, O dialectician: Therefore, medicine is the servant of money. It turned out well for you. I had intended to make you the servant of something worse, but modesty forbade it.

153   Sed, o gravis argumentator, quis te talia docuit? Assumis falsa
notorie, et ea de quibus principaliter discordamus; quod magnum
in argumentando vitium est. Primum enim, ut dixi, medicina ad
recte vivendum nichil omnino, nisi quantum una mechanicarum
corpori famulantium. Deinde quis illud diffinivit inter nos, de quo
ab initio litigamus? Preter enim quod circa medicinam nobis infinita dissensio est, nonne alius scrupulus premit occultior? Equidem ut tibi plane concesserim, quod medicina ars nobilissima,
tuque preclarus medicus. Illa, ut est mechanicarum penultima, sic
omnium prima artium. Tu, ut non tantum ultimus, sed hostis es,
sic medicorum omnium sis princeps.

154   Liceat vobis passim cuiuslibet necessarie artis obsequio uti, et
cuius utile obsequium fuerit, illa confestim vobis ancilla sit. Quid
futurum arbitramur? Ancillabitur forsan astrologia, que celestium
corporum notitia terrenis aliquam corpusculis opem ferat? Ancillabitur musica, que in hominum pulsu forte non inutiliter dimen-
siones temporum et intervalla consideret? Que res, vobis quia necessaria esse posset, ideo prorsus incognita et neglecta est. Illam
appetitis, quam nec consequi potest, et si possetis, deberetis nolle.
Rethores esse vultis, ridente Tullio, indignante Demosthene, flente
Ypocrate, populo pereunte.

155   Ne enim in singulis immorer, ad litis nostre summam venio. Si
omnes, inquam, artes, quamvis nobiles, quamvis ingenuas, tuo humili et mercennario artificio servas facis, eo ipso quod utiles aut
necessarie proposito tuo sunt — idque tibi nescio quo iure permittitur — nunquam profecto vel sic tibi rethorica serva fiet, quam
constat ad id, quo te intendere oportet, non modo nil prodesse,
sed obesse quam plurimum. Quid enim egro longa oratione opus
est, cui fere verbum omne molestum est, nisi ut iubeatur bono
animo esse, cureturque artis ope, si potest? An forsan apothecariis

But who taught you such things, O weighty syllogizer? You 153
make assumptions which are notoriously false, and which relate to
the principle subject of our dispute. This is a serious technical
fault in a debate. First of all, as I said, medicine contributes nothing to living well, except as one of the mechanical arts serving the
body. Second, who defined the subject that we have been debating
from the start? Besides our endless disagreement about medicine,
isn't there a hidden doubt that bothers you? Let me grant clearly
that medicine is a noble art, and that you are an excellent physician. Let me grant that medicine is first of all the arts, rather than
next to last. And let me grant that you are the prince of physicians, rather than their worst enemy.

Let me further grant that any art you find useful or necessary 154
will forthwith become your handmaid. What consequences do we
foresee? Will astrology perchance be a handmaid, as it uses its
knowledge of celestial bodies to aid earthly ones? Will music be a
handmaid, perhaps because it is useful in measuring the timing
and intervals of the human pulse? But precisely because this art
could be essential to you, it remains ignored and neglected. Instead, you physicians desire an art which you cannot master, and
which you should renounce if you could master it. When you seek
to be rhetoricians, you provoke Cicero's laughter, Demosthenes' indignation, Hippocrates' tears, and the death of our people.

Rather than dwell on particulars, I come to the crux of our de- 155
bate. I say that even if you enslave all the arts, however free, as servants of your humble and mercenary trade, because they are useful
and necessary to your goal—and I don't know what justifies
this—then rhetoric will never be your servant. For it is clear that
rhetoric not only does not aid you in achieving your ends, but in
fact thwarts you. Of what use is a lengthy oration to a sick patient? A sick person finds most talk annoying, except when he is
urged to take heart and to let medical science cure him, if possible.

persuadere propositum est, quibus pene maternis verbis sunt dictanda remedia?

156   Unum est—quoniam factum tuum, quam possum, excusare disposui—unum est quo in te alienum eloquentie studium excusem: si forte defectus tuos et medicine imperitiam, non dicam supplere, sed tegere putas eloquentia, et, cum aperte peremeris, ostendas culpam esse non tuam, sed egroti, sed astantium, sed nature; si, preterea, in morte manibus tuis ascita, vis superstites consolari. Utrunque enim oratorium et rethorici opus est, fateor.

157   Accusare, excusare, consolari, irritare, placare animos, movere lacrimas atque comprimere, accendere iras et extinguere, colorare factum, avertere infamiam, transferre culpam, suscitare suspitiones: oratorum propria sunt hec; medicorum esse non noveram. Sed si rethorica tibi servit, quicquid vero ancille tue est, tuum esse conceditur. Omnia hec, igitur, tua sunt, et quecunque alia oratoribus assignantur. Plusquam tibi permittitur quam putabam. Potes enim occidere—mirum dictu!—et quem occideris accusare. Sed quando hodie (nescio quomodo) de accusatore factus sum excusator tuus, quid te vetat, hoc tanto et tam capaci ingenio, ut philosophum et medicum, sic oratorem esse, atque actus oratorios exercere cum gloria?

158   Nonne ita homo es tu, ut Cicero? Accusat ille Clodium ac Verrem et in *Invectivis* Catilinam, et in *Philippicis* insectatur Antonium—magnos viros ac feroces, ad ultionemque promptissimos— et molem multorum criminum, ac reipublice ruinam illis opponit. Tu defunctum unum nec loqui valentem nec ulcisci, cur non fiden-

Or do you intend to harangue the apothecaries, even though they generally prescribe medications using vernacular terms?

There is one reason — since I have resolved to defend your actions as best I can — there is one reason, I say, that lets me defend your zeal for an eloquence that is foreign to you. Perhaps you think that eloquence can cover up your defects and incompetence, if it cannot compensate for them. Thus, after you have clearly killed a patient, you can prove that the fault was not yours, but lay with the patient, his attendants, or nature. Perhaps you also hope to console the survivors for a death caused by your hands. I confess that both these cases require the oratorical skill of a rhetorician. 156

Accusing, defending, consoling, exciting and assuaging passions, summoning tears and repressing them, inflaming anger and quelling it, casting a deed in a certain light, averting scandal, shifting blame, arousing suspicion — these are the proper tasks of orators, and not of doctors, as far as I know. But if rhetoric is your servant, we must grant that whatever belongs to your handmaid belongs to you as well. Therefore, all these things are yours, and anything else that is attributed to orators. You are permitted to do more than I thought. You can kill someone, and then — amazing to say — you can accuse the corpse. If I have today been changed somehow from your accuser to your defender, what is to prevent you with your vast intellect from becoming an orator, just as you are a philosopher and doctor, and from playing the part gloriously? 157

Aren't you just as human as Cicero? He accuses Clodius and Verres; and he assails Catiline in his *Invectives* and Antony in his *Philippics*. These are powerful, violent men, and quick to take revenge; but he charges them with a huge number of crimes and the ruin of the republic. So why can't you confidently accuse a dead patient, who is incapable of speech or revenge, alleging that he killed himself? Cicero in turn defends men accused of capital 158

ter accuses, quod se ipse necaverit? Excusat item Cicero capitalium rerum reos: Deiotarum regem, Plancium, Quintum Ligarium, Milonem, mille alios; tibi cur te ipsum non liceat excusare? Consolatur ille se se in morte unice carissimeque filie: tu in illorum morte, de quibus nichil ad te, cur non possis alios consolari?

159   Facile se ipsum excusat, quem non pudet; facile consolatur alium, qui non dolet. Et illud est certum: quod quisque promptius se, quam alium excusat. Contra autem quisque promptius alium consolatur, quam se ipsum. Si hec ergo te movent, stude in oratorum libris. Velis esse rethorice dominus: utilis est tibi, necessaria est, totum est: sine illa nullus es. Quotidie enim facis quo et excusator tibi sit necessarius, et consolator alteri. Sed, si es quod profiteris, non excusator tui, non consolator aliorum, imo medicus, si non vulgi plausum, sed, ut debes, egroti tui respicis salutem, quo pergis? quid cogitas? quid agis? aut quid tibi rei est extra terminos tuos longe? An non illud tibi semper conscientia ad aurem cordis immurmurat: 'Iste, cum quo ludis, eger est'. Tu te medicum dicis: quid opus est verbis? Cura, sepe tibi dixi, medice.

160   Rethorica, quam servam tibi vis efficere, hostis tua est; postquam rethores ac poete esse voluistis, medici esse desiistis. Sed hec michi tecum vetus est querela. Cogita et recogita sillogismos tuos: inanes et vacuos invenies. Non probant quod volunt; et, si probarent, tibi dedecus, egris tuis damnum ac periculum probarent. Proba potius rethoricam tibi incognitam, quam servam. Sed egros oculos lux serena prestringit, delectat videri quod esse nec expedit, nec licet. An autem solidum et universalem sillogismum recipis

crimes: Deiotarus the king, Plancius, Ligarius, Milo, and a thousand others. So why shouldn't you defend yourself? Cicero consoles himself for the death of his only, most precious daughter. So why can't you console others for the death of patients who mean nothing to you?

It is easy to defend yourself when you feel no shame, and easy 159 to console others when you feel no grief. And certainly one is quicker to defend oneself than someone else, and quicker to console someone else than oneself. If these topics interest you, study the books of the orators. You would like to be the master of rhetoric, which is useful to you, and even necessary. Rhetoric means everything; without it, you are nothing. Because of your actions, each day you need a defender, and someone else needs a consoler. But if you are what you profess — not your own defender or another's consoler, but a physician — and if you look not to the plaudits of the mob, but to your patient's health, as you should, where are you going? What are you thinking? What are you doing? What involves you with an art so far beyond your limits? Doesn't your conscience continually murmur in your heart's ear: "The fellow you are tricking is a sick man"? You say you are a physician. Why do you need words? Cure your patients, physician, as I have often said.

In fact, Rhetoric, whom you wish to make your servant, is your 160 enemy. When you all chose to be rhetoricians and poets, you ceased to be physicians. But this is my longstanding complaint against you. Think and rethink your syllogisms. You'll find them vain and empty. They fail in what they attempt to prove. And if they proved it, they would prove your dishonor and your patients' harm and danger. Instead, prove that rhetoric is a stranger to you, not a servant. But the pure light blinds your ailing eyes, and you delight in appearing to be something that is neither proper nor permissible. Will you accept a solid and all-embracing syllogism from someone who lacks logic? As long as a rational soul has its

unius logica carentis? Siquidem, sicut anima rationalis, nisi rationem amiserit, corpori suo imperat, corpus autem illi servit, sic
omnes artes, propter animam invente, imperant propter corpus in-
ventis; ille autem serviunt. Constat autem liberales propter animam, mechanicas propter corpus inventas. Conclude, dyaletice:
ergo medicine rethorica serva est.

161   Habes, medice, quod optabas. Sed an ego tecum ludo, cum tu
tamen sis iratus et iocosa conclusio in contrarium cadit? Dimo-
veantur ambages: dicam clare quod sentio, quamvis dentibus tuis
fremas, et tabescas, et michi fortassis anceps farmacum mineris.
Expediret tibi, sed multo magis egris tuis, ut mutus esses, non orator. Et quod natura non fecit, faceret homo aliquis reipublice amicus, linguamque precideret, sumpto forcipe de altari, linguam illam, insulso vix ore versatilem, qua superbis. Tum demum curare
cogitares: nunc cogitas predicare; et quicquid predicas in nichilum
finit. Fallor: imo vero, in tuam infamiam et in perniciem alienam.
Certe non ad artis ignominiam, nec a casu, medicinam Virgilius
mutam vocat, sed quoniam muta debet esse, non loquax.

162   Vos autem eo rem deduxistis, impudentia vestra, ut de mutis
parabolani dici merueritis. Hoc nomen, iure civili vobis imposi-
tum, nunquam cadet. Solebant medici veteres taciti curare: vos pe-
rorantes, et altercantes, et conclamantes occiditis. Hoc medicina,
hoc rethorica vestra est; et cum nulla gens magis rethoricis floribus
nuda sit, nulla minus illis indigeat, tamen rethorici, et oratores, et
poete, et philosophi, et apostoli, ac suscitatores corporum dici
vultis; et penitus nichil estis, nisi verba inania nugeque volatiles.

reason, it commands the body, and the body serves it. Thus all the arts invented for the soul's sake command those invented for the body's sake, and the latter serve the soul. It is clear that the liberal arts were invented for the soul, and the mechanical arts for the body. Draw the conclusion, O dialectician: Therefore, rhetoric is the servant of medicine!

Now you have what you wanted, physician. But should I joke 161 with you when you are still angry and my joking conclusion tells against you? Let us set aside circumlocutions. I shall say clearly what I think, even if you grind your teeth, waste away, or perhaps threaten me with a dangerous drug. It would be better for you, and even better for your patients, if you were mute and not an orator. Let some friend of the republic do what nature left undone. Let him cut off your tongue, "taking tongs from the altar"[147] — that tongue that almost sticks in your boring mouth but makes you proud. Then you might finally think of curing people, whereas now you think of preaching, and all your preaching comes to naught. I'm mistaken. In fact, it ends in your disgrace and in the ruin of others. It is clearly neither a slur on the profession nor an accident when Virgil calls medicine mute: it should be mute and not verbose.[148]

But in your shamelessness, you physicians have gone so far that 162 you deserve to be called palaverers (parabolani) rather than mute. This name, which civil law has imposed on you, will never fall into disuse.[149] Ancient physicians used to give care in silence. You kill while declaiming, arguing, and shouting. This is your medicine, and this your rhetoric. Although no group lacks rhetorical embellishments more, and needs them less, you still insist on being called rhetoricians, orators, poets, philosophers, apostles, and raisers of the dead. Yet you are absolutely nothing but empty words and fleeting trifles. In the past, patients were cured without syllogisms, and nearly raised from the dead, as you now falsely boast. This was the origin of the myth, I believe, that Aesculapius raised

Olim quidem sine sillogismis curabantur et prope, ut tu nunc falso gloriaris, suscitabantur infirmi. Hinc, arbitror, fabule locus fuit, Hipolytum ab Esculapio suscitatum: quod eum ab extremis efficax medicus et velut a morte media revocasset. Nunc quanta mutatio! Sillogizantibus vobis, pereunt qui sine vobis vivere potuissent. Sepe iam nequicquam dixi; curate, medemini; eloquentiam his quorum est propria relinquite; vestra esse non potest.

163   Et ut pro consilio consilium reddam tibi, sed aliquanto fidelius: tu me iubes in alienos fines irrumpere, ego te ad tuos redire moneo. Tu michi consulis ut, mutato adhuc vite genere, medicus fiam—rem neque magnificam et pene impossibilem. Ego tibi ne unquam rethorice studeas, ut tandem medicus esse incipias, quod diu te esse mentitus es. Tam decet ornatus medicum, quam asellum falere. Tibi sane ne hinc reprehendi posses, abunde provisum est. Quisquis te disertum dixerit, idem et nitidam suem, et volucrem testudinem, et candidum corvum dicat. In te ergo, non facundia, sed facundie studium male olet, et facundie inimica loquacitas. De aliis loquebar, dum dixi non esse medici ornatum: magis est mercatori necessarius, quamvis nec ille rethorice quidem studet, sed usu experientiam querit, ac promptitudinem colloquendi. Quam ob causam illud a te non sine certa ratione quesieram: cur non potius navigationi rethoricam subiecisses, si cogebas eam servire mechanice. Quem locum non intelligens (qui ignorantium mos est), non sine meo et multorum risu responsionem supervacuam diffinisti.

Hippolytus from the dead.[150] For that skillful doctor saved him at the last minute, as if from the jaws of death. How different things are now! As you spout syllogisms, those patients die who might have lived without your care. I have already said too often and in vain: cure and heal. Leave eloquence to its rightful owners. It cannot be yours.

Let me repay your advice with some of my own that is rather more trustworthy. You urge me to invade another's field. I enjoin you to return to your own. You advise me to change my former life and become a physician, a change which is neither attractive nor possible. I advise you never to study rhetoric, but to begin to act like a physician, which you have falsely claimed to be for so long. Ornate speech suits a doctor just as as a caparison suits a donkey. I have taken great care to prevent your being censured on this score. If someone calls you eloquent, let him also call the hog elegant, the turtle winged, and the crow snow-white. In sum, what reeks about you is not eloquence, but your pursuit of it, and your verbosity, which is its enemy. I spoke about others when I said that ornate speech is inappropriate for a physician. It is more essential for a merchant who, while not studying rhetoric, seeks by practice to acquire experience and ease in speaking. This is the reason I asked you rather pointedly why you don't subordinate rhetoric to navigation, if you must force it to be subject to a mechanical trade. As is the custom of ignorant people, you misunderstood my remark, and composed a gratuitous reply that made me and many others laugh.

163

164 Sciens gratissimam michi partem maledictorum tuorum ad ultimum reservavi, non quia tu quoque ultimam posuisses — de ordine
enim tuo, de ingenio, de stilo quid sentiam audivisti — sed ut,
prioribus exactis, in hac parte licentius immorarer, palamque omnibus fieret quam sis virtutis amicus, quam cupidus literarum, qui
michi solitariam vitam velut probrum aliquod obiectas. De qua
quidem duo mei libri extant, quos quoniam ad te nec pervenisse,
nec perventuros esse confido, neu perveniant velim, de hoc ipso
cogor aliquid hic etiam ignorantie tue loqui. Ita ne demens igitur
et excors, quos vituperare vis laudas? Non miror, quia et quos
curare vis interficis, et, puto, quos interficere velles efficeres immortales.

165 Tu michi ergo, vesane et omnis boni expers, inter acervos iurgiorum etiam solitudinem exprobrasti. Fecisti optime, quamvis
pessima voluntate. Libenter crimen hoc fateor: sum solitudinis
amicus; talem me genuit natura, accessit consuetudo nature emula,
accessit studium et iugis cura. Magno nisu animi semper incubui,
ut quantum fieri posset illa contemnerem, que te moribundum,
marcidum, semianimem in urbibus captum tenent. Solitarius sum,
fateor, imo profiteor, et solitarium esse iuvat, vixque ullam vite
dulcedinem urbano in strepitu ac fragore percipio. Addam quod
non postulas: vix de homine, presertim studioso, bene extimo, qui
non, si absque intermissione honesti officii datum sit, cupide interdum e procellis civilium curarum in solitudinem velut in portum
fugiat. 'Habes igitur quod est accusatori maxime optandum,' ut ait

Book IV

I have intentionally saved the most pleasant part of your insults   164
for last. This is not because you placed them last. You have already
heard my opinion of your sense of order, your intellect, and your
style. But having finished with the earlier arguments, I wished to
dwell more frankly on this part. In this way, I can make clear to
everyone how you love virtue and how you desire learning when
you object to my solitary life as a sort of disgrace. In fact, I have
written two books on the subject.[151] But I am sure that you have
not seen them and will not see them, nor would I want you to see
them. So here too I am forced to speak to you in your ignorance.
Are you so deranged and senseless that you praise the very people
you wish to disparage? I'm not surprised, since you kill the people
you wish to cure. I even think you could render immortal those
whom you wish to kill.

Now, amid the heaps of your vituperations, O madman lacking   165
all good qualities, you also reproach my solitude. You acted in the
best way, if with the worst intentions. I gladly confess this fault. I
am a friend of solitude, for such did nature create me. My inclina-
tion was compounded by habit, which emulates nature; and it was
further compounded by my studies and continual concerns. With
great spiritual effort, I have always striven as far as possible to despise the things that keep you in the cities as a moribund, rotting,
and half-alive captive. I am a solitary person, as I confess and even
profess. I enjoy being solitary, and take little pleasure in the clatter
and din of the city. Let me add something that you don't expect
me to say. I don't think much of someone, especially a scholar,
who doesn't occasionally flee the turmoil of the civic affairs to seek
out solitude as a haven, provided there is no interruption in his
honorable duties. As Cicero says: "You have then the benefit of
what is the dearest dream of counsel for the prosecution, a defen-

Cicero, 'confitentem reum'; neque confitentem modo, sed se se novorum insuper criminum coacervatione spontanea deferentem.

166   Sed expecta, noli victorie letitia inflari: sepe probavit actor quod non probasse prestabat, et, facti victor, in iure succubuit. Probas, me fatente ac favente, quod intendis; sed an hinc in meum, an in tuum caput redundet infamia, nondum probas. Proinde pedagogum tuum, senex puer, ut arcessas consulo. Multis hic tibi sillogismis claudicantibus opus est, ut vel irrisor vite solitarie clarus sit vel sectator obscurus.

167   Incipe, aude, noli trepidare! Logicus es, philosophia tua est, rethorica tibi servit, et, quod omnes titulos tuos transcendit, summus es medicus. Confice ridiculum sillogismum, qui sepe mortiferum poculum confecisti, et si nescis melius, dic ita: 'Quod nature adversatur, malum sit necesse est, cum natura ipsa sit optima; solitarie autem vivens nature adversatur, secundum quam politicum animal est homo. Mala igitur solitudo'. Ad hec: 'Constat quod carere bonis est miserum; multa vero in urbibus bona esse certum est, quibus solitarius caret. Misera igitur solitudo'. Adde, si placet: 'Ut utilis est qui multis prodest, sic inutilis qui nulli. Habitator vero urbium, vir bonus, multis prodest, saltem exemplo; solitudo autem seu sancta rusticitas nulli nisi sibi soli prodest, teste Ieronimo. Inutilis ergo rustica solitudo'.

168   Vides ut periculosum est cum stulto multum colloqui. Ecce iam ipse ludens sensim ad ineptias tuas labor, et dum te emulari studeo, prope tui similis factus sum. Sed quoniam ex persona tua loquor, excuser; et fatebor ingenue: nulla arte, nullo studio, simulare possem usqueadeo stilum tuum, quin prima fronte discerneremur.

dant who pleads guilty."[152] A defendant who not only pleads guilty, but comes forward volunteering a list of new charges.

But wait, don't puff yourself up yet with the joy of victory! Often a plaintiff will prove a point he should not have offered to prove, and will be victorious on the facts, but lose on the law. You prove what you want to, by my admission and with my assistance. But you haven't proved yet whether the disgrace falls on my head or yours. So I advise you to summon your tutor, O childish old man. You'll need a lot of your stumbling syllogisms to prove that someone is illustrious for deriding the solitary life, or obscure for pursuing it.

Begin, be bold, never fear! You are a logician; philosophy is yours; rhetoric is your servant; and you are a leading physician, a title that surpasses all your other ones. Concoct a ridiculous syllogism, just as you have often concocted lethal potions. If you can't think of anything better, say this: "Whatever contradicts nature is of necessity evil, for nature herself is what is best. Whoever lives solitarily contradicts nature, which made man a political animal.[153] Therefore, solitude is evil." Moreover: "Everyone agrees that a lack of goods is misery. And it is clear that cities offer many goods, which a solitary person lacks. Therefore, solitude is misery." And if you wish, you may add: "A person who benefits many people is useful, and a person who benefits no one is useless. A virtuous city-dweller benefits many people, at least by his example. But solitude or 'holy rusticity benefits itself alone', as Jerome attests.[154] Therefore, rustic solitude is useless."

You see how dangerous it is to converse at length with a fool. Behold, even as I jest, I gradually slip into your nonsense; and as I try to imitate you, I have nearly become your twin. But since I have spoken in your person, let me be excused. I must freely confess: no art or study allows me to reproduce your style so well that the difference would not be immediately apparent. Thus, you hiss at me about something called *Therapeuticum*, which could easily

Ita michi nescio quid terapenticum insibilas, quod e rostris pero-
rantem Tullium facile possit expellere. Sillogismos autem tibi
texui, ne a te texti farmacum oleant stomacumque subvertant. Ceterum hos ludos hasque tendiculas puerorum ridendo preterire
magnificum, puerile dissolvere. Tamen quia cum pueris pueriliter
et interdum, quod nutrices solent, bleso ore loquendum est, et hic
parumper insistam.

169   An nature semper obsequendum, an vero nonnunquam valde
etiam resistendum sit, non huius temporis est questio. Tu eam
forte, philosophorum princeps, in aliquo tuorum voluminum ven-
tilasti. Quem enim philosophie locum rear a tanto philosopho pre-
termissum? Sed sit nature obsequendum, sitque homo naturaliter
animal politicum, nichil tamen politie obesse solitudinem studiosorum hominum, qui proculdubio rari sunt, sepe etiam multum
prodesse compertum est, plusque unum solitarium conferre reipublice, quam centum qui latrinis aut tabernis ac lupanaribus obver-
sentur. Neque enim solitudinem loquimur cuntis hominibus in-
fensam, qualem Bellorophontis accepimus, qui universo generi
humano odium indixerat, aut Timonis nesciocuius (obscurum
enim nomen habet) qui ob id, quod omnem amicitiam sperneret
nullumque diligeret, ab Atheniensibus lapidatus traditur. Non
hanc solitudinem loquimur, sed tranquillam et mitem et ab hominum vitiis, non ab humanitate semotam.

170   Ecce nunc tu per vicos ruis ac plateas, et quasi ad currendum
nati simus, me in solitudine sedentem inhumanum putas. Crede
michi, si placet: plures te quotidie impellunt, plures melioresque
me diligunt; et nisi gloriari tibi importune nimium videar, dicam
quod multis est notum: tales ad me visendum viros in hanc solitudinem venisse, et propter me unum hic cupide fuisse, tales etiam

drive Cicero from the speaker's stand before he ends his oration. I have composed these syllogisms for you to prevent you from composing syllogisms that reek of drugs and turn one's stomach. Besides, it is noble to dismiss such jests and children's sophisms with laughter; just as it would be childish to refute them. Still, since one must speak childishly with children, and sometimes use baby-talk, as nurses do, I shall briefly dwell on this topic.

Whether we must always obey nature, or sometimes firmly re- 169
sist it, is not a question suited to this occasion. In one of your volumes, O prince of philosophers, you may have aired this question. Can I suppose that you have neglected any topic in philosophy? Let's say that nature must be obeyed, and that man is naturally a political animal. Even so, no harm comes to the polity from the solitude of scholars. Such men are doubtless quite rare, but in fact we often have seen that they benefit society. Indeed, one solitary figure may contribute more to the public good than a hundred who frequent latrines, taverns, and brothels. I am not speaking of that solitude which is hostile to all men. We read about such hostility in Bellerophon, who proclaimed his hatred of the entire human race.[155] And a certain Timon, whose very name is obscure, is said to have been stoned by the Athenians because he spurned all friendship and loved no one.[156] Rather than such solitude, I am speaking of the peaceful and gentle solitude which is remote from human vices but not from humanity.

See how you race through lanes and squares, and you think me 170
inhuman for sitting in solitude, as though we were born to run around. Please believe me. Every day you are beleaguered by many people, but I am beloved by many choice people. Unless you think I am boasting too relentlessly, I shall tell you what many already know. Such men have come to see me in my solitude, eager to be here for my sake alone, and have even sent from afar to exhort me and to find out what I am doing. If you approached these same men, they would be loath to see you, saying nothing, and scarcely

misisse de longinquo ad cohortandum me noscendumque quid
agerem, qui te, si ultro illos adeas, egre visuri sint, nichil dicturi,
modicum responsuri. Sed transeo, ne te nimis affligam. Hec autem non ut glorier, cum omnis honor in honorante sit, sed ut scias
multos ruris amatores etiam in urbibus caros esse, multos habita-
tores urbium ipsis in quibus habitant urbibus odiosos. Ita non ad-
versam solitudinem politie, meque, licet solitarium, et amare bonos noveris et ab illis non minus amari quam si, ceno oblitus ac
sudore, et nunc hac, nunc illac more tuo discurrens, prehensarem
homines, loquendo caput omnium obtunderem, nullum dormire
sinerem, cuntis liminibus insultarem, et quem semel arripuissem
tenerem, occideremque tenendo, ut ait Flaccus,

non missura cutem nisi plena cruoris hirudo.

171   In eo quidem quod bonis urbium carere solitarii videntur, nolo
questionem antiquissimam renovare, que inter Perypatheticos ac
Stoicos multis iam seculis fuit, eritque per secula, illis summum,
his solum bonum dicentibus esse virtutem. Que si vera sententia
est, quibus quantisque bonis careat solitaria vita, quisquis vera
bona urbium numerat ac metitur intelliget. Sed quia te, post Aristotilem, tempore, ingenio etiam, primum et cum additamento logice perypatheticum scio, concedam, ne de hoc ipso noviter liti-
gandum sit, esse preter virtutem bona, quibus urbes abundare non
negem, in quibus fornicem, balnea, macellum, mulsum, adipem,
pulmentum, et que sunt similia numeratis. Verum his carere apud
vere realiterque philosophantes non modo non miserum, sed magna etiam solitarie felicitatis accessio est, simul ut cum his vestris
bonis et aliis careat urbanis malis. 'Et quenam ista sunt?' inquies.
Quis cunta dinumeret? Illis caruisse non est parum, que, si ad lite-

replying to you. But I shall pass over this, lest I afflict you too harshly. I don't say this to boast, for honor belongs to the one who bestows it. But you should know that many lovers of the country are esteemed in the cities, whereas many city-dwellers are hateful to the very cities in which they dwell. And you should see that solitude is not the enemy of the polity. Despite my solitude, I love virtuous people, and am loved by them. For them to love me, I don't have to run here and there as you do, stained with mud and sweat, laying hold of people, deafening them with my chatter, letting no one sleep, and trampling all doorsteps. And if I catch someone, I don't hold him until he dies in my grasp, as Horace says,

A leech that will not let go the skin, till gorged with blood.[157]

Some think that solitary people lack the goods of the city. I 171 don't wish to revive the ancient question that divided the Peripatetics and Stoics for many centuries in the past, and will divide them for centuries to come. The Peripatetics said that virtue is the highest good, while the Stoics said that it is the only good. If this latter opinion is true, anyone who reckons and measures the true goods of the city will surely understand what great goods are lacking in the solitary life. But I know that after Aristotle, both chronologically and mentally, you are the foremost Peripatetic, and a great logician to boot. So to avoid arguing about this again, I shall grant that there are goods besides virtue, and I shall not deny that cities offer them in abundance: brothels, baths, food markets, honeyed wine, lard, appetizers, and other things of this kind. Yet for those who are really and truly philosophers, the lack of such things is not a source of misery. In fact, it even increases their solitary happiness, since their solitude lacks both your so-called goods and the other ills of the city. "What ills?" you will ask. Who could count them all? It is no small thing to avoid such ills, for if you

ram intelligas, non mediocris quemlibet fortune virum, sed David regem ex urbibus in solitudinem pepulerunt.

172   Quenam vero hec? Nempe iniquitas et contradictio in civitate, et labor in medio eius, et iniustitia, et non deficiens de plateis eius usura, et dolus. Iam quod sequitur responsione non eget. Sancta rusticitas sibi soli prodest: studiosa autem solitudo prodesse posse quamplurimis non negatur. Et ipse Ieronimus, qui hoc dixit, quantum solitudine delectatus et quantum ibi mundo utilis fuerit, sciunt omnes. Sed quia non possunt omnes esse Ieronimi, etsi magnum nichil in solitudine geratur, tantum ut vivatur innocue, vitentur incentiva libidinum, quibus porticus civitatum ac theatra flammescunt, parum ne tibi forsitan videtur? Apud me multo quidem optabilius est solum salvari, quam perire cum multis.

173   Sed iam satis est; iam te egrum egris tuis linquere meditor: illi te conficient, tu illos. Caret solitudo multis vulgi voluptatibus, sed abundat suis: quiete, libertate, otio; quamvis verum sit quod ait Anneus: 'Otium sine literis mors est, et vivi hominis sepultura', et profecto solitarius ydiota, nisi forte Cristus valde continue secum sit, quantolibet in spatio terrarum sine ullis vinculis vinctus est. Unde non miror id tibi vite genus invisum. Quid enim hic ageres, nisi numerare horas, et querere quando cenatum secundum regulas tuas, quando cubitum ires? Quem circumscribere, seu cum quo clamare posses? Nullus occurreret: tecum loqui nescires. Id enim est hominum paucorum, et tamen his eisdem in locis parva, fateor, seu verius nulla copia. Sed nonnullo nec parvo quidem amore literarum tam bene tamque predulciter michi est, ut si statum animi mei nosses, putem te horam, qua natus es, odio habiturum, que te in illam miseram et infelicem vitam proiecit, et propter pecunie parve spem permagnas rapit angustias.

read the text literally, they drove not just some fellow of moderate fortune, but King David himself, to flee the city into solitude.[158]

What ills, then? Clearly, iniquity, civil dissension, the hardship   172 in the center of town, injustice, the usury practiced in its squares, and fraud. The following charge needs no response. "Holy rusticity benefits itself alone." True, but no one can deny that studious solitude benefits a great many people. Take Jerome himself, who said this about rusticity.[159] Everyone knows how much he delighted in solitude, and how useful he was to the world by living there. Not everyone can be a Jerome. But even if one does nothing great in solitude, do you think it a small thing if one lives innocently and avoids the incitements of the lusts that burn in the colonnades and theaters of our cities? For me, it is far more desirable to be saved alone than to perish with many.

Enough of this. By now I contemplate leaving you as a sick man   173 to your sick patients. They will kill you, and you them. Solitude lacks many of the mob's pleasures, but it abounds in its own: quiet, freedom, leisure. Of course, what Seneca says is true: "Leisure without letters is death, and a tomb for the living man."[160] Indeed, unless Christ always attends him, a solitary ignoramus is fettered even without fetters, no matter how great the earthly space he occupies. Hence, I am not surprised that you hate this way of life. What would you do here but count the hours, and ask when you could eat and sleep according to your rules? Whom could you swindle, or at whom could you shout? You would meet no one, and would not know how to converse with yourself. Few people know how to do this. Even in these parts, I confess, such people are in short supply, or, to be frank, there is no supply of them at all. Yet because I have a great love of letters, my life here is so good and delightful that, if you knew my state of mind, I think you would hate the hour you were born. For it has cast you into a wretched and unhappy life, and has plunged you into great anguish in the hope of petty gain.

174   Quid ergo locutus es, miserabilis senex? Quid in me damnasti?
Amarunt solitudinem patriarche, prophete, sancti, philosophi,
poete, duces imperatoresque clarissimi. Imo vero solitudinem quis
non amat, nisi qui secum esse non novit? Odit solitudinem quisquis in solitudine solus est, timetque otium quisquis in otio nil
agit. Quantum vero habet unde tristetur qui, ut gaudeat, turbam
querit! Plane miser est qui felicitatem sperat a miseris. O mendice
medice, qui te, nature conscium, philosophum vocas, sic ubinam
sit vera felicitas didicisti? Certe non opus est turbis confusisque
clamoribus, non theatrico strepitu, non vulgo inter miserias plaudente, non quadrigis fundamenta quassantibus, non cruento foro,
non nidore fumantium popinarum, et olentium acie coquorum
atque aromata transmarina terentium, quos, vobis exceptis, nescio
an efficacissimos omnium ministros mortis appellem. Nichil his
omnibus est opus. Intus in anima est quod felicem et quod miserum facit. Hinc illud poeticum digne laudatur:

    nec te quesieris extra.

175   Constat autem nunquam melius esse anime quam dum, amotis
obstaculis viteque compedibus, in Deum atque in se ipsam libera
tandem et expedita convertitur. Enimvero id, dum sumus in terris,
nusquam melius quam in solitudine fieri posse, etsi tu non capias,
fatebuntur experti. Illud quoque platonicum, ab Augustino relatum et laudatum, notissime verum est: 'Non corporeis oculis,' ut
verba etiam ipsa ponam, 'sed pura mente veritatem videri. Cui
cum anima inheserit, eam beatam fieri atque perfectam; ad quam
percipiendam nichil magis impedire quam vitam libidinibus dedi-
tam'. Que sententia a Virgilio—quem tu spernis ut vespertilio
aquilam, simia leonem—elegantissime sub allegorica nube recon-

What did you say, wretched old man? What did you condemn   174
in me? Many people have loved solitude — patriarchs, prophets,
saints, philosophers, poets, generals, and famous emperors. Indeed, who would not love solitude, except a person incapable of
living with himself? Solitude is hated by people who feel solitary in it, and leisure is feared by people who are idle in it. By contrast, people who seek joy in the crowd have good reason to feel
sad. Truly wretched is the person who hopes for happiness from
wretches. O mendicant medic, as an expert on nature, you call
yourself a philosopher. Is this what you have learned about where
true happiness is found? Surely we don't need crowds and confused shouts, the racket of the theater, the applause of the miserable mob, the thundering chariot-races, the squares awash in blood,
the fumes of reeking taverns, the hosts of smelly cooks and grinders of exotic spices. (I would call the spice grinders the most effi-
cient ministers of death, with the exception of you physicians.)
There is no need for any of these. Deep within the soul lies what
makes us happy or wretched. Hence, the poet's phrase is justly
praised:

Look to no one outside yourself.[161]

Now, everyone agrees it is best for the soul to shake off life's   175
hindrances and shackles, and to turn free and unencumbered to itself and to God. While we are on earth, this can best be done in
solitude. This is a fact that experienced people will confess, but
that you don't understand. Plato's observation, which Augustine
cited and praised, is widely recognized as true. To cite his very
words: "We see the truth not with the body's eyes, but with a pure
mind. When the soul clings to the truth, it becomes blessed and
perfect; and nothing hinders our perception of the truth more
than a life devoted to sensual desires."[162] Virgil too, whom you despise as a bat despises an eagle, or an ape a lion, concealed this no-

ditur; quem locum pretereo, ne cerebellum tuum mole rerum opprimam.

176   Quam doctrinam ab Archita tarentino, magno in primis et preclaro viro, didicisse Plato ipse potuerat, dum illum pithagoreosque alios visendi discendique gratia in Italiam venisset. Ille enim, ut apud Ciceronem Cato meminit, 'nullam capitaliorem pestem quam corporis voluptatem hominibus dicebat a natura datam'. Deinde, enumeratis malis que ex voluptatis[13] radice nascuntur, illud addebat: 'Cum homini sive natura sive quis deus mente nichil prestabilius dedisset, huic divino dono nichil tam inimicum esse quam voluptatem. Nec enim, libidine dominante, temperantie locum esse, neque omnino in voluptatis regno virtutem posse consistere'. Quibus ita se habentibus nec illud ambigitur: et quod beatam perfectamque animam fieri vetat summo studio vitandum, et virtutem in proprio, non inimice sue regno esse querendam.

177   Iam illud ne probari quidem est necesse; civitatem libidinum esse sentinam, omniumque ibi turpium voluptatum illecebras scaturire. Piget nunc, pudetque conclusiunculas infantiles tuo more subnectere. Tu, qui logicam spuis, facile consequentiam vides. At ne nimis urgeam, excusare nunc etiam iudicium tuum libet. Profecto enim solitudinem odisse mechanici est. Facis, fateor, quod te decet. Ubi enim nisi inter turbas credulas fatuorum ingenioli tui mercimonium ostentares? Posses hic quidem esurire: totius anni mendacia una te luce non pascerent. Iure igitur locum fugis moribus tuis adversum. Illud iniuste agis, quod inter studiosos literarum ac mechanicos non discernis. Linque solitudinem his quibus nec falli nec fallere est animus, qui nec pauperiem timent nec divitias venerantur, sed utrinque paribus spatiis delectantur absistere, qui honestissimam voluptatem ex libris, ex ingenio, ex animi agitatione percipiunt.

tion most elegantly in a cloud of allegory; but I omit the passage to avoid crushing your little brain under such a weight.[163]

Plato himself may have learned this doctrine from Archytas of 176 Tarentum, a great and distinguished man, when Plato came to Italy to visit and study with him and his fellow Pythagoreans. As Cato observes in Cicero's dialogue, Archytas used to say that "physical pleasure was the deadliest plague that nature had given to humankind."[164] Then, having enumerated the ills that have their roots in pleasure, he would add: "Since nature or some god endowed humankind with nothing more excellent than intelligence, there is nothing more hostile to this divine gift than pleasure. For when lust commands, there is no place for temperance, and virtue cannot survive in pleasure's domain."[165] As this is the case, there can be no doubt that we must avoid at all costs whatever opposes the happy and perfect life, and that we must seek virtue not in its enemy's domain, but in its own.

By now it is pointless to show that the city is the bilge of lust, 177 and that from it spring the lures of all shameful pleasures. I am loathe and ashamed to weave infantile and flimsy syllogisms as you do. As one who spouts logic, you will easily draw the conclusion. But lest I press you too hard, let me now defend your point of view. Clearly, hating solitude is typical of a mechanic. I confess that you are only acting as is proper for you. Where but amid crowds of credulous fools could you display the wares of your small talent? Here in the country, you might go hungry. A year of lies wouldn't feed you for a single day. Thus you justly flee a place so contrary to your character. But you are unjust when you fail to distinguish between men of letters and mechanics. Leave solitude to people who wish neither to deceive nor to be deceived; who neither fear poverty nor worship wealth, but gladly steer a middle course between the two; and who take honest pleasure in books, in talent, and in mental exercise.

178   Tu autem, nullo prohibente, habita ubi te matutina muliercula-
rum cohors in publico sedentem adeat, circumstrepat, interpellet.
Tu pro tribunali, stricto pallido labello elatoque rugoso supercilio, suspirans examines quid ea nocte quis minxerit, et vix tandem quassanti capite sententiam feras: 'Ille peribit, iste curabitur.'
Quam cum falsam finis ostenderit, apud te non prius mendacium
quam excusatio sit inventa. Sin vera forsan evaserit—fieri enim
non potest, ut quisquam tam plenus mendaciorum sit, quin casu
saltem veri aliquid multiloquio misceatur—exultes ac tumeas, ipsumque te putes Apollinem et Delphis oraculum processisse.

179   Non es itaque totus amens: locum tibi aptissimum delegisti.
Habitant reges in urbibus, presidesque terrarum et iudices, quique
coercendis vulgi moribus presunt, quos reipublice necessitas excusat horum presentiam requirentis; habitant ibi aliquo gravi negotio
detenti: hos proprie ius necessitatis absolvit; habitant ibi volup-
tuosi atque cupidinarii, quibus placet 'fornix et uncta popina', ut
ait Flaccus; habitant ibi circumscriptores, mimi, fures, totumque
id genus; ibi postremo habitant mechanici, quibus omnibus propositum unum: vel fallere vel lucrari. Tibi utrunque propositum
est; quod intendis, alibi non potes: fuge igitur solitudinem, urbes
ama. Quinetiam, siquid michi credis, illic tibi non suburbium
elige, sed plateam. Quid multa? Doctos ut scopulum cave, habita
inter stultos. Venator nemora; piscator aquas; sequitur lupus inde-
fensum gregem; circulator, mimus, fur, impostor divites, stultos,
credulos insequitur: nichil sane circulatori gravius, quam ludum
suum ab astante cognosci.

180   Hinc—ne me omnino rusticum putes, quia rure habito—hinc
illud venenum visceribus tuis sparsum, quod te quiescere non si-

As for you, no one forbids you to live where each morning a co- 178
hort of little ladies will accost you as you sit in public, surrounding
you with importunate cries. Before this court, you will tense your
pallid lips, raise your wrinkled brow, and sigh as you examine the
urine samples of the previous night. Then shaking your head, you
will pronounce judgment: "That fellow will die; this one will re-
cover." When the outcome exposes your judgment as false, you'll
have an excuse as quick as a lie. But if your judgment proves
true — for even a person so full of lies must by chance mix some
truth into his wordy chattering — you'll exult and swell up, thinking that you are Apollo and that your oracle came from Delphi.

You're not completely crazy, then. You have chosen a place quite 179
suited to yourself. In cities, there dwell kings, local governors,
judges, and officials who oversee public behavior. Their presence
there is dictated by the needs of the commonwealth. In cities,
there dwell people occupied with important affairs. They are justified by the duty of their personal obligations. In cities, there
dwell voluptuaries and epicures — people who love "a brothel and a
greasy tavern," as Horace says.[166] In cities, there dwell swindlers,
mimes, thieves, and all their breed. And finally there dwell mechanics, who share a single goal: to deceive or make a profit. You
have both these goals, and cannot achieve them anywhere else. So
flee solitude, and love the cities. Indeed, if you take my advice, you
won't choose a suburb, but the town square. In short, avoid scholars like a perilous reef, and dwell among fools. A hunter seeks
woods, a fisher seeks waters, and a wolf seeks an unguarded herd.
A swindler, mime, thief, or impostor seeks out the rich, the foolish, and the credulous. Nothing grieves a swindler like a bystander
who sees through his game.

This is the source of the poison that has spread through your 180
bowels and gives you no peace. Don't take me for a bumpkin because I live in the country. When I saw that the pontiff was beset
by disease on one side and by fraud and ignorance on the other, I

nit. Cum enim pontificem maximum hinc morbo, hinc quorundam fraude vel ignorantia circumventum cernerem, eum certe fideliter sed, ut res docuit, frustra premonui. Licet enim tunc evaderet, in eosdem tamen laqueos mox reversus, utilisque consilii vel immemor vel contemptor, totum se vobis tradidit. Ubi, quod sepe accidit, melior pars numero victa est, tuaque et ceterorum ignorantium prevalente sententia, intempestivis remediis et immodica (ut fertur) senilis sanguinis rapina, illum, si sineretur adhuc forte victurum, pontificali solicitudine liberastis. Ita brevi tempore caput mutavit Ecclesia, et antequam nos nostre contentionis, is, unde contentio orta erat, vite sue finem repperit, te iuvante.

181   Hoc quenquam animadvertisse fers graviter? Sed certe non solus ego ludos vestros intelligo: quid soli michi irasceris? An quia solus e cuntis ludo astantibus mutire ausus sum, ut qui fallebatur adverteret? Habes prope iustam iracundie causam, circulator: pulverem tuum funiculumque detegere, quinetiam spargere atque confringere volui, fateor; fecissemque, si michi creditum fuisset.

182   Unum tibi satis inculcare nequeo; nec enim decies repetiisse sufficiet. Si in me rabies tua, ignorantie sibi conscia, linguam urgebat, quid poete meriti, quorum nec aliquem noscis nec aptus natus es noscere? Ut sim ego poeta—quod tu potius dicis, et ego patior, quam credam—quid tamen ideo? Non ego te carmine aut ullo poetico mucrone confixeram, sed pedestri solutoque sermone leseram, quodque maius impatientie tue signum fuerit, non ad te, sed ad alterum transmisso. Neque enim de te, sed de ignorantibus atque discordibus, quorum tunc ego te principem nesciebam. Quotiens tibi iam dixi: frustra despumas in poetas, aerem verberas, in ventum furis. Neque enim poetice lesus es. O cerebrum plumbeum! Hoc non potes intelligere, cum philosophia et logica

warned him in good faith but to no avail, as the event proved.[167] Although he recovered then, he soon fell into the old snares. Ignoring or disdaining my useful advice, he placed himself completely in your hands. As often happens, the better faction was defeated by the larger one. Your opinion, shared by other ignorant physicians, prevailed. Your ill-timed medications and your bloodletting (which people say were excessive) delivered this old man from his papal cares, although he might still be alive if he had been left alone. In this way, the Church changed its leader in a short time; and before our dispute had an end, the man who had inspired it had met his end, thanks to your help.

Are you distressed that someone noticed the fact? Clearly I am 181 not alone in recognizing your game. So why are you angry at me alone? Because I alone among all the bystanders dared to murmur against your game, in order to warn your dupe? You nearly have a just reason for your anger, you mountebank. I wished to expose your magic powders and your rope tricks, or rather to scatter and break them, I confess. And I would have succeeded, had I been believed.

There is one lesson that I cannot sufficiently hammer home. 182 Even repeating it ten times would not suffice. If rage and guilt for your ignorance urged your tongue against *me*, what fault was it of the poets, whom you neither know personally nor were born to know? Suppose that I am a poet as you say, and as I concede even without believing it. So what? I did not transfix you with a poem or poetic barb, but offended you with humble prose. And it is a clear sign of your hypersensitivity that my prose was addressed not to you, but to someone else. I was not writing about you, but about ignorant and contentious men. I didn't know then that you were their ringleader! How many times I have told you? You foam in vain against the poets. You beat the air, and rage against the winds. You weren't even offended in poetry. O leaden brain! You don't understand *this*, even though philosophy and logic belong to

tue sint? Et miraris si te surdum cecumque, aut si saxeum vocem! Quid tecum amplius quam cum aliquo ex his scopulis Sorgie impendentibus loqui iuvat? Nisi quod ille aliquid forte, tu nichil ad quesita respondes.

183 Leserim ego te: quid poetica meruit? Sim poeta: telum illud veritatis quod, ut video, alte descendit in cor tuum, non loro poetico, sed nuda manu et verbis puris atque simplicibus missum erat. Philosophe ingens, quero a te: an si te musicus non cantu, sed verbis offenderet, vel Aristoxenum vel ipsam musicam condemnares? An siquis astrologus non quadrantem eneum, sed baculum tibi quernum in calvitium impegisset, malediceres Ptholomeo? An si te vel agricola non stiva, sed saxo feriat, Hesiodum carperes aut Palladium? Vel piscator non hamo, sed gladio percutiat, Petro detrahes aut Andree? An ego, quia tu michi oles, Ypocratis vel Asclepiadis memoriam lacerabo?

184 Satis est adversarium ferire, etiam ne, ob unius hominis odium, humanum omne genus oderis, multosque tibi hostes feceris, impar uni. Hec repetere visum est, ut, quod ingenio non potes, crebra saltem repetitione concipias te, dum me invaderes, iratum fuisse, dum poeticam lacesseres,[14] furiosum: utrobique non modo mendicum literarum, sed omnis inopem rationis. Et cum poetis quidem deinceps, ut libet, michi iam parcere poteras: odii causa sublata est. Hactenus enim ludum tuum volui impedire, nec potui; posthac impedire nec cogito nec oportet. Hunc enim pontificem habemus, qui, si verum audio, nugas tuas non pluris faciat quam sint, quique vel innata prudentia vel exemplo novo et insigni tales facile vitet insidias.

185 Finis iam huius sermonis esse poterat et, ut arbitror, tempus erat; sed ubere ac pregnanti eloquio tuo retrahor: sic facete tan-

you? And you are surprised that I call you deaf, blind, and made of stone! There is no more point in talking to you than to some boulder overhanging the Sorgue river.[168] Except that the boulder might perhaps reply to my questions, while you remain silent.

Suppose that I offended you. Was poetry at fault? Suppose that I am a poet. The spear of truth that I see lodged deep in your heart was not launched by a poetic slingshot, but by a naked hand and by pure and simple words. O great philosopher, I ask you this. If a musician offended you by his words rather than his song, would you condemn Aristoxenus and the very art of music? If some astronomer had struck your bald pate, not with a bronze quadrant, but with an oak club, would you curse Ptolemy? If a farmer had hit you, not with a plow-handle, but with a rock, would you blame Hesiod or Palladius? If a fisherman had slashed you not with a hook, but with a sword, would you disparage Peter or Andrew? And if you stink, shall I tear to shreds the memory of Hippocrates or Asclepiades? 183

It is enough to strike one's opponent. Hatred for one man should not make you hate the whole human race. If you are no match for a single enemy, you should not make many enemies. These remarks bear repeating, so that frequent repetition teaches you what your intellect can't grasp. When you attacked me, you were angry; but when you challenged poetry, you were raving mad. In both instances, you were not only destitute of learning, but devoid of reason. You could have easily have spared me together with the poets, for the cause of your hatred had passed away.[169] Now we have a pontiff who values your nonsense no more than it deserves, if what I hear is true.[170] Warned by his native wisdom or by this recent and notable example, he will easily avoid similar traps. 184

This could have been the end of my discourse, and it was about time, I think. But your exuberant and fecund eloquence drags me back. You hold me with such wit and art that I cannot let you go. 185

taque arte me detines, ut abire nequeam abs te. Quis enim tam mutus, ut illi ioco non respondeat, quo desponsasse me dicis fontem Sorgie? Clare philosophe, non locum hunc aut illum, sed tranquillitatem mentis ac libertatem sequor, quas tu nescis. Illas ego non tantum ad Sorgie, sed ad Nili fontem querere non gravabor. Ibo quo nec Alexander mittere, nec Cambises potuit pervenire. Non me 'rubicunda perusti zona poli,' non 'epularum defectus' impediet, que causa duplex cepto arcuisse legitur tantos reges. Solus et esuriens et adustus, si illas ibi esse noverim, ad tranquillitatem animi libertatemque perveniam.

186   Scio tamen eas non in locis sed in animis inveniri; verum ad id conferre aliquid loca salubria et quieta non dubito. 'Cur,' inquies, 'asperiore loco habitas, cum mollioribus non veteris?' Si reddenda nunc etiam vite ratio est, necdum manum ferule subduximus. Dicam de multis unam causam legisse: nescio an intellexisse potes apud Senecam honestius Scipionem Literni exulasse quam Bais.

187   Non est unam rem amantis contrariam sponte sequi. Non est igitur aut virtutem adepti, qualem me non esse lugeo, aut ad virtutem suspirantis, qualem me, si permiseris, non nego — non est, inquam, ad virtutem aspirantis ultro degere ubi voluptas, inimica virtutis, imperet. 'Quid ergo? Nemo,' inquies, 'bonus in urbibus?' Non dico id quidem; sed innumerabiles mali, a quibus non modo proficientem sed profectum quoque, si possit, securius sit abesse. Accedit quod nec ita rure relegatus sum, quin sepius quam vellem amicorum precibus ad urbem retrahar, sepe etiam sponte mea vager, vitans locorum alternatione fastidium.

Is anyone so mute that he would not reply to your jibe that I am "married to the source of the Sorgue river"? O illustrious philosopher, I do not seek one place or another, but peace of mind and freedom, which are unfamiliar to you. I would be no more reluctant to seek these things at the source of the Nile than at the source of the Sorgue. I would go beyond where Alexander could lead, and Cambyses journey. Neither "the blazing zone of parched sky" nor "the shortage of provisions" would stop me, even though we read that these two causes kept such great kings from attaining their goals.[171] Alone and starving and burning, I would attain peace of mind and freedom, if I knew they were there.

Of course, I know that these things are found not in our habitats, but in our hearts. Yet I have no doubt that healthy and quiet places may contribute to attaining them. "Why do you dwell in a harsh place," you will ask, "when no one denies you milder locales?" If even now I must account for my life, I have not yet escaped the schoolmaster's rod. Let me explain that I chose one reason out of many. I don't know whether you can understand what Seneca means when he says that Scipio's exile was more honorable in Liternum than in Baiae.[172]

A person fond of one thing will scarcely choose to pursue its opposite. Now, take someone who has attained virtue—which, I regret, is not my case—or take someone who longs for virtue—as I admit I do, if you will allow me. Such a person, I say, will scarcely choose to live where pleasure, the enemy of virtue, is in command. "What then?" you will ask. "Is there no one good in the city?" I don't say that, but there are countless bad people. When possible, it is safer for both the beginner and the advanced student of virtue to avoid them. What's more, I have not been banished to the country so rigorously that my friends' entreaties don't summon me back to the city more often than I would like. And I often wander of my own accord, changing places to avoid boredom.

186

187

159

188   Facti mei causam audisti. O, si te nunc scisciter, vice versa, quid tu latrinas omnes ambire nunquam desinas, qualem michi expedies rationem? Dices te sanare rempublicam, quam egram fateor, a te sanari posse nego, nisi quantum te spero quotidie multis illam dementibus, veluti corpus infectum damnosis humoribus, exhaurire.

189   Quem vero non curis exonerent impleantque letitia speculationes ille tue pulcerrime? Quarum prima est: an, in solitudine habitans, sim deus an bestia; diffinisque non deum. Sed audite, queso, philosophi, rationem: quia poetas sequor, ut dicit et non probat. Ergo, si poetas non sequerer, deus essem. Tu, igitur, qui nec poetam nec ipsum poete nomen intelligis, quis deorum es? Certe si ignorantia deum facit, tu non solum deus, sed deus deorum iure vocaberis. Quero autem quod apud Lucanum de Nerone scriptum est:

    quis deus esse velis?

190   Non respondes, perplexus es. Dabo tibi consilium: lege Varronis vel, quia illos non habes, Augustini libros, inveniasque tibi placitum aliquod dei nomen. Deus enim esse non prohiberis, quia poetas negligis. Magna ibi deorum copia et nominum multa varietas. Si me rogas, quod in his paulo forsan exercitatior sum, tria tibi deorum nomina, utriusque sexus, excerpsi: esto vel Pallor vel Cloacina vel Febris. Hec te cito utinam, o stolidum caput, arripiat, ut et strepere desinas et tuo periculo experiaris quibus remediis abundes!

191   O insensate, non sum deus, nisi forte eo modo quo, propter intelligentiam et actum Aristoteli videtur homo mortalis deus. Quod, si beatus essem, utique deus essem, iuxta illud philosophi-

You have heard the reasons for my behavior. If I now asked you 188
in turn why you keep making the rounds of all the latrines, what
reason will you produce? You will say you are healing the body
politic, which I confess is sick. But I deny that you can heal it, except insofar as I hope that you rid it each day of many madmen,
like a body infected with noxious humors.

But who would not forget his cares and be filled with joy by 189
your exquisite speculations? The first of these is the following.[173]
Since I live in solitude, I must be either a god or a beast. You
won't define me as a god. Listen to his reasoning, ye philosophers.
The reason is that I emulate the poets, or so he alleges but does
not prove. Therefore, if I didn't emulate the poets, I would be a
god. And you, then, who understand neither a poet nor even the
name of poet, which god are you? Clearly, if ignorance made us
gods, you would justly be called not merely a god, but the god of
gods. I ask you the question that was posed to Nero in Lucan:

What god do you wish to be?[174]

You don't answer. You are perplexed. I shall give you a piece of 190
advice. Read Varro's books or, since you don't have them, read Augustine's books.[175] There you will find the name of some god that
pleases you. Since you neglect the poets, you are not forbidden to
be a god. There is a great abundance of gods, and a vast variety of
names. If you ask me, since I may have a bit more experience with
them, I have selected three divine names for you, of both genders:
Pallor, Sewer, and Fever.[176] May Fever quickly seize you, block-
head, so that you stop ranting and discover to your peril what sort
of remedies you offer so abundantly.

O senseless fellow, I am no god, except perhaps in the view of 191
Aristotle, who considers man a "mortal god" because of his intelligence and actions.[177] If I were blessed, I would certainly be a god,
according to Boethius' philosophical dictum: "Every happy person
is God. God is by nature one only, but nothing prevents the great-

cum Severini: 'Omnis beatus deus. Natura quidem unus; partecipatione vero quam plurimos esse nil prohibet,' quod ab Augustino habuit Psalmo centesimo decimo octavo: 'Non enim,' inquit, 'existendo sunt homines dei, sed fiunt partecipando illius unius qui verus est Deus'. Certe peccatis nostris effectum est ut, cum audissemus: 'Ego dixi dii estis et filii Excelsi,' omnes illud continuo tristius audiremus: 'Vos autem sicut homines moriemini'; ac ne quis principatui potentieque fideret additum est: 'Et sicut unus de principibus cadetis'.

192   Itaque, profundissime speculator, non sum deus, nec semideus quidem, qualem Lucanus Pompeium, Labeo describit Herculem, Romulum, et de philosophis Platonem. Nunquam miser in has insanias cecidisses, si aliquando cogitasses, quam grande negotium sit, licet excellentibus ingeniis, divinitatem non dicam assequi, sed etiam contemplari; si semel legisses illud preclare dictum a Platone, ab Apuleio relatum et ab Augustino in libro *De Civitate Dei* positum: 'Deum esse summum omnium creatorem, ipsumque solum esse qui non possit, penuria sermonis humani, quavis oratione vel modice comprehendi; vix saltem sapientibus viris, cum se vigore animi, quantum licuit, a corpore removent ad intellectum huius Dei. Id quoque interdum, velut in altissimis tenebris, rapidissimo coruscamine lumen candidum intermicare'. Quid tibi, medice, videtur? Quid de hac urina iudicas Platonis? Certe Augustinus, magnus medicus animorum, sani hominis eam censet. Quamobrem non sum deus, ut dixi, quippe nec idoneus contemplator Dei; non, si tam sapiens sim quam tu tibi sapiens videris. Quid ergo? Opus exiguum Dei sum, cultorque utinam! Bestie vero titulum nemo, te vivente, merebitur.

193   Sed eloquentie tue nichil est arduum: nomen tuum michi tentas ingerere. Et quem non exhilaret urbanitas tua, dum me inter-

est number possible sharing in that divinity."[178] Boethius derived this notion from Augustine's commentary on Psalm 118: "People are not gods by their act of existence, but become gods by sharing in the one true God."[179] Yet as a result of our sins, after we have heard, "I have said: You are gods, and all of you children of the Most High," we are all saddened to hear the next verse, "Yet you shall die like men." Then, warning us not to trust in princedoms and power, the Psalmist adds: "And you shall fall like any prince."[180]

Hence, O profound speculator, I am not a god, nor even a 192 demigod, which is how Lucan describes Pompey, and how Labeo describes Hercules and Romulus, and the philosopher Plato.[181] You would never have fallen into such insanity, poor wretch, if you had considered what a great labor it is, even for outstanding intellects, to contemplate divinity, much less to attain it. Or if even once you had read Plato's excellent teaching, which is reported by Apuleius and cited in Augustine's *City of God*: "God is the supreme creator of all things, and the only one who, 'because of the poverty of human speech, cannot be even passably described. Even when wise men have removed themselves by a powerful act of mind as far as possible from the body, the knowledge of this God hardly reaches them, and when it does on occasion, it darts at lightning speed like a flash of white light through the deep darkness.'"[182] What do you think, physician? What is your opinion of Plato's urine? Clearly Augustine, a great physician of souls, judges it that of a healthy person. This is why I am not a god, as I said, nor an ideal contemplator of God. Nor would I be even if I were as wise as you think you are. What then? I am merely a petty work of God. May I also be his worshiper! But no one else will merit the title of "beast" as long as you are alive.

Nothing proves too arduous for your eloquence: you even try to 193 impose your name on me. Who will not be cheered by your witticism when you ask me if I am a lion, since the opening of my reply

rogas an sim leo, quia scilicet id, ut dicis, responsionis mee principium preferebat? Atqui, conviciator mordax et frivole, sive me
leonem voces, non movebor, sciens quod in Scripturis Sacris—
quarum non ignarus modo, sed hostis es—Cristus leo dicitur, sive
me leonem neges, non irascar, memor quod in eisdem Scripturis
diabolus leo est. O insulsi sales, auctorique suo simillimi! Quid
ais? Non potes iocum tuum concludere, mime senex! Iam nemo
est qui aliud in te, nisi te, rideat. Explica lingue nodum, fac rideamus, dum egri interim tui plorant. Dic, age, dic secure, nil timue-
ris: tuam auream eloquentiam expectamus. Dic, rethorice imperator, dic, Galiene, Demosthenes, dic, bone Cicero et Avicenna; sum
leo vel quid aliud?

194   'Non es,' inquit, 'leo, sed noctua'. Ridete omnes, plaudite, fa-
bula acta est. Sed—heu! —non sacrarum tantum, verum omnium
literarum nescie, an non saltem audisti—talia enim legisse non
potes, quoniam extra *Terapenticam* tuam sunt—apud antiquos nostros ingeniosissimos, quod nemo ambigit, ac doctissimos quidem
viros avem hanc Minerve consecratam, que apud illos sapientie dea
est? Miraris, ydiota? Peregrina sunt hec. Velles audire rei causam?
Occulta est avis, et volucrum stupor; nocte vigilat, inter tenebras
videt, dormientibus cuntis volat. Mirari autem desines, si cogitare
ceperis ex persona Cristi, qui verus sapientie Deus et ipse sapientia
Patris est, in Psalmo centesimo primo dictum esse: 'Factus sum sicut nycticorax in domicilio'.

195   Vide autem quanti te faciam, philosophe. Quod ad irridendum
studio conquisisti, ad irrisionem tuam et gloriam meam facili lu-
dificatione conversum est. Videro qualiter upupam tuam, philosophie rethoriceque dominus, laudando, tuam vertes in gloriam.
Disce iam, iurgator, vel mordere profundius vel silere. Nunc enim

introduced the word, as you note? In fact, O mordant and frivolous slanderer, if you call me a lion, I shall not be troubled. I know
that Christ is called a lion in the Holy Scriptures, of which you
are not only ignorant, but an enemy as well.[183] And if you say I am
not a lion, I shall not be angry, since I recall that the devil is called
a lion in the same Scriptures.[184] What witless witticisms, so like
their author! What do you say? You cannot conclude your jest,
you decrepit buffoon! By now, nobody is laughing with you; they
are laughing at you. Untie the knot in your tongue. Make us laugh
while your patients weep. Speak up, speak freely, have no fear!
We await your golden eloquence. Speak, O emperor of rhetoric!
Speak, Galen and Demosthenes! Speak, my dear Cicero and
Avicenna! Am I a lion, or something else?

"You are not a lion, but an owl," he says. Laugh, everyone! Ap- 194
plaud! The comedy is over. Alas, you are not only ignorant of
Holy Scripture, but of all learning! Our ancient ancestors, who
were men of great genius and learning, as no one doubts, regarded
the owl as sacred to Minerva, the goddess of wisdom. You can't
have read about this, since it is not found in your *Therapeutica*. But
haven't you at least heard the fact? Are you surprised, ignoramus?
It's Greek to you. Would you like to hear the reason for this? The
owl is a secretive bird, and the wonder of flying creatures. It is
awake at night, sees in the dark, and flies around when all other
creatures are asleep. But you will cease to be surprised if you start
to reflect on Psalm 101. Speaking in the person of Christ, who is
the true God of wisdom and also the wisdom of the Father, the
Psalmist says: "I am like an owl that lives in its habitat."[185]

See how much I value you, O philosopher! Everything you 195
zealously assembled to deride me has turned, by simple mockery,
into your derision and my glory. Show me, O master of philosophy and rhetoric, how by praising the hoopoe you turn it into your
glory. Learn now, O reviler, either to bite more deeply, or to remain silent. For you see now how you barely scraped me with this

me noctue rostro vides quam leviter vellicasti! Veneni multum, virium nichil habes, quando michi, ut crimen aliquod solitudinem obiciens, ex actu laudabili conflare infamiam voluisti. Providebo ne me veris probris possis attingere; eritque tibi livor tuus ad penam, michi tum ad laudem, tum etiam ad cautelam.

196 Curabo ita vivere, ut boni gaudeant, tu medius crepes, sive in hac sive in alia solitudine, ut sors tulerit, sive in urbibus vivam, ubi vixi longe aliter ac tu, ubi nemo michi urinam suam, multi et magni secretum animi familiariter ostenderunt, contigitque, quod optabam, ut essem carus illustribus, vulgo ignotus. Libet enim gloriari, sed in Domino, cui semper tum pro multis, tum pro hoc nominatim gratias agam: quod me valde dissimilem tui fecit.

197 Interea dum hic sum—quod quamdiu sit futurum nescio—illud ne tibi videor mentitus quod, superbie michi datum, in principio literarum tuarum, huc sciens distuli: me florentes silvas et solitarios colles ambire solitum, vel scientie cupiditate vel glorie? Repeto enim, non dubitans ne lateat, ut tu fingis; notum enim spero non modo quid agam, sed quid cogitem. Dixi igitur ut doleres, et repeto ut doleas, tantam diversitatem nostre sortis agnoscens.

198 Dum certe oculos tuos ille mestus atque horrens pelvium ferit aspectus, meos grata serenitas et agrorum ac nemorum letissimus viror lenit; dum auribus tuis irati ventris murmur intonat, meas suavis volucrum cantus et dulcis aque strepitus delectat; dum naribus tuis inclusus aer et aure tristioris flatus ingeritur, meas florum circumfusa diversitas et calcatarum odor mirus herbarum recreat atque permulcet; dum lingua hebes infelixque palatum tuum deli-

owl's beak! You were all poison and no power when you reproached my solitude as a crime, and sought to contrive my disgrace from my laudable actions. I shall see to it that you cannot assail me with reproaches that are true. Your spite will bring you punishment, but it will win me praise and teach me caution.

I shall strive to live so that good men will rejoice. But you will 196 go on farting in your mediocrity — no matter whether I live in this solitude or another, as fate decrees, or in cities, where I have lived quite differently from you. No one has shown me his urine, but many great people have intimately revealed the secrets of their souls. My wishes came true. I was dear to illustrious people, and unknown to the masses. I like to boast, but in the Lord,[186] whom I always thank for many things, and to whom I give special thanks for making me so unlike you.

In the meantime, while I am here — for how long, I know 197 not — did you think I lied about my habit of strolling through flowering woods and solitary hills, desiring knowledge and glory? In the opening of your letter, you attributed this to my pride; and I intentionally postponed the topic until now. I repeat what I said, and I have no doubt that the fact is not a secret, as you pretend. I hope to make known not only my actions, but even my thoughts. I spoke, then, to grieve you, and I repeat myself to grieve you again, as you recognize the vast difference between our conditions.

While the gloomy and horrid sight of bed-pans surely offends 198 your eyes, mine are soothed by the pleasant serenity and cheerful verdure of fields and groves. While the rumblings of an angry stomach thunder in your ears, mine are delighted by the soft singing of birds and sweet babbling of water. While stuffy air and gusts of foul gas crowd your nostrils, mine are caressed and refreshed by a variety of flowers on all sides and by the wonderful scent of herbs beneath my feet. While samples of virulent potions besmear your dull tongue and unhappy palate, my tongue is engaged in some honorable colloquy or salubrious soliloquy. While

bandis atris potionibus inviscantur, michi lingua in aliquo vel ho-
nesto colloquio vel salubri soliloquio detinetur; dum manus tua
miserorum rimatur atque explicat purgamenta, mea aliquid scribit
gratum posteris, ut spero, dum legetur: quod certe scio, gratum
michi dum scribitur; et si nichil enim maius, at saltem oblivia
temporum malorum multarumque gravium et inutilium curarum
animo meo affert; denique, dum tu lucrum cogitas aut rapinam,
ego illud meditor, ut si possim, ex alto pereuntia lucra despiciam,
et, ut sepissime stomaceris, dum tu, captus vilis lucri cupidine,
grabatulos ambis ac latrinas, ego illa sola cupidine quam audisti
florentes silvas et solitarios colles lustro.

199   Sentis quam me non peniteat dixisse quod totiens repeto et
exaggero? Magnifice forsan et de me altius loqui videor, sed a quodam magnanimo literatoque viro didici 'magnifice loquendum adversus ignorantes.' Brutus hoc in epystolis suis ait: patere me uti
testimonio hominis incogniti apud te, notissimi apud doctos, et
quem Tullius ac Seneca cum veneratione suscipiunt. Quanto ergo
magnificentius atque altius loquendum adversus surdos? Alte locutus sum: sic oportuit ut audires. Hymnis quidem tuis carmen
breve reddideram, sed iniuriam Musis hanc inferre nolui, ut eas
insueto odore confunderem, tuumque ad limen cogerem, ubi se
nunquam fuisse glorientur.

200   Ecce multa michi que pene per dissuetudinem evanuerant ad
memoriam reduxisti; gratiam habeo conviciis tuis. Exercent ingenium: bonum opus, nisi malo more pessimoque animo fieret. Hoc
tibi examinandum linquo: ut libet, igitur. Ego et tacere possum et
loqui audeo, insultusque tuos nec opto, nec horreo; nec dum acu-

your hand is examining and interpreting the discharge of your wretched patients, mine is writing something which, I hope, will please posterity when it is read, and which, I know for certain, pleases me when I write. If my writing achieves nothing greater, it at least lets my mind forget bad times and many grave but pointless worries. Finally, while you meditate some profit or larceny, I meditate how I may rise above transient gains and despise them, if I can. And—this will set off your rage most of all—while you make your rounds amid pallets and latrines, driven by your desire for vile profit, I wander the flowering woods and solitary hills with the sole desire that you have heard me describe.

Do you sense how I have no regrets for stating what I repeat   199 and amplify so many times? Perhaps I seem to speak in too loud and lordly a fashion about myself, but I was taught by a magnanimous and cultured man that "we must speak in a lordly way in the presence of the ignorant." So Brutus wrote in his letters.[187] Allow me to cite the testimony of someone unknown to you, but quite well-known to men of learning, and a man whom Cicero and Seneca treat with veneration.[188] Well then, how much more magnificently and loudly must we speak in the presence of the deaf? I spoke loudly, since it was necessary to make you hear. I would have repaid your hymns with a brief poem. But I chose not to offend the Muses by disturbing them with strange odors, and to force them to your doorstep, which they boast of having never crossed.

Behold, you have revived in my memory many things that had   200 faded through disuse. I am grateful to you for your insults. They exercise my wits. This would be a noble work, if it were not done in a harmful way and with a hurtful spirit. I leave this for you to consider, so act as you wish. I can remain silent, but I also dare to speak. I neither desire nor fear your insults. I have not yet laid aside my stinging barbs. Even though you take my writing ill, I think you sense how truly I have spoken, unless your mind has

leos deposui; quod a te quoque graviter acceptum, quam vere dixerim puto sentias, nisi prorsus obtorpuisti. Ita tamen hoc accipias velim: si non post annum, sed ad iusti temporis spatium in aciem redis. Absit enim ut ab unius tempus non extimantis pendeam semper arbitrio: tempus michi carum est, fugamque eius intueor. Si ergo distuleris, tibi nichil, carte autem quod merebitur, que indignari non poterit, si illic posita fuerit, ubi auctor suus assidue cor, ingenium, manus, linguam, oculos, nares habet. Et tibi quidem in presens hec suffectura crediderim, ut aliquid in diem proximum reservemus.

201   Tibi autem, lector, quisquis, otio abundans, in has forte literulas incidisti, pauca dicturus sum. Duo sunt quidem ad que perraro, nunquamque nisi invitus, venio: ad utrunque nunc iste mordacissimus convitiator me coegit. Gloriari et de seipso predicare vanum ac superbum, alteri detrahere iniuriosum et molestum est. Non audeo te rogare, ut mea legas opuscula. Altiorem tibi fertilioremque lecturam opto; sed hoc dicere audeo: si quicquid ab ineunte etate scripsi et, ut puto, scribam, cum his conferatur, que michi detractor iste violentus extorsit, neque sermo tam fervidus, neque tantum in reliquis omnibus iurgiorum, neque decima vel proprie laudis vel aliene infamie pars legetur; nisi quod olim memini me alterius cuiusdam, et certe maioris emuli, quem in alio terrarum tractu atque alia etate perpessus sum, rabiem, invidie facibus accensam, coactum, similiter tribus aut quattuor epystolis contudisse. Sed ea contentio lege carminis iuveniliter actitata est. Hoc deerat iniurie: ut a sene iam senior soluta oratione lacesserer, utque in omni etate et in utroque stilo compellerer insanire. Unum me solatur: utrobique lacessitus sum.

202   Putabam aliquando fugisse latebris invidiam; fallebar. Illa me, ut video, vel subterraneis latitantem cavernis inveniet. Displicet

been numbed. But I want you to accept my writing it in this way. You'll return to the fray, if not in a year, at least after a proper interval of time. God forbid that I should wait upon the whims of a person who has no regard for time. Time is dear to me, and I contemplate its fleeting passage. So if you delay, nothing will happen to you, but your writings will get what they deserve. They will have no cause for indignation when they find themselves in the same place where their author keeps his heart, mind, hands, tongue, eyes, and nose. I would like to believe that these remarks suffice for the moment, so that I may reserve something for the future.

But now I must say a few words to you, O reader, whoever you 201 are, who in your abundant leisure have come across these little letters. This mordant detractor has driven me to two measures to which I seldom resort, and always against my will. Boasting and self-praise are vain and proud actions, just as disparaging others is injurious and obnoxious. I don't dare ask you to read my little works. I pray that you may find deeper and more rewarding readings. But I dare say one thing. Compare anything I have written since my youth, or shall ever write, to this reply, wrung from me by that violent detractor. You will not find in all my other works such heated language, so much vituperation, or even a tenth as much of my own praises or another's reproaches. You must except three or four epistles of mine that I remember being forced to write once to curb the rage, burning with envy, of a different man, clearly a greater rival, who attacked me in a different place and age. But the struggle was fought in verse and during my youth.[189] This insult was not enough. As an older man, I had to be attacked by another old man, and in prose. This forced me to act crazily at each age, and in both prose and poetry. My only consolation is that in both cases I was the one attacked.

I once thought that I could escape envy by staying out of sight, 202 but I was wrong. As I see now, envy will find me even if I hide in underground caverns. I dislike persecution, even if it perhaps

persecutio, quamvis forte non inutilis; displicet invidia; sed invidie causa non displicet. Neque velim talis esse, in quem illa nil cogitet; at in quem nil audeat esse velim, nisi putem impossibile. Ausa est in Cesares, in reges, in philosophos; penitusque paucis contigit, quod Salustius merito 'difficillimum' dicit 'inter mortales', ut 'gloria invidiam' superarent. Illud contra facillimum multis accidit, ut gloria invidiam irritarent. Unum miror: quod cum hec pestis inter pares unique studio intentos oriri soleat, michi semper unde non debuit orta est. Deum testor: non libens ad respondendum olim veni, sed multo nunc magis invitus ad hec redeo, quamvis inter utriusque lingue principes interque sanctos viros, quod multo mirabilius est, quenam verborum certamina frequenter exarserint non ignorem. In immortalibus enim scriptis memorieque mandata sunt.

203   Que probra, quas contumelias vel in Ciceronem Salustius non iacit, vel in eum ille non reiecit? Vivum ipsis in verbis odium cernas. Non mitior, sed multo quoque acrior inter Eschinem ac Demosthenem, capitaliorque dissensio. Quis Ieronimi contentiones non audivit cum Rufino aquilegiensi? Quasdam quoque cum Augustino, lenius quanquam reverentiusque habitas, duras tamen atque mordaces.

204   Verum hec et his similia in aliis quam in me libentius excusarem, sed cogor ubi nollem, et ad duo, michi in primis molestissima, per vim trahor. Quid enim — lector, oro te — quid est quod in me sponte glorier? Profecto, quamvis obtrectator meus quovis iusto extimatore rerum nichilo etiam, si dici liceat, minus sit, adeo ut stilus ipse meus, quodammodo frenum mordens, adversarii contemptu et ignobilitate superbiat, ego tamen, ut tibi verum fatear, meipso iudice, nichil sum, et si quid vel vere essem vel viderer michi — quorum alterum cupio, alterum abominor — an tamen

serves a purpose. I dislike envy, but not what causes envy. I would not like to be someone against whom envy has no designs. But if I didn't think it impossible, I would like to be someone envy dares not attack. Envy dared attack emperors, kings, and philosophers. Only a very few succeed in "overcoming envy by their glory," which Sallust rightly calls "a most difficult feat for mortal men."[190] By contrast, it proves quite easy for many to stir up envy by their glory. One thing surprises me. This plague usually arises among people of the same rank and interests. But in my case it always arises whence it should not. I call God as my witness. Earlier I was loath to reply, but now I return even more unwillingly to these charges. Still, I am not unaware that such verbal debates frequently burst out between the greatest authors in Latin and Greek and, more amazingly, between holy men. They have been preserved in immortal writings.

What reproaches, what insults does Sallust not hurl against 203 Cicero himself, or Cicero hurl back in reply? You can see the living hatred in their very words. The conflict between Aeschines and Demosthenes was no milder, but was even more bitter and deadly. Who has not heard of Jerome's disputes with Rufinus of Aquileia? Or his disputes with Augustine, which are milder and more reverent in tone, but still harsh and mordant?[191]

In fact, I would excuse these and similar debates more readily 204 in others than in myself. Yet I am compelled to take a position I dislike, and am dragged by force to these two measures that I find especially offensive. I ask you, O reader: Why should I willingly boast? In truth, any fair judge of things will find my detractor worth less than nothing, if it is possible to say so. Yet my very pen champs at the bit and grows proud at this contemptible and ignoble adversary. To tell you the truth, I am nothing in my own estimation. But suppose I were truly something—which I desire—or thought myself something—which I detest. Could I therefore forget the counsels of wise men that even children know? "Let an-

ideo possem oblivisci illa sapientum pueris etiam nota consilia
'Laudet te alienum, et non os tuum', et alius 'Tollite inanem iactantiam; res loquentur tacentibus nobis'?

205   Ex diverso autem, quid ego alterius nomen invadam? Iniuste
agam, si honestum nomen; si infame, supervacue. Quod si forte de
literis, ut fit, questio esset exorta—verum est enim non solum illud 'Quot capita tot sententie,' sed illud quoque: 'Cuiusque capitis
multas esse sententias'; unde sepe accidit, ut de una eademque re
aliud mane, aliud sero, imo et in eodem instanti nunc hoc nunc illud uni et eidem ingenio videatur — si ergo vel de scientiis inter se,
vel de unius scientie terminis, vel de re qualibet dissensio incidis-
set, dicente uno quod alius non probaret, an statim ad iurgia ve-
niendum et, quasi pugnando veritas quereretur, furore atque odio
decertandum erat?

206   Cur non potius meminisse illius sententie decebat, que in libro
De finibus a Cicerone posita est, quam si legisti, parces nota repe-
tenti, si minus, puto, non invitus leges? 'Dissentientium,' inquit,
'inter se reprehensiones etiam non sunt vituperande; maledicta,
contumelie, iracundie, contentiones concertationesque in disputando pertinaces indigne philosophia michi videri solent'. Et sequitur: 'Neque enim disputari sine reprehensione, nec cum iracun-
dia aut pertinacia recte disputari potest'. Neque in disputando
solum, sed etiam in atrocioribus causis doctrine huius meminisse
profuerit. Hinc idem alibi: 'Rectum est,' inquit, 'etiam in illis
contentionibus que cum inimicissimis fiunt, etiam si nobis indigna
esse videamus, tamen dignitatem retinere, iracundiam pellere'. Et
sequitur: 'Quo enim cum aliqua perturbatione fiunt, ea nec con-
stanter fieri possunt, neque his, qui assunt, probari'. Sane, quod
ad disputandum pertinet, Latinis iste non fuerat disceptandi mo-

other praise thee, and not your own mouth."[192] And someone else said: "Put aside vain boasting; the facts will speak even if we remain silent."[193]

By contrast, why should I attack someone else's reputation? For   205
me to attack an honorable name would be unjust, and to attack a disgraceful one would be pointless. Suppose that a literary question chanced to arise, as often happens. There is a true saying that "There are as many opinions as there are heads." But it is also true that "Each head has many opinions." As a result, we may hold one view of a question in the morning, and another in the evening. Indeed, one and the same mind will hold different views in the same instant. Suppose, then, that a disagreement arose between the sciences, or about the terminology of a science, or anything at all. If one person said something that another did not approve, should they fall to arguing and struggle with fury and hatred, as if the truth were sought by coming to blows?

Wouldn't it be more fitting to recall the opinion expressed by   206
Cicero in his book *On the Highest Good?* Forgive me for quoting something familiar, if you have read it. If not, I don't think you'll mind reading it. "You must not find fault with members of opposing schools for criticizing each other's opinions," Cicero writes, "though I feel that insult and abuse, or ill-tempered wrangling and bitter obstinate controversy are beneath the dignity of philosophy." And he continues: "It is impossible to debate without criticizing, but it is also impossible to debate properly with ill-temper or obstinacy."[194] Recalling this teaching would be useful not only in debates, but also in fiercer contests. Hence, Cicero later says: "The right course, moreover, even in our differences with our bitterest enemies, is to maintain our dignity and to repress our anger, even though we are treated outrageously."[195] And he continues: "For what is done under some degree of excitement cannot be done with perfect self-respect or the approval of those who witness it."[196] As far as debates are concerned, the Latins did not share this method

dus; licet, ut Cicero idem ait, 'sit ista in Grecorum levitate perversitas, qui maledictis insectantur eos, a quibus de veritate dissentiunt'.

207　　Que cum michi iampridem nota essent, et animus, natura quietis appetens, a contentionibus abhorreret, nunquam sponte fueram ad talia discensurus, nisi iste, quem alloquor, superbus, invidus, preceps, temerarius et ignorans, ut brevi eum tibi circumlocutione describam, me nolentem, procacis ut ita dicam lingue sue manibus, ad hunc velut pulvereum ac strepentem iurgiorum campum ex arce tranquilli silentii detraxisset, ut quem delectet, porcorum more, ceno semper immergi, et cui ego nichil, sed omnis veritas, omnis virtus offensa sit.

208　　Itaque, lector amabilis, a te veniam peto, si in volutabrum iniuriosi colloquii protractus, contra naturam moresque meos aliquid dixi, quod aures tuas leserit, sicubi gloriosius[15] de me, deque illo mordacius quam velles effatus sum. Magnificentius, fateor, fuisset utrunque contemnere, sed rara patientia est quam non penetret acutum convitium. Proinde, sique iacula primus ille contorserit in nomen meum, quod, quantulumcunque sit, augeri studeo, non minui; si preterea (quod molestius tuli) quot quantisque mendaciis aures veri avidas impleverit; quam denique importune sit et scurriliter debacchatus audieris et quis ipse sit noveris, spero tecum ipse dicturus sis: 'Gloriatus es necessario; detraxisti vere. Primum excuso, secundum probo, nisi quia rem verbis equare nequivisti'.

209　　Solebant equidem ingeniosi adolescentes ab insigni accusatione aliqua primum nomen auspicari, quasi victori accederet victi nomen, et fama multis quesita laboribus eventum unius iudicii se-

of disputation, whereas Cicero also says: "Let us leave to the frivo-lous Greeks the wrong-headed habit of attacking and abusing the persons whose views of the truth they do not share."[197]

I already knew this, and my mind by nature desires peace and 207 shrinks from contentions. Hence, I would never willingly have de-scended to such quarrels, if it had not been for this fellow whom I am addressing. To give you a brief portrait of him, he is a proud, envious, headstrong, reckless, and ignorant man. Laying hold of me, as it were, with his impudent tongue, he dragged me against my will from the citadel of my tranquil silence into this dusty and noisy arena of quarrels. Like a hog, he delights in wallowing con-stantly in the mud; and he has affronted every truth and every vir-tue, rather than me.

So, amiable reader, I ask your pardon. Having been dragged 208 into this wallowing-hole of injurious exchanges, I may have said things contrary to my nature or character that offended your ears. I may have spoken more boastfully about myself, and more mor-dantly about him, than you might wish. It would have been more lordly, I confess, to disregard both options, but patience that re-sists sharp insults is rare. He was the first to hurl darts at my rep-utation, which, as modest as it is, I desire to see increased rather than diminished. Then, to my great annoyance, he filled my ears with many mighty lies, when they hunger for the truth. You may have heard how rudely and boorishly he raved. In sum, if you know him for what he really is, then I hope you will say to your-self: "You boasted out of necessity, and disparaged him truthfully. I excuse your boasts, and commend your disparagements, except that your words could not do justice to the facts."

In fact, young men of genius used first to make a name for 209 themselves by accusing a prominent individual. They believed that the victor would inherit the renown of the vanquished, and that the outcome of a single verdict would bestow on them fame that had been won by many labors. As this was the custom, it was no

queretur. Non infame negotium, ut mos erat, sed unde quosdam
valde nobilitatos legimus. Hic si ex me lacerato senex idem sperat,
spero ego quod fallitur, atque utinam non magis ad votum cogitatio sibi ulla succedat. Inventus est qui solius fame cupidine Philip-
pum Macedonie regem interficeret, ut quidam putant (apud alios
enim causa cedis est iustior); inventus est qui Diane Ephesie templum incenderet, ut vel insueto facinore notus esset, qui, ne per
scelus assequi videretur quod optabat, Ephesii providerunt indicto
supplitio, siquis eum historicus nominasset. Certe convitiator
meus, qui non regem, non templum violavit, sed humilem soli-
vagumque ruricolam, non hinc nobilitabitur; neque hic per me
neque alibi nominandus, puto, nec per alios. Quis est enim tam
vili deditus negotio, qui circa tam ieiunum nomen tempus expen-
dat? Aut quis est qui, etsi eum antea dilexisset, non deinceps livi-
dis adversus immeritum scriptis eius perlectis adversetur atque
oderit? Ita, si fortassis hoc calle famam petit, necquicquam insa-
nierit.

210   Sin turbasse otium et silentium meum interrupisse contentus
est, quod decreverat implevit: aliquot michi dies eripuit quos nemo
nemo restituet, et a meis tramitibus abductum, ad durum et insolitum iter traxit. Quidni igitur turber, temporisque iacturam querar nec michi nec alteri fructuosam, nisi quantum studioso homini, modo animi crimen absit, et data sit occasio non quesita, in
omni genere orationis exercendus est stilus? En in demonstrativo
genere exerceor; mallem in laudibus exerceri. Ceterum, ut aliquando sit finis, is qui hanc michi necessitatem imposuit, in alienis
finibus non inveniens quod querebat, revertatur ad proprias febres;
tu lacessito faveas, lacessentem oderis, et valeas precor.

disgraceful affair. Indeed, we read that it rendered some men very famous.[198] Now, if this old man hopes to achieve the same by wounding me, I hope that he fails, and pray that none of his other designs succeed any better than this one. In history, we find that some believe Philip of Macedon was slain solely because he desired fame, although others give a juster reason for the murder.[199] We find that someone else burned the temple of Diana at Ephesus in order to become famous, even by means of so extraordinary a misdeed; but the citizens of Ephesus kept him from achieving his goal by threatening with capital punishment any historian who recorded his name.[200] Clearly, my detractor will gain no fame by violating a humble and solitary country-dweller, rather than a king or temple. And I believe that he should neither be named by me here, nor by others elsewhere. Is anyone engaged in such worthless affairs that he would waste his time on such a trivial reputation? Or is there anyone who, despite having loved him before, would not oppose and detest him after reading his spiteful attacks on a innocent man? If he seeks fame by this route, he has gone mad quite pointlessly.

But if he is content to have troubled my leisure and interrupted my silence, he has attained the goal he had proposed. He stole from me several days that no one can restore, and he dragged me from my usual path down a harsh and unaccustomed road. Why should I not be troubled? Why not regret this waste of time? It was fruitless for me and for him, unless perhaps a scholar should exercise his pen in every genre of oratory, provided he is morally blameless, and responds to circumstances he did not create. Behold, I exercise myself in the demonstrative genre, when I would have preferred an exercise in the laudatory genre. But to conclude at last, let the man who imposed this necessity on me return to his own feverish existence, since he has not found what he sought in another's territory. O reader, favor the man who was attacked, and hate the man who attacked him. Fare you well, I pray.

210

INVECTIVA CONTRA QUENDAM MAGNI STATUS HOMINEM SED NULLIUS SCIENTIE AUT VIRTUTIS

: I :

1 Eras, fateor, non indignus, cuius ab homine non insano facile temni posset insania; tua non virtus quidem, sed sola te dignitas dignum facit, qui verbis, non silentio feriare, quanquam ipsam illam quoque misereor, si modo dignitas, et non illusio potius ac ludibrium, dici debet. Solent qui insigni ridiculo in spectaculis destinantur auro tegi, purpura caput obnubi, equis comptis ac phaleratis impositi per plateas et compita urbium circunduci; ubi vero dies totos erraverint, et populum risu impleverint, se contemptu, ad vesperam deponuntur, exuuntur, repelluntur. Idem tibi accidet, nempe hos ludos, hec spectacula de te mundo exhibet Fortuna.

2 Iam populus tui satur; iam, si ad etatem respicis, lucis est terminus ac ludorum; iam detractis, quibus gaudes, amictibus, nudum te circi rector abiciet. Tunc quid esses et quid videreris intelliges, risum aliis qui relinquens, luctum tibi miseriamque repereris. Minime autem novum aut insolitum mali genus; nam et Eutropius consulatum tenuit et Eliogabalus imperium: spado ille vilissimus, hominum iste turpissimus. Verum nimis experimento deprehenditur illud satyricum: Tales summa

INVECTIVE AGAINST
A MAN OF HIGH RANK
WITH NO KNOWLEDGE
OR VIRTUE

: I :

You seemed so dignified, I confess, that a sane person might easily 1
have overlooked your insanity.[1] Yet it is not your virtue, but your
dignity that makes you deserve to be stung by words rather than
silence, although I pity your dignity—if dignity it is, rather than
an illusion and a sham. When people are assigned the role of egregious buffoons in public spectacles, they are usually dressed in
gold robes, cloaked in purple hoods, seated on plumed and capari-
soned horses, and then trotted through the squares and cross-
roads.[2] But after they wander around all day, filling the populace
with laughter and heaping contempt on themselves, in the evening
they are deposed, stripped, and expelled. The same thing will happen to you. Fortune will use you to offer such games and spectacles to the world.

By now, the populace is fed up with you. By now, if you con- 2
sider your age, the end of your days and your games is at hand. By
now, stripped of the clothes you delight in, the ringmaster throws
you out naked. Then you will understand what you were and how
you were seen: as you leave laughter to others, you will find grief
and misery for yourself. This is by no means a new or unusual
kind of evil. Eutropius became consul, and Heliogabalus emperor,
although the former was a vile eunuch and the latter the foulest of
men. All too often experience confirms what the satirist wrote:
Such are the men

> ad fastigia rerum
> extollit, quotiens voluit fortuna iocari.

De te quidem satis superque iam iocata est: deponat te precamur. Iam ad fastidium iocus spectat, neve his monstris immunem ipse tibi tuum hunc ordinem blandiaris, qui abs te multo facilius inquinandus fuerit, quam tu ab illo honestandus atque ornandus. Cogita quot non iniquos modo vel turpes nostra ille habuit etate, sed ineptos etiam et insanos; habet autem quo se ipsum consoletur, quando, inter patritios ac principes Romanorum, quibus nichil est clarius, Catilina et Nero, et inter apostolos Cristi, quibus nichil est sanctius, Iudas fuit.

3   Ad rem venio. Ego quidem sic presagiebam, atque ita futurum arbitrabar, siquid scriberem, ut doctorum hominum iudicio subiacerem; nec ferendus sim, nisi comunem hanc scribentium omnium sortem feram. Non scribere potui—si tamen id possumus, cuius in contrarium tota nos animi vis impellit, tota urget intentio—scribere autem et iudicia hominum effugere non magis potui, quam in luce positus a circumstantibus non videri. Sed cum ingeniorum, qui non minores quam patrimoniorum sunt aut corporum, casus fortunasque circumspicerem ac timerem, tuum certe iudicium non timebam; dicam melius: non sperabam.

4   Quo enim modo, quibus artibus de me michi vel aliis tantam spem dare potuisti, quantam obtrectando prebuisti? Fatebor ingenue quod res habet. Ubi primum crebro te meum nomen usur-

that Fortune raises to the heights of power
whenever she wishes to jest.[3]

She has jested with you more than enough; we pray she will depose you. By now, the jest is turning into disgust. Do not flatter yourself that your order is immune to such monstrosities, for you will pollute it more easily than it will honor and glorify you. Consider how many men it admitted in our day who were not only wicked and foul, but also foolish and insane. Yet it may find consolation in the fact that Catiline and Nero were patricians and leading men of Rome, who were the most illustrious of men; and that Judas belonged to the apostles of Christ, who were the holiest.

Let me come to the point. I foresaw, and even regarded as inevitable that writing something would expose me to the judgment of learned men. Indeed, I would myself be unbearable if I did not bear the fate common to all writers. I might have refrained from writing, if indeed it were possible to do something that runs completely contrary to all of one's instincts and aspirations. But I could no more write and escape the judgments of my fellow human beings than I could stand out in the open without being seen by the people around me. Still, while I observed and feared the mishaps and fortunes that befell great talents — which are no less serious than those affecting our estates or our bodies — I certainly did not fear your judgment; or to be more precise, I did not hope for it.

By what means or arts could you have stirred such great hopes about me, both in myself and in others, as by your disparagements? I shall freely confess how things stand. When I first heard that you went about citing my name, I was perplexed, fearing that you might be praising me. If you had done this, I would have been finished. You would be depriving me of any glory or credibility, since having a base and infamous man praise you is one of the

3

4

183

pare audivi, suspensus animo timui ne laudares; quod si faceres, actum erat: nullum glorie, nullum tu fiducie relinquebas locum, siquidem infamie non ultimum genus laudator turpis atque infamis. Nam quid, queso, laudares, nisi quod ingenio caperes? Quid caperes, nisi humile et exiguum et abiectum? Porro, ut intellectus et intellecte rei proportio, sic laudantis et laudati paritas quedam et ingeniorum cognatio esse solet; que siqua esset . . . o quid cogito? Parce, oro, anime, his te curis involvere. Nescio enim quid non potius, etiam nichil, quam huic similis esse maluerim: itaque ubi comperi meum nomen esse tibi materiam obtrectandi, Deum testor, non aliter sum affectus quam si me magnus aliquis vir laudaret.

5   Non magis enim opto esse michi similitudinem cum bonis ac doctis viris, quam cum malis dissimilitudinem atque indoctis. Una prorsus est ratio, et tanto quisque remotior fit vitio, quanto propinquior fit virtuti. Sentio igitur mali causam: dissimilis tui sum. Aliis fortasse tramitibus, sed non aliam in spem adduci poteram. Et sperarem et gauderem, si similis bonis essem; et spero et gaudeo, si dissimilis malis sim. Plus michi ergo quam crederes contulisti, quando tibi in mentem venit libido illa carpendi in conviviis meum nomen, quod profecto laudares, si quam loquor in me similitudinem deprehendisses. Tum de me autem optime meritus dignusque eris, cui debitor fame sim, quando hec convitia, quibus in absentem estuas, hasque tam operosas ardentesque detractiones ad sobria ac ieiuna colloquia transtuleris. Nunc enim quod vituperando me laudas, vereor ne vino potius quam iudicio tribuatur. Si plene igitur me laudatum cupis, siccus impransusque vitupera, aut post somnum e grabatulo tuo surgens, ubi crapulam digessisti; sic non meri fumus, sed animi tui cecitas ac caligo lucem aliquam meo dabit ingenio.

6   Sed ut tandem liqueat nostri pars una litigii, tu michi in primis ignorantiam obicis. Qua in re uno verbo multorum iudicia convel-

worst kinds of infamy.[4] For what, I ask, could you praise except what your mind could grasp? And what could you grasp except what is lowly, paltry, and worthless? Furthermore, just as there is a proportion between our understanding and the thing understood, so there is usually an equivalence between one who praises and one who is praised, and an affinity between their minds; and if this existed . . . but what am I thinking? Please refrain, my mind, from becoming entangled in such concerns. Rather than resembling this man, I would prefer to be anything at all, or even nothing at all. So when I learned that my fame was the subject of your disparagements, as God is my witness, I felt as if I had been praised by a great man.

For while I strive to resemble good and learned men, I strive no   5
less to avoid resembling evil and ignorant ones. The principle is one and the same. The further we are from vice, the closer we are to virtue. Here, then, I perceive the source of the problem. I am unlike you. I might perhaps have chosen a different path, but not a different goal. I would hope and rejoice to resemble good people, just as I hope and rejoice that I am unlike evil people. You did me a greater service than you imagined when you felt the urge at a banquet to disparage my name. (You should rather have praised it, if you had perceived in me that resemblance to good people that I am describing.) Still, you will earn my gratitude and place me in your debt for my reputation if, rather than raging against me in my absence, you will exchange your elaborate insults and fiery detractions for a sober and abstemious colloquy. As it is, when your censures win me praise, I fear they spring from wine rather than your judgment. So if you wish to praise me fully, censure me when sober and fasting, or when you rise from your pallet after sleeping off your inebriation. In this way, it will not be the fumes of wine, but the gloom and blindness of your mind, that illuminate my wit.

Now, to make clear one part of our dispute, you reproach my   6
ignorance in particular. With this one word, you undermine the

185

lis, qui interdum sentire aliquid visi erant. Quid respondeam? Credo te, quamvis non tam veri studio quam odio indulgentem, rectius tamen de me sensisse quam reliquos. Sepe casu aliquo vidit stultus unus, quod multi non viderant sapientes. Fieri potest, ut que ceca solet esse invidia, lincea meis in rebus sit, profundiusque oculos in meum pectus suis stimulis acta coniecerit. Utcunque se veritas rerum habet, meum arbitror, ut non tam laudatorum meorum, quam iudicio tuo stem: illi enim amore ad superbiam ac segnitiem, tu odio ad humilitatem ac diligentiam me impellis. Mira res, bonum esse nonnunquam mali causam, malum boni.

7   Nitar, etsi plena sit etas, adhuc discere, ut obiectum crimen, qua dabitur, vigilando diluam. Multa in senectute didicerunt multi; neque enim ingenium anni exstinguunt, et noscendi desiderium ultro accendunt, dum quid desit sibi senectus cauta circumspicit, quod insolens iuventa non viderat. Didicit in senio Solon, didicit Socrates, didicit Plato, didicit ad extremum Cato, qui quo senior, eo sitientior literarum fuit. Quod me prohibet horum vestigiis insistere, gressu licet impari, desiderio tamen pari? Nemo est tam velox, quem non longe saltem sequi valeas. Discam fortasse, magne censor; discam aliquid, quo non tam indoctus videar tibi. Vellem me in adolescentia monuisses, et iustum spatium pulcro conatui reliquisses. Instabo tamen, et, quod unum est iam reliquum, brevitatem temporis velocitate pensabo. Sepe in angusto seu temporum seu locorum magne res atque egregie geste sunt.

judgments of many people who seemed at times to know something. How shall I reply? Even though you indulge your hatred rather than any desire for the truth, I believe you understand me better than others. Often by some chance one fool will see what many wise men failed to see. It is possible that envy, which is usually blind, proves sharp-sighted in my affairs, and being stung by its own goads, directs its gaze deeper into my breast. Whatever the truth of the matter, I think it proper for me to accept your judgment rather than that of my praisers. Their love moves me to pride and indolence; but your hatred moves me to humility and diligence. It is remarkable how good is at times the cause of evil, and evil the cause of good.

Despite my advanced age, I shall strive to keep on learning, so that by vigilant efforts I may refute this charge as best I can. Many people have learned many things in old age. Rather than extinguishing our mental powers, the years inflame our desire to know. Prudent old men look around themselves and perceive deficiencies that insolent youth failed to see. Solon learned in old age, as did Socrates and Plato. To the very end, Cato learned; and the older he grew, the greater was his thirst for letters.[5] What prevents me from following in their steps, at a slower pace perhaps, but with equal desire? No one is so swift that he can't be followed, at least at a distance. I may well learn, great censor; I may learn something that makes me seem less unlearned to you. I wish you had warned me in my youth and left me the right amount of time for this noble enterprise. But I shall press onward, and as a last resort I shall make rapidity compensate for the brevity of the time that remains. Often great and outstanding deeds have been achieved in a narrow stretch of time or space.

: II :

8 Quomodo autem michi tunc ignorantiam obiectares, cuius in primis ingenium ac scientiam mirabaris! Oblitus es, puto; et presentia solum, quia extrinsecus clara sunt, aspicis, neque omnino quid fueris, exemplo Tiberii, meministi. Reddam tibi memoriam, quam prosperitas abstulit, que non mei tantum, sed te tui etiam fecit immemorem. Sedulo tibi offeram que maxime refugis, et velut amariusculam potionem egro ingeram respuenti. Nec semper damnosa que cruciant, nec semper utilia que delectant.

9 Flecte igitur te in tergum, mitte oculos retro illud in tempus, quod, umbre levis in morem, celi volubilis preceps cursus eripuit. Ibi, tribus iam lustris interiectis, prorsus alium te videbis, priusquam ab amentia in rabiem blandior te fortuna converteret; ibi invenies quanto tunc studio amicitiam meam (que cur tibi nunc adeo viluerit miror), ambieris, cum esses ea tempestate unus ex illorum cetu, quos protonotarios dicunt. Quod ipsum tam ineptum, tamque supra meritum tuum erat, ut non modo multum assidue indignantis populi murmur audires, sed bonorum stomacum fastidio iam implesset tua illa dignitas tam indigna. Quia tamen rutilare nondum ceperas obscurum caput, ut ignotior, sic remissior latebas; et erat in tenebris tuis multis una que placeret, humilitas. Quam tamen falsam simulatamque fuisse res docuit.

10 Et tunc quidem agente clare memorie Agapito Columnensi, suis tuisque victus precibus, manus dedi. Ibam nempe invitus in amicitiam illiterati hominis, in quo nulla—que una tunc michi cura erat—vel discendi vel docendi aliquid spes esset. Veni tandem, trahente illo verius quam ducente, cumque tu me ceu divinum munus ingenti gaudio excepisses, atque illud sepe dixisses, 'Scio me amicitia tua indignum, oro tamen illam michi ne neges,'

: II :

But how could you reproach my ignorance, when you used to be   8
among the first to admire my intelligence and knowledge? You
have forgotten, I suppose; and only look at what is present, which
is outwardly most clear. Like Tiberius, you can't remember what
you were before.[6] I shall restore your memory, which your prosperity had taken from you, causing you to forget me and even
yourself. I shall diligently offer you what you shun most, as if forcing a bitter potion on an unwilling patient. Things that hurt are
not always harmful, and things that delight are not always helpful.

So turn around, and direct your gaze back to that time which,   9
like a faint shadow, has been carried away by the precipitous
course of the shifting heavens. There, at a distance of fifteen years,
you will see a completely different you, before favorable fortune
had converted your madness to rage. There you will find how zealously you once courted my friendship, which to my surprise you
now hold so cheap. At that time, you were one of the group
known as protonotaries, but this was so absurdly beyond your
merit that you not only heard the mutters of an ever indignant
populace, but that undignified dignity of yours filled the best men
with irritation and loathing. Your obscure head had not begun to
glow red, and you escaped notice, being both unknown and humble.[7] In your obscurity the one thing that pleased many people was
your humility, which later events proved false and feigned.

Then, through the mediation of Agapito Colonna of glorious   10
memory, I yielded to his entreaties and to yours.[8] Unwillingly I
formed a friendship with an illiterate fellow who had no goals of
learning or teaching, which were my sole concern at the time. At
last I came to you, dragged rather than led by my friend. With immense joy, you welcomed me like a gift from heaven, and often
said "I know that I am unworthy, but I beg you not to deny me

rediens, dum ex me ille dux meus quereret, 'Quid tibi de hoc homine visum est?' respondi (nam et verba teneo): 'Verecundia in adolescente laudabilis, michi in hac etate non placet, cui nulla materia verecundie esse debet; humilitas autem ista, quanquam ex ignorantie proprie conscientia et pudore sui ipsius, malis utique radicibus orta, non displicet. Quid enim importunius ignorante superbia?'

11   De illo tempore nichil amplius dicam, nisi quod viderunt omnes quibus noti eramus quique, si superant, testabuntur, per eos annos tibi ex me non tam quesitam amicitiam quam stuporem. Ita, quotiens casu aliquo tibi occurrerem, quasi angelum Dei, non hominem invenisses, attonitus suspensusque animo herebas, quicquid loquerer intentus excipiens,

pendensque[1] iterum narrantis ab ore,

ut Maro ait. Quod quamvis ad infamiam, potius quam ad laudem michi a doctis verti animadverterem, caritas tamen que fert omnia, hoc tuum de me iudicium pium tibi, michi licet inglorium, ferebat. Certe per id tempus — quod michi forte negaveris, conscientie tue vel nolens invitusque fatebere — tibi ego cotidie novus stupor, nova semper admiratio; et que nunc subito apud te facta est ignorantia, monstrum erat.

12   Sed progredior. Ex illo quidem, nisi nunc pudet, amicitiam nostram studiosissime coluisti, non fructu aliquo, non spe ulla, nisi quod tam sciens tunc tibi videbar, quam nunc videor ignorans; magna vel ingenii mei mutatio vel iudicii tui. Atque usqueadeo tunc te parvi non penituit amici, ut cum post longum tempus, multo tamen ante meritum, ad romani cardinis apicem flexis preruptisque tramitibus conscendisses, meque, qui tunc aberam, sero ad curiam non mea voluntas sed amicorum necessitas revexisset, magnis me ad te confestim precibus evocares.

your friendship." When I returned, my guide asked me: "How does this fellow strike you?" And I replied in these very words: "Diffidence is laudable in a youth, but I am not pleased to see it in someone of this age, who should have no reason to be diffident. Still, his humility is not displeasing, even if it springs from bad sources, an awareness of his own ignorance and shame about himself. What could be more obnoxious than ignorant pride?"

I shall say no more about that time. Anyone who knew us saw   11
and will bear witness, if they are still alive, that in those years you sought in me not so much a friend as someone to idolize. Whenever I chanced to meet you, you froze thunderstruck, as if you beheld an angel of God, not a man, and stood in suspense waiting intently to hear my words,

again hanging on the speaker's lips,

as Virgil says.[9] I observed that this won me more infamy among learned men than praise. But charity, which endures all things, endured your esteem for me, which you thought pious, and I thought inglorious.[10] At that time — though you may perhaps deny it openly, in your conscience you must confess it even against your will — each day I caused you new astonishment and new admiration: once a prodigy, I have suddenly turned into an ignoramus.

But I proceed. From that moment, unless it shames you, you   12
most zealously cultivated our friendship, not for some profit, not for some hope, but because I then seemed as wise to you as I now seem ignorant — truly a great change, either in my intelligence or in your judgment! You clearly did not regret your little friend then. Indeed, a long time later, if earlier than you deserved, you rose by abrupt and devious paths to the Roman cardinalate. I was away at the time, but when at last I returned to the Curia, drawn back more by the bonds of friendship than by my will, you at once sent for me with urgent entreaties.

13 Ad quem cum invitus, fateor, venissem, ut qui nec moribus nec
fortune satis ascensuique tuo fiderem, in fronte quidem tua multa
signa dementie licentioris agnovi, in nullo tamen erga me muta-
tum animum tuum sensi. Idem michi qui fueras, eadem caritas,
idem sermo, pristino me favore vel honore complexus. Illud insuper addidisti, venisse tempus, quo meis saltem, quando ego nil cu-
perem, fructuosior atque utilior esse posses. Denique abeunti michi extremum illud insusurrasti: 'Amicum me, si experiri velis,
invenies; in tua quidem amicitia nulli me secundum faciens, unum
tibi experientie laborem linquo, quem si respuis, amicus non ero
minus, sed videbor, obtestorque te ne tuus iste contemptus hoc
michi glorie genus eripiat'.

14 His blanditiis atque hac spe plenus abii, cui quantum tua de-
mebat inconstantia, tantum simulata verbis ac gestibus addebat
humanitas. Itaque quid simplicitati latebras queram? Quid dissimulem? Sperabam, si quid dignum voluissem, promptis te promis-
sisque favoribus affuturum. Nunc quid accidit, aut quid feci, ut de
miratore amico detractor hostis evaseris? Tu in me olim ingenium,
doctrinam et eloquentiam mirabaris; que quanquam nulla ipse co-
gnoscerem et amori potius quam iudicio imputarem, quero tamen
ex te: quenam tibi mutande sententie causa fuit? Quid vel tu interim didicisti, cuius et etas iam tum prona in senium et hebes semper ingenium torporque ridiculus, vel ego dedidici, qui si per vale-
tudinem licuit, nullum diem sine studio atque animi intentione
traduxerim?

: III :

15 Sed scio quid rei est, et querenti michi ipse respondeo: ascendisti
in locum, unde tibi videaris posse de omnibus iudicare. Unus ex il-

I went to you unwillingly, I confess, since I distrusted your 13
character, your fortune, and your rise in the world. While I read
many signs of unbridled madness in your countenance, I sensed
that your feelings for me were unchanged. You had remained the
same, as had your affection and your language; and you embraced
me with the same favors and honors as before. In addition, you
told me that the moment had arrived when you could prove beneficial and useful to my friends, even if I myself desired nothing. As
I departed, you whispered one last remark: "If you wish to try me,
you will find me your friend. I consider you second to none of my
friends, and leave you the small effort of testing my offer. If you
reject me, I shall no less be your friend, even if seem so. I pray
you, don't let your contempt rob me of this kind of glory."

I went away filled with flattery and hopes, encouraged as much 14
by the kindness feigned in your words and gestures as I was dis-
couraged by your fickleness. Why then should I seek to hide my
ingenuousness? Why should I dissemble? I hoped that, if I desired anything worthy, you would respond with the prompt favors
you had promised. What has happened now, or what have I done,
to convert you from an admiring friend into a disparaging enemy?
You once admired my intelligence, learning, and eloquence — qualities which I failed to see, but I imputed to your love rather than
your judgment. I ask you: what caused you to change your opinion? What did you learn in the meantime, now that your age is
nearly senile, your intelligence dull, and your lethargy absurd? Or
what did I unlearn when, my health permitting, I spent no day
without study and mental exertion?

: III :

In fact, I know what the problem is, and shall therefore answer my 15
own question. You have risen to a place from which you think you

lorum sucessoribus quibus dictum est: 'Sedebitis et vos super duodecim sedes, iudicantes XII tribus Israel'. Atqui sedes alia, iudex idem. An vero quia altius sedes, aliter sapis? Solent quidem ex alto cernentibus que in imo sunt decrescere et minora videri; sed an propter unius gradus ascensum minima iudicas, que maxima iudicabas? Sic omnes habenas amentie relaxasti? Reserva tibi aliquid quo insanias, si, iocante nunc etiam fortuna, in summi pontificatus culmen ascenderis!

16   Triste omen auditu, sed, ut est seculi nostri stilus, ut sunt mores, nichil est impudentie desperandum. Nunc autem an quia maiusculus, ego nichil, an tuum hoc solium vel te alium, vel me fecit? Quod si penitus mutata sede mutari iudicium oportebat, cur, queso, peius et non, quo altius, eo et melius iudicandum de amicitiis extimasti? Non tibi ascendisse altius visus es, nisi que modo erant alta despiceres, quodque est durius, etiam lacerares. Tantum ne animi, tantum ne protervie attulisse lignum illud, sive est ebur, tantamque vertiginem tam repente rerum omnium incidisse?

17   I nunc, et Fortune regnum nega; dic errasse Virgilium, ubi ab illo 'omnipotens' dicta est, que non opes modo potentiamque tribuere possit indignis, sed censuram rerum ad se nullo iure pertinentium, momentoque temporis ex ignorantissimo hominum iudicem facere super ingeniis alienis. O magne Virgili, o vates eximie, an ista fortasse vaticinans Fortune omnipotentiam predicasti? An tu, Salusti, historicorum certissime, dum 'Fortunam in omni re dominari'? An tu, Cicero, oratorum princeps, quando illam dixisti 'rerum dominam humanarum'?

18   O Fortuna, si vera viri tales loquuntur, omnipotens, quid hoc est quod agis? Huccine etiam regni tui potestas extenditur? Nimis

can judge everyone. You are a successor of those to whom it was said: "Ye also shall sit upon twelve thrones, judging the twelve tribes of Israel."[11] True, the seat is different, but the judge is the same. Are you wiser because you sit higher up? To people who view things from above, what is below them usually appears to diminish and recede. But by virtue of a single step upward, must you now judge least what you once judged greatest? Have you given full rein to your madness? Keep some material for insanity in reserve, in case Fortune continues her jest and you ascend to the height of the papacy!

This is a dismal omen to hear, but given the style and customs of our generation, impudence need never despair. If you are now somewhat greater, and I am nothing, which one of use was changed by your throne, you or me? If a complete change of place entailed a change of judgment, why didn't you judge your friendships better for rising higher, rather than worse? You seem to have ascended no higher, except that what was lofty before, you now despise, and what is harsher, you tear to pieces. Were such arrogance and great impudence conferred on you by a mere piece of wood or ivory?[12] Have you suddenly been overcome by a great dizziness that upsets all things?

Go now, and deny the sway of Fortune. Say that Virgil was mistaken when he called her "omnipotent."[13] On the undeserving, Fortune can bestow not only wealth and power, but also control over matters they have no right to judge. In a single moment, she can set an ignoramus as judge over the intelligence of others. O great Virgil, O great prophet, were these perhaps the events you prophesied when you proclaimed Fortune's omnipotence? Or you, Sallust, most certain of the historians, when you wrote that "Fortune holds dominion over all things"?[14] Or you, Cicero, prince of orators, when you called her the "mistress of human affairs"?[15]

O Fortune, who are omnipotent if such men speak the truth, what are you doing? Does the power of your realm extend even

est. Nichil est autem quod non possit omnipotens, sed absit ut omnipotens sit Fortuna, neque est enim nisi unus omnipotens; imo vero mox ut virtutem ab adverso viderit, impos et imbecilla succumbit: veriusque illud et gravius alter, licet inferior, vates ait:

> Fortunaque perdit
> opposita virtute minas.

Itaque liceat illi ad te bonis debitos honores divitiasque transferre. Ingenium Deus dat, qui si tibi illud dare voluisset, an in senium distulisset? Non est istud ingenium, non eloquium, sed audacia et temeritas, et tui oblivio atque hinc nata procacitas, qua iudex omnium insperatus fieres, et ab adolescentia mutum saxum, subito non vocalis tantum senex evaderes, sed in picam loquacissimam vertereris — inaudita metamorphosis et quam Naso non noverit! Et fecisse quidem hoc Fortuna que dicitur, non negabo.

19   'Quid ergo ait?' dicat aliquis. 'Vide ne tecum pugnes, qui, cum fere cunta subtraxeris, hanc tantam illi vim tribuas naturalia transformandi'. Ego autem opes, potentiam, honores, cumque his stultitiam, superbiam, elationem, iactantiam, presumptionem, vaniloquium dare illam fateor, ne, si negem, te teste redarguar. Hec sunt Fortune munuscula, quibus te illa prelargiter circumfersit. Ea tibi dare non potuit que sui iuris non erant, que ve homini fortunato sepe quidem eripuit, nunquam dedit.

20   'Et quenam ista sunt?' inquies. Illa, inquam, quorum, nisi ultro te fallis, semper pauperrimum te fuisse, nunc mendicum prorsus ac nudum esse comperies. Non dat Fortuna mores bonos, non in-

here? It is too much. There is nothing omnipotence cannot accomplish, but God forbid that Fortune should be omnipotent. For there is only one who is omnipotent. Indeed, as soon as Fortune sees virtue approach, she surrenders, impotent and infirm. The verse of another, if lesser, poet says more gravely and truly:

When Virtue is her opponent,
Fortune wastes her threats.[16]

So let her transfer to you the honors and wealth that were due to good men. But our intelligence is a gift from God; and if he had chosen to give you intelligence, would he have waited for your old age? You have no intelligence and no eloquence, but only audacity, temerity, and the effrontery born of forgetting who you are. You have become an unexpected judge of everything. From a mute stone in your youth, you have suddenly turned into a talkative old man, and have been changed into a chattering magpie—an unheard-of metamorphosis, unknown even to Ovid! I can't deny that this is the work of what we call Fortune.

"What is he saying?" someone may ask. "Take care you don't 19 contradict yourself when, after stripping her of nearly everything, you grant her this great power of transforming human nature." But if in fact I concede that she bestows wealth, power, and honors—accompanied by folly, pride, elation, boastfulness, presumption, and idle chatter—it is so that your example may not refute me. These are the little gifts of Fortune, with which she has filled you so abundantly. But she could not give you things that were not in her possession, and she never gave you those things of which she often deprives a fortunate man.

"What are those?" you ask. They are the goods in which—un- 20 less you willingly deceive yourself—you will find that you were always poor, and are now completely destitute and naked. Fortune cannot grant good character, intelligence, virtue, or eloquence. When you quack like a duck rather than sing like a swan, the

genium, non virtutem, non facundiam. Unde hec qua nescio quid anserinum potius quam cycneum strepis, non eloquentia, ut dicebam, sed loquacitas tua est; neque profecto de ingenii fiducia, sed opum insolentia ac tumore oriens, quasi quibus opulentior, his ingeniosior factus sis. Quod quam verum fuerit, scies illico, ut ad ingenii tui arculam te converteris, cuius claves inter nummorum acervulos perdidisti, utque illam effringas, crede michi, nil intus invenies. Tum sentire incipies quam ineptus iudex alieni fueris ingenii, qui tam proprii sis egenus.

21   Nam, ut huic tandem controversie finis sit, humane mentis ingens malum ignorantiam non ignoro, ut sit tamen necessitas optionis, multo magis ignorantiam innocentem eligam, quam scientiam peccatricem. Inter hec autem quisque suo eligat arbitrio. Neque etiam nunc id ago, sed ut meo iudicio summum probrum noveris non ignorantiam, sed peccatum, etsi multi mortales non tam homicide vel adulteri quam illiterati hominis famam vereantur, veriusque in dies probem illud patris Augustini: 'Vide,' inquit, 'Deus meus,'[2] et patienter, ut vides, vide quomodo diligenter observent filii hominum pacta literarum et syllabarum accepta a prioribus locutoribus, et a te accepta eterna pacta perpetue salutis negligant; ut qui illa sonorum vetera placita teneat aut doceat, si contra disciplinam grammaticam sine aspiratione prime syllabe "ominem" dixerit, magis displiceat hominibus, quam si contra tua precepta hominem oderit, cum sit homo'.

22   Quod sanctissimi ac doctissimi viri dictum ab initio sic inhesit ossibus, sic ad ultimum medullis insedit, ut cum reliquis in rebus sepe unum probem et aliud concupiscam, in hoc unum semper probaverim ac semper optaverim: melior potius esse quam doctior.

cause is not eloquence but loquacity, as I said. And its source is not any confidence in your intelligence, but the insolence and pomp of your wealth—as if by growing wealthy, you grew more intelligent! You will see at once how true this is, if you turn to the small coffer of your intelligence. You have lost the keys to it in the little piles of your money; but if you break it open, believe me, you will find nothing inside it. Then you will begin to realize how foolish you are to judge others' intelligence when you are so destitute of your own.

Now, to put an end to this dispute, I am aware that ignorance is 21 a notable disease of the human mind. Yet if it were necessary to choose, I would by far prefer innocent ignorance to sinful wisdom. Let everyone choose between these two as he pleases. That is not my point here, but to make clear that, in my judgment, the greatest fault is sin, and not ignorance. Yet many people are less afraid of being called a murderer or adulterer than an illiterate. Indeed, every day I increasingly commend the truth of what St. Augustine wrote: "Behold, my God, behold with patience, as you do, how diligently the sons of humankind observe the conventions of letters and syllables that they receive from earlier writers; and yet observe not the eternal covenants of everlasting salvation that they inherit from you. For if someone holds or teaches the ancient rules of pronunciation, and contrary to grammar pronounces the word *omo* [*homo* 'human being'] without aspirating the first syllable, he will displease humankind more than if contrary to your precepts he hates a human being, when he himself is human."[17]

From the first, this most holy and learned man's saying pierced 22 me to the bone and lodged deep within my marrow. Hence, while in other matters I may approve one thing and desire another, in this regard I always desire and prefer the same thing: to be more virtuous rather than more learned. And in such cases I adapt Themistocles's remark about money, and say that I prefer to be a man without letters, rather than letters without a man.[18] For a

Semperque themistocleum illud de pecunia dictum huc inflexerim, ut quoniam a virtute vir dicitur, malim virum sine literis, quam literas sine viro. Ita enim sentio, ut literas male viventibus nil prodesse, sed improperio esse portumque omnem excusationis eripere, sic bene viventibus literarum ignorantiam nil obesse: esse quidem per literas ad salutem iter clarius atque sonantius, sed nec tutius, neque directius.

23   Ad summam ergo ignorantiam michi obiectam, ut excusem, non laboro, iudicem te recuso. Idque quam iuste faciam, si odium hactenus michi ignotum semperque notissimam ignorantiam tuam librabis, intelliges. Et odium quidem multi; odii causas, ut puto, tu solus nosti; ignorantiam vero omnes, nisi tu solus; quam si nosses, non totus esses ignarus; est enim scientie quedam pars ignorantiam suam scire. Quodsi fortassis illam discere teque ipsum nosse volueris, quod, ut aiunt, apollineo monemur oraculo, vel linguam illam salsamentis maceratam atque aromatibus delibutam exere vel scabrum illum et inertem calamum sume in manus, ut levia et inania ista discutias ac refellas. Mox videbis quam tuo turpiter ex ore sonuerit ignorantie mee nomen. Qua in re unum iure meo postulo, nequid michi aliena ope respondeas. Te ipsum excute, et invenies quid in sinu sit.

24   Et quoniam me de aliorum inventionibus furari solitum dicis, et a philosophis ac poetis ista decerpere, poteram tibi cum Tullio respondere: 'Metuebam ne a lenonibus diceres'; ego tamen id falsum esse conscientiam meam testem habeo, nisi quantum casu forsan inscius in aliena vestigia scrutatorque rerum vagus incido, vel apium more nonnunquam doctorum consilio de floribus favos fingo. Sed hec lis in tempus aliud differatur; tu furare undecunque libuerit et collige et stringe quod in me remittas, inclite ferventis eloquii iaculator, modo per te ipsum te te adiuves; cetera ut occur-

man, *vir*, is named for his virtue, *virtus*.[19] It is my belief that letters are of no use to people who live badly, but are rather a source of reproach that deprives them of any excuse in which they might seek refuge. By the same token, an ignorance of letters does no harm to people who live well. For if the path to salvation through letters is more glamorous and acclaimed than others, it is no more secure or direct.

In short, then, I am not at pains to excuse the vast ignorance 23 with which I am charged; and I refuse to let you be my judge. You will grasp how justly I do this, if you measure your hatred, previously unknown to me, and your ignorance, which was always well known. Many knew of this hatred, but you alone, I think, knew its causes. By contrast, everyone knew of your ignorance, except for you alone. If you had known of it, you would not be completely ignorant, for part of knowledge is knowing one's ignorance. If perhaps you decide to learn this and to know yourself — as we are urged, they say, by Apollo's oracle — then stick out your tongue, which is pickled with sauces and imbued with spices; take up your rusty and clumsy pen; and try to refute and dispel these frivolous and empty rumors. You'll soon see how obscene the charge of my ignorance sounds in your mouth. In this matter, I justly make only one demand: don't answer using others' help. Search your own person, and you'll find what is in your bosom.

Since you say that I often steal the inventions of others and 24 snatch bits from the philosophers and poets, I could answer you with Cicero's phrase: "I was afraid you'd say I steal from the panders."[20] But the charge is false, as my conscience bears witness, unless perhaps by chance I unwittingly retrace others' footsteps in my desultory researches, or sometimes follow the advice of scholars and fashion honeycombs from flowery passages, as bees do. But let us defer this dispute to another time. Steal wherever you please, collect, and draw forth weapons to cast at me, egregious hurler of burning eloquence, as long as you alone aid yourself! Whatever

rent, stilus saltem tuus sit, nec tibi tamen illorum cum quibus
dum digitulos tuos fricant, multa noctibus de voluptate disserere
solitus diceris, exoletorum tuorum auxilium interdico, cum tantum virum incomitatum ire non deceat in certamen.

: IV :

25 Sed parum est quod ignorantem me feceris; malum facis, grande si
verum crimen;[3] itaque nunquam esse, quam semper malum esse
prestiterit. Hic tu me, orator argutissime, silentio gravi et suspitionibus tacitis multis premis, plus auditoribus cogitandum linquens,
quam quod exprimis. Verum quia scelus proprium, quod aperte
obicias, vel non habes vel in aliud tempus differs, quo profundius
meam famam vulneres, nec, bellator callidus, primo congressu
pharetram missilibus cuntis exhaurias, sola me in presens malorum participatione diffamas. Iactas equidem et sepe iteras — nichil
est enim stultitia loquacius — sepe, inquam, repetis, tyrannos, quorum, ut ais, sub ditione vitam dego, de laboribus inopum vidua-
rumque vivere. Quodsi tibi concessero, comune tamen omnium
regnantium crimen erit. Unde enim nisi de sudore populorum
tantus hic sumptus, tantus cultus, tantus principum famulatus?
Ille melior innocentiorque, seu verius, minus nocens, qui hac licentia parcius modestiusque utitur. Ita quod in reliquis, et in hoc fa-
tendum erit, ut cum sine crimine nemo sit, ille optimus dici possit,
qui minus est malus.

26 Sed queso te primum, qui tam temere alios iudicas, caligantes
in te ipsum fige oculos, recordare preterita, contemplare presentia,

else occurs to you, let the style at least be yours. Still, I don't forbid you the aid of your cronies, who, it is said, massage your dainty fingers while you spout nightly discourses on pleasure. So great a hero cannot properly enter the combat unattended.

: IV :

It's not enough that you call me ignorant. You also call me bad, which is a serious charge, if it is true. For it would be preferable not to be at all, rather than to be a bad person. But here, O most clever orator, you burden me with grave silence and many tacit insinuations, leaving your audience to infer more than you state. Now, either you find no particular offense of mine to reprove openly; or else you temporize — either because you hope to inflict deeper wounds in my reputation later, or because as a cunning warrior you don't wish to empty your quiver of missiles in the first encounter. So for the moment, you accuse me only of frequenting evil men. Indeed, you exclaim and often reiterate — for folly is the greatest chatterbox — you often repeat, I say, that I live under the sway (as you put it) of tyrants who subsist on the labors of paupers and widows. I might grant you this, but the charge would prove common to all rulers. Could anything but the sweat of peoples produce the great luxury, the great magnificence, and the great households of our princes? The most virtuous and innocent ruler — or, more correctly, the least harmful one — is the one who is most sparing and moderate in exploiting his privilege. As in other matters, here too we must grant that, since no one is without fault, we may call best that person who is least evil.

But first I ask this of you, who so rashly judge others: turn your clouded vision toward yourself, recall the past, observe the present, and measure you and your affairs by that earlier measure. You are

teque tuasque res ad mensuram illam pristinam metire. Tu idem qui fuisti, nisi quod aliquanto superbior stultiorque, dicam verius, conspectior factus es. Non format animum Fortuna, sed detegit; eadem superbia inerat quando humillimus videbaris; idem virus, sed serpentum more hieme torpidum; Fortune mox ut radius fervide prosperitatis affulsit, venenosum animal exarsisti, meque in primis, quem lambere solebas, credo itidem alios, momordisti.

27   Res autem tue omnes alie. Unde hic, queso, tuus luxus et Petri moribus tam dissimilis victus? Unde hec laqueata inauratis trabibus domus tua, sanctis patribus in speluncis aut sub divo pernoctantibus? Unde hic ostro et mollibus plumis instratus lectulus, Iacob humi iacente et sacrum caput supra durum lapidem reclinante? Unde demum sonipes iste purpureus, Cristo super asinam sedente? Quamvis te natura, fortuna, usus, etas impudentem fecerit, pudebit forsan hunc movisse sermonem. Unde enim qui de aliorum vita iudicas, unde, oro te, vivis? Nempe vel mentiri oportet, quod coram veri consciis frustra fit, vel fateri hunc fastum, has delitias atque inanes pompulas tuas pasci solo de sanguine crucifixi, quo impinguatus calcitras, nec attendis quam hec tua turpis sagina, tam macro tamque arido Cristi grege, quam feda nausea in tanta pauperum Cristi fame, de quorum lacrimis ac sudore hunc quo tumes panem, si nescis, intrivisti, qui tibi morbos anime mortemque peperit.

28   Tu tamen — o verissime dictum: 'ceca fortuna, cecique illi quos ceca illa complectitur' — tu, inquam, hec tam manifesta non vides, et quorundam more qui, defecti oculorum viribus, peius quo iuxta sunt vident quam que longe de aliena conscientia remotissima oc-

the man you were before, except that you are somewhat more proud and foolish, or to speak more correctly, you are more conspicuous. Rather than shaping our minds, Fortune reveals them. You harbored the same pride when you seemed humblest, and the same venom, like a snake dormant in the winter. As soon as Fortune warmed you with the blazing ray of prosperity, you burned like a poisonous reptile, and struck — first biting me, whom you used to lick, and then others too, I'm sure.

Clearly, your estate is entirely changed. Why, I ask, do you live 27 in luxury, with a lifestyle so unlike Peter's? Why do you live in a house with paneled ceilings and gilded beams, when the holy fathers spent their nights in caves or under the open sky? Why this bed spread with purple dye and soft down, when Jacob lay on the ground and rested his holy head on a hard rock?[21] And why this steed with purple trappings, when Christ rode on an ass?[22] Even if nature, fortune, custom, and the age have rendered you shameless, you will perhaps still be ashamed that you provoked this lecture. You judge the lives of others; but what, may I ask, is the source of your living? Clearly, you must either lie, which serves no purpose when you face people who know the truth; or you must confess that your grandeur, your pleasures, and your empty pomp feed on the blood of the Crucified alone. Grown fat, you spur along, unaware how obscene your corpulence is amid Christ's thin and wasted flock, or how disgusting your bloated nausea is amid the great hunger of Christ's paupers. For, if you don't know it, it is in their tears and sweat that you have dipped the bread that swells you, breeding diseases and death in your soul.

How true is the saying: "Fortune is blind, and blind are those 28 whom she embraces in her blindness"![23] For you don't see what is obvious; rather, like people with poor vision who see close objects less clearly than distant ones, you pronounce judgment on your neighbor's conscience, which is something quite distant and hidden from you. Unaware of the log in your eye, you perceive quite

cultissimaque re sententiam fers, trabisque tue nescius, alieni fes-
tucam oculi claro cernis intuitu. Ego te, cece, vel nolentem diri-
gam; ego bacillum, siquem tibi cui insistas rationis arbor tuo
generi indecerpta largitur, vere considerationis in semitam manu
flectam. Quotiens ergo de laboribus populorum viventes arguere
visum erit, illud una mentem subeat, non te de mercatorum curis,
non de artificum industria, non de rerum publicarum proventibus,
sed de mendicantium tergo ac squalore vivere. Aliquanto, ni fallor,
honestius illos vulgi labor, quam te Cristi famelicorum pascit esu-
ries. Adde quod nemo omnium eorum, quos tyrannos vocas, aut
rapinis aut muneribus tam ieiune inhiat quam tu.

29   De primo aliis nichil dicam, ne te odio nimis acri urgere videar,
ac studio altercandi famam tuam conquisitis veris licet criminibus
insectari. Tibi ad excitandam conscientiam unum illud sufficit,
qualiter patroni illius famosissimi familiam in se scissam, sed pariter te fidentem inque hoc solo unanimem, longis litium anfractibus fatigatam mirisque elusam ambagibus, ad extremum magnis
hinc depositis librorum pretioseque supellectilis atque argenti et
auri, toto denique multis quesito vigiliis patrimonio, arbiter egregie, spoliasti: tuleruntque filii crimen patris, qui cum tam diu certa
omnibus consilia prebuisset, ita sibi et suis in amicitie talis elec-
tione consuluit, ut esset qui post suum obitum discordantes filios
novis artibus ad concordiam revocaret, ab illis in suam domum
omnem litigii materiam transferendo. Debebatur forsan illis opibus hic exitus, quoniam patronorum divitie sine multis mendaciis
non queruntur, dignumque est ut male parta male pereant,[4] et dolis exstructa dolis ruant; sed an tibi etiam deberetur rapinis ac
fraudibus amicorum litigio finem dare, tecum cogita.

clearly the speck in your neighbor's eye.[24] Blind man, I shall lead you, even against your will. If only the tree of reason — so seldom culled by your kind — will furnish a staff for you to lean on, my hand will guide you back to the path of true reflection. So the next time you decide to accuse others of living off the people's labors, remember that you do not live off the toils of merchants, the industry of craftsmen, or the revenues of the state, but off the backs and the squalor of mendicants. Unless I am mistaken, others feed more honorably on the labor of the masses than you feed on the hunger of Christ's starvelings. What's more, none of the men you call tyrants hungers as avidly as you do for either plunder or gifts.

Now, as for your plundering, I won't say a word to others, lest I seem to attack you with excessive hatred and, in my zeal for quarreling, to assail your reputation with recherché, if true, accusations. But to you personally, I shall cite one example that will suffice to rouse your conscience — how you treated the family of your celebrated patron, which, though torn by dissension, was united in their common trust of you.[25] At length, after they were exhausted by their protracted disputes and hoodwinked by your marvelous stratagems, O egregious arbiter, you despoiled them of their great stores of books, precious furnishings, silver and gold — indeed, of the entire patrimony that had been assembled through tireless labors. Thus, the sons suffered for the sins of their father. Just as he had offered sure advice to everyone for many years, so by choosing you as a friend he planned to provide for himself and his family after his death, when an arbiter might find new ways to create concord among his discordant sons, by moving the entire object of their dispute from their home to his own. Perhaps such wealth was bound to suffer this outcome, for the riches of the powerful are amassed through many falsehoods. It is fitting that "bad gains meet bad ends,"[26] and that what is built on deceit falls by deceit. But consider in your heart whether you were bound to resolve dispute between friends through theft and fraud.

30   De secundo autem, quid opus est testibus, cum de his ipsis iuvenibus, de quorum michi tyrannide conflare verbis invidiam niteris, quod erga te liberalitatem defuncti patrui senis intermisisse videantur, sepe multis audientibus questus sis? Quod equanimius ferres, si te ipsum unquam iusto librasses examine, cum nec ingenium, nec lingua, nec virtus, nec omnino aliquid te, non dicam magno precio comparandum faciat, sed, si gratis obtuleris, nec magnopere respuendum, quanquam munificentissimus ille senex et ecclesiasticis viris, quorum de grege erat, amicissimus, dum benignitati studet ac generose obsequitur nature, sepe iudicii negligens, dignos cum indignis uno sue largitatis torrente miscuerit. Hec tibi, tyrannorum pessime, pro veritate proque his optimis dominis, quos, quoniam spoliare nequis, accusas, hodie decursa suffecerint; plura, ni desinis, parantur. Quotiescunque te moveris, occurram tibi, nec verebor, nec fatigabor pro veritate certare, cum tu tam piger ad reliqua, ita sis semper pro mendacio indefessus.

:   V   :

31   Tempus est ut ad me ipsum sermo redeat, idque expurget quod michi obicis, convictum atque amicitiam tyrannorum, quasi simul agentibus omnia esse comunia sit necesse, cum sepe tamen inter bonos pessimi, inter pessimos boni habitent. An non inter triginta tyrannos Athenarum Socrates fuit? Plato cum Dyonisio, Callisthenes cum Alexandro, Cato cum Catilina, Seneca cum Nerone? Nec infecta est virtus in vicinitate nequitie; nam, etsi teneros animos sepe leves cause quatiant, solidas mentes morum contagia non

And as for your love of gifts, who needs witnesses, when you 30
yourself have complained about these young men in front of many
others? These are the same youths against whose "tyranny" you
strive to arouse my resentment, because they seem to have discontinued the generosity that their late uncle showed you in his old
age.[27] You would bear this with equanimity if you ever weighed
yourself in a just balance. For you have no intelligence, no eloquence, no virtue — in short, nothing to make anyone hire you at a
great price, rather than reject you with great disdain, even if you
offered your services for free. Nevertheless, that most beneficent
old man, a close friend of his fellow ecclesiastics, in practicing benevolence and indulging his generous nature, often neglected his
better judgment, and mixed worthy and unworthy men in the
flood of his munificence. O worst of tyrants, let these offhand remarks suffice today to defend both the truth and those worthy
lords whom you accuse because you cannot rob them. Unless you
stop, more arguments stand ready. No matter where you turn, I
shall confront you. I shall prove neither wary nor weary of fighting
for the truth, while you, who are so slothful in other matters,
prove untiring in the cause of falsehood.

: V :

It is time for the discussion to return to me, and to refute your 31
charge of my intimacy and friendship with tyrants. You act as if
people who live together must share everything, when in fact
wicked people often live among the good, and good people among
the wicked. Didn't Socrates live under the Thirty Tyrants of Athens? Didn't Plato live with Dionysius, Callisthenes with Alexander, Cato with Catiline, and Seneca with Nero? Virtue is not infected by the proximity of vice. Whereas trivial causes may disturb

attingunt. Huic tamen calumnie multisque aliis quibus non nunc primum me stultitia livorque impedit, uno pridem toto volumine respondisse videor et verborum inanium tendiculas confregisse.

32 Quod ad presens attinet, unum dicam, quod si credas, stupeas, si minus, irrideas. Animo quidem sub nullo sum, nisi sub illo qui michi animum dedit, aut sub aliquo quem valde illi amicum ipse michi persuaserim, rarum genus. Addam aliquot michi conformes animas, quibus me amor iugo subiecit amenissimo: non leve imperium sed tam rarum, ut ab adolescentia ad hanc etatem perpaucis talibus iugis obnoxius fuerim. Quo in genere et humiles et illustres et pontifices fuerant et reges, ita tamen ut in his fortuna nichil aut dignitas, sed totum virtus amorque ageret, quo illis sponte subicerer, graviterque doluerim quotiens tali me servitio mors absolvit. Unde accidit ut humilioribus sepe subiectior fuerim, quod in illis quidem eius, quam nec amo ne veneror, fortune minus cernerem, plus virtutis, quam michi, si in me non possum, at in aliis venerari atque amare propositum semper fuerit. His cessantibus, nullus est hominum, cui animo sim subiectus. Ita, ut vides, melior pars mei vel est libera, vel iucundis atque honestis ex causis libertate carens, aliter libera esse non vult, cogique metuit ac recusat. Sic est animus.

33 Pars autem mei altera hec terrestris terrarum dominis, quorum loca incolit, subdita sit oportet. Quidni enim, cum hos ipsos, qui minoribus presunt, maioribus subesse videam? Et ad illud cesareum rem redire:

Humanum paucis vivit genus;

quin et hi pauci quibus humanum genus vivere dicitur, non formidolosiores populis quam populi illis sunt. Ita fere nullus est liber;

tender spirits, the contagion of evil character does not affect strong minds. In answer to this slander, and to many others in which folly and envy have entangled me, and not for the first time, I seem to have replied recently in an entire volume that demolished the snares of their empty words.[28]

As for the present, I shall say one thing. If you believe it, you will be amazed; if you don't, you will mock me. In spirit, I am subject to no one but Him who gave me spirit, or to that rare kind of person who, I am convinced, is His close friend. I may add that there are some kindred souls, to whom love has subjugated me with the sweetest yoke. Such dominion is not lightly borne, but it is so rare that from my youth to the present age I have been subject to only a few such persons. These included both the humble and the illustrious, and even kings and popes. Yet it was not at all their fortune and rank, but their virtue and love that made me submit to them freely and completely, and to mourn them deeply when death released me from their service. This is why I often submitted to humbler persons: for I perceived in them less fortune, which I neither love nor revere, but more virtue, which I have always resolved to revere and love in others, if I could not in myself. Apart from these, there is no human being to whom my spirit is subject. Hence, as you see, the better part of me is free. Or if pleasant and honorable reasons cause me to forego freedom, I do not choose to be free in any other way, but both fear and refuse any coercion. Such is my spirit.

By contrast, the earthly part of me must perforce be subject to the lords whose lands it inhabits. Why shouldn't it, when I see that even those who rule their inferiors submit to their superiors? It all comes down to Caesar's observation that

The human race lives for a few.[29]

In fact, those few for whom the human race is said to live are no more terrifying to their peoples than their peoples are to them.

undique servitus et carcer et laquei, nisi fortasse rarus aliquis rerum nodos adiuta celitus animi virtute discusserit. Verte te quocunque terrarum libet: nullus tyrannide locus vacat; ubi enim tyranni desunt, tyrannizant populi; atque ita ubi unum evasisse videare, in multos incideris, nisi forsan iusto mitique rege regnatum locum aliquem michi ostenderis. Quod cum feceris, eo larem illico transferam, cumque omnibus sarcinulis commigrabo. Non me amor patrie, non decor ac nobilitas Italie retinebit; ibo ad Indos ac Seres et ultimos hominum Garamantes, ut hunc locum inveniam et hunc regem.

34   Sed frustra queritur quod nusquam est. Gratias etati nostre, que cum cunta pene paria fecerit, hunc nobis eripuit laborem. Frumenta mercantibus satis est modicum pugno excipere, illud examinant, inde notitiam totius capiunt acervi. Non est opus oras ultimas rimari et terrarum abdita penetrare: lingue, habitus, vultusque alii; vota, animi, moresque adeo similes, quocunque perveneris, ut nunquam verius fuisse videatur illud Satyrici ubi ait:

Humani generis mores tibi nosse volenti,
sufficit una domus.

Unus est, fateor, sacer locus, ubi tu degis, ubi tua presentia tuisque consiliis, Saturne alter vel Auguste, aureum seculum renovasti. Felix Rodanus tali incola, felix cardo romuleus tali duce, felix orbis terrarum tali cardine, felix Ecclesia tali consule! Vere, inquam, locus sacer quem inhabitas! Sic apud Virgilium, 'sacer ignis' insanabilis morbi, 'sacra fames auri,' 'sacre porte' dicuntur inferni.

35   Equidem de iuvenibus nostris quid sentiam, audivisti: rectores patrie, non tyranni; tamque omnis tyrannici spiritus quam tu

Hence, practically no one is free: slavery and prison and chains are found everywhere, unless some rare individual with heaven-sent virtue happens to untie the knots of human affairs. No matter where you turn on earth, you will find no place without tyranny. When there are no tyrants, the people tyrannize. So when you think you have escaped one tyrant, you fall into the hands of many, unless you can show me some place that is ruled by a just and benign ruler. If you can, I shall at once pack all my bags and move my home there. I shall not be hindered by my love of country, nor by Italy's grace and nobility. I shall travel to the people of India, China, and the remotest Sahara to find such a place and such a ruler.[30]

But it is pointless to seek what exists nowhere. We may thank   34 our age for making nearly all things equal and thus sparing us the trouble. Merchants find that examining a handful of grain is enough to judge an entire heap. We need not explore the remotest lands or penetrate into unknown regions. Wherever you travel, people's languages, clothes, and faces may differ; but their hopes, thoughts, and habits will be so similar that Juvenal's lines will seem truer than ever:

If you would know what humankind is like,
one house will suffice.[31]

But there is one "holy" place, I confess. It is where your presence and your counsels, O second Saturn or second Augustus, have restored the Golden Age. Happy the Rhone for such an inhabitant, happy the Roman cardinalate for such a leader, happy the world for such a cardinal, happy the Church for such a consul![32] Truly "holy," I say, is the place where you dwell.[33] Just so, Virgil calls an incurable disease a "holy fire," and he calls "holy" both the hunger for gold and the gates of hell.[34]

You have heard what I think about these youths, who are the   35 rulers of their country, but not tyrants. They know as little of the

equitatis ac iustitie sunt expertes. Ita sunt hactenus; quid futuri sint nescio. Est enim mobilis animus, eorum maxime quorum est immota felicitas stabilisque licentia. Sed ut illos vel tyrannos falso dixeris, vel tyrannos vere dies longior factura sit, seu quod usque nunc contegit, detectura sit, quid ad me? Cum illis, non sub illis sum, et in illorum terris, non domibus habito. Nil comune cum ipsis est michi, preter commoda et honores, quibus me largiter, quantum patior, continuo prosequuntur. Consilia et executiones rerum administratioque munerum publicorum committuntur aliis ad hec natis; michi autem nil penitus, nisi otium et silentium et securitas et libertas: hec cure, hec negotia mea sunt. Itaque ceteris palatium mane petentibus, ego silvas et solitudines notas peto. Nec me dominos ulla re alia quam liberalitate ac beneficiis habere sentio, nempe cui promissum servatumque bona fide ad hunc diem fuerit, ut nil ex me aliud requiratur quam presentia, et in hac urbe florentissima inque his amenissimis locis mora, quam sibi, ut dicunt, suoque dominio gloriosam putant.

36   Nota hec omnibus sunt, que loquor; tibi autem incredibilia videbuntur, quia nunquam tale aliquid sub te tuaque tyrannide visum est, quem nullus affectus, nulla caritas, nulla dulcedo tangit amicitie, qui solum ex hominibus, quasi ex pecudibus, lucrum queris, multoque pluris lenonem utilem facis, quam inutilem philosophum. Durum est tibi cogitare quod nosti; nichilo quidem plus inter abyssi fundum et celi verticem interesse crediderim, quam inter tuam senilem avaramque superbiam horumque mansuetudinem ac magnificentiam iuvenilem. Denique sic habeto: neque hos tyrannos, meque esse liberrimum. Et si, ut eunt res humane, servum esse sors adigat, hoc animo sum, ut nusquam male sim futurus, modo sub te non sim, longeque sit tibi, me iudice, preferendus Agathocles aut Phalaris aut Busiris.

tyrannical spirit as you do of equity and justice. Or at least until now: I can't predict their future. For the mind is changeable, especially in people whose happiness never changes and whose privileges are secure. But whether you falsely call them tyrants, or whether in the end time makes true tyrants of them, or reveals what it has hitherto concealed—how does this affect me? I live with them, not under them; and I reside in their lands, but not in their houses. I have nothing in common with them, except for the benefits and honors that they continue to lavish on me, as long as I allow it. Political deliberations and measures, as well as the administration of public funds, are entrusted to others, who were born for this purpose. To me, nothing is entrusted but leisure, silence, security, and freedom. These are my concern and my business. While others at dawn seek great palaces, I seek my familiar woods and solitude. I feel the presence of such lords only because of their generosity and benefits. For up to this time, they have promised in good faith that they require only my presence and my residence in this flourishing city and its charming quarters—a presence which, they say, glorifies both themselves and their realm.

What I am saying is common knowledge, but it will seem incredible to you, since nothing of the kind has ever been seen under you and your tyranny. You are moved by no affection, by no love, and by no sweet friendship. You only seek profit from human beings, as if from cattle; and you find a pimp more useful than a philosopher. It's hard for you to reflect on what you know. I believe that the distance between the bottom of the abyss and the vault of the heavens is no greater than that between your senile and greedy pride and the youthful mildness and magnificence of these youths. In sum, recognize that they are not tyrants, and I am completely free. And if, as happens in human affairs, my fate should make me a slave, I shall remain convinced that I am well off anywhere as long as I am not in your power, and that in my opinion Agathocles, Phalaris, or Busiris is far preferable to you.[35]

36

: VI :

37 Restat ut unius tibi falsissime opinionis velum ab oculis auferam,
quo sublato videas et liberius tecum tractes, an expediat inermem
in hec verborum bella descendere, an in silentio potius voluptatibus tuis frui. Tu me quidem, ut intelligo, magnitudine tua terri-
tum iri speras. Falleris; nullum timeo, nisi quem diligo. Te non
diligo, quia non sinis. Mores autem ac superbiam superbieque causam, magnitudinem tuam, odi. An vero forte non auditum tibi est
in illo quondam fame certamine, quod michi similis conflavit invidia, ubi, immeritis quoque convitiis lacessitus, non tantum iuste
sed propemodum necessarie ultionis seu verius defensionis arma
arripui, quam penitus illi viro tunc per Italiam formidato nichil
detuli? Et erat is, quod nemo ambigit, etsi non in eo apice literarum, quem sibi ipse, vel vanitate insita vel flatibus adulantum, falsa
de utique opinione confinxerat, attamen plusquam mediocri litera-
tura et eloquio supra comunem modum; accedebat viri potentia
fortuneque illi ad nutum famulantis ingens favor, mens preterea
omnis impatiens offense atque ulciscendi consuetudo notissima,
finitimis tunc late suspecta principibus.

38   Qui hunc igitur talem virum, tam potentem non tantum verbis
et calamo, sed vinculis et gladio, solius veritatis auxilio fretus non
timuerim, te timebo? Cui segne ingenium, obtusior calamus, lingua nodosior, imo cui penitus horum nichil, nisi forte pro his omnibus rubentem michi obicies galerum. Sed reverentia tui status
mei stili impetum cohibebit? Sed per omnes deos oro te, ubi me
tam stolidum deprehendisti, ut non equum credas extimare sed
phaleras? An vero nunc alius, alius tunc fuisti, dum vulgo quoque

: VI :

It remains for me to lift the veil of false opinion from your eyes.   37
Once it is removed, you shall see and reflect more freely whether
you ought to enter this war of words unarmed, or whether you
should enjoy your pleasures in silence. You hope to terrify me, I
perceive, by your greatness. You are mistaken. I fear no one but
the One whom I love. I do not love you, for you do not permit it.
And I hate your character, your pride, and the cause of your
pride — your greatness. But perhaps you have not heard how in
that previous dispute concerning fame, which was stirred up by
similar envy, I showed absolutely no deference to a great man who
was feared throughout Italy. Provoked then, too, by unwarranted
insults, I took up arms in just and even necessary retaliation, or
rather in my own defense. Yet my opponent, as no one doubts,
was a man of some learning — if not at the height which his innate
vanity or the empty praise of flatterers falsely caused him to imagine, yet of no little culture and of exceptional eloquence. Add to
this the man's power and the immense favor of fortune, which
served him at his beck and call; his mind intolerant of any offense;
and his well-known habit of taking revenge, which was widely suspected by neighboring rulers.[36]

If relying solely on the truth for assistance, I did not fear so   38
mighty a man, whose power lay not only in words and writings,
but in shackles and the sword, why shall I fear you? Your wit is
slow, your pen even duller, and you are tongue-tied. No, you have
none of that man's abilities, unless perhaps in their place you wave
your red biretta in my face. Will awe of your rank stay my stylus
from attacking you? By all the gods, I ask you, when did you catch
me being so stupid that you think I value a horse's trappings more
than the horse? Or are you now different from your former self,
whom the mob despised? How very precious and invaluable is the

contemptui habebare? Preciosissimus atque inextimabilis pannus
tui capitis, si tam cito sapientiam possessoribus suis daret! Crede
autem michi, non dat ille sapientiam, sed private vite latebras pan-
dit et latentia in apertum trahit.

39   Scio ego, sciunt omnes, nec tu nescis, quibus meritis, quibus
venatibus ad hunc gradum veneris. Certe si te excutis, si te inspi-
cis, si te libras, si te extimas, nec te fallis, nichil invenies, quamvis
et te multum ames et valde tibi placeas — dico iterum, nichil invenies, quo te possis attollere, nisi insanis. Nichil est tibi — quod ita
esse, nemo tam tardus est qui dubitet — sed totum generi unde te
ortum iactas ac familie datum fuit; cui, licet antiquum nichil, sunt
tamen ad claritatem et gratiam multa recentia. Que omnia, illo superstite cuius (credo) me tibi memoria odiosum facit, nunquam te
huc attollere potuissent, quo iam senex, sublato demum illo, tam
lente tamque miserabiliter subrepsisti, ut non cepisse pulcrius fuerit, quamvis ad nundinas Simonis, non ut serus, sic et piger mercator accesseris. Nemo liberalius, ideoque nemo crebrius, Spiritum
Sanctum vendit.

40   Sed ne te nimis affligam, omissa illius viri mentione, quem adhuc, ut reor, extinctum times, ad familiam tuam redeo, cuius merita, cum quasi quidam gradus ad ascensum tibi fuerint, nil est
quod familie detraham. Sed te illud interrogo: qua fronte, quo ve
animo statum tenes, non tibi utique, sed maioribus datum tuis?
Que ista impudentia, quis ve hic furor, ut de aliena potius virtute
superbias, quam de tuis vitiis erubescas? Miserebar equidem statum hunc tuum: donec a me amari passus eras, unus e numero te
ridentium evasi. Credebas me novis insignibus terruisse. Non sum
pavidus, ut rebaris; irritasti potius; inflammasti. Fulgentem galeam

cloth that covers your head, if it so swiftly imparts wisdom to its owners! Yet, believe me, it doesn't impart wisdom, but exposes the hidden places of private life and drags what is hiding out in the open.

I know, everyone knows, and even you yourself are aware what   39
merits and what hunting skills raised you to this degree. Certainly, if you search, examine, weigh, and evaluate yourself without self-deception, you will find nothing — no matter how much you love and please yourself — you will find nothing (I say again) for which you may extol yourself, unless you are insane. You have nothing, and no one is so dull-witted that he can doubt it. Instead, everything is due to the lineage that you vaunt and to your family, which (if not ancient) has many recent claims to fame and favor. If the man were still alive whose memory (I believe) makes me odious to you, these claims would never have advanced you so far.[37] But now that he is gone, you have in your old age crept to this height so slowly and miserably that you might more decorously have given up the attempt, even though you entered the bazaar of Simon Magus as a zealous if tardy merchant.[38] No one sells the Holy Spirit more generously, and hence more often, than you do.

Still, to avoid unduly distressing you, I shall not mention that   40
man, whom you fear even now, I think, although he is dead. Let me return to your family, whom I shall not disparage, although their merits provided the steps, as it were, for your ascent. But let me ask you: with what cheek and arrogance do you hold a rank that was granted, not to you, but to your forebears? By what impudence or madness do you take pride in others' virtue, rather than blush at your own vices? I for one pitied your high rank; and as long as you let me love you, I alone avoided the crowd of those deriding you. You believed that your new insignia had terrified me, but I am not the coward that you thought. Instead, you irritated and inflamed me. I had scorned a gleaming helmet and openly

sprevi, armatoque iuveni in frontem restiti: ut togati senis rutilum pilleum expavescam?

41   Nil vereor, verum loquens. Dixi iam: non metuo nisi quos diligo; metui dum dilexi; ne diligerem, coegisti. Vis autem, ni fallor, ut timeam, et mente volatili tragicum illud usurpas: 'Oderint, dum metuant'. Spernam ego, dum odero. Terribilis fieri optabas: contemptibilis factus es. Nolim, edepol, notum fiat quanti ego te faciam, ne ipse minoris fiam ab aliquo horum extimatorum, qui nichil magni faciunt nisi quod oculis lucet, inscii quid illo sub murice lateat, quo te simul et quadrupedem tuum tegis. Nec immerito una est vestis, quibus unus est sensus.

42   Imo, Hercle, omnibus notum velim quam ex alto teque tuosque despiciam miratores, ut alicuius rari extimatoris iudicio magni sim, ausus opes contemnere et me quoque dignum Deo fingere; interque umbras rerum resque ipsas et solida bona discernere; calcare aurum, virtutem colere; spernere Alexandrum, Dyogenem admirari. Proinde quere alium qui te metuat, et tua hec levia vereatur insignia: ego induci, fateor, non possum, ut hanc in auro tantam virtutis inopiam unquam colam, ut hanc tuam, non propriis fundamentis innixam, sed externis adminiculis male fultam, et casuram nutantemque iam ac ruine proximam, magnitudinem perhorrescam.

defied an armed youth.³⁹ Should I now be frightened by the bright red cap of an old man in robes?

I am afraid of nothing, for I speak the truth. As I said before, I 41 fear only those whom I love. I feared you while I loved you. But you forced me not to love you. Unless I am mistaken, you want me to fear you; and with your unstable mind, you quote the tragic verse "Let them hate, as long as they fear me."⁴⁰ And I shall despise you, as long as I hate you. You hoped to become terrible; you have become contemptible. By Jove, I would not want it known how little I value you, lest I should be little valued by those critics who only value what dazzles the eye, but are ignorant of what lies beneath the purple drapery that covers both you and your horse. It is only fair that beasts with equal sense should share the same cloak.

By heaven, I would rather have it known from what heights I 42 look down on you and your friends, so that I might be greatly valued in the judgment of some rare critic for "daring to scorn riches and fashion myself worthy of God."⁴¹ And for daring amid the shadows of things to discern the things themselves and solid goods, daring to trample down gold and worship virtue, and daring to spurn Alexander and admire Diogenes. So find someone else to fear you and to revere your petty insignia. Nothing can ever induce me, I confess, to worship your great dearth of virtue amid all that gold. When I see how your greatness — resting not on its own foundations, but weakly propped up on external supports — is ready to fall and already totters on the brink of ruin, I shudder.

DE SUI IPSIUS ET MULTORUM IGNORANTIA

[Epistola Dedicatoria]

Ad Donatum apenninigenam grammaticum[1]

1   Habes en, amice, iamtandem expectatum promissumque librum paruum de materia ingenti, mea scilicet ac multorum ignorantia, quam si ingenii incude[2] studii malleo extendere licuisset, crede michi, in cameli[3] sarcinam excreuisset. Nam que latior loquendi area, quis campus ingentior, quam humane tractatus ignorantie, et presertim mee?

2   Ita uero hunc leges, ut me ante focum hibernis noctibus fabulantem audire soles, et qua impetus fert uagantem. Liber quidem dicitur, colloquium est; nil de libro habet preter nomen, non molem, non ordinem, non stilum, non denique grauitatem, ut qui cursim in itinere approperante[4] conscriptus sit; sed ideo librum appellare mens fuit, ut paruo te munere, magno sed nomine promererer, et fisus licet nostra tibi omnia placere, tamen ita te fallere cogitaui.

3   Est et inter amicos hic fallendi usus, pauxillum[5] pomorum uel exiguum obsonium missuri, uase argenteo inclusum, candido linteo obuoluimus, nec plus nempe quod mittitur nec melius, sed accipienti gratius, honestius fit mittenti; sic et ego rem paruam pulcro uelamine honestaui, cum quod epystolam possem dicere, li-

ON HIS OWN IGNORANCE AND
THAT OF MANY OTHERS

[Letter of Dedication]

To the grammarian Donato, born in the Apennines[1]

My friend, at last you have the book that I promised and you ex-   1
pected, a small work on a vast subject, namely, on my own ignorance and that of many others. If I had used the hammer of study
to work it out on the anvil of my wit, believe me, it would have
grown into a load for a camel. Can there be any wider area or
vaster field for eloquence than a treatise on human ignorance, especially my own?

You will read it just as you often listen to my fireside chats on   2
winter nights, when I ramble as the impulse moves me. I have
called this work a book, but it is really a talk. Except for the name,
it has none of the qualities of a book—no amplitude, structure,
style, or gravity—for it was written rapidly during a journey made
in haste But I decided to call it a book, and thus to win your favor
by sending this small gift under a great name. Although I was
confident that you liked all my works, I intended to beguile you in
this way.

It is customary for friends to beguile each other in this way.   3
When we send someone a bit of fruit or a dainty snack, we wrap it
in white linen and place it in a silver bowl. This doesn't make the
gift larger or better, but it makes it more attractive to the recipient,
and more honorable for the sender. Just so, I have dignified my little work with an attractive covering, and have called it a book
when it might have been called a letter. You won't regard it as less
valuable if it is laced with numerous additions and corrections,

brum dixi, qui tibi non idcirco uilior fuerit, quod lituris et additio-
nibus plurimis intertextus et pleno undique margine circumfertus
est; etsi enim oculis demptum aliquid sit decoris, animo tamen
tantundem gratie additum uideri debet, quod hinc uel maxime te
michi familiarissimum intelligis, cui sic scribam, ut additiones ac
lituras ceu totidem signa familiaritatis ac dilectionis[6] aspicias.

4   Nec preterea dubitare possis meum esse, qui et manu mea tibi
olim[7] notisissima scriptus et quasi de industria tot cicatricibus
deformatus ad te ueniat, memorans tale aliquid de Nerone principe scripsisse Suetonium Tranquillum: 'Venere,' inquit, 'in manus
meas pugillares libellique cum quibusdam notissimus uersibus, ipsius cirographo scriptis, ut facile appareret non translatos aut dictante aliquo exceptos, se plane quasi a cogitante atque generante
exaratos, ita multa et deleta, et inducta et superscripta inerant'. Et
hec quidem ille. Nil tibi nunc aliud sum scripturus. Viue mei memor, et uale.

Pataui, idibus Januariis, mei doloris in lectulo, hora noctis xia.

⁝ I ⁝

5 Nunquam ne igitur quiescemus? Semper conflictabitur hic calamus? Nulle nobis erunt ferie? Quotidie amicorum laudibus,
quotidie emulorum iurgiis respondendum erit? Nec inuidiam aut
latebre excluserint aut tempus extinxerit? Nec quietem michi omnium ferme pro quibus humanum laborat atque estuat genus, rerum fuga pepererit? Nec uacationem denique iam deuexa ac de-
fessa etas attulerit? O uenenum pertinax! Que me pridem rei

and all of its margins are crammed with notes.[2] If this detracts from the work's beauty to the eye, your mind should find that it gains to that extent in grace. For you'll understand how special a friend you are to me when I write in this way, hoping that you regard my additions and corrections as so many tokens of our friendship and affection.

Besides, you can scarcely doubt that this is my work, since it is   4 written in a hand that has long been familiar to you. And it is almost purposely disfigured by many scars, to remind you of what Suetonius wrote about the emperor Nero: "Some tablets and short works have come to my hands which contain some celebrated verses, written in his own hand. It is clear that they weren't copied out or taken down in dictation, but obviously penned as they were born in thought, for there are numerous phrases cancelled, added, or written in above the line."[3] Thus wrote Suetonius. I write no more for now. Keep me in your thoughts, and stay well.

Padua, 13 January, on my bed of pain, at 5:00 in the morning.[4]

: I :

Shall I never have a moment's peace? Will my pen be harassed for-   5 ever? Shall I have no days of rest? Must I reply to the praises of friends each day, and each day to the insults of foes? Will no refuge exclude envy, and no length of time extinguish it? Shall I obtain no quiet by fleeing nearly everything for which humankind toils and burns? Will not my declining and decrepit age bring me some respite? O unrelenting poison! My age, which would have excused me long ago from serving the state, does not yet excuse me from envy. And although I am absolved by the state, to which I owe so much, I am tormented by envy, to which I owe nothing.[5] Once, I confess, there was a time for a friendlier style, and a

publice excusasset, nondum excusat inuidie, cumque illa cui multum debeo me absoluat, hec, cui nil debeo, me molestat. Olim, fateor, stili tempus erat amicioris, et naturam meam semper et etatem iam tranquillior decebat oratio. Date ueniam, amici; et tu,
lector, quisquis es, parce, oro. *Tuque ante alios, Donate optime, cui hec
loquor, ignoscito;*[8] loqui oportet, non quia id melius, sed quia contrarium difficile. Etsi enim ratio silentium suadeat, digna, nisi fallor,
indignatio et iustus dolor uerba extorquent. Auidissimus pacis, in
bellum cogor. Rursus ecce inuiti trudimur, rursus ad censorium
agimur tribunal — mirum! — nescio an inuide amicitie, an amice
dixerim inuidie.

6   Quid non potes, liuor improbe, si amicos etiam flamare animos potes? Multa experto, hoc mali genus inexpertum hactenus;
nunc primum michi mea sors obicit, omnium grauissimum pessi-
mumque. Nam cum hostibus congressus sepe prosperi; dulcis, ut
quibusdam placet, ira est; dulcis profecto uictoria; cum amicis de-
certanti et uincere et uinci miserum. Michi uero neque cum amicis
modo neque cum hostibus, sed cum inuidia bellum est. Non
nouus hostis, licet insolitum pugne genus; pharetrata *fere quidem*[9]
in aciem descendit, sagittis aggreditur, e longinquo ferit. Hoc boni
habet: ceca est, ut et facile declinetur, si prouisa sit, et sine delectu
iaciens sepe suos uulneret. Hoc michi nunc monstrum, salua amicitia, transfigendum.

7   Anceps sane negotium e duobus inuicem se complexis, illeso altero, alterum confodere. Tenes puto memoria ut apud Alexan-
driam Cesar inopino Marte circumfluus Ptholomeum regem secum in omnes belli casus trahit, ne sine illo pereat: que res sibi

calmer manner of speaking has always suited my nature and now suits my age. Forgive me, my friends. O reader, whoever you are, please pardon me. And you in particular, my worthy Donato, excuse what I say here. I must speak, not because it is the best course, but because the contrary is so difficult. Even though reason enjoins my silence, righteous indignation and pain wrest the words from me. Though I yearn for peace, I am forced into war. See how I am once more dragged forth against my will, and once more hauled, incredibly, into a court of censure which I am uncertain whether to call a tribunal of envious friendship or one of friendly envy.

Is there anything you cannot do, O shameless spite, when you 6 can inflame even the minds of our friends? I have known many evils, but this evil was unknown to me. Yet now my fate casts before me this gravest and worst of all evils. Often our clashes with enemies end favorably, and some maintain that our anger proves sweet: certainly victory is sweet. But when we struggle with our friends, both victory and defeat are distressing. Yet my war is not merely with friends or enemies, but with envy itself. This is no new enemy, but the nature of the battle is unusual. Armed with a quiver, envy generally takes the field, firing its arrows and striking from afar. But here's a good thing. Envy is blind, and you can easily avoid it if you see it coming. It shoots its arrows aimlessly, and often wounds its own troops. This is the monster I must slay, while saving my friendships.

When two people hold each other in an embrace, it is quite a 7 tricky business to stab one of them without harming the other. I think you will recall how, when Caesar found himself surrounded during unexpected fighting at Alexandria, he forced king Ptolemy to accompany him into all the dangers of battle as protection. It is thought that this played no small part in his escape, since the men who hated Caesar but loved Ptolemy deemed it impossible to kill the former while saving the latter.[6] Nor have you forgotten, I

227

non exigua euadendi, ut creditur, causa fuit, quod illum scilicet
mactare, simulque hunc seruare difficile censuissent qui illum ode-
rant, hunc amabant. Nec id, puto, excidit, ut die illo quo Persa-
rum regnum Hortanis uiri prudentis ingenio et septem uirorum
fortium uirtute seruili tyrannide liberatum est, Gophirus, unus ex
coniuratis, fusco in loco tyrannorum alterum amplexus, sotios ut
uel per suum corpus illum feriant hortatur, ne parcendo sibi ille
forsan euaderet. Et michi nunc igitur sancta clamat amicitia, ut uel
per suum latus stili acie impium feriam liuorem, quem ipsa non
equis amplexibus sinu fouet. Durum inter res tam iunctas tantis in
tenebris discernere. Nitar tamen, ut sicut tunc Gophiro incolumi
hostis occubuit, sic confutata nunc et perempta acri inuidia, dulcis
amicitia salua sit; que si uera est, ad quod necessaria uera est uirtus, ubi non aliter fieri possit, extincta inuidia ledi mauult, quam
illa superstite supraque se regnante non ledi.

: II :

8 Sed iam tandem ipsam rem aggrediar. Mox ut loqui cepero et, ni
fallor, antequam ceperim, notam tibi non aliter quam michi, eoque
fortasse notiorem, quo amici fame quam proprie studiosior est
amicus, et facilius quidem et honestius irascimur, siquid in amicos
dictum fuerit, quam si in nos. Itaque multi sua spreuere conuitia,
atque hinc laudati sunt. Amici nemo tranquillus iniurias uel spec-
tare potuit uel audire. Neque enim par animi magnitudo est, alie-

think, how the cunning of the prudent Hortanes and the valor of seven brave men once freed the kingdom of Persia from servile tyranny. On that day, a conspirator named Gophirus embraced one of the tyrants in a dim room, and urged his companions to strike, even through his own body, lest by sparing him they let the tyrant escape.[7] Just so, sacred friendship now calls on me to strike impious spite with my pen point, even if I wound friendship herself, who warms this monster in her bosom with unrequited embraces. It is difficult to distinguish between two things that are so closely joined in such darkness. But I shall try to do so. Just as Gophirus was unhurt while his enemy perished, so I shall strive to protect sweet friendship while confuting and destroying bitter envy. If friendship is true friendship, in which true virtue is indispensable, it would rather suffer injury and see envy destroyed, given no other choice, rather than remain unhurt while envy survives and triumphs.

: II :

But now let me finally address the matter at hand. Unless I am mistaken, as soon as I begin to speak, or even before I begin, the case will be as familiar to you as it is to me. It may be even better known to you than to me, since a friend is more concerned for a friend's reputation than for his own. Indeed, we are more readily and more justly angered by slurs directed against a friend than against ourselves. Thus, many people have ignored insults to themselves, and have been praised accordingly. But no one can calmly bear to see or hear a friend insulted. Ignoring personal affronts and affronts to others require different degrees of magnanimity. Besides, how could you not know what you yourself made known to me? Indeed, you grieved to see me treat the matter with

8

nis ac propriis offensionibus non moueri. Quomodo autem ignotum tibi esse potest, quod, ut michi notum esset, tu fecisti, de
quo me spernente ac ridente doluisti? Nota tibi igitur loquar, non
ut amplius innotescant, sed ut scias quo aduersus inuidiam sim
animo, et eodem esse incipias, nec grauius alienum uulnus quam
proprium ingemiscas; denique ut agnoscas quibus contra illam armis utor, qualiter longo usu atque acri studio et aduersus oblatran-
tium murmur obsurdui et aduersus liuidos dentes obdur⟨a⟩ui.

9   Et presentis quidem textus historie hic est. Veniunt ad me de
more amici illi quattuor, quorum nominibus nec tu eges, gnarus
omnium, nec in amicos, quamuis unum aliquid non amice agentes,
nominatim dici lex inuiolabilis sinit amicitie. Veniunt autem bini
et bini, ut illos seu morum paritas seu casus aliquis conglutinat.
Nonnunquam uero simul omnes, et ueniunt mira suauitate, letis
frontibus dulcibusque colloquiis. Nec sim dubius piis intentioni-
bus, nisi quod nescio quibus rimulis in illas meliori hospite dignas
animas infelix liuor obrepsit. Incredibile negotium, uerum licet,
atque utinam non tam uerum! Quem non saluum modo, sed felicem cupiunt; quem non solum amant, uerum etiam colunt, uisi-
tant, uenerantur; cui non tantum mites, sed obsequiosi ac liberales
esse omni studio nituntur. O natura humana, et patentibus et abditis plena langoribus! Eidem illi inuident!

10   Quid? Nescio, fateor, et inquirens stupeo. Non opes certe, quibus me tantum singuli superant quanto 'delphinis balena britan-
nica maior,' ut ait ille; quas preterea et maiores optant michi,
et mediocres easque non proprias sed comunicabiles, non super-
bas sed humillimas, sine iactantia, sine fastu, nec ulla prorsus inui-

scorn and laughter. I shall speak of things you know, then, but not to make them better known to you. Rather, I want you to see how I feel about envy, and to begin to feel the same way, so that you will not bewail my wounds more keenly than your own. And you will realize what arms I employ against envy; how by long practice and keen study I have deafened myself against the mutters of barking detractors; and how I have steeled myself against their spiteful backbiting.

Here is the context of the present story. I am often visited by 9 four friends, whose names you don't need to ask, since you know them all.[8] Besides, the inviolable law of friendship does not permit us to cite our friends by name, even when their actions are unfriendly. They arrive in pairs, as chance or their likeness of character binds them together. Occasionally they are all together, and arrive with marvelous charm, good cheer, and sweet conversation. I would not doubt their loyalty, except that wretched spite has crept through some chink into their hearts, which deserve a better guest. It's an incredible business, but true. If only it were not so true! They wish me both happy and healthy; they not only love me, but cultivate me, call upon me, and pay homage to me; and they strive to show me all kindness, deference, and generosity. Yet how human nature is filled with frailties, both apparent and concealed! I am the very one they envy!

What do they envy? I confess I don't know. The question leaves 10 me dumbfounded. Clearly they can't envy my possessions, for each of their estates exceeds mine by as much as "the British whale exceeds the dolphin," to quote the poet.[9] Indeed, they wish me greater wealth. They know that what I have is modest, and is not even mine, but is shared with others. What I have is not sumptuous but humble, lacking in pomp or ostentation, and completely undeserving of envy. They can't envy me my friends. Death has taken most of them from me, and like everything else I have, I generally share my friends gladly with others. They can't envy the

dia dignas norunt. Non amicos, quorum michi partem maximam mors abstulit, quosque, ut reliqua omnia, partiri libens cum amicis soleo. Non formam corporis, que, siqua unquam fuit, cunta uincentibus annis euanuit, et quamuis huic etati satis adhuc, Deo largiente *ac seruante*,[10] habilis, at certe inuidiosa iampridem esse desiit, *et si qualis unquam fuit adhuc esset, an uel hodie possem uel tunc poteram obliuisci, uel poeticum illud quod puerulus hauseram: 'forma bonum fragile est,' uel illud Salomonis in eo libro quo paruulum docet: 'fallax gratia, et uana est pulcritudo'? Quomodo igitur inuiderent michi quod non habeo, quod dum habui, ipse contempserim, quodque si redderetur, nunc uel maxime cognita et experta eius instabilitate, contemnerem?*[11]

11   Non denique scientiam aut eloquentiam, quarum primam penitus nullam michi esse confirmant; altera, si qua esset, apud illos hoc moderno philosophico more contemnitur et quasi literatis uiris indigna respuitur. Sic iam sola philosophantis infantia et perplexa balbuties, uni nitens supercilio atque oscitans, ut Cicero uocat, sapientia, in honore est, nec redit ad memoriam Plato eloquentissimus hominum, nec, ut sileam reliquos, dulcis ac suauis, sed ab his scaber factus Aristotiles. Sic a suo desciscunt seu deerrant duce, ut eloquentiam, quam ille philosophie ornamentum ingens ratus ei studuit adiungere, Ysocratis, ut perhibent, oratoris gloria permotus, hanc isti impedimentum probrumque extiment.

12   Ultimo, non uirtutem ipsam, optimam haud dubie, inuidiosissimamque rerum omnium, sed illis, ut puto, uilem, eo quod nec tumida nec elata est. Hanc michi ergo uere optarem, sed profecto concorditer ac libenter tribuunt, et cui parua negauerint, muneris instar exigui, quod est maximum largiuntur. Virum bonum, imo optimum dicunt, qui, o utinam non malus, utinamque non pessi-

beauty of my person. If this ever existed, it has vanished with the years, which conquer everything. And if by God's generosity and protection my appearance still becomes my age, it certainly ceased long ago to be enviable. Even if it were as it once was, could I forget today, or have forgotten then, the poet's phrase that I imbibed as a young boy? "Good looks are a fragile possession."[10] Could I forget Solomon's saying in the book where he teaches a small child? "Charm is deceitful, and beauty vain."[11] How, then, could they envy what I do not have, what I despised when I had it, and what I would disdain utterly if it were restored to me, having learned and experienced how unstable it is?

Furthermore, they can't envy my knowledge or my eloquence. 11 They assert that I have not a trace of knowledge. As for eloquence, if I have any at all, they despise it as our modern philosophers do, and reject it as unworthy of learned men. At present, the only things they honor in a philosopher are babyish and puzzled babbling, and that wisdom that relies on arrogant frowns and that "yawns drowsily," as Cicero puts it.[12] Nor do they call to mind Plato, the most eloquent of all humankind, or — to leave others aside — Aristotle, a sweet and pleasant writer to whom they have given a scaly hide.[13] They deviate and depart so far from their leader that they think eloquence an impediment and a disgrace to philosophy. But in fact Aristotle considered it a great ornament and strove to unite eloquence and philosophy, incited, we are told, by the glory of the orator Isocrates.[14]

Finally, they can't envy me for virtue, which is doubtless the 12 best and most enviable of all things. But to them it seems worthless, I think, because it is neither puffed up nor elated with pride. Virtue is the one thing that I truly wish for, and that they unanimously and freely grant me. Having denied me small things, they lavish this great gift on me as if it were insignificant. They say I am a good man, and even the best of men. If only I were not bad, if only I were not the worst, in God's judgment! At the same time,

mus in iudicio Dei sim! Eundem tamen illiteratum prorsus et ydiotam ferunt; cuius aliquando contrarium iudicio literatorum hominum diffinitum est, quam ueraciter non laboro. Neque enim magnifacio quod michi eripitur, modo quod conceditur uerum esset. Cupidissime cum his fratribus meis nature parentis *ac gratie celestis*[12] hereditatem sic partirer, ut ipsi quidem literati omnes, ego autem bonus essem. Literarum uero uel nichil, uel non nisi quantum quotidianis Dei laudibus oportunum est nouissem.

13　　Sed heu! uereor ne et humile me frustretur uotum et superba illos opinio. Ipsi autem mitem, bonis moribus et multa me asserunt amicitiarum fide; in quo quidem ultimo, nisi ego fallor, non falluntur. Ceterum ea est causa cur me in amicis habeant, non ingenium ullum, non industria, non doctrina, non studium honestarum artium aut spes ueri ex me unquam audiendi discendique. Ita plane eo reditum, quod de Ambrosio suo narrat Augustinus: 'Amare,' inquit, 'eum cepi, non tanquam doctorem ueri, sed tanquam hominem benignum in me'; *seu quod de Epicuro sentit Cicero, cuius cum multis in locis mores atque animum probet, ubique damnat ingenium ac doctrinam respuit.*[13]

14　　Quibus ad hunc modum sese habentibus, quid michi inuideant dubitari potest, cum inuidere aliquid non sit dubium; neque enim bene dissimulant, nec internis pulsas stimulis linguas frenant; quod in hominibus, alioquin non incompositis nec insulsis, quid nisi euidens passionis indomite signum est? Quod si inuident, ut faciunt, nec quod inuideant est aliud, utique latens uirus per se ipsum panditur. Unum enim hoc inane inuident, quantulumcunque est, nomen, et hanc famam, que uiuenti maior forsitan quam pro meritis aut pro comuni more obtigit, qui perraro uiuos celebrat. In

they call me completely illiterate and an ignoramus. Yet learned men once pronounced just the opposite judgment of me, how truthfully I don't care. I attach no importance to what is taken from me, as long as what I am granted is true. With these brothers of mine, I would gladly share what we have inherited from mother Nature and heavenly grace, so that they would all be men of learning, and I would be a good man. I would need no learning, or only enough to sing God's praises every day.

Alas, I fear that I shall be disappointed in my humble desire, 13 just as they will be in their haughty opinion. They say that I am kind, have a good character, and show great loyalty in my friendships. On this last point, they are not mistaken, unless I am mistaken. Now, this is the reason why they consider me a friend — and not my intelligence, diligence, and learning, my study of the liberal arts, or their hopes of hearing or learning the truth from me. In other words, it all boils down to Augustine's observation about his friend Ambrose: "I began to love him, not as a teacher of the truth, but as one kindly disposed toward me."[15] Cicero felt the same way about Epicurus. In many passages, he commends his behavior and courage, but he always condemns his intellect and rejects his doctrine.[16]

Given their attitude towards me, we may doubt what they envy, 14 but there is no doubt that they envy me something. They are poor at dissembling, and can't control their tongues, which are goaded by their inner impulses. In people who are otherwise decorous and sensible, can this be anything but a clear sign of unbridled passion? Now if they envy me, as they do, and there is only one thing they envy, inevitably this invisible poison is spreading itself everywhere. For there is one empty thing that they envy: my reputation, small as it is, and the fame I have won in this life, which is perhaps excessive when measured by my merits or by the general custom that rarely celebrates the living. It is on this fame that they have fixed their sidelong gaze. If only I could have foregone it,

hoc illi obliquos defixere oculos, quo et nunc et sepe utinam ca-
ruissem; crebrius enim damno id memini michi fuisse, quam usui,
cumque non paucos michi fecerit amicos, hostes fecit innumeros,
et ita michi accidit, ut his qui insigni casside, uiribus haud magnis
in pugnam eunt, quibus nil aliud chimere fulgor prestat, nisi ut a
pluribus feriantur. Hec michi olim pestis perquam familiaris uiridioribus annis fuit, nunquam uero molestior, quam que nunc exarsit, quod et ego delicatior ineundis bellis iuuenilibus ac talibus
subeundis oneribus, et illa unde nec mereor nec uerebar, et
quando uel meis moribus uicta uel euo iam consumpta esse debuerat, inopina renascitur.

15   Sed progredior. Cogitant se magnos, et sunt plane omnes diui-
tes; que nunc una mortalibus magnitudo est. Sentiunt, etsi in hoc
multi sese fallant, nullum sibi nomen partum, nullum, si rite pre-
sagiunt, speratum. Has inter curas anxii tabescunt, et — quanta uis
mali est! — rabidi uelut canes, in amicos quoque linguas exerunt
dentesque acuunt, uulnerantque quos diligunt. Quenam hec cecitas? Quisnam furor? Nonne enim sic et Pentheum furens mater
lacerat, et Hercules paruos natos? Amant isti me et mea omnia,
preter unum nomen, quod mutare non renuo, ut Thersites dicar
aut Cherilus, uel siquid aliud malunt, si uel sic obtineam, nequa
sit penitus tam honesti amoris exceptio.

16   Eo uero acrius uruntur et ceco estuant incendio, quod et ipsi
studiosi omnes et lucubratores magni sunt. Ita tamen, ut primus
literas nullas sciat (nota tibi loquor omnia), secundus paucas, tertius non multas, quartus uero non paucas, fateor, sed perplexas
adeo tamque incompositas, et, ut ait Cicero, 'tanta leuitate et iacta-
tione', ut fortasse melius fuerit nullas nosse.

both now and often in the past! For I recall that it has often done me more harm than good, winning many friends, but also countless enemies. What happens to me suggests a warrior who enters battle wearing an ostentatious helmet but possessing little strength: his chimerical crest serves only to attract more enemy blows. This curse was all too familiar to me in my more vigorous years, but it was never as vexatious as what has recently flared up. By now, I am too frail to enter such youthful battles or to assume such burdens. And this envy has unexpectedly revived where I least deserved and feared it, and when it ought to have been silenced by my conduct or consumed by time.

But I continue. They think they are great, and indeed they are 15 all rich, which is the only greatness mortals have today. Even though many people deceive themselves about fame, these men sense that they have won no name and that, if their foreboding is correct, they can hope for none. Anxious with such cares, they are wasting away. And so great is the power of evil that they stick out their tongues like rabid dogs and whet their fangs even against their friends, wounding the ones they love. What blindness! What fury! Isn't this how Pentheus's raving mother tore her son apart, and Hercules his small children? They love me and all that is mine, except my name alone. I am willing to change it. Let them call me Thersites or Choerilus or anything else they prefer, if I may thus remove this deep-seated objection from their honorable love.[17]

These men burn and rage with blind ardor all the more fiercely 16 because they themselves are all scholars and great burners of midnight oil. Nevertheless, and this is not news to you, the first of them has no learning, the second a little, and the third not much.[18] The fourth, I admit, has considerable learning.[19] But it is so confused and disordered, and filled "with such frivolity and vanity," as Cicero says, that none at all might perhaps have been better.[20]

17   Sunt enim litere multis instrumenta dementie, cuntis fere superbie, nisi, quod rarum, in aliquam bonam et bene institutam
animam inciderint. Multa ille igitur de beluis deque auibus ac pis-
cibus: quot leo pilos in uertice, quot plumas accipiter in cauda;
quot polipus spiris naufragum liget; ut auersi coeunt elephantes
biennioque uterum tument; ut docile uiuaxque animal et humano
proximum ingenio et ad secundi tertiique finem seculi uiuendo
perueniens; ut phenix aromatico igne consumitur ustusque renascitur; ut echinus quouis actam impetu proram frenat, cum fluctibus erutus nil possit; ut uenator speculo tigrem ludit, Arimaspus
griphen ferro impetit, cete tergo nautam fallunt; ut informis urse
partus, mule rarus, uipere unicus isque infelix; ut ceci talpe, surde
apes; ut postremo superiorem mandibulam omnium solus ani-
mantium cocodrillus mouet.

18   Que quidem uel magna ex parte falsa sunt — quod in multis horum similibus, ubi in nostrum orbem delata sunt, patuit — uel
certe ipsis autoribus incomperta, sed propter absentiam uel credita
promptius uel ficta licentius; que denique, quamuis uera essent,
nichil penitus ad beatam uitam. Nam quid, oro, naturas beluarum
et uolucrum et piscium et serpentum nosse profuerit, et naturam
hominum, ad quid[14] nati sumus, unde et quo pergimus, uel nescire
uel spernere?

19   Hec et alia huiusmodi aduersus hos scribas, non mosaica utique
nec cristiana, sed aristotelica, ut sibi uidentur, in lege doctissimos,
cum sepe liberius agerem quam soliti sint audire, idque fortassis

Learning is an instrument of madness for many, and of pride   17
for nearly everyone, unless, as rarely happens, it meets with a good
and cultured mind. This fourth fellow knows about wild beasts,
birds, and fish. He knows how many hairs a lion has in its mane,
how many feathers a hawk has in its tail, and how many coils an
octopus wraps around a castaway.[21] He knows that elephants mate
from behind, and are pregnant for two years; and that this docile
and vigorous animal, with its near-human intelligence, lives as
long as two or three centuries.[22] He knows that the phoenix is
burned on an aromatic pyre and is reborn from its ashes; that the
sea urchin can halt a vessel launched with great force, but is pow-
erless when taken out of the water; that a hunter can trick a tiger
with a mirror; and that an Arimaspean uses a spear to slay the
griffin.[23] He knows that sailors are fooled by the broad backs of
whales, that a she-bear gives birth to a formless cub, that a mule
rarely gives birth, and that a viper gives birth once and dies.[24] He
knows that moles are blind, that bees are deaf, and that the crocodile is the only animal that moves its upper jaw.[25]

In most cases, these things are false, as was revealed when many   18
such animals were brought to our part of the world. Clearly, the
facts were not verified by those reporting them, and they were
more readily believed or more freely invented because the animals
were not present. Yet even if they were true, they would contribute
absolutely nothing to the happiness of our life. What use is it, I
ask, to know the nature of beasts and birds and fish and snakes,
and to ignore or neglect our human nature, the purpose of our
birth, or whence we come and whither we are bound?[26]

I have often made these and similar objections to these scribes,   19
who consider themselves most learned, not in the law of Moses or
Christ, but in that of Aristotle. I spoke with greater freedom than
they are accustomed to hear, and perhaps with less caution, since I
foresaw no danger involved in speaking with friends. At first they
were amazed, and then angered, for they felt that my words ran

incautius, ut qui inter amicos loquens nichil inde periculi prouide-
rem. Mirari illi primum, post irasci. Et quoniam contra suam he-
resim ac paternas leges dici ista sentirent, collegerunt et ipsi conci-
lium, non ut me, quem profecto diligunt, sed ut famam meam,
quam oderunt, ignorantie crimine condemnarent. Vocassent utinam et alios! Fuisset forsitan in consilio dicende sententie con-
tradictum. Ipsi uero, ut concors esset et unanimis sententia, soli
quattuor conuenere. Ibi de absente atque indefenso multa et uaria,
non quod uarie animati essent, cum unum omnes sentirent
unumque dicturi essent, contra se tamen suumque iudicium, peri-
torum more iudicum, arguentes, ut uelut contradictionum angustiis eliquata et expressa ueritate coloratius diffinirent.

20   Dixerunt primum[15] famam publicam pro me stare, sed parum
fidei meritam responderunt; nec mentiti sunt, eo quod uulgus ra-
rissime uerum cernat. Dixerunt deinde maximorum atque doctis-
simorum hominum amicitias, quibus ornatam, quod in Domino
glorier, uitam egi, eorum sententie obstare. Quin et regum familia-
ritates plurimorum, nominatim Roberti Siculi regis, qui me iuuenem quoque crebro et claro scientie atque ingenii testimonio
honestasset. Responderunt—et hic plane mentita est, non dico
iniquitas, sed uanitas sibi—regem ipsum literarum magna etiam
fama, sed nulla fuisse notitia; reliquos, quamuis doctos, in me tamen non sat perspicaci fuisse iudicio, seu amor ille seu incuriositas
fuisset.

21   Illud sibi preterea obiecere, quod Romanos Pontifices[16] tres
proximos pro se quemque certatim me ad sue familiaritatis insignem gradum, *nequicquam licet*,[17] euocasse, et hunc ipsum qui nunc
presidet, *Urbanum*,[18] de me bene loqui solitum mitissimisque me
literis uisitasse iam; insuper et Romanum hunc principem—neque
enim alius etate hac legitimus princeps fuit—me inter familiares

counter to their sect and its ancestral laws. So they formed a council, not to condemn me, whom they love, but to condemn my fame, which they hate, on a charge of ignorance. If only they had summoned others! Perhaps someone in the council would have objected when they pronounced sentence. But to arrive at a harmonious and unanimous sentence, only these four convened. They voiced many different arguments concerning the accused, who was absent and undefended, but not because they held different opinions. They all held the same opinion and would vote the same way. But like experienced jurists, they entertained arguments against themselves and their own views, hoping to render a more plausible decision by sifting and refining the truth through the fine sieve of contradictions.

First of all, they said that public opinion was on my side, but they countered that it deserved little credence. This was no lie, for the masses very rarely discern the truth. Next, they said that the friendships with very powerful and learned men that have graced my life—glory be to God!—formed an objection to their views. They cited my intimacy with several kings, and specifically with King Robert of Sicily, who honored me in my youth with frequent and famous tributes to my knowledge and genius. To this, they countered that the king was greatly renowned for his learning, but was absolutely ignorant—a patent lie, inspired, I would say, not by their iniquity, but by their vanity. And the others, while they may have been learned, judged me with little discernment, whether from affection or carelessness.

Raising another objection against themselves, they said that the last three Roman pontiffs had competed to summon me—in vain—to high office in their households, and that the present pope, Urban, often spoke well of me and sent me kind letters.[27] Moreover, everyone knows and no one doubts that the present Roman emperor—who is the only legitimate emperor in our age—counts me among his friends, and often summons me by a

20

21

caros numerare, meque ad se multa quotidie precum ui et nuntiis repetitis atque epistolis solitum uocare, late notum nullique dubium est. Ex quibus aliquod michi nonnullius precii argumentum queri sentiunt. Sed et hunc obiectum dissoluentes, et pontifices, uel secutos famam aberrasse cum ceteris uel moribus, non scientia inductos ut id agerent, asseruere, et principem studio gestarum rerum atque historiis motum, quarum aliquam michi notitiam non negant.

22   Ad hec, obstare sibi dixerunt eloquentiam, quam ego mediusfidius non agnosco; ipsi autem persuasorem satis efficacem perhibent, quod, etsi rethorici siue oratoris officium *sit*[19] apposite dicere ad persuadendum, finis persuadere dictione, multis tamen indoctis contigisse aiunt; quodque est artis tribuunt fortune, uulgatumque illud afferunt: 'Multum eloquentie, parum sapientie';[20] nec aduertunt diffinitionem catonianam illam oratoris huic calumnie aduersantem.

23   Obstare demum et scribendi stilum, quem non solum uituperare, sed parcius laudare ueriti, elegantem prorsus et rarum, sed absque ulla scientia fassi sunt. Quod qualiter fieri possit, nec intelligo, nec intelligere illos reor; et, puto, si ad se redeant dictumque recogitent, tam futilis pudebit ineptie. Si enim primum uerum esset, quod ego rursum nec fateor nec opinor, secundum falsum esse non dubitem; nam quo pacto omnium ignaro stilus excellens sit, qui eis nichil ignorantibus nullus est? Itane fortuita omnia suspicantes, locum non linquimus rationi?

24   Quid uis autem, seu quid reris? Expectas, credo, iudicum sententiam. Omnibus igitur ad examen ductis, nescio quem deum—quoniam nec deus uolens iniquitatem, nec deus inuidie aut ignorantie ullus est, quam geminam ueri nubem dixerim—ante oculos

great number of daily requests and by repeated envoys and letters.[28] They sense that this affords some proof that I enjoy a certain prestige. But they refute this objection as well, asserting that,
like others, the popes were misled by my reputation, or that their
actions were motivated by my character rather than my learning.
And they say that the emperor was swayed by his passion for history and great deeds, a field with which they do not deny I have a
certain familiarity.

As another objection against themselves, they cited my elo-   22
quence, which in all faith I do not claim to possess. They call me
fairly effective at persuading others. But even if the office of the
rhetorician or orator is to speak effectively and persuasively, and
his aim is to persuade by his speech, they say that many ignorant
people have achieved this. Thus, they ascribe to chance what belongs to art, and quote the familiar saw, "Much eloquence, little
wisdom," failing to notice that Cato's famous definition of the orator contradicts this false claim.[29]

Finally, they cited my written style as another objection. They   23
were afraid to censure it or even to praise it too faintly, and confessed that it is elegant and exquisite, but devoid of any knowledge. How this can be I don't understand, nor do they understand, I imagine. If they came to their senses and reconsidered
their words, I think they would be ashamed of such empty nonsense. For if the first statement were true—which, again, I neither
claim nor believe—I have no doubt that the second statement is
false. How can someone who knows nothing have an excellent
style, and these men who know everything have none at all? Shall
we ascribe everything to chance and leave no room for reason?

What do you want then? Or what do you think? I suspect you   24
await the judges' verdict. Having examined all these points, they
fixed their eyes on some god—although there is no god that desires iniquity, nor any god of either envy or ignorance, which
might be called the twin clouds that dim the truth—and pro-

habentes,[21] breuem diffinitiuam hanc tulere: me sine literis uirum bonum. O utinam ueri nichil unquam preter hoc unum dixerint aut dicturi sint! Et, o alme salutiferque Iesu, uere literarum omnium et ingenii Deus ac largitor, uere rex glorie ac uirtutum domine, te nunc flexis anime genibus supplex oro, ut si michi non amplius uis largiri, hec saltem portio mea sit, ut uir bonus sim; quod, nisi te ualde amem pieque colam, esse non possum. Ad hoc enim, non ad literas natus sum; que si sole obuenerint inflant diruuntque, non edificant: fulgida uincula laboriosumque negotium ac sonorum pondus anime.

25   Tu scis, Domine, coram quo omne desiderium atque omne suspirium meum est, quod ex literis, quando his sobrie usus sum, nichil amplius quesiui quam ut bonus fierem. Non quod id literas aut, quamuis id ipsum polliceretur Aristotiles multique alii, omnino aliquem, nisi te unum facere posse, confiderem; sed quod per literas, quo tendebam iter honestius ac certius simulque iocundius extimarem, te duce, non alio. Tu scis, inquam, scrutator renium et medullarum, ita esse ut dico. Nunquam tam iuuenis nunquamque tam glorie cupidus fui, quod interdum me fuisse non inficior, quin maluerim bonus esse quam doctus. Utrunque, fateor, optaui, ut infinita est et inexplebilis humana cupiditas, donec in te sistat, supra quem quo se erigat, non est. Duo optabam; sed quoniam alterum eripitur seu negatur, gratiam iudicibus meis habeo, qui e duobus michi optimum reliquerunt, modo ne id quoque mentiti sint, et ut michi preriperent quod uolebant, quod non erat dederint. Quo iacturam ipse solarer meam, sed inani solatio, morem in me muliebris inuidie secuti, que si queritur de uicine forma, bonam illam et bene moratam dicit, omnes denique titulos, falsos licet, illi cedit, unum et fortasse uerum ut eripiat formose nomen.

nounced this concise verdict: I am a good man without learning. Would that this were the only truth they have spoken or will ever speak! O gracious savior Jesus, true God who bestows all learning and intelligence, true King of glory and Lord of virtues, I pray to You as a suppliant on my soul's bended knee. If You choose to grant me nothing else, let it at least be my portion to be a good man. This I cannot be unless I greatly love and devoutly worship You. I was born for this, and not for learning. If learning alone is granted us, it puffs up and ruins, and does not edify.[30] It becomes a gleaming shackle of the soul, a wearisome pursuit, and a noisy burden.

O Lord, to whom all my desires and sighs are open, You know 25 that when I used learning soberly, I sought only to become good. I did not trust in learning to make me good. And although Aristotle and many others have promised this, I trusted in You alone. I judged that under your guidance alone learning would make the path I chose more honorable, certain, and pleasant. You who examine our "hearts and reins" know that what I say is true.[31] I won't deny that at times I was youthful and eager for glory, but never so much that I did not prefer to be good rather than learned. I confess that I wished for both things, for human desire is infinite and insatiable until it rests in You, beyond whom it cannot raise itself. I wished for both goodness and learning. But since the one is snatched away or forbidden to me, I am grateful to my judges for leaving me the better of the two — unless they have lied about this too, and given me what was not mine, in order to deprive me of what they coveted. To let me console myself for this loss, if with an empty solace, they treated me in the manner of jealous women. When a woman is asked about a neighbor's beauty, she will say she is "good and well-mannered," and use all kinds of descriptions, even false ones, to rob her of the one title, "beautiful," which may be true.

26   At tu, Deus meus, scientiarum domine, extra quem non est
alius, quem et Aristotili et philosophis quibuslibet ac poetis, et
quicunque 'multiplicant loqui sublimia gloriantes', quem denique
literis ac doctrinis et omnino rebus omnibus[22] preferre debeo et
uolo, tu michi quod illi falsum tribuunt uiri boni nomen, tribuere
uerum potes, et ut uelis precor. Neque tam nomen bonum, quod
unguentis preciosis prefert Salomon, quam rem ipsam posco, ut
sim bonus, ut te amem amarique merear abs te — nemo enim sic
suis amatoribus uicem reddit — ut te cogitem, tibi obsequar, in te
sperem, de te loquar. Recedant uetera de ore meo, et tibi preparen-
tur cogitationes mee. Vere enim arcus fortium superatus est et
infirmi accincti sunt robore; feliciorque est multo unus ex pusillis
istis qui in te credunt, quam Plato, quam Aristotiles, quam Varro,
quam Cicero, qui suis omnibus cum literis te non norunt, et ad-
moti iunctique tibi, qui petra es, absorpti sunt iudices eorum, et li-
terata ignorantia patefacta est.

27   Litere igitur sint, uel horum qui illas michi auferunt, uel quia
horum, nisi fallor, esse non possunt, sint quorumcunque potuerint. Horum autem sit suarum opinio rerum ingens, et Aristotilis
nudum nomen, quod his quinque sillabis multos delectat ignaros;
insuper et inane gaudium, et elatio fundamenti inops ac ruine
proxima, omnisque quem inscii et inflati de suis erroribus fructum
uaga et facili credulitate percipiunt. Mea uero sit humilitas et
ignorantie proprie fragilitatisque notitia et nullius nisi mundi et
mei et insolentie contemnentium me contemptus, de me diffidentia, de te spes; postremo portio mea Deus, et, quam michi non
inuident, uirtus illiterata.

28   Ridebunt plane, si hec audiant, et dicent me ut aniculam quamlibet sine literis pie loqui. His enim literarum typo tumidis nil pietate uilius, qua ueris sapientibus ac sobrie literatis nichil est carius,

But You are my God, the Lord of knowledge, beyond whom 26
there is no other. I must and shall prefer You to Aristotle, to all
philosophers and poets, to all who "talk loudly and speak arrogance," and to all learning, all teaching, and all things.[32] You can
grant me the true name of "good man" which they have falsely
given me; and I pray that You will do so. More than a good name,
which Solomon prefers to precious ointments,[33] I ask to be truly
good. Let me love You and deserve to be loved by You — for no
one requites love as You do — and let me think of You, obey You,
hope in You, and speak about You. "Let the words of yore pass
from my lips, and let my thoughts be prepared for You: for truly
the bows of the mighty are broken, but the feeble gird on with
strength."[34] One of those weak ones who believes in You is far
happier than Plato, Aristotle, Varro, or Cicero, who for all their
learning knew You not. Brought before You, who are a rock, "their
judges were overthrown,"[35] and their learned ignorance was revealed.

Let learning belong to those who take it from me, then — or 27
rather, to those who can acquire it, for unless I am mistaken, these
men cannot. Let them keep their prodigious opinion of themselves and the bare name of Aristotle, whose five syllables delight
the ignorant. Let them also have their empty joy, their unfounded
elation that is near collapsing, and all the profit that ignorant and
conceited folk derive from the errors born of their flighty and
superficial credulity. As for me, let me have humility, an awareness
of my own ignorance and fragility, and contempt for nothing but
the world, myself, and the insolence of those who contemn me.
Let me have diffidence in myself, and hope in You, O Lord. In
short, let my portion be God and that unlearned virtue which they
do not envy me.

They will laugh when they hear this, and will say that I speak 28
piously and without learning, like a little old woman. There is
nothing baser than piety to people swollen with conceit in their

quibus scribitur: 'Pietas est sapientia,' meisque sermonibus magis ac magis in sententia firmabuntur, ut sine literis bonus sim.

: III :

29 Quid uero nunc dicimus, Donate fidissime? Te alloquor, quem magis horum liuoris aculeus quam meipsum, cui infligebatur, pupugit. Quid, inquam, amice, agimus? An equiores iudices prouocamus? An silemus et silentio sententiam confirmamus? Hoc satius. Imo ut scias quam nichil oblucter, ne decimus expectandus dies sit, nunc nunc qualiumcunque sententiis iudicum acquiesco, teque et reliquos quos res tangit, qui de me contrarias sententias tuleratis, obsecro ut et uos mecum pariter manum detis et uobis patientibus horum iudicium uerum sit. Verum utinam in eo quod michi tribuunt! Nam in eo quod eripiunt, ultro fateor, imo profiteor uerum esse, etsi iudices ydoneos plane negem.

30 Nisi forte eo iure niti uelint, quod istorum deus Aristotiles ait: 'unusquisque bene iudicat que cognoscit et eorum bonus est iudex'; melius nempe cognosci nichil posse uideatur, quam quo abundat ipse qui iudicat, ut scilicet hoc obtentu possint ignorantissimi homines de ignorantia iudicare. Non est autem ita; et de ignorantia enim et de sapientia et de re qualibet sapientis est iudicium, in eo, inquam, sapientis de quo iudicat. Neque uero ut de musica musici, de grammatica grammatici, sic de ignorantia ignorantes iudicant. Sunt quibus abundare inopia summa est, et que

learning. But there is nothing dearer to the truly wise and to men of sober learning. For them it is written: "Piety is wisdom."[36] But these remarks will only confirm my judges all the more in their view that I am a good man without learning.

: III :

What shall we say now, my faithful Donato? I turn to you, whom   29 the barb of their spite stung more than me, for whom it was meant. I ask you, my friend, what shall we do? Shall we appeal to fairer judges? Or shall we remain silent and confirm their verdict by our silence? This last course is better. Indeed, to show you that I put up no fight, I forego the ten days that are granted for appeal, and accept at once the verdict of any judges whatsoever.[37] As for you and the others involved in the matter, who arrived at a different verdict about me, I beg you to yield as well, and not to prevent their judgment from standing as true. If only it were true insofar as it grants me goodness! Insofar as it takes away my learning, I freely confess and even profess its truth, although I emphatically deny that they are proper judges.

But perhaps they choose to appeal to the principle enunciated   30 by their god Aristotle: "Each man judges well the things he knows, and of these he is a good judge."[38] Hence, a judge would seem to know nothing better than what he himself possesses in abundance. By this specious reasoning, the most ignorant men could best judge ignorance. But this is not the case. For concerning ignorance, wisdom, and anything else, judgment belongs to the wise man—wise, I mean, in whatever he judges. The ignorant cannot judge ignorance as musicians judge music, or as grammarians judge grammar. With certain things, abundance in fact means an utter lack, and practically anyone can judge such things better

melius a quolibet iudicentur, *quam ab eo*[23] qui maxime his abundat. Deformitatem nemo minus intelligit, quam deformis, cui cum illa familiaritas iam contracta est, ut que formosi oculos uulneraret, hanc iste non uideat. Eadem ratio reliquorum omnium defectuum: nemo peius de ignorantia iudicat quam ignorans.

31   Non hec dico, ut declinem forum, sed ut pudeat, si quis est pudor, iudicasse qui nesciunt. Ego etenim de hac re non modo sententiam amicabilis amplector inuidie, sed hostilis odii, et ad summam, quisquis ignarum me pronuntiat, mecum sentit. Nam *et*[24] ego ipse recogitans quam multa michi desint ad id quo sciendi auida mens suspirat, ignorantiam meam dolens ac tacitus recognosco. Sed me interim, dum presentis exilii finis adest, quo nostra hec imperfectio terminetur, qua ex parte nunc scimus, nature communis extimatione consolor. Idque omnibus bonis ac modestis ingeniis euenire arbitror, ut agnoscant se pariter ac solentur; his etiam quibus ingens obtigit scientia. Secundum humane scientie morem loquor, que in se semper exigua, pro angustiis quibus excipitur et collata aliis ingens fit.

32   Alioquin quantulum, queso, est, quantumcunque est, quod nosse uni ingenio datum est? Imo, quam nichil est scire hominis, quisquis sit, si, non dicam scientie Dei, sed sui ipsius ignorantie comparetur! Et hanc sui cognitionem ac proprie imperfectionis extimationem, suique ipsius quam dixi consolationem, his maxime qui plus sciunt plusque intelligunt inesse auguror. Felices errore suo iudices mei, qui huiuscemodi consolatione non indigent! Felices, inquam, non scientia, sed errore et ignorantia arroganti, qui

than the person who abounds in them. No one understands deformity less than a deformed person, who is inured to his defect and therefore cannot see what offends the sight of a handsome person. The same reasoning applies to all other defects: no one is a worse judge of ignorance than the ignorant.

I don't say this to reject their tribunal, but so that these igno- 31 rant men will be ashamed, if they have any shame, that they have passed judgement in their state of ignorance. In this matter, I warmly embrace not only the friendly verdict rendered by envy, but also the hostile verdict of enmity. In short, anyone who declares me ignorant agrees with me. When I reflect how far I am from learning all that my avid mind seeks to know, I sadly and silently acknowledge my ignorance. But in the meantime, until the end of this earthly exile arrives and ends this imperfection, by which "we know only in part," I am consoled when I reflect that this is our common nature.[39] I think this happens to all good and modest minds: they learn to know themselves and are consoled. It certainly happens to people with "vast" learning. I speak by the standards of human knowledge, which is always slight in itself, but which appears vast when we consider the narrow space that contains it, or compare it to that of others.

But see what a small amount is even the greatest knowledge 32 granted to a single mind! In any case, isn't the knowledge granted to one intellect still very small, whatever its amount? Indeed, human knowledge is as nothing compared with human ignorance, not to mention God's knowledge. I surmise that the people who know and understand the most possess in the highest degree this self-knowledge, this awareness of their own imperfection, and the consolation that I have described. Happy are my judges in their error, for they need no such consolation! Happy are they, I say, who believe they lack no part of angelic knowledge, not for their knowledge, but for their error and arrogant ignorance! In fact, all

sibi ad angelicam scientiam nil deesse autumant, cum ad humanam proculdubio desint multa omnibus et multis omnia.

33   Sed ad me reuertor. Et heu! amice, quid non mali affert uita
longior? Cui unquam tam firma prosperitas fuit, ut non quandoque uariauerit et quasi uiuendo senuerit? Senescunt homines,
senescunt fortune, senescunt fame hominum, senescunt denique
humana omnia; quodque aliquando non credidi, ad extremum
animi senescunt, quamuis immortales, uerumque fit illud Cordu-
bensis: 'Longius euum destruit ingentes animos.' Non quod animi
senium mors sequatur, sed discessus a corpore resolutioque illa,
quam cernimus et que uulgo mors dicitur, et est mors corporis
profecto, non animi.

34   Senuit ecce refrixitque animus meus. Nunc experior senex
quod iuuenis inexpertus et pastorium canens dixi: 'Quid uiuere
longum fert homini?' Quo enim ante hos non multos annos hec
tulissem animo, quibus nisibus obstitissem? Crede michi, bellum
graue inter ignorantiam et ignorantiam fuisset. Nunc senem inua-
dere eo turpius quo tutius; tollo manum, et mea illorum cedit
ignorantie.

35   Certe ego, quasi presagiens quid michi restaret, nunquam sine
compassione quadam Laberii historiam legi; qui, cum uitam omnem honesta militia exegisset, sexagenarius ad extremum, Iulii Cesaris blanditiis ac precibus, que de ore principum armate prodeunt, productus in scenam, de romano equite factus est mimus.
Quam iniuriam ipse quidem non tacitus tulit, imo multis interque
alia his questus est uerbis:

Ergo,[25] bis tricenis annis actis sine nota,
eques romanus ⟨e⟩ lare egressus meo,
domum reuertar mimus[que]:[26] nimirum hoc die
uno plus uixi michi quam uiuendum fuit!

of them lack much of human knowledge, and many of them lack all of it.

But I return to myself. Alas, my friend, what evil does long life 33 not bring us? Has anyone ever enjoyed prosperity so stable that it did not sometimes change and even grow old with age, so to speak? People grow old, fortunes grow old, and reputations grow old. In sum, everything human grows old. In the end, although formerly I disbelieved it, even our immortal souls grow old, and the words of the Cordovan prove true: "A long age destroys even great souls."[40] It's not that the old age of the soul is followed by its death. The release and separation from the body that we see and commonly call death is clearly the death of the body, not the soul.

Behold, my soul has aged and grown cold. As an old man, I ex- 34 perience what I sang in a pastoral poem as an inexperienced youth: "What does long life bring a man?"[41] How courageously I would have borne this only a few years ago! How sturdily I would have resisted! Believe me, there would have been a bloody battle between my ignorance and their ignorance. To attack me now as an old man is all the more disgraceful because it is safer. I raise my hands in surrender, and my ignorance capitulates to theirs.

In fact, as if foreseeing what awaited me, I have never read the 35 story of Laberius without compassion.[42] Having spent his entire life in honorable military service, this Laberius was in his sixties when he was persuaded by Julius Caesar's flattery and entreaties — requests that spring fully armed from a ruler's mouth — to appear on the stage, and was changed from a Roman knight into a mime. He himself did not bear this insult in silence, but protested in many words, including these:

Thus I lived twice thirty years without reproach,
and left my home as a Roman knight,
only to return as a buffoon. Clearly I have lived
one day longer than I should have![43]

Ego quidem—gloriari enim licet apud te—literatus nunquam uere, sed aliquando creditus, domo puer *egressus*[27] mea,[28] nec uel senex rediens, totum pene uite tempus in studiis triui.

36   Raro ulla unquam sano michi dies otiosa preteriit, quin aut legerem, aut scriberem, aut de literis cogitarem, aut legentes audirem, aut tacitos sciscitarer. Neque uiros tantum, sed et urbes quoque doctas adii, ut doctior inde meliorque reuerterer: Montempessulanum primo, quod per annos pueritie propinquior illi essem loco, mox Bononiam, post Tholosam, et Parisius Patauiumque, et Neapolim ubi tunc florebat—scio me multorum aures pungere—ille regum et philosophorum nostri eui maximus Robertus, non doctrine quam regni gloria inferior; quem mei iudices ignorantem uocant, ut infamiam tanto cum rege comunem pene michi arbitrer gloriosam (quanquam et cum aliis utrique nostrum possit esse comunis et fama et etate maioribus, de quo in fine dicturus sum); ceterum de hoc rege et orbis totus et ueritas in contraria fuere sententia.

37   Ego autem iuuenis senem illum non ut regem colui—reges enim passim plurimi—sed ut rarum ingenii miraculum uerendumque sacrarium literarum. Ego illi et fortuna et annis tanto impar—quod adhuc multis est notum, in illa urbe presertim—familiarissime carus fui, non meritis meis ullis aut meorum, neque militaribus aut aulicis artibus, que michi penitus nulle erant, sed ingenio, ut aiebat, ac literis. Aut ipse igitur iudex malus aut ego custos pessimus, qui studendo semper et laborando dedidicerim.

38   Maximam preterea atque optimam studiis uite partem illa in curia—quam romanam *nescio cur dicebant*,[29] leuam Rodani ad ri-

For my part, I may boast to you that I left my house as a boy, and never returned there even as an old man. Although I was never a true man of learning, I was once considered one, and spent nearly all my life in studies.

When I was in good health, I almost never let a day pass in 36 idleness. I read, wrote, or pondered some learned question. I listened to others as they read, or questioned them when they were silent. I sought out not only learned men, but learned cities as well, so that I would return more learned and more virtuous. First, I went to Montpellier, since it was near my home as a boy; and later to Bologna, Toulouse, Paris, and Padua. Finally, I went to Naples, where the famous Robert flourished, the greatest of our age's kings and philosophers, and a man no less glorious for his learning than for his kingdom.[44] I know that this will offend the ears of many. My judges call him ignorant, but I regard such defamation as glorious when I share it with such a great king. (And we may both share it with others whose fame and age are even greater, as I shall point out toward the end of this work.) At any rate, the truth and the entire world held quite the opposite opinion of this king.

As a youth, I honored this older man not as a king — for there 37 are many kings everywhere — but as a rare miracle of intellect and a venerable shrine of letters. Yet while no match for his fortune and age, I became his near and dear friend, as many people know, especially in Naples. This was not due to any merits of mine or my relations, or to any military or courtly skills, which I lacked, but to my intelligence and learning, as he himself said. Either he was poor at judging knowledge, or I was bad at keeping it, for my continual studies and labors have supposedly caused me to unlearn everything.

Now, I spent the greater part of my life, and the most studious 38 part, in that Curia which is called Roman, although I know not

255

pam, ubi quinquaginta uel eo amplius egit annos, atque unde nuper, hoc ipso anno (utinam irreditura!) digrediens, ductu et aus-
piciis sancti, si perseuerauerit, Urbani quinti, almam urbem et
sacratissimam Petri sedem (utinam permansura!) repetiit — nec
procul inde, transalpino in Elicone meo, ubi Sorgia oritur, rex fon-
tium, consumpsi. Quarum in altera omnium ferme nostri orbis literatorum hominum conuentus assiduus presto fuit; in altero, solitudo et silentium et quies meditantibus aptissima. Itaque illic
studendo et nunc scolas, nunc magistros adeundo; nunc amicis
que didiceram aut scripseram recitando; hic uagando et cogitando
et licet peccator sepe etiam orando, ac mecum semper raroque nisi
de studiis liberalibus conferendo, omne meum tempus in literis
actum est.

39   Mille interea doctis ac probatis senibus in notitiam et in gratiam ueni, quos si pergam numerare, commemoratio quidem dulcis, sed cathalogus haudquaquam breuis euaserit. His sane omnibus uel solam uel precipuam hanc ob causam placui, quod literati
famam studiosis in urbibus adolescens habui, quam nunc seni in
nautica ciuitate quattuor iuuenes per sententiam eripiunt. Ita et
michi ut Laberio accidit. Post sexagesimum annum meo de statu
excidi, non ut ille saltem mimus — quod artificium, imum licet, et
ingeniosum tamen querit artificem et suum inter mechanica locum
tenet — sed quod est ultimum, ignorans.

40   Sic res eunt: huc et studia, et labores nostri, nostreque uigilie
peruenere, ut qui iuuenis doctus a quibusdam dici soleo, profun-
diore iudicio senex ydiota reperiar. Dolendum forsitan, sed feren-

why, since it has spent more than fifty years on the left bank of the Rhone. Just this year, the Curia left that place (never to return, I hope!) under the guidance and auspices of Urban v, who will be a saint if he perseveres, and returned to its kindly mother city and the most holy seat of Peter, where I hope it may long abide.[45] And I spent these same years not far away, in my trans-Alpine Helicon, where the Sorgue river, the king of all springs, has its source.[46] In the first of these cities, I had continual contact with nearly all the learned men in the world. In the second, I had the solitude, silence, and quiet which are so conducive to meditation. In these two places, I spent all my time learning. In the first, I studied, at times frequenting schools and teachers, at times sharing with friends what I had learned or written. In the second, I devoted all my time to literature; I wandered and reflected, often praying, too—sinner though I am—and communed with myself, nearly always about liberal studies.

Meanwhile, I came to the attention of a thousand learned and revered old men, and won their friendship. If I tried to count them, the recollection would be sweet, but the list would be long. These older men loved me chiefly or wholly because as a younger man I had the reputation in scholarly cities of being a man of learning. Now that I am an old man in a maritime city, four younger men have by their verdict stripped me of my reputation. Thus I have met the same end as Laberius. After my sixtieth year, I have lost my status. Unlike Laberius, I did not become a buffoon. Despite its low status, the buffoon's trade at least requires a gifted performer, and holds its place among the mechanical arts. No, I became the lowest of all, an ignoramus.

So things go. This is the result of my studies and labors and vigils. In my youth, some used to call me learned. Now, as an old man, I am deemed an ignoramus by profounder judges. This may perhaps hurt, but it must be borne. Or perhaps it does not hurt,

dum; *forsitan nec dolendum, ferendum sane*,[30] ut reliqua omnia que hominibus accidunt: damnum, pauperies, labor, dolor, tedium, mors, exilium, infamia. Que si falsa est, spernenda est; nam et contradictores inueniet, et eundo deficiet; si uera autem, recusanda non est, ut nec alia culpis hominum inuenta supplicia. Equidem, si scientie uerum decus michi uerbis eripitur, ridebo. At si falsum, non feram modo, sed gaudebo, non meis sarcinis excussus et indebite fame laboriosa custodia liberatus. Melius cum predone agitur, dum iniustis spoliis exuitur, quam dum impune furto utitur. Iniusti possessoris exclusor iniustus[31] esse potest, at exclusio utique iusta est. Quod ad me attinet, ut dixi, non iustam modo sententiam, sed iniustam probo, nec iudicem quemlibet nec raptorem renuo.

41   Operosa ac difficilis res est fama, et precipue literarum. Omnes in eam uigiles atque armati sunt; etiam qui sperare illam nequeunt habentibus nituntur eripere; habendus calamus semper in manibus; intento animo erectisque auribus semper in acie standum est. Quisquis quocunque proposito me his curis atque hoc fasce liberauerit, assertori meo gratiam habeo, et seu falsum seu uerum, certe laboriosum ac solicitum literati nomen, quietis atque otii auidus, libens pono, memorans illud Annei: 'Magno impendio temporum, magna alienarum aurium molestia laudatio hec constat: "o hominem literatum!" Simus hoc titulo rusticiore contenti: "o uirum bonum!" '

42   Consilio tuo sto, preceptor morum optime; titulo rusticiore, ut tu ais — ut ego arbitror, meliore ac sanctiore atque ob eam rem etiam nobiliore — contentus sum, *quando presertim michi hunc mei iudices relinquunt*.[32] Illud tamen metuo, ut dicebam, ne hic ipse titulus

but it still must be borne, like other ills that befall humankind: loss, poverty, labor, pain, boredom, death, exile, defamation. Now, if a defamation is false, you should spurn it. It will meet with contradiction, and collapse as it runs its course. But if it is true, it must be accepted, like the other punishments devised for human misdeeds. For my part, I shall laugh if their words strip me of the true glory of my knowledge. But if this glory is false, then I shall not only bear the loss, but shall rejoice to shake off baggage that is not mine, and to be released from the wearisome custody of undeserved fame. We do better to despoil a robber of his illegal booty than to let him enjoy his stolen goods unpunished. Even if the person who confiscates illegal goods is still more unjust, the confiscation remains just. In my case, as I said, I approve their verdict, whether it is just or unjust, and accept any sentence or seizure whatsoever.

Fame is a laborious and difficult affair, especially literary fame. 41 Everyone is alert and armed against it. Even those who cannot hope for it strive to wrest it from those who have it. One must constantly keep one's pen in hand, and stand in the front lines with one's mind intent and one's ears open. If for any purpose whatsoever someone frees me from these cares and this burden, I shall be grateful to him as my deliverer. I gladly set aside the name of scholar, which, whether true or false, is certainly troublesome and distressing. I long for quiet and repose, and recall the words of Seneca: "It is at the cost of a vast outlay of time and of vast discomfort to the ears of others that we win such praise as this: 'What a learned man you are!' Let us be content with this humbler title: 'What a good man you are!' "[47]

I agree with your advice, O most excellent teacher of morals. I 42 am content with what you call a simpler title, which I call a better and holier one, and therefore a nobler one, especially since my judges leave it to me. But as I said, I still fear that this title may be false. Yet I shall strive to make it true, and shall not cease or weary

falsus sit. Nitor tamen ut sit uerus, neque hinc desinam nec lassabor usque ad extremos alitus nouissimumque singultum. Et si—quod idem alibi dixisti—ut sim bonus, opus est uelle, siue hoc perficit, bene erit, siue inchoat et 'pars est bonitatis uelle bonum fieri':[33] pro ea saltem parte titulum uerum spero.

: IV :

43 Redeo ad censores meos, de quibus et multa dixi, et ut nil te lateat, nunc etiam aliquid est dicendum. Neque enim ut illiteratus sic et amens ac stupidus dici uelim. Litere enim sunt aduentitia ornamenta, ratio autem insita ipsiusque hominis pars est; non ergo ut illis, ita et hac non me pudeat caruisse. Neque uero hec defuit, qua illorum tendiculas declinarem. *Circumueniri eorum artibus non facile potuissem; mea ipse puritate et*[34] uelo honestissimo fidelis, ut rebar, amicitie obuolutus sum. Fidentem fallere perfacile est.

44 Dixi et repeto. Ad uisendum me, ut multi alii illius pulcerrime maximeque urbis ciues, soliti uenire, bini sepius, et interdum simul omnes. Ego autem letari et quasi totidem Dei angelos excipere, oblitus rerum omnium nisi illorum, qui totum animum occupabant et miris serenabant modis. Ibi confestim, ut inter amicos, multa et diuersa colloquia. Michi autem nichil cure esse qualiter seu quid dicerem, seu omnino aliud, quam ut leta frons letiorque animus esset talium hospitum aduentu, ita ut interdum gaudio in silentium cogerer, interdum reuerentia quadam, ne concursu, ut fit, loquendi auidos impedirem, et nunc nichil, nunc uulgaria loquerer.

even to my last breath and final gasp. If being good requires my willing it, as you once said, then I shall improve, whether my will achieves goodness or merely begins to. "Part of goodness is the will to become good,"[48] and to that extent at least I hope the title is true.

: IV :

I return to my critics, about whom I have said much and must 43 now say more, so that nothing may be hidden from you. I wouldn't like to be called stupid and demented as well as un-learned. For learning is an external ornament, but reason is an in-nate part of humanity. Hence, I would be more ashamed to lack reason than learning. Indeed, reason has not failed me in avoiding their little snares. Of course, it would not have been easy for them to trick me with their wiles. Rather, I was tripped up by my own innocence and entangled in the decorous veil of a friendship that seemed trustworthy. It is quite easy to trick a trusting soul.

I have said this before, and repeat it now. Like many other citi- 44 zens of their great and beautiful city, they used to visit me, most often two at a time, but sometimes all at once. I would rejoice and welcome them like so many angels of God, forgetting everything but their affairs, which occupied all my attention and cheered me immensely. We would at once engage in many various discussions, as happens among friends. I gave no thought to what I said or how I said it. My only thought was to show them a happy face and an even happier spirit at the arrival of such guests. Sometimes I was forced to remain silent by my joy, and sometimes by a cer-tain deference, when I feared that my remarks would interrupt their heated conversation, as often happens. Hence, I would either say nothing or merely utter commonplaces.

45   Nichil enim in amicitiis comere didici, nichil dissimulare, nichil
fingere, sed in lingua atque in fronte animum habere, neque aliter
cum amicis, quam mecum ipse loqui omnia — quo, ut ait Cicero,
nichil est dulcius. Quid enim ostentare amicis eloquentiam aut
scientiam opus est, qui animum, qui affectus, qui ingenium ipsum
uident? Nisi forte aliquid non tentandi, sed discendi gratia quesie-
rint. Ubi tamen nec ostentatio ulla nec ornatus exigitur, sed fidelis
ut *reliquorum omnium*,[35] sic scientie participatio, exceptionis expers
et inuidie.

46   Itaque sepe miror Cesarem Augustum, tantum principem, tantam tam exigue rei curam inter tot maximarum rerum curas alias
suscipere potuisse, ut *non modo ad populum aut senatum seu ad milites,
sed*[36] cum uxore etiam *atque amicis nil nisi*[37] deliberate et crebro in
scriptis loqueretur. Fecit hoc forsitan, ne quid superuacuum aut
insulsum casu aliquo sibi excideret, quo celestis oratio reprehendi
posset aut sperni. Licuerit hoc illi summo de culmine subditos
scriptis uelut oraculis alloquenti.

47   Michi autem sermo uagus inter amicos inelaborateque sententie. Valeat eloquentia, si tam iugi studio querenda est; indiser-
tus malim esse, quam solicitus semper ac tristis. Hoc proposito
cum semper inter caros ac familiares uti solitus, mee presertim
facultatis conscios, tum precipue nuper usus inter hos nostros,
amica fiducia in hostilem calumniam inaduertens incidi. Nichil
enim accurate, nichil anxie, ut quidque in animum utque ad os
primum uenisset prius erumpere. Illi ex composito circumfusi singula trutinare, quicquid dicerem sic excipere tanquam nec melius a
me quicquam nec id ipsum comptius dici posset. Id semel idque
iterum atque iterum cum fecissent, in sententia[38] quam ueram op-

In my friendships, I am unable to embellish, dissemble, or 45
feign. Both my face and my tongue express my feelings, and I
speak to my friends as I do with myself—something that Cicero
calls the sweetest thing of all.[49] Why should we ostentatiously display our eloquence or knowledge to our friends, when they can see
our hearts, our feelings, and our temperament? Or perhaps they
ask questions in order to learn, rather than to test us. But even
then no ostentation or ornamentation is necessary, but only a
faithful sharing of all things, including our knowledge, without exception or envy.[50]

Hence, I often wonder why the great emperor Augustus took 46
such great care over such a trifling matter, even in the midst of his
other important affairs. When he spoke to the people, the senate,
or the army, and even to his wife and friends, he spoke only after
careful consideration, and frequently in written form. Perhaps he
did so in order to avoid letting slip some gratuitous or insipid remark which might cause his sublime speech to be criticized or
scorned. From his lofty height, Augustus was entitled to speak to
his subjects in nearly oracular writings.

When I speak to my friends, I use a rambling sort of speech 47
and avoid elaborate sentences. Farewell to eloquence if it must be
won by such continuous study! I would prefer to be ill-spoken
rather than always anxious and solemn. This is the style I have always used with my friends and loved ones, who are especially familiar with my talents. But recently, when I used it with these
companions, my trust in my friends led me to fall victim, un-
awares, to hostile slander. I spoke neither carefully nor cautiously,
but blurted out whatever first came to my mind or to my lips. As
they had planned, these men surrounded me; and weighing my every word, they noted everything I said as if I spoke with the greatest precision and elegance. After they had done this time and time
again, they were easily convinced of the verdict they wished to find
true. For there is nothing easier than to persuade people who are

tabant facile confirmati sunt. Nil nempe facilius quam persuadere *uolentibus iamque*[39] credentibus. Eo illi fidentius, ut ignarum alloqui, credo insuper, quod tunc minime suspicabar, et inscitiam ridere. Sic incautus unus, plurium insidiis circumuentus, ignorantium gregibus ignorans misceor.

48   Solebant illi uel aristotelicum problema uel de animalibus aliquid in medium iactare. Ego autem uel tacere uel iocari uel ordiri aliud, interdumque subridens querere quonam modo id scire potuisset Aristotiles, cuius et ratio nulla esset et experimentum impossibile. Stupere illi, et taciti subirasci, et blasphemum uelut aspicere, cui *ad fidem rerum*[40] aliud quam uiri illius autoritas quereretur, ut iam plane de philosophis et sapientie studiosis amatoribus Aristotelici seu uerius Pithagorici facti simus, renouato illo more ridiculo quo querere aliud non licebat, nisi an ille dixisset. Ille autem erat Pithagoras, ut ait Cicero.

49   Ego uero magnum quendam uirum ac multiscium Aristotilem, sed fuisse hominem, et idcirco aliqua, imo et multa nescire potuisse arbitror; plus dicam, si per istos liceat non tam ueri amicos quam sectarum: credo *hercle*,[41] nec dubito, illum non in rebus tantum paruis, quarum paruus et minime periculosus est error, sed in maximis et spectantibus ad salutis summam aberrasse tota, ut aiunt, uia. Et licet multa Ethicorum in principio et in fine de felicitate tractauerit, audebo dicere — clament ut libuerit censores mei — ueram illum felicitatem sic penitus ignorasse, ut in eius cognitione, non dico subtilior, sed felicior fuerit uel quelibet anus pia, uel piscator pastorue fidelis, uel agricola.

50   Quo magis miror quosdam nostrorum tractatum illum aristotelicum sic miratos quasi nefas censuerint — idque scriptis quoque

willing to be persuaded or who already believe. They were bolder in addressing me because I was unaware; and I believe they even laughed at my ignorance in suspecting nothing. Unwary and alone, I was surrounded by several men in ambush, and in my ignorance I was assigned to the ranks of the ignorant.

They used to propose some Aristotelian problem or some ques- 48 tion about animals for discussion. I would remain silent, or joke, or introduce some other topic. Sometimes I would smile and ask how Aristotle could have known things that obey no reason and cannot be tested experimentally. They would be amazed and silently angered, and would look at me as a blasphemer for requiring more than that man's authority as proof of a fact. It was clear that, instead of philosophers and eager lovers of wisdom, we had become Aristotelians, or more truthfully, Pythagoreans. For we had revived the ridiculous custom of the Pythagoreans, who were only allowed to ask whether *he* had said so — and "he" meant Pythagoras, as Cicero writes.[51]

Now, I believe that Aristotle was a great man and a polymath. 49 But he was still human and could therefore have been ignorant of some things, or even of many things. I shall go further, if I am allowed by these men who are greater friends of sects than of the truth. By heaven, I believe without a doubt that he was "quite on the wrong road," as the phrase has it[52] — not only in minor questions, in which any error is minor and scarcely dangerous, but also in the major questions that concern our ultimate salvation. To be sure, he discusses happiness at length in the beginning and at the end of his *Ethics*. Let my critics cry out as they like. Yet I daresay that he was so completely ignorant of true happiness that any devout old woman, or any faithful fisherman, shepherd, or peasant, is happier, if not more subtle, in recognizing it.

Hence, I marvel all the more that some of our Latin authors 50 have admired this treatise by Aristotle so much that they think it sacrilegious to discuss happiness after him, and have said so in

testati sint—de felicitate aliquid post illum loqui, cum michi tamen—audacter forsan hoc dixerim, sed, ni fallor, uere—ut solem
noctua, sic ille felicitatem, hoc est lucem eius ac radios, sed non ipsam uidisse uideatur; nempe qui illam non suis in finibus nec soli-
dis in rebus edificium uelut excelsum procul in hostico tremulaque
in sede fundauerit, illa uero non intellexerit, siue intellecta ne-
glexerit, sine quibus prorsus esse felicitas non potest: fidem scilicet
atque immortalitatem. Quas ab illo uel non intellectas uel neglec-
tas dixisse iam me penitet; alterum enim tantum dicere debui.
Non intellecte erant, nec nouerat eas ille, nec nosse potuerat aut
sperare; nondum enim uera lux terris illuxerat, que illuminat omnem hominem uenientem in hunc mundum.

51   Fingebant sibi ille et reliqui quod optabant, et quod naturaliter
optant omnes, cuiusque contrarium optare potest nemo, felicitatem dico, quam uerbis ornatam, absentem uelut amicam canentes,
non uidebant, gaudebantque de nichilo, prorsus quasi somnio
beati, uere autem miseri uicineque mortis tonitru ad miseriam ex-
citandi, apertisque oculis conspecturi quenam esset illa felicitas,
de qua somniando tractauerant. Que quidem, nequis ex me dici
omnia, atque ideo nimis temerarie dici putet, tertiumdecimum De
trinitate Augustini librum legat, ubi de hoc ipso contraque philosophos qui fecerunt sibi, suo utor uerbo, sicut eorum cuique pla-
cuit, uitas beatas suas, multa grauiter atque acriter disputata reperiet.

52   Hoc, fateor, dixi sepe, et dicam quoad loqui potero, quia uerum
me dixisse ac dicturum esse confido. Si hoc sacrilegum opinantur,
uiolate me religionis accusent, sed Ieronimum simul, non curan-

266

their writings. Perhaps I speak boldly, but unless I am mistaken, I speak truthfully when I say that he seems to me to have seen happiness as an owl sees the sun—that is, its light and rays, but not happiness itself. For he did not establish happiness within its own boundaries and on a solid foundation, as befits a lofty edifice, but far away in enemy territory and on a shaky site. He either failed to understand, or understood but ignored, the two things that are absolutely essential to happiness, namely, faith and immortality. But I already regret having said that he either failed to understand these two things or ignored them, when I should have simply said the former. He neither understood nor knew faith and immortality, nor could he know them or hope to know them. For the world was not yet illuminated by "the true Light, that enlightens everyone coming into this world."[53]

He and the rest of the philosophers fabricated what they de- 51 sired, and what everyone naturally desires, and whose opposite no one can desire, namely, happiness. They celebrated this happiness the way one sings of an absent lover. But they could not see her, and they rejoiced over nothing, like people happy in their dreams. In fact, they were miserable, and the thunderclap of imminent death would wake them to their misery. Once their eyes had been opened, they would see what sort of happiness they had pondered in their dreams. Let no one think that I say all this on my own and thus rashly. Read Augustine's book *On the Trinity*, where in Book Thirteen you will find many weighty and insightful arguments on this subject, refuting the philosophers who, in his words, "created their own blessed lives" according to their own beliefs.[54]

I confess that I have said this often, and shall continue to say it 52 as long as I can speak, for I am certain that I have spoken the truth and shall speak it again. If they think I am sacrilegious and accuse me of profaning our religion, then at the same time they must accuse Jerome, who is concerned with what Christ says, not Aristotle.[55] For my part, I have no doubt that it is they who are

tem quid dicat Aristotiles, sed quid Cristus. Ego contra, illos, si
diuersum sentiunt, impios sacrilegosque non dubitem, priusque
michi uitam et quicquid carum habeo Deus abstulerit, quam sententiam hanc, piam, ueram, salutiferam, aut quam amore Aristotilis Cristum negem. Sint plane philosophi, sint aristotelici, cum
proculdubio neutrum *sint*,⁴² sed ut sint utrunque; neque enim clara
hec nomina illis inuideo, quibus falsis⁴³ etiam tument; non michi
inuideant humile uerumque cristiani nomen et catholici.

53   *Sed quid peto*,⁴⁴ quod ultro facere illos et facturos esse scio? *Non
quidem*⁴⁵ nobis hec inuident, sed contemnunt tanquam simplicia et
abiecta, ingeniisque suis imparia et indigna. Secreta igitur nature,
atque altiora illis archana Dei, que nos humili fide suscipimus, hi
superba iactantia nituntur arripere; nec attingunt, nec adpropiant
quidem, sed attingere et pugno celum stringere insani extimant; et
perinde est eis ac si stringerent, propria opinione contentis et
errore gaudentibus. Neque illos ab insania retrahit, non dico uel
rei ipsius impossibilitas, ad Romanos apostolicis uerbis expressa:
'Quis enim cognouit sensum Domini, aut quis consiliarius eius
fuit?' uel illud Ecclesiasticum ac celeste consilium: 'Altiora te ne
quesieris, et fortiora te ne scrutatus fueris; sed que precepit Deus
tibi, illa cogita semper, et in pluribus operibus eius ne fueris curio-
sus; non est enim tibi necessarium ea que abscondita sunt uidere.'
Non hec dico; ex equo enim spernunt quicquid celitus, *imo, ut dicam quod est, quicquid catholice*⁴⁶ dictum sciunt.

54   At saltem *et Democriti non ineptus iocus: 'Quod est, inquit, ante pedes
nemo spectat; celi scrutantur plagas'*;⁴⁷ et facetissima illa Ciceronis irri-

impious and sacrilegious if they believe otherwise. I would sooner let Christ take from me my life and what I hold dear than I would deny this belief, which is pious, true, and brings salvation — or deny Christ out of love for Aristotle. Let them be philosophers and Aristotelians, even though they are obviously neither. Let them be both. I don't envy them these distinguished names, which falsely cause them to swell with pride. And let them not envy me the humble and true name of Christian and Catholic.

Why do I ask something that I know they freely do and will 53 continue to do? They don't envy me these names, but despise them as simple-minded and pitiful, and as unequal to and unworthy of their genius. In their haughty conceit, they strive to seize the secrets of nature and the even profounder mysteries of God, which we embrace in our humble faith. Yet while they fail to attain or even approach them, in their madness they think they have reached heaven and clutch it in their fist. Satisfied with their own opinion and rejoicing in their error, they feel as if they grasp it. They are not deterred from their madness, I say, by the mere impossibility of the task, as expressed in the Apostle's words to the Romans: "For who has known the mind of the Lord, or who has been his counselor?"[56] Or by the heavenly wisdom of Ecclesiasticus: "Seek not what is above you, and search not what is beyond your strength; but meditate on what the Lord has commanded; and be not curious of His many works; what He has kept hidden need not concern you."[57] As I say, they are not deterred by these things. In the same manner, they disdain anything that they know was expressed in heaven or, to speak correctly, in a Catholic spirit.

But at least they should recall the clever jest of Democritus: 54 "No one looks at what lies at his feet; they scan the regions of the sky."[58] Or they should recall Cicero's witty mockery of those who debate rashly and have no doubts on any subject. He described them "as if they had just come down from the assembly of the

sio temerarie disputantium, nullaque de re dubitantium, 'tanquam modo *deorum ex concilio*[48] descendentes,' quid ibi agatur oculis suis aspexerint *auribusque perceperint;*[49] uel illud antiquius atque acrius: apud Homerum Iupiter non mortalem hominem, non e comuni grege deum aliquem, sed Iunonem illam suam coniugem ac sororem reginamque deum graui comminatione deterrens, ne secretum suum intimum auderet inquirere aut sciri posse presumeret.

55   Sed ad Aristotilem reuertamur, cuius splendore lippos atque infirmos perstringente oculos multi iam erroris in foueas lapsi sunt. Scio eum unitatem principatus posuisse, quam iam ante posuerat Homerus; sic enim ait, quantum nobis in latinum soluta oratione translatum est: 'Non bonum multidominium: unus dominus sit, unus imperator.' *Iste autem: 'Pluralitas principatuum non bona, unus ergo princeps.'*[50] Sed ille humanum, hic diuinum, ille Grecorum, iste omnium principatum, ille Atridem, hic Deum principem statuebat, eousque sibi ueri fulgor illustrauit *animum.*[51] Quis hic princeps, qualisue, et quantus, nescisse eum, et qui multa de minimis curiose admodum disputasset, unum hoc et maximum non uidisse crediderim, quod uiderunt multi literarum nescii, uidentque *luce non altera, uerum aliter illustrante.*[52] Idque amici isti mei ita esse si non uident, cecos ego illos planeque exoculatos esse uideo, et sic omnibus uideri, quibus oculi sani sint, non magis hesitauerim, quam smaragdum uiridem, niuem candidam, coruum nigrum.

56   Utque audaciam meam equanimius aristotelici nostri ferant, non de uno tantum ita sentio, etsi unum nominem. Lego, quamuis

gods," and thus had seen with their eyes and heard with their ears what is done there.[59] Or they should recall an ever more ancient and severe injunction. In Homer, when Jupiter seeks to deter anyone from daring to inquire into his intimate secrets or from presuming to know them, he uses a terrible threat to frighten not a mere mortal or a god of the common herd, but Juno, who is his wife and sister, and the queen of the gods.[60]

But let us return to Aristotle, whose splendor has so blinded 55 many people's feeble and bleary eyes that they have fallen into the pits of error. I know that he asserted the unity of rule, which had previously been asserted by Homer. This is what Homer says as it has been translated into Latin prose for us: "The lordship of many is not a good thing; let there be one lord and one commander."[61] And Aristotle writes: "A plurality of rulers is not good, so let there be one ruler."[62] Now Homer described a human ruler, and Aristotle a divine one. Homer called Agamemnon the ruler of the Greeks, and Aristotle called God the ruler of all prinicipalities. To such an extent had the brilliance of the truth illuminated Aristotle's mind, even if he did not know who this ruler was, and did not understand his nature and greatness. And although he had subtly discussed many topics, I think he failed to see this one great truth, which many unlearned people have seen and continue to see, not because the light is different but because it illuminates them differently. If these friends of mine fail to see this, I see that they are clearly blind and sightless. And I would not hesitate to say that it must be obvious to everyone whose eyes are sound, just as they see that an emerald is green, snow is white, and a raven black.

Still, let our Aristotelians bear my insolence with greater equa- 56 nimity, for even though I name Aristotle alone, he is not the only one I judge in this way. Although I am ignorant, I read much; and until these men discovered my ignorance, I thought I understood something. I read now, but in my younger years I read more care-

ignorans, et antequam isti nostram ignorantiam deprehendissent, intelligere aliquid uidebar. Lego, inquam, sed uiridioribus annis attentius legebam. Adhuc tamen poetarum et philosophorum libros *lego*,[53] Ciceronis ante alios, cuius apprime et ingenio et stilo semper ab adolescentia delectatus sum. Inuenio eloquentie plurimum et uerborum elegantium uim maximam. Quod ad deos ipsos, de quorum ille natura nominatim libros edidit, quodque omnino ad religionem spectat, quo disertius dicitur, eo michi inanior est fabella; Deoque gratias tacitus mecum ago, qui hoc michi seu iners seu modestum dedit ingenium animumque non uagum, neque altiora se querentem neque his scrutandis curiosum, que quesitu difficilia, pestifera sint inuentu. Sed quo plura contra Cristi fidem dici audio, eo et Cristum magis amem et in Cristi fide sim firmior.

57 Ita nempe michi accidit, ut siquis in patris amore tepentior, de illo audiat obloquentes, amorque qui sopitus uidebatur illico inardescat; ita enim eueniat necesse est, si uerus est filius. Sepe me, Cristum ipsum testor, de cristiano cristianissimum hereticorum fecere blasphemie; pagani enim illi ueteres, etsi multa de diis fabulentur, non blasphemant tamen, quia ueri Dei notitiam nullam habent; neque enim Cristi nomen audierunt; 'fides' autem 'ex auditu' est; et quamuis 'in omnem terram exiuerit sonus eorum, et in fines orbis terre uerba eorum,' apostolorum tamen uerbis ac doctrinis toto orbe sonantibus illi iam mortui ac sepulti erant, miseri magis quam culpabiles, quorum aures, quibus haurire fidem salutiferam potuissent, inuida iam tellus obstruxerat.

58 Inter cuntos tamen potentissime illi tres libri Ciceronis, quos De natura deorum inscriptos supra memini, sepe me excitant. Ubi scilicet tantum illud ingenium de diis agens, ipsos sepe deos irridet ac despicit, non quidem serio (forte supplicium timens, quod ante

fully. I still read the books of poets and philosophers, and above all the works of Cicero, whose intelligence and style have given me special pleasure ever since my youth. In them I find the height of eloquence and a great abundance of elegant language. But concerning religion in general and the gods in particular, about whose nature he published the books with that name, the more eloquently he writes, the more vapid I find his old wives' tales about them. I give silent thanks to God for granting me this intelligence, as dull and modest as it is, and a spirit that is not restless for seeking higher things or curious to investigate things that are difficult to seek out and harmful when found. The more I hear said against the faith of Christ, the more I love Christ and the more firmly I abide in his faith.

The same happens to me as to a son whose love for his father 57 has cooled: when he hears people speaking ill of him, the love that seemed to lie dormant is instantly rekindled, as must perforce happen if he is a true son. As Christ is my witness, the blasphemies of heretics have often turned me from a mere Christian into the most Christian of men. The ancient pagans may tell many tales about the gods, but they do not blaspheme, for they have no knowledge of the true God. They never even heard Christ's name, and "faith comes from hearing."[63] Even though "their sound has gone out to all the earth, and their word unto the end of the world,"[64] by the time the Apostles' words and teaching sounded throughout the globe, these pagans were already dead and buried. They were more unfortunate than culpable, for the envious earth had stopped their ears from taking in the faith that brings salvation.

Among all these writers, I am often very powerfully moved by 58 Cicero's three books entitled *On the Nature of the Gods*, which I mentioned above. When this great genius discusses the gods, he often mocks and scorns them, if not in a serious way. Perhaps he feared punishment, which even the Apostles feared until the Holy Spirit descended upon them. Cicero employs very effective jests, of

aduentum Sancti Spiritus ipsi etiam apostoli timuerunt), sed his
quibus abundat iocis efficacissimis, quibus clarum fiat intelligentibus, de eo ipso quod tractandum assumpserat quid sentiret. Ut
sortem suam sepe inter legendum miseratus, ipse mecum tacitus
dolensque suspirem quod uerum Deum uir ille non nouerit. Paucis enim ante Cristi ortum annis obierat oculosque mors clauserat,
heu! quibus e proximo noctis erratice ac tenebrarum finis et ueritatis initium, uereque lucis aurora et iustitie sol instabat.

59   Qui tamen Cicero ipse suis in libris, quos innumeros *scripsit*,[54]
etsi errorum torrente uulgarium lapsus sepe deos nominet et sepe
illos tamen irridet, ut dixi, et iam inde a iuuentute sua, libros
Inuentionum[55] scribens, dixerat eos qui philosophie dent operam
non arbitrari deos esse. Nempe Deum nosse, non deos, ea demum
uera et summa philosophia est; ita dico, si cognitioni pietas et fidelis cultus accesserit.

60   Idem quoque iam senior, his ipsis in libris, quos de diis, non
de deo scribit, ubi sese colligit, quantis ingenii alis attollitur, ut interdum non paganum philosophum, sed apostolum loqui putes;
quale est illud in primo contra Velleium, epycuree sententie defensorem: 'Eos,' inquit, 'uituperabas, qui ex operibus magnificis atque
preclaris — cum ipsum mundum, cum eius membra, celum, terras,
maria, cumque eorum[56] insignia, solem et lunam stellasque uidissent, cumque temporum maturitates, mutationes uicissitudinesque
cognouissent — suspicati sunt[57] aliquam esse excellentem prestantemque naturam, que hec effecisset, moueret, regeret, gubernaret'.

61   In secundo autem: 'Quid,' inquit, 'potest esse tam apertum
tamque perspicuum, celum si aspeximus[58] celestiaque contemplati
sumus, quam esse aliquod numen prestantissime mentis, quo hec

which he had a rich supply, to make clear to perceptive readers his real opinions about the subject he has chosen to discuss. When I read him, I often pity his fate, and lament in silent grief that he did not know the true God. He passed away only a few years before the birth of Christ. Alas, death closed his eyes just when the night of error and its darkness was nearly over, and when the starting-point of truth, the dawn of true light, and the sun of justice were fast approaching.

In his countless books, Cicero often mentions the gods, engulfed as he was by the torrent of popular misconceptions, and often mocks them, as I said. Even in his youth, when he wrote *On Rhetorical Invention*, he said that people who study philosophy do not believe that gods exist.[65] In fact, to know God, rather than the gods, is the true and highest philosophy — provided, of course, that such knowledge is accompanied by piety and faithful worship.

When he was older, Cicero wrote his books on "the gods," rather than on God; and when he summons up his powers, how high he soars on the wings of his genius![66] At times you would think that an Apostle is speaking, not a pagan philosopher. Take the passage in Book One which refutes Velleius for defending the Epicurean position: "You censured those who argued from the splendor and the beauty of creation, and who, observing the world itself and the parts of the world, the sky and earth and sea, and the sun, moon, and stars that adorn them, and discovering the laws of the seasons and their periodic successions, conjectured that there must exist some supreme and transcendent being who had created these things, and who imparted motion to them and guided and governed them."[67]

Then in Book Two he writes: "When we gaze upward to the sky and contemplate the heavenly bodies, what can be so obvious and so manifest as that there must exist some power possessing transcendent intelligence by whom these things are ruled?"[68] And in the same book: "Extremely acute of intellect as is Chrysippus,

59

60

61

regantur?' Et eodem libro: 'Crisippus quidem,' inquit, 'quanquam
est acerrimo ingenio, tamen ea dicit, ut ab ipsa natura didicisse,
non ut ipse repperisse uideatur. "Si enim," inquit, "est aliquid in
rerum natura quod hominis mens et ratio,[59] quod uis, quod potestas humana efficere non possit, est certe id quod[60] effecit homine
melius. Atqui[61] res celestes, omnesque he, quarum est ordo sempi-
ternus, ab homine confici non possunt; est igitur id quo illa conficiuntur homine melius. Id autem quid potius dixeris quam
Deum?"'

62   Dein, paucis interiectis: 'Quod si omnes,' inquit, 'mundi partes
ita constitute sunt, ut neque ad usum meliores, neque ad speciem
pulcriores effici potuerint,[62] uideamus utrum ea fortuita[63] sint, an
eo statu quo coherere nullo modo potuerint, nisi sensu moderante
diuinaque prouidentia. Si igitur meliora sunt que[64] natura, quam
que[65] arte perfecta sunt, nec ars efficit quicquam sine ratione, nec[66]
natura quidem rationis expers est habenda; non[67] igitur conuenit,
signum aut tabellam pictam cum aspexeris, scire adhibitam esse
artem, cumque procul cursum nauigii uideris, non dubitare quin
id ratione atque arte moueatur, aut cum solarium uel descriptum
aut[68] ex aqua contemplere, intelligere declarari horas arte, non
casu, mundum[69] qui et has ipsas artes et earum artifices et cunta
complectatur, consilii et rationis expertem[70] putare. Quod si in
Scithiam aut in Britanniam speram aliquis tulerit hanc quam nuper familiaris noster effecit Possidonius, cuius singule conuersio-
nes idem efficiunt in sole et luna[71] et in quinque stellis errantibus,
quod efficitur in celo singulis diebus et noctibus, quis in illa bar-

nevertheless his utterance here might well appear to have been learned from the very lips of Nature, and not discovered by himself. 'If, he says, there is something in the world that man's mind and human reason, his strength and power are incapable of producing, that which produces it must necessarily be superior to man. Now the heavenly bodies and all those things that display a never-ending regularity cannot be created by man; therefore that which creates them is superior to man; yet what better name is there for this than God?'"[69]

Soon thereafter we read: "But if the structure of the world in all its parts is such that it could not have been better whether in point of utility or beauty, let us consider whether this is the result of chance, or whether, on the contrary, the parts of the world are in such a condition that they could not possibly have cohered together if they were not controlled by intelligence and by divine providence. If then the products of nature are better than those of art, and if art produces nothing without reason, nature too cannot be deemed to be without reason. When you see a statue or a painting, you recognize the exercise of art; when you observe from a distance the course of a ship, you do not hesitate to assume that its motion is guided by reason and by art; when you look at a sundial or a water-clock, you infer that it tells the time by art and not by chance. How then can it be consistent to suppose that the world, which includes both the works of art in question, the craftsmen who made them, and everything else beside, can be devoid of purpose and reason? Suppose a traveler carried into Scythia or Britain the orrery recently constructed by our friend Posidonius, which at each revolution reproduces the same motions of the sun, the moon, and the five planets that take place in the heavens every twenty-four hours—would any single native doubt that this orrery was the work of a rational being? These thinkers however raise doubts about the world itself from which all things arise and have their being, and debate whether it is the product of

62

barie dubitet, quin ea spera sit perfecta ratione? Hi autem dubi-
tant de mundo, ex quo oriuntur et fiunt omnia, casu ne sit ipse
effectus aut necessitate aliqua, an ratione ac mente diuina. Archi-
medem arbitrantur plus ualuisse in imitandis spere conuersioni-
bus, quam naturam in efficiendis, presertim cum multis partibus
sint illa perfecta, quam hec simulata solertius'.

63   Hec, ut audis, apud Tullium scripta sunt. Quibus dictis rudem
mox pastorem illum sumit ab Accio poeta et ad propositum suum
trahit, nauim nunquam antea sibi uisam, illam scilicet qua in Col-
chon[72] uehebantur Argonaute procul e monte cernentem, atque
attonitum nouitate miraculi pauentemque et multa secum opinan-
tem, montem aut saxum terre uisceribus erutum, ac uentis im-
pulsum pelago rapi, aut atros turbines conglobatos fluctuum concursu, aut tale aliquid; uisis inde iuuenibus quorum ope atque
opera nauigium agebatur, et cantu nautico audito, heroumque uul-
tibus conspectis, *ad se reuersum*,[73] et errore ac stupore deposito,
quidnam rei esset intelligere incipientem.

64   Post que statim infert Cicero: 'Ergo,' inquit, 'ut hic primo as-
pectu inanime quiddam sensuque uacuum se putat cernere, post
autem signis certioribus quale sit illud,[74] de quo dubitauerat, incipit suspicari, sic philosophi debuerunt, si forte eos primus aspectus mundi conturbauerat, postea, cum uidissent motus eius finitos
et equabiles, omniaque ratis ordinibus moderata immutabilique
constantia, intelligere inesse aliquem, non solum habitatorem in
hac celesti ac diuina domo, sed etiam rectorem ac moderatorem, et
tanquam architectum tanti operis tantique muneris'.

65   *Quod ipsum alio loco pene iisdem uerbis posuit Tusculanarum questio-*
num libro primo: 'Hec,' inquit, 'et alia innumerabilia cum cernimus, possu-

chance or necessity of some sort, or of divine reason and intelligence. They think more highly of Archimedes' achievement in making a model of the revolutions of the firmament than of nature's achievement in creating them, although the perfection of the original shows a craftsmanship many times greater than the copy."[70]

All this is written in Cicero, as you hear it. Next he cites the 63 rustic shepherd of the poet Accius to illustrate his point.[71] This fellow had never seen a ship before, when one day from a distant mountain he beheld the famed ship in which the Argonauts sailed to Colchis. Struck dumb and terrified by the novelty of this amazing sight, his mind was filled with many thoughts. He thought it might be a mountain or a boulder ripped from the bowels of the earth and borne across the sea by the winds, or dark waterspouts formed by clashing currents, or something of the sort. But when he saw the young men whose efforts propelled the ship, heard their sailor songs, and beheld the faces of the heroes on board, he came to his senses, banished his astonishment and error, and began to understand what was happening.

Right after this, Cicero adds: "So then, even as the shepherd at 64 first sight thinks he sees some lifeless and inanimate object, but afterwards is led by clearer indications to begin to suspect the true nature of the things about which he had previously been uncertain, so it would have been the proper course for the philosophers, if it so happened that the first sight of the world perplexed them, afterwards when they had seen its definite and regular motions, and all its phenomena controlled by fixed system and unchanging uniformity, to infer the presence not merely of an inhabitant of this celestial and divine abode, but also of a ruler and governor, the architect as it were of this mighty and monumental structure."[72]

In Book One of his *Tusculan Disputations*, Cicero says the same 65 thing in nearly the same words: "When we behold all these things

mus ne dubitare quin his presit aliquis uel effector, si hec nata sunt, ut Pla-
toni uidetur, uel si semper fuerunt, ut Aristotili placet, moderator tanti
operis et muneris?[75] Vides ut *ubique*[76] unum deum gubernatorem ac
factorem rerum omnium non philosophica tantum, sed quasi catholica circumlocutione describit. Itaque magis hoc probo, quam
quod *in ipso Nature deorum libro*[77] sequitur, auctore quidem Aristotile; quamuis nanque sententia una sit, ibi tamen mentio est deorum, quorum nomen in omni ueritatis inquisitione suspectum est.

66   Sic enim ait: 'Preclare ergo Aristotiles: "Si esset,"[78] inquit, "qui
sub terra semper habitasset bonis et illustribus domiciliis, que essent ornata signis atque picturis instructaque rebus his omnibus,
quibus abundant hi qui beati putantur, nec tamen exisset supra[79]
terram, accepisset autem fama et auditione esse quoddam numen
et uim deorum, deinde aliquo tempore patefactis terre faucibus, ex
illis abditis sedibus euadere in hec loca, que nos colimus,[80] atque
exire potuisset, cum repente terram et maria celumque uidisset,
nubium magnitudinem et pulcritudinem,[81] uentorumque uim cognouisset, aspexissetque solem, eiusque magnitudinem et decorem, quem tum[82] etiam per[83] efficientiam cognouisset, quod is
diem efficeret toto celo luce diffusa, cum autem terras nox opacas-
set, tum celum totum[84] cerneret astris distinctum et ornatum lu-
neque luminum uarietatem tum crescentis, tum senescentis, eo-
rumque omnium ortus et occasus, atque in omni eternitate ratos
immutabilesque cursus — que cum uideret, profecto et esse deos, et
hec tanta deorum opera esse arbitraretur." Atque hec quidem ille,'
Aristotiles scilicet.

and countless others, can we doubt that some being is over them, or some author, if these things have had a beginning, as Plato holds; or if they have always existed, as Aristotle thinks, some governor of so stupendous a work of construction?"[73] You see how Cicero consistently describes a single God as governor and creator of all things, using terminology that is not only philosophical but almost Catholic. As a result, I commend this passage more than what follows in Book Two of *On the Nature of the Gods*, which also cites Aristotle's authority. For although the viewpoint is the same, in the latter he refers to many gods, and mentioning them is suspect in any inquiry into the truth.

He writes: "So Aristotle says brilliantly: 'If there was someone 66 who had always lived beneath the earth, in comfortable, well-lit dwellings, decorated with statues and pictures and furnished with all the luxuries enjoyed by persons thought to be supremely happy, and who, though he had not come forth above the ground, had learned by report and by hearsay of the existence of certain deities or divine powers; and then if at some time the jaws of the earth were opened and he were able to escape from his hidden abode and to come forth into the regions which we inhabit; when he suddenly had sight of the earth and the seas and the sky, and came to know of the vast, lovely clouds and mighty winds, and beheld the sun, and realized not only its size and beauty, which neverthe-less he also recognized from its potency in causing the day by shedding light over all the sky; and if after night had darkened the earth, he then saw the whole sky spangled and adorned with stars, and the changing phases of the moon's light, now waxing and now waning, and the risings and settings of all the heavenly bodies and their courses fixed and changeless throughout all eternity—when he saw these things, surely he would think that the gods exist and that these mighty marvels are their handiwork.' Thus far he writes." And "he" is Aristotle.[74]

67   Cuius exemplum quod peregrinum nimis et ab experientia se-
motum uideretur, factam et non fictam rem memorieque proximam in medium deducit *idem Cicero*:[85] 'Et nos autem,' inquit, 'tenebras cogitemus tantas quante quondam eruptione Ethneorum
ignium finitimas regiones obscurasse dicuntur, ut per biduum
nemo hominem homo agnosceret, cum autem die tertio sol illuxis-
set, ut[86] reuixisse sibi uiderentur. Quod si hoc idem externis[87]
contingeret ut subito lucem aspiceremus, quenam species celi uideretur? Sed assiduitate quotidiana et consuetudine oculorum as-
suescunt animi, neque admirantur neque requirunt rationes earum
rerum quas semper uident, perinde[88] *quasi*[89] nouitas[90] magis quam
magnitudo rerum debeat ad exquirendas causas excitare. Quis
enim hunc hominem dixerit, qui cum tam celi motus certos, tam
ratos astrorum ordines, tamque inter se omnia connexa et apta uiderit, neque[91] in his ullam inesse rationem eaque casu fieri dicat,
que, quanto consilio gerantur, nullo officio[92] assequi possumus?
An cum machinatione quadam moueri aliquid uidemus ut speram,
ut horas, ut alia permulta, non dubitamus quin illa opera sint rationis; cum autem impetum celi admirabili cum celeritate moueri
uertique uideamus constantissime conficientem uicissitudines an-
niuersarias, cum summa salute[93] rerum omnium, dubitamus quin
ea non solum ratione fiant, sed etiam excellenti quadam diuinaque
ratione? Licet enim, iam remota subcilitate disputandi, oculis quodammodo contemplari pulcritudinem earum rerum quas diuina
prouidentia dicimus constitutas'.

68   Audis, amice, quod predixeram, non quasi philosophum loquentem, *sed apostolum*.[94] Quid enim aliud tibi sonare uidentur hec

Since this example seems too far-fetched and remote from ex- 67
perience, Cicero adduces an event that was factual rather than
fictional, and of recent memory: "And let us for our part imagine a
darkness as dense as that which is said to have once covered the
neighboring districts on the occasion of an eruption of the volcano
Etna, so that for two days no man could recognize his fellow, and
when on the third day the sun shone upon them, they felt as if
they had come to life again. Well, suppose that this same thing
had happened to us outsiders, so that we suddenly beheld the light
of day, what should we think of the splendor of the heavens? But
daily recurrence and habit familiarize our minds with the sight,
and we feel no surprise or curiosity as to the reasons for things
that we see always; just as if it were the novelty and not rather the
importance of phenomena that ought to arouse us to inquire into
their causes. Who would not deny the name of human being to a
man who, on seeing the regular motions of the heaven and the
fixed order of the stars and the accurate interconnection and inter-
relation of all things, says that there is no rational design in these
things, and that these phenomena, the wisdom of whose ordering
transcends the capacity of our wisdom to understand it, take place
by chance? When we see something moved by machinery, like an
orrery or clock or many other such things, we do not doubt that
these contrivances are the work of reason. When therefore we behold the whole compass of the heaven moving with revolutions of
marvelous velocity and executing with perfect regularity the annual changes of the seasons with absolute safety for all things, how
can we doubt that all this is effected not merely by reason, but by
a reason that is transcendent and divine? For we may now put
aside elaborate argument and gaze as it were with our eyes upon
the beauty of the creations of divine providence, as we declare
them to be."[75]

As I said earlier, my friend, you hear how he speaks more 68
like an Apostle than a philosopher. You see how everything he

omnia et singula, quam apostolicum illud ad Romanos: 'Deus enim manifestauit illis; inuisibilia enim ipsius a creatura mundi per ea que facta sunt intellecta conspiciuntur; sempiterna quoque *eius*[95] uirtus ac diuinitas, ita ut sint inexcusabiles, quia cum cognouissent Deum, non ut Deum glorificauerunt aut gratias egerunt, sed euanuerunt in cogitationibus suis'. Quid, queso, aliud sibi uult Cicero, totiens repetendo mundum diuina prouidentia constitutum, diuina etiam prouidentia gubernari, idque uelut manu lingue oculis hominum ingerendo, nisi ut auctore ac factore rerum cognito, puderet uiros ingeniosos, a fonte uere felicitatis auersos, per opinionum deuia uanis atque aridis cogitatibus circumuolui?

69   Posses autem admirari, ni me nosses, quod a Cicerone uix diuellor; sic me illud delectat ingenium. Ecce nunc rerum stilique dulcedine quadam non insolita raptus quo non soleo, ut alieno mea inferciam opuscula, patientiam non tam tuam quam lectoris imploro. Equidem, dum habere meum aliquid uisus eram, de proprio uestiebar. Mercator inops literarum, ab his quattuor scientie fameque predonibus spoliatus, cum michi iam proprium nichil sit, si aliena mendicem, importunitatem atque impudentiam paupertas excusat. Et quam putas? Magna animi paupertas ignorantia est, et qua nulla maior preter uitium.

70   Sed ne tres illos libros in libellum hunc unicum coangustem, ciceronianum nichil amplius hodie transcribam, quamuis et sepe alibi et illic presertim plurima studiose operosissima disputatione perstrinxerit, ad hunc ipsum finem, ut ex his omnibus que uidemus, esse Deum et factorem *et rectorem*[96] omnium cogitemus.

says, each single word, expresses what the Apostle wrote to the Romans: "God has shown it to them. For the invisible things of Him from the creation of the world are clearly seen, being understood by the things that are made, even his eternal power and divinity, so that they are without excuse, for though they knew God, they did not honor Him as God or give thanks to Him, but they became vain in their imaginations."[76] What is Cicero's purpose, I ask, in repeating so many times that the world was founded by divine providence and is governed by divine providence, and in thrusting this fact, as it were, upon the hands, tongues, and eyes of humankind? Only this: when gifted people recognize the author and maker of the world, they will be ashamed that they were misled by vain and sterile notions, and turned away from the source of true happiness to pursue the dead end of false opinions.

If you didn't know me, you might be surprised that I can't tear   69
myself away from Cicero, so much pleasure do I take in his genius. Even now you see how the usual charm of his subject and style inspires me to an unusual act: I cram my little works with another's words, for which I beg your indulgence as well as the reader's. For as long as I seemed to possess something of my own, I dressed in what was mine personally. But now I have become a poor peddler of learning, robbed of my knowledge and fame by these four brigands. Now that I have nothing of my own, poverty must excuse my importunity and impudence in begging from others. What poverty do you think I mean? Great ignorance is a poverty of the mind, the worst there is except for vice.

I shall not squeeze all three of Cicero's books into this little   70
tract, and shall transcribe no more Ciceronian passages today. Nevertheless, in many other works and especially in this one, he has thoroughly examined many arguments that lead to this single conclusion: everything we see leads us to believe that God exists as the creator and ruler of the universe.

71   *Hec enim fere disputationis illius summa est, ut celestibus atque terres-*
tribus pene cuntis expositis, celi scilicet speris ac sideribus, tum stabilitate ac
fecunditate terrarum, maris ac fluminum oportunitatibus temporumque ua-
rietatibus ac uentorum, herbis quoque et plantis et arboribus atque animan-
tibus, miris uolucrum et quadrupedum et piscium naturis, deque his omni-
bus commoditate multiplici, cibo, labore, uectura, remedioque morborum,
uenatuque et aucupio, et architectura, et nauigatione, et artibus innumeris,
omnibusque uel ingenio uel natura inuentis, denique corporum ac sensuum
et membrorum compage ac dispositione mirabili, ad ultimum ratione et in-
dustria, in quorum explicatione curiose admodum ac facunde uersatur, sic
ut nesciam, an scriptorum aliquis tam anxie unquam tamque acriter ista
tractauerit,[97] *semper una sit conclusio: omnia quecunque cernimus oculis*
uel percipimus intellectu, pro salute hominum et diuinitus facta[98] *esse et*
diuina prouidentia ac consilio gubernari.

72   *Imo etiam ad indiuidua condescendens, cum quattuordecim, nisi fal-*
lor, insignes Romanos duces nominasset, addidit: 'Quorum neminem, nisi
adiuuante Deo, talem fuisse credendum est'. Et post pauca: 'Nemo,' inquit,
'uir magnus sine aliquo afflatu diuino unquam fuit'. Quem afflatum quid
aliud quam Spiritum Sanctum homo pius intelligat? Itaque preter eloquen-
tiam, que nulli hominum par fuit, quid hic in sententia tractator quicunque
catholicus immutaret?[99]

73   Quid nunc igitur? Ciceronem ne ideo catholicis inseram? Vellem posse. Et o utinam liceret! Utinam qui tale illi ingenium dedit,
et se ipsum cognoscendum prebuisset, ut querendum prebuit! Etsi
enim Deus uerus nec nostrarum laudum nec mortalis eloquii
egens sit, haberemus tamen nunc in templis, ut arbitror, Dei nos-

Here is the gist, more or less, of his argument. He describes 71
nearly all the celestial and terrestrial phenomena, to wit, the
spheres and stars of the heavens; the stability and fecundity of the
earth; the benefits offered by the seas and rivers; the varieties of
the seasons and the winds; herbs and plants and trees and animals; the marvelous nature of birds and quadrupeds and fish, and
the manifold advantages that they all offer us: food, labor, trans-
port, and remedies for disease. Then he describes hunting, fowl-
ing, architecture, navigation, and all the countless arts devised by
human genius or by nature; next, the marvelous construction and
composition of our bodies, members, and senses; and finally, human reason and industry. He expounds all this with such great
diligence and eloquence that I can think of no other writer who
has treated these subjects so meticulously or so subtly. His discussion always leads to one conclusion: whatever we see with our eyes
or discern with our intellect was divinely created for the well-being
of humankind, and is governed by divine providence and counsel.

Even when he descends to individuals, and names outstanding 72
Roman generals — fourteen, if I'm not mistaken — he comments:
"None of these could conceivably have been what he was without
God's aid."[77] Soon thereafter, he writes: "No great man ever existed who did not enjoy some portion of divine inspiration."[78] Can
this divine inspiration be interpreted by a pious person as anything
but the Holy Spirit? Besides his eloquence, which no one has
equaled, could any Catholic writer modify anything in the opinion
Cicero expresses?

What, then? Should I therefore place Cicero among the Catho- 73
lics? I wish I could. Alas, if only it were possible! If only the God
who gave him such genius had allowed Himself to be known, as
He allowed Himself to be sought! Even though the true God has
no need of our praises or our mortal eloquence, I believe that our
temples would perhaps resound, if not with truer or holier praises

tri non quidem ueriora nec sanctiora — id enim nec fieri potest nec sperari debet — at forsitan dulciora et sonantiora preconia.

74   Verum absit ut uno aut altero bene dicto totum quicquid est ingenii unius amplectar, *nam philosophos non ex singulis uocibus spectandos, sed ex perpetuitate atque constantia, ab eodem ipso Cicerone, imo a ratione insita didici. Quis tam rudis, ut non quandoque gratum aliquid dicat? An id uero satis est? Sepe una uox ad tempus multam tegit ignorantiam;*[100] sepe splendor oculorum aut flaua cesaries fedas corporum mendas uelat. Qui totum tuto uult laudare, totum oportet ut uideat, totum examinet, totum libret. Fieri potest ut iuxta illud quod delectat, aliud lateat, quod tantundem uel multo etiam magis offendat.

75   Ecce idem Cicero ibidem, ubi multa pergrauiter disseruit et pietati simillima, mox ad deos *suos*[101] ut ad uomitum redit, expeditisque nominibus et qualitatibus singulorum, nec iam de unius dei, sed deorum prouidentia acturus; audi, queso, quid interserat: 'Quos deos et uenerari,' inquit, 'et colere debemus. Cultus autem deorum est optimus, idemque castissimus,[102] plenissimusque pietatis, ut eos semper pura, integra, incorrupta et mente et uoce ueneremur'.

76   Heu, mi Cicero, quid ais? Tam cito dei unius et tui ipsius obliuisceris? Ubi excellentem illam prestantemque naturam numenque illud prestantissime mentis? Ubi meliorem deum homine atque eorum que humana uel ratione uel potentia fieri nequeunt, celestium scilicet huius ue quem cernimus sempiterni ordinis effectorem? Ubi illum denique celestis ac diuine domus habitatorem, insuper et rectorem ac moderatorem et tanquam architectum

of our God — which can neither be nor be hoped for — then with more melodious and resonant ones.

Yet heaven forbid that one or two fine phrases would cause me   74
to embrace a thinker's entire system! I have learned from Cicero himself, or rather from innate reason, that "philosophers must be judged not by isolated utterances, but by the coherence and consistency of their thought."[79] Who is so uncouth that he does not occasionally utter a pleasing phrase? But is that enough? Often a timely phrase will disguise great ignorance; and often dazzling eyes or blond tresses will cover up ugly physical defects. If you wish to praise the whole safely, then you must view the whole, examine the whole, and weigh the whole. For it may happen that, side by side with what is pleasing, there lies hidden something that offends as much or even more.

Here is the same Cicero later in the same book. After many   75
weighty observations that smack of piety, he suddenly returns to his gods, like a dog to its vomit.[80] Having explained the names and characteristics of each of them, he begins to discuss the providence not of a single god, but of many gods. Listen, please, to his comment at this point: "It is our duty to revere and worship these gods. But the best and also the purest, holiest, and most pious way of worshiping the gods is ever to venerate them with purity, sincerity, and innocence both of thought and of speech."[81]

Alas, dear Cicero, what are you saying? Have you so quickly   76
forgotten yourself and the one true God? Where is that excellent and outstanding nature, that divinity of outstanding intellect? Where is the God superior to man, and where is the creator of those celestial things that human reason and power cannot create, and of this sempiternal order that we behold? Where, finally, did you leave the inhabitant of the celestial and divine dwelling, the director and moderator and architect, as it were, of such a great work? You have fairly evicted him from the starry dwelling which you offered him with a flattering acknowledgment. You have as-

tanti operis reliquisti, et quasi e domo illa siderea quam grata sibi confessione prebueras depulisti, dum tam fedos tamque indignos ei[103] comites dares aspernanti atque ore prophetico proclamanti: 'Videte quod ego sum solus et non *est*[104] alius deus preter me'? Qui sunt igitur hi noui recentesque et infames dii, quos in domum Domini conaris intrudere? *Sunt ne hi de quibus propheta alter ait:* 'Omnes dii gentium demonia, Dominus autem celos fecit'?

77   *Tu nunc michi de hoc celorum rerumque omnium factore et creatore loquebaris, meritoque pii auditoris aures atque animum delectabas; sic repente illum creaturis rebellibus atque immundis spiritibus miscuisti.*[105] Euertisti uno uerbo omnia que sapienter ac sobrie dixisse uidebaris. Sed quid dixi: uno uerbo?[106] imo compluribus; sepe enim, imo passim, eodem, quasi dormitans, uestigio nutante relaberis, et quos modo deos irriseras, ueneraris. *Quin et solem et lunam et stellas et postremo palpabilem hunc mundum*[107] ipsum quem uidemus, quem tangimus, quem calcamus, sensu preditum, animantem, et—quo nichil est stultius—deum facis.

78   Idque licet non tu tibi, sed Balbo tribuas apud te loquenti, quod ipsum achademice fuerit cautele, in fine tamen libri illius, Balbi disputationem non ausus, *ne in Achademie legem pecces,*[108] ueriorem dicere, uerisimiliorem dixisti, ut quicquid ille disputauerat approbando tuum fecisse uidearis, uere autem tuum sit, quod platonicum secutus morem alteri tribuere tuasque sententias proferre ficto alterius ore malueris.

79   Quanquam sane quodam loco dicti operis deum unum plurinomium Balbus idem afferre uideatur; quo uelut errorum clipeo uti solent Stoici ad excusandas insanias deorum turbe, quasi diuersis uocabulis non nisi rem unicam designari uelint et intelligi, ut sit scilicet exempli gratia deus unus, isque in terra Ceres dictus, Nep-

signed him such foul and unworthy companions that he spurns them and declares in a prophetic voice: "See now that I alone am God, and that there is no god besides me."[82] Who are these new, recent, and abominable gods that you seek to thrust into the house of the Lord? Aren't these the gods of whom another prophet says: "All the gods of the nations are demons; but the Lord made the heavens"?[83]

Only now you spoke to me about this maker and creator of the 77 heavens and of all things, and you justly delighted the ears and mind of a devout listener. Suddenly you confuse him with rebellious creatures and unclean spirits. With a single word, you subverted everything that you seemed to say wisely and reasonably. But why did I say "with a single word"? In fact, you used many words. Often, or rather everywhere, as if dozing off, you stumble and relapse into worshiping the gods you have just mocked. The sun, the moon, the stars, and even this tangible world that we see, touch, and tread upon — all these you endow with sense and soul, and in the height of your folly, you make gods.

True, you display typical Academic caution in attributing this 78 view not to yourself, but to your spokesman Balbus. But at the end of the work, you dared not call Balbus's discussion truer, fearing to violate the laws of the Academics; so you called it more like the truth.[84] By your approval, you seem to be adopting *his* position. In fact, you followed the Platonic custom of assigning *your* true position to someone else, and chose to have your own views voiced by a fictional speaker.

Still, in a certain passage of this work Balbus himself seems to 79 assert the existence of a single god with many names. This is a shield against errors that the Stoics generally use to excuse the folly of imagining a host of gods, as if they chose to denote and conceive a single entity under different names. For example, there is one deity, who is called Ceres on land, Neptune in the sea, Jupiter in the heavens, and Vulcan within fire.[85] Yet this excuse and

tunus in pelago, in ethere Iupiter, in igne Vulcanus. Tamen hec excusatio et ueritatis adumbratio quam sit friuola, quis non uidet,
qui, ut reliqua sileam, apud scriptores gentium preeminentiam inter se deo-
rum discordiasque et bella sacrorumque diuersitatem uiderit?

80   *Deus enim uerus, qui nisi unus esse non potest, neque se maior neque se*
minor alicubi, cum semper et ubique idem ipse sit, neque aliquando secum
discors esse potest aut fuisse, neque nunc oue nunc thauro, sed uno semper
laudis ac iustitie et contribulati spiritus ac lacrimarum sacrificio delectatur.
Unus ille in celo et in terra, una illi utrobique substantia, unum nomen.[109]

81   Illa quoque diuersoria ac fictionum subterfugia, quod uidentes
philosophi que de Ioue dicerentur Deo non conuenire, duos Ioues,
unum naturalem, alterum fabulosum, ut Lactantius ait, seu potius
tres Ioues, ut ait Cicero, numerant hi qui theologi nominantur —
deorum, inquam, theologi, non unius dei — quantas uires habeant
et quanti extimanda sint precii, ne nimis a proposito deerrem,
apud ipsum Lactantium Formianum qui queret, inueniet Institutionum suarum libro primo. Nam illud piget etiam attigisse quod
et soles quinque totidemque Mercurios, totidem Dyonisios totidemque Mineruas, quattuor uero Vulcanos, quattuor Apollines,
quattuor Veneres, tres Esculapios, tres Cupidines, tres Dyanas dicunt, *sex Hercules, ut Cicero ait, at, ut Varro, tres et quadraginta.*[110]

82   *Neque illos pudet ea dicere, que nos pudeat audire, ne dicam credere.*
Rogo enim,[111] quis has non stomacetur ineptias? Quis has ferat ambages? Omnia non errorum modo, sed sic inanium somniorum
plena undique ac referta *sunt,*[112] ut miserear interdum atque indigner nobile illud eloquium in his positum et consumptum curis.
Nam de reliquis ut libet. At que circulatio, quis hic ludus, quenam he fa-

pretense of the truth is utterly frivolous, as one will see by observing how pagan authors — to cite one case — describe the contentions of the gods, their battles for supremacy, and the diversity of their rites.

The true God can only be one. Nowhere is he either greater or 80
lesser than himself, for he is always the same everywhere. He cannot sometimes be at odds with himself, neither in the past nor in the present. He does not delight by turns in the sacrifice of sheep or bulls, but at all times solely in our offering of praise and justice, of a contrite spirit and our tears. He is one in heaven and on earth; and in both places he has but one substance and one name.

The philosophers who are called theologians — meaning the 81
theologians of the gods, not of God — observed that the attributes of Jupiter were unsuited to one God. Hence, they imagined two Jupiters — one natural, and one mythical, as Lactantius tell us[86] — or three Jupiters, as Cicero tells us.[87] If you wish to gauge the strength and value of such evasive fictions and subterfuges, you will find the answer in Book One of Lactantius's *Divine Institutions*, so that I needn't wander too far from the subject at hand.[88] I am loath even to mention that the ancients said there were five Suns, five Mercuries, five Dionysuses, and five Minervas; four Vulcans, four Apollos, and four Venuses; three Aesculapiuses, three Cupids, and three Dianas.[89] As for versions of Hercules, Cicero says there were six, and Varro forty-three.[90]

Yet the ancients are not ashamed to say such things, which we 82
are ashamed to hear, much less to believe. Who, I ask, would not be disgusted by such follies? Who could tolerate such convoluted notions? All their writings are so full and laden not only with errors, but also with vain dreams, that I sometimes feel both pity and indignation that their noble eloquence was wasted on such concerns. In other matters, let them write as they wish. But why this quackery, this farce, and these old wives' tales? They create five suns, even thought they say that the sun (*sol*) is so-called be-

belle? Quinque soles facere, cum ab eo quod solus luceat solem dici uelint, et cum plures non fuisse quidem unquam, sed oculorum uitio fortassis aut animorum consternatione uisos esse, nonnunquam inter prodigia numeratum sit.

83   *Pace ueterum sit dictum, Ciceronis ante alios: nec scribenda hec fuisse censeo, nec legenda*[113] censerem, quibus conscribendis ille uir tantus incubuit, nisi ut lecte et cognite deorum nuge, uere diuinitatis et unius Dei amorem et contemptus superstitionis externe, nostre religionis reuerentiam legentium animis excitaret. Nullo enim clarius modo unaqueque res quam contrario admota cognoscitur; nil magis amabilem lucem facit, quam odium tenebrarum.

84   Que si de Cicerone meo dixi, quem in multis miror, quid de aliis me dicturum speras? Scripserunt multi multa subtiliter, quidam etiam grauiter, dulciter, eloquenter; sed in his, quasi uenenum in melle, miscuerunt quedam falsa, periculosa, ridicula, de quibus nunc agere longum nimis et impertinens. Neque enim in omnibus ea michi excusatio fuerit, que fuit in Cicerone: non sic omnes alliciunt, quibus, etsi materia alta sit, non est eloquii par dulcedo. Sepe cantus idem pro uarietate canentium nunc delectabilis, nunc molestus fuit, et eandem musicam longe uariam uox ostendit. Ne tamen res egeat exemplo, Pithagoram summi uirum ingenii fuisse quis non nouit? Eius est tamen nota illa ΜΕΤΕΜΨΙΚΟΣΙΣ[114] quam in caput non dicam philosophi, sed hominis scandere potuisse supra fidem stupeo. Scandit tamen et a magno ingenio profecta, magna etiam, ut perhibent, infecit ingenia.

85   *Dicerem hic aliquid, si auderem; quod quia non audeo, audentior pro me dicet Lactantius Formianus, qui in libris Institutionum, hunc ipsum de*

cause it alone (*solus*) shines.[91] At times it has been reported as a miracle that several suns appeared to be seen — but were not really seen — but this was perhaps caused by a defect of the eyes or by a disturbance of the mind.

Let this be said with all respect to the ancients, and to Cicero 83 above all. This great man labored to compose things that I believe should never have been written. I wouldn't believe they should be read either, except that reading and understanding such trifles about the gods awaken our love of true divinity and the one God, and that, as we read, our contempt for foreign superstition awakes reverence for our religion in our minds. The clearest possible means of understanding a thing is to place it next to its opposite. Nothing makes light more lovely than our hatred of darkness.

If I have said this about my Cicero, whom I admire for many 84 things, what do you expect me to say of others? Many of the ancients wrote a great deal with subtlety, and some even wrote with gravity, charm, and eloquence. But into their work, like poison in honey, they have mixed false, dangerous, and ridiculous elements, which it would be tedious and irrelevant to discuss here. I cannot claim Cicero's excuse for all these writers, for even when they treat important subjects, not all of them are so appealing, since they lack the charm of his eloquence. The same song can be either delightful or tiresome, depending on who sings it. A different voice can make the same music sound quite different. If this point needs an example, doesn't everyone know that Pythagoras was a man of the greatest genius? Yet his doctrine of metempsychosis is also well-known, and I am amazed beyond belief that such a notion could have occurred not just to a philosopher but to any human being at all. Yet it occurred to him, and from this great genius, we are told, it proceeded to infect other great geniuses.

I would add more on this point if I dared. But since I don't 85 dare, the more daring Lactantius will speak for me. In his *Divine*

quo loquimur Pithagoram, uanum senem et ineptum, hominemque leuissimum deridende uanitatis appellare non ueritus, totum hoc fabulosum et inane mendacium, atque illud in primis, quod se in priore uita Euphorbium fuisse mentitus est, generosa stili atque animi libertate despicit ac refellit. Hoc est autem unum illud electissimum inter pithagorica dogmata, quibus ille uir aduena apud Methapontinos credulos, ubi diem obiit, tantum meruit nomen, ut domus eius pro templo, ipse pro deo cultus atque habitus sit.[115] Et quamuis hec ipse non scripserit—nichil enim scripsisse traditur—dixit tamen, et post eum scripsere alii.

86   Quis athomorum turbas concursusque fortuitos non audiuit? Ex quibus in unum coeuntibus celum et terram et uniuersa constare uult Democritus, secutusque Democritum Epycurus, qui, nequid penitus deesset insanie, mundos innumerabiles posuere. Quod cum audisset, suspirasse fertur Alexander Macedo, quod nondum unum ex innumeris subegisset. Vani uastique animi suspirium! Certe hi duo *philosophice*[116] heresis huius auctores millesimam nondum partem mundi unius agnouerant, dum mundos innumerabiles somniabant. *I nunc, et non solum doctos, sed sobrios etiam ac discretos, quodque est euidentissimum, otiosos nega, quibus uacauerit talia cogitare!*[117]

87   Quid de aliis dicam, qui non mundorum innumerabilitatem infinitatemque locorum, ut hi proximi, sed mundi huius eternitatem astruunt? In quam sententiam, preter Platonem ac platonicos, philosophi fere omnes, et cum illis mei quoque iudices, ut philosophi potius quam cristiani uideantur, inclinant; et ut illum famosissimum siue infamem Persii uersiculum defendant:

Institutions, he does not hesitate to call this same Pythagoras we are discussing a "vain and foolish old man," and a shallow person swollen with ludicrous vanity.[92] With a noble freedom of style and spirit, Lactantius repudiates and refutes all of this fantastic and empty lie, especially Pythagoras's mendacious claim that in a former life he had been Euphorbus.[93] Yet this was the choicest of the Pythagorean dogmas, for which this [Greek] immigrant won such fame among the credulous people of Metapontum that after his death his house was revered as a temple, and he was worshiped as a god.[94] Although he himself never put these ideas into writing — he is said to have written nothing — he spoke them, and others wrote them down after his death.[95]

Who has not heard of the dense masses of atoms and their ran-   86
dom collisions? Democritus and his follower Epicurus maintained that the earth, the sky, and the universe are formed by the combination of these atoms.[96] In order to complete their insanity, they further postulated the existence of countless worlds.[97] They say that when Alexander of Macedon learned of this, he sighed because he had not yet conquered even a single one of these countless worlds.[98] Truly the sigh of a vain and vast spirit! Yet while they were dreaming of countless worlds, the two authors of this philosophical heresy had not yet understood the thousandth part of our one world. Go now, and deny that the men who had time to imagine such things were not only learned, but sober and discreet, and most obvious of all, men of leisure!

What shall I say about the other philosophers? Unlike these   87
two, they do not affirm the existence of countless worlds and of boundless regions, but the eternity of this world. Except for Plato and the Platonists, nearly all the philosophers tend toward this view, together with my four judges, who wish to appear philosophers rather than Christians. They would defend that famous or rather infamous verse of Persius:

gigni

de nichilo nichil,[118] in nichilum nil posse reuerti,

non modo mundi fabricam Platonis in Thimeo, sed mosaicam Genesim fidemque catholicam, totumque Cristi dogma sanctissimum ac saluberrimum et celesti rore mellifluum oppugnare non metuant, nisi humano magis quam diuino supplicio terreantur. Quo cessante submotisque arbitris oppugnant ueritatem et pietatem, clanculum in angulis irridentes Cristum atque Aristotilem, quem non intelligunt, adorantes, meque ideo, quod cum eis genua non incuruo, accusant, quod est fidei ignorantie tribuentes.

88   Fidem enim ipsam incusare ueriti, sectatores fidei insectantur, obtususque et ignaros dicunt; neque quid alii sciant aut quid nesciant, sed in quo secum sentiant aut dissentiant attendunt; omnisque dissensio apud illos ignorantia est, cum ab errantibus dissentire summa sit sapientia. *Ita autem proposito insistunt, ut quoniam ex nichilo fieri aliquid impossibile sit natura, Deo ipsi impotentiam hanc ascribant, ceci ac surdi, qui non saltem naturalium philosophorum antiquissimum audiant Pithagoram, solius hanc dei fore uirtutem ac potentiam asserentem, ut quod natura efficere nequeat, deus facile possit, ut qui sit omni uirtute potentior atque prestantior, et a quo natura ipsa uires mutuetur. Non miror, si Cristum, si apostolos, si doctores catholicos non audiunt, quos contemnunt; hunc philosophum non audire uel spernere illos miror.*

89   *Sed nec non legisse hec tantos aliorum iudices fas est suspicari; que si tamen forsitan non legerunt, legant, si quis est pudor, apud Calcidium, in*

Nothing is born of nothing, and nothing can return to
nothing.[99]

And if they didn't fear human rather than divine punishment,
they would not hesitate to attack not only the structure of the
world set forth in Plato's *Timaeus*,[100] but the book of Genesis written by Moses, the Catholic faith, and all the sacred and saving
teaching of Christ that flows with the honey of celestial dew. But
when there is no threat of punishment, and there are no witnesses,
they attack the truth and piety, and in their private dens they secretly mock Christ. They worship Aristotle, whom they don't understand; and they accuse me for not bending my knee before him,
ascribing to ignorance what stems from my faith.

While fearing to blame faith itself, they persecute those who 88
pursue the faith, calling them dull and ignorant. They pay no attention to what others know or do not know, but only whether
they are in agreement or disagreement. All dissent is ignorance,
when in fact to dissent from people in error is the highest wisdom.
Since it is supposedly impossible for anything in nature to be born
of nothing, they insist on this view to the point of ascribing such
impotence to God himself. They are so blind and deaf that they
don't even heed the most ancient of the natural philosophers, Pythagoras, who "asserts that this virtue and power belongs to God
alone: for what nature cannot do, God can easily do, since he is
more powerful and pre-eminent in every virtue, and nature derives all her strength from him."[101] I am not surprised that they do
not heed Christ, the Apostles, and the Doctors of the Catholic
Church, whom they despise. But I am surprised that they do not
heed this philosopher, and even spurn him.

We can scarcely suppose that these great judges of others have 89
not read these things. But if perhaps they have not read them before, let them read the second part of Calcidius's commentary on
Plato's *Timaeus*, if they have any shame.[102] Yet I admonish them in

Thimeum Platonis secundo commentario. Sed nequicquam moneo. Omne quod ad pietatem tendit, a quocunque dictum, pari temeritate atque impietate despiciunt, et ut docti uideantur, insaniunt,[119] *quod ancille humili negatum sit, omnipotenti quoque domino uetitum opinantes.*[120] Quinetiam — quod in horum tumultibus aduertere potuisti — ubi ad disputationem publicam uentum est, quia errores suos eructare non audent, protestari solent se *in presens*[121] sequestrata ac seposita fide disserere. Quod quid, oro, est aliud, quam reiecta ueritate uerum querere, et quasi, sole derelicto, in profundissimos et opacos terre hiatus introire, ut illic in tenebris lumen inueniant? Quo nichil amentius fingi potest. Ipsi autem ne nil agere illos putes *seu quid agant ignorare.*[122] Quod aperta professione non audent, protestatione clandestina fidem negant, nunc seriis sophisticisque blasphemiis, nunc ludicris et male salsis,[123] et olentibus iocis atque impiis.

90 Atque magno audientium assensu apud ipsum Ciceronem loquens Balbus: 'Mala,' inquit, 'et impia consuetudo est contra deos disputandi, siue ex animo id[124] siue simulate,' loquebatur ut deorum cultor pie, quanquam pietas illa impia esset ac pestifera. Quam ergo mala quamque impia consuetudo ueri Dei cultoribus uideri debet, contra deum suum, hoc est contra unum, uerum, uiuum celi Deum disputandi quocunque proposito? Nam si ex animo fiat, scelus ingens et impietas; si ludendo autem, ineptissimus ludus et censoria dignus est nota.

91 Non hoc tamen aspiciunt iudices mei, quorum in iudicio non ignorans adeo uiderer, ni cristianus essem. Quomodo enim cristianus homo literatus uideretur his, qui ydiotam Cristum, magistrum et dominum nostrum, dicunt? Non facile rudis magistri discipulus

vain. They despise everything that tends toward piety with equal degrees of rashness and irreverence, no matter who says it. Striving to appear learned, they madly believe that whatever is denied to the humble handmaiden is likewise forbidden to her omnipotent Lord. Indeed, when it comes to a public debate—and you have observed their brawling—since they dare not belch forth their errors, they usually declare that they will separate and seclude our faith from the present discussion. Isn't this the same, I ask you, as seeking what is true while rejecting the truth? Or the same as leaving behind the sun, entering into the profound and obscure abysses of the earth, and hoping to find light in the darkness there? Nothing more insane can be imagined. But don't think that these fellows do nothing or are unaware of what they do. Not daring to make overt professions, they deny our faith in covert protestations, at times using serious and sophistical blasphemies, and at times using distasteful jests or rank and impious jokes.

In Cicero, Balbus finds his companions in complete agreement 90 when he says: "Disputing against the gods is an evil and impious practice, whether sincere or simulated."[103] As a worshiper of many gods, Balbus spoke piously, even though this piety was impious and pernicious. How evil and impious, then, must worshipers of the true God find the practice of disputing on any subject against our own God, the one, the true, and living God of heaven? If it is done sincerely, it is an enormous crime and impiety. If it is done in sport, it is a foolish sport and deserves the censor's condemnation.[104]

But this is not how my judges view it. In their judgment, I 91 would be less ignorant if I were not a Christian. For how must a Christian man of letters appear to men who say that our lord and master Christ was an ignoramus? It is not easy for the disciple of an uncouth master to become erudite if he follows in his master's footsteps. But these men cry out eagerly, boldly, and rudely against both the teacher and his disciples, or rather they bark insults.

eruditus fiet, ab illius uestigiis non diuertens. Cupide igitur et audacter et importune contra preceptorem contraque discipulos eius
clamant, imo latrant et insultant, inque eo maxime gloriantur, si
confusum aliquid ac perplexum dixerint, nec sibi nec aliis intellectum. Nam quis, precor, intelligat non intelligentem se? *Nec audiunt
Cesarem Augustum, inter multa animi ingeniique bona, disertissimum
principem, qui, ut de illo scribitur, 'genus eloquendi secutus est elegans et
temperatum', 'precipuamque curam duxit sensum animi quam apertissime
exprimere', et amicos irrisit uerba insolita et obscura captantes, et hostem
increpuit, 'ut insanum, ea scribentem, que mirentur potius audientes*[125]
quam intelligant'.

92   *Vere ergo*[126] miri homines, qui hinc doctrine gloriam aucupentur,
unde apud doctos ignorantie merentur infamiam. Summum enim
ingenii et scientie argumentum claritas. Nam quod clare quis intelligit, clare eloqui potest, quodque intus in animo suo habet, auditoris in animum transfundere. Ita uerum fit, quod his dilectus
nec intellectus Aristotiles ait in primo Methaphisice: scientis signum posse docere. Quamuis hoc ipsum artificio non uacet, quia,
ut ait Cicero secundo De legibus: 'non solum scire aliquid artis est,
sed quedam ars est etiam docendi'. At ars hec nimirum in intellectus ac scientie claritate fundata est. Etsi enim ars huiusmodi preter scientiam exigatur, ad exprimendum scilicet imprimendumque
animi conceptus, nulla ars tamen de obscuro ingenio claram pro-
met orationem.

93   Amici autem nostri, nos luce gaudentes neque secum in tenebris palpitantes, quasi nostre scientie diffisos, et ob id omnium
ignaros, quia non de omnibus per compita disputamus, ex alto
despiciunt, tumentes inauditis ambagibus, sibique precipue hinc
placentes, quod cum nichil sciant, profiteri omnia et clamare de

Their greatest glory is to make some confused and baffling state-ment which neither they nor anyone else can understand. And who, I ask, can understand someone who doesn't understand him-self? Nor do they heed Caesar Augustus, a ruler who besides his other qualities of character and intellect was well-spoken. We read that "he cultivated a style of speaking that was chaste and elegant" and "made it his chief aim to express his thoughts as clearly as possible." Indeed, he laughed at friends who collected unusual and obscure words, and reproached an adversary as "a madman for writing things his hearers would marvel at rather than under-stand."[105]

These fellows are truly amazing. They pursue the glory of 92 learning in ways that cause learned men to brand them as igno-rant. Now, clarity is the supreme proof of one's understanding and knowledge. Whatever is clearly understood can be clearly ex-pressed, so that one person's inner thoughts can be transferred to the mind of his listeners. Hence the truth of the saying found in Book One of the *Metaphysics* of Aristotle, whom they love but do not understand: "The ability to teach is a sign of one's knowl-edge."[106] Of course, teaching requires some skill since, as Cicero writes in Book Two of *On Laws*: "An art consists not merely in possessing knowledge, but also in teaching it to others."[107] Such an art must be based on clarity in one's intelligence and knowledge. Besides our knowledge, we need such an art to express our mental concepts and to impress them on others. But no art can produce clear speech from a clouded intellect.

All the same, these friends of mine look down with disdain on 93 those of us who rejoice in the light and do not grope with them in darkness. They affect to despair of our knowledge, seeing us as ig-norant of everything because we do not debate everything out in the street. Puffed up with their outlandish fabrications, they are particularly pleased with themselves for having learned the art of lecturing and declaiming about everything, when in fact they

omnibus didicerunt. Neque illos hinc retrahit pudor ullus, aut
modestia, et conscientia latitantis inscitie, neque non dicam ille
Publii mimus: 'Nimium altercando ueritas amittitur,' sed illud Salomonis autenticum: 'Verba sunt plurima multamque in disputando habentia uanitatem'; aut illud Apostoli: 'Siquis autem uidetur contentiosus esse, nos talem consuetudinem non habemus,
neque ecclesia Dei'; atque illud eiusdem: 'Videte nequis uos decipiat per philosophiam et inanem fallaciam, secundum traditionem
hominum, secundum elementa mundi, et non secundum Cristum'.

94   Quid est autem hoc quod loquor, aut quomodo Paulo unquam
credituros sperem? An non ipse Cristi discipulus, quo magistro
gratior, eo istis inuisior contemptiorque? Quis aurem odioso unquam prebuit consultori? Non si amicus, non si ipse frenum
stringat Aristotiles, quiescent: tantus est impetus, tanta animi temeritas, tantus tumor, tanta philosophici nominis et tam uana iactantia, tanta denique opinionum peruicacia, et peregrinorum dog-
matum uentoseque disputationis improbitas!

95   Cuius illud supra positum inter multa damnabile, quod coeternum Deo mundum uolunt. Ubi profanas illas cautiunculas[127] graui
non sine stomaco solitus sum audire, quas hi nostri in triuiis passim; apud Ciceronem uero Velleius, Epycuri partium defensor,
querit his uerbis: 'Quibus enim,' inquit, 'oculis *animi*[128] intueri potuit Plato fabricam illam tanti operis, qua construi a deo *atque edificari*[129] mundum facit?' Potest utcunque hec interrogatio tolerari,
nisi quod iam querendo responsum est, quibus hec[130] oculis uidit
Plato: nempe animi, quibus inuisibilia cernuntur, et quibus ipse,
ut philosophus fretus acerrimis atque clarissimis, multa uidit,
quamuis ad hanc uisionem *nostri*[131] propius accesserint, non uisu
quidem sed lumine clariore.

know nothing. Neither shame nor modesty nor any awareness of their hidden ignorance restrains them. Nor do any maxims restrain them. I don't mean what the mime of Publius said: "By too much arguing the truth is lost;"[108] I mean the authoritative statement of Solomon: "There are many words, which reveal their great vanity in disputation."[109] Or the words of the Apostle: "But if anyone is disposed to be contentious — we have no such custom, nor do the churches of God."[110] Or these words of his: "See that no one ensnares you through philosophy and empty deceit, according to the tradition of men, according to the elements of the world, and not according to Christ."[111]

But what am I saying? How can I hope they will believe Paul? 94 Don't they find this disciple of Christ as hateful and contemptible as his master found him pleasing? Has anyone ever lent his ear to a counselor he despises? No, they will not relent, not even if they were reined in by a friend or by Aristotle himself. So great is their vehemence, their reckless spirit, and their swollen pride! So great and vain are their vaunted title of philosopher, their obstinacy in their own views, and the depravity of their outlandish doctrines and windy disputes!

Among many other views, we must condemn their notion, cited 95 earlier, that the world is co-eternal with God. I am generally revolted when I hear their petty comments on this subject, which they mouth on every street corner. And in Cicero, Velleius, the defender of the Epicurean school, asks: "With what eyes was your Plato able to see the construction process of that vast work, by which he says God assembled and built the world?"[112] We could tolerate his asking this, if his question didn't already imply its own answer. "With what eyes did Plato see?" The eyes of the mind, of course, by which we discern what is invisible, and by which Plato with his keen and clear mental acuity saw many things, although our eyes behold this vision more closely by virtue of their greater illumination than their powers of sight.

96   At quod sequitur quis ferat? 'Que molitio,' inquit, 'que ferramenta? qui uectes? que machine? qui ministri tanti muneris[132] fuerunt? Quemadmodum autem obedire et parere uoluntati architecti aer, ignis, aqua, terra potuerunt?' Questio diffidentis et irreligiosi animi. Ita enim quasi de lignario aut ferrario fabro querit, non de illo, de quo scriptum est: 'Ipse dixit, et facta sunt'.

97   Dixit autem non uerbo uolatili, ne laborasse uel iubendo somnient, ut multa sunt soliti, sed per uerbum internum sibique coeternum, quod erat in principio apud Deum, 'Deus uerus de Deo uero, consubstantialis patri, per quem facta sunt omnia'. Hic profecto mundum fecit ex nichilo; uel si, ut philosophi quidam uolunt, ex informi materia, quam 'ylen' Grai quidam, alii 'siluam'[133] uocant, factus est mundus, hec ipsa, ut ait Augustinus, facta est de omnino nichilo. Fecit, inquam, Deus igitur mundum Verbo illo, quod Epycurus et sui nosse non poterant, nostri uero philosophi non dignantur; eoque sunt priscis illis inexcusabiliores. Potest etiam linx in tenebris non uidere; qui in luce apertis oculis non uidet, plane est cecus.

98   At, quod apud ipsum Ciceronem in processu queritur, quomodo 'qui mundum natum' seu factum 'introduxerit, is eum dixerit fore sempiternum', haud iniuste quidem queritur. Nos autem et principium habuisse et finem habiturum mundum dicimus. Illa que sequitur uana magis, sed uulgaris est questio. 'Sciscitor,' inquit, 'cur mundi edificatores repente exciti ante[134] innumerabilia secula dormierunt'. Qui hoc interrogant, non attendunt, si ante centum milia — uel quia id quoque apud Tullium scriptum est, Babilonios quadringenta septuaginta annorum milia numerare — ante hec omnia seu multo plura milia factus esset hic mundus, idipsum similiter queri posse, cur non prius, cum mille annorum milia infi-

But who can bear the passage that follows? He says: "What 96
method of engineering was employed? What tools and levers and
derricks? What workers carried out so vast an undertaking? And
how were air, fire, water, and earth enabled to obey and execute
the will of the architect?"[113] This is the question of an unbelieving
and irreligious mind. He sounds as if he is asking about a carpen-
ter or blacksmith, rather than the One of whom it is written: "He
spoke, and it was done."[114]

But God spoke not in transient words. Let them not dream, 97
as they so often do, that commanding wearied him! He spoke
through his internal and co-eternal Word, which "in the beginning
was with God."[115] For he is "true God from true God, one in substance with the father, through whom all things were made."[116] He
made the world from nothing. Or if, as some philosophers believe,
the world was made from the formless matter that some Greeks
call *hyle* and the Latins call *silva*, this very matter was made out of
absolute nothing, as Augustine says.[117] God made the world, I say,
through the Word which Epicurus and his followers could not
know, and which our philosophers do not deign to know, so that
they are more culpable than the ancients. In the darkness even a
lynx may not be able to see, but anyone who opens his eyes in the
light and sees nothing must be blind.

In Cicero, as the discussion proceeds, the following question is 98
rightly posed. If you say that the world was born or created, how
can you call it eternal?[118] By contrast, we say that the world had a
beginning and will have an end. The next question is an empty
but familiar one. "I ask you," he writes, "why did these builders of
the world suddenly awake after sleeping for countless ages?"[119]
Those who ask this question don't perceive that, even if the world
was created a hundred thousand years ago or even many thousands of years earlier—Cicero writes that the Babylonians reck-
oned the earth's age as 470,000 years—one could still ask why it
had not been created even earlier.[120] For even a million years,

nito collata nichil amplius quam totidem dies sint, dicente psalmo-
grapho: 'Quoniam mille anni ante oculos tuos tanquam dies hes-
terna que preteriit'; uel multo etiam minus, seu uerius nil penitus.

99   Unius enim diei, *uel unius hore*,[135] ad mille annos siue ad mille
milia annorum, sicut unius exigue stille leui imbre delapse ad omnem Occeanum, cuntaque maria, perquam minima quidem, aliqua
tamen est comparatio et nonnulla proportio. At multorum, et
quotcunque uolueris milium annorum usque dum numero nomen
desit, ad eternitatem ipsam prorsus nulla. Illa enim supra modum,
hinc maxima et hinc parua, utrinque certe finita sunt. Hec autem
contra, hinc infinita, hinc finita, licet maxima, que illis admota
non *exigua*[136] existimanda esse, sed nulla, ait ille uir magnus Augustinus, qui de hoc ipso ualidissime disputat, libro duodecimo
Ciuitatis Dei.

100   Et hec est illa perplexitas, que philosophos coegit eternitatem
mundi ponere, ne tam diu otiosus fuisse uideatur Deus. Quam
multorum sententiam paucis uerbis stringens Theodosius Macrobius secundo commentario in sextum ciceroniane Rei publice:
'Mundum quidem,' inquit, 'fuisse semper philosophia autor est,
conditore quidem deo, sed non ex tempore; siquidem tempus ante
mundum esse non potuit, cum nichil aliud tempora nisi cursus solis efficiat'. Que tamen apud ipsum Ciceronem his uerbis eliditur:
'Non enim, si mundus nullus erat,[137] secula non erant. Secula
nunc[138] dico, non ea que dierum noctiumque numero anni[139] cursi-
bus conficiuntur; nam fateor ea sine mundi conuersione effici non
potuisse. Sed fuit quedam ab infinito tempore eternitas, quam
nulla[140] temporum circumscriptio metiebatur; spatio tamen qualis
ea fuerit intelligi potest, quod ne in cogitationem quidem cadit, ut
fuerit aliquod tempus, cum nullum esset'. Que uerba pene ad
contextum ibidem Augustinus interserit.

when compared to infinity, are no more than a day, as the Psalmist writes: "For a thousand years in your sight are like yesterday when it is past."[121] They are even less, or more correctly, nothing at all.

Now, if you compare a single day or a single hour to a thousand or even a million years, it is like adding a single raindrop to all of the ocean and seas. It may be infinitesimal, but there is a ratio or proportion between them. But if you then take many thousands of years, or even a number so large that it has no name, and compare them to eternity there can be no such ratio. In the first case, the quantities, however excessively large or small, are still finite numbers. In the second case, eternity is infinite; and compared to it, any finite quantities, however large, must be judged not merely insignificant but non-existent, as the great Augustine says, who quite persuasively discusses the subject in Book Twelve of his *City of God*.[122]

This was the paradox that forced philosophers to postulate the eternity of the world, lest God appear to have remained idle for so long. In Book Two of his commentary on Cicero's *Republic*, Macrobius summarizes this widespread opinion in a few words: "Philosophy teaches us that the world has always existed, created by God, but not within time: for time could not exist before the world, since only the sun's movement marks the shifts in time."[123] But Cicero demolishes this view in the following words: "For although the world did not exist, it does not follow that ages did not exist—meaning by ages, not periods made up of a number of days and nights in annual courses, for ages in this sense I admit could not have been produced without the circular motion of the firmament; but from the infinite past there has existed an eternity not measured by limited divisions of time, but of a nature intelligible in terms of extension; since it is inconceivable that there was ever a time when time did not exist."[124] Augustine inserts these words nearly verbatim in the passage mentioned above.[125]

99

100

101   Addunt sane ingeniosi magis homines quam pii, ad eternitatem ipsam, de qua dictum est, mutationes rerum uarias ex incendiis ac diluuiis terrarum mundo inuectas, quibus et temporalis et quodammodo nouus uideatur, cum eternus sit. Quo in genere *to-to*[141] — ut iamtandem, sero licet, unde discessi redeam; euectus enim *sum*[142] rerum coherentium cathena — maxime uitandus Aristotiles, non quod plus errorum, sed quod plus autoritatis habet ac sequacium.

102   Fatebuntur forsitan, seu uero seu uerecundia coacti, diuina non satis Aristotilem uidisse, *neque eterna, quod a puro ingenio semota sint;*[143] sed humanorum *atque pretereuntium*[144] nichil non peruidisse contendent. Ita eo reuertimur, quod contra hunc ipsum philosophum disputans Macrobius, siue ioco siue serio: 'Videtur,' ait, 'michi uir tantus[145] nichil ignorare potuisse'. Michi autem prorsus contrarium uidetur; neque ulli hominum humano studio rerum omnium scientiam fuisse concesserim. Hinc laceror, et quamuis alia sit inuidie radix, hec tamen causa pretenditur: quod Aristotilem non adoro.

103   Sed alium quem adorem habeo, *qui michi non inanes rerum fallentium ac friuolas coniecturas, ad nil utiles, nulli subnixas fundamento, sed sui ipsius notitiam pollicetur; quam si prestat, ceterarum ab eodem conditarum rerum et accessio superuacua et apprehensio facilis et inquisitio ridiculosa uidebitur. Hunc igitur habeo, de quo sperem; hunc habeo, quem adorem;*[146] quem pie utinam et iudices mei colant! Quod si faciunt, sciunt philosophos multa mentitos, eos dico qui philosophi dicuntur; ueri enim philosophi uera omnia loqui solent. Horum tamen ex numero nec Aristotiles, certe nec Plato est,[147] quem ex omni

In explaining the eternity described here, certain men who are   101
more ingenious than devout add that, because of various changes
caused on earth by fires and floods, the world seems temporal and
recently created, when it is in fact eternal. Let me return at last, if
late, to where I started before I was diverted by a chain of related
subjects. On this entire question, we should particularly avoid Aristotle, not because he committed more errors, but because he has
more authority and more followers.

Perhaps my judges will be compelled by truth or shame to ad-   102
mit that Aristotle did not adequately see what is divine and eternal, since such things are far removed from pure intellect. But they
will maintain that he had comprehensive insight into what is human and transitory. Thus we come back to what Macrobius said
against this philosopher, whether he wrote in jest or in earnest: "It
seems to me that such a great man could not have been ignorant
of anything."[126] But it seems to me that just the opposite is true. I
would not concede that any human being can attain knowledge of
everything by merely human study. For this they harass me; and
although the root of their envy is something else, this is the cause
they allege: that I do not worship Aristotle.

But I have someone else whom I worship. He does not promise   103
me empty and frivolous conjectures about fallacious things, which
serve no purpose and rest on no solid basis. He promises the
knowledge of Himself. And if He grants this, it will appear
superfluous to concern myself with the things He has created. For
it will prove easy to comprehend them, and ridiculous to investigate them. He is the one in whom I hope, and the one whom I
worship. It is He whom I wish my judges would devoutly revere.
If they do, they will know that the philosophers lied about many
things. I mean the so-called philosophers, since true philosophers
generally speak only what is true. But clearly Aristotle is not in
their number, and certainly not Plato, who of all the host of an-

prisca illa philosophorum acie ad uerum propius accessisse nostri dixere philosophi.

104　　Isti uero, ut diximus, sic amore solius nominis capti sunt, ut secus aliquid quam ille de re qualibet loqui sacrilegio dent. Hinc maximum nostre ignorantie argumentum habent, quod nescio quid aliter de uirtute neque sat aristotelice dixerim. En crucibus dignum crimen! Perfacile fieri potest, ut non diuersum modo aliquid, sed aduersum dixerim, nec male illico dixerim,

　　nullius addictus iurare in uerba magistri,

ut de se loquens Flaccus ait. Illud quoque possibile est,[148] ut idem, licet aliter, dixerim, atque his omnia iudicantibus, sed non omnia intelligentibus, dicere aliud uisus sim. Magna enim pars ignorantium, ut ligno naufragus, uerbis heret, neque rem bene aliter atque aliter dici putat; tanta uel intellectus uel sermonis, quo conceptus exprimitur, inopia est!

105　　Equidem fateor me stilo uiri illius, qualis est nobis, non admodum delectari, quamuis cum in sermone proprio et dulcem et copiosum et ornatum fuisse, Grecis testibus et Tullio autore, didicerim, ante quam ignorantie sententia condemnarer. Sed interpretum ruditate[149] uel inuidia ad nos durus scaberque peruenit, ut nec ad plenum mulcere aures possit, nec herere memorie; quo fit ut interdum Aristotilis mentem non illius, sed suis uerbis exprimere et audienti gratius et promptius sit loquenti.

106　　Neque illud dissimulo, quod persepe cum amicis dixi, nunc ut scribam cogor, non ignarus magnum hinc michi fame periculum

cient philosophers "came closest to the truth," according to our
Christian philosophers.[127]

Still, as I noted, my judges are so captivated by their love of the   104
mere name of Aristotle that they consider it a sacrilege to differ
with whatever "He" said on any subject. Hence, as the greatest
proof of my ignorance they cite some remark I made about virtue
that was insufficiently Aristotelian. Behold a crime worthy of the
death penalty! It could easily be that I said something different
from and even contrary to their view. But that doesn't mean that I
spoke wrongly, for I was

not bound to swear by the words of any master,

as Horace says of himself.[128] It's also possible that I said the
same thing as Aristotle, but in a different way, so that these men,
who judge everything without understanding everything, thought
I meant something else. Most ignorant people cling to words the
way the shipwrecked cling to a plank, and don't believe that the
same thing can be said well in two different ways. Such is the poverty of their intelligence or of the language in which they express
their thoughts!

Now, I admit that I take no great pleasure in the style of the fa-   105
mous man, as it comes down to us. But before I was condemned
on a charge of ignorance, I learned from Greek witnesses and from
Cicero's writings that Aristotle's personal style was sweet, copious,
and ornate.[129] Yet because of the coarseness or the envy of his
translators, the text of Aristotle has come down to us so harsh and
rough that it scarcely charms the ear or sticks in the memory. This
is why it is often easier for the speaker and more pleasant for
the listener to express Aristotle's thought in words different from
his own.

I shall not conceal what I have often told my friends and am   106
now compelled to write, even though I am aware that it may do
great harm to my reputation and offer great and new proof of the

instare, magnumque et nouum eius, que michi obicitur, argumentum ignorantie. Scribam tamen, nec iudicia hominum uerebor.
Audiant me licebit omnes qui usquam sunt Aristotelici. *Scis quam
facile solum hunc peregrinum et exiguum conspuent libellum — est enim in
conuitia pronum genus — sed de hoc libellus ipse uiderit, quo se linteo deter-
gat: modo ne me conspuant, sat est michi. Audiant aristotelici, inquam,
omnes,*[150] et quoniam Grecia nostris sermonibus surda est, audiant
quos Italia omnis, et Gallia et contentiosa Pariseos[151] ac strepidu-
lus Straminum uicus habet.

107　　Omnes morales, nisi fallor, Aristotilis libros legi, quosdam
etiam audiui, et antequam hec tanta detegeretur ignorantia, intelligere aliquid uisus eram, doctiorque his forsitan nonnunquam, sed
non, qua decuit, melior factus ad me redii. Et sepe mecum et
quandoque cum aliis questus sum illud rebus non impleri, quod in
primo Ethicorum philosophus idem ipse prefatus est, eam scilicet
philosophie partem disci, non ut sciamus, sed ut boni fiamus. Video nempe uirtutem ab illo egregie diffiniri et distingui tractarique
acriter, et que cuique sunt propria, seu uitio, seu uirtuti. Que cum
didici, scio plusculum quam sciebam; idem tamen est animus qui
fuerat, uoluntasque eadem, *idem ego.*[152]

108　　Aliud est enim scire atque aliud amare, aliud intelligere atque
aliud uelle. Docet ille, non infitior, quid est uirtus; at stimulos ac
uerborum faces, quibus ad amorem uirtutis uitiique odium mens
urgetur atque incenditur, lectio illa uel non habet, uel paucissimos
habet. Quos qui querit, apud nostros, precipue Ciceronem atque
Anneum, inueniet, et, quod quis mirabitur, apud Flaccum, poetam quidem stilo hispidum, sed sententiis periocundum. Quid
profuerit autem nosse quid est uirtus, si cognita non ametur? Ad
quid peccati notitia utilis, si cognitum non horretur? Imo hercle, si
uoluntas praua est,[153] potest uirtutum difficultas et uitiorum illece-

ignorance with which I am charged. Still, I shall write it and shall not fear the judgments of my fellow men. Let all the Aristotelians everywhere hear me. You know how readily they will spit on this lonely, strange, and meager booklet, for their breed is prone to insults. But let this booklet find a cloth to wipe itself clean. I shall be content if they do not spit on me. Let all the Aristotelians hear me, I say. Since Greece is deaf to our speech, let those hear who live throughout Italy and in Gaul, contentious Paris, and the noisy Street of Straw.[130]

Unless I am mistaken, I have read all of Aristotle's book on ethics, and have heard lectures on some of them.[131] Indeed, before my great ignorance was discovered, I seemed to understand some of his teaching. At times they perhaps made me more learned, but never a better person, as was proper. I often complained to myself and sometimes to others that the goal announced by the philosopher in Book One of his *Ethics* is not realized in fact—namely, that we study this branch of philosophy not in order to know, but in order to become good.[132] I see how brilliantly he defines and distinguishes virtue, and how shrewdly he analyzes it together with the properties of vice and virtue. Having learned this, I know slightly more than I did before. But my mind is the same as it was; my will is the same; and I am the same. 107

For it is one thing to know, and another to love; one thing to understand, and another to will. I don't deny that he teaches us the nature of virtue. But reading him offers us none of those exhortations, or only a very few, that goad and inflame our minds to love virtue and hate vice. Anyone looking for such exhortations will find them in our Latin authors, especially in Cicero and Seneca, and (surprisingly) in Horace, a poet coarse in style but very pleasant for his maxims. What good is there in knowing what virtue is, if this knowledge doesn't make us love it? What point is there in knowing vice, if this knowledge doesn't make us shun it? By heaven, if the will is weak, an idle and irresolute mind will take 108

brosa facilitas, ubi innotuerit, in peiorem partem pigrum nutantemque animum impellere. Neque est mirari si in excitandis atque
erigendis ad uirtutem animis sit parcior, qui parentem philosophie
huius Socratem 'circa moralia negotiantem,' ut uerbo eius utar, ir-
riserit, et, siquid Ciceroni credimus, contempserit; *quamuis eum ille
non minus.*[154]

109   Nostri autem — quod nemo nescit expertus — acutissimos atque
ardentissimos orationis aculeos precordiis admouent infliguntque,
quibus et segnes impelluntur, et algentes incenduntur, et sopiti ex-
citantur, et inualidi firmantur, et strati eriguntur, et humi herentes
in altissimos cogitatus et honesta desideria attolluntur; ita ut terrena iam sordeant et conspecta uitia ingens sui odium, uirtus *internis*[155] spectata oculis *formaque et 'tanquam honesti uisa facies,' ut uult
Plato, miros sapientie,*[156] miros sui pariat amores. Que licet preter
Cristi doctrinam atque auxilium omnino fieri non posse non sim
nescius, *neque sapientem neque uirtuosum neque bonum aliquem euadere,
nisi largo haustu, non de fabuloso illo Pegaseo, qui est inter conuexa Par-
nasi, sed de uero illo et unico et habente in celo scatebras fonte potauerit
aque salientis in uitam eternam; quam qui gustat, amplius non sitit.*

110   *Ad hec tamen ipsa pergentibus illi ipsi, quos dicebam,*[157] multum
conferunt multumque adiuuant, quod et de multis eorum libris
multi sentiunt, et de Ciceronis Hortensio nominatim in se expertus grate admodum*[158] profitetur Augustinus. *Etsi enim non sit in uirtute finis noster, ubi eum philosophi posuere, est tamen per uirtutes iter rectum eo ubi finis est noster; per uirtutes, inquam, non tantum cognitas, sed
dilectas.*[159] Hi sunt ergo ueri philosophi morales et uirtutum utiles
magistri, quorum prima et ultima intentio est bonum facere audi-
torem ac lectorem, quique non solum docent quid est uirtus aut
uitium preclarumque illud, hoc fuscum nomen auribus instrepunt,

the wrong path when it discovers the difficulty of the virtues and the alluring ease of the vices. We should not be surprised if Aristotle barely arouses and excites our minds to virtue, for he mocked Socrates, the father of moral philosophy, as a "peddler of morality," to use his own words; and if we believe Cicero, he "despised" him, and Socrates despised him no less.[133]

By contrast, everyone who has read our Latin authors knows   109 that they touch and pierce our vitals with the sharp, burning barbs of their eloquence. By these, the sluggish are aroused, the frigid are inflamed, the drowsy are awakened, the weak are strengthened, the prostrate are raised, and the earthbound are lifted up toward lofty thoughts and noble desires. Then earthly matters seem squalid, and the sight of vices inspires great loathing. Virtue in turn is revealed to our inner eyes; and its beauty and what Plato calls "the visual aspect of the good" engender a wonderful love of both wisdom and virtue.[134] I know that this cannot happen without the teaching and the aid of Christ. No one can become wise, virtuous, or good without drinking a deep draft, not from the mythical spring of Pegasus that lies between the peaks of Parnassus, but from that true and unique source that springs from heaven and gushes upward toward eternal life. Whoever tastes these waters will never thirst again.

Yet to those who seek this goal, the writers I have mentioned   110 offer much encouragement and much assistance. Many readers have found this true of many books. Augustine in particular gratefully acknowledges his personal debt to Cicero's *Hortensius*.[135] Although our ultimate goal does not lie in virtue, where the philosophers placed it, yet the straight path toward our goal passes through the virtues, and not through virtues that are merely known, I say, but loved. Thus the true moral philosophers and valuable teachers of virtues are those whose first and last purpose is to make their students and readers good. They not only teach the definitions of virtue and vice, haranguing us about virtue's

sed rei optime amorem studiumque pessimeque rei odium fugamque pectoribus inserunt.

III   Tutius est uoluntati bone *ac pie quam capaci et claro*[160] intellectui operam dare. Voluntatis siquidem obiectum, ut sapientibus placet, est bonitas; obiectum intellectus est ueritas. Satius est autem bonum uelle quam uerum nosse. Illud enim merito nunquam caret; hoc sepe etiam culpam habet, excusationem non habet. Itaque longe errant qui in cognoscenda uirtute, non in adipiscenda, et multo maxime qui in cognoscendo, non amando Deo tempus ponunt. Nam et cognosci ad plenum Deus in hac uita nullo potest modo, amari autem potest pie atque ardenter; et utique amor ille felix semper, cognitio uero nonnunquam misera, qualis est demonum,[161] qui cognitum apud inferos contremiscunt. Et quanquam prorsus incognita non amentur, satis est tamen Deum eatenus, *quibus ultra non datur,*[162] ac uirtutem nosse, ut sciamus illum omnis boni fontem lucidissimum, sapidissimum, *amenissimum,*[163] inexhaustum, a quo et per quem et in quo sumus quicquid sumus boni, hanc post Deum rerum optimam. Quo cognito, totis Illum precordiis ac medullis propter se, hanc autem propter Illum amemus et colamus, uite Illum unicum[164] auctorem, uite hanc precipuum ornamentum.

II2   Que cum ita sint, non est forsitan his philosophis nostris, etsi non sint greci, de uirtute presertim credere, ut iudices mei putant, reprehensibile. Et siquidem uel hos ipsos uel meum forte iudicium secutus, dixi aliquid, quamuis Aristotiles aliter aut aliud dixerit, non ideo apud equiores rerum iudices sim infamis. Notus enim mos aristotelicus, in Thimeo Platonis a Calcidio expressus: 'Hic,'

splendor and vice's drabness. They also instill in our breasts both love and zeal for what is good, and hatred and abhorrence of evil.

It is more prudent to strive for a good and devout will than a 111 capacious and clear intellect. As wise men tell us, the object of the will is goodness, while the object of the intellect is truth. But it is better to will what is good than to know what is true. Willing the good always has merit, but knowing the truth often involves some fault and is "without excuse."[136] Hence, people make a grave mistake when they devote their time to knowing virtue rather than to attaining it. And they make the greatest mistake of all by seeking to know God rather than loving him. For God can never be fully known in this life, but he can be devoutly and ardently loved. Loving God always brings us happiness, but knowing him sometimes causes misery: witness the demons in hell who know God and tremble. We cannot love what is entirely unknown; but it suffices to know God and virtue to the extent that is granted us. Then we know God to be the most radiant, savory, charming, and inexhaustible source of every good thing, from whom, through whom, and in whom we become as good as we can be. And we know that virtue is the best thing after God. Knowing this, we shall love and worship God in Himself with all our heart and being, and we shall love virtue for God's sake. For God is the sole creator of our life, and virtue its principal ornament.

As a result, it is perhaps not reprehensible, as my judges think, 112 to believe our Latin philosophers—even if they are not Greek— especially what they say about virtue. If I followed them or my own judgment, and said something that differed or departed from Aristotle, I don't think that fairer judges would think me a disgrace. Everyone is familiar with Aristotle's custom, which Calcidius describes in his commentary on Plato's *Timaeus*: "Given his method of establishing a complete and perfect doctrine, Aristotle selects what suits him, and neglects other views with disdainful indifference."[137] Suppose, then, that I said something that Aris-

inquit, 'suo quodam more pleni perfectique dogmatis electo quod uisum sit, cetera fastidiosa incuria negligit'. Si ab illo igitur *fastiditum aut*[165] neglectum aliquid dixi, uel non forsitan cogitatum—fieri enim potest, nec humane dissonum est nature, quamuis, *si hos sequimur*,[166] nec consonum uiri fame—si hoc dixi, quicquid id est— neque enim satis quid sit illud noui, *neque hi satis ingenue ueris me certisque criminibus impetunt, sed suspitionibus ac susurris*[167]—hecne sufficiens causa est, qua fluctibus sic demergar ignorantie, ut in uno errans—in quo ipso possum, his errantibus, non errasse— factus sim omnium reus, et in omnibus semper errare nilque omnium scire damnandus sim?

113   'Quid ergo?' dicat aliquis, 'An et tu contra Aristotilem mutis?' Contra Aristotilem nichil, sed pro ueritate aliquid, *quam licet ignorans amo*,[168] et contra stultos aristotelicos multa quotidie in singulis uerbis Aristotilem inculcantes, solo sibi nomine cognitum, usque ad ipsius, ut auguror, audientiumque fastidium, et sermones eius etiam rectos ad obliquum sensum temerarie detorquentes. Nemo uero me amantior, nemo reuerentior illustrium uirorum, et, quod ait Naso:

Quotque aderant uates rebar adesse deos,

ad philosophos et maxime ad theologos ueros traho. Ipsum uero Aristotilem—nisi maximum quemdam uirum scirem, non hec dicerem—scio maximum, sed, ut dixi, hominem. Scio in libris eius multa disci posse, sed et extra sciri aliquid posse credo, et ante quam Aristotiles scriberet, ante quam disceret, ante quam nasceretur, multa aliquos scisse non dubito: Homerum, Hesiodum, Pithagoram, Anaxagoram, Democritum, Dyogenem, Solonem, Socratem, et philosophie principem Platonem.

114   'Et quis,' inquient, 'principatum hunc Platoni tribuit?' Ut pro me respondeam, non ego, sed ueritas, ut aiunt; etsi non appre-

totle had disdained or neglected or perhaps never even considered—which is possible and in harmony with human nature, if
not harmonious with Aristotle's fame in the opinion of these
judges. Suppose I said something of the kind. (In fact, I am rather
uncertain what I said, and these fellows rather disingenuously assail me, not with true and certain charges, but with suspicions and
whispers.) Is this sufficient cause to sink me beneath a flood of ignorance? If I erred in but one respect—but the error may possibly
be theirs, rather than mine—must I be guilty in all respects? Must
I be condemned as always in total error and as knowing nothing
at all?

"Well, then?" someone may ask. "Aren't you too muttering   113
against Aristotle?" I have nothing to say against Aristotle, but
something to say on behalf of the truth, which I love despite my
ignorance. And I have much to say against our foolish Aristotelians. In every single sentence, they daily pound us with Aristotle, whose name alone they grasp, until I suspect that both he
and their listeners are disgusted; and they recklessly distort even
his most direct statements into twisted meanings. No one loves or
reveres men of distinction more than I do. Ovid says,

All the poets that were there I regarded as so many gods.[138]

I apply his words to philosophers and theologians above all others.
Aristotle himself I know to be a great man, but a human one; and
I wouldn't say this if I didn't know his greatness. I know that one
can learn many things from his books, but I also know that one
can learn many things elsewhere too. Before Aristotle wrote, studied, or was even born, I have no doubt that others knew many
things: Homer, Hesiod, Pythagoras, Anaxagoras, Democritus,
Diogenes, Solon, Socrates, and the prince of philosophy, Plato.

"And who," they will say, "assigned this supremacy to Plato?"   114
To speak on my own behalf, I did not, but the truth did, as they
say. Now, Plato could not fully grasp the truth, but he saw it and

hensa, uisa tamen illi propiusque adita quam ceteris. Dehinc magni tribuunt auctores,[169] Cicero primum et Virgilius (non hic
quidem nominando illum, sed sequendo), Plinius preterea, *et Plotinus*,[170] Apuleius, Macrobius, *Porphirius, Censorinus, Iosephus*,[171] et ex
nostris Ambrosius, Augustinus *et Ieronimus*,[172] multique alii. Quod
facile probaretur, nisi omnibus notum esset. Et quis non tribuit,
nisi insanum et clamosum scolasticorum uulgus? *Nam quod*[173]
Auerrois omnibus Aristotilem prefert, eo spectat, quod illius libros exponendos assumpserat et quodammodo suos fecerat; qui
quanquam multa laude digni sint, suspectus tamen est laudator.
Ad antiquum nempe prouerbium res redit: mercatores omnes
suam mercem solitos laudare.

115   Sunt qui nichil per se ipsos scribere audeant et, scribendi auidi,
alienorum expositores operum fiant, ac uelut architectonice inscii,
parietes dealbare suum opus faciant et hinc laudem querant, quam
nec per se sperant posse assequi, nec per alios, nisi illos in primis et illorum libros, hoc est subiectum cui incubuere, laudaue-
rint, animose id ipsum, et immodice, ac multa semper yperbole.
Quanta uero sit multitudo — aliena dicam exponentium, an aliena
uastantium? — hac presertim tempestate, Sententiarum liber, ante
alios, mille tales passus opifices, clara, si loqui possit, et querula
uoce testabitur.

116   Et quis unquam commentator non assumptum ceu proprium
laudauit opus? Imo eo semper uberius, quo alienum urbanitas,
suum opus laudare uanitas atque superbia est. Linquo eos qui tota
sibi delegere uolumina, quorum unus est aut primus Auerroys.
Certe Macrobius, non tantum licet expositor, sed scriptor egregius, cum tamen ciceroniane Rei publice non libros quidem, sed

came closer to it than the rest. Many great authors confirmed this, above all Cicero, and Virgil too, who follows Plato without naming him; also, Pliny, Plotinus, Apuleius, Macrobius, Porphyry, Censorinus, and Josephus; and among our Christian writers, Ambrose, Augustine, Jerome, and many others.[139] This would be easy to prove, if the fact weren't known to everyone. Who ever denied Plato his supremacy, except for the mad and brawling mob of Scholastics? Now, if Averroes prefers Aristotle to all others, the reason is that he undertook to comment on his works and in a way made them his own. These works deserve great praise, but the man who praises them is suspect. It all comes down to the old adage: "Every merchant praises his own merchandise."

There are people who dare not write anything of their own. In 115 their desire to write, they turn to expounding the works of others. Like people who know nothing of architecture, they make it their job to whitewash walls. From this, they seek praise which they cannot hope to win on their own or with others' help, but only by praising authors and books in their chosen field — and by praising them impetuously, immoderately, and always with great hyperbole. Our age in particular offers a multitude of people who expound others' works or, should I say, who devastate them? If it could speak, the *Book of Sentences* would bear witness to this in a loud and complaining voice, since it has suffered at the hands of a thousand such workmen.[140]

What commentator has ever failed to praise his chosen text as 116 if it were his own? Or to praise it all the more lavishly, because praising another's work is courtesy, while praising one's own work is vanity and pride? I omit those who chose to expound entire volumes, one of whom, and perhaps the foremost, is Averroes. Indeed, Macrobius, who was not only a commentator but an outstanding writer too, chose not to expound all of Cicero's *On the Republic*, but only part of one book. Everyone knows the note he added at the end of his commentary: "I must truly declare that

unius libri partem exponendam decerpsisset, expositionis in fine quid addiderit notum est: 'Vere,' inquit, 'pronuntiandum est nichil hoc opere perfectius, quo uniuerse philosophie continetur integritas'. Finge hunc non de libri parte, sed de totis philosophorum omnium libris loqui: pluribus quidem uerbis, non plus *autem*[174] dicere potuisset; siquidem nichil integritati potest nisi superfluum accedere. *Quid uero philosophorum libris omnibus, qui uel scripti uel scribendi sunt, contineri amplius potest quam philosophie integritas? Si tamen hec ipsa uel omnibus contineri potuit aut poterit libris, et non aliquid deest primis, et nouissimo defuturum est.*[175]

117   Sed hec hactenus. Scio, ut dixi, durum me fame scopulum adisse, tantorum non modo mentione philosophorum, sed comparatione proposita. Stilum tamen obiecta, nec reiecta, excuset ignorantia, audaces facere solita et loquaces. Metus amittende glorie aut nominis minuendi frenare solitus oratores, amicorum michi demitur sententia: quid metuam, queso? Non potest perdi, nec *michi iam*[176] minui quod amissum est. Quicquid dixero, aut id erit quod amici *mei*[177] iudicant, aut plus aliquid: minus nichilo, nichil est. Quando ergo, quolibet flatu pulsus, huc prodii, emergam ut potero, et id dicam quod me sepe et interdum magnis quesitoribus respondisse memor sum.

118   Siquidem de Platone et Aristotile si queratur, quisnam maior clariorque uir fuerit, non michi tanta *est*[178] ignorantia, etsi multam iudices mei *tribuant*,[179] ut tanta de *re*[180] precipitare ausim sententiam, que de rebus licet paruis continenda ac libranda est. *Neque uero me fugit quanta sepe de doctis hominibus inter doctos concertatio sit exorta, de Cicerone ac Demosthene, deque ipso itidem Cicerone ac Virgilio, de Virgilio insuper atque Homero, de Salustio ac Tuchidide, denique de Platone ipso et condiscipulo eius Xenophonte,*[181] *deque aliis multis. Quo-*

there is nothing more perfect than this work, since it contains the whole of universal philosophy."[141] Imagine that he spoke not just about part of a book, but about the complete works of all the philosophers. Even if he used more words, he could not have said more: for anything added to a whole must be superfluous. How could all the books of the philosophers, those written and those yet to be written, contain more than the whole of philosophy? The question presumes that such a perfect whole could never be attained in all the books, past and future, without something missing in both the first books and the very last.

But enough on this subject. As I said, I know that by naming   117
such great philosophers, and daring to compare them, I have run ashore on the rocky cliff of their fame. Yet my pen is excused by this ignorance of mine, which has been imputed but not refuted. Ignorance tends to make people audacious and loquacious. Orators are usually restrained by fear that they may lose their glory or see their reputation impaired. But the verdict of my friends relieves me of this fear. What should I fear, I ask you? What has been lost cannot be destroyed or diminished. Anything I say now will have the value my friends assign it, or a bit more: nothing can be less be than nothing. No matter what wind drove me to this pass, I shall extricate myself as best I can. I shall relate how I replied, as I recall, to questions that have sometimes been asked by great men.

Suppose we ask: "Who was greater or more famous, Plato or   118
Aristotle?" Even if my judges say that my ignorance is considerable, it is not so great that I would dare render a hasty judgment. Even on a minor question, our judgments should be controlled and balanced. I have not forgotten that great controversy often arises between scholars when they judge men of learning, such as Cicero and Demosthenes, Cicero and Virgil, Virgil and Homer, Sallust and Thucydides, Plato and his fellow-student Xenophon, and many others. If investigating and evaluating these cases is

rum omnium si indago difficilis atque extimatio anceps est, inter Platonem
atque Aristotilem quis sedens iudiciaria autoritate pronuntiet?[182]

119   At si queritur uter sit laudatior, incunctanter expediam inter hos
referre, quantum ego arbitror, quod inter duos, quorum alterum
principes proceresque, alterum uniuersa plebs laudet. A maioribus
Plato, Aristotiles laudatur a pluribus. Et a magnis et a multis, imo
ab omnibus dignus uterque laudari. Eo enim ambo naturalibus
atque humanis in rebus peruenerunt, quo mortali ingenio ac studio perueniri potest. In diuinis altius ascendit Plato ac platonici,
quanquam neuter peruenire potuerit quo tendebat.

120   Sed, ut dixi, propius uenit Plato, de quo nullus Cristianorum et
in primis Augustini librorum fidelis lector hesitauerit; quod nec
Greci, quamuis hodie literarum nescii, dissimulant, maiorum per
uestigia Platonem diuinum, Aristotilem demonium nuncupantes.

121   *Neque me rursum fallit, quanta in libris suis in Platonem Aristotiles dis-*
putare sit solitus. Quod quam honeste et quam procul a suspitione inuidie
faciat (quamuis alicubi[183] *amicum Platonem, sed amiciorem asserat uerita-*
tem) ipse uiderit, simulque hoc sibi dictum audiat: facile est cum mortuo li-
tigare. Quem tamen multi uiri maximi post obitum[184] *defenderunt, nomi-*
natim in ydeis, contra quas ualide omnes ingenii sui neruos ille acerrimus
disputator intenderat, notissima Augustini ipsius ac secura defensio est, cui
pium quoque lectorem non minus assensurum rear quam uel Aristotili uel
Platoni.[185]

122   Unum incidenter hic dixerim, ut errorem meorum iudicum
hisque similium refellam, qui, uulgi uestigiis insistentes, opinari
solent et insolenter nec minus ignoranter obicere multa scripsisse
Aristotilem. Neque hic errant: multa enim scripsit proculdubio,

difficult and doubtful, who may sit and pronounce between Plato and Aristotle with judicial authority?

But suppose we ask, "Who has been more praised?" I would say without hesitation that the difference between the two is this: Plato was praised by princes and nobles, and Aristotle by the entire populace. Plato is praised by the greatest people, Aristotle by the most. Each of them deserves to be praised by magnates and the masses, or rather by everyone. In the natural and human sciences, they both achieved as much as mortal intellect and study can achieve. Plato and the Platonists ascended higher in divine matters, but neither he nor his followers could achieve the goal they sought. 119

Still, as I said, Plato came closer. No Christian will doubt this, especially if he is a faithful reader of Augustine's works.[142] Even the Greeks, despite their present ignorance of letters, do not disguise the fact, and follow in the footsteps of their ancestors by calling Plato "divine" and Aristotle "daemonic."[143] 120

I am aware that Aristotle often argues against Plato in his works. In doing so, let him consider how honest he appears, and how free from any suspicion of envy. Although in one passage he says that "Plato is my friend, but the truth a closer friend,"[144] he might at the same time apply to himself that other saying, "It is easy to argue with a dead man." Still, after Plato's death many excellent men defended him, and particularly his doctrine of Ideas. Against this doctrine, that sharp disputant Aristotle vigorously strained all the might of his intellect. But Augustine himself provided a famous defense of it, and I think any devout reader will agree with him no less than with Aristotle or Plato.[145] 121

Incidentally, I must say one thing to rebut the error of my judges and people like them. They customarily form their opinions by following in the footsteps of the masses, and they insolently and ignorantly object that Aristotle wrote many books. They are not mistaken in this, for he doubtless wrote many books, 122

plura etiam quam cogitent, quippe quorum aliqua nondum habeat
lingua latina. At Platonem, prorsum illis et incognitum et inui-
sum, nil scripsisse asserunt preter *unum*[186] atque alterum libellum.
Quod non dicerent, si tam docti essent quam me predicant indoc-
tum.

123   Nec literatus ego nec Grecus, sedecim uel eo amplius Platonis
libros domi habeo; quorum nescio an ullius isti unquam nomen
audierint. *Stupebunt ergo si hec audiant.*[187] Si non credunt, ueniant et
uideant. Bibliotheca nostra, tuis in manibus relicta, non illiterata
quidem illa, quamuis illiterati hominis, neque illis ignota est,
quam totiens me tentantes ingressi sunt. Semel ingrediantur et
Platonem tentaturi, an et ipse *sine literis sit famosus.*[188] Inuenient sic
esse ut dico, meque licet ignarum, non mendacem tamen, ut arbitror, fatebuntur. Neque Grecos tantum, sed in latinum uersos aliquot nunquam alias uisos aspicient literatissimi homines.

124   De qualitate quidem operum iure illi suo iudicent; de numero
autem nec iudicare aliter quam dico, nec litigare litigiosissimi homines audebunt. Et quota ea pars librorum est Platonis? Quorum
ego his oculis multos uidi, precipue apud Barlaam Calabrum, mo-
dernum graie specimen sophie, qui me latinarum inscium[189] docere grecas literas adortus, forsitan profecisset, nisi michi illum
inuidisset mors, honestisque principiis obstitisset, *ut solita est.*[190]

in fact, even more than they think, since some of them have not been translated into Latin. As for Plato, of whom they know nothing but whom they hate, they assert that he only wrote one or two little books. They would not say this if they were as learned as they say I am unlearned.

Although I am no scholar and not a Greek, I have in my home   123
at least sixteen of Plato's books, whose titles I doubt they have ever heard. They will be dumbfounded to hear this. If they don't believe it, let them come and see. My library, which I left in your care, is not an unlearned collection, even if it belongs to someone unlearned.[146] They are familiar with this library, for they entered it many times when they put me to the test. So let them enter once more and put Plato to the test, and see whether he too is famous without learning. They will find that what I say is true, and I think they will admit that I may be an ignoramus, but I am not a liar. These great men of letters will view not only Greek texts, but several Latin translations, none of which they have seen before.

They may judge the quality of such works as they see fit. But as   124
to their number, they will not dare judge differently from me. These quarrelsome fellows will not dare to quarrel with me. Yet what small part of Plato's works do I have? With my own eyes I have seen a great number of them, especially in the collection of Barlaam the Calabrian, that modern paragon of Greek wisdom.[147] He once began to teach me Greek, despite my ignorance of Latin letters, and perhaps he might have succeeded, if death had not spitefully taken him from me and cut short this noble undertaking, as often it does.

: V :

125 Nimis iam[191] post ignorantiam meam uagor, et animo et calamo nimis indulgeo. Redeundum est. He sunt igitur, amice, atque harum similes cause, que me amico, sed iniquo (mirum dictu) meorum iudicio sodalium obiecere. Quarum, ut intelligo, nulla potentior quam quod, licet peccator, certe cristianus sum. Etsi enim forsitan audire possim quod obiectum sibi Ieronimus refert: 'Mentiris, ciceronianus es, non cristianus. Ubi enim thesaurus tuus, ibi et cor tuum'. Respondebo et thesaurum meum incorruptibilem et supremam cordis mei partem apud Cristum esse. Sed propter infirmitates ac sarcinas uite mortalis, quas nedum ferre sed enumerare difficile est, non possum, fateor, ut uellem, sic inferiores partes anime, in quibus est irascibilis et concupiscibilis appetitus, attollere, quin adhuc *terris*[192] inhereant. Et quotiens, quanto nisu humo illas auellere mestus et indignans retentauerim, et, quia non successit, quid hinc patiar, solus ipse quem testor et quem inuoco Cristus nouit, qui fortasse miserebitur, ut salubrem conatum adiuuet imbecillis anime et peccati mole obrute ac depresse.

126   Interim non nego multis me curis uanis ac noxiis deditum. Sed in his non numero Ciceronem, quem michi nunquam nocuisse, sepe etiam profuisse cognoui. Quod dictum ex me nemo mirabitur, Augustinum si audierit de se similia profitentem — de quo me *supra proxime, sed*[193] alibi pluribus egisse memini, ideoque nunc unum hoc dixisse contentus sim. Non dissimulo equidem me Ciceronis ingenio et eloquentia delectari, quibus, ut innumeros si-

: V :

I have been rambling on too long about my ignorance, and overin-   125
dulging both my mood and my pen. Let me return to the subject.
These causes, my friend, and others like them exposed me to the
friendly but strangely unfair judgment of my companions. Now, as
I understand it, the most compelling of these reasons is that I am
clearly a Christian, if a sinful one. To be sure, I might hear the
words in which Jerome says that he was reproached: "You lie. You
are a Ciceronian, not a Christian. For where your treasure is, there
your heart will be also."¹⁴⁸ I shall answer that my incorruptible
treasure and the highest part of my heart are with Christ. But because of the infirmities and burdens of our mortal life—which are
difficult not only to bear, but even to number—I confess that I am
unable to lift up the lower parts of my soul, which are still bound
to the earth by their passions and fleshly appetites.¹⁴⁹ How often
and how mightily I have tried again and again to tear them away!
How sad and indignant I feel, and how I suffer because I fail!
Christ alone knows, whom I invoke and call to witness! Perhaps
he will pity my feeble soul, oppressed and sinking under the
weight of its sin, and will aid it in its struggle for salvation.

At times, I don't deny it, I am occupied with vain and harmful   126
concerns. But I do not number Cicero among them. In my experience, he has never harmed me, but has often done me good. No
one will be surprised at my saying this, if he has heard Augustine
confess much the same about himself.¹⁵⁰ (I recall having mentioned this earlier, and elsewhere at greater length, so I limit myself here to this one statement.) I shall not conceal how much
pleasure I take in Cicero's intellect and eloquence. I see that
Jerome himself, not to mention countless others, took such pleasure in them that neither his terrifying dream nor Rufinus's invectives could make him change his style. He was aware that his writ-

leam, Ieronimum ipsum usque adeo delectatum uideo, ut nec ui-
sione illa terribili nec Ruphini iurgiis sic stilum inde dimouerit,
quin ciceronianum aliquid redoleret. Quod ipsemet sentiens de
hoc ipso alicubi se excusat. Nec uero Cicero fideliter ac modeste
lectus aut illi nocuit, aut cuique alteri, cum *ad eloquentiam cuntis, ad
uitam*[194] multis ualde profuerit, nominatim, ut diximus, Augustino.
Qui ex Egipto egressurus, Egiptiorum auro et argento sinum sibi
gremiumque compleuit, ac tantus pugil Ecclesie, tantus propugnator fidei futurus, ante diu quam in aciem descenderet, sese armis
hostium circumfulsit.

127　　Ubi ergo de his, de eloquentia presertim, queritur, Ciceronem
fateor me mirari inter, imo ante omnes, qui scripserunt unquam,
qualibet in gente, nec tamen ut mirari, sic et imitari, cum potius in
contrarium laborem, ne cuiusquam scilicet imitator *sim nimius*,[195]
fieri metuens quod in aliis non probo. Si mirari autem Ciceronem,
hoc est ciceronianum esse, ciceronianus sum. *Miror eum nempe;
quinetiam non mirantes illum miror. Siqua hec ignorantie noua confessio
uideri potest, hoc sum animo, fateor, hoc stupore.*[196]

128　　At ubi de religione, id est de summa ueritate et de uera felicitate deque eterna salute cogitandum incidit aut loquendum, non
ciceronianus certe nec platonicus, sed cristianus sum; quippe cum
certus michi uidear, quod Cicero ipse cristianus fuisset, si uel Cristum uidere, uel Cristi doctrinam percipere potuisset. De Platone
enim *nulla*[197] dubitatio est apud ipsum Augustinum, si aut hoc
tempore reuiuisceret aut, dum uixit, hec futura prenosceret, quin
cristianus fieret; quod fecisse sua etate plerosque platonicos idem
refert, quorum ipse de numero fuisse credendus est. Stante hoc
fundamento, quid cristiano dogmati ciceronianum obstet eloquium aut quid noceat ciceronianos libros attingere? cum libros

ing still smacked of Cicero, and he defended the fact in another work.[151] Indeed, when Cicero was read with piety and moderation, he did no harm to Jerome or anyone else. Rather, he did much good to everyone pursuing eloquence and to many seeking to live well, especially to Augustine, as I have said. When Augustine was about to leave Egypt, he filled his pockets and bosom with the gold and silver of the Egyptians.[152] This man, who would become a great fighter for the Church and a great champion of the faith, arrayed himself with the arms of the enemy before he went into battle.

When we examine such things, especially eloquence, I confess 127 that I admire Cicero as much or even more than all the authors that have ever written. As much as I admire him, I do not imitate him, but strive rather to do the opposite. For I fear that if I too closely imitate anyone, I may become something that I don't condone in others. If admiring Cicero means being a Ciceronian, then I am a Ciceronian. For certainly I admire him, and I marvel at others who do not admire him. If this seems to be a new confession of my ignorance, I confess that it reflects my feelings and my wonder.

But when it comes to pondering or discussing religion — that is, 128 the highest truth, true happiness, and eternal salvation — then I am certainly neither a Ciceronian nor a Platonist, but a Christian. I feel certain that Cicero himself would have been a Christian if he had been able to see Christ or grasp his teaching. As for Plato, we find that Augustine himself does not doubt that he would have become a Christian if he had come back to live in our age or if he had foreseen the future in his lifetime.[153] Augustine relates that most of the Platonists in his day did so, and we may believe that he himself was among these.[154] With such a foundation as this, how can we regard Ciceronian eloquence as an obstacle to Christian dogma? Or what harm can there be in consulting Cicero's books? Reading the books of heretics does no harm, and in fact

hereticorum legisse non noceat, imo expediat, dicente Apostolo: 'Oportet hereses esse, ut et qui probati sunt, manifesti fiant in uobis'. Ceterum multo hac in parte plus fidei apud me habiturus fuerit pius quisque catholicus, quamuis indoctus, quam Plato ipse uel Cicero.

129   Hec sunt igitur argumenta ualidiora nostre ignorantie; que uera esse gaudeo, hercle, utque in dies ueriora sint cupio. Profecto enim, de quo michi cum magnis uiris liquido conuenit, si quemcunque philosophum, quamlibet famosum, si denique deum suum Aristotilem, reuixisse et cristianum factum esse audiant, ruditatis et inscitie arguent, et quem ante suspexerint, superbi despicient ignorantes — *tanta penuria tantumque odium ueri est*[198] — quasi dedidicerit, eo ipso quod ad sapientiam Dei patris a caliginosa et loquaci mundi huius ignorantia sit conuersus!

130   Neque michi dubium est, quin Victorinus, dum rethoricam docuit clarissimus habitus, ita ut in romano foro statuam meritus accepisset, illico ut Cristum et ueracem fidem clara et salutifera uoce confessus est, ab illis superbis demonicolis, quorum *offense*[199] metu aliquandiu conuersionem distulisse *eum*[200] in Confessionibus suis Augustinus refert, hebes ac delirantissimus haberetur. Quod de ipso etiam Augustino eo magis suspicor, quo et ipse uir clarior fuit clariorque conuersio, et quanto fidelibus utilior gratiorque, tanto Cristi et Ecclesie *sue*[201] hostibus inuisior mestiorque, quando apud Mediolanum, ut in eisdem Confessionibus idem ipse commeminit, magisterio rethorice deposito, sub illo fidelissimo ac sanctissimo precone ueritatis Ambrosio, scientiam celestem atque iter salutis arripuit, et de Ciceronis expositore factus est predicator Cristi.

131   De quo quid semel audierim narrabo, ut intelligas quantus hic morbus, quam pestifer, quam profundus sit. Audiui uirum magni

does us good, as the Apostle says: "There must be heresies among you, that those who are approved may be made manifest among you."[155] All the same, in this matter I would place more trust in any devout Catholic, no matter how unlearned, than in Plato or Cicero.

Such, then, are the more convincing proofs of my ignorance. By heaven, I am glad that they are true, and I hope that each day they will prove truer. It is clear, and great men certainly agree with me, that if my judges learned that some famous philosopher — even their god Aristotle — had come to life and become a Christian, they would accuse him of boorish ignorance. In their pride and ignorance, they would look down on someone to whom they had formerly looked up. So great is their lack of truth and their hatred of it, that they would regard him as ignorant, as though he had unlearned everything precisely because he had been converted from the murky and verbose ignorance of this world to the wisdom of God the father! 129

Consider Victorinus, a teacher of rhetoric so famous that he deserved to have his statue placed in the Roman forum. I have no doubt that, as soon as he confessed Christ and the true faith in the clear voice of salvation, he was judged an imbecile and a madman by the proud devil worshipers, so that he delayed his conversion in fear of offending them, as Augustine relates in his *Confessions*.[156] I suspect that Augustine himself did the same, especially since this famed rhetorician's famed conversion proved the more beneficial and welcome to the faithful, the more hateful and grievous it was to the enemies of Christ and his Church. As he himself recalls in his *Confessions*, he quit his position as rhetorician in Milan. Then, under the faithful and holy guidance of Ambrose, he turned to heavenly knowledge and the way of salvation, and was changed from a commentator on Cicero to a preacher of Christ. 130

Let me tell you what I once heard someone say about Augustine, so that you understand how great, how deadly, and how 131

nominis, dum de Augustino placitum sibi nescio quid dixissem, cum suspirio respondentem: 'Heu! quam dolendum, quod ingenium tale fabellis *inanibus irretitum fuerit!*'[202] Cui ego: 'O te miserum, qui hec dicas, miserrimumque si sentias!' Contra ille subridens: 'Imo uero stultum te, inquit, si sic credis ut loqueris, sed melius de te spero'. Quid de me autem speraret, nisi ut contemptor pietatis in silentio secum essem?

132   Pro[203] superum atque hominum fidem! Sic[204] iam nemo[205] igitur literatus horum iudicio esse potest, nisi sit idem hereticus et insanus, superque omnia importunus et procax, qui per uicos ac plateas urbium de quadrupedibus ac beluis disputans, bipes ipse sit belua! Quid autem miri, si delirum me, non modo ignarum iudicant amici mei, cum de hoc proculdubio sint grege, qui pietatem quolibet ingenio cultam spernunt, et religionem diffidentie ascribunt, neque ingeniosum putant neque satis doctum, qui non aliquid contra Deum loqui audeat, *in Aristotilem solum mutus,*[206] aliquid contra fidem catholicam disputare?

133   Quam quo quisque animosius oppugnare presumpserit (expugnari enim nullo potest ingenio, nulla ui), eo ingeniosior apud istos doctiorque; quo fidentius fideliusque defenderit, eo habetur obtusior atque indoctior, et ignorantie conscientia fidei uelum assumpsisse, quo se contegat atque inuoluat, creditur — prorsus quasi non discordes ac trepide fabelle et nugelle inanes ac *uacue sint illorum, nec scientia certa de ambiguis aut ignotis, sed opiniones uage et libere et incerte!* Vere autem[207] fidei notitia et altissima et certissima et postremo felicissima sit scientiarum omnium. Qua deserta, relique omnes non uie, sed deuia, *non termini, sed ruine,*[208] non scientie, sed errores sunt.

deep-rooted this disease is. I once cited some saying of Augustine to a man of great fame. He replied with a sigh: "Alas, that such an intellect was ensnared by these empty fables!" At this, I said: "How wretched you are to say this! And how utterly wretched to think so!" He answered with a smile: "No, it is you who are foolish, if you believe as you say. But I have better hopes of you." Yet what hope could he have, except that I would join him in his silent disdain of piety?

By the honor of the gods and mankind, in their judgment, no 132 one is a man of learning unless he is also a heretic and a madman, and above all, aggressively perverse, a two-legged beast who disputes about four-legged beasts as he wanders the city streets and squares! Is it surprising that my friends judge me not only ignorant but crazy? For they clearly belong to that breed of people who spurn piety, no matter how it is practiced, and who ascribe religious feeling to insecurity. They consider someone ingenious and learned only if he dares speak out against God and dispute against the Catholic faith, remaining silent about Aristotle alone.

The more spiritedly someone presumes to assail our faith— 133 which no intellect or force can conquer—the more ingenious and learned they consider him. And the more confidently and faithfully someone defends it, the more dull-witted and unlearned he is thought to be. They believe that such a person, being aware of his ignorance, has sought to hide it by wrapping himself in the cloak of faith. As if their own fables were not contradictory and wavering, and their frivolities empty and vain! Or as if they had certain knowledge about ambiguous and unknown questions, rather than vague, licentious, and uncertain opinions! In fact, the knowledge of the true faith is the most profound, certain, and blessed of all the sciences. Once we abandon this knowledge, all others are not paths, but dead-ends; not goals, but ruins; not sciences, but errors.

337

134   His tamen isti animis hisque sunt iudiciis, ut nesciam an non solum duo illi, de quibus supradictum est, uel siqui sunt similes, sed supremus omnium Paulus ipse, *non dico, ceperit displicere Iudeis, quibus ante placuerat, quod Ieronimus, epistolam eius ad Galathas exponens, ait; sed omnino et*[209] Phariseis et pontificibus insanire uisus olim sit, quod de lupo agnus, de persecutore cristiani nominis factus esset apostolus Cristi, et his nostris nunc etiam uideatur. Possum ergo ignorantiam michi obiectam—possim et si obiciatur insaniam—magnis comitibus consolari, et sic facio. Quin interdum et delector et gaudeo honestis ex causis non ignorantie tantum, sed amentie reus esse.

135   Ceterum de me letus, de amicis doleo; etsi enim alie iudicio pretendantur cause et forsitan leuiores, he quidem scelere et impietate non uacant, illis mortifere et infames, michi etiam gloriose, ut pro his causis non solum fama, sed uita insuper spoliari, si res tulerit, equissimo sim passurus animo. Illud angit in primis, quod uerissima omnium uel unica uel inter cuntas eminens obliqui causa iudicii liuor est, qui multos semper, sed *nullos unquam*[210] sanos ac lucidos infecit oculos, coegitque falsum cernere. Res stupenda *et noua,*[211] neque michi unquam hactenus audita, nunc (quod nolim) in meo capite experta et cognita, amicis inuidiam inesse pectoribus. Amicis, inquam, sed non plena ac perfecta amicitia, que est ita amicum ut se amare.

136   Amant isti me, sed non toto pectore. Dicam melius: toto amant pectore, sed non totum me. Vitam certe, corpusque et animam, et quicquid habeo, preter famam, eamque duntaxat literarum, horum ego uel omnium uel singulorum in manibus fidenter nilque hesi-

Given the attitudes and views of my judges, I suspect they dis- 134
like not only the two thinkers I have mentioned, or others like
them, but even Paul, who was the greatest of them all.[157] Jerome
tells us in his commentary on the Epistle to the Galatians that in
the same way Paul began to displease the Jews, whom he had formerly pleased.[158] What's more, the Pharisees and high priests once
thought him mad for changing from a wolf to a lamb, from a per-
secutor of the Christians to an apostle of Christ. This is how he
now strikes our friends. Hence, I may console myself for this
charge of ignorance, as I could if charged with insanity. And I do
console myself, for I am in the company of great men. At times, I
both delight and rejoice that for honorable reasons I am accused
not only of ignorance, but of madness as well.

At any rate, I am happy with myself, but my friends cause me 135
pain. To excuse their verdict, they allege other, less serious reasons; but the true ones are wicked and impious. My judges find
them deadly and disgraceful. I find them so glorious that I would
bear it with perfect equanimity if for these reasons they deprived
me of my reputation and, if necessary, of my life as well. It particularly distresses me that spite is the essential reason for their bi-
ased judgment, the only true reason or the main one at least. Spite
has infected many people's eyes, if never healthy and clear ones,
and has forced them to see what is false. Here is a novel and perplexing state of affairs, which I had never heard about, but which I
have now unwillingly experienced and understood to my peril.
Envy lurks in the breasts of one's friends. I say "friends," but I am
not referring to that complete and perfect friendship that consists
in loving a friend as oneself.

My friends love me, but not wholeheartedly. More exactly, they 136
love me wholeheartedly, but not all of me. To all of them, or any
one of them, I would entrust my life, my body and soul, and all
that is mine with confidence and without hesitation. But not my
fame, or my literary fame, at least. This exception is not due to ha-

tans posuerim. Neque hec exceptio aut odii aut amicitie lentioris, sed inuidie est, ut dixi, etiam in amicitiis habitantis, uel si hoc auditu durum est, et hoc quoque melius aliter est dicendum, ut non liuoris sit exceptio, sed doloris. Dolent forsitan, imo dolent utique apud doctos, apud quos michi, uere ne an falso, literati hominis partum nomen audiunt, se nec literatos esse nec cognitos. Hinc ereptum michi cupiunt quod non habent, neque, si sapiunt, sperant.

137   Magna uotorum conflict*atio rerumque*[212] discordia, cui bonum omne uel maximum uelis, eidem nolle uel minimum, non tam puto quia id michi esse, quam quod sibi doleant deesse. Querunt, neque id fateor iniuste, in amicitia pares esse, et id agunt, ut quoniam clari omnes esse non possumus, quod facilius censent, simus omnes obscuri. Est, non inficior, in amicis paritas pulcerrima. Ubi enim insigniter pars una preponderat, non bene uidentur amicorum animi quasi impares iuuenci sub amicitie iugum mitti. Verum ea paritas amoris ac fidei esse debet; fortunarum et glorie non ita. Idque, ut ignotos sileam, Herculis ac Philotete, Thesei ac Pirothoi, Achillis et Patrocli, Scipionis et Lelii probat imparitas. Ipsi tamen, ut libet, uiderint quo animo erga meum nomen fuerint, qui erga me, *ni fallor,*[213] hauddubie sunt optimo.

⁚ VI ⁚

138   Ego autem, amice, nequid nescias, et ut noris unde et quo animo tibi hec scribo, inter Padi uertices parua in naui sedeo. Ne mireris si uel manus scribentis uel oratio fluctuat; per aduersum hunc in-

tred or lukewarm friendship, but to the envy that dwells in some friendships, as I have said. Or, if this is too unpleasant to hear, and should be expressed more pleasingly, this exception is not due to spite, but to grief. They are perhaps grieved; no, they are certainly grieved that in learned circles they appear unlettered and obscure, while I appear to be a man of letters, whether rightly or wrongly. Hence they want to deprive me of that which they lack and which, if they are wise, they will not hope to attain.

There is a great conflict in their desires and a great discrepancy 137 in their actions. They wish me the greatest boons, and at the same time to begrudge me a trifle. I suppose that they are grieved less by my fame than by their lack of it. They seek equality in our friendship, and rightly so, I admit. Since we cannot all be famous, they strive to see that we are all obscure, which they think is the easiest solution. Now, I don't deny that equality is a fine thing in friendship. For whenever part of a group conspicuously dominates the others, the minds of such friends seem ill matched under the yoke of friendship, like unequal bullocks.[159] Yet this equality should be an equality of love and trust, not of fortunes and glory. This is proved by the inequality between Hercules and Philoctetes, Theseus and Pirithous, Achilles and Patroclus, and Scipio and Laelius, not to mention obscure men. So if they are willing, let these men consider their feelings toward my reputation. Unless I am mistaken, their feelings toward me personally are excellent.

: VI :

I want you to know everything, my friend: where I am writing 138 this, and in what mood. I am seated in a small boat amid the swirling currents of the river Po.[160] So don't be surprised if my

gentem amnem tota cum ignorantia mea nauigo, cuius olim in ripis multa scripsi iuuenis multaque meditatus sum, que illorum temporum senibus probarentur, priusquam hi iuuenes senilem ignorantiam deprehendissent. O sors hominum instabilis! Padus ipse quodammodo michi compati uisus est, quasi studii nostri memor et ueterum conscius curarum, quod quem iuuenem—si sine superbia dici potest—gloriosum uidit, senem cernat inglorium fameque prefulgidis exutum uestibus; meque retro assidue ad ius meum ab iniquis iudicibus reposcendum magno impetu et toto gurgite reimpellit.

139 Verum ego, laboriosam michi et quibus minime suspicabar inuidiosam fame sarcinam perosus, et litium fugitans et contemptus spretor, exuuias meas raptoribus caris linquo. Habeant sibi, me cedente, si ut pecunia, sic et fama, dum habenti eripitur, ad raptorem transit. Habeant sibi uel scientiam, uel huic apud stultos parem, scientie opinionem. Ego uel utraque uel profecto altera, hoc est opinione scientie, nudus eo, felicior fortassis ac ditior nuditate humili, quam superbis illi spoliis et, ut arbitror, non suis. Vado igitur letus, claro et graui fasce deposito, et obstantem Padum remis, uelis ac funibus supero, Ticinum repetens, studiosam et antiquam urbem, ubi non modo uestimentum fame uetus inter nautas perditum inueniam, si ea cura sit; sed carere illo, etsi ualde cupiam, nequibo.

140 Ego autem nitar semper et optabo illiteratus dici, dum uir bonus aut non malus sim, ut uel sic quiescam: fesso nil dulcius est quiete. Hanc michi semper ad hunc diem mendax, ut nunc audio, literarum fama preripuit, et hanc ipsam, seu falsa seu uerax, igno-

hand or my words falter as I write. I am sailing up this mighty river with all my ignorance on board. As a youth, I wrote many things on its banks and pondered many ideas that were lauded by older men. In those days, the ignorance of my old age had not yet been discovered by my youthful friends. How unstable is human destiny! Even the Po seems to pity me, as if mindful of my studies and aware of my long-standing cares. For if I may speak without arrogance, in my youth the Po beheld my glory, but now it sees only an inglorious old man stripped of fame's dazzling raiments. With the vast might of its great current, it constantly pushes me back to demand justice from my unfair judges.

I detest the laborious burden of fame, which arouses envy in   139
those I least suspected. Fleeing their disputes and spurning their contempt, I leave my spoils to these dear brigands. Let them have my fame. I hand it over, if fame can be given to a robber as money is snatched from its owner. Let them have my knowledge, or my reputation for knowledge, which fools regard as the same thing. Freed of both, or at least of my reputation for knowledge, I shall go my way naked. In my humble nakedness, I shall be happier and richer perhaps than they are with their proud spoils, which in my view do not belong to them. I travel happily, having laid down this illustrious but weighty bundle. With oars, sails, and ropes, I overcome the current of the Po, returning to the Ticino river and its ancient city of scholars.[161] There, if I choose to, I shall not only resume the mantle of my former fame, which has been lost among the seamen, but I shall not be able to renounce it, even if I should really want to.

Still, I shall always strive and hope to be called unlearned, so   140
long as I am good or at least not bad; and so long as this brings me rest, for nothing is sweeter to the weary than rest. Such rest has been stolen from me by a literary reputation that is false, as I now learn. It will only be restored to me by a reputation for ignorance, whether true or false. At last, I shall at last feel better, even

rantie fama restituet. Atque ita uel sero, tandem aliquando, bene
erit. Id tamen, ut uereor, frustra nitar atque optabo. Tam multi
contra meos iudices sentiunt, ut non illic tantum, quo michi nunc
iter est, sed ubicunque per hunc nostrum orbem suam hanc sententiam promulgarint. Quamuis apud me in rem iudicatam iam
transierit, ut audisti; apud alios tamen in suum caput, plurium ac
maiorum iudicio, recasura sit, preter illam unam[214] forsitan, ubi
hec audent, urbem nobilissimam atque optimam; ubi propter populi magnitudinem multiplicemque uarietatem multi sunt qui sine
literis philosophentur ac iudicent.

141   Multa enim rerum omnium, et quod unicum ibi uel maximum
malum dixerim, uerborum longe nimia est libertas; qua freti sepe
ineptissimi homines claris nominibus insultant, indignantibus quidem bonis, qui ibidem quoque tam multi sunt, ut nesciam an in
ulla urbe tot boni modestique uiri sint; sed tanto maior est ubique
stultorum acies, ut sapientium indignatio frustra sit. Tam dulce
omnibus libertatis est nomen, ut temeritas et audacia, quod illi similes uideantur, uulgo placeant. Hinc impune aquilam noctue, cignum corui, leonem simie lacessunt; hinc honestos fedi, doctos
inscii, fortes ignaui, bonos mali lacerant; nec malorum licentie
boni obstant, quod et numero illi superant et fauore publico, expedire credentium ut quicquid loqui libet et liceat. *Ita prorsus insedit illud Tiberii Cesaris, 'in ciuitate libera linguam mentemque liberas esse debere'. Libere quidem esse debent; ita tamen ut libertas uacet iniuria.*[215]

142   Viden ut ad finem propero, neque peruenio? Multa enim in-
terueniunt, que cursum orationis impediant. Non quod ego ignorem multo sapientius multoque grauius futurum fuisse, quod hec

if it is too late. Yet I fear that I shall strive and hope in vain, for many people disagree with my judges. They will proclaim this verdict not only in the city to which I travel, but throughout our world. As you have heard, I consider the case closed; but the judgment of more numerous and greater men will cause my judges' verdict to fall back on their heads. Perhaps this won't happen in the one most noble and excellent city where they dare judge me. Because of the magnitude and manifold variety of its populace, many people there philosophize and judge who are without learning.[162]

This city enjoys great freedom in many things, including an excessive freedom of speech, which I would call its only or its greatest evil. Protected by this, foolish people there often insult renowned figures. This stirs the indignation of good men, who are so numerous there that perhaps no other city has so many good and moderate citizens. But the host of fools is everywhere so much greater that the indignation of the wise proves vain. The name of freedom is so sweet that the mob welcomes temerity and audacity, which resemble it. Hence, owls safely bait the eagle, crows bait the swan, and apes the lion. Hence, the corrupt abuse the honest, the ignorant abuse the learned, the cowardly the brave, and the wicked the good. In turn, the good do not oppose this license of the wicked. Since wicked men outnumber them and command public favor, they believe that it is best when one is free to say anything one pleases. So entrenched is the view expressed by Tiberius Caesar: "In a free city, our tongues and minds must be free."[163] Yes, they should be free, as long as they cause no injustice.

You see how I hasten toward the end, but never reach it? Many things occur to me that interrupt the flow of my discourse. I know that it would have been far more prudent and dignified to remain silent about such topics. But it is difficult to remain unmoved while being bitten, and so I was often forced to crush these fleas, or shake them off. But I could easily have tolerated these men if I

et alia sepe similia tacuissem; sed difficile est inter aculeos non moueri. Sepe ergo tales pulices uel conterere necesse michi fuit uel excutere. Facile autem hos tulissem, si te facile perferentem cognouissem. In his enim non inscitiam meam, quam libenter amplector, sed illorum insolentiam egre fero, sed, ut dixi, tacitus hanc laturus, nisi tu fuisses. Tue equidem et non mee indignationi tam longis sermonibus morem gessi; de ignorantia mea[216] tibi non epystolam iam, sed librum scribens. *Addidi de multorum ac pene omnium ignorantia que se obtulerant festinanti, de quibus cogitare studiosius si detur, non libellus exiguus, sed ingentes texi queant libri. Quid enim, queso, comunius ignorantia? Quid uberius? Quid latius? Quocunque me uertam, in me illam et in aliis, sed nusquam exundantius quam in meis iudicibus inuenio. Que si tam illis nota esset ut michi, aliene forsan ignorantie ferendis sententiis abstinerent, essetque ad tribunal illud iniquissimum atque ineptissimum perenne iustitium. Quis enim, nisi impudentissimus, quod in se uidet, damnat in altero? Excusatio una est: docti sibi uidentur, eo presertim tempore; nam quod constat, post cenam illa sentententia lata est.*

143 *Videri autem prima fronte potuerit De mei ipsius ignorantia, nisi aliud addidissem,*[217] nouus libri titulus, non stupendus tamen ad memoriam reuocanti ut *De ebrietate sua* librum scripsit Antonius triumuir. Tanto enim hoc turpior titulus ille est, quanto morum quam ingenii turpiora sunt uitia. Ignorantia quidem uel desidie cuiuspiam fuerit uel insite tarditatis, at ebriositas uoluntatis *peruersique animi.*[218] Sicut autem ibi Antonius omnium ebriosissimum se fatetur, unum duntaxat excipiens magni — pro[219] pudor! — filium Ciceronis, sic et ego omnium ignorantissimum me non nego; sed non unum, imo quattuor fortassis excipiam.

144 Sed iam satis est, uereorque ne nimium; iamque uelut e turbidis fluctibus portum specto. Iam demum igitur alto animo fera-

had seen that you easily tolerated them. What I can scarcely tolerate in them is not my own ignorance, which I gladly accept, but their insolence; but, as I said, I was going to bear this in silence if it hadn't been for you. In this lengthy disquisition, I have tried to appease your indignation, rather than mine, and have now written a book on my ignorance rather than a letter. To it I have added many observations about the ignorance of many people and of nearly everyone, which occurred to me in my haste. If I had time to ponder them more carefully, I might have composed not just this booklet, but massive volumes. For what, I ask, is more common than ignorance? What more flourishing? What more widespread? Wherever I turn, I find it in myself and in others, but nowhere more abundantly than in my judges. If they knew their own ignorance as well as I know mine, perhaps they might refrain from passing judgment on the ignorance of others; and their unjust and incompetent tribunal would be perpetually adjourned. Who but an impudent scoundrel condemns in others what he sees in himself? They only have one excuse. They think themselves learned in this particular moment. They clearly pronounced their sentence after dinner!

If I hadn't added another phrase, my title page would have read 143 *On My Own Ignorance*.[164] This title is strange, but it would not surprise those who recall that the triumvir Mark Antony wrote a book *On My Drunkenness*.[165] His title is more shameful than mine, just as moral vices are more shameful than mental ones. Ignorance stems from indolence or natural stupidity, but drunkenness stems from the will and a perverted mind. In his book, Mark Antony confesses that he is the greatest drunkard of all, with the sole exception—for shame!—of great Cicero's son. I do not deny that I am the greatest ignoramus of all, but I note the exception of four men, rather than one!

But enough for now. I fear I have said too much. Yet even now, 144 tossed as I am by churning waves, I see the port. Now let me no-

mus hanc seu falsam infamiam, seu ueram famam ignorantie.
Nam neque falsum metuit, nisi qui parum uero fidit; neque uerum
odit, nisi qui falsum amat. Si falsa est infamia, cito desinet apud
ipsos etiam auctores infamie, *dum quid dixerint ruminantes pudor
inuaserit.*[220] Apud alios enim nec incipiet quidem, nec ad quem
diuertat patens limen docti hominis repertura est. Sin uera est
fama, quid tergiuersamur? An amore uani nominis labefactare so-
lidam nitimur ueritatem? Quid est autem in hoc ipso, quod magnopere generosum animum et humana noscentem et celestia sus-
pirantem torqueat, dum cogitat metiturque quantulum est, quam
nichilo proximum — quod non dicam unus alterque philosophus,
eorum quoque qui clarissimum scientie nomen habent, sed simul
omnes norunt — quamque exilis rerum portio omnium hominum
scientia uel humane ignorantie uel diuine sapientie comparata?

145   *Dabis hic michi, amice, aurem, dabis fidem, atque hoc non recens et
nunc primum ad os ueniens, sed sepe dictum, sepius cogitatum credes:
quemcunque horum qui magna scientie fama sunt, seu ueterum seu nouo-
rum, ex illo illustrium grege et nominum luce secreueris et diligenter excus-
seris, inuenies, si rerum ueritas, non hominum clamor inspicitur, scientie
modicum, ignorantie plurimum habuisse. Quod ipsos, si adsint,[221] nec inge-
nuus pudor absit, plane fassuros michi ipse persuadeo; et hoc Aristotilem
morientem ingemuisse quidam ferunt, 'ut nemo sibi blandiatur, aut scientie
opinione superbiat, sed deo gratias agat, siquid ei forsitan supra comunem
modum obtigit. Ad quod ipsum credendum non sit uelox, potiusque sibi
quam aliis de se credat, sibique non plausoris blandi, sed censoris in se ri-
gidi uice fungenti'. Vere enim quisquis, fauore seposito, quo et fallimus et*

bly bear this charge of ignorance—whether it is an infamous false-hood or a famous truth. We fear what is false only when we mis-trust the truth. And we hate what is true only when we love falsehood. If this infamous charge is false, it will soon be dropped even by those who brought it, when they ponder their statements and feel shame. Others will not even admit the charge; and no man of learning will open his door to receive it. But if this fame is true, why should I turn my back on it? Should I try to undermine the solid truth out of love for a vain reputation? There is nothing here that can profoundly torment a noble mind which understands what is human and longs for what is celestial. Such a mind pon-ders its own insignificance, and gauges how near it is to nothing. (The truth of this is recognized, not only by one or two philoso-phers, even the most widely renowned for their learning, but by all people everywhere.) The noble mind sees how paltry human knowledge is when compared to human ignorance or divine wis-dom.

Lend me an ear, my friend, and your trust too. Believe me, I 145 say nothing that is new here for the first time, but I repeat what I have often said and thought. Take anyone famous for his wisdom, ancient or modern. Remove him from the company of the illustri-ous, and from the limelight of renown. Then, if you consider the actual truth, rather than popular acclaim, you will find that he had little knowledge, and abundant ignorance. If such men were pres-ent and did not lack candor and modesty, I am convinced that they themselves would openly admit this. They say that Aristotle, as he lay dying, groaned: "No one should flatter himself or take pride because he believes in his own knowledge. He should rather give thanks to God if he chanced to possess more than the com-mon measure. But let him not be hasty to believe such a thing. As for his abilities, let him trust himself more than others, and act as a severe censor rather than as a fawning flatterer."[166] Truly, anyone who examines his affairs with open eyes, but without that appro-

349

uicissim fallimur, apertisque oculis res suas aspexerit, multa in se flenda,
pauca admodum plaudenda reperiet.

146   *Sed omissis quorum grauior est querela—de uirtutibus loquor—ad*
scientiam reuertamur. Iam quid inops perdere metuat, ubi qui habentur
ditissimi uere inopes sunt? Siquidem²²² in hac *ipsa*²²³ portiuncula scibi-
lium rerum philosophamur tumidissimi, *et inquietissimi disside-*
*mus,*²²⁴ et magne uelut specie scientie²²⁵ superbimus. Inque his ipsis angustiis qui maximi etiam sunt uersantur, et pauca scientes
multa nesciunt, et nescire se, nisi insaniant, non nesciunt. Verissi-
mumque est ciceronianum illud, quod quisque grauis philosophus
multa sibi deesse cognoscit. Quem defectum, quo quisque minus
intelligit, minus sentit et curat minus; ideoque doctissimos maxime uideas discendi auidos, et maxime ignorantiam negligentem.

147   Sane *in hac tanta scientie inopia,*²²⁶ ubi implumes alas uento aperit
humana superbia, quam frequentes et quam duri scopuli! Quot
quamque ridicule philosophantium uanitates! Quanta opinionum
contrarietas, quanta pertinacia, quanta proteruia! Qui sectarum
numerus, que differentie, quenam bella, quanta rerum ambiguitas,
que uerborum perplexitas! Quam profunde, quamque inaccessibi-
les ueri latebre, quot insidie sophistarum omni studio ueri iter
uepribus ceu quibusdam obstruentium, ut nequeat internosci quis
illuc rectior trames ferat! Quam ob causam Cato maior, ut noui-
mus, pellendum censuit urbe Carneadem. Quenam postremo hec
inter *hinc temeritas, hinc*²²⁷ diffidentia maximorum hominum et des-
peratio quedam apprehendende ueritatis! Pithagoras ait de omni
re ad utranque partem equis argumentis disputari posse, et de hoc
ipso, an res omnis ex equo disputabilis sit.

148   *Sunt qui dicant alte obrutam ueritatem et profundo uelut in puteo de-*
mersam, quasi ex imis terre latebris, et non potius e summo celi uertice, pe-

bation by which we deceive and are deceived, will find many things worthy of lament, and quite few worthy of applause.

But let us leave aside a more heated debate, namely, the one 146 concerning the virtues, and return to the question of knowledge. What should a pauper be afraid of losing, when those who are thought rich are themselves truly paupers? Within our small share of what can be known, we haughtily philosophize, we feverishly disagree, and we swell with pride at our great display of specious knowledge. Even reputedly great thinkers are confined by these limits. They know a little, and are ignorant of a lot; and unless they are mad, they are not ignorant of their own ignorance. Hence the perfect truth of Cicero's observation that every serious philosopher recognizes how much knowledge he lacks.[167] By contrast, the less one is aware of this lack, the less one feels it or worries about it. As a result, you'll find that the most learned people are most eager to learn, but that ignorance is most indifferent to learning.

In this dire lack of knowledge, human pride spreads its un- 147 fledged wings to the wind. How many rough cliffs there are! How many ridiculous vanities of philosophizers! What great discrepancy of opinions, what obstinacy, what impudence! What a number of factions, what differences, what wars! What uncertainties about things, what perplexity about words! What deep and impenetrable lairs of the truth! How many traps the sophists set with their thorns to block the way toward truth, hiding the straight path! As we know, this is the reason why Cato the Elder voted to banish Carneades from Rome.[168] What temerity on the one side, and what diffidence and desperation on the other, as great men attempt to grasp the truth! Pythagoras says that we may argue with equal force on both sides of any question, and that we may even debate whether this last assertion itself is true, namely, that everything is equally debatable.[169]

Some say that the truth lies deeply buried and sunk in a deep 148 pit, so to speak. As if it must be extracted from the obscure

tenda ueritas et uncis ac funibus eruenda, non scalis gratie et ingenii gradi-bus[228] *adeunda sit!*[229] Socrates ait: 'Hoc unum scio, quod nichil scio'. Quam humillimam ignorantie professionem ceu nimis audacem reprehendit Archesilas, ne id unum sciri asserens, nichil sciri. En gloriosa philosophia, que uel ignorantiam profitetur, uel ignorantie saltem notitiam interdicit! Circulatio anceps! Ludus inextricabilis!

149 *Contra Gorgias Leontinus, rethor uetustissimus, non modo aliquid, sed sciri omnia posse credit, non a philosopho tantum, sed ab oratore. Nempe qui, ut ait Cicero, omnibus de rebus oratorem optime posse dicere existi-mauit, quod certe ipse non potuit.*[230] *Non posset autem optime de rebus omnibus dicere, nisi optime omnes nosset. Idem sensit Hermagoras, qui non modo rethoricam, sed philosophiam omnem rerumque omnium notitiam tribuit oratori. Magna mediocris ingenii fiducia. Sed longe omnibus fiden-tior*[231] Hippias, scire se omnia profiteri ausus, ut non modo de li-beralibus studiis deque uniuersa philosophia, sed de mechanicis quoque plenam sibi gloriam usurparet. Dicerem diuinum homi-nem, nisi insanum crederem.

150 Sed quoniam iam nec sciri omnia, imo[232] nec multa per homi-nem certum est, et confutata iampridem atque explosa Achade-mia, ac reuelante Deo sciri aliquid posse constat, sit satis scire quantum sufficit ad salutem. Multi plus sapientes quam oportet periere, et dicentes se esse sapientes, ut ait Apostolus: 'stulti facti sunt, et obscuratum est insipiens cor eorum'. Michi ad sobrieta-tem sapere si contingat — quod sine multis, imo et sine ullis literis fieri posse illiterata utriusque sexus sanctorum cohors indicat — sa-tis erit, et feliciter agi mecum extimabo, neque unquam mei me

depths of the earth with hooks and ropes, rather than approached in the heights of heaven by ascending the stairs of grace and the steps of the intellect! Socrates says: "I know one thing: that I know nothing."[170] Arcesilaus criticizes this humble admission of ignorance as too bold, and says that we cannot even know that we know nothing.[171] What a glorious philosophy! It either confesses its own ignorance or forbids us to know our ignorance. O vicious circle! O inextricable riddle!

By contrast, the ancient rhetorician Gorgias of Leontini be-   149
lieved that both the philosopher and the orator could know not just one thing, but everything. According to Cicero, Gorgias "thought that the orator could speak perfectly about all subjects," although Gorgias himself clearly failed to do so.[172] And the orator could only speak perfectly about all things if he knew them all perfectly. Hermagoras agreed with him, and claimed for the orator not only rhetoric, but all of philosophy and human knowledge.[173] What great presumption in a mediocre intellect! By far the most confident of all was Hippias, who boldly declared that he knew everything, and who claimed consummate glory not only in liberal studies and in all branches of philosophy, but in the mechanical arts as well.[174] I would call the fellow divine, if I didn't think he was insane.

It is clear that we cannot know everything, or even know many   150
things. But the Academy was refuted and rejected long ago, and we can know something through God's revelation. Let us then be content to know what suffices for our salvation. Many people have perished who knew more than they should and who called themselves wise men. As the Apostle says: "They became fools, and their foolish heart was darkened."[175] It will suffice that I am able "to think soberly."[176] This can be achieved with little or no learning, as is proved by the legions of unlearned saints of both sexes. If I succeed in this, I shall consider myself fortunate and not regret my studies. As for these chattering ignoramuses, who are swollen

studii penitebit. Et hos garrulos ydiotas, qui, falso literarum nomine turgidi, dici amant quod non sunt, aut miserebor, aut odero,
aut ridebo, de rebus inanibus atque incognitis altercantes. Neque
illis iactantiam, nec tumorem pestiferum, nec omnino aliquid, non
ipsas certe diuitias, inuidebo, nunquam ad se se redeuntibus, semper foras effusis seque extra querentibus.

151   In finem literati nomen libens pono, et iam posui. Si indignum,
ut ueritati conscientieque satisfaciam, alioquin ut inuidie. De re
autem posteritas uiderit, si ad illam fame passibus peruenero; si
minus, obliuio. Viderit, inquam, posteritas incorrupta, quam ab
equitate iudicii non animorum perturbatio ulla, non odium, non
ira, non amor, liuorque, ueri hostes, impedient. Viderit illa, si me
nouerit. Iudices enim meos proculdubio non agnoscet; quippe
quos nec etas hec nouerit, uix uicinie notos sue. Viderit iudi-
cetque, et si horum sententiam approbet, acquiesco; si rescindat,
non ideo his irascor, sciens quanta sit in animis hominum potestas
affectuum. Hi sunt autem qui in me sententiam hanc dictarunt.
Fallor: unus enim, quem sepe hodie nomino, liuor fuit. Ille hanc
digitis suis scripsit, quam nec amor potuit mutare nec ratio. Cur
ergo irascerer amicis pro eo quod ab illorum hoste commissum
est? Si iniquitatem filii non fert pater, nec filius patris, quanto minus hostis iniquitas nocere debeat amico, presertim illius carcere ac
uinclis astricto, qui siquando sibi redditus fuerit, et suas et amici
iniurias sit ulturus.

152   Sunt multa preterea, que iracundiam, siqua esset, exemplorum
comprimant compescantque remediis. Nam que[233] unquam uel
doctrina uel sanctitas, *aut uirtus quelibet*[234] tam excellens fuit, ut ob-

with their false show of letters and who like titles they don't deserve, I shall pity or detest or deride them for wrangling about empty and obscure questions. And I shall not envy their boasting, their deadly arrogance, or anything else—especially their wealth. For they never look inside themselves, but constantly rush outwards and seek self-knowledge in external things.

In the end, I gladly renounce, and have already renounced, the 151 title of scholar. If it is undeserved, I thus satisfy the truth and my conscience; if it is deserved, I placate their envy. Posterity will decide the question, if the steps of fame carry me that far; if not, oblivion will resolve it. Let posterity decide, I say, for it is uncorrupted and its fair judgments unswayed by any passion like hatred, anger, love, or spite, which are the enemies of truth. Let posterity decide, if it hears about me. Without a doubt, it will not recognize my judges. The present age does not know them, and even their neighbors scarcely know them. Let posterity decide and judge. If it approves their verdict, I shall assent. If it overturns the verdict, I shall not be angry with these men, for I know what power the passions wield over human minds. These passions framed the verdict against me. No, I am mistaken. It was one passion, spite, which I keep naming so often today. Spite itself wrote this verdict in its own hand, and neither love nor reason could alter it. Why, then, should I be angry with my friends, when the evil was committed by their enemy? A father is not responsible for his son's unfairness, nor a son for his father's unfairness. So even less should an enemy's unfairness harm a friend, especially one who lies imprisoned and shackled by that very enemy! When he is liberated, this man will avenge both his own injury and that of his friends.

There are many examples that can repress anger, when it arises, 152 and remedies to restrain it. Has there ever been any learning or holiness or virtue so excellent that it escaped detractors? Indeed, as Livy writes, "the greater the glory, the nearer there is envy."[177] And so it is. Envy is a sluggish evil that cannot rise up into noble

trectatoribus non pateret? Imo quidem, ut Liuius ait, 'quo gloria
maior, eo propior inuidia'. Et sic est. Quanquam enim iners malum sit inuidia et altos in animos non ascendat, sed uipere in morem, iuxta Nasonis sententiam, humi serpat, familiare tamen illi
est alte glorie radices auidius insequi clarisque nominibus suum uirus infundere; non aliter quam subterranei quidam uermes, qui
proceras arbores radicum morsibus clandestinis et tacita labe per-
tentant. *Sic sepe tacitus seuit liuor; sed interdum magnis estuat passione*
animi silentium frangente clamoribus. Et Thersiten pede claudum, distor-
tum cruribus, humeris gibbosum, pectore concauum, caluastrum uertice,
atque pruriginosum, et Agamenoni Grecorum regi, et Achilli Grecorum for-
tissimo detrahentem publice Ylias narrat homerica, et Drancem Turno uer-
bis iniuriantem Eneys uirgiliana testatur. Sed hic miri nichil; est enim con-
trariis inter se naturale odium. Quanta in diuum Iulium et Augustum
Cesares uel ab amicis uel ab hostibus dicta sunt! Illud supra fidem stupeo,
quod Pescennius Niger, uir fortissimus, progeniem Scipionum, toto Romano
orbe precipuam, fortunatam potius dicebat esse quam fortem. Nullus hic
proculdubio liuor erat, sed libertas inconsulta iudicii. Verum hec et simi-
lia[235] *peregrina nobis atque longinqua sunt; ad propinquiora ueniamus.*[236]

153   Possem sanctos memorare, precipueque Ieronimum; sed pro-
fana materia et de solis literis sermo est. Itaque illos attingam, sed
non omnes, qui nostre propius sunt querele. Quis ergo in primis
Epycurum, intoleranda superbia siue inuidia siue utraque, detrahentem omnibus non audiuit, Pithagore, Empedocli, Timocrati,
quem, amicum licet, totis uoluminibus lacerasse traditur, quod in
philosophia paululum a se suisque insanis opinionibus discorda-
ret? Habent tamen et hi tres, et alii quos discerpsit, patientie materiam, quando idem et mire Platonem spernit, et contumeliosis-
sime Aristotilem uexat, ac Democritum, a quo ultimo que sciebat
in philosophicis cunta didicerat, et quem exigua mutatione uerborum in omnibus sequebatur, *hunc acrius*[237] infamabat, nempe qui
magistro caruisse gloriaretur et uideri uellet.

minds, but creeps on the ground like a viper, to cite Ovid.[178] But envy has a habit of pursuing the roots of lofty glory, and of injecting its venom into famous names, like certain underground worms that gnaw unseen at the roots of tall trees and secretly strive to topple them. Thus spite often rages in silence, but sometimes seethes with passion until it breaks its silence with loud cries. Homer's *Iliad* describes how Thersites — who is lame, crippled, hunchbacked, hollow-chested, bald, and mangy — openly disparages Agamemon, the king of the Greeks, and Achilles, their bravest hero.[179] And Virgil's *Aeneid* portrays Drances as insulting Turnus.[180] This is not surprising, for there is a natural hatred between opposites. How many things were said against the deified Julius Caesar and Augustus by both friends and enemies! But I am amazed beyond belief to read that Pescennius Niger, a very brave man, said that the family of the Scipios, illustrious throughout the Roman empire, was lucky rather than brave.[181] Still, he spoke not in spite, but from an irresponsible freedom of judgment. But these and similar examples are foreign to us and quite remote. Let us consider what is closer to home.

I could cite various saints, especially Jerome; but my topic is a 153 secular one, and we are only talking about learning. So I shall only mention some, and not all, who are related to the present dispute. To begin with, who has not heard how Epicurus, in his intolerable pride or envy, maligned everyone, including Pythagoras, Empedocles, and even his friend Timocrates? It is said that he disparaged them all in many works for disagreeing slightly with him and his insane opinions.[182] Yet these three philosophers, and others he reviled, have reason to be patient, for he treats Plato with extraordinary disdain, heaps abuse on Aristotle, and viciously defames Democritus. In fact, Epicurus had learned everything he knew about philosophy from Democritus, and had adopted the latter's teaching with only slight changes of terminology. But he boasted that he had no master, and wished to give this impression.

154　　*Secuti sunt in hac detrahendi libidine preceptorem suum Metrodorus*
　　　　atque Hermacus, supradictos quoque philosophos lacerantes, nec ullius ma-
　　　　gnitudini parcentes aut glorie.[238] Fuit et Zeno ipse maledicus atque ir-
　　　　risor, qui Crisippum, uirum acutissimum et eiusdem secum secte,
　　　　contemptim nominans, non Crisippum, sed Crisippam semper
　　　　diceret. Et non modo coetaneos, sed parentem philosophie Socra-
　　　　tem conuitiis ac maledictis incesseret, latinoque usus uerbo, credo,
　　　　ut peregrine lingue mordacior iocus esset, scurram Atthicum uoci-
　　　　taret.

155　　Quod ipsum scomma—si sic illud et non potius ledoria dici de-
　　　　bet—in eundem, apud quem hec scripta sunt, Ciceronem post ab
　　　　emulis uersum[239] est; quem ob insignem lingue festiuitatem dixere
　　　　aliqui consularem scurram: dignus iocus non illius uiri auribus ac
　　　　moribus, sed ore potius et scurrilitate iocantium. Iam Annei Se-
　　　　nece in Quintilianum atque in Senecam Quintiliani detractio nota
　　　　est. Erantque ambo uiri egregii, ambo Hispani; mutuis tamen
　　　　morsibus se se carpunt, atque alter alterius stilum damnat. Mirum
　　　　prorsus in tantis ingeniis!

156　　Solent enim docti indoctis esse odio ac stupori; horum illi igi-
　　　　tur, modo facultas affulserit, famam rodunt. Doctis, facie licet in-
　　　　cognitis, inter se cognatio multa est, nisi hanc liuor aut excellentie
　　　　appetitus abruperit (quod in his proximis duobus, inque aliis de
　　　　quibus ante diximus, euenisse credibile est). *Quibus quandoque ces-*
　　　　santibus, nouum dictu, claros inter uiros esse uidetur emulatio quedam,
　　　　quasi uentis quiescentibus tumens mare, cuius duplicem rei[240] *causam apud*
　　　　quosdam lego. Una est fauor discipulorum atque sequacium, qui libentius
　　　　quieturos contrariis sententiis in certamen trahit; altera uero paritas ipsa,
　　　　que, sine sensu eorum qui in comparationem adducuntur, spectantium iudi-
　　　　cia in diuersum agit, ut quamuis in se concordes duo uiri et passionibus

In this lust for disparaging, Metrodorus and Hermarchus fol- 154
lowed their teacher by abusing the above-mentioned philosophers
with no respect for their greatness or glory.[183] Zeno too was a
foul-mouthed scoffer, and he contemptuously referred to Chrysippus, a brilliant philosopher of the same school, always calling him
"Chrysippa." He not only heaped insults and curses on his con-
temporaries, but even on Socrates, the father of philosophy. He
called him "the Athenian buffoon," using the Latin word *scurra*, I
think, so that this foreign expression would give the jibe more
bite.[184]

This same taunt — or should it be called abuse? — was later 155
turned by rivals against Cicero himself, who relates these cases.
On account of his remarkable wit, some Romans called him "our
consular buffoon" — a jest worthy not of the orator's ears and character, but of the scurrilous mouths of the jesters.[185] The exchange
of insults between Seneca and Quintilian is well-known.[186] Both
men were distinguished, and both Spaniards, but they snap at
each other and each condemns the other's style. An amazing display in men of such intellect!

Men of learning usually inspire the hatred and wonder of the 156
ignorant, who carp at their fame, if given the chance. But even
when they don't know each other personally, men of learning feel a
certain kinship, unless their spite or their desire to excel destroys
it. (This was probably the case with the last two orators mentioned, and with the others discussed earlier.) But even when
these passions sometimes cease, wondrous to say, a sort of rivalry
arises between famous men, like a sea that still swells when the
winds are calm. In my reading, I find two reasons for this. The
first is the partiality of the disciples and followers of great men.
Their conflicting opinions draw into confrontation their masters,
who would prefer tranquility. The second is the equal validity of
great men's views, which inspires divergent judgments in their followers. Even if two men may be in agreement and free of passions,

liberi, uideantur tamen inter se taciti,[241] *quasi duo propinqui montes, aut totidem turres excelse, de altitudine eminentiaque contendere.*

157 *Cuius exemplum, nisi memoria me frustratur, est supra memoratum par uirorum Plato et Xenophon. Incidunt uero nonnunquam non his modo, sed superioribus etiam acriores dissensionum cause, non inuidia studiorum, sed profundis flammate odiis.*[242] Nam Salustii in Tullium atque Eschinis in Demosthenem, horumque in illos inuectiue, non ingenia neque stilos arguunt, sed mores, amarumque aliquid et hostile, imo uero pacatum nichil in se continent. Nulle ibi facetie, nullus iocus, sed certamen longe aliud, quam quod de literis aut pro gloria sumi solet. Cui collati omnes meorum iudicum aculei ludi sunt equissimo animo ferendi, dum preter hos ipsos quos audisti, mille alios memini de solis literis concertantes, nominatim homericos Aristarcum[243] ac Zoilum, uirgilianos Cornificium et Euangelum, ciceronianos Asinium et Caluum, dumque in animum Gaius uenit, ferox (fateor) sed minime rudis princeps, qui cogitauit, ut scriptum est, de Homeri carminibus abolendis, cur enim sibi non licere dicens, quod Platoni licuisset, qui eum e ciuitate quam constituebat eiecerit. Sed et Virgilii et Titi Liuii scripta et imagines parum abfuit quin ex omnibus bibliothecis amouerit, quorum alterum ut nullius ingenii minimeque doctrine, alterum ut uerbosum in historia negligentemque carpebat. *At Anneum Senecam, et tum quidem, et nunc maxime placentem, arenam esse sine calce dicebat.*[244]

158 *Et loquimur uiros, cum Leuntium, Greca mulier, imo, ut Cicero ait, meretricula, contra Theofrastum tantum philosophum scribere ausa sit.*[245] Quis hec audiens indignetur in se aliquid dici, cum in tales *a talibus*[246] talia dicta sint?

159 Nil superest aliud, nisi, ut non dicam te et aliquot *paucos, qui ad amandum non egetis stimulis, sed amicos reliquos*[247] censoresque[248] simul

they seem to contend silently for stature and eminence, like two neighboring mountains or two lofty towers.

Unless my memory deceives me, we see an example of this in 157 Plato and Xenophon, two men mentioned earlier. But sometimes even more bitter reasons for dissension affect men like these and others I have discussed, who are inflamed not by scholarly envy but by profound hatred. The invectives exchanged by Sallust and Cicero, and by Aeschines and Demosthenes, do not attack an opponent's intelligence or style, but his character; and they contain elements of bitter hostility rather than reconciliation. There are no witticisms or jests, but a struggle far different from those concerning letters or glory. Compared to this, all the stinging barbs of my judges are easily tolerated jests. For besides the examples you have heard, I recall a thousand other disputes solely concerned with literary questions: the Homeric scholars Aristarchus and Zoilus, the Virgilian critics Cornificius and Evangelus, and Cicero's friends Asinius and Calvus. Then I remember Caligula, an admittedly fierce emperor who was by no means uneducated. Yet it is recorded that he contemplated destroying the Homeric epics, and asked why he couldn't act as Plato had in banishing them from his imagined republic.[187] He nearly removed the writings and images of Virgil and Livy from all the libraries, censuring the former as a poet of no talent and little learning, and the latter as a verbose and sloppy historian.[188] As for Seneca, who was popular then and is even more popular today, Caligula called him "sand without lime."[189]

We are discussing men. But a Greek woman named Leontium, 158 whom Cicero calls a prostitute, dared to write against the great philosopher Theophrastus.[190] Hearing this, could one be indignant when attacked, when such figures were so attacked by such critics?

Nothing remains but to pray and beseech, not you and the few 159 friends who need no incentive to love me, but the rest of my

meos precer atque obsecrem, ut deinceps me, etsi non ut hominem literatum, at ut uirum bonum, si ne id quidem, ut amicum, *denique si amici nomen pre uirtutis inopia non meremur, at saltem ut beniuolum et amantem ament.*[249]

EXPLICIT[250]

friends and my censors. If they cannot love me as a man of letters, or as a good man, or even as a friend, at least let them love me, if my lack of virtue denies me the name of friend, as a benevolent and loving person.

THE END

INVECTIVA CONTRA EUM
QUI MALEDIXIT ITALIE

: I :

1 Nuper aliud agenti michi, et iandudum certaminis huius oblito, scolastici nesciocuius epystolam, imo librum, dicam verius ome-liam ingentem pariter atque ineptam, multo (ut res indicat) sudore confectam et magni iactura temporis, attulisti, dum e longinquo veniens, amice, hanc exiguam domum tuam, me visurus, adisses. Vix fuit tempus raptim trepidante oculo tantam nugarum conge-riem percurrendi, in quibus cum multa essent risu tacito digna po-tiusquam responso, heserunt tamen nonnulla memorie, quibus respondendum credidi, ut ostenderem illum sibi.

2 Qui quoniam michi nec vultu nec nomine notus est, nec quem percussus repercutiam scio, tu lues immeritus. Nec res nova est, ut culpa unius in supplitium vergat alterius. Quibusdam nocuit ve-nena gestasse, et in caput alterius comparata, alterius in perniciem reciderunt. Tulisti tu quo me ille conficeret: temetipsum confece-ris. Ille te verbis et fastidio sue ruditatis implevit: ego, siquid de-fuerit, reimplebo. Tu, etate iuvenis moribus senex et professor iu-ris, sede medius et iudica. Si suspectum Gallis natio te reddit italica, veritas ipsa et quicunque iustus iudex iudicet.

3 Primum quidem miror unde hec nunc, quo ve a demone meri-diano. Epystola enim mea, quam hic Gallie propugnator et oppu-

INVECTIVE AGAINST
A DETRACTOR OF ITALY

:   I   :

Recently, while I was busy with other things, and had long since   1
forgotten about the dispute, my friend, you brought me a letter,
having traveled a long way to visit me in this small house of
yours.[1] Written by some Scholastic, this letter was in fact a book,
or more truthfully, a massive and maladroit sermon, quite obviously composed at the cost of much sweat and a great waste of
time.[2] I scarcely had time for a fleeting glance to skim this vast
heap of nonsense, much of which deserves silent ridicule rather
than any reply. But a few passages stuck in my memory, and I
thought I must reply to them in order to reveal the author to himself.

Now, since I don't know this fellow either by sight or by name,   2
and thus whose blows I am returning, you may undeservedly pay
the price. Of course, it's nothing new for one person to be pun-
ished for another's offense. Merely conveying poisons has harmed
some people, and what was devised to take one person's life has
caused another's destruction. By bearing his letter, which sought
to ruin me, you have ruined yourself. He burdened you with his
verbiage and cloying boorishness; and whatever he omitted, I shall
supply. While you are young in years, you are old in character and
are a professor of law; so I ask you to sit between us and judge. If
your Italian birth renders you suspect to the Gauls, let the truth
itself and any just judge pass judgment.[3]

To begin with, I wonder why this question arises now, and   3
what noonday demon inspires it.[4] For unless I am mistaken, it has
been four years since I sent to the Roman pontiff Urban V, of holy

gnator Italie lacerandam sibi — difficilem certe provinciam — elegit, ad felicis sancteque memorie Urbanum quintum, Romanum Pontificem, ante hoc, ni fallor, quadriennium missa erat. Quid igitur rei est, ut vel tot annis orator iste tacuerit, vel nunc tandem caput extulerit, nisi quod parum sue iustitie tunc fidebat, sicut obstare sue iracundie nunc non potest? Dolent enim estuantque dum veritate tanguntur; more autem segnium bellatorum differunt, dum se clanculum adversus incautos ulciscantur.

4   Hec profecto et longi silentii et intempestivi alloquii causa fuit. Tum clarissima veri luce superatus obstupuit, atque ideo, veritus se commisisse impari duello, substitit; donec, emendicatis ostiatim stipendiariis, ut sic dixerim, auxiliis, omnesque quos invenire potuit libros, sive unum *Manipulum florum*, opus vere Gallicum, et quod Gallica levitas pro omnibus libris habet, in prelium secum trahens, auderet in aciem venire, nilque adversario denuntians e transverso sagittas fragiles iaculari. Qui, ne parum scolasticus videatur, et capitula et paragraphos et externe longam seriem scripture suis nugis interserit tanto nisu, ut ridiculus labor suus pene omnes qui illas audierunt aut legerunt hieme media sudare coegerit.

5   Compatior homini contra verum tam anxie laboranti; et tamen — mirum dictu — quisquis eum suscepte concertationis eventus exceperit, ipse iam se de adversariis suis fastidio vindicavit. Vinci potest, non inultus tamen; ita omnes affecit, sic capita omnium obtudit, ut pro se quisque neroneum illud exclamaret: "Utinam literas nescirem!" unusque omnium sermo esset. Literato stulto nichil est importunius; habet enim instrumenta quibus late suam ventilet ac diffundat amentiam, quibus ceteri carentes parcius insaniunt.

and happy memory, a letter which this defender of Gaul and attacker of Italy has chosen to tear apart, which is quite a difficult task.[5] Now, if this orator remained silent for so many years, and has only now reared his head, can there be any reason but this: that he had little faith then in the justice of his cause, just as now he cannot contain his anger? Some people feel pain and rage when they are stung by the truth. But like weary combatants, they put off the battle, hoping later to take revenge secretly on their unwary opponents.

This was clearly the reason for his long silence and his untimely address. Back then, the bright light of the truth overwhelmed him and struck him dumb, so that he stood fast, afraid that he had joined a mismatched battle. But eventually, by begging door to door, he called up mercenary reserves, as it were, and led into battle all the books he could find — or rather one volume, *A Handful of Flowers*, a truly Gallic work which the shallow Gauls consider a substitute for all other books.[6] Then he dared enter the field of battle, and without openly declaring war on his adversary, he shot his fragile arrows from an unexpected quarter. To avoid seeming insufficiently Scholastic, he laced his nonsense with paragraphs, chapters, and a long series of extraneous quotations. As a result of his great effort, his ridiculous labor caused nearly everyone who heard it or read it to break into sweat, even though it was midwinter.

I feel sorry for a man who labors so anxiously against the truth. And yet, strange to say, no matter how this controversy turns out, he has already taken revenge on his adversaries by disgusting them. He can be defeated, but he will not go unavenged. He so tormented everyone, pommeling their brains, that each cried out in Nero's words, "Would that I couldn't read!"[7] And everyone said the same thing. There is nothing more nauseating than an educated fool. He has the means of venting and spreading his madness, whereas people without such means spare us their insanity.

4

5

6   Ut vero iantandem his preludiis modus sit, prolocutor iste, non scribentis epystolam sed sermocinantis in morem, pro fundamento sui sermonis evangelicum illud assumit: "Homo quidam descende-bat a Ierusalem in Ierico," et reliqua. Ei michi, quid est quod ego audio, ex ore presertim literati hominis? Pro superum fidem, o ineptum ac turpe principium fabelle! Eo ne igitur miseriarum ac vesanie ventum est, ut quicunque cristicola, maximeque Pontifex Romanus, Avinione digrediens Romam petat, a Ierusalem descen-dere dicatur in Ierico, et non potius e sentina profundissima vitio-rum omnium, imo quidem ex inferno illo viventium, in Ierusalem dicatur ascendere? Huccine igitur res prolapsa est, ut Avinio, pro-brum ingens fetorque ultimus orbis terre, Ierusalem dicatur, Roma vero, mundi caput, urbium regina, sedes imperii, arx fidei catho-lice, fons omnium memorabilium exemplorum, Ierico nuncupetur?

7   O cor saxeum! o lubrica et effrenis lingua! Quenam hec fera-lis monstra licentie? Quenam ista temeritas, ne dicam rabies lo-quendi, dicam minus improprie, blaterandi? utque sermone utar homerico, "quod verbum sepem dentium transivit"? Debuit fauci-bus vox herere neque in apertum erumpere, doctis piisque omni-bus stomacum concussura! Dicam certe quod sentio: siquid fuisset ingenii, pudor e manibus calamum extorsisset, ne fede prorsus ora-tionis tale iaceret fundamentum, super quo boni nichil posset edificari. Quid enim, nisi pessimum, queso, dicturus sit qui, in ipso sermonis exordio, Petri sedem — Romam! — deprimens verbis inanibus, celotenus illam mundi fecem turpemque barbariem nita-tur attollere?

8   Sensi equidem in verbis illius hominis descendentis, imo vero habitantis in Ierico, seu Romanum Pontificem descendere facien-

But to set a limit now to my preface, this prosecutor speaks not   6
like a letter-writer but like a preacher, taking as the theme of his
sermon that familiar passage in the Gospel: "A man was going
down from Jerusalem to Jericho," etc.[8] Woe is me! What is this I
hear, and coming from the mouth of a learned man? May the gods
protect me, what a silly and shameful way to start a tale! Have we
sunk to such misery and madness that when a Christian — indeed,
the Roman pontiff — leaves Avignon to go to Rome, he is said to
"go down from Jerusalem to Jericho"? Shouldn't we rather say that
he has gone up to Jerusalem from the deepest dregs of all vices,
or indeed from the very hell of the living? Have we sunk so far
that Avignon — that immense disgrace and extreme stench of the
earth — should be called Jerusalem, while Rome — the capital of
the world, the queen of cities, the seat of empire, the citadel of the
Catholic faith, and the source of all remarkable models of virtue —
should be named Jericho?

O heart of stone! O slippery and unbridled tongue! What   7
monstrous products of bestial license are these? What is this rashness, not to say frenzy, in your speech or (more precisely) your
blathering? To use Homer's expression, "What word has crossed
the hedge of your teeth?"[9] Your voice should have stuck in your
throat, and not burst out into the open, stirring the displeasure of
all learned and pious men. I shall state plainly what I think. If the
man had any intelligence, shame would have wrested the pen from
his hands, and kept him from laying such a foundation for his foul
speech that nothing good could be built on it. Pray, can someone
utter anything but the worst rubbish, when from the very outset
he disparages Rome, the see of Peter, in empty words, and then
strives to praise to the sky the dregs of the world and its filthy barbarism?

Indeed, I sensed from the words of this man, who goes down to   8
Jericho, or rather dwells there, and who makes the Roman pontiff
go there, that he finds the name of barbarian painful and unpleas-

tis, grave sibi ac molestum barbari nomen. Sic deformes quoque formose dici amant ac videri, nec ulla est tam turpis, que obiectam sibi turpitudinem non in contumeliam trahat. Non mutatur autem veritas rerum humanis affectibus; alioquin quis non et nature bonis ornatissimus esset et fortune? Non habet autem quo michi suscenseat ille vir. Hanc ob causam dico: si ad barbari nomen irascitur, irascatur non michi—neque enim ego nominis huius inventor sum—sed historicis omnibus atque cosmographis, qui tam multi sunt, ut eos epystola una vix capiat. Quorum quis est omnium, qui non barbaros Gallos vocet? Rei huius indaginem sibi linquo, ut industriam eius exerceam. Historias evolvat, inveniet— credo—unde mecum in gratiam revertatur.

9   Iste autem declamator, multiplicibus verbis herentem ossibus barbariem tentat excutere, multa de Gallica morum elegantia disputans, quorum omnium ut scias quam vera sint cetera, victus temperantiam primam ponit. In quo michi quidem tam aperto mendacio irridere visus est, potius quam laudare. Quid enim nisi irrisio est, in aliquo id laudare, cuius contrarium publice notum sit? Atqui omne humanum genus interroget, una voce contrarium respondebit. Si, preter suos, nulli hominum fidem habet, querat a Sulpicio Severo et inveniet ab illo, omnium—meo quidem iudicio—Gallorum disertissimo, obiectam Gallis edacitatem: ea vero, nisi fallor, ab hoc barbaro laudate victus temperantie est adversa.

10   Mitto alia, non enim Gallicos mores damno, et de eis quid sentiam satis in epystola ad Urbanum videor dixisse. Quamvis enim et a feritate morum Franci olim dicti et feroces aliquando habiti,

ant. In the same way, unattractive women like to be called beautiful, and to appear so; and no woman is so ugly that she does not take as an affront any reproach of her ugliness. But the true state of affairs is not altered by human feelings. Otherwise, wouldn't every one of us be well endowed with the blessings of nature and fortune? This fellow has no reason to be angry with me, and I'll explain why. If the name of barbarian angers him, let him not be angry with me—I didn't invent the name—but with all our historians and cosmographers, who are so many that they can scarcely be named in a single epistle. Is there any one of them who does not call the Gauls barbarians? I leave it to him to explore the question, which will put his industry to the test. Let him peruse the history books. I think he will find reason for being reconciled with me.

Yet with his multitudinous words, this rhetorician attempts to 9 shake off the barbarism bred in his bones by expatiating at length about the elegance of Gallic behavior. You may judge the truth of his other arguments by the fact that he begins by citing the Gauls' moderation in eating. This is such an obvious falsehood that I thought he was mocking them rather than praising them. For isn't it mockery to praise someone for a quality when the public knows just the opposite is true? So let him ask the entire human race. With one voice, everyone will say just the opposite. If he only trusts his countrymen, let him consult Sulpicius Severus. He will find that this man—who in my opinion was the most eloquent of the Gauls—reproaches the voracity of the Gauls.[10] Unless I am mistaken, voracity is the antithesis of the moderation in eating praised by this barbarian.

I say no more than this, for I am not condemning Gallic behav- 10 ior. I think I fully expressed my opinion concerning them in my letter to Urban. Although they were once called Franks because of their feral behavior, and were considered quite fierce, they are now completely different.[11] They are a lightheaded and lighthearted

nunc tamen longe alii, leves letique homines sunt, facilis ac iu-
cundi convictus, qui libenter adsciscant gaudia, curas pellant ludendo, ridendo, canendo, edendo et bibendo— puto—intelligen-
tes ad literam illud Sapientis Hebreorum, quod semel dixisse non
contentus, perquam sepe repetiit: 'Nonne melius est,' inquit, 'co-
medere et bibere et ostendere anime sue bona de laboribus suis?'
Et iterum: 'Omnis enim homo qui comedit et bibit et videt bonum de labore suo, hoc donum Dei est.' Et rursus: 'Hoc itaque
michi visum est bonum, ut comedat quis et bibat et fruatur letitia
ex labore suo.' Et preterea: 'Vade ergo,' inquit, 'et comede in letitia
panem tuum, et bibe cum gaudio vinum tuum.' Et non solum
quod hoc bonum esset, sed quod bonum aliud non esset, adiecit:
'Laudavi,' inquit, 'igitur letitiam, quod non esset homini bonum
sub sole, nisi quod comederet et biberet atque gauderet, et hoc solum secum afferret de labore suo.' Quis, queso, tanti viri consilio
non ederet libenter ac biberet et gauderet? Sapientes Galli, qui et
per se ipsos hec sapiunt et sapientibus crediderunt, inque consuetudinem naturamque verterunt. At quod eodem libro ait idem:
'Cogitavi in corde meo abstrahere a vino carnem meam,' ceu Galli-
canis legibus contrarium adversantur ac respuunt.

: II :

II Hactenus excusasse sufficiat epystole mee principium illud improprium, ut ipse asserit, et ineptum. Ego quidem de re maxima
summo hominum scripturus, magis proprium, fateor, non inveni;
nec adhuc video, preter hominem illum suum descendentem a Ierusalem in Ierico, quid accomodatius materie, quid in rem aptius

people, whose company is easygoing and cheerful. They gladly indulge in pleasures, and drive away their cares by playing, laughing, singing, eating and drinking. I think they take literally the counsel given by the Jewish Sage.[12] Not content with saying this once, he often repeated it: "There is nothing better for a man than to eat and drink and show his soul the goods of his labors."[13] And again: "For every man who eats and drinks and sees the good of his labor, this is the gift of God."[14] And once more: "Thus it seemed good to me for to eat and drink and take joy from one's labor."[15] Further he says: "Go then and eat your bread with joy, and drink your wine with a merry heart."[16] And not only because this is good, but the only good, he adds: "Therefore I praised joy, for there is nothing better under the sun but to eat and drink and be merry, and this alone shall he take with him from his labor."[17] Who, I ask, on this great man's advice would not gladly eat and drink and be merry? The sages of Gaul, endowed with their own wisdom and believing the ancient sages, converted these words into their custom and their nature. But when in the same book it says "I thought in my heart to withdraw my flesh from wine," they oppose and reject the passage as contrary to their Gallic laws.[18]

: II :

Let this suffice to defend the opening of my letter, which he declares "improper and inept."[19] For my part, since I was writing to the highest of men about the greatest matter, I confess I could find no more proper beginning. Even now, I fail to see what could be said more appropriately on the subject or more aptly in the situation, unless it was his man going down from Jerusalem to Jericho. Nor do I understand at all what was missing from my exordium, except perhaps for the authority of the writer. Let the Gauls in-

dici possit; nec prorsus intelligo, quid principio illi desit, nisi sola forsitan scribentis autoritas. Fingant enim Galli se credantque quod volunt; licet enim cuique de se suisque de rebus opiniones favorabiles atque magnificas animo fabricari; suntque qui hoc faciunt, ut ille ait, 'felices errore suo.' Ad hoc opus sane nulla gens promptior quam Galli. Ceterum opinetur ut libet, barbari tamen sunt, neque de hoc inter doctos dubitatio unquam fuit; quamvis ne id quidem negem, nec negari posse arbitrer: esse Gallos barbarorum omnium mitiores.

12   Sed hic barbarus, nostrarum rerum vituperationes suarum laudibus intermiscens, non irati tantum sed furentis in morem, nullo ordine multa in nos, stomaci impos, evomuit, magnum, credo, aliquid se se existimans, cui impune maximis obtrectare malitia temporum sit permissum. Quorum ego partem magnam sciens transeo, quod nec responso certe, nec audientia dignam duco.

13   Atque in primis varietates urbis Rome, quas hic quidem usque ad curiositatem ridiculam prosecutus est, figuras lune varias Romano statui comparando, quasi Roma sola, et non urbes ac regna omnia, multoque magis singuli homines, mutentur assidue, et temporali vicissitudini tam diu simus obnoxii, donec pervenerimus ad eterna. Babilon illa vetustior funditus ruit, Troia itidem et Carthago, Athene insuper et Lacedemon et Chorintus, iamque nil penitus nisi nuda sunt nomina. Roma non in totum corruit, et quanquam graviter imminuta, adhuc tamen est aliquid preter nomen. Muri quidem et palatia ceciderunt: gloria nominis immortalis est.

14   Quid hic, velut in re insolita, tot lune varietatibus opus erat, nisi ut astrologum, imo ut lunaticum, se probaret? Indignetur Gallus ut libet. Non prius alme urbis quam totius orbis fama deficiet; semper altissimus mundi vertex Roma erit. Et si propter invi-

vent and believe what they choose about themselves. We are all free to construct favorable and exaggerated notions about ourselves and our affairs. Indeed, people who do so are "happy in their own error," as the poet says.[20] Truly there is no race more prone to this than the Gauls. In any case, let him believe as he pleases. They are still barbarians, and among the learned there has never been any doubt about this. Still, I would not deny one thing, nor do I think it can be denied. Of all the barbarians, the Gauls are the mildest.

But this barbarian mixes his criticisms of my views with his 12 own praises in a confused order that betrays more rage than anger. Unable to control his bile, he has vomited many charges against me, apparently considering himself someone great, who is licensed by the wickedness of our times to disparage the greatest men with impunity. I intentionally pass over a large part of these charges, for I don't think they deserve my attention, much less a reply.

First of all, he cites the vicissitudes suffered by the city of 13 Rome, which he details with a ridiculous extreme of pedantry, comparing the Roman state to various phases of the moon, as if Rome alone changed constantly — and not all cities and realms, and even more, individual persons — and as if we were not all subject to the vicissitudes of time until we pass to eternity. Ancient Babylon collapsed utterly; so did Troy and Carthage, as well as Athens, Sparta, and Corinth; and today they are absolutely nothing but mere names. But Rome did not entirely collapse, and even though severely diminished, she is still more than a mere name. True, her walls and palaces have fallen; but the glory of her name is immortal.

Why did he need to cite so many phases of the moon, as if this 14 were an unusual case, except to prove that he is an astrologer, or rather a lunatic? Let the Gaul vent his indignation as he likes. The fame of our kindly mother city will last as long as the globe.[21] Rome will always be the highest summit of the world. Even if

diam aut odium aut segnitiem causam ve aliam et pontifices et
principes illam sui deserant, gloria illam comitabitur; illi autem,
ubicunque et undecunque fuerint, Romani pontifices Romanique
principes vocabuntur. Quid hic Gallus strepit? Quid barbarus fre-
mit? An mentior? Negabit magnum aliquid fuisse, cuius post tot
secula reliquie nunc etiam tante sunt, ut nec Gallia nec Germania
nec ulla barbaries se illarum glorie conferre audeat? Non presumet
id, credo, quamvis natio sit contemptrix omnium et miratrix sui.

15   Sed quid aget? Scio. Laudabit Gallie tabernas — pulcra laus so-
brii hominis — quas ego tamen illac nuper transiens et eversas vidi
et desertas. Laudabit patrie quietem, quam profecto turbidam in-
quietamque prospexi. 'Sed non est ibi mutatio, quanta est Rome.'
Quis hanc rem reique causam non videt? Minutarum rerum ruina
magna esse non potest; procul absunt ab hoc metu: nunquam cadet ex alto, qui in imo iacet. Roma igitur ex alto cecidit, non cadet
Avinio. Unde enim caderet, aut quomodo decresceret, que est
nichil?

16   Pudet me, fateor, erroris eius, qui cum videatur aliquid legisse,
non erubuit summis ac preclaris infima rerum et abiectissima comparare, quodque est stultius, anteferre. Sed excuset eum utcunque
natalis zone dulcedo quedam feminea, non virilis, et qui multum
in rebus hominum usus valet, ac presertim rudium. Viri enim
egregii virtutis ope vincunt omnia. Certe magni homines fuerunt,
qui in media orti barbarie et nutriti, pudore tamen originis, se Romanos dici voluerunt, splendore nominis gloriosi, quos, quoniam
omnibus noti sunt, enumerare non attinet.

17   Gallus noster, ut video, nollet esse non barbarus, et libenter in
ceno, ubi educatus est, residet. Parcendum imbecillitati animi,

envy, hatred, indolence, or other reasons cause Rome's pontiffs and princes to desert her, glory will still attend her. And no matter where they are or whence they come, they will be called Roman pontiffs and Roman princes. Why is this Gaul bawling? Why is this barbarian howling? Do I lie? Will he deny that Rome was something great, when even after so many centuries her ruins are still so vast that neither Gaul nor Germany nor any barbarous nation dares rival their glory? He won't presume as much, I believe, even though his nation despises others and admires itself.

But what will he do, then? I know. He will praise the taverns of 15 Gaul. Fine praise from a sober fellow! Yet on a recent trip there, I found them ruined and deserted. He will praise the quiet of his homeland. Yet it was utterly confused and unquiet when I saw it. "But there is no change of fortune in Gaul as great as that in Rome." Does anyone fail to see this, and the reason for it? Minor things can suffer no major ruin, and are far removed from fearing this. Nothing that lies in the depths can fall from a height. Rome fell from her height, but Avignon will not fall. Whence could she fall? Or how could she decrease, when she is nothing?

I confess that his delusion fills me with shame. For although he 16 appears to have done some reading, he did not blush to compare the lowest and basest things with the highest and grandest, and more foolishly, to prefer the former. But in any case he may be excused by the charm of his native clime — a feminine charm, not a manly one — as well as by the force of habit, which wields great power over the affairs of men, especially the ignorant. Aided by virtue, outstanding men overcome all obstacles. Clearly there have been great men who were born and raised in the midst of barbarism, but who were ashamed of their origin and chose to be called Romans, proud of this splendid name. Yet since they are known to everyone, there is no point in listing them.

But our Gaul, I see, would prefer to remain a barbarian, and is 17 happy to stay in the mud where he was reared. We must forgive

consuetudine obruti atque assurgere non valentis; nam et lutum suibus et palus ranis et tenebre vespertilionibus grate sunt. Illud autem quis excuset aut quis ferat, quod vilissimi loci studio optimis nobilissimisque detrahere et, affectu incondito atque insulso, veritatem tentet opprimere? Ita enim querit, quasi nesciat id quod omnibus cristicolis notum est, atque utinam non Saracenis paganisque etiam notum esset, ne tam late ludibrio haberemur.

18   'Et quam,' inquit, 'angustiam Ecclesia passa sit in Gallia, ego sine dubio non audivi.' Surdaster est, imo surdus omnino, qui tonitrum non audit. Multa hic de quieto et prospero Ecclesie statu, intra cloacam illam palpitando, prosequitur. O carnalis homuncio, nichil habens spirituale, vere unus ex illorum grege, de quibus agens Cicero: 'Nichil,' inquit, 'animo videre poterant, ad oculos omnia referebant.' Ergo nec angustia nec molestia ulla est, nisi dum corpus in carcerem et vincula conicitur? Quid si animus, peccatorum nexibus coartatus, miseri servitii iugum subit? De hoc barbarus iste non cogitat. Non vidit hec igitur, nec audivit, quia scilicet aures oculosque in carne habuit; quos si in spiritu habuisset, audisset utique vidissetque miras et miseras angustias, quas nulla compedum durities, nullus carcer equaverit; vidisset morum veterum ruinam, que multo est gravior ac funestior quam murorum.

19   Et querit, quasi solus in Ierusalem peregrinus, quam angustiam Ecclesia passa sit in Gallia. Ego autem quero: ubinam gentium parem pati potuisset angustiam? Et, o quam multa se hic stilo offerunt! Sed frenandus est, ne prodeat quo non decet; imo quidem

the weakness of his mind, which is weighed down by custom and unable to rise up: for hogs love mud, frogs love the swamp, and bats love darkness. But who could forgive or tolerate it, when in his zeal for this vile place he disparages excellent and noble cities, and when in his confused and senseless devotion he attempts to suppress the truth? He poses questions as if he didn't know what is known to all Christians. I only wish the facts were unknown to the Saracens and pagans, so that we weren't a laughing-stock throughout the world.

"I have certainly not heard that the Church suffered any dis-   18
tress in Gaul," he writes. A person must be hard of hearing, or rather completely deaf, if he can't hear thunder. Then he goes on at length about the tranquil and prosperous state of the Church, groping in that sewer. O carnal little man who lack any shred of spirituality, you are truly one of the herd described by Cicero: "They could see nothing with the mind, but judged everything by their eyes."[22] So is there no distress or discomfort, except when the body is cast into chains and prison? What if the mind is constrained by the bonds of sin, and submits to the yoke of wretched servitude? This barbarian gives it no thought. He has not seen or heard any of this, no doubt because his eyes and ears were trapped in the flesh. Using the eyes and ears of the spirit, he would have seen and heard astounding and appalling forms of distress that no harsh chains or prison could equal. He would have seen the ruin of ancient morals, which is far more serious and deadly than the ruin of ancient walls.[23]

He asks what distress the Church suffered in Gaul, as if he   19
were the only pilgrim in his Jerusalem. But I ask this: where in the world could the Church have suffered such distress? How many thoughts occur to my pen! Yet I must keep my pen from venturing where it is improper to go — or rather, where it is proper to go, but pointless, for one simple reason. As Cicero writes in his *Letters to Atticus*: "Hippocrates forbids administering medicine to the des-

379

decet, sed non expedit, eo maxime quia, ut in *Epystolis ad Athicum*
ait Cicero, 'desperatis Hippocras vetat adhiberi medicinam,' et michi satis odiorum veritas invisa conflavit. Neque ideo mentiri inci-
piam, sed tacere, et orationis hanc partem sponte pretervehar;
quodsi boni discipuli habet ingenium, qui magistri titulo gloriatur,
multa ex his paucis eliciet, quibus intelligat Romana Ecclesia quid
in Gallis angustie passa sit, meque vera locutum vel invitus in silentio fateatur.

20   Est tamen laudatoris illius certa quidem, utque est mos presens, non insulsa calliditas. Licet enim. Turpibus blanditiis bonum
opus, epyscopium, aucupatur, ad quod obtinendum sciat se aliis,
quam verborum, retibus indigere. Nedum enim salse nuge et inanes, sed omnis illic eloquentia Ciceronis hac in parte succumberet.
Unum ei posset opitulari. Posset , ut ego mentitus videar, epyscopus fieri. Quod si accidat, gaudebo quamvis verborum adversario
profuisse. Homo enim prodesse homini, dum possit, fatigari nunquam debet, quoque minus est gratie, minor amicitie nexus aut
sanguinis, eo maius est meritum. Sit epyscopus igitur, me favente,
candidamque (ut aiunt) togam sui habitus nigris atque deformibus
maculis inquinet, dum vel turpibus placitisque mendaciis, falsis
laudibus, adulationibus viro indignis, denique vel eorum gratia, vel
mei verique odio, perveniat quo suspirat. Sit epyscopus Placenti-
nus aut Laudensis, sit epyscopus Mentiensis, sit epyscopus Adu-
lensis, et mitram falsariis debitam mereatur. Michi, qui epyscopatum nolo, quique eum gradum sepe olim michi non oblatum
modo, sed ingestum, semper recusavi, preferens cuntis opibus libertatem, nichil blanditiis opus est. Loquor ergo liberius, ca-
riusque michi est odium veritate quesitum, quam barbaro illi erit,
si successerit, dignitas parta mendacio.

perately ill."[24] Telling the odious truth has already stirred up enough hatred against me. So rather than beginning to lie, I shall be silent, and gladly pass over this part of his treatise. Now, if this fellow, who vaunts the title of master, has the intelligence of a good pupil, a few words will offer him many indications of what distress the Roman Church suffered in Gaul; and he will confess that I spoke the truth, even if he does so unwillingly and in silence.

Still, this eulogist displays a certain cunning which is scarcely 20 dull-witted, in keeping with current customs. And well he may. With his base flattery, he sets his traps for a fine position — a bishopric. Still, he should know that he will need other nets, not merely verbal ones, to obtain the post. In this cause, not only his witty and empty trifles, but even all of Cicero's eloquence would suffer defeat. One thing alone would help him. He might be named a bishop, so that I am proved a liar. Should this happen, I shall rejoice that I have aided him, even if I opposed him in words. When it is in their power, people should not weary of aiding others. Indeed, the less goodwill he enjoys, and the weaker the bonds of friendship or blood, the greater is his merit. So let him become a bishop, with my approval. And let him defile the so-called "candid toga" of his official garb with black and unseemly stains. By using base and flattering lies, false praise, and unbecoming flattery, let him attain the rank he desires with the favor of such means, and with hatred of me and the truth. Let him become bishop of Piacenza or Lodi, bishop of Metz, or bishop of Adula; and let him earn the miter that is assigned to counterfeiters.[25] For myself, I never desired a bishopric: preferring freedom to all riches, I often refused the office when it was offered to me, and even thrust upon me.[26] Hence, I have no use for flattery, and speak more freely. Hatred bred by the truth is dearer to me than any high rank bought with lies will be to that barbarian, if he succeeds.

: III :

21 His omissis, ad id venio quod adversus urbem Romam convitiator
hic murmurat. Ubi illud mirum: quod vulgares homines atque
inopes rationis, suas non dicam iniurias, sed offensas quaslibet,
magni existimant, cum sic negligant alienas. Ubi enim populum
barbarum nominavi — quod etsi non blande, iuste tamen feci — ceu
gladio ictus exclamavit; nec in me nunc aliter excandescens quam
in Cristum olim princeps sacerdotum: 'Audistis,' inquit 'blasphemiam.' Nec advertit, qui videri doctus vult, in solam Divinitatem
esse blasphemiam. Ipse autem, alme urbi venenose detractionis
contumelias irrogando, esse credit excusabilis — tanta est barbari et
tam temulenta presumptio! — quamvis non ego blasphemiam ut
ille, sed blasphemie proximum dico urbem sacram profano convitio lacerare.

22 Quanta servorum audacia et quanta protervia, ubi semel forte
dominorum vinculis elapsi sunt! Non valentes aliter se ulcisci,
contra dominos maledictis insurgunt, effunduntque in ventos dolorem animi ulcerosi et, quasi canes invalidi metu, latrant. Recor-
datur hic barbarus antiqui servitii et, adhuc pene callosum Romano iugo collum habens, fugitivus servus de domina sua procul
tremebundus obloquitur. Que, o si filiis suis — illis dico maioribus — Deus omnipotens pacem daret fraternamque concordiam,
quam cito, quam facile rebellantem barbariem iugo illi veteri, itali-
cis ut olim viribus adiuta, compesceret!

23 Id si antea fuisset incognitum, nuper apparuit, dum vir unus,
obscurissime originis et nullarum opum atque, ut res docuit, plus

: III :

Leaving this topic, I come to the slurs that this reviler mutters   21
against the city of Rome. Here's an oddity. Vulgar and weak-
brained people take seriously the insults and slights that affect
them, but ignore those that affect others. When I called his people
barbarians — an observation that was not flattering, but was just —
he cried out as if he had been struck by a sword. Burning with anger against me, as the high priest once raged at Christ, he said:
"You have heard his blasphemy."[27] Although he wishes to appear
learned, he doesn't realize that blasphemy can only be uttered
against the Divinity. But this same man, who inflicts the con-
tumely of his poisonous detractions on our kindly mother city, believes he will be pardoned — so great and so intemperate is this
barbarian's presumption! Unlike him, I do not call it blasphemy,
but something near blasphemy, when his profane insults tear at
the holy city.

How great is the temerity and impudence of slaves, once they   22
have slipped from the bonds of their masters! Unable to take revenge in any other way, they rise up with curses against their masters, pour forth to the winds the pain of their ulcerated spirit, and
bark like dogs paralyzed with fear. Our barbarian recalls his ancient servitude. With his neck still callous from the Roman yoke,
this fugitive slave trembles as he slanders his mistress from afar. If
only omnipotent God would grant peace and brotherly harmony
to her sons — her oldest sons, I mean — how quickly and easily
Rome would reduce the rebellious barbarians to their ancient
yoke, aided as of old by Italian forces!

If this was unclear before, it recently took shape when one   23
man — a person of obscure origin, without wealth, and possessing
(as events showed) more courage than constancy — dared to support the state on his weak shoulders and to proclaim the defense

animi habens quam constantie, reipublice imbecillos humeros sub-
icere ausus est et tutelam labentis imperii profiteri. Quam subito
erecta omnis Italia! Quantus ad extrema terrarum Romani nominis terror ac fama pervenit! Et quanto gravior pervenisset, si tam
facile esset perseverare quam incipere! Eram ego tunc in Galliis, et
scio quid audierim, quid viderim, quid eorum, qui maximi habe-
bantur, in verbis inque oculis legerim. Negarent modo forsitan,
negare enim eculeo absente perfacile est; vere autem omnia tunc
pavor oppleverat: adeo adhuc aliquid Roma est! Sed de his nil amplius, ne barbarum meum, forte acriter cogitantem quid est Italia,
quid sua barbaries, quamque nulla rerum paritas, nulla proportio
vero indicio metientem, ad desperationem metus impelleret.

24   Quanquam, quomodo ego illum vel cogitare vel sapere aliquid
rectum credam, qui quodam loco sui sermonis interroget, quid per
nomen 'sacre urbis' intelligam? Nec videtur audivisse, civili cautum
lege, ut is locus, ubi non dicam liberi, sed servi etiam corpus, nec
corpus modo integrum, sed pars corporis humo condita est, reli-
giosus habeatur. Quam religiosa igitur videri debet urbs Roma,
ubi tot virorum fortium atque illustrium, ubi tot principum integra corpora, ubi denique—quod in hac re maxime estimandum
censeo, ut urbs ante omnes alias sacra sit—tot apostoli gloriosi,
tot sancti martires, tot almi pontifices atque doctores, tot sacrate
virgines requiescunt!

25   Omnis profecto sacri nescius et profanus hauddubie totus est,
qui Romam merito 'sacram' dici seu dubitat seu miratur. Et certe,
si civili iure leges 'sacratissime' nominantur, idque nemo sane mentis unquam arguit, quam 'sacra' dici potest urbs, legum domus
augustissima, et eorum omnium qui latinas condiderunt leges aut
altrix aut genetrix! Quid notissime autem rei argumenta conquiri-

of the tottering empire.[28] How suddenly all of Italy was aroused! What great terror and rumors, inspired by the name of Rome, spread to the ends of the earth! And how much greater the effect would have been, if persevering in his plan had been as easy as undertaking it! Since I was in Gaul at the time, I know what I heard, what I saw, and what I read in the words and the eyes of those who are considered great. Today they might deny it: when the rack has been removed, it is quite easy to deny the facts. But at the time, fright truly took hold of everyone and everything, for Rome still means something! But no more on this subject. If my barbarian were to examine closely the true nature of Italy and his own barbarous land, measuring them by a true standard, he would find how unequal and disproportionate they are, and fright would drive him to desperation.

All the same, how can I believe that he has any correct ideas or 24 knowledge, when at one point in his treatise he asks what I mean by the "holy city"? He seems not to have heard the stipulation of the civil law that wherever a body is buried — the body not only of a free man, but of a slave, and not merely an entire body, but even part of one — that place is considered "religious."[29] How religious, then, the city of Rome must appear! In it repose the integral remains of so many valorous and illustrious men and rulers! In it, indeed, there lies at rest — and this I consider the crowning point that makes Rome the holy city *par excellence* — a mighty host of glorious apostles, sainted martyrs, kindly pontiffs and doctors, and holy virgins.

A person must be completely ignorant of all holiness and in- 25 deed entirely profane to doubt or marvel that Rome is justly called "sacred." Clearly, if in civil justice laws are called most "sacrosanct" — and no one in his right mind ever contested the fact — then the city of Rome can be called "sacred," since she is the most venerable home of laws, and the mother or nurse of all the jurists who framed our Latin laws![30] Why should we search for proofs of

mus, cum expresse 'sanctissimam et temperantissimam' urbem Seneca, et non sacram modo, sed 'sacratissimam' civitatum nuncupet lex civilis? Quam hic fortasse despiciet, quia non Avinione per protonotarios pape, nec est dictata Parisius per magistros scilicet parlamenti.

26   Sed quid illi facias ineptie? Querit enim curiose admodum Gallus noster quid est quod Urbani felicitatem verbis extulerim, an quia secundum virtutem operari felicitas una sit, an quia in suam sedem reduxit Ecclesiam exulantem; primum namque fatetur, at secundum negat. O cervicositas Deo et hominibus odiosa! O cristati Gallorum vertices ac superbi, eque falsum asseverare et verum negare dispositi! Ego autem utrunque confiteor. Nam, et secundum virtutem agere felicitas vite huius et ad felicitatem vite alterius via est, et virtuosius quicquam nego fieri ab homine potuisse quam Ecclesiam, pro qua Cristus sanguinem suum fudit, de sanguinibus liberasse, suamque in sedem, e ceno illo erutam, reduxisse, modo in finem generosum illud sanctumque propositum tenuisset. Quidni igitur mirer virtutem viri illius? Que tanta fuit, ut vix michi possibile videretur, virum talem in illa natum esse barbarie, nisi a Satyrico didicissem

summos posse viros et magna exempla daturos
vervecum in patria crassoque sub aere nasci.

Neque illud ignorarem: humani generis rerumque omnium creatorem paris ubique potentie atque ad illam exercendam, nec impediri locis aut temporibus nec iuvari.

27   Ceterum, ut norit hic barbarus quantum ab eius opinione dissentio, ego et virtutem viri illius et in primis sanctum propositum illud miror, et contrarium sentientis, non sani hominis, sed Galli

this well-known fact, when Seneca expressly calls the city "most sacred and most temperate," and when civil law calls her "the most sacrosanct" of cities?[31] But this fellow will perhaps despise the civil law because it was not dictated at Avignon by the pope's protonotaries, or at Paris, if you please, by the masters of parliament.

But how can you deal with such stupidity? Our Gaul asks very   26
curiously why I praised Urban's happiness. Was it because our sole happiness consists in acting virtuously, or because he moved the exiled Church back to its own home?[32] He admits the first reason, but denies the second. O stiff-necked obstinacy, hateful both to God and to humankind! O proud and crested Gaulish heads, ready to assert what is false and to deny what is true! I admit both reasons. Living virtuously is both our happiness in this life, and the path to our happiness in the next life. And I say that no one could have acted more virtuously than this pope. For if only he had carried out his noble and holy plan, he would have freed from bloodshed the very Church for which Christ shed his own blood, and would have plucked it from the mud and led it back to its seat. Why shouldn't I admire the man's virtue? It was so great that it seemed impossible that such a man had been born in that barbarous land, if I hadn't learned from the Satirist:

> Men of high distinction and destined to set great examples
> May be born in a dullard air and in the land of mutton-
>   heads.[33]

Nor was I unaware that the Creator of the human race and of all things has equal power everywhere, and that time and place neither aid nor hinder him in exercising his power.

But so that this barbarian knows how strongly I disagree with   27
his opinion, I admire the man's virtue and particularly his holy project. (Anyone who thinks the opposite I regard as having the brain not of a sane person, but of a rooster suffering from a severe

caput egrotantis ac pituita gravissima laborantis existimo, nec omnino illi aliquid, preter constantiam, defuisse.

28   Itaque sepe nunc michi ad memoriam redeuntem acri simul ac fideli increpatione compello: 'Heu, pater beatissime, quid fecisti? Unde ista mollities? Quis te fascinavit ut principium tam grande desereres? Quis te autem clarior, si quod gloriosissime ceperas ad extremum spiritum perduxisses, ad quem, ut patuit, iam propinquum veniens, grabatulumque tuum ante proximam Petri aram, cuius hospes ac successor eras, ferri iubens, Cristoque et sibi gratias agens, qui tibi hunc animum atque hoc consilium prebuissent, in loco illo sanctissimo felicissimam animam emisisses? Quis te, oro, vixisset honestius? Quis equanimius obiisset? Siquis enim forte post te ad oscenum illum fornicem Ecclesiam reduxisset, culpe ille reus sue rationem Cristo redderet: tu, facti conscius eximii, recto calle isses ad superos. Nunc tu ipse — heu, quis te perdidit? — tu, inquam — dicam quod in animo est — sponte ad vomitum redisti, non audiens Petrum iterum exclamantem: "Domine, quo vadis?"'

29   His illum horumque similibus lamentis exagito, que sibi scribere meditabar, et iam ceperam, si mori paululum distulisset. Valde enim eum, facie licet incognitum — dicam verius virtutem eius, michi mundoque notissimam — amavi, et familiaritatem secum, quanta esse poterat in tanta rerum omnium imparitate, contraxeram. Uti ergo tota eius patientia atque humanitate decreveram, utranque feliciter iampridem, dum adhuc in illa miseria moras traheret, acri quadam expertus epystola, quam ipse non patienter modo, sed gratanter ac benigne recepisse, seque illam diligenter perlegisse, et in ea 'multa bene et eleganter dicta' — utor ad

case of the pip.)[34] I think that the only thing the pope lacked was constancy.

Often now, when he returns to my memory, I address him with a sharp but devoted reproach: "Alas, blessed father, what have you done? Whence comes this weakness? Who cast a spell on you to make you desert your great undertaking? Who would have been more renowned than you, if only you had persisted in your plan, so gloriously begun, to your final breath? And who more renowned if, as you approached your end—which was clearly at hand—you had ordered your bed carried to the altar of Peter (whose guest and successor you were), had rendered thanks to him and to Christ (who had given you this courage and counsel), and had released your happy soul in that most holy place? Who, pray, would have lived more honorably? Who would have died more serenely? If anyone after you had brought the Church back to that obscene brothel, the guilty party would have accounted to Christ for his misdeed; while you, conscious of your lofty deed, would have gone straight to heaven. But now you (alas, who corrupted you?) —yes, you!—and I shall speak my mind—have yourself of your own will returned to that vomit, and did not hear Peter again exclaiming "Lord, where are you going?"[35]

In my mind, I scold him with these and similar laments, which I intended to write—I had already begun a letter—if only he had put off dying a little longer.[36] For even if I didn't know him personally, I loved him greatly. Or more truly, I loved his virtue, which was known to me and to the whole world, and I had formed as close a friendship with him as the great disparity in our conditions allowed. I had therefore decided to take full advantage of his patience and humanity, two qualities that I had happily experienced while he lingered in that miserable place. At that time, he received a rather sharp letter of mine not merely with patience, but with gratitude and courtesy; and having read it through carefully, he replied that it contained "many fine and elegant things"—

28

29

literam verbis suis — et tam verborum elocutione quam sententiarum pondere laudanda comperisse respondit.

30   Atque in finem (ut Gallo nostro bilem excitem) dignatus est
meam, ut ipse ait, prudentiam et eloquentiam, quas ego, fateor,
non agnosco, ac zelum, quem ad comune bonum me habere et ipse
dicit et ego non dissimulo, multipliciter commendare, seque me videndi avidum, et gratiis ac favoribus prosequi dispositum profiteri.
Que profecto non diceret aut dixisset, si tam male loqui visus essem sibi, arguendo moram eius ad quem spectabat in loco illo pessimo atque turpissimo, et hortando ut ad sedem sibi et Ecclesie
debitam se transferret, quam barbaro huic nostro, ad quem omnino nil pertinet, visus sum. Et litere quidem apostolice thesauri
instar penes me sunt eruntque dum vixero, non tam quia pape,
quam quia optimi ac sanctissimi viri sunt, nec tam ideo quia laudes meas, quam quia illius pie testimonium voluntatis evidentis-
sime protestantur.

: IV :

31   Post hec autem, anno elapso, cum et ipse Romam petisset et ego,
voti compos, illam sibi alteram epystolam misissem, que hunc barbarum in furorem vertit, scripsit ille michi iterum. Quibus in literis, parumper questus quod, cognito eius desiderio, ad visitandum
eum essem tardior, deinde eam ipsam tarditatem excusans sub obtentu mee adverse valetudinis, ad extremum iubere regibus solitus
me rogavit ut, quam primum sine persone mee periculo aut in-
commodo possem, ad se pergerem, cupide tunc etiam me visurum
et animi mei quieti consulere intendentem. Et ego, parendi avidus,
ibam, nisi me casus horribilis ex itinere medio retraxisset.

I am quoting his very words—and that he found it praiseworthy
both for my choice of words and for the gravity of my thoughts.[37]

And in conclusion (I say this to stir the bile of our Gaul), 30
he deigned to commend in many ways my "wisdom and eloquence"—these were his words, although I don't profess to claim
such qualities—as well as my zeal for the common good, which he
cited and which I don't disguise. He declared that he was eager to
meet me, and was disposed to shower me with kindnesses and favors. Clearly he wouldn't say this, or wouldn't have said this, if in
reproving his lingering on in that evil and filthy place—a matter
that concerned him personally—and in urging him to move to the
seat worthy of himself and the Church, I spoke as ill as it seems to
this barbarian, whom it does not concern. I keep this apostolic letter with me like a treasure, and shall keep it as long as I live, not
because it is the pope's letter, but because it is the letter of a noble
and saintly man, and not because it sings my praises, but because
it bears unmistakable witness to the man's pious intentions.

: IV :

Then a year later, when he traveled to Rome, and I saw my wish 31
fulfilled, I sent the pope another epistle—one that drives our Gaul
into a rage—and he wrote to me again.[38] In his letter, he briefly
complained that I had been slow to visit him after learning of his
wishes, but he forgave my slowness with the excuse of my ill
health. In the end, this man who was wont to command kings
asked me to come to him as soon as I could without incurring personal danger or inconvenience: for he said that he desired to see
me and intended to set my soul at ease. Eager to obey, I would
have gone to him, if a terrible mishap had not forced me to turn
back halfway in my journey.[39]

32   Ita michi tantum illum patrem, quem videre non contigit, amare saltem licuit ac vereri atque eius acta laudare, illud in primis quod hic barbarus nec laudare vult nec vituperare audet; quamvis, ut sentio, libenter id faceret, nisi quod nondum sic omni ex parte depuduit; inter barbaros quoque adhuc reverentie aliquid, sed perexiguum est virtutis. Quem ipse ego uberius laudarem, nisi perseverantiam defuisse conspicerem. Illum tamen, in silentio respondentem audio, non potuisse unum se tot susurronibus obstare, contra Cristum atque eius Ecclesiam coniuratis. Quam excusationem nec admitto nec respuo, quod et verum scio et, si fundatus esset super firmam petram, non dubito flatus tales alto animo potuisse contemni.

33   Parcat illi Cristus, cuius negotium agenti ea trepiditas intercessit, illi vero gaudeant et triumphent, qui nunc in inferno viventium Beunense vinum bibunt, nec Prophetam audiunt exclamantem: 'Expergiscimini, ebrii, et flete et ululate omnes qui bibitis vinum in dulcedine, quoniam periit ab ore vestro.' More prophetico rem futuram quasi presentem, imo iam preteritam[1] narrat, et quasi iam evenerit quod necessario eventurum est; etsi enim nondum periit, peribit illico. Tempus est, enim, ut iamiam vilissime iste dulcedines in amaritudines convertantur. Et an ego cecutiens (ita enim iste me vocat), qui hec quasi presentia iam hinc video, an ipse magis exoculatus, qui fulgore panni captus exigui nichil videt aut cogitat preter epyscopatum, quem, mendacio fidens, stulta et cupida mente preoccupat? Non autem facile dictu est quam me delectaverit viri huius ingenium: tam recte, tam proprie Phariseorum usus est verbo, qui veritatem Deique opera predicanti responderunt: '"In peccatis natus es totus, et tu doces nos?" et eiecerunt eum foras.' Quid, queso, convenientius poterat secte illius defensor acerrimus contra eum qui quem factis expugnare non potest, verbis

Thus, although I didn't get to see that great father, I could at   32
least love and revere him, and praise his actions—especially the
one action that our barbarian neither wants to praise nor dares to
blame. (Still, I sense that he would gladly blame it, except that he
hasn't yet completely lost his sense of shame. Even barbarians have
a modicum of respect, if scarcely a drop of virtue.) I would praise
the pope even more lavishly, if I hadn't witnessed his lack of perse-
verance. Still, despite his silence I hear him answer that by himself
he was no match for the mutterers who conspire against Christ
and his Church. I neither accept nor reject this excuse: for I know
that it is true. If the pope had stood on a foundation of solid rock,
I don't doubt that he would have been able to despise their blus-
tery pride.

May Christ spare this man, who was overcome by trepidation   33
while doing the Lord's business. And let those rejoice and triumph
who now drink the wine of Beaune in their living hell, and who do
not hear the prophet's cry: "Wake up, you drunkards, and weep;
and wail, all you wine-drinkers, over the sweet wine, for it is cut
off from your mouth."[40] In his prophetic way, he describes a future
event as present, or rather as past, and what must necessarily occur as having already occurred. Even if the wine is not yet cut off,
it will soon be cut off. For it is time that the sweetness turned to
bitterness. Am I perhaps blind—as this fellow calls me—when I
see these things as if they were present? Isn't it he, rather, who is
sightless because he is enthralled by the splendor of the cloth, and
sees nothing but a bishopric which, confident in his lies, he foolishly and avidly anticipates usurping? It is hard to describe how
much this fellow's genius delighted me, when he so justly and
properly cited the words of the Pharisees. In response to a man
who proclaimed the truth and God's works, they said "'You were
born entirely in sin, and you would teach us?' and then they drove
him out."[41] I ask you, could our staunch defender of this sect have
spoken more aptly, deafening with words an enemy he cannot de-

oppugnat, si vel sic ubi nec paradisi amor proficit nec inferni metus aliquid saltem pudore proficeret?

34   Hec sibi pro responso Gallus noster accipiat, cur Urbanum
dixerim felicem, tunc scilicet dum virtuosissime operando non se
solum, sed totam felicitaret Ecclesiam. Atque ut me in sententia
fixum norit, unum istis adiciam, modo cautum michi sit ne lese
maiestatis accuser. Non equidem sic insanus sim, ut Romano Pontifici legem ponam, cum ipse sit legifer omnium cristianorum, aut
sibi sedem statuam qui sedium dominus est cuntarum. Si enim, ut
apud Cordubensem legimus,

> Veios habitante Camillo,
> illic Roma fuit,

quanto magis ubi Romanus Pontifex habitat, ibi quoque concesserim Romam esse? Unum hoc, si celitus datum esset, optarem: uti,
sicut tunc Camillus, ubi primum licuit, Veiis omissis, Romam rediit, ita nunc pontifex.

35   Audebo enim dicere, temerarie forsitan sed fideliter, et ni fallor
vere, quod si hoc sibi placeret, cui divinitas rei huius arbitrium dedit, non modo honestius sanctiusque, sed tutius ibi esset quam in
ulla penitus parte terrarum, neque ingenti pretio cogeretur a predonibus redimere suam et Ecclesie libertatem, quod predecessor
suus in sancta fecit Avinione, de quo et ipse tunc graviter in
consistorio questus est, et ego, dum sibi scriberem, non silui.
Quam Romane sedis angustiam Gallus iste non vidit, dum ad
enarrandas felicitates avinionicas magno nisu implumes alas expli-
cuisset? Sed recentis magneque miserie vel oblitos alios credidit,
vel oblitus est.

36   Unum his nunc etiam fide ac simplicitate subnectam: non opor-
tuisse nec oportere Pontificem Romanum armata manu Romam

feat with facts, so that he might achieve by shame what he could not achieve through the love of heaven or the fear of hell?

Let our Gaul take this for my reply, when he asks why I called 34 Pope Urban happy, precisely when his virtuous deeds rendered both him and the entire Church happy. And to show him that I remain firm in my opinion, I shall add one more point, on condition that I cannot be accused of *lèse majesté*. I am not so mad as to legislate to the Roman pontiff, who is himself the legislator for all Christians; nor would I determine the pope's see, when he is the lord of all sees. If the Cordovan poet tells us that

> when Camillus lived at Veii,
> Rome was there,

then how much more should I recognize as Rome the place where the Roman pontiff lives?[42] I would only wish for one thing, if heaven would grant it. Just as Camillus left Veii and returned to Rome as soon as he could, so too may the pontiff![43]

Speaking boldly but loyally, and truthfully, unless I am mis- 35 taken, I am bold to say that if the idea pleased the pope, to whom divine power assigned the decision, he would live there not only with greater honor and sanctity, but also with greater safety than anywhere else on earth. And he would not be forced to ransom his liberty and that of the Church by paying an immense sum to brigands, as his predecessor did in holy Avignon — an outrage that he earnestly bewailed in consistory, and that I mentioned in writing to him.[44] Didn't our Gaul behold the distress of the Roman see, when he spread his unfledged wings with great effort to sing the felicities of Avignon? But he believed that others had forgotten its recent great misery, or he had himself forgotten it.

Let me now add a further remark, made with equal loyalty and 36 sincerity. The Roman pontiff had no need, and has no need, to travel to Rome under armed guard. His authority protects him better than swords, and his sanctity better than breastplates. The

petere, tutiorem illum facit autoritas quam gladii, sanctitas quam
lorice. Arma sacerdotum sunt orationes et lacrime et ieiunia et virtutes et boni mores: abstinentia, castitas, humanitas, mansuetudo
actuum ac verborum. Quid signis militaribus opus est? Satis est
crux Cristi: illam solam tremunt demones, homines reverentur.
Quid tubis aut bucinis? Sufficit alleluia. Certe Iulius Cesar post
tot bella, tot victorias, non armatus urbem Romam, sed cum
inermi exercitu inermis victor introiit. Cesarem loquor, ut ad id de
quo agitur efficacius argumentum sit. Si sic enim venit Cesar, quid
putemus Petrum?

37   Scio autem quid calumniator noster obiciet. 'Inermis,' inquiet,
'venit Petrus atque ideo interfectus est.' Ita enim quodam *Apologe-*
tici sui loco, Romam multos innocentes homines iugulasse ait,
atque ideo merito a Satyrico 'sevam' dici. Nec intelligit, nolo dicere
ydiota, 'sevum' pro 'magno' poni solitum, iuxta illud *Eneydos* primo:

> sevus ubi Eacide telo iacet Hector

cum fuisse magnum Hectorem, non crudelem constet, et illud
eiusdem:

> maternis sevus in armis
> Eneas,

quem ubique scilicet pium dicit, hic 'sevum' dixit, id est 'magnum.'

38   Et est hauddubie non artificiosa quidem, sed insidiosa prorsus
et hostilis obiectio. 'Multi,' inquit, 'perierunt Rome sancti viri.'
Sed et multi quoque aliis in urbibus. 'Plures tamen Rome.' Quis
non videt unde hoc? Plures eo conveniebant, nempe ad mundi caput et imperii sedem. Pereundi autem causa fuit non regionis atro-
citas, sed religionis adversitas. Et volebat Cristus urbem suam,

arms of priests are their prayers, tears, and fasts as well as their
virtues and good morals: abstinence, chastity, humanity, and mildness in words and deeds. Why do they need military ensigns? The
cross of Christ is enough: before it demons tremble, and mankind
worships. Why do they need trumpets and bugles? The Alleluia is
enough. We know that Julius Caesar, after his many wars and
many victories, did not enter the city of Rome armed, but entered
as an unarmed victor with an unarmed army.[45] I mention Caesar
as a most effective argument on the present topic. For if Caesar
came unarmed, what shall we think of Peter?

But I know what our slanderer will object. "Peter came un-   37
armed," he will say, "and therefore was killed." In a passage of his
Apology, he writes that Rome slaughtered many innocent men, and
is therefore rightly called "fierce" by the Satirist.[46] This fellow —
not to call him an ignoramus — doesn't know that "fierce" is often
used to mean "great," as in Book One of the *Aeneid:*

> Where under the spear of Aeacides fierce Hector lies
> prostrate.[47]

Everyone knows that Hector was great, not cruel. In the same
poem, he writes:

> Aeneas fierce in his mother's armor.[48]

Everywhere else, he calls Aeneas "pious," but here he wrote
"fierce," meaning "great."

Then there is an objection which is clearly not ingenious, but   38
utterly insidious and hostile. "Many holy men," he says, "died in
Rome." But many also died in other cities. "Yet more died in
Rome." Who doesn't see why? More people were gathered there,
for it was the capital of the world and the seat of the empire. And
the cause of their death was not the hatefulness of the region, but
the hatred of their religion. It was with the martyrs' abundant
blood that Christ chose to consecrate as his own this city, which

quam et temporalium dominam iam fecerat et spiritualium facere
disponebat, uberiori sanguine suorum martirum consecrare.

39   Romanus fuit, non infitior, Nero qui occidit Petrum; sed Romani fuerunt qui Neronem occiderunt. Idem de Domitiano deque
aliis dici licet. Vertat se quocunque libet detractoris ingenium
atque odium: paucos fuisse Romanos inveniet qui sanctos con-
demnaverint, multosque qui vindicaverint; nec tantum apostolorum et martirum, sed sui proprii sanguinis, quamvis ignarum rei,
romanum tamen ultorem sibi Cristus elegit. Romanus fuit utique
Cristi ultor, cum Gallus fuerit flagellator, ut post dicam.

: V :

40 Audiamus nunc Gallum, seu verius corvum nostrum, qui candidam plumam fusco mendacio denigravit et didicit Cesarem atque
Antonium salutare. Audiamus, inquam, crocitantem et rauco strepitu suas amentias repetentem. Quia enim vinum Beunense vitupero, ut ipse ait—ut ego fateor, non adoro—rursus exclamat: 'et
audistis,' inquit 'blasphemiam!' O indigna viro, et pudenda prorsus, exclamatio! Verum minus forsan impropria, quam superior
fuit. Nam quid scimus, an iste sit illorum unus, 'quorum Deus
venter est,' ut ait Apostolus? Si sic est enim, qui contra vinum loquitur, utique contra ventrem, atque ita contra Deum suum loquitur; et videri potest species blasphemie.

41   Ego autem nec contra vinum, nec contra aliquod Dei donum
loquor, sciens quoniam que fecit Deus bona sunt omnia; sed ebrie-
tatem gulamque vitupero, quam non Deus, sed humana sibi fecit
improbitas. Et quoniam sepe bona aliqua, culpa abutentium, mali

he had already made the mistress of temporal affairs and which he was preparing to make mistress of things spiritual.

I don't deny that Nero, who killed Peter, was a Roman. But 39 those who killed Nero were also Romans. And the same may be said of Domitian and others. Let this detractor direct his wit and hatred wherever he likes. He will find few Romans who condemned the saints, and many who avenged them. As the avenger not only of the Apostles and martyrs, but also of his own blood, Christ chose a Roman, if one unaware of his role.[49] Christ's avenger was a Roman, then, but his scourger was a Gaul, as I shall later show.[50]

: V :

Now let us hear our Gallic rooster, or more truly, our raven, who 40 has blackened his white feathers with dark lies and learned to hail Caesar and Antony.[51] Let us hear him croaking, I say, and repeating his madness in hoarse squawks. Since I disparage the wine of Burgundy,[52] as he says — and I admit that I don't love it — he again exclaims: "You have heard his blasphemy!" What an utterly shameful exclamation, unworthy of a man! Yet it is perhaps less improper than the first. Do we know whether this fellow is one of those "whose God is their stomach," as the Apostle says?[53] If this is the case, someone who speaks against wine also speaks against the stomach, and thus against his God; and this can appear to be a sort of blasphemy.

Now, I say nothing against wine or any other gift of God, since 41 all things created by God are good. But I blame drunkenness and gluttony, which were not created by God but by man's wickedness. It has been found that some good things, through the fault of those who misuse them, often furnished material for evil — as wine

materiam fuisse compertum est, ut vinum ebrietatis, aurum ava-
ritie, ferrum sevitie formaque libidinis, optavi ego, ut cum damnosa quorundam Beunensis vini sitis et noceret Ecclesie et fre-
nari aliter non posset, vinum ipsum, unde ea nascitur, e medio
tolleretur.

42   Hanc potor egregius blasphemiam vocat, quasi (quod absit)
contra Cristum aliquid sim locutus, pro cuius reverentia et amore
vinum illud, quamvis in se bonum, odi, fateor. Et quid michi iratus Gallus occinat, non impertinens est audire. 'O nobilis vindemia,' inquit 'o venenum preciosum,' et hoc unum forsitan non
inepte, 'venenum', inquam, non corporum, sed mentium. His addidit: 'super omnia vina dulce, salutiferum et iucundum.' Hoc
utique non ineptum modo, sed falsum est. Sed omittamus de vinis
loqui, ne quem despicimus imitemur.

43   'Quam misera est,' inquit, 'et inepta tuae maledictionis occasio!'
O quam flebiliter sue felicitatis iniuriam fert! I nunc, nega vini
dolium loqui, nega Bacchi sacerdotem, qui contra vinum suum
suasque delitias hiscere ausum dicat esse blasphemum. O celum, o
terra, o humanum genus, o catholica plebs fidelis Cristo! Deo nostro sueque fidei vinum Beunense preponitur, nec ipsius Cristi decus aut voluntas, sed vini illius oportunitas ad summe rerum
consilium evocatur; et ego, tanti mali causam perosus, pene sacri-
legii reus agor, cum non solum tamen vinum illud accusem. Sunt
et alia quedam, de quibus tacere iubet Plato, iubet pudor. Transea-
mus igitur hinc, et id potius audiamus, qua se suumque bonum
summum imprecatione fraterculus hic flammatus ulciscitur.

44   'Propter quod,' inquit, 'non intres in os eius et dulcis sapor tuus
per eius fauces non transeat.' Quid vobis videtur? An non satis

for drunkenness, gold for greed, iron for cruelty, and beauty for lust. And since certain men's pernicious thirst for the wine of Burgundy was harmful to the Church and could not be slaked in any other way, I wished that we could get rid of the very wine that caused this problem.

Our illustrious toper calls this blasphemy, as if I had said some- 42
thing against Christ. Heaven forbid! It is because of my reverence and love for Him that I detest this wine — I confess it — no matter how good it is in itself. But what this angry Gaul croaks at me deserves to be heard. "O noble vintage," he says, "O precious poison!"[54] (This last word alone may be apt, in the sense that it poisons the mind, rather than the body.) Then he adds: "More than all other wines, it is sweet, healthful, and delicious." A statement that is not only foolish, but false as well. But let us stop talking about wine, lest we imitate a man we despise.

"What a wretched and foolish pretext for your slanders!" he 43
says. O how dolefully he endures this affront to his happiness! Go now, and deny that a barrel of wine can speak. Deny that he is the priest of Bacchus, since he calls blasphemer anyone who dares speak out against his wine and his delights. O heaven, O earth, O human race, O Catholics faithful to Christ! This fellow prefers the wine of Burgundy to our God and his faith; and to decide the greatest matters, he summons not the glory or will of Christ, but the merits of his wine. And for detesting this cause of such great evil, I nearly stand charged with sacrilege, although my accusations were not aimed at wine alone. There are other things which Plato and shame forbid me to mention.[55] Instead, let us move on, and hear what curse this inflamed little friar utters to avenge himself and his highest good.

He writes: "Enter not into his mouth, then, and let not your 44
sweet savor pass through his throat." What do my readers think of this? Hasn't he avenged himself splendidly? Truly, he could wish me nothing worse than what he judged worst for himself. But this

magnifice ultus est? Et sane nil peius optare michi poterat, quam
quod sibi pessimum iudicaret. Michi autem affecto aliter ac nu-
trito ea imprecatio levis est. Si nec Beunense nec omnino vinum
ullum biberem, tamen lete viverem. Itaque de gustu fideliter respondeo, quod pater Augustinus de olfactu, ciceroniano pene usus
verbo: 'De illecebra,' inquit, 'odorum non satago nimis: cum absunt, non requiro; cum adsunt, non respuo, paratus eis semper[2]
carere. Ita michi videor, nisi forsitan fallor.' Ita ego de omni vino
michi videor, quamvis et ipse multo facilius falli possim. Ab experientia quidem et sanctorum patrum ab exemplis, ab Anneo demum Seneca didicisse potui, quod satis est vite hominum panis et
aqua—vite hominum dixit, sed non gule. Quam sententiam carmine nepos eius expressit:

> satis est populis fluviusque Ceresque.

Sed non populis Galliarum. Neque ego, si essem Gallus, hoc dicerem, sed Beunense vinum pro summa vite felicitate defenderem,
hymnis et metris et cantibus celebrarem.

: VI :

45 Sum vero Italus natione, et Romanus civis esse glorior, de quo non
modo principes mundique domini gloriati sunt, sed Paulus apostolus, is qui dixit: 'non habemus hic manentem civitatem.' Urbem
Romam patriam suam facit, et in magnis periculis se Romanum
civem, et non Gallum natum esse, commemorat; idque tunc sibi
profuit ad salutem. Sed hic barbarus ad vituperium sacre urbis,
cuius laudibus nec lingue omnium disertorum nec libri omnes
sufficiunt, os impurum aperire ausus, multa dicit, que nec relatu
quidem digna sunt.

curse has little effect on someone with different views and tastes. If I never drank any Burgundy, or any other wine at all, I would still live happily. I may boldly answer about this taste, as St. Augustine did about the sense of smell, nearly borrowing Cicero's words: "I don't bother much about the charms of perfumes. When there are none, I don't seek them; when there are some, I don't avoid them; but I am always prepared to forego them. This is how I feel, unless perhaps I am deceived."[56] And thus I too seem to feel about all wines, although I too may be more easily deceived. From my own experience, from the example of the holy Fathers, and from Seneca, I have learned that bread and water suffice for human life — for life, I say, not gluttony.[57] And Seneca's nephew Lucan expressed the same view in his poem:

A river and Ceres suffice for the peoples.[58]

But not for the peoples of Gaul. And if I were a Gaul, I would not say this, but would defend the wine of Burgundy as the greatest happiness in life, and would celebrate it in hymns, poems, and songs.

: VI :

In fact, I am Italian by birth, and glory in being a Roman citizen, 45 just as the rulers and lords of the world gloried, and even the apostle Paul, the same man who said: "Here we have no lasting city."[59] He makes the city of Rome his homeland, and in moments of great danger recalls that he is a Roman citizen, not a Gaul — a fact that helped save him.[60] Yet in order to disparage the sacred city, which cannot be praised sufficiently by the tongues of all eloquent men or by all the world's books, this barbarian has dared to open his impure mouth, saying many things that are not even worth repeating.

46   Quod gravissimum Romane glorie vulnus est, contra illam Bernardus, durissimis convitiis armatus, inducitur. Nota res est. Qui de consideratione agens, forte si diligentius cunta considerasset, gentem famosissimam omnium, que sub celo sunt, parcius infamasset. Fecit tamen, et licere sibi debuit calamo suo scribere quod occurrit. Quid hic dicam? Non ego contra sanctum virum loqui velim, eum maxime, quem in quibusdam scriptis meis valde aliquando laudaverim. Qui si sanctus non esset, quantumlibet magnus in reliquis, facilis esset et expedita responsio. At nunc quidem, etsi non contra sanctum, de sancto tamen loqui nichil prohibet. Multa quidem, loquendo et scribendo, multa redeunt in animum, que dilapsa videbantur.

47   Damnavit iste (nunc recolo) Bernardus Claravallensis abbas, de quo sermo est, Petrum Abelardum, literatum quendam virum. Hinc iratus Berengarius Pictavensis, vir et ipse non infacundus ac discipulus Petri, contra Bernardum librum unum scripsit, non magni quidem corporis, sed ingentis acrimonie, de quo postmodum a multis increpatus se excusat, et quod adolescens scripsisset, et quod sibi viri sanctitas nondum penitus nota esset. Horum certe neutrum michi competit, nam nec de Bernardi sanctitate sum dubius et adolescens esse dudum desii. Sed illud dico, quod—licet hodie procul dubio sanctus sit—fieri potest ut, dum ad Eugenium scripsit, nondum forsitan sanctus esset. Sanctitas enim, sicut omnis virtus, non cum homine nascitur, sed studio queritur et augetur, et frequentatis actibus in habitum transit. Itaque michi aliud assumo, quod in quadam excusatoria epystola ad epyscopum Mimatensem Berengarius idem ait: 'Nonne abbas homo est? nonne nobiscum navigat "per hoc mare magnum et spatiosum inter reptilia, quorum non est numerus"? Cuius navis etsi prosperiori feratur navigio, tamen serenitas maris in dubio est.'

As the gravest wound to Rome's glory, he introduces St. Ber-   46
nard to attack her, armed with harsh rebukes. The story is well-
known. Perhaps if Bernard had considered all the facts more carefully in writing his *On Consideration*, he might have been more
moderate in defaming the most famous people on earth.[61] But he
defamed them, and he was clearly entitled to write down whatever
occurred to him. What can I say about this? I would not like to
speak against a saintly man, especially a man whom on occasion I
have highly praised in some of my writings.[62] If he weren't a saint,
no matter how great he was in other respects, answering him
would be an easy and effortless matter. But as it is now, nothing
forbids me to speak about this saint, if not against him. As I speak
and write, may things now return to my mind that I thought had
faded away.

This Bernard of whom we are speaking was the abbot of   47
Clairvaux. As I now recall, he once condemned a certain man of
letters named Peter Abelard.[63] Angry at this, Berengar of Poitiers,
who was himself an eloquent man and Abelard's student, wrote a
book against Bernard—not a long book, but one filled with enormous bitterness.[64] Later, when many reproached Berengar, he
apologized by saying that he had written as a young man and that
he had not yet fully recognized Bernard's saintliness.[65] Neither of
these excuses applies to me, for I have no doubts about Bernard's
saintliness, and I ceased to be young a long time ago. But I say
this. Bernard is doubtless a saint today, but he was perhaps not yet
a saint when he wrote to pope Eugene.[66] For like other virtues,
saintliness is not innate in a person, but is acquired; it increases
with practice, and becomes a habit through repeated actions. So I
borrow another passage that this same Berengar wrote in an apol-
ogetic letter to the bishop of Mende: "Isn't an abbot a man?
Doesn't he sail with us through 'this great and wide sea, wherein
are things creeping innumerable'? Even if his ship makes a prosperous voyage, the calm of the sea is in doubt."[67]

48   Ego vero Bernardi navim portum iam tenere non ambigo; sed, dum scriberet, haud dubie non tenebat. Homo erat et, in carne positus, passionibus subiacere poterat. Notum est illud Iohannis Osaurei non de sanctis quibuslibet, se de ipsis apostolis: 'Nam etsi sancti sunt,' inquit, 'homines tamen sunt: etsi vinci a carne non possunt, quasi iam spirituales, tamen percuti possunt, quasi adhuc carnales.' Potuit, aliqua forte lacessitus iniuria, Bernardus illa scribere; et multa irati homines dicunt, quorum postea illos pudet. Esto autem. Cesset ira, animi repens motus ex aliqua ortus offensa. An non naturale inter aliquas nationes est odium? Et profecto Gallorum gentem infestissimam nomini Romano apud Crispum, et de immanitate gentis Gallorum et de infestissimo odio in Romanum nomen apud Livium legimus, et sic esse realiter experimur.

49   Ut cessent tamen haec omnia, nec ira ulla nec odium Bernardum impulerit, et fuerit plane sanctus, dum id scriberet, quamvis ambrosiane sententie sit adversum, ubi ait: 'quis autem vivens tutus possit ac sine trepidatione laudari, qui et de preterito meminit se habere quod doleat, et de futuro videt sibi superesse quod timeat? Quis vero hominum in hoc corpusculo positus debeat sibi quicquam vendicare de meritis?' Nota sunt reliqua. Sed ita fuerit sanctus in vita, quid hic responsionis inveniam? Non reprehendam Bernardum, sed laudatores — hoc vituperatore eodem ipso nec negante nec indignante — maiores obiciam.

50   Ambrosius, in proemio epystole *ad Romanos*, de eis loquens: 'Hi enim,' inquit, 'caput sunt omnium gentium.' Mirum valde; nec excepit Gallos. Mox, super textu, gaudium suum testari dicit apostolum, quod cum Romani regnent in mundo — nec excepit Galliam — subiecerunt se fidei Cristiane. Dicet autem Gallus: 'Romanorum iste potentiam et imperium, non virtutem laudat.' Audiat

By now, I am sure, Bernard's ship has safely reached port,   48
but clearly it had not yet reached port when he wrote. He was human and, dwelling in the flesh, he may have been subject to passions. Everyone knows what John Chrysostom said not only about
saints, but about the apostles themselves: "Even if they are saints,
they are still human. Even if they are nearly spiritual and cannot
be overcome by the flesh, they are still carnal and can be stirred by
it."[68] It may be that Bernard wrote this after being provoked by
some insult. Angry men say many things that later they regret.
Well and good. Let us leave anger aside, since it is a sudden emo-
tion that springs from some insult. Doesn't hatred naturally exist
between certain nations? Indeed, in Sallust we read that the people of Gaul hated the name of Rome. And in Livy we read of the
ferocity of the Gauls and of their hatred toward the name of
Rome — something that our experience bears out in reality.[69]

But let us leave all these charges aside, and suppose that Ber-   49
nard was not motivated by anger or hatred, but was a perfect saint
when he wrote. This contradicts the observation of Ambrose, who
writes: "Who among the living can accept praise safely and without fear who has memories of the past that trouble him, or foresees future events that scare him? What human being, dwelling in
this little body, ought to claim any merits for himself?"[70] The rest
of the passage is well-known. But if in life Bernard was truly a
saint, what reply can I find? I shall not reproach him, but must rebut him by citing even greater eulogists — even if this disparager
objects indignantly.

In his preface to the Epistle to the Romans, Ambrose writes of   50
them: "They are the head of all nations."[71] How very strange! He
made no exception for the Gauls! Then in his commentary on the
text, he says that the Apostle expresses his joy that the Romans
bowed to the Christian faith, even though they ruled the world —
and he made no exception for Gaul.[72] But our Gaul will say: "He
is praising the might and empire of the Romans, not their virtue."

ergo quod sequitur: 'Erant enim,' inquit, 'doctrina memorabiles et boni operis cupidi, studiosique magis agendi bene, quam sermonis.' Sed ecce iterum strepet Gallus: testi domestico non credendum, quoniam sit civis Romanus Ambrosius; quod negari nequit. Nec intellego tamen quid irato hosti plus sit fidei quam placato civi.

51   Hieronymo autem quid opponet, qui et Romam laudat et laudatam dicit ab Apostolo? De quo, quoniam in ipsa epystola ad Urbanum scripsi, nil nunc amplius dico, sed ipsius Hieronymi dictum aliud adiungo, qui secundo libro in epystola *ad Galatas:* 'Romane plebis,' inquit, 'laudatur fides. Ubi tanto studio et frequentia ad ecclesias et martyrum sepulcra concurritur, ubi sicut ad similitudinem celestis tonitrui amen resonat, et vacua idolorum templa quatiuntur? Non quod aliam habeant Romani fidem, nisi hanc quam omnes Cristi Ecclesie, sed quod devotio in eis maior et simplicitas ad credendum.'

52   Quid hic Gallus dicet? An consonat hic Bernardo, in eo maxime quod ille incredulos primum, dehinc impios, tandem etiam proditores vocat, nimis (si dici licet) hostiliter? Ubi est autem ista proditio? Ubi non potius observata, et publice et privatim, etiam hostibus Romana fides, cuius omnis historia plena est? Illud quoque, quod his interposuit, temerarios in sancta illos dicens, contrarium est fere omnibus scripturis que Romanis attribuunt gravitatem. Quid est enim tam temeritati dissonum quam gravitas? Sed audire Gallum hic videor protestantem: 'Nisi Romanum hostem in testimonium adduxeris, non credam.' Est plane hostis ex ore laus ingens, nec immerito Virgilius ait:

ipse hostis Teucros insigni laude ferebat.

Then let him hear what follows: "They were notable for their learning, and eager to do good works, and more zealous for good deeds than fine words."[73] But here too our Gaul will squawk that we must not believe a domestic witness: for Ambrose was a Roman citizen, a fact that no one can deny. Still, I don't see why an angry enemy should be more trustworthy than a calm citizen.

And what objection can he make against Jerome, who praises 51 Rome and notes that she is praised by the Apostle?[74] Since I wrote about this in my letter to Urban, I say no more now, but add a further remark that Jerome makes in Book Two of his commentary on Galatians. "The faith of the Roman populace is praised here," he writes. "Where else do people flock to churches and martyrs' tombs with such zeal and in such numbers? Where does the 'Amen' ring out like heavenly thunder, and where are the vacant temples of idols demolished? It is not that the Romans' faith differs from that of all believers in Christ's Church, but that they have greater devotion and sincerity in believing."[75]

What does our Gaul say to this? Does he agree here with Ber- 52 nard, especially when he first calls the Romans unbelieving, then impious toward God, and finally traitors?[76] This last charge is overly hostile, if I may say so. For where is their treason? Rather, where do we not see the Romans keeping faith—both publicly and privately, to friend and foe alike—the faith that fills our histories? And when Bernard adds that the Romans are careless about what is sacred, this runs contrary to nearly all written records, which make gravity their chief attribute. For can anything be less compatible with carelessness than gravity? But I seem to hear our Gaul protesting here: "Unless you summon an enemy of Rome to testify, I shall not believe you." Praise from the mouth of an enemy is immense, and Virgil rightly says:

Even the foe often lauded the Trojans with highest praise.[77]

53   Aperiat nunc aurem Gallus et cristam insolentie demittat, ut non semper placita, sed interdum vera incipiat audire; atque ut veris tandem opinionibus locus sit, concretum pulverem erroris e cauda gallice levitatis excutiat. Pyrrhus Epyrotarum rex, hostis populi Romani, cum Cineam, doctissimum illum virum et insignis memorie laude conspicuum, pro componenda pace Romam misisset, et infecto negotio redeuntem, qualis esset Roma interrogarret, ille regum urbem sibi visam, sive (ut alii perhibent) regum patriam se vidisse respondit, scilicet illic fere omnes tales esse, qualis Pyrrhus in Grecia, quem regum sane optimum fuisse constat et mitissimum.

54   Videat Gallus et Bernardus videat, inter reges optimos atque mitissimos — et non amicis modo, sed hostibus minime odiosos — et immitem atque intractabilem gentem et in extraneos inhumanam, quid intersit. Nam quod emulos ait in vicinos, directe opponitur ei, quod in libro *Macchabeorum* de Romanis legitur, quod non est invidia neque zelus inter eos. Nec ego nunc tamen Gallo meo transcribere librum illum cogito, ut ipse mihi Iustinum, quo (ut verum fatear) non egebam. Locum signasse suffecerit. Legat ergo operis illius librum ⟨tricesimum⟩ primum, capitulum octavum, et abunde laudatam virtutem ac potentiam inveniet Romanorum.

55   Iam quidem grandiloquentiam parvificentie coniunctam Romanis obicit. Improprie dictum a Bernardo nunquam dixerim, sed improprie et inepte ab hoc barbaro refricatum dico. Prima namque Grecis datur. Iungo ego Grecis Gallos, qui licet inferiores ingenio, iactantia et loquacitate superiores sunt. Romanis hoc vitium non convenit, boni operis cupidis (ut repetam quod premisi) studio-

Now let our Gaul open his ears, and lower his insolent cocks- 53
comb, so that he can begin to hear the truth for a while, rather
than always hear what he likes. To make room for true beliefs, let
him shake off the dust of error that has accumulated on the tail-
feathers of his Gallic shallowness. An enemy of the Roman people, King Pyrrhus of Epirus, once sent the great scholar Cineas, a
man famous for his remarkable memory, to Rome to negotiate a
peace.[78] When the mission failed and Cineas returned, Pyrrhus
asked him what Rome was like. Cineas replied that he had seen a
city of kings, or (as others report) a country of kings.[79] In other
words, nearly everyone at Rome resembled Pyrrhus of Greece,
who was recognized as the best and mildest of kings.

Let our Gaul see, and let Bernard see too, what difference there 54
is between the best and mildest kings of Rome — those least hateful both to friends and foes alike — and their own intractable people, who are so inhuman to foreigners. When Bernard says that
the Romans are jealous of their neighbors, he is directly contra-
dicted by the Book of Maccabees, where we read that there is no
envy or jealousy among the Romans.[80] But I don't intend to transcribe Bernard's book for my Gaul, even if he transcribes Justin
for me, which wasn't necessary, to tell you the truth.[81] It would
have sufficed to indicate the passage. But let him now read Book
Thirty-one, Chapter Eight, in Justin's work. There he will find
both the virtue and power of the Romans abundantly praised.[82]

Next he charges that the Romans accompanied their pompous 55
words with petty deeds. I would never say that Bernard spoke improperly; but I do say that our barbarian rehashes the charge
improperly and ineptly. Grandiloquence is associated with the
Greeks. And I add the Gauls to the Greeks: for while inferior in
wit, they are superior in boasting and loquacity. But this vice is incompatible with the Romans, who — to repeat what I quoted
above — were eager to do good works, and more zealous for good
deeds than fine words. We read of them: "The best citizens pre-

sisque magis agendi bene, quam sermonis. De quibus scriptum est: 'Optimus quisque facere quam dicere malebat.' Secundum vero illis affricuisse perridiculum. Audeo enim dicere, quod me verum dicere certus sum; et nichil facile affirmare solitus hoc affirmo, quod totius humane magnificentie supremum domicilium Roma est, nec est ullus tam remotus terrarum angulus, qui hoc neget. Quod si barbarus hic ignorat, aut torpet aut stertit, aut plene desipit et insanit.

56   Quis enim magnificum, queso, legit unquam aliquid, aut audivit, sine nomine et gloria urbis Rome, ex quo Urbs ipsa condi cepit et crescere? De quo tempore scriptum est:

> nunc quoque Dardanidum fama est consurgere Romam
> ⟨ . . . ⟩
> quanta nec est, nec erit, nec visa prioribus annis.

Et ab ingenio altiore:

> illa inclyta Roma
> imperium terris, animos equabit Olympo
> septemque una sibi muro circumdabit arces,
> felix prole virum.

Et rursus idem:

> verum hec tantum alias inter caput extulit urbes,
> quantum lenta solent inter viburna cupressi.

De qua alter vir magnus: 'nulla unquam respublica nec maior, nec sanctior, nec bonis exemplis ditior fuit.'

57   Vellem scire, quid nunc agit Gallus noster. Sed sat scio, stupet hec ignota, que nec a Gallis, nec a gallinis, addisci possunt. Discuntur ab historicis et poetis ac scriptoribus rerum. Nec stupet modo, sed irascitur, quoniam hec tam multa, tam magna de Avinione ac Parisius non scribuntur, quarum altera significatorem non habet in celo, alteram laudat Architrenius, de quo post videbimus.

ferred action to words."[83] And to smear them with the second charge — petty deeds — is completely ridiculous. I dare say this, since I am certain that I speak the truth; and while I am used to affirming nothing lightly, I affirm this: Rome is the supreme domicile of all human magnificence, and no one even in the farthest corner of the world would deny this fact. If our barbarian doesn't know this, he is either dull-witted, snoring in his sleep, or utterly demented and crazed.

For who, I ask, has ever read or heard of anything magnificent 56 that didn't involve the name and glory of Rome, ever since that city was founded and began to grow? About this age we read:

And now fame has it that Dardanian Rome is rising . . .
A city than which none greater is or shall be, or has been in
    past ages.[84]

And a poet of greater genius wrote:

That glorious Rome
Shall bound her empire by earth, her pride by Olympus;
And with a single city's wall shall enclose her seven hills,
Blessed in her brood of men.[85]

And he also wrote:

But this city has reared her head as high among all others
As cypresses oft do among the bending osiers.[86]

And another great man wrote of her: "No republic was ever greater, or holier, or richer in noble examples."[87]

I'd like to know what our Gaul will do now. But in fact I know 57 full well: he is gawking at these unfamiliar things, which cannot be learned from cocks or hens, but only from historians, poets and writers.[88] Not only does he gawk, but he is angry that such great things are not written about Avignon and Paris. The former has no "significator" in the heavens, while the latter is praised by Architrenius, about whom we shall see later.[89]

413

: VII :

58 Ante tamen quam ad laudes alias procedam, convitiis respondendum est, que, nisi fallor, nunc etiam duo supersunt: inverecundos
Romanos ad petendum, ingratosque cum acceperint ille vir sanctus ait. Unum a tergo relinquebam: frontosos scilicet ad negandum. Hec est fere, nisi me fallit numerus, obiectorum summa.

59   Nam quod his additur, insuetam paci gentem assuetamque tumultibus ac bellis, si negare velim, Ianus ipse fatebitur a Numa
rege in Cesarem Augustum nonnisi ter clausus. Quibus exercendis
in utraque fortuna tanta fuit virtus, ut preter hunc barbarum pa-
trio more tergiversantem, nil in terris simile unquam extitisse,
fidenter addiderim, nec futurum esse, omnibus notum sit; et videatur in omnibus Romanis bellis cum fortitudine certasse iusti-
tiam, sintque illa verissima que in libris autenticis scripta sunt: 'ut
omnes gentes sciant populum Romanum et suscipere iusta bella et
finire,' atque in omni fortuna eosdem animos habere; imo vero,
'magnitudinem populi Romani admirabiliorem prope adversis rebus quam secundis esse'; et illud etiam ab hoste predicatum: 'populum Romanum eo invictum esse, quod in secundis rebus sapere
et consulere meminerint, et³ mirandum fuisse si aliter facerent. Ex
insolentia, quibus nova bona fortuna sit, impotentes letitie insanire: populo Romano usitata ac prope iam obsoleta ex victoria
gaudia esse, ac plus pene parcendo⁴ quam vincendo imperium
auxisse.'

60   Quanquam quid ego minutiora ista perstringo, que si velim
cunta complecti, omnes michi scriptorum secularium libri illustres

: VII :

Yet before I proceed to other praises, I must answer further in-   58
sults, two of which remain, unless I am mistaken. This saint says
that the Romans are shameless in asking favors, and ungrateful in
accepting them. I was leaving out another charge, namely, their
effrontery in refusing requests. Unless my counting is wrong, these
are the sum of his accusations.

He adds that they are a people unaccustomed to peace, but ac-   59
customed to uprisings and wars. Now, if I tried to deny this, the
very temple of Janus would concede that its doors were closed only
three times between the reigns of Numa Pompilius and the emperor Augustus.[90] In waging wars, their valor was so great, in victory and defeat, that everyone knows — except for this barbarian,
who is cowardly and evasive in the manner of his countrymen —
there has never been anything like it on earth, and, I would confidently add, there never will be. In all of Rome's wars, justice
seemed to vie with courage, and we see the truth of what is written in genuine histories: "All nations should know that the Roman
people start and end just wars."[91] The Roman people faced every
kind of fortune with the same spirit; indeed, "the greatness of the
Roman people is nearly more admirable in adversity than in prosperity."[92] As an enemy observed: "The Roman people are invincible because in prosperity they remember to act with wisdom and
prudence; and it would be surprising if they did otherwise. When
people's good fortune is new to them, its novelty makes them lose
control and go mad in their elation. But the joys of victory are
usual and almost worn-out for the Roman people, and they have
increased their dominion nearly more by sparing the vanquished
than by conquering them."[93]

But why should I review these minor details? If I wished to in-   60
clude every one of them, I would have to transcribe all the illustri-

transcribendi erunt? Quid est enim aliud omnis historia, quam
Romana laus? Unum inter alia est quod non modo acceptare, sed
acervare propositum est: gentem subdi nesciam, fateor, sed sub-
dere alias et preesse, ne, si hoc negare voluero, magnitudo convin-
cat imperii. Quod, licet inter manus barbaricas imminutum atque
debilitatum et pene consumptum sit, Romanas inter manus tale
fuit, ut omnia mundi imperia illi admota pueriles ludi fuisse videantur et inania nomina.

61   Quanquam non sim nescius quosdam levissimos Grecorum,
'qui,' ut Titus ait Livius, 'Partorum quoque contra Romanum nomen glorie favent,' dictitare solitos maiestatem Alexandri Macedo-
nis, vix tenui fama Rome cogniti, non laturum fuisse populum
Romanum: videlicet non tot duces egregios, tot prudentium ac
fortium virorum milia, uni furioso adolescenti potuisse resistere.
Neque solum levissimi Grecorum, sed quod Titus Livius nosse
non potuit, levissimus quidam nuper vanissimusque Gallorum
idem dixit, et sic omnis pudor periit, ut non tantum literis vilissi-
mam hanc nugellam, sed numeris etiam carminibusque mandaret.
Nescio quidem cur, nisi quod insignem, nec tam Grecum quam
Gallicum, potorem noverat Alexandrum. Et sic similitudo morum
parit amicitias, ac partas nutrit.

62   Iratus iocor:[5] imo quidem causam aliam scio; tantum est enim
odium Romani nominis, ut non Alexandrum modo, sed Sardana-
palum Iulio Cesari prelaturi sint. Nempe illos nisi per famam non
noverunt, hunc senserunt eorum ferro ulcera resecantem atque in-
solentias castigantem. Dissecentur, tamen, et crepent medii: nunquam sibilis vipereis veritas quatietur. Adamantino monte solidior

ous books of the pagan authors. For what is all of history but the praise of Rome? Among others, there is one point that I intend not only to accept, but to pile onto to the list. Lest the greatness of the Roman empire prove me wrong for denying it, I confess that the Romans were a people unused to subjection, but used to subjecting and governing others. And although at the hands of the barbarians this empire was reduced, weakened, and nearly destroyed, in the hands of the Romans it was so great that in comparison all the world's empires seem like childish games and empty names.

Of course, I am not unaware that some shallow Greeks, who 61 "favored the glory of the Parthians to spite the name of Rome," as Livy writes,[94] were fond of repeating that the Roman people could not bear comparison with the majesty of Alexander the Great, who was practically unknown at Rome except by some faint rumors. In other words, so many outstanding generals, and so many thousands of wise and courageous men, could not stand up to one crazed youth! The shallow Greeks were not alone in saying this. What Livy could not have known is that a very shallow and vain Gaul has recently said the same thing. And all sense of shame has so utterly perished that he not only committed this bit of nonsense to writing, but even versified it in a poem.[95] I don't know why he did this, unless he recognized Alexander as a notable toper, in this respect more Gallic than Greek. Thus similar habits breed friendships, and afterwards nourish them.

Despite my anger, I jest. In fact, I know that there is another 62 reason. So great is their hatred of the name of Rome that they would prefer not only Alexander, but even Sardanapalus to Julius Caesar.[96] In fact, they only know the first two by rumor, whereas they have felt the latter's sword cut through their sores and punish their insolence. But let them be cut to ribbons, and sputter in our midst. The truth will never be shaken by their viperous hissing. More solid than a mountain of diamond, the glory of Rome will

semper Romana gloria toto orbe resonabit, semper invidentium illi
nomen erit inglorium, imo infame. Sed de hoc, ne in longum nimis exeam, nil amplius; de tota enim ista materia ab ipso Tito Li-
vio *Ab Urbe condita* libro nono preclarissime disputatum est. Ibi legat barbarus, et crepabit.

63   Hoc igitur quem confiteor articulo pretermisso, ad eos redeo
quos negabo. Obicitur Romanis impudentia ad petendum ingrati-
tudoque accepti: duo magna, si vera sunt, vitia. Quis nunc tantis
obiectionibus nisi Veritas nuda respondeat? Et contra primum
quidem mille sunt testes. Sufficiant tamen in presens tres populi,
duo reges. Bello punico secundo, afflictis pene ad ultimum Romanis rebus, atque erario exhausto, Neapolitani legatos Romam cum
muneribus miserunt, in quibus erant quadraginta patere auree magni ponderis. Quibus in Capitolium invectis, et ante patrum pedes
expositis, orabant legati ut munus de se parvum, ingens tamen devotione mittentium, dignarentur accipere, et Neapolitanorum rebus omnibus tanquam propriis suis uti. Neapolitanis gratie acte
sunt, legatique cum muneribus remissi, nichil acceptum preter
unam, eamque minimi ponderis, pateram, ne amicorum munus
sprevisse crederentur. Eodem tempore et Pestani legati ipsi quoque
pateras aureas attulerunt, et gratiis actis remissi sunt; auri nichil
acceptum est.

64   Post id tempus, durante adhuc bello, cum Carthaginienses ad
conducenda stipendiaria auxilia cum immenso pondere auri et argenti in Hispaniam misissent, capti nuntii a Saguntinis, cumque
omni eo quod attulerant Romam missi per legatos. Quibus gratie
acte, aurum et argentum quod hostibus ereptum, et in suam perniciem missum suo quodam iure retinere poterant, legatis reddi-
tum, insuper addita munera; soli nuntii hostium retenti coniec-

always resound throughout the world; and the name of those who envy her will always be inglorious, or rather infamous. But enough on this topic, lest I digress too long: for the entire subject has been brilliantly discussed in Book Nine of Livy's *History of Rome*.[97] Let this barbarian read it, and he will sputter with rage.

Leaving aside the charge of the Romans' warlike spirit, which I concede, I return to those I shall deny. The Romans are accused of shamelessness in asking favors, and ingratitude in accepting them. Certainly, these are two great vices, if they are true. Now, who can answer such great charges but naked Truth? Against the first charge, we have a thousand witnesses; but let three peoples and two kings suffice for the moment. During the second Punic War, when the Roman state had been nearly destroyed and the treasury depleted, the people of Naples sent envoys to Rome with gifts, including forty massive goblets of gold. Having carried the gifts to the Capitol and set them at the feet of the senators, the envoys begged them to accept this gift—which, though small in itself, was an immense token of the donors' devotion—and to use all of the Neapolitans' possessions as their own. The senators thanked the people of Naples, and sent the envoys back with gifts; but they accepted only a single goblet, and the smallest one at that, so that they would not seem to disdain a gift from their allies.[98] Around the same time, envoys from Paestum also brought golden goblets, and were sent back with thanks; but none of their gold was accepted.[99]

Some time later during the same war, the Carthaginians sent envoys to Spain with an immense horde of gold and silver for the hiring of mercenary troops. These envoys were captured by the people of Saguntum, who sent them and all their booty to Rome escorted by their own legates. The Romans thanked them, and since the gold and silver intended to harm them had been seized from the enemy, they claimed it by rights and gave it back to the Saguntine legates, adding other gifts besides. Only the enemy en-

tique in carcerem, ut advocata in consilium non avaritia, sed inimicitia videretur.

65   Pyrrhus ille, cuius mentionem fecimus, sentiens Romanos armis indomitos muneribus aggredi instituit; itaque pro pace cum Cineam mitteret, magnos illi contulit thesauros, quibus patricios ac senatum, dehinc ordinem equestrem, postremo plebem humilem tentaret. Quid autem? Neminem cuius domus muneribus pateret invenit. Qui si missus esset Avinionem, puto aliquod apertum ostium invenisset! Per eosdem dies Ptholomeus, rex Egypti, legatis Romanis ad se profectis, magna munera miserat, que cum illi alto animo recusassent, ad cenam postridie invitatis, singulas aureas coronas in convivio destinavit. Quas cum ob honorem magni et amici hospitis recepissent, die illas proximo statuis regiis impresserunt, ut intelligi daretur caritatem eos et honorificentiam regis acceptasse, non aurum. Quam inverecundi essent igitur ad petendum negata, qui tam obstinati erant ad oblata renuendum, viderit ipse qui dixit.

66   Contra secundum vero obiectum, scilicet indignis ingratitudinem, multi quoque et reges et populi testes sunt. Massinissa in primis rex Numidie, Attalus et Eumenes Pergami, Hiero Sicilie, Deiotarus minoris Armenie, Mamertini, preterea Tusculani, innumerique alii quos attingere longum est. Sed ad summam, etsi adversus quosdam cives severi patris in morem durior non negetur, quam vel suum reique publice decus vel illorum merita postularent, erga amicos tamen, non solum reges et populos, sed humillimas quoque personas nil gratius populo Romano; de quo

voys were detained and thrown into prison, to show that the
Romans had acted not from greed, but as a nation at war.[100]

When Pyrrhus, whom I mentioned before, heard that the   65
Romans were invincible in battle, he decided to assail them with
gifts. So when he sent Cineas to negotiate a peace, he furnished
him with great treasures with which to tempt first the patricians
and senate, then the order of knights, and finally the lowly plebe-
ians. What happened? He found that no one opened his door to
such gifts.[101] (Had he been sent to Avignon, I think he would
have found the door open!) Around the same time, King Ptolemy
of Egypt sent huge gifts to some visiting Roman envoys, who no-
bly refused the gifts. The next day, the king invited them to a dinner, where he presented each of them with a golden crown, which
they accepted in honor of their great ally and host. But the following day, they placed these crowns on the king's statues so that everyone could see that they had accepted his friendship and homage, but not his gold.[102] How were they shameless in asking for
what was denied them, when in fact they were obstinate in refusing what was offered them? Let their accuser decide.

As for the second charge—namely, their ingratitude toward   66
people who didn't deserve it—here too, many kings and peoples
bear witness. First of all, there is king Massinissa of Numidia,
then Attalus and Eumenes of Pergamum, Hieron of Sicily,
Deiotarus of Armenia Minor, the Mamertines, the people of
Tusculum, and countless others whom it would be tedious to
mention. In short, although Rome, like a severe father, was unde-
niably harsher towards some citizens than was required by the
honor of the republic or the merits of their case, still no one was
ever more grateful than the Roman people to their friends, including not only kings and nations, but even the lowliest persons. It
has been written with great truth that "The senate and the Roman people is wont to remember both a benefit and an injury."[103]
And further: "Intent on their domestic and military affairs, the

verissime scriptum est: 'Senatus populusque Romanus beneficii et
iniurie memor esse solet.' Et iterum: 'Romani domi militieque in-
tenti, festinare, parare, alius alium hortari, hostibus obviam ire, libertatem, patriam parentesque armis tegere. Post, ubi pericula virtute propulerant, sociis atque amicis auxilia portabant, magis[6]
dandis quam accipiendis beneficiis amicitias parabant.' Et rursus:
'Hoc in pectus tuum demitte: nunquam populum Romanum beneficiis victum esse; nam bello quid valeat tute scis.'[7]

67   Hoc proprie sibi dictum Gallus accipiat. Scit enim, et si nescit
expertos milites suos maiores interroget, et dicent sibi; ante alios
ille—sic enim de illo scriptum est—'corpore, armis spirituque terribilis, nomine etiam quasi ad terrorem composito, Vercingetorix.'
Alvernus, Galliarum rex, qui fortuna multis sepe et magnis preliis
atque conatibus retentata, novissime in deditionem redactus, et—
maximum victorie decus—supplex cum in castra venisset, et fale-
ras et sua arma ante Cesaris genua proiecit. Et 'Habes,'[8] inquit,
'fortem virum, vir fortissime, vicisti.' Non muto aliquid hac in re:
Flori, illustris historici, verba sunt.

68   Unum superest: Romana illa durities, sive (ut verbo eius utar)
frontositas ad negandum. Et est sane difficile in universum pro-
nuntiare: tam dissimiles, tam diversi sunt hominum mores. Dabo
autem e tot milibus duos viros Romanos ac principes, qui insimu-
lationem publicam singulari sua laude discutiant: Iulium Cesarem
Titumque Vespasianum. De quorum primo scriptum est: 'Cesar
in animum induxerat laborare, vigilare; negotiis amicorum intentus sua negligere, nichil denegare quod dignum dono esset.' Alter,
et ipse nichil solitus negare, '"non oportere," aiebat,[9] "quenquam a
sermone principis tristem discedere." Atque enim, recordatus

Romans made haste, prepared, encouraged one another, went to meet the enemy, and defended their freedom, their country, and their parents under arms. Later, when their valor had averted the danger, they lent aid to their allies and friends, and won friendships more by conferring benefits than by receiving them."[104] And again: "Let this thought sink into your heart: the Roman people has never been outdone in kindness; its prowess in war you know."[105]

Let our Gaul consider these words addressed to him. He knows 67 this fact; and if he doesn't know it, let him ask his ancestors, who were experienced soldiers. They will tell him, especially about the famous Vercingetorix, who is described as "a man fearfully built and armed, whose very name seemed devised to inspire fear."[106] This king of the Gauls, who came from the tribe of the Arverni, tried his fortune in many great battles and contests, but in the end he was forced to surrender. He arrived at the Roman camp as a suppliant — paying the greatest honor to the victor — and cast his armor and medals at Caesar's feet, saying, "They are yours: you have conquered a brave man, o bravest of men." I have changed nothing in this account: the words are those of the illustrious historian Florus.[107]

One last charge remains: the Romans' harshness or, to use Ber- 68 nard's word, their effrontery in refusing requests. It is quite difficult to make a universal pronouncement, for human behavior is so various. From so many thousands, I shall cite two great Roman rulers whose singular merits dispel this collective accusation: Julius Caesar and the emperor Titus. About Caesar, we read: "He had schooled himself to work hard and sleep little, to devote himself to the welfare of his friends and neglect his own, to refuse nothing that was worth giving."[108] And Titus was likewise accustomed to refusing no request, and "used to say: 'No one should ever go away sad after speaking with the ruler.' Indeed, once when he recalled at dinner that he had given no gifts the entire day, he uttered that

quondam super cenam quod nichil cuiquam tota die prestitisset, memorabilem illam meritoque laudandam vocem edidit: "Amici, diem perdidi".' Sic enim de illo scribitur. Et rursus: 'Neque negavit quicquam petentibus, et ut que vellent peterent ultro adhortatus est.' Non prosequor utriusque clementiam morumque dulcedinem. Sufficit ad obiectam negandi duritiem respondisse; sed occurret, et 'non sunt,' inquiet, 'omnes tales.' Certe. Nam, si essent, non tanta esset horum gloria. Magnum rerum atque hominum decus est raritas, magnum imparitas ornamentum. Si pares essent omnes, nullus excelleret. Det michi autem adversarius unum Gallum vel omnino unum barbarum similem his duobus, et vicerit.

: VIII :

69 Nescio quidem an ad cunta responderim, nec tanti illa facio, ut in hac inquisitione multus sim. Optarem ego, si fieri posset, ut ille vir tantus discussisset exactius non modo quid diceret, sed et contra quos diceret. Fortasse etenim tacuisset, nec perpetuam illam fame notam immeritis inussisset. Sed si irrevocabile verbum, quanto irrevocabilior est scriptura, presertim post obitum scribentis. Itaque quod scripsit scripsit. Eat ut potest et rerum veritas cum contradictione linguarum suo marte contendat, sub incorruptis — non sum dubius — victura iudicibus, aliorum sententias contemptura. 'Non potuit vir sanctus errare.' Sed si homo, si Gallus, si Burgundio, si iratus errasset, non esset, ut arbitror, inter prodigia numerandum.

memorable and truly praiseworthy sentence: 'Friends, I have lost a day.'" [109] That's what is written about him. And again: "He refused nothing that anyone asked, and himself urged others to ask for what they wished."[110] I shall not go into detail about the clemency and charming nature of both men. It suffices that I have answered the charge of Roman harshness. But this fellow will reply, saying "Not all of them are like this." Of course. If everyone were like them, their glory would not be so great. Rarity is a great distinction in people and things, and singularity is a great ornament. If all were equal, no one would excel. But let my adversary cite one Gaul or even one barbarian similar to these two, and he will win the argument.

: VIII :

I don't know whether I have answered all Bernard's charges, nor do I value them enough to spend much time in this inquiry. If it were possible, I would wish that this great man had more carefully examined not only what he said, but against whom he said it. In that case, he would perhaps have remained silent, and not branded a mark of infamy on those who didn't deserve it. But if the spoken word is irrevocable, [111] how much more irrevocable is the written word, especially after the death of the writer. Thus, what is written, is written.[112] Let him proceed as he is able, and let the truth of the facts rely on its own strength to combat the contradictions of rash tongues. I doubt not that, with impartial judges, the truth will conquer, and contemn the opinions of others. "A saint could not err." But if he had erred as a human being, a Gaul, a Burgundian, or an angry man, we would not count this as a miracle, I suspect.

69

70   Ceterum quocunque res vergat, non efficiet barbarus quin in loco famosissimo Iuris Civilis ita scriptum non sit: 'Summa Reipublice tuitio de stirpe duarum rerum, armorum atque legum, veniens vimque suam exinde muniens, felix Romanorum genus omnibus anteponi nationibus omnibusque dominari, tam preteritis effecit temporibus, quam Deo propitio in eternum efficiet.' Mirum valde, Romanorum dixit, non Gallorum. Et ita 'secundum Salvii Iuliani scripturam, que indicat debere omnes civitates consuetudinem Rome sequi' et legem, 'que est caput orbis terrarum, non ipsam alias civitates.' Romam dixit, non Parisius; et preterea legum corpus, non Avinionensis, sed 'Romane iustitie templum' dicit. Quin et 'legum originem' et 'summi Pontificatus apicem' Rome tribuit, deque hoc dubitare neminem ait; neque enim dubitantem de hoc, imo aperta prorsus impudentia reluctantem barbarum istum norat, cum eandem urbem 'legum patriam, sacerdotii fontem' vocat. Ego autem, petita venia, occiduam hanc Ierusalem, unde homo ille descendit, felicissimus ni rediisset, patriam potorum et vini multiplicis fontem voco. Confer nunc titulos, vincet Avinio, maxime si alios addidero mundo notos, michi autem a pueritia longe notissimos, quos ut taceam verecundia persuadet.

71   Sed iam sensim fatigari incipio, Romane urbis preconia colligendo; quibus si diutius immorari velim, tempus michi prius defuturum quam materiam, intelligo. Parcendum et scribentis tedio et legentis, atque in primis barbari illius, qui quam amaro animo, quam tristis hec videat audiatque, quam cupide, si facultas detur, ex libris hec omnibus erasurus sit, non aliter scio quam si oculis viderem: ita illum ex animoso nimis alloquio nosse michi videor. Et quoniam in uno eodemque homine galli cristam atque anseris

Besides, no matter which way the question turns, this barbarian   70
cannot cancel what is written in a famous passage of our Civil
Law: "The supreme guardianship of the republic, which springs
from two things—arms and laws—and derives its force from
them, has in ages past, and with God's aid shall forever, set the
happy race of the Romans above all nations to dominate them."[113]
How very strange! It says Romans, and not Gauls. Likewise, "according to the text of Salvius Julianus, which indicates that all cities should follow the custom" and law "of Rome, which is the capital of the whole world, and not vice versa."[114] It says Rome, not
Paris, and speaks, not of the legal code of Avignon, but of the
"temple of Roman justice."[115] Indeed, it ascribes the "origin of
laws" and the "crown of the supreme Pontiff" to Rome.[116] It says
that no one doubts this. For when it calls this city the "homeland
of laws and source of the priesthood," it does not know of this
barbarian who doubts all this and indeed resists it with brazen impudence.[117] By your leave, I shall call this sinking Jerusalem—
from which the pope went down to Rome, and which would have
been most fortunate if he had never returned—the "homeland of
topers and the source of many wines."[118] Now compare their
claims to distinction. Avignon will win, especially if I add the
others known to all the world, and known to me since childhood,
but modesty urges me to remain silent.

But little by little I begin to tire as I compile these eulogies of   71
the city of Rome. I realize that, if I chose to dwell longer on this
subject, I would sooner run out of time than material. Both the
author and his reader should be spared such tedium. Above all, I
must spare this barbarian, who sees and hears my words with such
bitterness and gloom, and who would cancel my name from every
book if he had the chance. I know this as if I saw him with my
own eyes: so well do I think I understand him from his haughty
address. In a single person, I have found a cock's comb and a
goose's tongue—O monstrous species!—combined with the stub-

linguam—monstri genus!—et contentiose gentis pervicaciam
novi, illum exclamantem hinc exaudio: 'vera erant ista, dum scribe-
rentur, sed mutata sunt tempora.'

72   Mutata inquam et tempora, mutatos homines, mutataque omnia et in peius fateor. Cui enim queso, non illud lirici vatis auditum est:

> damnosa quid non imminuit dies?
> Etas parentum, peior avis, tulit
> nos nequiores, mox daturos
> progeniem vitiosiorem?

73   Sed universalis ista mutatio est, quamvis necessario (ut dixi) in
rebus maioribus maior sit, et non solum in tot seculis, sed in paucis annis. Et in nostra etate mutatio mirabilis et miserabilis facta
est; et si res prodeunt ut ceperunt, valde (ut reor) ad mundi exitum propinquamus. Quis, non dicam Gallus, sed asellus hoc nesciat? Et, si loqui valeat, fateatur.

74   Ego quidem mutationes temporum legens, nonnunquam tardior ad credendum; ex his que ipse nuper oculis meis vidi, nil iam
incredibile existimo. Verumtamen in hoc statu rerum nunc etiam
Romanos viros bonos, et si amice, si paterne, non hostiliter, non
tyrannice tractarentur, satis affabiles expertus dico. Multis annis
cum eisdem et Rome et alibi conversatus, in uno plane fateor in-
tractabiliores esse Romanos, quam Ierosolymitanos Rodani, quod
non tam equis animis coniuges suas sibi eripi pati possunt, omnia,
prius quam dedecus id, laturi; nempe quorum in auribus adhuc
sonat verbum illud vetus Icilii civis sui. 'Sevite in tergum et cervi-
ces nostras, pudicitia saltem in tuto sit.' Que vox, toto orbe dignis-

bornness of his contentious nation, and I can hear him cry out: "Such things were true when they were written, but the times have changed."

Changed are the times, I admit; changed are the people, and all 72 things are changed—for the worse, I confess. Who has not heard the words of the lyric poet?

What do the ravages of time not injure?
Our parents' age, worse than our grandsires',
Has borne us, more wicked still, and destined soon
To yield yet more depraved offspring.[119]

This change is a universal one, even if, as I have said, it neces- 73 sarily appears greater in greater things, not only over many centuries, but even within a few years. In our own age, there has been a miraculous and miserable change; and if things continue as they have begun, I think we are quickly nearing the end of the world. Is there anyone, not just a Gallic rooster, but even a jackass, who is ignorant of this? And if he could speak, he would admit the fact.

For myself, while reading about the changes in our times, I was 74 sometimes slow to believe it; but after what I recently saw with my own eyes, I no longer find anything incredible. Yet even in the present state of affairs, I may speak from experience and say that I have found that, even now, the men of Rome are good. If you treat them in a friendly or paternal manner, rather than as enemies or tyrants, they are quite courteous. I have spent many years with them in Rome and elsewhere, and I admit that on one point they are more intransigent than the Knights of Jerusalem on the Rhone.[120] They will not patiently allow their wives to be taken from them, and will suffer anything rather than this disgrace. Indeed, the ancient cry of their citizen Icilius stills rings in their ears: "Vent your rage upon our backs and our necks; let our chastity at least be safe."[121] But this statement, most worthy of hearing

sima exaudiri, propter distantiam forte in Gallias et ad ripam Rodani non pervenit.

75 Et quamvis iste convitiator, non contentus Bernardi convitiis, avaritiam illis obiciat, dicens eos, semper lucris temporalibus inhiantes, nichil aliud cogitare, nichil aliud somniare, ego (pace eius) nichil hoc falso falsius dico. Nulla gens minus lucro dedita est, nunquam magna in urbe tam pauci mercatores, tam nulli feneratores invenientur. Itaque preter principes, qui plures sunt quam Gallus hic cogitet, et maiores, nullus fere in populo tanto dives est. Utinam non magis voluptatibus quam lucris incumberent! Et de viris quidem hactenus. Sin autem saltatrices suas claudas ac potrices Romanis matronis comparare voluerint, sol eclipsabitur, mare tumultuabitur, terra tremet, ego attonitus obmutescam.

76 Cogitet Gallus et recogitet, odiique velum ab oculis mentis amoveat, videre fortassis incipiet quid intersit inter Romanam gravitatem et Gallicam levitatem. Sed ipse, ut auguror, Rome semper pavens — sic enim scripta eius indicant — ideoque iudicii inops fuit, unus ex illis de quibus ait Psalmista: 'Illic trepidaverunt timore, ubi non erat timor.' Nec enim amicis formidabiles, sed amabiles sunt Romani. Gallus autem qui illos, nulla quidem alia causa, nisi hereditario quodam iure, oderat, se ab illis amari non posse existimabat. Non iniustus metus, fateor, sed iniustum odium odisse, qui nichil mali sibi fecerint. Etsi patres eius ab illorum patribus victi, domiti, triumphati ac tributarii facti sint, sed illa transierint, non est causa odii; nisi 'mala mens, malus animus,' ut ait Comicus, implacatus, inflexibilis, ad malivolentiam obstinatus. Et o utinam, quando amori nullus est locus, esset saltem vicissitudo

in all the world, never reached Gaul or the banks of the Rhone, perhaps because of the distance.

Not content with Bernard's insults, this calumniator reproaches 75 the Romans for their avarice, and says they are always intent on temporal profits, and neither think nor dream of anything else. By his leave, I say that there is nothing falser than this falsehood. No people is less devoted to profit; in no other great city will you find so few merchants, and practically no moneylenders. Except for their rulers, who are more numerous than our Gaul thinks, and their leading citizens, there are hardly any rich men in their vast population. If only they pursued pleasures as little as they do profit! So much, then, for the men of Rome. As for the matrons of Rome, if the Gauls choose to compare them to their own lame and tippling dancing-girls, the sun will be eclipsed, the sea will churn, the earth will tremble, and I shall fall silent as if thunder-struck.[122]

Let our Gaul think and think again. Let him remove the veil of 76 hatred from his mind's eyes. Perhaps then he will begin to see the difference between Roman gravity and Gallic levity. Yet I surmise that he himself has always been afraid of Rome, as his writings indicate. Hence, his judgment was deficient, like one of those people of whom the Psalmist says: "There were they in great fear, where no fear was."[123] For the Romans are not terrifying, but kindly, to their friends. Our Gaul, who hated them for no reason but a sort of hereditary birthright, supposed that they could not love him. Not an unjust fear, I confess, but it is an unjust hatred when he hates those who have done him no harm. To be sure, his ancestors were conquered and subdued by their ancestors, who triumphed over them and made them pay tribute. But these events have long since passed away, and are no reason for hatred, unless you are a "bad mind, bad heart," as the comic poet says,[124] implacable, inflexible, and stubborn in your malevolence. Since there is no place for love, I only wish this hatred were mutual and equal! Then we

et paritas odiorum; ut sicut illi nos oderunt ex toto corde suo, in tota anima sua et in tota mente sua, ita nos illos odissemus: aut ego fallor augurio aut e vestigio litium omnium finis esset idem ille, qui maioribus nostris fuit.

: IX :

77   Progredior autem meo quidem, non illius ordine. Quid nunc agit igitur inquietus et impatiens veritatis homuncio? Et quid putas? Aggravat crimina, blasphemias coacervat; et primo 'populum barbarum' dixisse arguor, quem dicere aliter non poteram nec debeam, nisi nova vocabula rebus imponere voluissem; insuper et Beunense vinum, de quo satis est dictum, et Rodanum blasphemasse. Mirum si inter tot blasphemias vestimenta non scidit. Ego vero nil penitus blasphemavi, sed optavi ut cause malorum ingentium tollerentur, venenose damnoseque vindemie tristis exilii. Quid Gallicus noster strepit? 'Quod,' inquit, 'exilium Avinione passa est Ecclesia?' Responsio odiosa, non operosa est: ipse sibi respondeat. Quid scit enim penitus, qui hoc nescit? Scit utique. Sed precipitem in locum astu barbarico me impellit ut cadam.

78   At quod Rodanum exilii locum dixi, non debet quasi rerum inscius stupere. Turpe est enim docto viro de communibus admirari. Legat Bede librum *De temporibus*, legat et Iosephum, Scholasticam denique notam omnibus evolvat Historiam; inveniet filium Herodis Archelaum ab Augusto, propter eius scelera, exilio dam-

would hate them, just as they hate us—with all their heart, with all their soul, and with all their mind. Either I am mistaken in my prediction, or all these quarrels would soon end in the same way as they did for our ancestors.

: IX :

But I proceed following my own order, rather than his. What does 77 he do now, this restless fellow who cannot stand the truth? What do you think? He heaps up further accusations, and piles on more blasphemies. First, I am accused of calling his people "barbarous," but I could not justly have called them anything else, unless I had chosen to assign them new names. I am also accused of blaspheming the wine of Burgundy—about which enough has been said— and the Rhone river. It's a wonder that amid so many blasphemies he didn't tear his clothes.[125] In fact, I in no way blasphemed. I only hoped that the causes of enormous ills—the poisonous and ruinous harvest of this unhappy exile—could be eliminated. What does our Gaul squawk now? "What exile," he asks, "did the Church suffer in Avignon?" The answer is troubling but not troublesome; so let him answer himself.[126] What does one know at all, if one doesn't know this? And he surely knows. Still, with barbaric cunning he pushes me to a precipitous height, hoping to make me fall.

And if I called the Rhone a place of exile, he should not be 78 amazed, as if he knew nothing about the facts.[127] It is shameful when a man of learning is amazed by what is common knowledge. Let him read Bede's *Chronology*; let him read Flavius Josephus; and finally let him leaf through the *Scholastic History* that is familiar to everyone.[128] He will find that Herod's son Archelaus was condemned by Augustus and sent into exile for his crimes. Where was he banished? Why, to Vienne, a city on the Rhone.[129] Then

natum. Quo autem deportatum? Nempe Viennam, Rodani civitatem. Procedat Gallus noster ulterius et videbit Herodem illum, qui cognominatus est Antipas, similiter relegatum: quo autem opinemur, nisi ad locum exilii, Viennam? Procedat nunc etiam et videbit Herodem alterum, tetrarcham scilicet, a Gaio principe Lugdunum Rodani relegatum, ubi cum uxore, que illum ad exilium coniugali pietate prosecuta erat, misera morte consumptus est. Sed nimis accelero. Ubi Pontium Pilatum linquimus, qui iam antea magnorum reus criminum Lugdunum quoque a Tiberio fuerat deportatus?

79   Dicat nunc Gallus, quanquam sit dicaculus, me mentitum, in epystola ubi ad Urbanum scripsi Rodanum non Romanorum Pontificum sedem esse, sed reorum atque exilio damnatorum. Potest quidem (non infitior) Romanus Pontifex, si velit, non in Galliis modo, sed in Hispaniis aut Britanniis habitare. At quid expediens, quid honestum, pro sua ipsum sapientia non dubitare non dubito. Sibila vereor. Qui enim potuerunt unum senem verbis e propria opinione convellere, quanto poterunt facilius unum iuvenem in communi omnium sententia detinere. De hoc tamen Cristus viderit, sua res agitur. Ego, quia plus non datur, dum loqui potero, non tacebo. Potest Avinionem caput mundi presentia sua facere. Quidni enim possit omnipotentis Domini vicarius et Cristiani caput populi? At si eam velit gloria et honore ac devotione fidelium Rome parem facere, illi ipso Domino erit opus, ut arbitror, 'qui facit mirabilia magna solus.'

80   Ecce autem inter loquendum michi, quod sepe accidit, in animum venit de quo nichil, incipiens, cogitaram. Gaudeant nunc igitur et exsultent Galli, parvis et frivolis ex causis soliti gaudere. Magna, imo maxima res inventa est. Gaudeant, inquam, et qui

let our Gaul proceed further, and he will see that the Herod who was surnamed Antipas was likewise banished. Where shall we suppose, if not to Vienne, that place of exile?[130] Now let him proceed even further, and he will see that the other Herod, the tetrarch, was banished by the emperor Caligula to Lyon on the Rhone, where he died a wretched death, together with his wife, who in her conjugal devotion had followed him into exile.[131] But I am going too fast. Where did we leave Pontius Pilate who, already guilty of great crimes, was likewise banished to Lyon by Tiberius?[132]

Now let our Gaul, for all his glibness, declare that I lied when in my letter to Pope Urban I wrote that the Rhone was not the seat of the Roman pontiffs, but of criminals condemned to exile! I don't deny that the Roman pontiff may, if he chooses, live not only in Gaul, but even in Spain or Britain. Yet in his wisdom Urban clearly had no doubts about what was convenient and honorable. Still, I fear the mutterings of the Curia. For if they could shake an old man from his personal viewpoint, how much more easily can they make a young man adhere to their common view![133] Yet Christ will see to this, since it is his affair. For my part, since I can do no more, I shall at least not remain silent while I am still able to speak. The pope's presence may make Avignon the capital of the world. Why not? He is the vicar of almighty God and the head of the Christian people. Still, if he chooses to make Avignon the equal of Rome in glory and honor and the devotion of the faithful, he will need God's help, I think, for "He alone does great wonders."[134]

As often happens, while I am speaking, something occurs to me that I never imagined when I began. So let the Gauls now rejoice and exult! They usually rejoice for small and trivial reasons, but I have discovered a great fact—or rather, the greatest fact of all. Let them rejoice, I say. And since they boast in their cups, let them boast when the historians mention the exile of Pontius Pilate in

435

gloriantur in poculo, glorientur, si quidem ubi apud historicos est mentio de hoc exilio Lugdunensi, his utuntur verbis: 'pro iis omnibus deportatus est in exilium [Pontius videlicet Pilatus] Lugdunum.' Et sequitur: 'unde oriundus erat, ut ibi in obbrobrium gentis sue moreretur.' Parva ne igitur gaudendi causa est, tantum civem invenisse? O mens hominum obliviosa et improvida! Ego quidem ex Evangelio mirabar, quomodo in passione Iesu Cristi Pontius Pilatus tam prompte manus lavisset, quasi innocens a sanguine iusti illius. Nunquam facere hoc scivisset, ni fuisset Gallus — gens argutula, promptula, facetula. Miror quod non etiam lotis manibus semel bibit, ut innocentior videretur.

81   Noveram ab adolescentia Pontium Pilatum Gallum esse, sed tempore michi elapsus, in tempore rediit, ut, cum hoc precone Gallorum communicato gaudio, gratularer Gallicis nationibus tanto duce nobilitatis, ut iam frustra Roma suos Cesares loquatur, suos Scipiadas, suos Emilios, suos et Marcellos et Fabios et Metellos et Pompeios et Catones et Curios et Fabricios et Corvinos et Decios et Torquatos et Flaminios et Valerios et Appios et Papirios et Camillos. His aliisque omnibus respondebit Pontius, qui non de Hanibale neque de Carthaginiensibus, non de Pyrrho, non de Macedonibus, non de Gallis, de Germanis, de Britannis, de Hispanis, de Volscis, de Samnitibus, collatis signis, sed de Iesu Nazareno lotis manibus illoto animo triumphavit. Nominatim Gallo nostro gratulor, qui bellum mecum et cum Italia et cum veritate suscepit; nusquam, credo, triumphaturus de nobis, nisi in arcu parvi pontis et in vico Straminum, famosissimis nunc locorum omnium nostri orbis, mulierculis puerisque plaudentibus et quicquid contra Italiam dictum fuerit consona voce laudantibus.

82   Felix natio, que de se optime, de aliis omnibus pessime opinatur, grato saltem semper leta mendacio. Sed nonne ego sim iniu-

Lyon in these words: "For all these reasons, he was sent into exile in Lyon, whence he had come, so that his death would bring his people greater shame."[135] Can the discovery of such a great citizen be a minor reason for rejoicing? How forgetful and shortsighted the human mind is! When I used to read the Gospel account of Christ's passion, I wondered how Pontius Pilate could wash his hands so quickly, as if he were innocent of a just man's blood. He would never have been able to do this, if he hadn't been a Gaul, for they are a clever, glib, and witty race. I am surprised that, once he had washed his hands, he didn't take a drink, in order to seem more innocent.

In my youth, I knew that Pontius Pilate was a Gaul. With 81 time, he faded away, only to return to me at the right moment, so that I could share my joy with this herald of the Gauls and congratulate the Gallic nations on their great and noble leader. By comparison, Rome speaks in vain of her Caesars and of men like Scipio, Aemilius, Marcellus, Fabius, Metellus, Pompey, Cato, Curius, Fabricius, Corvinus, Decius, Torquatus, Flaminius, Valerius, Appius, Papirius, and Camillus. Pontius Pilate is a match for these men and all the others. He did not triumph over Hannibal and the Carthaginians, over Pyrrhus and the Macedonians, over the Gauls, Germans, Britons, Spanish, or over the Volscians and Samnites in close combat. But Pilate triumphed over Jesus of Nazareth with clean hands and an unclean heart.[136] I must personally congratulate our Gaul for declaring war on me and on Italy and on the truth. Yet I think he will not triumph over us anywhere, except perhaps under the arches of the Petit Pont and in the Street of Straw—the most notorious places in the entire world today.[137] There the foolish women and children will applaud, unanimously praising whatever he says against Italy.

O happy nation, which has the highest opinion of itself and the 82 lowest of all other nations, and which is always cheered at least by a gratifying falsehood! But isn't it unfair of me to belittle the fame

437

rius, qui sic famam Gallice gentis extenuem, quasi non sit eis alius vir illustris nisi Pontius Pilatus? Imo quidem et alii multi sunt, quos hic vir iratus in oculos michi ingerit et queritur me dixisse quod 'nullus doctus in Gallia.' Quomodo ego hoc dicerem de tam magna provincia, tot studiis ornata? Nondum sic insanio ut hoc dicam. Sed cum de quattuor illis doctoribus agerem, quos post apostolos et evangelistas primos fidei nostre duces Sancta habet Ecclesia, nullum eorum vel in Gallia ortum, vel in Gallia doctum dixi.

83   Quid igitur, an erravi? Bene autem me Gallus intelligit, sed calumniam sciens struit, ex me querens, nunquid essem oblitus Hilarium Pictaviensem. Minime. Magnus quidem vir, sed non unus ex quattuor. Profert dehinc sancto agmine multa suorum plebeia nomina, quos ego non existimo ultra suam viciniam nota esse. Misertus sum hominis, magna clarorum sive nominum penuria laborantis. Et quam multos ad furtum credimus traxisse pauperiem, quos cupiditas non traxisset? Nempe inter ceteros, quos ad Gallie ornamentum trahit invitos, unus est Hugo de Sancto Victore, cuius si sepulcri legisset epygramma, sciret non Gallum cum fuisse, sed Saxonem, nisi forte quadam cognatione barbariei omnes barbaros Gallos dicat. Sed disputator argutus advertere debuit, non omnem propositionem esse versatilem. Certe enim omnis Gallus est barbarus, sed non barbarus omnis est Gallus. At fortasse non homines aspicit iste, sed studium, ut quisquis Parisius studuerit, Gallus sit.

84   Invitus dicam, sed urget veritas. Est illa civitas bona quidem et insignis regia presentia. Quod ad studium attinet, ceu ruralis est calathus, quo poma undique peregrina et nobilia deferantur. Ex quo enim studium illud, ut legitur, ab Alcuino preceptore Caroli regis institutum est, nunquam (quod audierim) Parisiensis quisquam ibi vir clarus fuit; siqui fuerunt, externi utique et, nisi odium

of the Gallic nation, as if Pontius Pilate were its only illustrious citizen? Indeed, there are many others whom this angry Gaul thrusts before my eyes, complaining that I said "There is no one of learning in Gaul." When would I have said this about such a great province, and one distinguished for its many studies? I am not yet mad enough to say such a thing! Still, when I discussed those four Doctors who, after the apostles and evangelists, are the holy Church's foremost guides in faith, I said that none of them was born or educated in Gaul.[138]

What, then—was I mistaken? Our Gaul clearly understands 83 me; but he knowingly contrives to slander me when he asks whether I have forgotten Hilary of Poitiers. A great man, to be sure, but not one of the four Doctors! Then he marshals a host of plebeian names from his people, who I believe are unknown outside their own neighborhoods. I felt sorry for the fellow, struggling with this great dearth of famous names. How many people shall we think have been driven to stealing by their poverty, rather than by greed! Thus, among several men whom he reluctantly presses into service to glorify Gaul, one is Hugh of St. Victor. But if he had read the inscription on his tomb, he would know that he was a Saxon, not a Gaul—unless perhaps some barbaric affinity moves him to call all barbarians Gauls. But this shrewd debater should have observed that not every proposition can be reversed. Clearly, every Gaul is a barbarian, but not every barbarian is a Gaul. Or perhaps he less regard for the person than for his university, so that anyone who has studied in Paris is a Gaul.

I am loathe to speak, but the truth compels me. Paris is indeed 84 a fine city, and one ennobled by the king's presence. As for the university, it is like a rustic basket into which exotic and precious fruits are gathered from many places. We read that it was founded by Charlemagne's tutor Alcuin, but to my knowledge no Parisian since that time has ever become famous there. If any were famous men, they were in fact foreigners. And unless hatred shuts this

barbari oculos perstringeret, magna ex parte Itali fuere: Petrus Lombardus Novariensis (quem ipsi Petrum Lombardi solent dicere, ut videatur patris nomen esse, non patrie); Thomas de Aquino, Bonaventura de Balneo Regio atque Egidius Romanus multique alii.

85   At ne semper accusem, excusabiles Gallos non negaverim, si modice literati sunt. Nempe contra naturam niti, sepe labor est irritus. Natura autem Galli sunt indociles. Iratus est barbarus: non michi autem irascatur, sed Hilario suo, qui primus hoc dixit. Testis est Hieronymus libro in epystolam *ad Galatas* secundo. Fatebitur forsan, quod negare nequit; sed occurret: 'et quanquam Galli sint,' inquiet, 'indociles et indocti, habent tamen alias virtutes (neque enim solis in literis est humana felicitas): fortissimi viri sunt atque victoriosissimi.' Vellem hercle ita esset. Etsi enim vere barbarus nullus amabilis multum sit, minus tamen odibiles sunt, qui parcius barbarizant. Sed contrarium sepissime, et olim et presertim nuper, apparuit, verumque experimento his temporibus deprehensum est, quod libro tertio *Belli Gallici* Iulius Celsus ait: 'nam ut ad bella suscipienda Gallorum alacer ac promptus est animus, sic mollis ac minime resistens ad calamitates perferendas mens eorum est.' Et quid ait princeps historie? 'His corporibus animisque omnis in impetu vis est, parva eadem languescit mora.'

86   Sed expecta, ne properes. Audiamus Iustinum. Nec obiciam Augustinum, qui quarto libro *Civitatis Dei* de Iustino et Trogo, quem Iustinus abbreviavit, mentione oborta, 'quedam,' inquit, 'illos fuisse mentitos, alie fideliores litere ostendunt.' Sed ut nil mentiti fuerint et omnia vera sint, quibus hic barbarus totam fabulam suam replet, quid inde conficiet? Verset et reverset, ut libet, nichil

barbarian's eyes, the majority of them were Italians: Peter Lombard of Novara—whom they like to call Peter Lombardi, so that his surname seems to be his father's rather than his country's—Thomas of Aquino, Bonaventure of Bagnoregio, Giles of Rome, and many others.

But lest I continually accuse the Gauls, I won't deny that they 85 may be excused if their learning is but modest. To strive against nature is always a bootless effort; and by nature the Gauls are unteachable. Now my barbarian is angry. But let him direct his anger not at me, but at his own Hilary, who was the first to say this, as Jerome bears witness in Book Two of his commentary on Galatians.[139] Perhaps he will admit what he can't deny. But then he will counter: "Even if the Gauls are unteachable and untaught, they still have other virtues, for happiness does not consist solely in learning. They are very brave and victorious men." By heaven, I only wish this were true. For if no barbarian is truly lovable, less hateful are those who restrain their barbarous behavior. Yet the contrary has often been the case, both long ago and especially in recent times. In our age, we have experienced the truth of what Julius Celsus wrote in Book Three of the *Gallic War*: "Just as the temper of the Gauls is impetuous, ready to engage in war, so their mind is weak and by no means resolute in enduring calamities."[140] And what does the prince of historians say? "All their strength and courage lie in attacking, but they languish as soon as there is a slight delay."[141]

But wait, don't hurry. Let us hear Justin. Now, I won't object by 86 citing Augustine, even though in Book Four of his *City of God* he mentions Justin and Trogus, whom Justin abridged, and says: "Other more reliable sources show that they sometimes lied."[142] Instead, let us suppose that they didn't lie, and that everything is true that this barbarian crams into his fable. What will he prove by this? Let him read and re-read as much as he wants. He will find no great praises there, except that the population of the Gallic

ibi magne laudis inveniet, nisi quod multitudo Gallici populi ingens fuit, ut eos scilicet Gallia ipsa non caperet. Quid hic, queso, laudabile? Nempe et musce multe sunt et culices et formice, pauci leones, paucissimi elephantes. Phenix est unicus, et omnino signum nobilitatis est paucitas. Quis autem, queso, tanto in populo unus aut alter illustris est habitus? Relegat illum historie locum, et quos invenerit nobis, qui hoc nescimus, annuntiet.

87   Est et aliud in ea multitudine gloriosum, quod mercenarii regum orientalium fuere. Atqui stipendiariorum nulla vita miserior, corpus atque animam parva mercede vendentium. Eat nunc, et comparandi studio ponat hos miseros contra

Romanos rerum dominos gentemque togatam.

At Gallos, ferro omnia prosternentes, multas provincias peragrasse commemorat. Ut sit ita, finem respicere sapientes iubent. Eorum certe, qui in Italiam venerunt, nullus omnino superfuit. Tribus magnis preliis ad unum deleti omnes, ne quis in ea gente, ut ait Florus, exstaret, qui incensam a se Romanam Urbem gloriaretur. Eorum vero, qui in Greciam perrexerunt, nichilo melior sors fuit. Primum mero, qui peculiaris genti mos, dehinc ferro victi, omnes occubuere. Brennus, dux illorum, qui solus in ea hominum colluvie nomen habet, vulnerum impatientia gladio se transfixit. Reliqui fugientes, et incommodis multis afflicti atque attriti et preventi ab hostibus, periere, 'ut nemo ex tanto exercitu, qui paulo ante fidutia virium etiam Deos contemnebat, vel ad memoriam tante cladis superesset.' Testem ab adversario citatum in iudicium adduco, Iustinum ipsum, cuius hic est quarti et vicesimi libri finis: 'Et hec sunt Gallorum expeditiones, hec bellica gloria: pro virtute impetus, postque impetum ruina.'

race was so immense that Gaul could not contain them all.[143] What is praiseworthy in that, I ask? Clearly, there are many flies and gnats and ants, but only a few lions and very few elephants. The phoenix is unique, and in general rarity is a mark of nobility. And in this vast nation, I ask, did even one or two become illustrious? Let him re-read the passage in Justin's history, and report any that he finds to us, who know of none.

Another glorious achievement of this multitude was their 87 service as mercenaries for Eastern kings.[144] Yet no life is more wretched than that of hired soldiers, who sell their bodies and souls for a pittance. Let him go now, and in his zeal for comparisons let him set these wretches beside the

Romans, lords of the world and the nation of the toga.[145]

Still, the Gauls, he reminds us, traversed many provinces, and put everything to the sword.[146] This may be true, but wise men bid us consider the end result. Of those who came to Italy, absolutely none survived. In three great battles, they were wiped out to a man. In this way, as Florus says, "none would survive to boast of burning the city of Rome."[147] And the fate of those who went on to Greece was no better. They all perished, overcome first by wine — a custom peculiar to this nation — and then by the sword.[148] Their leader Brennus, who alone is named in that cesspool of humankind, ran himself through with a sword, unable to bear his wounds.[149] The others fled; and wearied and wasted from many hardships, they were overtaken by the enemy and perished. "Thus, none of this vast army, which had lately been so confident in its own strength as to despise the very gods, survived even to commemorate its great defeat."[150] I call to the stand the very witness cited by my opponent, Justin. Here is the conclusion of his Book Twenty-Four: "These were the expeditions of the Gauls, and their military glories: fury instead of valor, and ruin after their fury."[151]

: X :

88 Credo ego iam barbarum suscepti sponte certaminis penitere; sentit enim, nisi cerebrum bovis atque asini habet auriculas, se ratione succumbere. Quid faciat igitur, nisi quod obsessi solent, quibus ad defendendam urbem non satis est animi? In arcem confugiet et, quia Galliam non potest, urbem illam unicam, famosissimam ac fabulosissimam defendet; atque ad id ipsum, Deus bone, quam frivola implorantur auxilia! Multo quidem illaudatus esse maluerim, quam a tali laudatore laudari. Verum equidem hoc michi videor asserturus, licet forsitan inurbane. Ex omnibus, quos legerim, nullus usquam tediosior Architrenio illo est, quem hic ad Parisiense preconium velut alterum Ciceronem aut Virgilium implorat. O que monstra sermonis, que verborum inculcatio, non tantum lectori nauseam incutiens ac dolorem capitis, sed risum eliciens ac sudorem! Usque adeo, dum vult omnia dicere, nichil dicit. Unum ex omnibus attingendum est, quo cunta conicias: 'Rosa,' inquit, 'mundi, balsamus orbis.' O fetidum balsamum, o olentem rosam! Equidem ex omnibus civitatibus, quas multas ab ineunte etate, nunc negotio tractus, nunc videndi discendique desiderio circuivi, olentiorem nullam vidi. Una excipiatur Avinio, que hac in parte miserie principatum tenet.

89 Pudeat vero iantandem de tam nota veritate contendere, ne non tam rei obscuritas videatur, quam cecitas contendentis. Piget nunc illas ad insanias respondere. Avinionem carpsi, laudat iste Massiliam, urbem, fateor, haud ignobilem, et tranquillo portu et equoreo prospectu, et, quod precipuum habet, Romana fide ac devo-

: X :

I believe that our barbarian now regrets having chosen to engage 88
in this contest. For unless he has the brain of an ox and the ears of
an ass, he senses that he must properly concede defeat. What can
he do, then, except what besieged people do when they lack the
courage to defend their city? He will seek refuge in the citadel.
Unable to defend all of Gaul, he will defend its one famous and
fabulous city. Good God, what trifling reinforcements he calls up
in its defense! By far, I would prefer to be unsung, rather than
praised by such a praiser. What I am about to say seems true to
me, if not very polite. Of all the authors I have read, no one anywhere is as tedious as the famed Architrenius, whom he summons, like a second Cicero or Virgil, to sing the praises of Paris.
What monstrosities of speech, what a pounding din of words!
They not only give the reader nausea and a headache, but provoke
his laughter and sweat. So little does he say by trying to say everything! We need only sample one phrase from many to form an
idea of the whole: "Rose of the world, balsam of the globe."[152] O
fetid balsam, O malodorous rose! Since my youth, I have toured
many cities, whether on business or from a desire to see and learn.
And of all these, I have seen none more malodorous than Paris,
with the sole exception of Avignon, which takes first place in this
regard.[153]

By now, we should be ashamed of contesting a well-known 89
truth, lest we expose not so much the obscurity of the question as
the blindness of the one who contests it. I am reluctant to reply to
his madness. Since I found fault with Avignon, he praises Marseilles. I admit that Marseilles is a noble city that deserves praise
for its tranquil harbor and its view of the sea, as well as for its
fidelity and devotion to Rome. Without its aid, Cicero says, our
Roman generals would never have triumphed beyond the Alps.[154]

tione laudabilem, sine qua, ut dicit Cicero, nunquam nostri imperatores ex transalpinis bellis triumpharunt. Sed quo, queso, vir hic prudens, quo progreditur? Ut inter barbaros suos scire aliquid videatur, nichil ad rem pertinentem illius urbis originem interserit, que narratio — ut plerunque ignorantibus evenit — contra ipsum vertitur. Nam et feras Gallorum gentes et Gallicam continet feritatem, et postremo sic Massilienses adventu suo Gallicam mansuefecisse barbariem, 'ut non Grecia in Galliam emigrasse' (ipsius historici verbis utor), 'sed Gallia in Greciam translata videretur.' De quorum adventu, in libro *De consolatione ad Helviam matrem,* agens Seneca: 'maxime trucibus,' inquit, 'et inconditis Gallie populis se interposuerunt.'

90   Hec disputator callidus non vidit, contentus multa dicere, sed qualia non advertens. Iam illud quale est, duos proferre non Italos poetas, quasi quoscunque subtraxerit Italie sui sint, Statium scilicet et Claudianum, quem facere nititur Viennensem. Risi legens dixique mecum: 'O quam male tegeris inscitia, nisi velo silentii tegaris! Certe nichilo melius quam tussis aut scabies. Emergeris enim, teque ipsum tuo prodis indicio.' Viennensis est igitur Claudianus? Errat Gallus in re Gallica; imo quidem Lugdunensis. Sed excusat errorem urbium vicinitas. Illud inexcusabile, quod, de quo loquitur, ipse idem non intelligit. Duo enim fuerunt Claudiani, poeta alter et paganus, alter presbyter cristianus. Hic, fateor, Lugdunensis fuit disputator, acer satis, qui magnorum hominum, inter ceteros Hilarii Pictaviensis, deprehendit errores. Ille autem unde fuerit, etsi sciam, non dicam; ne Gallus insultet, velle me patriam meam — satis per se ipsam, Deo gratias, florentem — uno Pyerio cive nobilitare.

91   Statium origine Gallum non infitior; addo, si libet, et Lucanum ex Hispania. Ceterum, undecunque ipsi fuerint, stilus est Italus,

But how, I ask, how does this prudent man proceed? To lend his barbarians an air of learning, he introduces the origin of Marseilles, which is completely irrelevant. As often happens to the ignorant, this narrative turns against him. For it describes the savage tribes of Gauls and their Gallic savagery. Then it relates how the arrival of people from Marseilles domesticated their Gallic barbarity, so that, as the historian puts it, "rather than Greece migrating to Gaul, Gaul seemed transformed into Greece."[155] In his *Consolation to his Mother Helvia*, Seneca discusses this migration and says that the people of Marseilles "established themselves in the midst of what were then the most savage and uncivilized peoples of Gaul."[156]

Our wily disputant fails to see this, and is content to voice many arguments, heedless of their quality. For example, as if anyone he steals from Italy becomes one of his people, he cites two non-Italian poets, namely, Statius and Claudian, and tries to make the latter a native of Vienne. As I read this, I laughed and said to myself: "How poorly you conceal your ignorance, unless you cover it in a veil of silence! It's like trying to conceal a cough or the mange. You'll be discovered, betrayed by your own testimony." Claudian was from Vienne, you say? Our Gaul is in error on a Gaulish question. No, Claudian was from Lyon.[157] But the proximity of the two cities excuses his error. What is inexcusable is that he talks about things he fails to understand. There were two Claudians. One was a pagan poet, and the other a Christian priest. The priest was from Lyon, I admit, and a sharp disputant who detected the errors of many men, including Hilary of Poitiers. As for the poet, I won't say where he was from, although I know, lest our Gaul insults me for exploiting a citizen-poet to ennoble my homeland, which is quite flourishing, thank God.[158]

I don't deny that Statius was of Gallic origin.[159] If you like, I may add that Lucan was from Spain. But wherever they came

90

91

nempe aliter nullus esset; verumque deprehenditur, quod ego ipse
in pastorio iuvenili carmine olim dixi:

> Tiberina Latine
> docti omnes per rura loqui.

Itaque se Lucanus multis in locis Romanum vult videri; nec, ut
reor, ullam patrui graviorem habet iniuriam, quam quod is in operis sui principio, si vera est fama, verbum illud apposuit:

> Corduba me genuit.

Norat enim quanto nobilius Rome civem esse quam Cordube.
Statius vero, suum poema concludens, iubet, ut poetam Italum
longe sequatur et

> vestigia semper adoret.

92   Quid sibi igitur vult Gallus? An non videt quid alienigene
quoque de se ipsis et de nostris senserint? Sufficiat sibi *Anticlaudianus* Alani sui, paulo minus tediosus Architrenio. Poete ambo bar-
barici multum pariter se diffundunt, multum frustra se torquent,
mirum nisi multum etiam sudent. His contentus, de Claudiano altero non laboret.

93   Quale illud est enim, quod inter Romanos et Latinos differen-
tiam ut inducat atque ita latinarum literarum gloriam Romanis
eripiat, dicit inter eos fuisse discordias! Nec fallitur. Quid tamen
ad rem ipsam, cum inter Romanos ipsos et in eisdem menibus et
discordie fuerint et bella civilia? An non omnes ideo Romani?
Odia atque discordie civitatem[10] ac patriam non mutant, quamvis
imminuant vel eripiant caritatem. Certe de bello inter eas gentes
orto agens Livius: 'Bellum,' inquit, 'utrinque summa ope paraba-

from, their style is Italian, nor could it be otherwise. Indeed, we perceive the truth of what I wrote in an early pastoral poem:

In the fields by the Tiber
They all learned to speak Latin.[160]

Hence, in many passages Lucan wishes to appear Roman. I suspect that he considered it the gravest offense possible when, if the report is true, his uncle prefaced his epic poem with the phrase

Cordoba gave me birth.[161]

For he knew how much nobler a citizen of Rome is than a citizen of Cordoba. And when Statius concludes his epic, he urges it to follow our Italian poet at a distance and

always worship his footsteps.[162]

So what does our Gaul want? Doesn't he see how foreigners   92
felt about themselves and our countrymen? He need only read the
Anticlaudianus by his countryman Alan of Lille, which is slightly
less tedious than his Architrenius. Both these barbaric poets are
greatly prolix and pointlessly contorted, and it is no wonder if they
sweat a great deal. Let him be content with these authors, and not
trouble himself about the other Claudian.

And what kind of argument is his next one? In order to distin-   93
guish between the Romans and the Latins, and thus to rob the
Romans of the glory of Latin literature, he says that there were
dissensions between them! He's not mistaken. But what difference
does this make, when there were dissensions and civil wars between the Romans within their own city walls? Does this mean
that they weren't all Romans? Feuds and dissensions do not
change one's city or country, even if they weaken or destroy the
bonds of amity. Indeed, when Livy describes a war between the
two peoples, he says: "Both sides prepared for a war with the
greatest energy—a civil war, as if between fathers and sons."[163] In

449

tur, civili simillimum bello, prope inter parentes natosque.' Denique quotiens inter eos ferro certatum traditur, non tanquam duarum, sed unius gentis, et belli civilis mentio est. Si testem alium Gallus querit, audiat Augustinum libro XVIII *Civitatis Dei*, haud procul a principio de Grecis historiis agentem: 'Per Grecos,' inquit, 'ad Latinos, deinde ad Romanos, qui etiam ipsi Latini sunt, temporum seriem deduxerunt, qui gentem populi Romani in originis eius antiquitate rimati sunt.' Et iterum: 'Ex Grecis, inquit, 'et Latinis, ubi est ipsa Roma.'

94   Equidem literas latinas a Carmenta Evandri regis matre repertas invenio, et quantum opinari est, Palatino in monte, qui est unus e septem, quos hodie Romane urbis murus amplectitur. Illic enim filii sedes fuit, ubi nondum Roma erat. Et preterea docti viri, in omni sermone ac scriptura, Romanam facundiam Latinam vocant, atque e converso, ut duo sint nomina, sed res una. Esto autem. Probet Gallus quod intendit, non Romanas esse quibus utimur literas, sed Latinas. Quid hinc tamen efficiet? Utraque gens Itala est: ut non sint Romane, Itale tamen sunt. Neque ego in epystola, quam iste sibi delegit oppugnandam, Rome sed in Italia ortas dixi. Contentionis autem studio bene armatum hostem plumbeo etiam pugione diverberat, ne nil agere videatur.

95   Quid rursus igitur illi faciam, iam non ineptie dicam, sed insanie? Tantus est enim ardor, tantus impetus obtrectandi, ut quid loquitur non attendat. 'Ubi, queso,' inquit, 'legitur Tulli *Phisica*, ubi Varronis *Methaphisica?*' O stulta percontatio! Barbarus insolens grecis nominibus delectatur, et ita hoc dicit tanquam qui hos libros scripsit, Aristotiles, Gallus sit. Legi librum fraterculi cuiusdam, cui nomen est *Prosodion*. In hoc ille grammaticali opusculo impertinentissime evagatus, et patrie sue vano ebrius amore, hispanum fuisse ait Aristotilem, quem fortassis nunc iste freneticus

fact, whenever we read of armed conflict between these two peoples, reference is made to one people rather than two, and to "civil war." If our Gaul wants another witness, let him hear Augustine's discussion of Greek history near the beginning of Book Eighteen of his *City of God*: "Those who have explored the descent of the Roman people from their most ancient origins have traced their succession through the Greeks to the Latins, then to the Romans, who themselves are Latins."[164] And he also writes "from the Greeks and from the Latins, where Rome itself is."[165]

I find that the Latin alphabet was invented by Carmenta, the   94
mother of King Evander, presumably on the Palatine, which is one of the seven hills enclosed today by Rome's city walls.[166] For it was the dwelling of her son even before Rome existed. In all their speech and writing, moreover, learned men call Roman eloquence Latin, and vice versa, so that the two names refer to one thing. Be that as it may, suppose our Gaul proves his point, that we use Latin letters, not Roman ones. What will he accomplish by this? Both peoples are Italian. If their alphabet is not Roman, it is still Italian. And in my letter, which he has singled out for attack, I said that this alphabet arose in Italy, not in Rome.[167] Eager to combat, he strikes his well-armed adversary with but a leaden dagger, to avoid seeming idle.[168]

In turn, how can I deal with what I no longer call folly, but in-   95
sanity? So great is his ardor, so great his vehemence in disparaging, that he pays no attention to what he is saying. "Tell me," he asks, "where do we read about Cicero's *Physics* or Varro's *Metaphysics*?" What a stupid question! This insolent barbarian delights in Greek words, but then speaks of Aristotle, who wrote these books, as if he were a Gaul. Now, I have read a book by a certain Franciscan titled *Prosodion*.[169] In this little work on grammar, the friar wanders far from his subject and is so drunk with vain patriotism that he says that Aristotle was a Spaniard.[170] And now our madman apparently makes him a Gaul. His words can only mean

Gallum fecit. Quid enim aliud sonant verba Tullio, Italo ac Romano, quid nisi ut Gallum obiciat illum, qui Galliam nunquam vidit (credo equidem) nec audivit, natione Grecus aut Macedo, patria Stagirites?

96   Fatetur hic quidem Gallus—non, ut reor, ex animo, sed urbanitate quadam Gallica—'Italiam magnam partem et bonam orbis esse': ipsius enim verba transcribo. Agamus ergo Gallo gratias, imo quidem veritati, que fateri illum cogit, quod ab alio dici fert moleste, et id valde laudare quod vehementer odit. Fatetur insuper et nostrorum quosdam scripsisse libros multos humane vite utiles, 'longe tamen *Ethice* Aristotelis posthabendos.' Mirum pugne genus! Cum uno ceperam duellum; is iam fessus, labante vestigio, alium fortiorem michi velut inadvertenti obicit. Quid enim comune habet Aristotelis *Ethica* cum Gallorum ignorantia? Ut vincat Aristotiles: quid ad Gallos? Nisi quod intensum odium, quicquid hosti detrahitur, sibi ascribit. Ego tamen externo et valido bellatore non moveor, sed in mea opinione persisto, quam, ut reor, experientia veritasque adiuvant. De qua quoniam multa nuper, materia cogente, disserui, brevibus nunc attingam.

97   Scio Aristotelis *Ethicam* librosque alios viri illius ab alto ingenio profectos. Quantum tamen ad id spectat, ad quod philosophie pars moralis inventa est, hoc est, ut fiamus boni, sicut idem ipse diffinit, nego ullos seculares libros nostrorum libris ne dicam preferendos esse, sed equandos; atque illud esse verissimum, quod Tullius ipse confirmat multis in locis, sed in uno maxime: 'Meum,' inquit, 'semper iudicium fuit omnia nostros aut invenisse per se sa-

that he dismisses Cicero, an Italian and a Roman, by citing this alleged Gaul, Aristotle—who I am sure never saw or even heard of Gaul, since he was Greek or Macedonian by birth, and a native of Stagira!

Now, our Gaul admits that "Italy is a large and goodly part of the globe." I transcribe his own words, although he may not be speaking sincerely, but merely out of Gallic politeness. Let us thank our Gaul, or rather the truth, which forces him to admit things that irk him when expressed by someone else, and to praise strongly what he violently detests. He further admits that some Italians have written many books that are useful to human life, but are "far inferior to Aristotle's *Ethics*." What a strange kind of battle! I had entered a duel with one man. But now that he is weary and staggering, he sends a stronger combatant against me, as if I wouldn't notice. What does Aristotle's *Ethics* have in common with the ignorance of the Gauls? Suppose Aristotle wins: what does this have to do with the Gauls? Unless his intense hatred claims as its own everything he strips from his adversary. Yet I am not shaken by this foreign and formidable warrior, but hold fast to my own opinion, which I believe is confirmed by experience and truth. Since I recently spoke at length about this, as the occasion required, I shall only briefly touch on it here.[171]

I know that Aristotle's *Ethics* and his other works are the products of a great mind. But if we look at the purpose for which the ethical branch of philosophy was devised—namely, to become good, which is his own definition—I deny that any secular books are superior or even equal to those of our Latin authors.[172] I believe the absolute truth of what Cicero affirms in many passages, but especially in this one: "It has always been my conviction that our countrymen have shown more wisdom everywhere than Greeks, either in making discoveries for themselves, or else in improving upon what they had received from Greece, in such subjects at least as they had judged worthy of the devotion of their

pientius quam Grecos, aut accepta ab illis fecisse meliora, que quidem digna statuissent in quibus elaborarent.' Et hoc igitur meum quoque iudicium est, non ideo minus verum quia Gallo forsitan non probetur: plus Aristotilem docere, plus Tullium animos movere; plus in illius moralibus libris acuminis, plus in huius efficacie inesse. Ille docet attentius quid est virtus; urget iste potentius ut colatur virtus. Quid sit utilius vite hominum Gallus ipse diffiniat.

98   Et cum Tullio Senecam pono, de quo Plutarchus, magnus vir et grecus, ultro fatetur nullum in Grecia fuisse, qui sibi posset in moralibus comparari. Sed occurret Gallus, et dicet origine hunc Hispanum. Respondebo dignitate et conversatione, stilo insuper ac studiis Romanum esse; et michi sufficere, quod Gallus utique non est, sicut adversario sufficit Aristotilem Italum non fuisse. 'Non scripsit Tullius *Phisicam*'; addo ego: nec *Ethicam*; 'non scripsit Varro *Methaphisicam*'; addo ego: nec *Problemata*. Sumus enim non Greci, non barbari, sed Itali et Latini. At scripsit Tullius *Officiorum* libros: illa *Ethica* sua est; scripsit de re familiari sive de domo sua: illa *Yconomica*; scripsit *De re publica*, de re militari: illa *Politica* sua est.

99   At Galliculus titulos Grecos amat, et quamvis scientiam forte nec Grecam habeat nec Latinam, magnum se aliquid credit, dum 'Phisicam' ructat, 'Methaphisicam' spuit. Non scripsit *Phisicam* Tullius; scripsit autem *De legibus, De academicis, De laude philosophie* librum, quo se ad rectum iter vite et ad studium veritatis adiutum ingenue predicat Augustinus; quod de Aristotile nunquam dixit. An de philosophorum Gallicorum aliquo dixerit, ego nescio; adversarius forsitan meus scit, laudum auceps solicitus Gallicarum. Non scripsit Tullius *Phisicam*, sed scripsit *De essentia mundi, De natura deorum, De divinatione, De fato, De senectute, De amicitia, De consolatione, De gloria, De tusculanis questionibus, De fine bonorum et*

efforts."[173] This is my view too, and it is no less true because this Gaul may disagree. Aristotle teaches more, but Cicero moves our minds more. Aristotle's books on ethics hold greater insights; Cicero's have a greater effect. Aristotle teaches the nature of virtue more precisely; Cicero urges the pursuit of virtue more persuasively. Let our Gaul define for himself which is more useful to human life.

Next to Cicero, I place Seneca, of whom the great Greek Plutarch confessed that Greece had produced no comparable thinker in moral philosophy.[174] But our Gaul will confront me and say that Seneca's origins were Spanish. I shall reply that his rank and social circles, as well as his style and his studies, made him a Roman; and that it is enough for me that he was no Gaul, just as it is enough for my opponent that Aristotle was no Italian. "Cicero wrote no *Physics*." And no *Ethics*, I would add. "Varro wrote no *Metaphysics*." And no *Problems*, I would add. For we are not Greeks or barbarians; we are Italians and Latins. Yet Cicero wrote books *On Moral Duties*, which are his *Ethics*. He wrote works on householding, or on his home, which are his *Economics*. He wrote *On the Republic* and works on military science, which are his *Politics*.

But our little Gaul loves Greek titles; and although he may have no Greek or Latin learning, he thinks he is someone great when he belches forth the word "Physics" or spits out "Metaphysics." Cicero wrote no *Physics*, but he wrote *On Laws, On the Academics*, and a book *In Praise of Philosophy*. Augustine candidly states that this last work helped guide him toward the right path in life and toward the pursuit of truth.[175] This is something he never said about Aristotle, and I don't know whether he ever said this about a Gallic philosopher. Perhaps my opponent knows, since he tirelessly hunts for praises of Gaul. Cicero wrote no *Physics*, but he wrote *On the Essence of the Universe, On the Nature of the Gods, On Divination, On Fate, On Old Age, On Friendship, On Consolation, On Glory, Tusculan Disputations, On the Ultimate Good, Rhetorical Parti-*

98

99

malorum, Partitionum, Topicorum, De oratore, De optimo genere orato-
rum, De optimo genere dicendi, Rethoricorum duo volumina, tria autem
Epystolarum, orationes innumeras, quibus par eloquium nunquam
fuit.

100   Stupet Gallus ad hec nomina peregrina, cum tamen et pauca de
multis attigerim, et maior multo rerum quam nominum fulgor sit.
Quid quod nec *Methaphisicam* Varro scripsit? Ingens accusatio
docti viri! At scripsit libros viginti quinque rerum humanarum, sedecim divinarum. 'Sed in his ultimis multa vana congessit, et a
cultu vere divinitatis abhorrentia.' Agat divine providentie divi-
neque misericordie gratias Gallus noster, que erroribus eum priscis eductum ad meliorem etatem verique Dei notitiam reservavit.
Nam et maiores suos, Druides sacerdotes, multis deorum nominibus falsorum et vanissima superstitione obrutos habuisse non
ignorat, qui omnes Gallos Dite prognatos assererent; et credulita-
tem publicam inanis assertio merebatur. Nullo enim modo divinarum rerum veritas apparere illis poterat, quibus nondum verus sol
iustitie illuxerat.

101   Elucebant tamen inter errores ingenia, neque ideo minus viva-
ces erant oculi, quamvis tenebris et densa caligine circumsepti, ut
eis non errati odium, sed indigne sortis miseratio deberetur; et
quod ydolis servierunt, ut Hieronymus ait, non obstinationi mentis, sed ignorantie tribuendum esset. Magni quidem erant illi, sed
in imo positi; nos parvi, autem in excelso, Deo gratias, collocati
sumus. Intempesta fuit illis nox: nobis est lucidus meridies; nec
propterea meliores, quia sine meritis, sed profecto feliciores dici
possumus. Idque non de his duobus tantum, quos in manibus habeo, sed de omnibus gentium philosophis ac poetis intelligo, quibus inter oculos mentis et veritatis obiectum nubes impenetrabilis
intercessit.

tions, Topics, On the Orator, On the Best Kind of Orator, On the Best Kind of Style, two volumes of *Rhetoric*, three volumes of *Letters*, and countless speeches whose eloquence has never been equalled.[176]

Hearing these strange names, our Gaul is dumbfounded, even though I only cited a few from his many works, and the brilliance of their content far outshines their titles. What if Varro wrote no *Metaphysics*? Truly a prodigious charge against this great scholar! All the same, he wrote twenty-five books on human institutions, and sixteen on divine ones.[177] "But in the latter he compiled many falsehoods at odds with the worship of the true divinity." Let our Gaul thank divine providence and God's mercy, which kept him for a better age and a knowledge of the true God, releasing him from ancient errors. For he is aware that his ancestors were Druid priests who, mired in a vast host of false gods and in the vainest superstition, asserted that all the Gauls were descended from Dis—an empty assertion that won their people's credulity.[178] The truth of divine things could in no wise appear to people who were not yet illuminated by the true sun of justice.

Yet even among their errors some intellects shone forth. Their eyesight, although enshrouded in darkness and dense fog, was still vigorous, so that we should not display hatred for their error, but compassion for their undeserved plight. As Jerome says, if they served idols, we must ascribe this to ignorance rather than to obstinacy.[179] They were great men, but placed in the depths. We are small, but placed on the heights, thanks to God. They lived in the dead of night; we live in a bright noonday. We cannot therefore claim to be superior—for we are without merit—but merely more fortunate. I consider that this applies not only to the two authors I have before me, but to all the pagan philosophers and poets, whose mind's eyes were blocked by an impenetrable cloud from any vision of the truth.

102   Sed redeo ad Varronem. Non scripsit *Methaphisicam*; scripsit tamen de philosophia, de poetica, de lingua latina, de vitis patrum.
Et quo feror? An Terrentianum illud oblitus sum, cuius meminit
Augustinus? 'Vir,' inquit, 'doctissimus undecunque Varro, qui tam
multa legit, ut aliquid ei scribere vacavisse miremur; tam multa
scripsit, quam multa vix quenquam legere posse[11] credamus.' Libet
igitur indignari. O viri maximi, o Latini eloquii preclarissima sidera, o ingeniorum rerumque omnium sors immitis! Huc ne igitur
vestri labores vestreque vigilie pervenerunt, ut Gallicum ad tribunal barbarico iudicio rei essetis, quod *Phisicam* et *Methaphisicam*
non scripsistis?

: XI :

103   Iam vero deliramenta illa non prosequor, ut res adducit innumeras, nil ad propositum pertinentes; atque inops mercator omnes
suas merces simul explicat, inter alia Iustini sui partem non exiguam transcribendo. Urbium Italicarum narrat auctores, de quo
Hyginus quidam integrum librum fecit. Legat autem quem dixi
Senece librum ad Helviam: ibi reperiet omnes ferme gentes, alteram ex altera ortas. Sic more celestium et terrena volvuntur.

104   'Multi alienigene in Italia urbes condiderunt.' Quis hoc nescit?
Quid ve ad rem? Que autem mundi pars est, ubi non Itali urbes
quoque condiderint? 'Romanum imperium,' ut ait Seneca, 'nempe
auctorem exulem respicit, quem profugum capta patria, exiguas
reliquias trahentem, necessitas et victoris metus longinqua que-

But I return to Varro. He wrote no *Metaphysics*, but he wrote   102
about philosophy, poetics, the Latin language, and the lives of the
Roman fathers. Where does this lead me? Have I forgotten the
words of Terentian cited by Augustine? "Varro was most learned
in every field. He read so much that we are amazed that he had
time to write, and wrote so much that we can hardly believe anyone could read it."[180] There is reason, then, for my indignation. O
illustrious men, O shining stars of Latin eloquence, O fate implacable to every genius and to all our affairs! Have all your toils and
vigils come to this: that you are found guilty by barbarian judges
in a Gallic tribunal, simply because you wrote no *Physics* or *Metaphysics?*

: XI :

But I no longer pursue his delirious ravings. He adduces countless   103
examples that are completely irrelevant. Like an indigent peddler,
he displays all his wares at once, transcribing *inter alia* long excerpts from his beloved Justin. He lists the founders of Italian cities, a subject to which a certain Hyginus dedicated an entire
book.[181] But let him read Seneca's book to Helvia, which I mentioned earlier, where he will find that nearly all nations descend
from others.[182] Like heavenly bodies, earthly affairs have their cy-
cles.

"Many foreigners established cities in Italy." Who doesn't know   104
this? But what difference does it make? Is there any part of
the world where Italians did not found cities? As Seneca says:
"The Roman empire itself, in fact, looks back to an exile as its
founder—a refugee from his captured city who, taking along a
small remnant of his people and driven by fear of the victor to
seek a distant land, was brought by destiny into Italy."[183] Then see

rentem in Italiam deduxit.'[12] Dehinc vide quid addidit: 'Hic demum,'[13] inquit, 'populus quot colonias in omnem provinciam misit! Ubicunque vicit, Romanus habitat.' Hec Seneca. Ubi autem, queso, non vicit, nisi forsan in Gallia? Roma in Italia a Troianis est condita; Troiam vero quis condidit? Nempe Italus fuit et Tuscus. Unde est illud apud Virgilium sub Troianorum ad Italiam adventum:

> Hinc Dardanus ortus,
> huc repetit.

105   Coloniam Agrippinam Marcus Agrippa, Augusti gener, ad sinistram Rheni ripam condidit, similiter et alias multas per diversa terrarum; sed hec una nomen nunc etiam servat auctoris. Lugdunum, de quo multa hodie diximus, Plancius, Romanus civis, extruxit; Tarraconem in Hispania Scipiones; Parisiorum urbem—et pene Gallis invideo tantum sue sedis auctorem—Iulius Cesar creditur condidisse. Idem de Gandavo, dum adolescens ibi essem, a civibus audiebam: sic a patribus per manus proditum memorie. Totam preterea Rheni vallem colonis ab Augusto missis habitatam invenio.

106   Verum hec sedium mutatio non patriam, ad quam pergitur, sed pergentes immutat. Itaque et Galli in Asiam Asiatici, et Itali in Phrygiam profecti Phryges, et post Troie excidium in Italiam reversi Itali iterum facti sunt. Sic nostri in Galliam aut Germaniam translati naturam illarum partium imbiberunt moresque barbaricos. Et Mediolanenses a Gallis conditi, atque olim Galli, nunc mitissimi hominum, nullum servant vestigium vetustatis. Ita vis celestis humana vincit ac moderatur ingenia. Conditarum sane a

what he adds: "This people, in turn—how many colonies has it sent to every province! Wherever the Roman conquers, there he dwells."[184] Thus Seneca writes. And where, I ask, did it not conquer, except perhaps in Gaul? In Italy, Rome was founded by Trojans; but who founded Troy? In fact, it was an Italian from Tuscany. This accounts for Virgil's phrase describing the Trojans' arrival in Italy:

Hence was Dardanus sprung,
And hither he returns.[185]

Marcus Agrippa, the son-in-law of Augustus, founded Colonia Agrippina on the left bank of the Rhine, and many other colonies too throughout the world, although only this one still retains its founder's name.[186] A Roman citizen named Plancus built Lyon, about which I have said a great deal today.[187] The Scipios founded Tarragona in Spain.[188] Julius Caesar is believed to have established the city of Paris; and I nearly envy the Gauls for this great founder of their capital.[189] I heard the same about Ghent from its citizens when I was there as a young man; such was the tradition handed down by their forefathers.[190] In addition, I find that the entire Rhine valley was populated by colonists sent by Augustus.[191]

Yet such a change of settlement changes the people who migrate, rather than the country to which they migrate. Hence, the Gauls migrating to Asia Minor became Asians; and the Italians migrating to Phrygia became Phrygians, but reverted to Italians when they returned to Italy after the fall of Troy.[192] Thus, our own Italians who moved to Gaul or Germany have imbibed the nature of those regions and their barbaric customs. But the inhabitants of Milan, whose city was founded by Gauls and who were themselves formerly Gauls, are now the gentlest people on earth, and retain no trace of their ancient past.[193] So much does the power of the heavens dominate and influence human minds. No one can count all the cities that the Romans founded in Italy: Bologna, Modena,

Romanis in Italia non est numerus: Bononia, Mutina, Pollentia, Parma, Cremona, Placentia, et decus urbium Florentia. Nolo nunc in alias mundi partes stilum cogere, neque in hac curiositate diutius istum sequi, ne, in quo alium rideo, ipse ab aliis sim ridendus.

107   Quonam vero progreditur? Dicit Massilienses aurum misisse, quo a Gallis Roma redimeretur. Insulse dictum, ut alia multa. Ita enim loquitur, quasi salutem urbis Rome Massilie tribuat et redemptionem ignominiosam Romanis improperet. Contra ego aurum missum non infitior; idque eam, de qua dixi, urbis illius in Romanos promptissimam fidem probat. Ceterum qui captam Romam et incensam fateor, auro redemptam nego; ferro nempe redempta est et Gallico sanguine expiata. Historie patrem legat, ex hac ipsa urbe oriundum unde hec scribo, illum lacteo eloquentie fonte manantem, ad quem visendum usque Romam de extremis Hispanie Galliarumque finibus nobiles veniebant viri, unius aspectum urbi regie preferentes: illum, inquam, legat et luce clarius suum videbit errorem.

: XII :

108   Dicit Rome multos esse malos et fuisse. Quis hoc etiam nescit? Tres soli homines in mundo erant: unus fuit malus. Cum illo qui mundum creaverat fuerunt duodecim: unus fuit proditor. An non igitur meminit illud Iulii Cesaris apud Crispum? 'In magna civitate multa et varia ingenia sunt.' Fuerunt Romani ingrati, non id quidem nego. Non est autem is mos magis populi Romani, quam

Potenza, Parma, Cremona, Piacenza, and that glory of our cities, Florence. I don't want to force my pen to traverse other parts of the world, or to pursue this fellow's pedantry any further, lest others mock me for what I mock in another.

But where does he lead us now? He says that the people of 107 Marseilles sent gold to ransom Rome from the Gauls.[194] An absurdity, like many of his statements! He speaks as if he attributes Rome's survival to Marseilles, and reproaches the Romans for this shameful ransom. Now, I don't deny that they sent gold, an act that proves the unfailing allegiance of Marseilles to Rome, which I have already mentioned. But while I grant that Rome was captured and burned, I deny that it was ransomed with gold; in fact it was ransomed with iron and expiated with Gallic blood. Let our Gaul read the father of history, who was a native of the city from which I write.[195] This milky font of eloquence was visited in Rome by noblemen from furthest Spain and Gaul, who preferred viewing this one man to the imperial city.[196] Let our Gaul read Livy, I say, and he will see his error more clearly than daylight.[197]

: XII :

He also says that many bad men lived in Rome, and still live there. 108 Who doesn't know this? There were once just three men in the world, and one of them was bad.[198] There were twelve men in the company of Him who created the world, and one was His betrayer. Has our Gaul forgotten the words of Julius Caesar quoted by Sallust? "In a great city, there are many different natures."[199] The Romans were ungrateful, I don't deny it. But such behavior is no more peculiar to the Roman people than to other peoples. What people was ever grateful? Gratitude is practiced by a few, not by all. "They were ungrateful." But to whom? "Towards their

omnium populorum. Quis unquam populus gratus fuit? Grati-
tudo non omnium, sed paucorum est. 'Ingrati fuerunt': contra
quos? 'Contra cives optimos.' Illi autem cives unde erant? Roma
una omnibus patria. Erant ibi et boni et mali: 'at plures mali.' Ubi,
queso, unquam contrarium visum est? Ubi unquam pro uno bono
non fuerunt—vellem dicere multi, cogor dicere mille mali? 'Fuit
Rome proditor patrie Catilina'; aliique, quos odio dictante dinu-
merat. Sed proditio illa quorum potius, quam Gallorum fulciebā-
tur auxilio? Gens radicitus inimica, contra invisam urbem per se
nichil ausura, ab ipsis civibus, ut audere aliquid inciperet, exci-
tanda erat.

109   'Fuit Rome Catilina,' sed et Cato fuit, qui de proditoribus sententiam tulit; fuit et Cicero, vigil consul, qui sententiam exsecutus
est; fuerunt et mille alii, quibus parem unum non habuit orbis
terre. 'At non fuit in Gallia aliquis Catilina.' Credo edepol. Fuit
enim Catilina, quamvis ingenio malo pravoque, magna tamen vi
animi et corporis. Hec profecto vis non habitat inter Gallos. Res
illarum partium undique fragiles exsanguesque sunt: nec boni nec
mali fame aliquid merentur. Sunt ibi, ut apud gentes alias, mali,
sed obscuri. Quomodo enim mali cognoscerentur, ubi boni etiam
sunt ignoti? Voluptatis ex regno ingens fama exulat.

110   Desinat, oro, iam barbarus conferre summis infima, fusca clarissimis. Et quid illud erroris, quod Italicum Satyricum de Romanis
moribus questum dicit? An de Serum rectius atque Indorum moribus quereretur? De his queritur, quos agnoscit, quibus tangitur.
At quis unquam pater non interdum de filii moribus est conques-
tus?

111   Addit etiam duos Rome lenones illo tempore fuisse, Artorium
et Catulum. Credidi primum, et sic scriptum erat, quod leones di-

worthiest citizens."[200] But where did these citizens come from? All of them had one homeland — Rome. Both good and bad men people lived there. "But more bad ones." Where, I ask, has anyone seen the opposite? Where in the world hasn't a single good individual been outnumbered — not only by *many* bad ones, as I wish I could say, but by *thousands*, as I perforce must say? "As traitor to his country, Rome had Catiline," and others listed by this Gaul, driven by his hatred. On whom did the traitors count for support more than the Gauls?[201] Despite their deep-rooted enmity, this race dared not act on their own against the hated city of Rome, but had to be goaded by Roman citizens into daring.

"Rome had Catiline." But it also had Cato, who pronounced 109 sentence on the traitors.[202] It also had Cicero, the vigilant consul who carried out the sentence.[203] And it had thousands of others, whom the entire globe could not equal. "But Gaul had no Catiline." I truly believe it. Despite his evil and corrupt nature, Catiline possessed great mental and physical strength.[204] Such strength does not dwell among the Gauls. The natures of that region are frail and feeble, and neither good nor bad men win any fame. As in other nations, there are bad people, but they remain obscure. For how should the bad be recognized where even good people are unknown? Great fame is banished from pleasure's domain.

Let our barbarian cease now, I pray, to compare the lowly with 110 the lofty, and the drab with the illustrious. Isn't he off the mark, when he says that an Italian satirist complains about Roman behavior?[205] Would the satirist have been more justified in complaining about the behavior of the Indians or Chinese? He complains about the behavior that he knows and that affects him. Was there ever a father who never complained at times about his son's behavior?

Then our Gaul adds that there were two panders in Rome at 111 the time, Artorius and Catulus.[206] At first, I thought he meant two lions (as was written), and I wondered what lions were doing

ceret. Et mirabar, quid sibi vellent hi leones. Intellexi illico de lenonibus esse sermonem, et subridens dixi, 'volo subcubuisse huic
barbaro (quod invitus facerem), nisi cum in magna Roma duo fuerint lenones, in parva Avinione sunt undecim.' Scit enim ipse (et
utinam nescirent alii!) quantus ibi illi artificio locus sit.

112   Obicit nobis, inter multa, patientiam tyrannorum. Vellem hoc
negare, sed nequeo in aliqua scilicet Italie parte; nam in aliis est libertas, quanta nusquam alibi terrarum, quod ego quidem noverim.
Vera autem libertas ac perfecta, dum in hoc exilio degimus, fateor,
nulla est. Si autem michi locum aliquem sub celo omnis expertem
tyrannidis hic iactator ostenderit, illuc raptim cum omnibus sarcinulis commigrabo, ibique relique vite mee sedem eligam ac sepul-
crum. Qua in re noverit, me non facile falli posse, ut qui in his locis, in quibus iste felicitatem statuit, a prima pueritia educatus
sim. Sane si species tyrannidum explicare voluero, occurreret stilo
longa nimis atque odiosa materia. Sit satis taciturnus intelligi.

113   Iam quod usque adeo miratur equestrem statuam marmo-
ream — idolum vocat ipse — super altare Dei vidisse Mediolani,
longe rudis est admiratio. Non enim super, sed secus altare et in
capella domestica illam vidit. Quanto ego dignius mirer, vidisse
Parisius insignium choros ecclesiarum sic confertas bustis et cada-
veribus peccatorum, quodque est fedius peccatricum, ut vix quisquam possit ibi se flectere vixque iter pateat ad altare. Si Gallo,
censori rigido alienarum rerum, molli (ut auguror) suarum, responsio ista non sufficit, illum interroget, cuius est statua. Ille sibi
summarie respondebit, paratus etiam maioribus respondere.

114   Sed iam satis, superque satis est; cavendumque ne, dum stulti
sequor ineptias, ipse sim stultior: contagiosus morbus est amentia.

here.[207] But I quickly understood that he was talking about panders, and I said with a smile: "May I succumb to this barbarian—however unwillingly—if there aren't eleven panders in little Avignon for the two panders in great Rome!" He himself knows what great opportunities the trade finds there. I only wish that others didn't know!

Among many other charges, he reproaches us for our tolerance 112 of tyrants. I would like to deny this but can't, at least for certain parts of Italy. Yet in other regions there is more freedom than exists in the rest of the world, as far as I know. There is no true and perfect freedom, I confess, as long as we live in this exile. But if this boaster will show me a place on earth that knows no tyranny, I shall at once pack my bags and move there, and choose to live the rest of my life and be buried there. In this matter, he should know that I am not easily deceived, since from childhood I was raised in those places that he regards as the seat of happiness. And if in fact I chose to explain the different kinds of tyranny, the subject would prove too vast and too odious for my pen. Let it suffice that I am understood even in my silence.

Now, when he says he was amazed to see a marble equestrian 113 statue—which he calls an "idol"—placed above a divine altar in Milan, his amazement is that of a boor. He didn't see the statue above the altar, but in a private chapel to one side.[208] How much more justly should I be amazed, for I have seen the choirs of famous churches in Paris so crowded with tombs of sinners, both men and—even more revolting—women, that there is scarcely room to kneel or approach the altar. If this reply fails to satisfy our Gaul, who is a rigid censor of others' affairs, but soft on his own nation, let him ask the man portrayed in the statue, who will reply brusquely, for he is ready to reply to even greater authorities.[209]

But this is enough, and more than enough, on the subject. I 114 must be careful not to chase after the nonsense of this fool and thus become more foolish myself. Madness is a contagious disease.

Exclamabit Gallus in fine, ut grex illum audiat ignorantium, et Gallice glorie defensorem vocet. Multa igitur me mentitum dicet. Intus autem—velit, nolit—clara voce fatebitur, nil verius dici posse, quanquam paratus ad omnia. Nempe Bruti factum non est veritus damnare, qui amore virtutis et libertatis et patrie, sese oblitus, patrios affectus exuerit. Nescio hercle an res ulla unquam hac virilior facta sit, quam iste vituperat, teste fretus Orosio, qui licet non inelegans scriptor, tamen—quod legentibus pronum est advertere—in vituperatione Romanorum totum pene suum expendit ingenium, intentione forsitan non mala—ad nobilitandam scilicet Cristi fidem, quamquam nec ab ipso nec ab ullo hominum sat laudari possit—quia tamen nec suo, nec cuiusquam mendacio veritas indigebat, supervacue. Neque enim, ut in Bernardo, michi obstat reverentia sanctitatis, sancto licet scripserit Augustino.

115 Iam quidem Romulo obiciunt, et violentas nuptias illum celebrasse et in reliquis ardentissimi virum spiritus fuisse. Excusari potest facilius quam negari. Et nuptias quidem pene excusat ipsa necessitas. Quis est enim tam modestus qui, si fame ultima laborans panem humili prece poposcerit, negatum non, si possit, eripiat? Atqui populus virorum erat, ita enim scriptum est, unius duntaxat etatis: ad perpetuitatem nuptiis opus erat. Hec a finitimis expetite, non duriter modo, sed contumeliose etiam denegate erant, credo, presagientibus iam vicinis nova ex urbe venturos, qui eos reliquosque mortales et terrarum orbem iugo premerent. Ea negatio ac repulsa viros fortes ac magnanimos incitavit. Occasione itaque mox arrepta, non ad stuprum, sed ad coniugium et divine atque humane domus sotietatem, negatas virgines rapuerunt.

In the end, this Gaul will cry out so that the herd of the ignorant will hear him and call him the defender of Gallic glory. He will say that I told many lies. Yet whether he wants to or not, deep inside he will confess distinctly that no greater truth can be told, even though he is ready to do anything. For example, he did not scruple to condemn the actions of Brutus, who loved virtue, liberty, and his country so much that he forgot himself and renounced all his paternal affection for his sons.[210] Forsooth, I cannot imagine a more manly deed than this one. But our Gaul disparages it, relying on the witness of Orosius, a writer who is by no means inelegant, but who expends nearly all his wit on disparaging the Romans, as his readers will easily discover. He did this with good intentions perhaps — since he sought to ennoble our faith in Christ, although neither he nor anyone else can sufficiently praise it — but pointlessly, since the truth had no need of lies, neither his nor anyone else's. Unlike Bernard, he has no sainthood to awe me, even though he wrote at the request of St. Augustine.

Then Romulus is reproached for celebrating nuptials by force 115 and for his extreme ardor in other matters.[211] The charge is easier to excuse than to deny. Necessity itself practically excuses the forced nuptials. If someone starving to death humbly asked for bread and was refused, would he would not steal it if he could? In fact, we read that Romulus's people consisted only of men, all of the same age: marriage was necessary to perpetuate the race.[212] The neighboring peoples refused such marriages not only harshly but with insults. (I believe these neighbors foresaw that this new city would give rise to a race that would subjugate them, together with the rest of humankind and the entire world.) This refusal and rebuff provoked the strong and great-spirited Romans. Seizing the first opportunity, the Romans abducted the young women who had been denied them, not to rape but to marry them and to make them partners in their human and divine family.

116   Quod hic, queso, tam nefarium scelus est? An vero vel primus ille, vel insolitus virginum raptus fuit? An non sic tribus Beniamini uxores sibi rapuerant, idque de consilio maiorum natu, dicata et responsione adversus earum patrum seu affinium querelas? 'Rogantibus ut acciperent, non dedistis, et a vestra parte peccatum est.' Hoc primum in Iudea, postmodum Rome actum est, cogente utrobique necessitate. Et quot aliis in urbibus, quas nominare non est necesse, nuptas quoque ad adulterium raptas, et depulsos insuper maritos audivimus! Quid est quod Romulus solus arguitur, nisi quod

nulli gravis est percussus Achilles?

117   Reliquum sane viri illius ardorem Florus excusat. 'Quid,' inquit, 'Romulo ardentius? Tali opus fuit, ut invaderet regnum.' Et profecto, quandocunque usquam regnum cernimus, aut regis invadentis ardor fecit aut ignavia populi patientis. Non fecit natura reges primos, sed industria. Ad id denique quod Camillum patria pulsum dicit, quid respondeam nisi Ciceronianum illud: 'novum crimen et ante hunc diem inauditum'? Novum, inquam, et mirabile crimen exilium!

: XIII :

118   Ecce quam multa vir doctus accumulat pro defensione mendacii, quod oppugnare pro viribus suum erat. Sed amicum Gallis est mendacium, et amicum suum nullus oppugnat. Ego autem veritatis non me sat amicum rear, nisi eius fidele patrocinium, qua celitus datum erit, contra quoslibet suos hostes proque eius amore prompto animo et multorum et magnorum odia inimicitiasque

What horrible sin is this, I ask? Was this perhaps the first ab- 116
duction of young women, or an unusual one? Didn't the tribes of
Benjamin seize wives for themselves in this way, as their elders ad-
vised them, and prepare an answer to the protests of the fathers
and brothers? "When we asked, you did not give them, and so
you incurred the guilt."[213] This was first done in Judaea, and later
in Rome. Both cases were dictated by necessity. In how many
other cities, which I need not name, have we heard of brides
abducted by adulterers and their husbands repudiated! Why is
Romulus alone accused? Is it because

it will hurt no one's feelings to hear how Achilles was slain?[214].

Florus excuses Romulus's ardor in other matters: "Was anyone 117
as ardent as Romulus? Such a man was needed to usurp the kingdom."[215] Indeed, any kingdom we see anywhere in any age was either established by the ardor of a usurping king or through the
cowardice of a passive population. Industry created the first kings,
not nature. When our Gaul remarks that Camillus was banished
from his country, how can I reply? I can only cite Cicero's phrase:
"A novel crime, never before heard of!"[216] I say, exile is truly a
novel and amazing crime!

: XIII :

See, then, how many arguments this learned man piles up in de- 118
fense of a falsehood which he ought rather to have attacked with
all his might. But falsehood is a friend of the Gauls, and no one
attacks a friend. For my part, I would think myself a poor friend
of the truth, if I did not seek to defend her faithfully against all
her enemies, as heaven allows me, and if in my love for her I did
not endure the hatred and enmity of many powerful opponents.

suscepero. Quod cum facere iuvenis inceperim, non desistam senex.

119   Tu, amice, hec in barbari notitiam ut veniant curabis. Sibi quidem, quoniam nichil michi scripserat, nil rescribo, sed in literis tuis illius procacitatem contudisse suffecerit. Sin fortassis eum videris, quem credo illo adulationum atque mendaciorum in regno esse, unde utinam tu abesses, admone eum non ut barbarum, sed ut hominem, quando aliquid scribit pro certamine glorie, ut nunc fecit, caveat saltem ab aperto mendacio. Nam que contra rationem aut sine ratione dicuntur, utcunque nonnunquam oratione defenduntur; palam falsa nulla defendit oratio. Adducit ergo vir ille, pueriliter satis, Lucani versiculum, non integrum et impertinentem ad rem, probationis non egentem:

humanum paucis vivit genus.

Vulgatam illam vult probare sententiam: naturam paucis esse contentam.

120   Qui quidem versiculus, etsi seorsum per se ipsum sensum ad quem trahitur non respuat, ubi tamen est positus, longe aliud sonat. Hoc enim vult dicere, quod humanum genus vivit paucis, id est, ad obsequium paucorum, regum videlicet et principum, qui numero pauci sunt. Cesar enim ibi loquitur, qui alibi hoc ipsum expressius attigit, non paucos, sed unum mundi dominum se se dicens, ut non paucis, sed uni sibi vivere humanum genus ostenderet, ubi ait:

frustra civilibus armis
miscuimus gentes, si qua est hoc orbe potestas
altera quam Cesar, si tellus ulla duorum est.

Romanum enim, non Gallicum animum habebat. In eo igitur doctus hic fallitur, quod 'paucis' eo loco sextum casum credidit esse,

Having begun to act thus in my youth, I shall not desist in my old age.

My friend, you shall see that my words come to the attention of 119 this barbarian. Since he did not write directly to me, I shall not write back to him, but shall content myself with having crushed his arrogance in this letter to you. I believe that he lives in the realm of flattery and falsehood, where (God willing) you never go. But if you chance to see him, warn him not as a barbarian, but as a human being, to avoid open lies whenever he writes something in his quest for glory, as he has done now. Statements made contrary to reason or without good reason can sometimes be defended in speech, but no speech can defend what is patently false. Rather childishly, this fellow cites an incomplete and irrelevant verse by Lucan which needs no proof:

for the sake of a few the human race lives.[217]

He wants to prove the familiar saying that "nature is content with little."

While not in itself contradicting the meaning he gives it, this 120 verse has a completely different sense in its original context. In fact, it means that the human race lives "for the sake of a few," that is, obedient to a few, meaning kings and rulers, who are few in number. Indeed, the phrase is spoken by Caesar, who more expressly touches on this subject in another passage. There he says that there is but one lord of the world, Caesar himself, rather than a few: he wants to show that the human race should not live under a few, but under one man:

In vain with civil war
Have I convulsed the world, if there is any power on earth
Beside Caesar's, if any land belongs to more than one.[218]

Caesar's spirit was Roman, not Gallic. Hence, our man of learning errs in taking the noun "few" as an ablative, when it is a dative.

cum sit tertius. In eo quoque quod Numitorem a nepotibus inter-
fectum dicit, pace tanti viri dixerim, in historie comunis labitur
notitia: Numitoris enim frater Amulius interfectus, Numitor autem restitutus in regnum fuit, unde a fratre pulsus exulabat.

121   Credo ibi plura esse talia, sed hec se legenti statim obtulerunt.
Sperabat, ut auguror, barbaris suis loqui, atque ideo sibi licere omnia, non discreturis quid veri in rebus et quid falsi sit. Iamque vale,
equisque auribus hinc multiloquium meum, illinc strepitum Galli
fer.

Patavi, Kalendis Martiis [1373].

And when he says that Numitor was killed by his nephews, let me observe, with all due respect, that this great man slips up in a detail of well-known history. It was Numitor's brother Amulius who was killed, whereas Numitor was restored to the kingdom from which his brother had banished him.[219]

I believe there are similar errors in his work, but these are the 121 first that strike a reader. He hoped to speak to his fellow barbarians, I presume, and thus supposed he could write anything for people who would not distinguish between what is true or false in actual fact. Farewell now. With impartial ears, hear both my lengthy discourse and the squawking of our Gaul.

Padua, 1 March [1373].

Note on the Texts and Translations

తిఎిస

The text of *Invectives Against a Physician* is based on Francesco Petrarca, *Invective contra medicum, Testo latino e volgarizzamento di ser Domenico Silvestri*, ed. Pier Giorgio Ricci, with an appendix by Bortolo Martinelli (Rome, 1978).

The text of *Against a Man of High Rank* is based on Francesco Petrarca, *Invectiva contra quendam magni status hominem sed nullius scientie aut virtutis*, ed. Pier Giorgio Ricci (Florence, 1949).

The text of *Against a Detractor of Italy* is based on Francesco Petrarca, *Invectiva contra eum qui maledixit Italie (In difesa dell'Italia)*, ed. Giuliana Crevatin (Venice, 1995).

For the translation of *On His Own Ignorance and That of Many Others*, I have consulted the version by Hans Nachod found in *The Renaissance Philosophy of Man: Selections in Translation*, edited by Ernst Cassirer, Paul Oskar Kristeller, and John Herman Randall, Jr. (Chicago, 1948).

The text of *On His Own Ignorance and That of Many Others* is the work of the series editor, James Hankins, who describes his procedure as follows.

The text is based on a fresh collation *in situ* of the two autograph manuscripts:[1]

B   Berlin, Staatsbibliothek (Haus Zwei), Hamilton 493, begun in
        May, 1367 and completed around June 1370
V   Vatican City, Biblioteca Apostolica Vaticana, Vat. lat. 3359, dated
        from Arquà, 25 June 1370.

B shows four layers of additions and corrections which are almost always clearly distinguishable *in situ* on the basis of the color of the ink and the thickness of the penstroke. The four layers are identified in the apparatus as follows:

B   *Petrarch's original text, begun in May, 1367*
Ba   *Additions contemporaneous with the copying of the original*

Bb   Additions made at some later date before 1370, but before Bc

Bc   Additions made at some later date before 1370, but after Bb

(Since Bc in several places adds to or corrects Bb, it is clear that it repre-
sents a later stage of revision.)

Though Petrarca clearly copied V from B, in some cases he made additions and corrections to V which were also, contemporaneously, entered
in B as well. In most cases they appear to have been made first in the
margins of B, then added to V, but in one or two cases (probably while in
the process of copying) he seems to have corrected or added to V first,
and only later entered the corrections into B (see Fenzi's edition, pp. 112–
114). Petrarca's additions to V are indicated by the sigla *Va*.

In order to help the reader form a clearer idea of the process of revision, the corrections and additions of *Ba, Bb,* and *Bc* are shown in italics.
Not recorded in the apparatus are the interventions of *Bc* when *Bc* is
merely retracing faded letters written by *B, Ba* or *Bb*. It is evident that the
interventions of *Ba* and *Va* are often simply corrections of banal tran-
scription errors rather than genuine revisions. Further details about
Petrarca's scribal interventions in V can be found in the edition of
Capelli. For the modern editions of Capelli, Ricci-Bufano, Buck and
Fenzi referred to in the apparatus, see the Bibliography.

The *Epistola Dedicatoria* is preserved in two redactions, (a) the version
presumably sent to the dedicatee, Donato Albanzani, preserved in B and
other manuscripts (but not in V), and (b) the slightly revised text included as *Ep.* XIII.5 of the *Seniles* (Petrarca's *Letters of Old Age*). In B, the
dedicatory letter is written on a bifolium (f. 2r) which was probably at-
tached to the main block of text after the latter was written; it is not autograph. Version (b) is preserved in the canonical collection of the *Seniles*,
Florence, Biblioteca Laurenziana, MS Acq. e doni 266[2] and numerous
other manuscripts of this collection. Version (a) is given here, but the
variants of (b) are indicated with the siglum *Lac* (see Fenzi, pp. 120–121).

The apparatus employs the following abbreviations: *Marg.* = text written in the margin; *s.s.* = text written superscript. *After correction* means
the original text has been erased and replaced with revised text. In almost
every case the original text beneath the correction is no longer legible, but

in the few cases where the original text can be read the apparatus specifies the original reading with the note: *before correction.*

The text follows the spelling of *V,* but capitalization and punctuation are those of the editor.

NOTES

1. For the manuscripts, see A. C. de la Mare, *The Handwriting of the Italian Humanists,* vol I.1 (Oxford, 1973), pp. 10, 12, with references to the various published descriptions. For the extensive literature on philological issues arising from this text, see Fenzi's edition, pp. 105–127 and 141–169.

2. See *Codici latini del Petrarca nelle biblioteche fiorentine,* ed. Michele Feo (Florence: Le lettere, 1991), pp. 178–180 (no. 150, described by Teresa De Robertis).

Notes to the Text

≈§?≈

1. immeritos *Ricci, Bufano*

2. attollas] accolas *Ricci, Bufano* (possi . . . lodare *Silvestri*)

3. perituris] preituris *Ricci, Bufano* (che perirebbono *Silvestri*)

4. nudos videbis omni vera laude, vanitatibus obsitos] nudos videbis, omni vera laude vanitatibus obsitos *Ricci, Bufano*

5. princeps hostium, Maometus, deterrente scilicet omnium linguas ac calamos nominis maiestate] princeps hostium, Maometus deterrente, scilicet omnium linguas ac calamos nominis maiestate *Ricci*

6. sentis, logice, quam] sentis logice quam *Ricci* ('Tu, loycho, comprendi bene' *Silvestri*; cf. §89: logice nobilis)

7. res ipsa vobis tribuit, et omnium mortalium <iudicium> et comune proverbium] res ipsa vobis tribuit, et omnium mortalium, et comune proverbium *Ricci* (Cf. *Silvestri*: 'la cosa medesima l'oppenione di tucti e il comune proverbio.' Cf. also *Contra quendam magni status hominem*, §3, 'hominum iudicio . . . iudicia hominum' and *De sui ipsius ignorantia*, §79, 'iudicia hominum')

8. princeps *Ricci, Bufano:* i principi *Silvestri*

9. qui *Ricci, Bufano:* di quelle cose *Silvestri*

10. indicio *Ricci, Bufano:* giudicio *Silvestri*

11. accuses *Bufano:* accusas *Ricci:* non sono da essere accusati *Silvestri*

12. infuderunt *Bufano:* infuderant *Ricci:* concedette *Silvestri*

13. voluptatis *Bufano:* voluptatibus *Ricci:* dalla radice di quegli (desideri) *Silvestri*

14. lacesseres *Bufano:* lacesserer *Ricci:* tu m'assalisti *Silvestri*

15. gloriosus *Ricci, Bufano:* più gloriosamente *Silvestri*

INVECTIVE AGAINST A MAN OF HIGH RANK

1. pendetque *Virgil*

2. Deus meus] domine Deus *Augustine*

3. *Ricci punctuates:* malum facis grande, si verum crimen. (Cf. *Against a Detractor of Italy*, §51: 'duo magna, si vera sunt, vitia'.)

4. male partum, male disperit *Plautus*

ON HIS OWN IGNORANCE

1. Ad Donatum . . . grammaticum *is omitted here in B, but the text proper in both B and V has the title:* Francisci Petrarce laureati de sui ipsius et multorum ignorantia liber incipit, ad Donatum apenninigenam grammaticum. *The Epistola Dedicatoria is absent from V, and is omitted by Ricci-Bufano.*

2. in incude *Fenzi (see his p. 121)*

3. cameli aut elephantis *Lac (see Fenzi, p. 121)*

4. cursim in itinere properante] cursum a properante in itinere scriptus *Lac*

5. pausillum *B*

6. dilectionis] pignora dilectionis *Lac*

7. tibi olim] olim tibi *Lac*

8. *marg. Ba*

9. *marg. Ba*

10. *marg. Bb, Va*

11. *marg. Bc*

12. *marg. Bc*

13. *marg. Bc*

14. quid *BV*: quod *Capelli, Ricci-Bufano, Buck, Fenzi*

15. primo *B*

16. *marg. Va*

17. *marg. Bc*

18. *marg. Bc*

19. *marg. Ba*

20. satis eloquentiae, sapientie parum *Sallust*

21. quam geminam . . . habentes *in marg. Va*

22. *marg. Va*

23. *marg. Ba*

24. *s.s. Ba*

25. Ego Macrobius, *Buck (and see Fenzi, p. 111)*

26. mimusque *BV, Capelli, Ricci-Bufano, Fenzi (see his p. 111):* mimus *Macrobius, Buck*

27. *marg. Bc*

28. *marg. Va*

29. nescio *after correction by Bc;* cur dicebant *marg. Bc*

30. *marg. Bc*

31. iniustius *Ricci-Bufano*

32. *marg. Bc*

33. pars magna bonitatis est uelle fieri bonum *Seneca*

34. *marg. Bc*

35. *after correction by Bc, Va*

36. *marg. Bc*

37. *after correction by Bc*

38. sententia *BV:* sententiam *Capelli, Ricci-Bufano, Buck, Fenzi*

39. *marg. Ba*

40. *marg. Bc*

41. *marg. Bc*

42. *marg. Ba*

43. falsit *Ricci-Bufano*

44. *marg. Bc*

45. *after correction by Bc (and Va?)*

46. *marg. Ba*

47. *marg. Ba*

48. ex concilio deorum *before correction by Ba*

49. *marg. Bc*

50. *marg. Bc*

51. *marg. Bc*

52. *marg. Bc*

53. *marg. Ba*

54. *after correction by Bc*

55. *marg. Ba*

56. horum *Cicero*

57. essent *Cicero*

58. celum si aspeximus] cum caelum aspeximus *Cicero*

59. et ratio] quod ratio *Cicero*

60. id quod] id quod illud *Cicero*

61. Atqui *BV, Cicero:* Atque *Capelli, Ricci-Bufano, Buck, Fenzi*

62. ad usum . . . potuerint] ad usum meliores potuerint esse neque ad speciem pulchriores *Cicero*

63. fortuitane *Cicero*

64. ea quae *Cicero*

65. illa quae *Cicero*

66. ne *Cicero, Buck*

67. Qui *Cicero*

68. uel *Cicero*

69. mundum autem *Cicero*

70. esse expertem *Cicero*

71. in luna *Cicero*

72. Colchos *Cicero, Buck (see Fenzi, p. 111)*

73. *marg. Ba*

74. id *Cicero*

75. *marg. Bb*

76. *s.s. Bc*

77. *marg. Bc*

78. essent *etc. Cicero; Petrarca changes Cicero's plural subject to the singular throughout this paragraph.*

79. super *Capelli, Ricci-Bufano, Buck, Fenzi*

80. colimus *BV, edd.*: incolimus *Cicero*

81. et pulcritudinem *is not in modern texts of Cicero*

82. magnitudinem et decorem quem tum *BV, Fenzi*: magnitudinem et decorem, quem tamen *Capelli, Ricci-Bufano*: cum magnitudinem pulchritudinemque, tum *Cicero, Buck*

83. *om. Cicero, Buck*

84. *marg. Va*

85. *marg. Bb, Va*

86. tum ut *Cicero*

87. externis] ex aeternis tenebris *Cicero*

88. proinde *Cicero*

89. *marg. Bc*

90. nos *after* nouitas *Cicero*

91. neget *Cicero*

92. consilio *Cicero*

93. salute et conseruatione *Cicero*

94. *marg. Ba*

95. *marg. Ba*

96. *marg. Ba*

97. sic ut nesciam . . . tractauerit *added by Bc to the long marginal addition of Bb*

98. facta *V:* factum *B*

99. §§71–72 *marg. Bb*

100. *marg. Bc*

101. *s.s. Bc*

102. castissimus atque sanctissimus *Cicero*

103. ei *BV, Capelli:* et *Ricci-Bufano, Buck, Fenzi*

104. *after correction by Bc*

105. *marg. Bc*

106. uno uerbo *marg. Va*

107. Quin et solem *after correction by Bc;* et lunam . . . mundum *marg. Bc:* et lunam . . . hunc *marg. Va*

108. *marg. Bc*

109. *marg. Bc*

110. sex Hercules . . . quadringinta *marg. Va*

111. sex Hercules . . . Rogo enim *marg. Bc*

112. *s.s. Bc, marg. Va*

113. Nam de reliquis . . . scribenda hec *marg. Bc;* fuisse . . . legenda *after correction by Bc*

114. *Written in Greek capitals in the text of BV: BV also add* metempsicosis *in the margin*

115. *marg. Bc, Va*

116. *marg. Bc*

117. *marg. Bc*

118. nihilum *Persius*

119. Ita autem . . . insaniunt *marg. Bb*

120. quod . . . opinantes *marg. Bc*

121. *after correction by Bc*

122. *marg. Bc*

123. falsis *Capelli, Ricci-Bufano*

124. id fit *Cicero*

125. homines *Suetonius*

126. Nec audiunt . . . Vere ergo *marg. Bc*

127. cautiunculas *BV, Ricci-Bufano, Fenzi (see his p. 111):* cantiunculas *Capelli, Buck (see his p. XXIII)*

128. *marg. Ba*

129. *marg. Ba*

130. hoc *B*

131. *marg. Ba*

132. *marg. Va (after correction)*

133. *marg. Ba*

134. exciti ante] extiterint *Cicero*

135. *marg. Ba*

136. *marg. Ba*

137. *marg. Va*

138. nunc *V, Cicero:* non *B (?)*

139. annuis *Cicero, Buck*

140. *s.s. Va*

141. *marg. Bc*

142. *marg. Ba*

143. *marg. Bc*

144. *marg. Bc*

145. *marg. Va*

146. *marg. Bc*

147. nec Aristotiles, certe nec Plato est *Petrarca's punctuation in V:* nec Aristotiles certe, nec Plato *edd.*

148. *s.s. Va*

149. *marg. Va*

150. *marg. Bc*

151. Pariseos *BV* (*a Graecism*): Parisius *Ricci-Bufano, Buck, Fenzi*

152. *marg. Bc*

153. est] sit *B*

154. *marg. Bc*

155. *after correction by Bc*

156. formaque . . . uult *marg. Bc*; Plato miros sapientie *after correction by Bc*

157. neque sapientem . . . pergentibus *marg. Bc*; illi . . . dicebam *after correction by Bc*

158. *after correction by Bc*

159. *marg. Bc*

160. *marg. Bc*

161. *marg. Va*

162. *marg. Bc*

163. *marg. Bc*

164. *s.s. Va*

165. *marg. Bc*

166. *marg. Bc*

167. *marg. Bc*

168. *marg. Bc*

169. autores *B*

170. *marg. Bb*

171. *marg. Bb*

172. *marg. Bb*

173. *after correction by Bc*

174. *marg. Bc*

175. *marg. Bc, Va*

176. *marg. Bb*

177. *marg. Bc*

178. *s.s. Bc*

179. *after correction by Bc*

180. *marg. Bb*

181. *Bc later added the phrase* denique . . . Xenophonte *to the longer marginal addition*

182. *marg. Bc*

183. *Bc later added* -uis alicubi *to the longer marginal addition*

184. *Bc later added* post obitum *to the longer marginal addition*

185. *marg. Bc, Va*

186. *marg. Ba*

187. *after correction by Bc*

188. *after correction by Bc*

189. *De Nolhac and others correct* inscium (*wrongly*) *to* inscius (*see Finzi, pp. 109–110*); *the phrase needs to be read as sarcastic.*

190. *added by Bc and Va in the space at the end of the sentence*

191. *s.s. Va*

192. *marg. Ba*

193. *marg. Bc*

194. *marg. Bc*

195. nimius sim *before correction by Bc*

196. *marg. Bc*

197. *after correction by Bc*

198. *marg. Bc*

199. *marg. Bc*

200. *s.s. Bc*

201. *s.s. Bc*

202. *after correction by Bc*

203. Proh *before correction by Ba*

204. Sic V, Capelli: Si B, Ricci-Bufano, Buck, Fenzi

205. Si iam nemo] *corrected to* Sine istis nec *by a fifteenth-century Italian hand in B*

206. *marg. Bc, after correction in Va*

207. *marg. Bc*

208. *marg. Bc*

209. *marg. Bb*

210. nullos umquam] numquam *before correction by Bc* (nullos *in marg.*)

211. *marg. Bc*

212. *after correction by Bc* (confligatio B: conflictatio V)

213. *marg. Bc*

214. unam illam B

215. *marg. Bc, Va*

216. *marg. Va*

217. Addidi . . . addidissem *marg. Bc*

218. *after correction by Bc*

219. proh *before correction by Ba*

220. *marg. Bc*

221. assint B: adsint V

222. Dabis . . . Siquidem *marg. Bc*

223. *after correction by Bc*

224. *marg. Bc*

225. *marg. Va*

226. *after correction by Bc*

227. *marg. Bc, after correction Va*

228. gratibus *Ricci-Bufano*

229. *marg. Bc*

230. *Bc later added* quod . . . potuit *to the longer marginal addition of Bb*

231. *marg. Bb*

232. *marg. Va*

233. Nam que *BV*: Namque *edd*.

234. *marg. Bc*

235. et similia *marg. Va*

236. *marg. Bc*

237. *marg. Bc, Va*

238. *marg. Bb*

239. usum *B*

240. rei *BV, Buck, Fenzi*: re *Capelli, Ricci-Bufano*

241. *Bc later added the word* taciti *to the longer marginal addition*

242. Quibus quandoque . . . odiis *marg. Bc*

243. Aristarchum *B*

244. At Annaeum . . . dicebat *marg. Va*

245. At Annaeum . . . ausa sit *marg. Bc*

246. *marg. Bc*

247. *marg. Bc*

248. *after correction by Bc*

249. *added by Bc after the last sentence of B*

250. *Petrarca adds at the end in V (f. 38v):* Hunc libellum, ante biennium dictatum et alibi scriptum a me ipso, scripsi hic iterum manu mea et produxi ad exitum, Arquade inter colles Euganeos, 1370 Jun. 25, vergente ad occasum die.

INVECTIVE AGAINST A DETRACTOR OF ITALY

1. futuram quasi presentem, imo iam preteritam *Bufano*: futuram quasi iam preteritam *Crevatin*

2. eis etiam semper *Augustine*

3. et hercle *Livy*

4. parcendo victis *Livy*

5. iocor *Bufano*: ioco *Crevatin*

6. magisque *Sallust*

7. tute scis] *Sallust (and cf. §69: "Scit enim, et si nescit . . .")*: tu testis *Bufano, Crevatin*

8. Habe *Florus*

9. ait *Suetonius*

10. civitatem] civilitatem *Bufano, Crevatin (but cf. Petrarch's pointed contrast to* caritatem).

11. potuisse *Augustine*

12. detulit *Seneca*

13. deinde *Seneca*

Notes to the Translation

ABBREVIATIONS AND QUOTATIONS

References to works by classical authors use the abbreviations found in the *Oxford Classical Dictionary*, ed. Simon Hornblower and Antony Spawforth, 3d ed. (Oxford: Oxford University Press, 1999). Most of the citations from classical authors are adapted from the Loeb Classical Library.

PG   *Patrologia graeca*, ed. J. P. Migne, 162 vols. (Paris: Migne, 1857–1866).

PL   *Patrologia latina*, ed. J. P. Migne, 221 vols. (Paris: Migne, 1844–1864).

Most citations from the Bible follow the New Revised Standard Version, occasionally modified to match the Vulgate or Petrarca's context. Citations of the Psalms give the Vulgate number followed by the modern number in parentheses.

INVECTIVES AGAINST A PHYSICIAN

1. On 12 March 1352, Petrarca wrote a letter to the ailing pope Clement VI, which he later included in his collection *Familiar Letters* 5.19. Petrarca describes the origins of these invectives in a later epistle to the Sienese doctor Francesco Casini: see his *Letters of Old Age* 16.3.

2. Petrarca, *Familiar Letters* 5.19.5.

3. "Manipulator": Petrarca uses the Latin noun *palpator* as connoting both flattery and the medical procedure of palpation.

4. Doctors commonly examined the urine of their patients.

5. Juvenal 10.22.

6. According to ancient and medieval medicine, body fluids were composed of "humors" whose imbalance caused illness. When the illness

reached a crisis — the "critical" day — a discharge of the offending humors was thought to restore balance and lead to recovery.

7. Juvenal 1.161: Petrarca reads *verum*, "the truth," for *verbum*, "a word."

8. Terence, *An.* 68.

9. Source unknown.

10. Cf. Hugh of St. Victor, *Didascalicon* 2.20, in *PL* 176.760; and 2.23, in *PL* 176.761: "Mercurius, quasi mercatorum kirrios."

11. Cf. Psalm 72(73).9: "They set their mouths against heaven."

12. Cf. Cicero, *Tusc.* 3.1.

13. Ecclesiasticus 38.4. Petrarca reads *medicinam*, "medicine," for the Vulgate *medicamenta*, "medicines."

14. Ibid. 1.1.

15. Ibid. 7.16.

16. Macrobius, *Sat.* 5.1.7.

17. Varro: In fact, Petrarca apparently refers to Isidore of Seville, *Etym.* 8.7.2: cf. §137, n. 129, below.

18. Cicero, *Arch.* 8.18.

19. The anecdote is recounted in Cicero, *De Or.* 2.18.75.

20. Ibid. 2.76.

21. Boethius, *Consol.* 1.1.

22. Ibid.

23. Averroes (1126–1198) was a Muslim physician and philosopher.

24. Lactantius, *Div. inst.* 1.11.24–25.

25. "The very scum:" *pars ultima*, an echo of Juvenal 8.44.

26. The "old man of Maeonia" (*meonius senex*) is Homer: an echo of Ovid, *Ars Am.* 2.4.

27. Proverbs 17.28.

28. Apuleius, *Flor.* 2.

29. Ecclesiastes 12.12.

30. The famed Roman actor Quintus Roscius Gallus (d. 62 BC) wrote a treatise on acting.

31. Cicero, *Inv. rhet.* 1.5.6.

32. Habakkuk 3.13.

33. Luke 21.25.

34. Augustine, *Conf.* 5.13.23.

35. Seneca the Elder, *Controv.* 3.pr.16: "If you were a sewer, you'd be a Great Sewer," alluding to the Cloaca Maxima in Rome.

36. Valerius Maximus 3.7.3, quoting Publius Cornelius Scipio Nasica, consul in 138 BC.

37. Livy 38.50.11.

38. Ibid. 38.50.12.

39. Ibid. 38.51.6–14.

40. Augustine, *Commentaries on the Psalms* 144.7, in *PL* 37.1873–74.

41. Virgil, *Aen.* 1.378–379.

42. Homer, *Od.* 9.19–20.

43. Cf. Terence, *Phorm.* 506; Suetonius, *Tib.* 25.

44. Apuleius's Latin novel called *Metamorphoses* or *The Golden Ass*.

45. Petrarca refers to the medieval Latin comedy *Geta* (ca. 1150) by Vitalis of Blois. Imitating a passage in Plautus's *Amphitryon*, the title character Geta sophistically persuades the servant Birria that he does not exist.

46. Wisdom of Solomon 4.8.

47. Ibid.

48. Ibid. 4.9.

49. Cicero, *Sen.* 26.

50. Ibid. 62.

51. Cf. Aristotle, *Rhet.* 2.12–14,1388b-1390b; and Horace, *Ars P.* 158–179.

52. Psalm 77(78).34.

53. Ecclesiastes 1.15.

54. Pliny, *HN* 29.7.17–18, previously cited in Petrarca's letter to Pope Clement VI, *Familiar Letters* 5.19.

55. Ibid.

56. Cicero, *Tusc.* 1.31.75.

57. Suetonius, *Aug.* 80.6.

58. In the classical trivium, the logical or verbal arts included grammar, rhetoric, and dialectic.

59. Cicero, *Deiot.* 6.17.

60. Cicero, *Fin.* 3.12.41.

61. Cf. Psalm 13(14).1: "The fool has said in his heart: there is no God."

62. Cf. Ecclesiastes 12.12: "Of making many books there is no end."

63. Cf. Juvenal 7.51–52: "The incurable disease of writing."

64. The Stoic philosopher Chrysippus (280–207 BC) was renowned as a logician.

65. Cf. Cicero, *Tusc.* 1.30.74, which paraphrases Plato, *Phd.* 67D and 80E.

66. Cf. Hugh of St. Victor, *Didascalicon* 2.1, in *PL* 176.752: "Philosophia est meditatio mortis, quod magis convenit Christianis, qui saeculi ambitione culcata . . . similitudine futurae patriae vivunt." ("Philosophy is a meditation upon death, a thing highly appropriate for Christians, who having stamped out worldly ambition live in the likeness of their future homeland.")

67. Literally a "horned enthymeme." The adjective refers to the ancient paradox known as "the Horns" (cf. Aulus Gellius *NA* 18.2.9): "What you never lost, you have; since you never lost them, you therefore have horns."

68. The hoopoe is a European woodland bird with a prominent crest which is considered unclean in the Bible (Leviticus 11.19; Deuteronomy 14.18).

69. The hoopoe was supposed to feed on graves and human feces: cf. Isidore of Seville, *Etym.* 12.7.66. Cf. also Jerome, *Adversus Jovinianum* 2.37 (*PL* 23.336): "Et quia opulentus paterfamilias es, in aviariis tuis non turtures, sed upupae nutriuntur, quae tota foetidae voluptatis lustra circumvolent" ("And since you are a wealthy paterfamilias, hoopoes, not turtledoves are raised in your aviaries, a bird which flies about for whole periods of filthy pleasure").

70. Augustine, *De Civ. D.* 18.18.

71. Apuleius, *Met.* 10.33.

72. Ovid, *Ars Am.* 1.729.

73. Horace, *Carm.* 3.10.14.

74. For the handsome appearance of various philosophers, cf. Apuleius, *Apol.* 4.5–9.

75. Herodes Atticus, cited in Aulus Gellius, *NA* 9.2.4.

76. Augustine, *De Civ. D.* 8.1.

77. Cicero, *Amic.* 18.

78. In Genesis 30.32–42, Jacob breeds speckled goats by exposing them to mottled tree branches.

79. Virgil, *Aen.* 1.335.

80. Cicero, *Inv. rhet.* 1.29.46.

81. Petrarca cites Galen's work by its medieval title *Terapentica.* The treatise in question is Galen's *De methodo medendi,* a text first translated into Latin by Burgundio of Pisa (ca. 1110–1193) and later revised by Pietro d'Abano (1257–1315). Twenty-six codices of the work survive: see Pearl Kibre, "A List of Latin Manuscripts containing Medieval Versions of the *Methodus Medendi*," in *Galen's Method of Healing: Proceedings of the 1982 Galen Symposium,* ed. F. Kundlien and R. Durling (Leiden and New York, 1991), pp. 117–22.

82. Sallust, *Jug.* 85.32.

83. In this passage, Petrarca plays on *unctioribus verbis . . . unguentarii,* "unctuous words . . . vendors of ointments," and uses the verb *mulcere,* "to

caress, soothe, beguile," in order to suggest the physical massaging already implied in §6: cf. n. 3 above.

84. Cf. Horace, *Ars P.* 374–378: "As at a pleasant banquet an orchestra out of tune, an unguent that is thick, and poppy-seeds served with Sardinian honey give offense, because the feast might have gone on without them; so a poem, whose birth and creation are for the soul's delight, if in aught it falls short of the top, sinks to the bottom."

85. This Sicilian logician has not been identified.

86. Petrarca's friend is Tommaso Caloria of Messina, whose death is mourned in Petrarca, *Familiar Letters* 4.10 and 4.1.

87. I translate *lanista* in the medieval sense of wool-worker, rather than the classical sense of gladiator trainer. Cf. the pairing of wool-working and armor in §17 above — trades discussed by Hugh of St. Victor in *PL* 176. 760–61.

88. Aristotle, *Metaph.* 1.2, 983a.

89. Cf. Hugh of St. Victor, *Didascalicon* 2.21, in *PL* 176.760.

90. Livy 35.14.12.

91. Petrarca's opponent had evidently repeated the broadly Aristotelian argument that rhetoric and poetry could not be considered theoretical sciences (the highest kind of science) because their subject matter was subject to time and change, unlike the objects of metaphysics, physics or biology. Petrarca (see 3.115) chooses to emphasize Aristotle's statements in the *Rhetoric* emphasizing the possibility of treating poetry and rhetoric systematically.

92. Horace, *Ars P.* 70–72.

93. Isidore of Seville, *Etym.* 9.2.84.

94. Suetonius, *Aug.* 97.2.

95. Cf. Aristotle, *Rhet.* 3.1–3, 1404a-1406b.

96. Statius, *Theb.* 12.816–817. Cf. also Petrarca's *Against a Detractor of Italy*, §96.

97. Aristotle, *Rhet.* 3.1.1404a.

98. Petrarca's opponent had evidently brought up an old chestnut of the opponents of poetry: Boethius' comparison (placed in the mouth of Phi-

losophy in the *Consolation*) of dramatic poetry to "whores of the stage", *scenicae meretrices*.

99. Cf. Boethius, *Consol.* 1.1.11.

100. Ibid. 3.7.6 (Euripides); 4.6.33 (Lucan).

101. Petrarca seems here to reject the view, common in his day, that Seneca the philosopher and Seneca the author of tragedies were two different persons. See Giannozzo Manetti's life of Seneca in his *Biographical Writings*, ed. Stefano U. Baldassarri and Rolf Bagemihl, ITRL 9 (Cambridge, Mass., 2003).

102. Plato, *Tim.* 21D.

103. Alluding to Horace, *Epist.* 1.4.16: "Epicuri de grege porcum" ("a pig from Epicurus' herd").

104. Colossians 2.8.

105. Augustine, *De Civ. D.* 8.10, citing Romans 1.19–20.

106. Augustine, *Conf.* 8.2.3.

107. Augustine, *De Civ. D.* 8.10, citing Acts of the Apostles 17.28.

108. Romans 1.21–23.

109. Cf. Augustine, *De Civ. D.* 2.14, citing Plato, *Rep.* 3.398A and 10.607B.

110. Augustine, *De Civ. D.* 8.13, referring to Plato, *Rep.* 3.398A.

111. Augustine, *Soliloquies* 1.15.27, in PL 32.883.

112. Cicero, *De Or.* 1.3.11.

113. Horace, *Ars P.* 372–73.

114. Aristotle, *Eth. Nic.* 5.5, 1133a 16–17.

115. Cf. Hugh of St. Victor, *Didascalicon* 2.21, in PL 176.760.

116. Psalm 24(25).17.

117. Aristotle, *Metaph.* 1.2, 983a 1–4.

118. All of these are familiar Latin poets, except for Lucius Varius Rufus, Virgil's literary executor and a poet praised several times by Horace (in *Satires* 1.5.41 he is named as one of several "candid" souls).

119. The cryptic aphorisms of Heraclitus won him the nickname "the obscure": cf. Cicero, *Fin.* 2.5.15.

120. Augustine, *Conf.* 9.5.13 and 4.16.28, referring to Aristotle, *Categories*.

121. "Jealous rather than zealous": Petrarca puns on the contrasting verbs "invidisse" and "providisse."

122. Augustine, *Conf.* 11.15.19.

123. Augustine, *Commentary on the Psalms* 126.11, in *PL* 37.1675.

124. Augustine, *Commentary on the Psalms* 146.12, in *PL* 37.1907.

125. Ibid.

126. Gregory the Great, *Homilies on Ezechiel* 6.1, in *PL* 76.829.

127. Petrarca sarcastically suggests that, even after much study, the physician might still think that Aeneas was a woman.

128. Cf. Matthew 7.6.

129. On the poets as the first theologians, cf. Aristotle, *Metaph.* 1.3, 983b 27; and Augustine, *De Civ. D.* 18.14. On the name "poet," cf. Isidore of Seville, *Etym.* 8.7.1–3, and §26, n. 17 above.

130. Augustine, *De Civ. D.* 18.24.

131. Augustine, *De vera relig.* 1.1, in *PL* 34.123.

132. In the spurious dedication by Cornelius Nepos to the Latin *Fall of Troy* attributed to Dares of Phrygia.

133. Augustine, *De vera relig.* 1.2, in *PL* 34.123.

134. Psalm 95(96).5.

135. Wisdom 2.24.

136. Cf. Aristotle, *Rhet.* 3.1–3, 1404a-1406b; *Metaph.* 1.2, 983a 15; 11.10, 1076a 4–5.

137. Proverbs 26.4.

138. Ibid. 26.5.

139. In 1356, Petrarca fled Parma, leaving a number of literary projects there.

140. Augustine, *De Civ. D.* 1.3, citing Horace, *Epist.* 1.2.69–70.

141. Cf. Augustine, *Conf.* 8.2.5.

142. Cf. Isaiah 65.20 ("child of a hundred years"); and Seneca, *Ep.* 36.4, where the phrase "elementarius senex," which Petrarca takes to mean "old man in first grade," merely means an old schoolteacher.

143. Petrarca's allusion to straw perhaps evokes the Rue du Fouarre, site of the Paris theological faculty: cf. *On His Ignorance* §95, and *Against a Detractor of Italy* §66.

144. Cf. Isidore of Seville, *Etym.* 6.8.2.

145. Pliny, *HN* 29.5.11, remarks that for centuries the Romans lived without physicians.

146. When a cobbler offered his "artistic" criticism of a painting of Apelles, the painter told him: "Stick to your last." See Pliny, *HN* 35.10.84–85; and Valerius Maximus 8.12.ext.3.

147. Isaiah 6.6.

148. Cf. Virgil, *Aen.* 12.396–397.

149. Cf. *Codex Theodosianus* 16.2.42; and *Codex Justinianus* 1.3.18, where *parabolanus* means "sick-nurse." Petrarca is punning on the root *parabola*, from which the Romance languages derive *parola, parole, palabra*: "word."

150. Cf. Servius, *Commentary on the Aeneid* 7.761.

151. Petrarca's treatise *De vita solitaria*.

152. Cicero, *Lig.* 2.

153. Aristotle, *Pol.* 1.2.

154. Cf. Jerome, *Ep.* 53.3: "sancta rusticitas sibi soli prodest" ("holy rusticity is profitable to oneself alone").

155. Cf. Cicero, *Tusc.* 3.26.63.

156. Cf. Cicero, *Tusc.* 4.11.25 and *Amic.* 23.87.

157. Cf. Horace, *Ars P.* 475–476.

158. Cf. 1 Samuel 19–24, where David flees from Saul into the "wilderness" (*solitudo* in the Vulgate).

159. See n.147 above.

160. Seneca, *Ep.* 82.2.

161. Persius 1.7.

162. Cf. Augustine, *De vera relig.* 3.3, in *PL* 34.123–34, citing Plato, *Phd.* 80D–81E.

163. Cf. Virgil, *Aen.* 2.604–606.

164. Cf. Cicero, *Sen.* 12.40–41.

165. Ibid.

166. Horace, *Epist.* 1.14.21.

167. On Petrarca's *Familiar Letters* 5.19 to pope Clement VI, see n. 1 above.

168. The Sorgue is the river near Petrarca's retreat at Vaucluse.

169. The ailing Clement VI, who died in 1352.

170. Innocent VI (1352–1362).

171. For the failed Nile expeditions of Alexander and Cambyses, see Lucan 10.272–282, from which Petrarca quotes "the blazing zone of parched sky" (274–275) and "the shortage of provisions" (281).

172. Seneca, *Ep.* 51.11. Liternum was a simpler, less exclusive resort than Baiae.

173. The following argument is based on Aristotle, *Pol.* 1.2, which says that someone who doesn't live in a polis is either subhuman or a divinity.

174. Lucan 1.52.

175. Cf. Augustine, *De Civ. D.* 7 *passim*, a discussion of pagan gods based on Varro's *Divine and Human Institutions*, a text lost already in Petrarca's day.

176. Pallor is masculine, while Cloacina and Febris are feminine. Despite Petrarca's satirical tone, all three were actual Roman deities. A shrine dedicated to Pallor and Pavor (Fright) is mentioned in Livy 1.27.7. Cloacina was a cult-title of Venus the Purifier (cf. Lactantius *Div. Inst.* 1.19), which Petrarca associates with *cloaca*, "sewer." And Febris, worshiped to avoid fevers, had an altar on the Palatine: cf. Cicero, *Leg.* 2.28; Pliny, *HN* 2.16, and Valerius Maximus 2.5.6.

177. Cf. Cicero, *Fin.* 2.13.40.

178. Boethius, *Consol.* 3.10.25.

179. Augustine, *Commentary on the Psalms* 118.16.1, in *PL* 37.1545.

180. Psalm 81(82).6–7.

181. Cf. Lucan 7.793–872 on Pompey; and Augustine, *De Civ. D.* 2.14, citing the jurist Marcus Antistius Labeo: "The philosopher Plato has been elevated by Labeo to the rank of a demigod, and thus on a level with Hercules and Romulus."

182. Augustine *De Civ. D.* 9.16, citing Apuleius, *De deo Soc.* 3. Cf. Plato, *Tim.* 28C: "The father and maker of all this universe is past finding out, and even if we found him, to tell of him to all men would be impossible."

183. Revelation 5.5.

184. 1 Peter 5.8.

185. Psalm 101(102).7. Cf. Peter Lombard, *Commentary on Psalm 101*, in *PL* 191, 907. The Vulgate text reads: 'adsimilatus sum pelicano deserti factus sum, quasi bubo solitudinum': "I am made like a pelican of the desert, like an owl of the waste places." Petrarca's version seems to be literally translated from the Greek.

186. Cf. 1 Corinthians 1.31; and Jeremiah 9.24.

187. Cf. Cicero, *Ad Brut.* 24(1.16).2.

188. Cf. Cicero, *Orat.* 10.33; *Brut.* 6.22, 97.331; and Seneca the Elder, *Controv.* 10.1.8.

189. In 1344, while living in Parma, Petrarca received a letter attacking him and his poetic ambitions. The author proved to be Brizio Visconti, son of Luchino Visconti, who was the lord of Milan from 1339 to 1349; and Petrarca replied to the attack in his *Metrical Epistles* 2.11 and 2.18: see P. G. Ricci, "Il Petrarca e Brizio Visconti," in *Leonardo* 16 (1947): 337–345; and cf. also *Against a Man of High Rank*, n. 36.

190. Sallust, *Jug.*10.2: "quod *difficillumum* inter *mortalis* est, gloria invidiam vicisti."

191. Between 395 and 405, Jerome and Augustine exchanged letters offering different views on the laws of the Old Testament.

192. Proverbs 27.2.

193. Source unknown.

194. Cicero, *Fin.* 1.8.27–28.

195. Cicero, *Off.* 1.38.137.

196. Ibid.

197. Cicero, *Fin.* 2.25.80.

198. Cf. Suetonius, *Jul.* 55, for Julius Caesar attaining fame in this way.

199. Cf. Valerius Maximus 8.14.4 for the first view; and Justin, *Epit.* 9.6–7 for the second.

200. Cf. Valerius Maximus 8.14.5 for the burning of the temple by Herostratus (356 B.C.).

INVECTIVE AGAINST A MAN OF HIGH RANK

1. Petrarca's invective is directed against Jean de Caraman, a grandnephew of Pope John XXII, who was elevated to the cardinalate by Pope Clement VI on 17 December 1350. He died of plague in Avignon on 1 August 1361.

2. Petrarca's description of the buffoon—*auro tegi, purpura caput obnubi . . . circunduci*—recalls the potentates described in Jerome's *Commentary on Zechariah* 4.8–9, in PL 25.1444: 'potentes saeculi fulgere *auro, purpura, gemmis rutilare, circumdari* exercitu . . .'

3. Juvenal 3.39–40 (slightly abridged by Petrarch).

4. Petrarca's phrase 'infamie *non ultimum* genus *laudator* turpis' echoes Horace, *Epist.* 1.17.35: 'principibus placuisse viris *non ultima laus* est'.

5. Cf. Cicero, *Sen.* 1.3.

6. In his earlier years, Tiberius had a distinguished military career, but as emperor he became vindictive and dissolute. Petrarca implies that high rank has similarly corrupted Cardinal de Caraman.

7. "Glowing red" refers to a cardinal's hat. For the verb *rutilare*, cf. the passage from Jerome cited in n. 2 above.

8. Agapito Colonna, the brother of Giovanni Colonna, died shortly after being named bishop of Luni (1344).

9. Virgil, *Aen.* 4.79.

10. Charity, which endures all things: 1 Corinthians 13.7.

11. Matthew 19.28.

12. "A mere piece of wood or ivory" means the crosier, symbol of a bishop's office.

13. Virgil, *Aen.* 8.333.

14. Sallust, *Cat.* 7.1.

15. Cicero, *Tusc.* 5.9.25.

16. Lucan 9.569–570.

17. Augustine, *Conf.* 1.18.

18. Cf. Valerius Maximus 7.2.9: "I prefer a man without money to money without a man." Petrarca makes the same point in his *Letters to his Friends* 19.17.12.

19. Petrarca reverses the etymology given by Cicero, *Tusc.* 2.18.43: "virtue is so called from 'vir.'"

20. Cf. Cicero, *Parad.* 3.23.

21. Genesis 28.11.

22. Cf. Luke 19.29–36; John 12.14.

23. Cicero, *Amic.*15.54.

24. Cf. Matthew 7.3–5; Luke 6.41–42.

25. Presumably the Visconti of Milan.

26. Plautus, *Poen.* 844.

27. Petrarca alludes to the sons of Stefano Visconti and to their late uncle, Giovanni Visconti (1290–1354), archbishop of Milan (1339–1354).

28. Petrarca apparently refers to his unfinished *Letter to Posterity*, in which he defends his association with powerful friends.

29. Lucan 5.343. Cf. Petrarca, *Against a Detractor of Italy*, §119.

30. I use "Sahara" to translate "Garamantes," a remote African tribe of Saharan Libya.

31. Juvenal 13.159–160.

32. Happy the Rhone: Avignon, the seat of the papacy in Petrarca's day, lies on the Rhone river.

33. Cf. Joshua 5.15: "The place where you stand is holy."

34. Virgil, G. 3.566; Aen. 3.57, 6.573–574.

35. Agathocles and Phalaris were Greek tyrants noted for their cruelty; Busiris was a legendary king of Egypt who according to Herodotus habitually slaughtered all foreigners who entered Egypt.

36. In 1344, Petrarca received a letter attacking his poetic ambitions, written by Brizio Visconti, the son of Luchino Visconti, the ruler of Milan. Petrarca replied to the attack in his Metrical Epistles 2.11 and 2.18; cf. also Against a Physician, n. 171.

37. Apparently, Giovanni Colonna.

38. Cf. Acts of the Apostles 8.18. Petrarca is accusing de Caraman of practicing the sin of simony, or the purchase of church offices.

39. Brizio Visconti.

40. A fragment of the Latin tragedian Accius (170–86 BC), infamously quoted by Caligula: see Suetonius, Calig. 30.3.

41. Virgil, Aen. 8.365, paraphrased by Petrarca.

ON HIS OWN IGNORANCE

1. Donato Albanzani (ca. 1328–1411), born in Pratovecchio in the Apennines, was a friend and correspondent of Petrarca: cf. the latter's Letters of Old Age 5.4–6, 8.6, 10.4–5, 13.5, and 15.9. He translated Petrarca's De viris illustribus and Boccaccio's De claris mulieribus into Italian. After teaching in Ravenna and Venice, he became tutor to Nicholas III d'Este in Ferrara, where he died. This letter is Petrarca, Letters of Old Age 13.5.

2. Petrarca's letter to Albanzani, now the Berlin, Staatsbibliothek, MS Hamilton 493, is indeed filled with such corrections.

3. Suetonius, Ner. 52.

4. The letter was written in 1371. Petrarca's phrase "bed of pain" echoes Psalm 40(41).3.

5. The "state" is the Venetian republic, for which Petrarca occasionally served as a diplomat until ill health forced his retirement in the late 1360s.

6. Cf. Caesar, *BCiv.* 3.107–11 and Lucan 10.460–464.

7. Cf. Justin, *Epit.* 1.9.9–23, where the best manuscripts give the names as Ostanes and Gobryas. Valerius Maximus 3.2.ext. 2 relates a similar anecdote about Darius.

8. The four friends are the soldier Leonardo Dandolo, the merchant Tommaso Talenti, the nobleman Zaccaria Contarini, and the physician Guido da Bagnolo; on them, see Fenzi, pp. 105–107.

9. Juvenal 10.12.

10. Ovid, *Ars Am.* 2.113.

11. Proverbs 31.30.

12. Cicero, *De Or.* 2.33.144.

13. Petrarca is referring to the crude medieval translations of Aristotle; see below.

14. Cf. Cicero, *Orat.* 1.11; *Tusc.* 1.4.7.

15. Augustine, *Conf.* 5.13.23.

16. Cicero, *Fin.* 2.30.96.

17. Thersites is a repulsive soldier in Homer, *Iliad* 2.214; Choerilus (of Iasus) a mediocre Greek epic poet mocked in Horace, *Epist.* 2.1.232–234 and *Ars P.* 357–358.

18. Petrarca alludes to Leonardo Dandolo, Tommaso Talenti, and Zaccaria Contarini, respectively: cf. n. 8 above.

19. Giovanni da Bagnoli, the physician, whose knowledge of the natural world Petrarca especially derides.

20. Cicero, *Tusc.* 2.4.12.

21. For the hairs of a lion, cf. Pliny the Elder, *NH* 11.99.2, and Vincent of Beauvais, *Spec. Nat.* 19.66–75. For the feathers of a hawk, cf. Pliny *NH*, 10.79.6, and Vincent of Beauvais, *Spec. Nat.* 16.8.18, 21. For the coils of

the octopus, cf. Pliny *NH*, 9.48, and Vincent of Beauvais, *Spec. Nat.* 17.123–26.

22. On the mating and gestation of elephants, cf. Isidore of Seville, *Etymologies* 13.2.16, cited by Vincent of Beauvais 19.44. On their intelligence and lifespan, cf. Pliny, *NH* 8.10.1 and Vincent of Beauvais, *Spec. Nat.* 19.39–40.

23. On the phoenix, cf. Isidore of Seville 12.7.22 and Vincent of Beauvais, *Spec. Nat.* 16.74. On the sea urchin's powers, cf. Pliny, *NH* 9.51.4 and Vincent of Beauvais, *Spec. Nat.* 17.49. On the tiger captured by a mirror, cf. ibid. 19.112. On the Arimaspeans, legendary inhabitants of central Asia, cf. Pliny, *NH* 7.2.2 and Vincent of Beauvais, *Spec. Nat.* 16.9.

24. On whales mistaken for islands, cf. Isidore of Seville 12.6.8 and Vincent of Beauvais, *Spec. Nat.* 16.41. On bear cubs, cf. Pliny, *NH* 8.54.1 and Isidore of Seville 12.2.22. On the birth of mules, cf. Pliny, *NH* 8.69 and Vincent of Beauvais, *Spec. Nat.* 18.63.65. On vipers giving birth, cf. Pliny, *NH* 10.82.2, Isidore of Seville 12.4.10–11, and Vincent of Beauvais, *Spec. Nat.* 20.50.

25. On the blindness of moles, cf. Isidore of Seville 12.3.5 and Vincent of Beauvais, *Spec. Nat.* 19.137. On the deafness of bees, cf. ibid. 20.75. On the crocodile's jaw, cf. ibid. 17.106.

26. Petrarca seems to echo Jerome, *Apology Against Rufinus* 3.28 in *PL* 23.478; cf. Saint Jérôme, *Apologie contre Rufin*, ed. Pierre Lardet (Paris, 1983), pp. 288–92.

27. The three pontiffs are Benedict XII (1335–1342), Clement VI (1342–1352), and Innocent VI (1352–1362). The present pope Urban is Urban V (1362–1370), to whom Petrarca wrote urging the return of the papacy to Rome: cf. Petrarca, *Letters of Old Age* 9.1 (1368), which occasioned his invective *Against a Detractor of Italy*.

28. Charles IV of Luxembourg (1316–1378), crowned Holy Roman emperor in 1355.

29. "Much eloquence, little wisdom": cf. Sallust, *Cat.* 5.4. "Cato's definition": "An orator is a good man skilled in speaking" (Quintilian, *Inst.* 12.1.1).

30. Cf. Corinthians 8.1: "Knowledge puffs up, but love edifies."

31. Cf. Psalm 7.9 (King James): "The righteous God trieth the hearts and reins."

32. Cf. 1 Samuel 2.3 (Hannah's prayer): "Talk no more so very proudly, let not arrogance come from your mouth; for the Lord is a God of knowledge."

33. Cf. Ecclesiastes 7.1.

34. Petrarca echoes the text of 1 Samuel 2.3–4 as found in the Vulgate.

35. Psalm 140(141).6.

36. Augustine, *De Civ. D.* 14.28.

37. According to Justinian, *Novellae Constitutiones* 23.1, a convicted person has ten days to appeal a verdict.

38. Aristotle, *Eth. Nic.* 1.3, 1094b 27–28.

39. 1 Cor. 13.9.

40. Lucan 8.27–28.

41. Petrarca, *Bucolicum Carmen* 9.38–39 (written in 1348).

42. Decimus Laberius (ca. 106–43 B.C.), author of Latin mimes.

43. Cf. Macrobius, *Sat.* 2.7.2–3. Petrarca misinterprets the anecdote. Laberius was a playwright of equestrian rank, rather than a soldier. In 46 B.C., Caesar forced him to appear in a mime competing against his rival Publilius Syrus, and he complied by portraying a "Syrian" slave who was flogged. His verses protest this theatrical degradation.

44. In 1341, when Petrarca was "examined" for the poet's laurel. For a recent assessment of Robert's learning, see Samantha Kelly, *The New Solomon: Robert of Naples (1309–1343) and Fourteenth-Century Kingship* (Leiden: Brill, 2003), esp. pp. 41–49, on Petrarca's 1341 examination for the laurel wreath.

45. From 1305 to 1377, Avignon was the seat of the papacy. Petrarca avoids naming the city here, merely saying that it lies on the left (sinister) bank of the Rhone river. Urban V temporarily restored the Curia to Rome in 1367, the year in which Petrarca wrote.

46. In Vaucluse.

47. Seneca, *Ep.* 88.38.

48. Cf. Seneca, *Ep.* 34.3.

49. Cf. Cicero, *Amic.* 6.22.

50. Cf. ibid., 17.61, where Cicero say that friends should share all things *sine ulla exceptione*, "without any exception."

51. Cicero, *Nat. D.* 1.5.10.

52. Cf. Terence, *Eun.* 245: "tota erras via" ("you've mistaken the entire road").

53. John 1.9.

54. Augustine, *De Trin.* 13.4.7, in *PL* 42.1018–19.

55. Jerome, *Contra Pelag.* 1.19, in *PL* 23.512–13.

56. Romans 11.34.

57. Ecclesiasticus 3.22–23.

58. Cicero, *Div.* 2.13.30.

59. Cicero, *Nat. D.* 1.8.18.

60. Cf. Homer, *Iliad* 8.399 and 15.13.

61. Homer, *Iliad* 2.204–205, which Petrarca cites in Leonzio Pilato's Latin version.

62. Aristotle, *Metaph.* 11.10, 1076a 4–5, citing the same Homeric passage as in n. 59. Cf. also Aristotle, *Pol.* 4.4, 1292a 13.

63. Romans 10.16.

64. Romans 10.18.

65. Cf. Cicero, *Inv. Rhet.* 1.29.46, written around 85 BC, when Cicero was twenty-one.

66. Cicero wrote *On the Nature of the Gods* in 44 BC, when he was sixty-two.

67. Cicero, *Nat. D.* 1.36.100.

68. Ibid. 2.2.4.

69. Ibid. 2.6.16.

70. Ibid. 2.34–35.86–88.

71. Ibid. 2.35.89, where Cicero cites Accius's *Medea*.

72. Ibid. 2.35.90.

73. Cicero, *Tusc.* 1.28.70.

74. Cicero, *Nat. D.* 2.37.95. When Petrarca comments that "he" (*ille*) is Aristotle, he echoes the phrase that followers of Pythagoras used to cite his authority: cf. §48 above and n. 51. Here as elsewhere Petrarca's text of Cicero differs slightly from modern texts; here Petrarca's text makes the subject of the thought-experiment singular, while modern texts use the plural.

75. Ibid. 2.38.96–98.

76. Romans 1.19–21.

77. Cicero, *Nat. D.* 2.66.165. In fact, Cicero lists fifteen generals.

78. Ibid. 2.66.167.

79. Cicero, *Tusc.* 5.10.31.

80. Cf. Proverbs 26.11 and 2 Peter 2.22.: "Like a dog that returns to its vomit."

81. Cicero, *Nat. D.* 2.28.71.

82. Deuteronomy 32.39.

83. Psalm 95(96).5.

84. Cicero, *Nat. D.* 3.40.95.

85. Ibid. 2.23.60.

86. Lactantius, *Div. inst.* 1.11.37.

87. Cicero, *Nat. D.* 3.21.53.

88. Lactantius, *Div. inst.*1 *passim*.

89. Cf. Cicero, *Nat. D.* 3.22–23.54–60.

90. Cf. Cicero, *Nat. D.* 3.16.42; and Servius, *Commentary on Virgil's Aeneid* 7.564, for the 43 Herculean figures named by Varro.

91. Cf. Cicero, *Nat.D.* 3.21.54, 2.17.68.

92. Lactantius, *Div. inst.* 3.18.16–17.

93. Lactantius, *Div. inst.* 3.18.15. Euphorbus was a Trojan warrior slain by Menelaus. On Pythagoras, cf. also Petrarch, *Familiar Letters* 10.3.8.

94. Justin, *Epit.* 22.4.16. Cf. also Cicero, *Fin.* 5.2.4, and *Tusc.* 4.1.2. Pythagoras was said to be an immigrant from mainland Greece to the southern Italian town of Metapontum, on the Bay of Tarento.

95. Cf. Augustine, *On the Consensus of the Evangelists* 1.7.12, in PL 34.1047.

96. Cf. Cicero, *Acad.* 2.17–18.55–56.

97. Ibid., 1.2.5–6, 2.40.125. For the countless worlds, cf. Lactantius, *On God's Wrath* 10.10.

98. Cf. Valerius Maximus 8.7.ext. 2.

99. Persius 3.83–84.

100. Petrarca read Plato's *Timaeus* in the Latin version by Calcidius; his copy is now Paris, Bibliothèque Nationale, Par. lat. 6280.

101. Calcidius, *Commentary on Plato's Timaeus*, ch. 295: see *Timaeus a Calcidio translatus commentarioque instructus*, ed. J. H. Waszink (London— Leiden: E. J. Brill, 1962), p. 298.

102. Ibid., ch. 276, ed. cit., pp. 280–81.

103. Cicero, *Nat. D.* 2.67.168.

104. The censor was an ancient Roman magistrate charged with the oversight of public morals.

105. Suetonius, *Aug.* 86.1–5; and cf. §46 above. The collector of unusual and obscure words is Maecenas; the madman is Mark Antony.

106. Aristotle, *Metaph.* 1.1, 981b 7–8.

107. Cicero, *Leg.* 2.19.47.

108. Actually, Publilius Syrus, cited in Aulus Gellius, *NA* 17.14, and Macrobius, *Sat.* 2.7.11.

109. Ecclesiastes 6.11.

110. 1 Corinthians 11.16.

111. Colossians 2.8.

112. Cicero, *Nat. D.* 1.8.19.

113. Ibid.

114. Psalm 32.9.

115. Cf. John 1.1.

116. Petrarca quotes the Latin Creed, in which the last phrase echoes John 1.3: "All things were made through him."

117. On *hyle* (Greek for "matter"), cf. Isidore of Seville, *Etym.* 13.3.1 (*hyle*) and Papias, *Vocabulista* (Venice, 1496; rpt. Turin, 1966), p. 145: "Hylen vocant rerum quandam primam materiam . . ."). On God's creation *ex nihilo*, cf. Augustine, *Conf.* 12.7.7; for his discussion of *hyle*, cf. *Against Faustus* 20.14, in *PL* 42.379–80.

118. Cicero, *Nat. D.* 1.8.20.

119. Ibid. 1.8.21.

120. Cicero, *Div.* 1.19.36.

121. Psalm 89(90).4.

122. Cf. Augustine, *De Civ. D.*12.13.

123. Macrobius, *In somn, Scip.* 2.10.9.

124. Cicero, *Nat. D.* 1.9.21.

125. Cf. Augustine, *De Civ. D.* 12.16: ". . . when we say there was a time when time did not exist, we speak incongruously. . . ."

126. Macrobius, *Somn. Scip.* 2.15.18.

127. Augustine, *De Civ. D.* 8.9.

128. Horace, *Epist.* 1.1.14.

129. Cf. Cicero, *De Or.* 3.35.141.

130. The Street of Straw is the Rue du Fouarre in Paris, site of the theology faculty of the University of Paris: cf. *Against a Detractor of Italy*, §84, and n. 137.

131. Presumably, Petrarca heard lectures on Aristotle while a student at the University of Bologna.

132. Aristotle, *Eth. Nic.* 2.2, 1103b 27–28.

133. "A peddler of morality": a mistranslation of Aristotle, *Metaph.* 1.6, 987b1–2. The alleged enmity between Aristotle and Socrates is based on faulty readings in Cicero, *Off.* 1.1.4, which alludes to the enmity between Aristotle and the orator Isocrates.

134. Ibid. 1.5.15, citing Plato, *Phdr.* 250D.

135. Cf. Augustine, *Conf.* 3.4.7, and 8.7.17. Cicero's dialogue *Hortensius*, now lost, promoted the study of philosophy.

136. Cf. Romans 1:20, cited above in n. 74.

137. Calcidius, *In Tim.* ch. 250, ed. Waszink, p. 260.

138. Ovid, *Tr.* 4.10.42.

139. The supremacy of Plato in philosophy was widely acknowledged in antiquity. Fenzi, nn. 486–498, provides a detailed list and analysis of sources quoted by Petrarca.

140. The *Book of Sentences*, compiled in 1148–1151 by Peter Lombard (1100–1160), became the standard university textbook on theology and the subject of numerous commentaries.

141. Macrobius, *In somn. Scip.* 2.17.17.

142. Cf. Augustine, *De Civ. D.* 8.11.

143. "daemonic": In classical Greek, *daimonios* means "semi-divine, miraculous," an adjective that Petrarca may have found in a medieval translation of the Neoplatonist Proclus (cf. Fenzi, p. 488, n. 519, citing Nachod). But in Christian writers, the term denoted demons and the devil: cf. Petrarca's use of *demonicolae* in §119 below.

144. Cf. Aristotle, *Eth. Nic.*1.6, 1096a 14–17: "Piety requires us to honor truth above our friends."

145. Cf. Augustine, *De Civ. D.* 8.5 and 11; *De vera relig.* 3.3, in *PL* 34.123–24.

146. In 1367, when Petrarca was summoned from Venice to Pavia by Gian Galeazzo Visconti, he entrusted his library to Donato Albanzani.

147. Born near Reggio Calabria, Barlaam (1290–1347) became a monk of the order of St. Basil. As ambassador for the Byzantine emperor Andronicus, he traveled in 1339 to the papal court in Avignon, where he

met Petrarca, who aided him in being named bishop of the Calabrian see of Gerace.

148. Jerome, *Ep.* 22.30, in *PL* 22.416. "Where your treasure is, there will your heart be also": Matthew 6.21.

149. Petrarca, following the Platonic tradition, assumes a tripartite structure of the soul, consisting of reason, the passions *(irascibilis appetitus)*, and corporeal appetites *(concupiscibilis appetitus)*, ranked hierarchically in that order.

150. Augustine, *Conf.* 3.4.7 and 8.7.17.

151. Jerome, *Apology Against Rufinus* 1.30, in *PL* 23.440–41.

152. Cf. Augustine, *De doctr. Christ.* 2.40.61, in *PL.* 34.63.

153. Augustine, *De Civ. D.* 8.5,11; 10.2; 11.4–6; *De vera relig.* 3.3, in *PL* 34.123–34.

154. Augustine, *De vera relig.* 4.7, in *PL.* 34.126.

155. 1 Corinthians 11.19.

156. Augustine, *Conf.* 8.2–5.

157. The two thinkers are Cicero and Plato.

158. Jerome: *Commentary on Galatians* 1.1, in *PL* 26.345–56.

159. Petrarca borrows this image from Ovid, *Heroides* 9.29–30, as is noted by Fenzi, p. 510, n. 574.

160. In late May 1367, Petrarca traveled by boat from Venice to Pavia.

161. Pavia, located on the Ticino river just north of the Po, was the site of an ancient law school which was granted an imperial charter in 1361 at the request of Galeazzo Visconti, Petrarca's patron.

162. The noble city is Venice.

163. Suetonius, *Tib.* 28.1.

164. The other phrase is *And That of Many Others.*

165. Cf. Pliny, *HN* 14.28.148.

166. Source unknown.

167. Cicero, *Tusc.* 3.28.69.

168. Cf. Pliny, *HN* 7.30.112.

169. Cf. Seneca, *Ep.* 88.43, where the best texts read "Protagoras" rather than "Pythagoras."

170. Cf. Cicero, *Acad. Post.* 1.4.16; *Acad. Pr.* 2.23.74.

171. Cf. Cicero, *Acad.* 1.12.45; Lactantius, *Div. inst.* 3.6.7.

172. Cicero, *Inv. rhet.* 1.5.7.

173. Ibid. 1.6.8.

174. Cf. Cicero, *De Or.* 3.32.127.

175. Romans 1.21–22.

176. Cf. Romans 12.3.

177. Livy 35.10.5.

178. Ovid, *Pont.* 3.3.102.

179. Homer, *Iliad* 2.212–277.

180. Virgil, *Aen.* 11.121–131, 336–375.

181. Cf. *Historia Augusta (Pescennius Niger)* 12.2.

182. Cf. Cicero, *Nat. D.* 1.33.93.

183. Ibid.

184. Ibid. 1.34.94.

185. Cf. Macrobius, *Sat.* 2.1.12.

186. Like other medieval authors, Petrarca conflated Seneca the Elder—who criticizes an obscure orator named Quintilian in the preface to Book 10 of his *Controversies*—and the younger Seneca—who is criticized in Book 10 of the *Education of the Orator* by the famed rhetorician Quintilian.

187. Suetonius, *Calig.* 34.3.

188. Ibid. 34.4.

189. Ibid. 53.3.

190. Cf. Cicero, *Nat. D.* 1.33.93.

INVECTIVE AGAINST A DETRACTOR OF ITALY

1. Uguccione da Thiene, a papal nuncio in Avignon, who visited Petrarca in Padua in January 1373.

2. The scholastic is Jean de Hesdin (ca. 1320–1400), a Paris-trained cleric and theologian: cf. Beryl Smalley, "Jean de Hesdin O. Hosp. S. Ioh.," *Recherches de théologie ancienne et médiévale* 1 (1961): 283–330. Hesdin's invective and Petrarca's reply were published by Enrico Cocchia in *Atti della Reale Accademia di Archeologia, Lettere e Belle Arti di Napoli* 7 (1920): 92–202, with Hesdin's text at 112–39.

3. Following classical usage and Hesdin's example, Petrarca writes *Galli, Gallia* 'Gauls, Gaul' for 'French, France,' evidently savoring the Latin forms as suggesting barbarians hostile to Rome. (In §10, he writes *Franci* 'Franks,' citing an unflattering etymology: see n. 11 below.)

4. Cf. Psalm 90(91).6, which in the Vulgate reads *daemonium meridianum*.

5. Cf. Petrarca, *Letters of Old Age* 9.1, written to Urban V in the spring of 1368.

6. The anthology *Manipulus Florum* by Thomas of Ireland, professor at the Sorbonne from 1302; see Beryl Smalley, "Jean de Hesdin," p. 303.

7. Suetonius, *Ner.* 10.2; Seneca, *Clem.* 2.2.3.

8. Luke 10.30 (beginning of the story of the Good Samaritan), quoted by Hesdin.

9. Homer, *Iliad* 4.350, which Petrarca cites in the recent Latin version by Leonzio Pilato.

10. In Sulpicius Severus's *Dialogues*, the presence of a man named Gallus occasions three references to Gallic voracity (*edacitas*): see his *Dialogue I*, 4.6, 8.5, and 9.2; English translation in *The Western Fathers*, ed. F. R. Hoare (New York, 1954), pp. 61–144.

11. Cf. Isidore of Seville, *Etym.* 9.2.101.

12. Solomon.

13. Ecclesiastes 2.24.

14. Ibid. 3.13.

15. Ibid. 5.18.

16. Ibid. 9.7.

17. Ibid. 8.15.

18. Ibid. 2.3 (following the Vulgate reading).

19. Petrarca's letter to the pope begins by quoting Psalm 113(114).1: "When Israel went out from Egypt, the house of Jacob from a barbarous people." In reply, Hesdin exclaimed: "O verbum improprium, vere admirabile et ineptum."

20. Lucan 1.459.

21. Petrarca plays on the traditional Latin phrase "urbs et orbis."

22. Cicero, *Tusc.* 1.15.37.

23. Petrarca puns on *mores* "morals" and *muri* "walls."

24. Cicero, *Att.* 16.15.5.

25. Piacenza, Lodi, Metz, Adula (Rheinwaldhorn, in the Swiss Alps); a series of Latin puns on the *placita [mendacia], laudes, mendacia, adulationes* ("flattering [lies], praise, lies, and flattery") to which Petrarca has just attributed Hesdin's advancement. Miter: In medieval Paris, convicted counterfeiters were placed in the pillory wearing a special cap.

26. Petrarca in fact refused bishoprics six times: in 1346, 1351, 1361, 1363, 1369, and 1371.

27. Mark 14.64.

28. Cola di Rienzo, the "consul" who attempted to reform the Roman state in 1347.

29. Digesta Justiniani 11.7.2.

30. Codex Justinianus 1.14.9.

31. Seneca, *Ep.* 87.41.

32. Urban V was born around 1310 as Guillaume de Grimoard in the south of France.

33. Juvenal 10.49–50.

34. Petrarca puns on *gallus*, "rooster," and *Gallus*, "Gaul." The pip is a disease of fowl causing mucous discharge in the mouth and throat.

35. Cf. Proverbs 26.11 and 2 Peter 2.22.: "Like a dog that returns to its vomit." The anecdote of Peter encountering Jesus and asking "Domine, quo vadis?" is recounted in the apocryphal Acts of Peter.

36. Petrarca refers to his incomplete epistle to Urban V: *Various Letters* 3.

37. Cf. Petrarca, *Letters of Old Age* 7.1, dated 29 June 1366.

38. Petrarca's *Letters of Old Age* 9.1 (1368) instigated the controversy with Hesdin.

39. Petrarca set out for Rome in April of 1370, but turned back after suffering a fainting spell at Ferrara in May: see his *Letters of Old Age* 11.17.

40. Joel 1.5.

41. John 9.34, cited by Hesdin.

42. Lucan 5.28–29.

43. Camillus conquered Veii in 396 BC, and lived there in exile until 390, when he returned to Rome. Pope Gregory XI (1370–1378) in fact restored the papacy to Rome in 1377.

44. In 1365, Urban V paid an immense sum to ransom the constable of France, Bertrand du Guesclin (1320–1380): cf. Petrarca, *Letters of Old Age* 7.1.

45. Caesar, *BCiv.* 1.32.1.

46. Juvenal 3.8–9.

47. Virgil, *Aen.* 1.99. Petrarca follows the commentary of Servius, who glosses *saevus*, "fierce," in this passage as meaning *magnus*, "great."

48. Ibid. 12.107–08.

49. Petrarca's avenger is the emperor Titus, who captured Jerusalem in 70 AD.

50. Christ's scourger, Pontius Pilate, was from Lyon in Celtic Gaul, according to Peter Comestor, *Scholastic History* 53, in PL 198.1680.

51. According to Ovid, *Met.* 2.534–631, Apollo changed the raven's white feathers to black. Pliny, *HN* 10.55.120, describes a talking raven that greeted Tiberius and his sons. Cf. Martial's distichs 14.73 (on a parrot

that says "Hail Caesar") and 14.74 (on a raven who greets guests: *corvus salutator*).

52. Where I translate "Burgundy," Petrarca writes "Beaune," a noted wine-producing center, 35 km southwest of Dijon, long the capital of the Burgundy region.

53. Philippians 3.19.

54. Hesdin wrote this odd phrase—*venenum pretiosum*, perhaps meaning "precious potion"—in reply to Petrarca's description of Burgundy wine as a poisonous vintage, *venenosa vindemia*.

55. Presumably carnal pleasures, like the prostitution that flourished at Avignon: cf. §III below.

56. Augustine, *Conf.* 10.32.48. No close model in Cicero's surviving works has been identified, but Augustine's expression *cum absunt non requiro* echoes Cicero, *Sen.* 10.33, where Cato, speaking of youthful strength, says *cum absit ne requiras*, "when it is gone, do not seek it."

57. Seneca, *Ep.* 25.4.

58. Lucan 4.381.

59. Hebrews 13.14.

60. Acts of the Apostles 16.37–38.

61. Bernard's treatise on papal duties *On Consideration* (1153), which he dedicated to pope Eugene III (himself a former Cistercian of Clairvaux), contains a violent denunciation of the Roman curia and populace; text in PL 182.727–808. Petrarca ironically notes that Bernard did not give the city all the "consideration" it deserved.

62. Petrarca's *On the Solitary Life* and *On Religious Leisure*.

63. Previously condemned at the Council of Soissons (1121) for his treatise *On the Divine Unity and Trinity*, Peter Abelard (1079–1142) was again condemned at the council of Sens (1141) largely at Bernard's instigation.

64. Berengar of Poitiers's *Apology against Bernard of Clairvaux*, written after the Council of Soissons; text in PL 178.1857–70.

65. Berengar apologized in his *Letter to the Bishop of Mende*; text in PL 178.1871–74. Both of Berengar's works and several by Abelard are found

in Paris, Bibliothèque Nationale de France, MS Par. lat. 2923, which belonged to Petrarca.

66. Pope Eugene III (1145–1153), a former Cistercian of Clairvaux, and the dedicatee of Bernard's *On Consideration*.

67. Berengar, *Letter to the Bishop of Mende*, in PL 178.1871, citing Psalm 103(104).25.

68. John Chrysostom, *Homily* 1.6, in PG 49.24.

69. Sallust, *Cat.* 40; Livy 5.33.

70. In fact, the passage is by Eusebius Gallicanus, whose works often circulated under Ambrose's name: see Eusebius Gallicanus, Sermon 51, in *Collectio homiliarum: Corpus Christianorum, Series Latina* 101.595.

71. *Commentary on Paul's Epistle to the Romans*, in PL 17.47.

72. Ambrose, *Commentary on Romans* 1.8, in PL 17.51.

73. Ibid.

74. Jerome, *Commentary on Paul's Epistle to the Galatians*, in PL 26.355, citing Romans 1.8.

75. Ibid.

76. Cf. Bernard, *On Consideration* 4.2, in PL 182.773–74.

77. Virgil, *Aen.* 1.625.

78. Cf. Seneca the Elder, *Controv.* 1.pr.19; Pliny, *HN* 8.24.88.

79. Cf. Justin, *Epit.* 18.2.10, and Eutropius, *Breviary of Roman History* 2.13.3. Cf. also Florus, *Epit.* 1.13.20, where the Roman senate is called an assembly of kings.

80. 1 Maccabees 8.16.

81. Hesdin's chapters 8 and 9 cite three paragraph-length excerpts from Justin.

82. Justin, *Epit.* 31.8.

83. Sallust, *Cat.* 8.5.

84. Ovid, *Met.* 15. 431: "*Dardaniam* fama est consurgere Romam." Dardanian refers to the Trojans, descended from Dardanus.

85. Virgil, *Aen.* 6.781–784.

86. Virgil, *Ecl.* 1.24–25.

87. Livy, pr. 11.

88. Petrarca puns on Latin *Galli*, "Gauls" or "cocks," and *gallinae*, "hens."

89. "Significator" is the Latin astrological term for a heavenly body that influences one's character or destiny. Petrarca earlier mocks Hesdin's appeal to astrology in comparing Rome to the inconstant and mutable moon: cf. §§13–14 above. (It is perhaps worth noting that during the 1360s a college of medicine and astrology was founded at the University of Paris.)

Architrenius ("arch-threnodist" or "great bewailer") is the title character of a satirical poem in Latin hexameters written in 1184 by the Norman poet Johannes de Hauvilla: see the edition and translation by Winthrop Wetherbee (Cambridge, 1994). Hesdin had cited the encomium of Paris in *Architrenius* 2.484–93.

90. The doors to the temple of Janus at Rome were closed during peacetime. For the three closings, see Florus, *Epit.* 2.34.

91. Livy 30.16.9, also cited in Petrarch, *Letters of Old Age* 16.7.

92. Ibid. 22.37.3.

93. Ibid. 30.42.16–17.

94. Ibid. 9.18.6.

95. The poem is the Latin *Alexandreis* in ten books by Walter of Châtillon, ca. 1135–1184.

96. Sardanapalus was the last king of Assyria, legendary for his devotion to the pleasures of the table; see Cicero, *Tusc.* 5.101.

97. Livy 9.18–19.

98. Ibid. 22.32.4–9.

99. Ibid. 22.26.9.

100. Ibid. 30.21.35.

101. Cf. Florus, *Epit.*1.13; Justin, *Epit.* 18.2.7.

102. Justin, *Epit.* 18.2.9.

103. Sallust, *Jug.* 104.5.

104. Sallust, *Cat.* 6.5.

105. Sallust, *Jug.* 102.11.

106. Florus, *Epit.* 1.45.21.

107. Ibid. 1.45.26.

108. Sallust, *Cat.* 54.4.

109. Suetonius, *Tit.* 8.1.

110. Ibid. 8.2.

111. The phrase "irrevocable word" echoes Horace, *Epist.*1.18.71: *inrevocabile verbum.*

112. Cf. Pilate's words in John 19.22: "What I have written, I have written."

113. Codex Justinianus, preface.

114. Codex Justinianus 1.17.1.10.

115. Ibid. 1.17.2.20.

116. Justinian, *Novellae Constitutiones* 9.

117. Ibid.

118. "Sinking Jerusalem" (*occiduam Ierusalem*), meaning Avignon, is a play on Hesdin's "Western Jerusalem" (*occidentalis Ierusalem*); the pope is Urban V.

119. Horace, *Carm.* 3.6.45–48.

120. The Knights of Jerusalem were officially known as the Knights Hospitaller of St. John of Jerusalem, and later as the Knights of Malta. According to H. J. A. Sire, *The Knights of Malta* (New Haven and London, 1994), p. 120, "The fourteenth century was the great age of florescence of the Order of St John in southern France; its principal communities ranked among the most important religious houses in the country."

121. Cf. Livy 3.45.9. Lucius Icilius was a Roman plebeian who in 449 BC defended his fiancée Virginia when she was abducted by the patrician Appius Claudius. The story was retold by Boccaccio in *Famous Women*,

ed. Virginia Brown (Cambridge, Massachusetts: Harvard University Press, 2001), pp. 242–248 (LVIII).

122. Cf. Petrarca, *Familiar Letters* 16.8, dated 24 April 1353, "on the noble character of Roman matrons."

123. Psalm 52(53).5.

124. Terence, *An.* 164.

125. Cf. Matthew 26.65.

126. Troubling but not troublesome: *odiosa non operosa.*

127. Cf. Petrarca, *Letters of Old Age* 9.1.

128. Petrarca read Josephus in Latin translations: see Pierre de Nolhac, *Pétrarque et l'Humanisme,* 2d ed., 2 vols. (Paris, 1907), 2:152–56. The *Scholastic History* was written by the French theologian Peter Comestor (1100–1179).

129. Cf. Bede, *De temporum ratione* 66, in *PL* 90.545; Josephus, *History of the Jewish War* 2.7.3 and *Jewish Antiquities* 17.13.344.

130. Cf. Peter Comestor, *Scholastic History* 53 in *PL* 198.1680.

131. Cf. Josephus, *Jewish Antiquities* 18.7.252 (but this tetrarch is the same as Herod Antipas).

132. Cf. Peter Comestor, *loc. cit.*

133. In 1371, the 61-year-old Urban V was succeeded by the 42-year-old Gregory XI.

134. Psalm 135(136).4.

135. Cf. Peter Comestor, *loc. cit.*

136. Petrarca alludes to Pilate's washing of his hands: cf. Matthew 27.24.

137. Petrarca refers to two principal landmarks of the medieval University of Paris. The Petit Pont links the Île St.-Louis and the Latin Quarter; in medieval times there were classrooms built on it where scholastic logic was taught. (Alternatively, Crevatin, p. 172, n. 171, and Fenzi, p. 448, n. 446, identify this "small bridge" with the Pont Saint Bézénet in Avignon.) The Street of Straw is the Rue du Fouarre (or Feurre), site of the Faculty of Arts and so called because students sat on benches covered

with straw. Dante refers to it as the "vico delli strami" in *Paradise* 10.137. Cf. also *On His Own Ignorance*, §106 and n. 130.

138. In *Letters of Old Age* 9.1, Petrarca mentioned the four Doctors of the Church—Ambrose, Augustine, Jerome, and Gregory—and said that none of them was a Gaul, and "none of them instructed in Gaul": *nullus doctus in Gallia*—a phrase that Hesdin misinterpreted.

139. See Jerome, *Commentary on Paul's Epistle to the Galatians* 2.427–28, in *PL* 26.355: "In one of his hymns, Hilary calls the Gauls hard to teach."

140. Cf. Julius Caesar, *B Gall.* 3.19.6. During the Middle Ages, the work was often attributed to Julius Celsus, who had revised and signed the text in certain manuscripts.

141. Livy 7.12.11.

142. Augustine, *De Civ. D.* 4.6.

143. Cf. Justin, *Epit.* 24.4.1, a passage cited by Hesdin.

144. Ibid. 25.2.9, cited by Hesdin.

145. Virgil, *Aen.* 1.282.

146. Justin, *Epit.* 24.4.1, cited by Hesdin.

147. Florus, *Epit.* 1.8. The three great battles were fought at the Anio river (361 B.C.), in the Pomptine marshes (350 B.C.), and at Lake Vadimo (283 B.C.).

148. Cf. Justin, *Epit.* 24.6–8.

149. Ibid. 24.8.11.

150. Ibid. 24.8.11.2–16.

151. This passage is not found in the extant text of Justin. Crevatin, p. 174, n. 196, suggests that it may be a gloss that Petrarca found in one of his sources.

152. Johannes de Hauvilla, *Architrenius* 2.486.

153. In *Canzoniere* 136.14, Petrarca alludes to the stench ("lezzo") of Avignon.

154. Cicero, *Off.* 2.8.28.

155. Justin, *Epit.*43.4.2.

156. Seneca, *Helv.* 7.8.

157. The priest and theologian Mamertus Claudianus (d. 474) — not the poet Claudian — was variously said to be from Vienne or Lyon.

158. Petrarca's "flourishing" homeland is of course Florence. The poet Claudian was in fact from Alexandria, but a passage in one of his poems was misconstrued to make him a Florentine.

159. In fact, Statius was from Naples, but he was confused (by Dante among others) with a rhetorician from Toulouse.

160. Petrarca, *Buccolicum carmen* 10.344–345.

161. In many manuscripts, Lucan's epic *Pharsalia* (*The Civil War*) is prefaced by an epigram supposedly written by his uncle Seneca, which begins *Corduba me genuit*, echoing a similar verse attributed to Virgil: *Mantua me genuit*, "Mantua gave me birth."

162. Statius, *Theb.* 12.816–817: the Italian poet is Virgil. Cf. also Petrarca, *Against a Physician*, n. 87.

163. Livy 1.23.1.

164. Augustine, *De Civ. D.* 18.2.

165. Ibid.

166. Cf. Livy 1.7.8; Ovid *Fasti*, I-461–542; Servius 8.51; and Isidore of Seville, *Etym.* 1.4.1. Boccaccio's short biography of her is in *Famous Women*, ed. Brown, pp. 104–113 (XXVII).

167. Petrarca, *Letters of Old Age* 9.1.

168. The phrase "leaden dagger" (*plumbeus pugio*) for a weak argument is from Cicero; see *Fin.* 4.48.

169. Juan Gil of Zamora (Joannes Aegidius Zamorensis), a Spanish Franciscan (d. 1318), who was advisor to Alfonso X and tutor of king Sancho IV of Castile and Leon.

170. See Fray Juan Gil de Zamora, *De preconiis Hispanie*, ed. Manuel de Castro y Castro (Madrid, 1955), p. 175: "De Hispania siquidem fuit Aristoteles. . . ." Cf. Francisco Rico, "Aristoteles Hispanus: Entorno a Gil de Zamora, Petrarca y Juan de Mena," *Italia Medioevale e Umanistica* 10 (1967): 143–54.

171. Presumably a reference to Petrarca's invective *On His Own Ignorance*.

172. Aristotle, *Nicomachean Ethics* 2.2, 1103b 27–28: "We are inquiring not in order to know what virtue is, but in order to become good."

173. Cicero, *Tusc.* 1.1.1.

174. Source unknown. Petrarca makes the same observation in his *Familiar Letters* 25.5.2–3 (addressed to Seneca).

175. Augustine, *Conf.* 3.4.7.

176. Petrarca cites most of Cicero's works by the standard titles, with two exceptions. The title *On the Essence of the Universe* refers to Cicero's translation of part of Plato's *Timaeus*, called *De universo* or *De essentia mundi* in medieval manuscripts. The "two volumes of *Rhetoric*" are today called the *De Inventione*. For a similar list of works, see Petrarca, *Familiar Letters* 24.4.12–13 (addressed to Cicero).

177. Cf. Augustine, *De Civ. D.* 6.3.

178. Cf. Caesar, *B Gall.* 6.18.1.

179. In his *Commentary on Paul's Epistles* (*PL* 111.1278), Rabanus Maurus cites Jerome as writing: "quod si idolis servivimus, non obstinationi mentis, sed ignorantiae deputandum." The same sentence is later quoted by Lanfranc of Canterbury (*PL* 150.105) and St. Bruno (*PL* 153.14).

180. Cf. Augustine, *De Civ. D.* 6.2.

181. The Augustan historian Hyginus was the author of many lost works including *The Origins and Sites of Italian Cities*, which is cited by Servius.

182. Seneca, *Helv.* 7.1–9.

183. Ibid. 7.7, with reference to Aeneas, who escaped the fall of his native Troy.

184. Ibid.

185. Virgil, *Aen.* 7.240. In this version of the myth, Dardanus came from Corythus in Etruria (later, Cortona in Tuscany).

186. Colonia Agrippina or Agrippinensis (now Cologne) was founded in 38 B.C. by Marcus Vipsanius Agrippa; cf. Tacitus, *Germ.* 28, and *Ann.* 12.27.

187. Lugdunum (now Lyon) was founded in 43 B.C. by Lucius Munatius Plancus; cf. Seneca, *Ep.* 91.14.

188. Cf. Livy 21.61.

189. Cf. pseudo-Boethius, *De disciplina scholarium*, ed. O. Weijers (Leiden, 1976), 2.4.

190. Petrarca visited Ghent in 1333; cf. his *Familiar Letters* 1.4 (on Ghent, 1.4.5).

191. Cf. Suetonius, *Aug.* 21.

192. The Galatians (Gauls) invaded Asia Minor in 278 B.C. The legendary Dardanus migrated to Phrygia, where his descendants founded Troy.

193. Cf. Livy 5.34.49.

194. Cf. Justin, *Epit.* 43.5.8–9, cited by Hesdin.

195. The Roman historian Livy was born in Padua, where Petrarca resided at this time.

196. Livy, whose eloquence is described by Quintilian, *Inst.* 10.1.32 as "Livy's milky richness" *(lactea ubertas)* was visited in Rome by a nobleman from Cadiz, who was uninterested in the other attractions of the city; see Jerome, *Ep.* 53.1.

197. See Livy 5.49.

198. The three men were Adam, Abel, and Cain.

199. Sallust, *Cat.* 51.35.

200. Hesdin cites the unhappy ends of Scipio Africanus, Scipio Aemilianus Numantinus, and Scipio Nasica.

201. Cf. Sallust, *Cat.* 40.

202. Ibid. 52.36.

203. Ibid. 54.1–6.

204. Ibid. 5.1.

205. Juvenal's third satire on Rome is quoted several times by Hesdin.

206. Cf. Juvenal 3.29–30.

207. Evidently, Petrarca's copy of Hesdin's letter read *leones*, "lions," rather than *lenones*, "panders." *Leo* is also a medieval word for a "john" or hirer of prostitutes.

208. Petrarca seems to be mistaken. The chronicler Pietro Azario describes the equestrian statue of Bernabò Visconti (d. 1385) as being placed above the principal altar in the Milanese church of San Giovanni in Conca: see Azario, *Liber gestorum in Lombardia*, ed. C. Cognasso, in *Rerum italicarum scriptores*, vol. 16 (Bologna, 1939), p. 133. The statue is now in the Castello Sforzesco.

209. Bernabò Visconti, whose haughty reply to an imperial vicar was drafted by Petrarca himself.

210. Junius Brutus ordered and observed the execution of his two sons for conspiring to restore the Tarquinian monarchy: cf. Livy 2.5 and Orosius 2.5.1.

211. Hesdin cites Orosius 2.4.2, which blames Romulus for the rape of the Sabine women.

212. Cf. Livy 1.9.1; Florus, *Epit.*1.1.10.

213. Cf. Judges 21.22.

214. Juvenal 1.163–164, meaning that it is safe to talk about the dead.

215. Florus, *Epit.* 1.8.2.

216. Cicero, *Rab. Post.* 4.10.

217. Lucan 5.343; cf. Petrarca, *Against a Man of High Rank*, §33.

218. Ibid. 9.1076–1078.

219. Cf. Livy 1.5.7; and 1.6.2.

Bibliography

❧❧❧

EDITIONS

Librorum Francisci Petrarchae Basileae Impressorum Annotatio. Basel: per Magistrum Ioannem de Amerbach, 1496. Includes *Contra medicum* (*Contra medicum obiurgantem Invectivarum libri IIII*).

Librorum Francisci Petrarchae Impressorum Annotatio. Venice: per Simonem de Luere, 1501. Includes *Contra medicum* (*Contra medicum obiurgantem Invectivarum libri IIII*) and *De sui ipsius et multorum ignorantia.*

Librorum Francisci Petrarchae Impressorum Annotatio. Venice: per Simonem Papiensem dictum Bivilaquam, 1503. Includes *Contra medicum* (*Contra medicum obiurgantem Invectivarum libri IIII*) and *De sui ipsius et multorum ignorantia.*

Francisci Petrarchae Florentini *Opera quae extant omnia.* 4 vols. Basel: excudebat Henrichum Petri, 1554. Anastatic reprint, Ridgewood, New Jersey, 1965.

Francisci Petrarchae Florentini *Opera quae extant omnia.* 4 vols. Basel: per Sebastianum Henricpetri, 1581.

Hermann Müller. "F. Petrarcas Invectiva contra quendam Gallum innominatum sed in dignitate positum." *Jahrbücher für Philologie und Paedagogik,* vol. 108 (1873): 569–83. First edition of *Contra quendam magni status.*

Le traité "De sui ipsius et multorum ignorantia," publié d'après le manuscrit autographe de la Bibliothèque Vaticane. Ed. L. M. Capelli. Paris: H. Champion, 1906.

M. Vattasso, *I codici petrarcheschi della biblioteca Vaticana.* Rome: Tipografia Poliglotta Vaticana, 1908. Includes *Contra quendam magni status,* pp. 207–28.

Enrico Cocchia. "La polemica del Petrarca col maestro Giovanni da Hesdin per il trasferimento della sede pontificia da Avignone a Roma." *Atti della reale Accademia di Archeologia, lettere e belle arti di Napoli.* Nuova serie, VII (1919), 93–202. Includes Petrarch's *Contra eum qui maledixit Italie* and the treatise that provoked it.

Francesco Petrarca. *Invectiva contra quendam magni status hominem sed nullius scientie aut virtutis.* Ed. Pier Giorgio Ricci. Florence: Le Monnier, 1949.

Francesco Petrarca. *Invective contra medicum.* Testo latino e volgarizzamento di ser Domenico Silvestri. Ed. Pier Giorgio Ricci. Rome: Edizioni di Storia e Letteratura, 1950.

Francesco Petrarca. *Prose.* Ed. Guido Martellotti, Pier Giorgio Ricci, Enrico Carrara, and Enrico Bianchi. Milan and Naples: Ricciardi, 1955. Selections from the invectives edited by Ricci, pp. 647–807.

Francesco Petrarca. *Opere latine.* Ed. Antonietta Bufano. With Italian translation. 2 vols. Turin: U.T.E.T., 1975. Invectives, pp. 817–1253. The text published by Bufano of the *De sui ipsius ignorantia* was prepared by P. G. Ricci, of which only a part was published in the 1955 edition.

Francesco Petrarca. *Invective contra medicum.* Testo latino e volgarizzamento di ser Domenico Silvestri. Ed. Pier Giorgio Ricci. With an appendix by Bortolo Martinelli. Rome: Edizioni di Storia e Letteratura, 1978.

Francesco Petrarca. *Invective contra medicum, Invectiva contra quendam magni status sed nullius scietie aut virtutis.* Ed. Francesco Bausi. Florence: Casa Editrice Le Lettere, 2005. With Italian introduction, translation, and notes.

Francesco Petrarca. *De sui ipsius et multorum ignorantia. Über seine und vieler anderer Unwissenheit.* Ed. August Buck. Tr. Klaus Kubusch. Hamburg: Felix Meiner, 1993.

Francesco Petrarca. *Invective contra eum qui maledixit Italie (In difesa dell'Italia).* Ed. Giuliana Crevatin. With Italian introduction, translation, and notes. Venice: Marsilio, 1995.

Francesco Petrarca. *Contra eum qui maledixit Italie.* Ed. Monica Berté. Florence: Casa Editrice Le Lettere, 2005. With Italian introduction, translation, and notes.

Francesco Petrarca. *De sui ipsius et multorum ignorantia (Della mia ignoranza e di quella di molti altri).* Ed. Enrico Fenzi. With Italian introduction, translation, and commentary. Milan: Mursia, 1999.

Pétrarque. *De sui ipsius et multorum ignorantia. Mon ignorance et celle de tant d'autres, 1367–1368.* Préface d'Olivier Boulnois. Traduction de Juliette Bertrand (1929) revue par Christophe Carraud (1999). Notes de

Christophe Carraud. Grenoble: Éditions Jérôme Millon, 2000. The essay by Boulnois is essential reading.

Pétrarque. *Invectives. Invective contra medicum. Contre un médecin, 1352–1353. Contra eum qui maledixit Italie. Contre celui qui maudit l'Italie, ou France-Italia, 1373. Invectiva contra quendam magnis status hominem sed nullius scientie aut virtutis. Contre un homme de haut rang, mais de petite vertu et faible intelligence, 1355.* Texte traduit, présenté et annoté par Rebecca Lenoir. Grenoble: Éditions Jérôme Millon, 2003.

SELECTED MODERN STUDIES

Ariani, Marco. *Petrarca.* Rome: Salerno Editrice, 1999.

Bernardo, Aldo S., ed. *Francesco Petrarca, Citizen of the World.* Padua: Antenore, and Albany: State University of New York Press, 1980.

Billanovich, Giuseppe. *Petrarca letterato. I. Lo scrittoio del Petrarca.* Rome: Edizioni di Storia e Letteratura, 1947.

Bosco, Umberto. *Francesco Petrarca.* 3d ed. Bari: Laterza, 1965.

Buck, August, ed. *Petrarca.* Darmstadt: Wissenschaftliche Buchgesellschaft, 1976.

Dotti, Ugo. *Vita di Petrarca.* Bari: Laterza, 1987.

Hoffmeister, Gerhart. *Petrarca.* Stuttgart and Weimar: Metzler, 1997.

Foster, Kenelm. *Petrarch: Poet and Humanist.* Edinburgh: Edinburgh University Press, 1984.

Mazzotta, Giuseppe. *The Worlds of Petrarch.* Durham, North Carolina, and London: Duke University Press, 1993.

Nolhac, Pierre de. *Pétrarque et l'humanisme.* 2 vols. 2d ed. Paris: Champion, 1907. Reprint, Paris: Champion, 1965.

Scaglione, Aldo, ed. *Francis Petrarch, Six Centuries Later: A Symposium.* Chapel Hill: Department of Romance Languages, University of North Carolina, 1975.

Schalk, Fritz, ed. *Petrarca 1304–1374. Beiträge zu Werk und Wirkung.* Frankfurt am Main: Klostermann, 1975.

Wilkins, Ernest Hatch. *Life of Petrarch.* Chicago: University of Chicago Press, 1961.

Index

⚜⚜⚜

References are to paragraph numbers. D = *Contra eum qui maledixit Italie* (*Against a Detractor of Italy*); H = *Contra quendam magni status* (*Against a Man of High Rank*); I = *De sui ipsius et multorum Ignorantia* (*On His Own Ignorance*); M = *Contra Medicum* (*Against a Physician*).

Publication of this volume has been made possible by

The Myron and Sheila Gilmore Publication Fund at I Tatti
The Robert Lehman Endowment Fund
The Jean-François Malle Scholarly Programs and Publications Fund
The Andrew W. Mellon Scholarly Publications Fund
The Craig and Barbara Smyth Fund
for Scholarly Programs and Publications
The Lila Wallace–Reader's Digest Endowment Fund
The Malcolm Wiener Fund for Scholarly Programs and Publications